1 and 2 Corinthians

Problematic, Apostolic Leadership

CLINTON'S BIBLICAL LEADERSHIP COMMENTARY SERIES

J. Robert Clinton, D. Miss., Ph.D.

BARNABAS PUBLISHERS

Copyright © J. Robert Clinton, November 2003
All Rights Reserved

No Part of this publication may be reproduced, stored in a retrieval system, or transmitted in any form or by any means - electronic, mechanical, photocopy, recording, or any other - except for brief quotations embodied in a critical article or printed reviews, without prior permission of the publisher.

Barnabas Publishers
P.O. Box 6006
Altadena, CA 91003-6006
ISBN No. 0-9741818-7-0

BARNABAS PUBLISHERS

Printed in the United States of America

Series & Title Cover Design: D.M. Battermann, R&D Design Servies
Book Design & Layout: D.M. & R.D. Battermann, R&D Design Services

Table of Contents

Page　Contents
vii　Abbreviations
ix　List of Tables
xi　List of Figures
xiii　Introduction to Clinton's Leadership Commentary Series

xv　Preface

1　Approach to 1,2 Corinthians in Perspective

3　Overview First Corinthians
6　General Reflections on First Corinthians

7　Leadership Topics and Leadership Lessons, 1 Corinthians
7　　1. COMPLEXITY OF LEADERSHIP
7　　2. GIFTEDNESS
8　　3. STEWARDSHIP MODEL
9　　4. LEADERSHIP STYLES
9　　5. SERVANT LEADERSHIP
10　　6. PERSONAL DISCIPLINE
10　　7. STRUCTURE

11　1 Corinthians Commentary

39　For Further Study

41　Overview Second Corinthians
43　General Reflections on Second Corinthians

44　Leadership Topics and Leadership Lessons, 2 Corinthians
44　　1. MINISTRY PHILOSOPHY AND VALUES
45　　2. FINANCIAL SAFEGUARD
46　　3. SPIRITUAL AUTHORITY INSIGHTS
46　　4. AUTHORITY/POWER
47　　5. PERSONAL EXPERIENCE/ SPIRITUAL AUTHORITY
48　　6. MOTIVATIONAL LESSONS
48　　7. TEACHING ON GIVING
49　　8. APOSTOLIC LEADERSHIP FUNCTIONS
50　　9. ACCOUNTABILITY

51　2 Corinthians Commentary
79　For Further Study

Leadership Articles[1]

Page	#	Articles Title (In the Ebook Version, these are linked; just click on them and go there.)
83	1.	Accountability—Standing Before God As A Leader
85	2.	Apostolic Functions
89	3.	Apostolic Functions—Comparison of Titus and Timothy
91	4.	Apostolic Giftedness—Multiple Gifted Leaders
98	5.	Barnabas—Significant Mentoring
103	6.	Bible Centered Leader
106	7.	Conscience, Paul's Use of
110	8.	Constellation Model, Mentoring Relationships
114	9.	Day of Christ—Implications for Leaders
115	10.	Destiny Pattern
121	11.	Entrustment—A Leadership Responsibility
123	12.	Figures and Idioms in the Bible
129	13.	Finishing Well—Five Factors Enhancing
132	14.	Finishing Well—Six Characteristics
135	15.	Finishing Well—Six Major Barriers Identified
137	16.	Followership—Ten Commandments
140	17.	Gender and Leadership
142	18.	Giving—Paul's View in 2 Corinthians
145	19.	God's Shaping Processes With Leaders
149	20.	Impartation of Gifts
151	21.	Influence, Power, and Authority Forms
156	22.	Integrity—A Top Leadership Quality
161	23.	Isolation Processing—Learning Deep Lessons from God
168	24.	Jesus—5 Leadership Models: Shepherd, Harvest, Steward, Servant, Intercessor
176	25.	Leaders—Intercession Hints from Habakkuk
181	26.	Leadership Act
184	27.	Leadership Eras in the Bible—Six Identified
187	28.	Leadership Functions—Three High Level Generic Priorities
191	29.	Leadership Genre—7 Types
193	30.	Leadership Lessons, Seven Major Lessons Identified
198	31.	Leadership Levels-Looking At a Leadership Continuum
202	32.	Leadership Selection
207	33.	Leadership Transition Concepts
212	34.	Leadership Tree Diagram
215	35.	Macro Lessons Defined
218	36.	Macro Lessons—List of 41 Across Six Leadership Eras.
221	37.	Mentoring—An Informal Training Model
224	38.	Ministry Entry Patterns
229	39.	Ministry Philosophy
234	40.	Motivating Factors For Ministry
236	41.	Motivating Principles: Pauline Influence
238	42.	Paul—A Sense of Destiny
242	43.	Paul—And His Companions
249	44.	Paul—Deep Processing
255	45.	Paul—Developer Par Excellence
257	46.	Paul—Intercessor Leader

---

[1] Throughout the commentary Articles listed with numbers are included with this commentary and refer to the numbered articles listed above. Some articles, without numbers occur in other commentaries. I will be publishing a series called, **Clinton's Leadership Encyclopedia**, which will contain all the articles in all the leadership commentaries. Those articles not included in this commentary will be available also there. Some of the articles included here were written later, some time after the 1,2 Corinthians commentary was already done. But in reviewing all of the leadership articles I felt that some were very appropriate to Paul's ministry with the Corinthians. In any case, I introduce each article with a short paragraph telling how the article is relevant to the Corinthian ministry. All of these articles were revised at least somewhat for this issue of the 1,2 Corinthian Leadership Commentary.

261	47.	*Paul—Mentor For Many*
264	48.	*Paul—Modeling as An Influence Means*
269	49.	*Pauline Leadership Styles*
275	50.	*Pauline Leadership Terms*
280	51.	*Pauline Leadership Values*
284	52.	*Prayer Macro Lesson*
285	53.	*Principles of Truth*
289	54.	*Problems—The N.T. Church*
293	55.	*Promises of God*
296	56.	*Receptor Oriented Communication*
299	57.	*Reciprocal Living—The One-Another Commands*
303	58.	*Social Base Issues*
307	59.	*Sovereign Mindset*
310	60.	*Spiritual Authority—Defined, Six Characteristics*
313	61.	*Spiritual Benchmarks*
314	62.	*Spiritual Disciplines—And On-Going Leadership*
319	63.	*Spiritual Gift Clusters*
323	64.	*Spiritual Gifts, Giftedness and Development*
326	65.	*Spiritual Warfare—Satan's Tactics*
328	66.	*Spiritual Warfare—Two Extremes To Avoid*
330	67.	*Spiritual Warfare—Two Foundational Axioms*
333	68.	*Time-Lines—Defined For Biblical Leaders*
335	69.	*Timothy A Beloved Son in the Faith*
337	70.	*Union Life—Intimacy With God*
342	71.	*Value Driven Leadership*
343	72.	*Vanishing Breed, Needed, Bible Centered Leaders*
347	73.	*Variations on His Theme—Paul's Salutations--Harbingers of His Epistles*
352	74.	*Vulnerability and Prayer*

355   Glossary of Leadership Terms

389   Bibliography

(This page deliberately left blank)

Abbreviations

Bible Books

Genesis	Ge	Nahum	Na
Exodus	Ex	Habakkuk	Hab
Leviticus	Lev	Zephaniah	Zep
Numbers	Nu	Haggai	Hag
Deuteronomy	Dt	Zechariah	Zec
Joshua	Jos	Malachi	Mal
Judges	Jdg	Matthew	Mt
Ruth	Ru	Mark	Mk
1 Samuel	1Sa	Luke	Lk
2 Samuel	2Sa	John	Jn
1 Kings	1Ki	Acts	Ac
2 Kings	2Ki	Romans	Ro
1 Chronicles	1Ch	1 Corinthians	1Co
2 Chronicles	2Ch	2 Corinthians	2Co
Ezra	Ezr	Galatians	Gal
Nehemiah	Ne	Ephesians	Eph
Esther	Est	Philippians	Php
Job	Job	Colossians	Col
Psalms	Ps	1 Thessalonians	1Th
Proverbs	Pr	2 Thessalonians	2Th
Ecclesiastes	Ecc	1 Timothy	1Ti
Song of Songs	SS	2 Timothy	2Ti
Isaiah	Isa	Titus	Tit
Jeremiah	Jer	Philemon	Phm
Lamentations	La	Hebrews	Heb
Ezekiel	Eze	James	Jas
Daniel	Da	1 Peter	1Pe
Hosea	Hos	2 Peter	2Pe
Joel	Joel	1 John	1Jn
Amos	Am	2 John	2Jn
Obadiah	Ob	3 John	3Jn
Jonah	Jnh	Jude	Jude
Micah	Mic	Revelation	Rev

Other

BAS	Basic English Version
CEV	Contemporary English Version
fn	footnote(s)
KJV	King James Version of the Bible
LB	The Learning Bible—Contemporary English Version
NEB	New English Bible
NLT	New Living Translation
N.T.	New Testament
O.T.	Old Testament
Phillips	The New Testament in Modern English, J.B. Phillips
TEV	Today's English Version (also called Good News Bible)
Vs	verse(s)

(This page deliberately left blank)

List of Tables for the 1,2 Corinthian Leadership Articles

Page	Table (In the Ebook version all these items are linked)
87	2-1. Apostolic Functions
89	3-1 Apostolic Functions--Paul's, Timothy's and Titus
90	3-2 Comparison of Apostolic Functions--Timothy and Titus
93	4-1. Apostolic Functions and Related Giftedness Needed.
99	5-1. The Biblical Data on Barnabas
100	5-2. Five General Mentor Functions Underlying Sponsorship
100	5-3. Sponsor Functions And Empowerment
103	6-1. Bible Centered Material O.T./ N.T.
105	6-2. Bible Centered Leader Components Explained
107	7-1. Paul's Use of Conscience—Relating it To Leadership Issues
108	7-2. Paul's Use of Conscience—in Corinthians
112	8-1. Nine Mentoring Relationships in the Four Quadrants
117	10-1. Four Categories of Destiny Experiences
124	12-1: 11 Figures in the Bible Defined
125	12-2. 13 Patterned Idioms
126	12-3: 15 Body Language Idioms
127	12-4: 14 Miscellaneous Idioms
133	14-1. Categories of Lasting Legacies—13 Specific Types Identified
143	18-1. 10 Guidelines Underlying Paul's Thoughts on Giving
146	19-1. Early Shaping Processes Identified and Defined
147	19-2. Middle Ministry Shaping Processes—Identified and Defined
147	19-3. Latter Ministry Shaping Processes—Identified and Defined
15	20-1. Passages—Laying On Of Hands
153	21-1. Influence, Power, Authority Concepts Defined
158	22-1. Kinds of Integrity Checks
159	22-2. The Ways that God Uses Integrity Checks
162	23-1. Isolation Results
163	23-2. Common Happenings in Isolation
163	23-3. Job and Type I Isolation
164	23-4. Moses and Type II Isolation
164	23-5. Elijah's Type I Isolation Experience, 1Ki 17:1-6—Some Observations
165	23-6. Elijah's Type II Isolation Experience, 1Ki 19—Running For His Life
165	23-7. Nine Observations from Paul's Isolation Experiences
168	24-1. Nine Radical Macro Lessons Seen in Jesus Ministry
174	24-2. The Three Archetype Church Leaders and Philosophical Models
176	25-1. 5 Prayer Observations Seen in Habakkuk
181	26-1. How To Study a Leadership Act
182	26-2. Lessons Drawn from Joshua 3,4—Crossing the Jordan
185	27-1. Basic Questions To Ask About Leadership Eras
186	27-2. Six Leadership Eras in the Bible—Brief Characterizations
188	28-1. Typical Task-Oriented Leadership Functions
188	28-2. Typical Relational-Oriented Leadership Functions
189	28-3. Typical Inspirational Leadership Functions
191	29-1. Six Leadership Eras in the Bible
192	29-2. Seven Leadership Genre—Sources for Leadership Findings
199	31-1. Five Types of Leaders Described
205	32-1. Leadership Selection Concepts Illustrated
209	33-1. Examples of Biblical Leadership Transitions Providing Insights
209	33-2. Observations on the Moses/ Joshua Leadership Transition
213	34-1. When Each Component Was In Focus in Leadership Eras

List of Tables for the 1,2 Corinthian Leadership Articles

Page	Table
213	34-2. Elements of the Tree Diagram Described
216	35-1. Leadership Eras and Number of Macro Lessons
216	35-2. Top Three Macro Lessons in O.T. Leadership Eras
217	35-3. Top Three Macro Lessons in N.T. Leadership Eras
222	37-1. Nine Mentor Functions
222	37-2. Five Mentoring Dynamics
225	38-1. Pattern A—Early Ministry Entry
226	38-2. Pattern B—Ministry Assignment First Full Time Ministry
227	38-3. Pattern C—New Ministry Attempts
234	40-1. Motivational Factors for Paul's Ministry
236	41-1. Paul's Motivational Principles and Techniques
240	42-1. Paul's Life Purpose Unfolding
243	43-1. Paul's Companions—Reflected in His Epistles
258	46-1. Paul's Prayer Concerns for the Churches
261	47-1. Nine Mentor Functions
262	47-2. Mentor Functions of Paul With Timothy
263	47-3. Five Features About Paul's Mentoring
275	50-1. Pauline Terms for Leaders
281	51-1. Pauline Leadership Values Summarized—2 Corinthians
281	51-2. Pauline Leadership Values Summarized—1 Timothy
282	51-3. Pauline Leadership Values Summarized—2 Timothy
282	51-4. Pauline Leadership Values Summarized—1 Corinthians
282	51-5. Pauline Leadership Values Summarized—Philippians
283	51-6. Pauline Leadership Values Summarized—Philemon
289	54-1. Problems in the Corinthian Church
291	54-2. Problems in the Other Churches
295	55-1. God The Promise Keeper—Examples
299	57-1. Harville's Four Categories of Reciprocal Commands
300	57-2. Commands Bearing Upon Inter-Relationships
301	57-3. The Negative Commands
301	57-4. The Mutual Edification Commands
302	57-5. Mutual Service Commands
304	58-1. 4 Social Base Needs
304	58-2. Three Elements Involved In Singles Social Bases
305	58-3. Social Base Profiles—Three Major Ones for Marrieds
311	60-1. Six Characteristics of Spiritual Authority
315	62-1. Abstinence Disciplines Defined
316	62-2. Abstinence Disciplines—Some purposes
316	62-3. Abstinence Disciplines—Applicational Ideas
326	65-1. Spiritual Warfare—Satanic Tactics
333	68-1. 12 Steps For Doing Biographical Study
335	69-1. Paul and Intimate Relationships
339	70-1. Seven Characteristics of Union Life Modeled By Paul in Php
350	73-1 Functions Identified in Paul's Salutations
350	73-2 Foreshadowing Phrases
352	74-1. Paul's Sharing

List of Figures for the 1,2 Corinthian Leadership Articles

Page	Figure (In the Ebook version all these items are linked)
95	4-1. Venn Diagram--Apostolic Core
96	4-2. Venn Diagram--Apostolic Core Modified for Phase 2
96	4-3. Venn Diagram--Apostolic Core Modified for Phase 3
111	8-1. The Constellation Model
117	10-1. Destiny Continuum—A Pictorial Display of the Destiny Pattern
118	10-2. Joseph's Destiny Processing and Three-Fold Destiny Pattern
119	10-3. Moses' Destiny Processing and Three-Fold Destiny Pattern
120	10-4. Paul's Destiny Processing and Three-Fold Destiny Pattern
124	12-1. 11 Common Figures of Speech
146	19-1. Some Major Shaping Processes Across The Time-Line
152	21-1. Leadership Influence Components—(Adapted from Wrong)
162	23-1. Three Types of Isolations
162	23-2. Isolation Sovereignty Continuum
185	27-1. Tree Diagram Categorizing the Basics of Leadership
187	28-1. Three High Level Leadership Functions
199	31-1. Five Types of Leaders—Expanding Sphere of Influence
204	32-1. Leadership Selection Process Viewed Pictorially Over a Time-line
207	33-1. Leadership Transition Continuum
212	34-1. Display of Three High Level Generic Leadership Components
215	35-1. Leadership Truth Continuum/ Where Macro Lessons Occur
221	37-1. Three Training Modes
225	38-1. Three Types of Ministry Entry
239	42-1. Paul's Destiny Processing and Three-Fold Destiny Pattern
262	47-1. Paul's Mentor-Mix with Timothy
269	49-1. Influence Behavior Along a Continuum
286	53-1. The Certainty Continuum
315	62-1 Tree Diagram of Spiritual Disciplines
321	63-1. Power, Love And Word Gifts Pictured
322	63-2. Three Example of Corporate Mixes of Word, Power, Love
324	64-1. Giftedness Development Over Time
334	68-1. The Apostle Paul's Time-Lines

(This page is deliberately blank)

Introduction

This leadership commentary on 1,2 Corinthians is part of a series, **Clinton's Leadership Commentary Series.** For the past 14 years I have been researching leadership concepts in the Bible. As a result of that I have identified the 25 most helpful Bible books that contribute to an understanding of leadership. I have done fourteen of these commentaries to date and am continuing on the rest. I originally published eight of these leadership commentaries in a draft manuscript for use in classes. But it became clear that I would need to break that large work (735 pages) into smaller works. The commentary series does that. Titus was the first in the series. Haggai was the second of the series that is being done as an individual work. Habakkuk was the third. Jonah was the fourth. Nehemiah, was the fifth. 1,2 Corinthians will be the sixth.

This is a leadership commentary, not an exegetical commentary. That means I have worked with the text to see what implications of leadership it suggests.

A given commentary in the series is made up of an *Overview Section*, which seeks to analyze the book as a whole for historical background, plan, theme, and fit into the redemptive story of the Bible. In addition, I identify, up front, the basic leadership topics that are dealt with in the book. Then I educe leadership observations, guidelines, principles, and values for each of these leadership topics. This *Overview Section* primes the reader to look with leadership eyes.

Then I present the *Commentary Proper*. I use my own translation of the text. I give commentary on various aspects of the text. A given context, paragraph size, will usually have 3 to 4 comments dealing with some suggestions about leadership items.

The *Commentary Proper* suggests *Leadership Concepts* and connects you to leadership articles that further explain these leadership concepts. The emphasis on the comments is not exegetical though we do make those kinds of comments when they are helpful for my leadership purposes.

The *Leadership Articles* (in 1,2 Corinthians there are 74 totaling more than 265 pages) in the series carry much of what I have learned about leadership in my years of ministry. In one sense, these articles and others in the series are my legacy. I plan to publish all of the articles of the total series in a separate work, **Clinton's Encyclopedia of Biblical Leadership Insights,** which will be updated periodically as the series expands. A leader at almost any level of leadership can be helped greatly by getting leadership perspectives from these articles.

I also include a *Glossary* which lists all the leadership concepts labeled in the comments.

Introduction to 1,2 Corinthians

Other books in the series, to be released over the next five years, include:

1,2 Timothy--Apostolic Leadership Picking Up the Mantle;
Daniel--A Model Leader in Tough times;
Philemon--A Study in Leadership Style;
Philippians--A Study in Modeling;
John--Jesus' Incarnational Leadership.

All of the above were previously done in the large manuscript and used in classes. And they are available as the original single work on CD in PDF format. Now I will break these out as individual commentaries in the series. And then I will do other books anticipated in the series over the next five years. One of these will be,

Malachi—Renewal Lessons Needed to Face Nominality Head-On.

My long-term thinking includes developing the following:

Acts—Apostolic Leadership in Transition Times (a multi volume project)
Deuteronomy—A Study in Moses' Inspirational Leadership
Numbers—Moses, Spiritual Authority, and Maintenance Leadership
Mark—Jesus' Power Ministry
Joshua—Courageous Leadership
Mathew--A Study in Leadership Selection and Development
1,2 Samuel—Comparative Study of Leaders In An Emerging Kingdom

I have already done a study of each book in the Bible from a leadership standpoint and have identified and written up a number of leadership topics for each book. This analysis is captured in my book, **The Bible and Leadership Values**.

In an age of relativity, we believe the Bible speaks loudly concerning leadership concepts offering suggestions, guidelines, and even absolutes. We, as Christian leaders, desperately need this leadership help as we seek to influence our followers toward God's purposes for their lives.

J. Robert Clinton
Fall 2003

Preface

Every Scripture inspired of God is profitable for leadership insights (doctrine), pointing out of leadership errors (reproof), suggesting what to do about leadership errors (correction), and for highlighting how to model a righteous life (instruction in righteousness) in order that God's leader (Timothy) may be well equipped to lead God's people (the special good work given in the book Timothy to the young leader Timothy).
(2 Timothy 3:16,17—Clinton paraphrase—slanted toward Timothy's leadership situation)

The Bible--a Major Source of Leadership Values and Principles

No more wonderful source of leadership values and principles exists than the Bible. It is filled with influential people and the results of their influence—both good and bad. Yet it remains so little used to expose leadership values and principles. What is needed to break this *leadership barrier*? Three things:

1. A conviction that the Bible is authoritative and can give leadership insights
2. Leadership perspectives to stimulate our findings in the Bible—we are blind in general to leadership ideas and hence do not see them in the Bible.
3. A willful decision to study and use the Bible as a source of leadership insights

These three assumptions underlie the writing of this leadership commentary series. **1,2 Corinthians** is one of a series of books intended to help leaders cross the *leadership barrier*.

Leadership Framework

Perhaps it might be helpful to put the notion of leadership insights from 1,2 Corinthians in the bigger picture of leadership in the Bible. Three major leadership elements give us our most general framework (cross-culturally applicable as well) for categorizing leadership insights. The study of leadership involves:

1. **THE LEADERSHIP BASAL ELEMENTS** (The *What* of Leadership)
   a. leaders
   b. followers
   c. situations

   In 1,2 Corinthians we will see:
   a. leaders— like Paul, Barnabas, Sosthenes, Crispus, Gaius, Chloe, Cephas (Peter), Stephanas, Apollos, Fortunaus, Achaicus
   b. followers— The church at Corinth, as a whole, are the followers in this book; some individuals are actually mentioned by name; but the leadership influence of Paul was intended for the whole church
   c. situations— In 1,2 Corinthians we will see that Paul was addressing a whole series of problems; Paul sought to give wisdom as to how to solve

Preface

these problems: concerning wisdom, divisiveness, tolerance of immorality, lawsuits among believers, marriage and divorce issues, Christian behavior, worship practices, wrong perspectives on spiritual gifts, doctrinal issue about the resurrection, finances for Christian workers, undue influence by false apostolic leaders.

2. **LEADERSHIP INFLUENCE MEANS** (The *How* of Leadership)
   a. individual means—this concept involves identifying leadership styles of individual leaders influencing the situation.

In 1, 2 Corinthians we see that Paul uses several leadership styles in getting at these problems in the Corinthian church. . In 1Co I point out his Father-initiator style (4:14,15), his Apostolic leadership style (9:1,2), his confrontation style (1Co 5:1-5), his indirect conflict leadership style (1Co 5:1-4) and his imitator leadership style (1Co 4:16). In 2Co I point out maturity appeal (6:9,10), obligation persuasion (8:8), Father-initiator (2Co 10:14). Paul is a multi-style leader—a very modern concept in leadership style theory.

   b. corporate means—this refers to organizational structures or group pressures that influence followers in a corporate sense.

In 1 Co there are a number of groups, which are claiming to be followers of different leaders (Apollos, Paul, Peter, etc.). These groups are splitting the church. In 2 Co we see that a traveling group of "so-called apostles" are exerting powerful influence on the church seeking to get them to break away from Paul's influence.

3. **LEADERSHIP VALUE BASES** (The *Why* of Leadership)
   a. cultural
   b. theological

In 1,2 Co we will see several outward indications that flow from Corinthian values.
   a. We'll see Corinthian values underlying the aberrant views on wisdom and especially the tolerance of immorality.
   b. In 1 Co Paul has to clarify ecclesiology (the nature of what the church is), especially in regards to spiritual gifts. He does this also with regard to the doctrine of the resurrection. In both cases, Paul inserts theological values into the Corinthian situation. In 2 Co Paul gives context after context in which he explicitly identifies personal values he has regarding ministry. I identify 19 of these.

It is through using these major leadership elements that we are able to analyze leadership throughout the whole Bible. Using these major notions we recognize that leadership, at different time periods in the Bible, operates sufficiently different so as to suggest leadership eras—that is, time periods within which leadership follows more closely certain commonalities than in the time preceding it and following it. This allows us to identify six such eras in the Bible.

Preface

Six Bible Leadership Eras

The six leadership eras include,

1. **Patriarchal Era**

2. **Pre-Kingdom Era**
   A. Desert Years
   B. The War Years
   C. The Tribal Years

3. **Kingdom Era**
   A. United Kingdom
   B. Divided Kingdom
   C. Southern Kingdom

4. **Post-Kingdom Era**
   A. Exilic
   B. A Foothold Back in the Land

5. **Pre-Church Era**

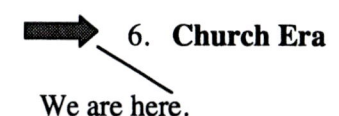

6. **Church Era**

We are here.

For each of these major eras we are dealing with some fundamental leadership questions.[1] We ask ourselves these major questions about every leadership era. Usually the answers are sufficiently diverse as to justify identification of a unique leadership era.

Where does 1,2 Corinthians fit?

The books of 1,2 fits in the sixth leadership era, *The Church Era*. It is a pioneering time in which the Gospel is spreading to the Gentile world. Churches have been started in about 5 separate city/town locations in Asia minor, and Greece. The churches are new. Leadership is in its infancy. Ecclesiology is not yet very well defined. It is a time of great challenges for Paul.

What do 1,2 Corinthians say?

Before we can look at leadership insights from 1,2 Corinthians we need to be sure that we understand why they are in the Scriptures and what they are saying in general. Having done our homework, hermeneutically speaking, we are free then to go beyond

---

[1] The six questions we use to help us differentiate between leadership eras includes: 1. What is the major leadership focus? 2. What are the influence means used? 3. What are the basic leadership functions? 4. What are the characteristics of the followers? 5. What was the existing cultural forms of leadership? 6. Other? I comment on each of these in the **Clinton's Encyclopedia of Biblical Leadership Insights**.

Preface

and look for other interpretative insights—such as leadership insights. But we must remember, always, first of all to interpret in light of the historical times, purposes of, theme of, and structure of the each of these epistles. Lets look at 1 Co first in terms of Paul's organization of the book and his thematic intent and hoped for purposes. Then we will do the same three items for 2 Co.

One way of analyzing the structure, that is, the way that Paul organizes his material to accomplish his purposes, in 1 Co would be:

Structure

I.	(Ch 1,2)	Problem About Wisdom
II.	(Ch 3,4)	Problem About Divisions
III.	(Ch 5)	Problem on Toleration of Immorality
IV.	(Ch 6)	Problem of Lawsuits Among Believers
V.	(Ch 7)	Problems About Marriage
VI.	(Ch 8-10)	Problem on Disputed Practices
VII.	(Ch 11)	Problem on Worship Practices
VIII.	(Ch 12-14)	Problems About Spiritual Gifts
IX.	(Ch 15)	Problem About Resurrection
X.	(Ch 16)	Problem About Supporting Christian Workers

The overall thematic intent could be represented by a subject, which permeates all of what God is doing through the book of 1 Co and several ideas about that subject. Here is my analysis of such a theme.

Theme **Church Problems, in Corinth,**
- involve multiple/ complex issues: problem about wisdom; problem about divisions; problem on toleration of immorality; problem of lawsuits among believers; problems about marriage; problem on disputed practices; problem on worship practices; problems about spiritual gifts; problem about resurrection; problems in supporting Christian workers.
- were dealt with by Paul in highly directive leadership styles, and
- are seen as solvable if people respond to God's revelation about them.

Purpose
It is always difficult to synthesize statements of purpose when the author does not directly and **explicitly** give them. But it seems reasonable to imply that the following are some of the purposes of 1 Co:

- to answer the questions posed about the many problems arising in the Corinthian church,
- to defend Paul's apostolic conduct,
- to demonstrate how leadership confronts and resolves problems in the church,
- to show that belief and conduct are both important in the life of the church,

Preface

- to stress the interaction between a church and its culture and thus highlight the need for the church to impact its surrounding environment or else be impacted by it.

One way of analyzing the structure, that is, the way that Paul organizes his material to accomplish his purposes, in 2 Co would be:

Structure
    I. (Ch 1-7)   Paul's Apostolic Ministry and Motives
    II. (Ch 8,9)   Paul's Financial Appeal to the Corinthians
    III. (Ch 10-12)   Paul's Defense of His Authority

Again, the overall thematic intent could be represented by a subject, which permeates all of what God is doing through the book of 2 Co and several ideas about that subject. Here is my analysis of such a theme.

Theme   **PAUL'S APOSTOLIC DEFENSE,**
- involved an explanation of his personal conduct, motives, and view of the ministry,
- was in harmony with his plea for the Jerusalem gift, and
- concluded with an overwhelming refutation of arguments opposing his Apostolic authority.

It is likely that some of the following were certainly the purposes of this letter.

Purposes
- to correct the over correction the Corinthians had made in regards to the immorality problem mentioned in the 1st letter,
- to explain his motives and ministry among the Corinthians so as to correct misrepresentations being circulated about him,
- to establish his spiritual authority among them,
- to give further instruction about the offering,
- to bring to light ministry values that ought to undergird a leader.

Having done our overview of the book, hermeneutically speaking, we can now focus on leadership issues seen in 1, 2 Co.

Approach To 1,2 Corinthians In Perspective

With this background in mind, we can now proceed to the leadership commentary including its *General Reflection*, *Leadership Lessons*, *Commentary Notes*, *Articles*, and *Glossary*.

Today, we live in the Church Leadership Era.[1] It is not difficult to place ourselves back hundreds of years into the 6th leadership era—Church Leadership. Though quite removed from us in time and certainly culturally, we can still identify with Paul and his church planting ministry. Most of us have studied well the New Testament. We are relatively familiar with the Acts and the Pauline epistles. So then, when Paul deals with church problems, such as the problems in Corinth, we are eager to learn about the problems. We want to see how Paul dealt with them. We want to learn about his solutions. For we live in the church leadership era. We will be facing these exact same problems or some similar to them. Paul will model for us both how to deal with church problems and actually give us some answers—at least when we are dealing with the same problems. Understanding Paul's apostolic ministry with this problematic church at Corinth is a must for present day leaders.

Suggested Approach for Studying The 1,2 Corinthian Leadership Commentary

Read through the overview to get a general feeling for what 1 Corinthians is about. Note particularly the *Theme* of the book and its *Plan* for developing that theme, i.e., the outline for developing that theme. Then note the various purposes I suggest that the books of 1 Corinthians is seeking to accomplish. Then read through each of the leadership topics that I suggest are in 1 Corinthians. This is all preparation for the first reading of the text.

Read the text of 1 Corinthians, preferably at one sitting, without referring to any of the commentary notes. Just see if you can *see what of the overview information* and the *leadership lessons* are suggested to you as you read the text.

Then reread the text, probably a chapter at a time and note the comments I give.[2] From time-to-time, go back and read a leadership lesson again when it is brought to your mind as you read the text and the commentary. Also feel free to stop and go to the **Glossary** for explanation of leadership terms suggested by the commentary. And do the same thing with the **Articles**. The articles capture what I have learned about leadership over the years as I have observed it, researched it, and taught it. It is these articles that will enlighten your leadership understanding. Obviously because of the uniqueness of the

---

[1] See **Article**, *27. Leadership Eras In The Bible— Six Identified;* This is probably an important prerequisite for you before approaching the commentary.

[2] From time-to-time in the comments, we will use the abbreviation SRN. SRN stands for Strong's Reference Number. Strong, in his exhaustive concordance, labeled each word in the Old Testament (dominantly Hebrew words but also some Aramaic/Chaldean) and New Testament (Greek words mostly) with an identifying number. He then constructed an Old Testament and New Testament lexicon (dictionary). If you have a **Strong's Exhaustive Concordance** with lexicon, you can look up the words we refer to. Many modern day reference works (lexicons and word studies and Bible Dictionaries and encyclopedias) use this Strong's Reference Number.

Approach To 1,2 Corinthians In Perspective   page 2

book, dealing primarily with apostolic problem solving dealing with a local church ministry, there will be some hopefully helpful leadership articles.

After finishing your whole study on 1 Corinthians then move on to 2 Corinthians and repeat the same procedure described above. You, like Paul, will be thrilled that the Corinthians responded to Paul's advice in his first epistle, at least somewhat. And 2 Corinthians puts further demands on them as Paul defends his spiritual authority and right to influence the Corinthian church.

Further Study

I have provided some *note space* at the conclusion of the textual comments, for both books, where you can jot down ideas for future study. Have fun as you work through 1,2 Corinthians, and by all means learn something about *apostolic problem solving*. Let these two books inspire your own problem solving as you minister for God during this church leadership era. And also learn the important lesson of learning vicariously by studying other leaders' lives.[3] Paul is exemplary in his modeling for church leaders. It was deliberate. And it was impactful then and can be impactful now.

The overview follows. It gives a summarized version of the hermeneutical background studies for 1 Corinthians. Later I will repeat the same thing for 2 Corinthians.

---

[3] The old adage, *experience is the best teacher* is true, **if you learn from it**. Personal experience is a great way to learn. But in terms of leadership, you will never have enough time to learn, *by personal experience alone*, all you need to know for your leadership. I suppose that is why God gave us the leadership mandate—Hebrews 13:7,8. He emphatically reminds us that vicarious learning is crucial for our leadership. And we have three whole books (Job, Habakkuk, Jonah) in the Bible devoted exclusively to illustrating God's shaping of leaders. And that is their main purpose for being in the Bible. Paul's leadership is in view throughout the church leadership era. We can learn leadership practices vicariously from his model.

Overview of First Corinthians   page 3

BOOK	**1 CORINTHIANS**		**Author: Paul**
Characters	People mentioned or involved: Paul, Sosthenes, Crispus, Gaius, Chloe, Cephas (Peter), Stephanas, Apollos, Fortunatus, Achaicus		
Who To/For	The young church at Corinth		
Literature Type	A letter containing teaching and exhortation		
Story Line	Paul got wind that the church at Corinth was having many problems[4] including improper view of wisdom, divisions, immorality, lawsuits, disputes over marriage and its dissolution, disputes over certain practices, impropriety in worship, misunderstanding and improper stress of certain spiritual gifts, an incorrect doctrinal view of the resurrection. He wrote to correct perspective on these various issues.		
Structure	I.	(Ch 1,2)	**Problem About Wisdom**
	II.	(Ch 3,4)	**Problem About Divisions**
	III.	(Ch 5)	**Problem on Toleration of Immorality**
	IV.	(Ch 6)	**Problem of Lawsuits Among Believers**
	V.	(Ch 7)	**Problems About Marriage**
	VI.	(Ch 8-10)	**Problem on Disputed Practices**
	VII.	(Ch 11)	**Problem on Worship Practices**
	VIII.	(Ch 12-14)	**Problems About Spiritual Gifts**
	IX.	(Ch 15)	**Problem About Resurrection**
	X.	(Ch 16)	**Problem About Supporting Christian Workers**

---

[4] A look at the following structure shows the number of problems Paul was dealing with. See **LEADERSHIP TOPIC 1. COMPLEXITY OF LEADERSHIP.**

Overview of First Corinthians page 4

Theme **Church Problems, in Corinth,**
- involve multiple/ complex issues: problem about wisdom; problem about divisions; problem on toleration of immorality; problem of lawsuits among believers; problems about marriage; problem on disputed practices; problem on worship practices; problems about spiritual gifts; problem about resurrection; problems in supporting Christian workers.
- were dealt with by Paul in highly directive leadership styles, and
- are seen as solvable if people respond to God's revelation about them.

Key Words grace (10); emphasis carried by repeated diverse problems not so much by actual repeated words though there are repeated words within treatment of a problem

Key Events none

Purposes
- to answer the questions posed about the many problems arising in the Corinthian church,
- to defend Paul's apostolic conduct,
- to demonstrate how leadership confronts and resolves problems in the church,
- to show that belief and conduct are both important in the life of the church,
- to stress the interaction between a church and its culture and thus highlight the need for the church to impact its surrounding environment or else be impacted by it.

Why Important

This is an urban book full of great warnings for our modern church today. Churches, which fail to impact their surrounding areas, are usually impacted by them. And because this is so, such churches will be problematic churches. And most of the leadership effort will be spent on correcting the church rather than carrying out the task of the church to those around. The Corinthian church illustrates this and is a warning to others.

Many of the problems in the Corinthian church were problems in the society: religious license, moral laxity, social disorder. Morgan (**Handbook for Preachers and Bible Teachers** page 210, see **For Further Study Bibliography**) points out two central truths of this letter. (1) A church ,which fails to fulfill her task in the city, will be invaded by the spirit of the city. Such a thing happens when a church is not what it ought to be, that is, is untrue to her essential nature of being and developing toward the potential God intended. (2) The secret of an effective church lies in its progress toward realization of its life in Christ. It is an interdependent body, united in one Spirit and under the organizing influence of that Spirit. That same Spirit gives gifts individually to members of that church that the church as a whole may fulfill its task of bringing glory to God.

The book of 1 Corinthians also points out one of the major functions of leadership—problem solving. It shows how an apostolic leader deals with problems in local churches. It also gives teaching on each of the problems—some of which we would

Overview of First Corinthians page 5

not get anywhere else in the Scriptures. But apart from this direct teaching there is this indirect and powerful overtone of the book, which is essentially then one of the major lessons of the Corinthian letter—the church is responsible for the religious life of the city, for the moral standards of the city, and for the social life of the city. And the church will only be as strong as its leaders.

Where It Fits

This is one of the earlier of Paul's epistles, written probably on his Third Missionary Journey--perhaps in the spring of 57 A.D. In the drama of redemption framework:

      Introduction—Genesis 1-11
      Chapter 1. The Making of A Nation
      Chapter 2. The Destruction of a Nation
      Chapter 3. Messiah
--->   **Chapter 4. The Church**
      Chapter 5. Kingdom

1Co occurs in Chapter 4, The Church.

In terms of the leadership era framework:

      1. Patriarchal Leadership Era
      2. Pre-Kingdom Leadership Era
      3. Kingdom Leadership Era
      4. Post-Kingdom Leadership Era
      5. Pre-Church Leadership Era
--->   **6. Church Leadership Era**

1Co occurs in the sixth era, the Church Leadership Era. It is one of the most helpful books in dealing with important lessons for N.T. Church leadership since it shows a mature apostolic leader dealing with a series of problems in the church. Both the answers given and the process of dealing with the problems are very instructive for church leaders today

General Reflections On First Corinthians

The church leadership era is dominated by Paul's leadership. His finest hour as an apostolic church leader occurred with the crisis at Corinth. Paul had been a Christian leader about 21 or so years. He was probably in his early 50s. He was a mature leader. His whole ministry was threatened by this crisis at Corinth. If this crisis could not be solved he would be discredited and his ministry as we now know it would never have happened. He would be finished.

Someone has said, "What we are in a crisis is what we really are!" The Good News Bible translates Proverbs 24:10 as, "If you are weak in a crisis, you are weak indeed." Well, Paul proved strong. In fact, this was his finest hour, except perhaps for his great finish seen in 2Ti.

Paul's solutions to the many problems, especially his own leadership crises, stand as models for how to approach problems faced in church leadership. The two epistles written to the Corinthian church are filled with leadership insights. The first epistle is structured around his apostolic advice concerning some major problems: divisions in the church, epistemology and over emphasis on secular wisdom, immorality in the church, lawsuits among believers, marriage issues, Christian practice/ legalistic tendencies, irregularities in worship, improper priorities on certain spiritual gifts/ gift projection and their abuse in services, teaching about the resurrection, failure to support Christian workers. Paul's letter not only gives answers about these issues (content/ Principles/ values/ processes) but also demonstrates for us how to solve these and the many other problems we will face as leaders in the church.

Paul is under great pressure—physical problems, burdens for the churches he related to, his own reputation at stake, his life purpose and achievements on the line. And he comes through with flying colors. Read these lessons and realize you are getting the best from the best. Paul, a mature Christian leader under pressure, is modeling for us and teaching us, as well as solving some first century problems. Without doubt we can claim the principle of 2Ti 3:16,17 for these two epistles to the Corinthians.

Every Scripture (1,2 Corinthians) inspired of God is profitable for
- leadership insights (doctrine),
- pointing out of leadership errors (reproof),
- suggesting what to do about leadership errors (correction),
- for highlighting how to model a righteous life (instruction in righteousness)

in order that God's leaders (us) may be well equipped to lead God's people.   (Clinton paraphrase—slanted toward any leadership situation)

1 Corinthians—Leadership Lessons/Topics

1. COMPLEXITY OF LEADERSHIP (Complexity Macro Lesson)

A major macro lesson occurring across all the leadership eras can be simply stated as: *Leadership is complex, problematic, difficult and fraught with risk—which is why leadership is needed.* Leadership is complex. Paul deals with a whole range of problems including moral issues, philosophical issues, practical everyday issues, theological issues, conceptual issues, methodological issues. Problems in a situation are a main reason for the existence of leaders. Leaders must see problems not as hindrances to leadership but as the warp and woof of leadership responsibility. Problems actually can become challenges to those who can carry a positive attitude. It is in the midst of problem solving that much creative thinking emerges. Problem solving is one of the major functions of Apostolic Ministry. This notion of Apostolic Ministry is discussed more in detail in the 2nd Corinthians Leadership Lessons. But do note that Paul identifies himself as an Apostle in both salutations—1st Co and 2nd Co. See **Articles**, *35. Macro Lesson Defined; 36. Macro Lessons—List of 41 Across Six Leadership Eras; 4. Apostolic Giftedness— Multiple Gifted Leaders; 2. Apostolic Functions; 3. Apostolic Functions—Comparison of Titus and Timothy; 73. Variations on His Theme, Paul's Salutaions...*

Leadership Principles/ Values Suggested by this concept:
a. Problems are opportunities for creative leadership to take place.
b. Problems are part of the responsibility of leaders. They come with the territory. If you are a leader you must expect to constantly deal with problems.
c. Apostolic leaders must be problem solvers since major problems occur in all three phases of apostolic ministry. The Corinthian church is dominantly a phase two Apostolic Ministry situation; but on its way to phase 3.

2. GIFTEDNESS (1Co 12-14 and other passages).

Leadership has much to do with giftedness. Both personally and corporately, giftedness is important. This book shows that leaders need to know the doctrine of giftedness and especially the sub-set of spiritual gifts thoroughly. Ministry problems will arise because of misunderstandings on giftedness. Leaders must deal with these problems in a balanced way.

This book should be studied in depth for its contribution to teaching on giftedness. There are references to giftedness throughout the book, not just chapters 12-14. The topic of giftedness is much broader than 1Co. There are some 24 or so lists in the Scripture referring to gifts—eight major passages and 16 minor passages. A major passage refers to any context in the New Testament epistles in which two or more gifts are listed either specifically or by a generic label and/or the passages deals with the use or abuse of a gift or gifts. Of the eight major gifts lists in the N.T., six occur in 1Co: 12:8-10; 12:28; 13:1-3; 13:8; 14:6; 14:26,27. Perspective on gifts only comes when all the passages are brought together and looked at from a leadership perspective. Detailed specific lessons on giftedness are left for comparative treatment.

This topic is particularly important when a leader begins to think of deliberate development in his/her own life or in the life of emerging leaders. The first Corinthians gifts passage 12:8-10 emphasizes come-and-go i.e. *non-vested gifts*. See **Glossary**. The second list and others which follow also emphasize permanent gifts. It shows that when the body gathers, the Holy Spirit imparts gifts as are needed. See **Article**, *63. Spiritual Gift Clusters; 64. Spiritual Gifts, Giftedness and Development.*

Leadership Observations/ Principles/ Values Suggested by this concept:
   a. The topic of spiritual gifts must be studied comparatively across the many passages on them in the Scriptures. None were given to teach comprehensively on gifts. All were given in a context of some special need or problem being dealt with.[5]
   b. Gifts are dominantly given for corporate use in the body or for extending the ministry of that body into the world.
   c. Gifts cannot be ignored simply because they are problematic. It is leadership's responsibility to correct abuses. To ignore or legislate away gifts because they are problematic is to introduce new problems in the church.
   d. The test of true spirituality involves submission to the lordship of Christ, not the possession of gifts.
   e. All gifts are important because they come as a direct result of the Holy Spirit's sovereign ministry.
   f. All gifts are important because of the interdependent nature of the church.
   g. Gifts, operating harmoniously together, each contributing its function, should have as its purpose the edification of the church as a whole.
   h. The possession of no single gift is a test of one's spiritual maturity. Not all church members can be expected to have any one particular gift.
   i. There should be no spiritual pride associated with having any gifts, even though the leadership gifts are prioritized as the top gifts.
   j. The proper attitude behind exercising gifts is that of love and is essentially more important than the gifts or results of exercising those gifts.
   k. Love is an enduring quality and will last into eternity—gifts will be used in time.
   l. The relative value of spiritual gifts is to be tested by their usefulness to the church as a whole (Paul contrasts prophecy and tongues in chapter 14 to illustrating this).
   m. Orderliness in public worship is consistent with the way God does things.

3. STEWARDSHIP MODEL (4:1-5).

One of the important N.T. philosophical leadership models is the stewardship model. The model is given in the Gospels, particularly in the stewardship parables. Paul amplifies and affirms that model in 1Co. Leaders who operate with a stewardship model must see themselves as servants of Christ, and as those entrusted with God-given resources. See **Articles**, *24. Jesus' Five Leadership Models: Shepherd, Harvest, Steward,*

---

[5] I researched the topic of spiritual gifts from a Biblical analysis viewpoint from the years 1968-1975. I returned to this analysis in 1985. I produced a book called **Spiritual Gifts**. From 1983-1993 I studied the topic empirically—studying contemporary cases of leaders and discovering how they developed in terms of giftedness. The Biblical findings of **Spiritual Gifts**, and the results of the 10 years of empirical studies were enfolded in a book, **Unlocking Your Giftedness**. In that work I do the detailed comparative study referred to. I identified all the major passages and minor passages dealing with gifts. I drew out findings. The sub-title of the book, somewhat boldly, captures the thrust of this work—*What Leaders Need to Know to Develop Themselves and Others.*

Servant, Intercessor; 1. Accountability—Standing Before God As a Leader; 11. Entrustment—A Leadership Responsibility.

Leadership Principles/ Values Suggested by this concept:
a. A leader leads first of all by serving Christ. A leader leads by serving and serves by leading. It is a dynamic balance.
b. A leader should see his/her leadership as a responsibility given by God.
c. The prime trait of a leader with respect to the stewardship model is faithfulness to God to operate that entrustment and develop it for God.

4. LEADERSHIP STYLES.

When dealing with problems leaders often have to come down with directive or highly directive leadership styles. Paul does so here using a *father-initiator style* (4:14,15). This style is related to the *apostolic leadership style*. This style uses the fact that the leader founded the work as a lever for getting acceptance of influence by the leader. Paul also uses the *apostolic style* (9:1,2), which is described as a method of influence in which the leader assumes the role of delegated authority over followers, receives revelation from God concerning decisions, and commands obedience based on this delegated role and revealed truth. One of the most important leadership styles illustrated in this book is the *confrontation style*—another highly directive leadership style. The *confrontation style* is an approach to problem-solving which brings the problem out in the open with all parties concerned, which analyzes the problem in light of revelation, and which brings force to bear upon the parties to accept recommended solutions. Since this book is filled with problems there are many instances of this leadership style. Note that all three of the highly directive leadership styles are used. This is often the case when a leader is faced with many problems or crises in a church and the followership is not very mature. Two other leadership styles are seen in the book: the *indirect conflict leadership style* (1Co 5:1-4); the *imitator leadership style* (1Co 4:16). See **Glossary** for leadership styles. See **Article, 49. *Pauline Leadership Styles***. See also my booklet, **Coming To Conclusions on Leadership Styles** listed in the Bibliography.

Leadership Principles/ Values Suggested by this concept:
a. Leaders must vary their leadership styles according to situation, personal ability, and follower maturity.
b. Problematic situations will frequently need highly directive leadership styles such as *father-initiator*, *apostolic*, *confrontation* in order to solve them and bring about unity and purpose in a situation.
c. Sometimes the *indirect conflict* style must be used first, before anything else can happen.
d. The *imitation style* is a modeling style. We use this whether or not we want to. Paul goes a step further; he deliberately and proactively uses it as a means of influence.

5. SERVANT LEADERSHIP.

Another of the N.T. Philosophical Leadership models is the servant leadership model. Christ introduced this model and practiced it in the Gospels and carefully announced that it contained one of the distinguishing leadership qualities between Christian leadership and secular leadership. *Leaders lead by serving and leaders serve by leading.* One of the strong testimonies to this dynamic balance and tension is given by Paul in the 1Co 9. Here Paul shows that he gives up his rights as a strong leader in order to serve those being led. Yet he does so with strong leadership exerted. See **Article**, *24. Jesus' Five Leadership Models: Shepherd, Harvest, Steward, Servant, Intercessor.*

Leadership Principles/ Values Suggested by this concept:
  a. Leadership must be exercised primarily as service first of all to God and secondarily as service to God's people.
  b. Service does not mean abrogating leadership. Leaders must lead. But they do so with a servant heart.
  c. Service should require sacrifice on the leader's part.

6. PERSONAL DISCIPLINE. (9:24-27)

Paul advocates discipline in a leader's life in order that a leader may finish well. Few leaders finish well. One enhancement to finishing well includes spiritual disciplines and other disciplines. Paul here shows that these will be needed throughout one's leadership. At the time of this book, Paul is about 50+ years of age. Discipline is still needed. One of the disciplines needed is that of Bible study. In the very next chapter, Paul gives one of the more important reasons for Bible study of the O.T. It is to derive lessons and values which will enable us to be better leaders. Paul advocates discipline in the body as a whole in order to purify it (ch 5). See **Article**, *13. Finishing Well—Five Factors Enhancing It; 62. Spiritual Disciplines—And On-Going Leadership.*

Leadership Principles/ Values Suggested by this concept:
  a. Leaders who finish well must maintain disciplines during the stressful middle stages of leadership in order to continue well.
  b. Bible study and prayer are major disciplines that leaders should maintain, especially in the plateauing years (ages 40-60).

7. STRUCTURE.

Paul, in his explanation of giftedness in the local church, helps leaders understand the structure of the local church. It is an interrelated group of people with diverse gifts, which serve to complement each other. Further, Paul shows that orderliness is compatible with the ministry of the Holy Spirit through this structure. These people meet and exercise their gifts with one another. They worship. They communicate truth to each other. The church also met in small house group clusters. One could see how there could be divisions along the lines of different house church leaders—a problem which arose.

Leadership Principles/ Values Suggested by this concept:
  a. Structure is secondary to ministry.
  b. The body as a whole is capable of solving problems. This epistle is not written specifically to leaders but to the church as a whole.
  c. In the early stages of the development of a church or organization, structure is usually very flexible. It becomes less flexible with time.

1 Corinthians 1:1,2

Note:
For longer Bible books, like 1 Corinthians, I will not print all the Bible text but only those passages, which have leadership comments. However, when I omit Scripture I will indicate the length of text left out and give contextual statements for the omitted verses.

I. (Ch 1- 2) Problem About Wisdom[1]
Chapter 1
1 Paul,[2] called as an apostle of Jesus Christ as God[3] willed it, and Sosthenes,[4] our brother, 2 To the

---

[1] This is Problem #1 of 10 problems that Paul has to deal with in the Corinthian situation. And some of the 10 have multiple issues—problems within problems. This repetitive dealing with various problems highlights the complexity macro lesson, **Macro Lesson 41:** *Leadership is complex, problematic, difficult and fraught with risk—which is why leadership is needed.* The many problems also allow us to see Paul's leadership style, *confrontation*, which he uses often in 1,2 Co. See **LEADERSHIP TOPIC 1. COMPLEXITY OF LEADERSHIP; LEADERSHIP TOPIC 4. LEADERSHIP STYLES.** See *confrontation style*, **Glossary.** See **Articles**, *35. Macro Lessons Defined; 36. Macro Lessons—List of 41 Across Six Leadership Eras.* See *49. Pauline Leadership Styles.*

[2] Paul wrote 13 epistles. See **Article,** *68. Time-Lines—Defined for Biblical Leaders.* Verses 1-3 form the salutation proper. Verses 4-9 form the salutation extension. Paul is foreshadowing in the salutation and salutation extension some important things (problems) he will be dealing with in the epistle. See *salutation, salutation extension,* **Glossary.** See **Article,** *73. Variation on His Theme, Paul's Salutations— Harbingers of His Epistles.*

[3] Paul had a strong sense of appointment to ministry from God. Paul needs apostolic authority if he is to clean up the messes in this Corinthian church. Straight away he claims this authoritative backing. This conviction is part of his sense of destiny. 2Co in general and 2Co 10-12 in particular are dealing with Paul's apostolic authority. Value 1 is in focus here—*Value 1: Divine Appointment. Leaders ought to be sure that God appointed them to ministry situations.* The Corinthian church is in a Phase II Apostolic ministry situation. See also 15:8-11 and Paul's salutations : Ro 1:1; 1Co 1:1; 2Co 1:1; Gal 1:1; Eph 1:1; Col 1:1; 1 Ti 1:1; 2 Ti 1:1; Tit 1:1. See *leadership value, spiritual authority, apostolic ministry—phase I, apostolic ministry— phase II, apostolic ministry— phase III,* **Glossary.** See also **Articles,** *42. Paul—A Sense of Destiny; 2. Apostolic Functions; 3. Apostolic Functions—Comparison of Titus and Timothy; Apostolic Giftedness; 4. Apostolic Giftedness—Multiple Gifted Leaders; 51. Pauline Leadership Values.*

[4] Sosthenes' name occurs twice, here as a co-author and in Acts 18:17. In the Acts reference we learn he was the chief ruler of the synagogue. In an unusual turn of events, he was beaten by a Gentile mob instead of Paul, the intended victim. In this reference we learn that he, formerly a Jewish religious leader, became a Christian leader, a fellow missionary with Paul. He would certainly have credibility with the Corinthian church people. Paul probably is not so much sponsoring him here (like he does Timothy and Silas in other salutations). But here he is using Sosthenes' name to lend credibility to his own letter. See **Article,** *43. Paul and His Companions.*

1 Corinthians 1:3-8

church of God which is at Corinth,[5] to those who are especially set apart in union with Christ Jesus, to live holy lives, with all who in every place call on the name of Jesus Christ our Lord, and theirs too. 3 Grace to you and peace from God our Father and the Lord Jesus Christ.

4 I am always thanking my God for you.[6] I am especially thankful for the grace[7] of God which was given to you by Christ Jesus. 5 I'm thankful also because you were enriched[8] in everything by Him in all utterance and all knowledge.[9] 6 Christ's testimony was confirmed in you with the result 7 that you are not lacking any spiritual gift. You have what you need as you eagerly wait for the second coming of our Lord Jesus Christ.[10] 8 He will also will keep you firm to the end—without fault in the day of our Lord Jesus

---

[5] Compare with what Paul calls other churches—usually location orientation only. See salutations for Pauline epistles. Paul, even in his salutations, often begins to deal with the issues at hand. Here he uses this special title to show that the work in Corinth is God's, not belonging to any of the popular charismatic leaders who are causing divisions and leading various groups astray. See ch 3 where this problem is dealt with directly. This is a motivational technique. See *change dynamics principle—getting it on the agenda*, **Glossary**. See **Article**, *73. Variations on His Theme: Paul's Salutations—Harbingers of His Epistles*.

[6] Paul illustrates a macro lesson on prayer first seen in Abraham's ministry (*Patriarchal Leadership Era*) in Moses' and Samuel's ministry (*Pre-kingdom Leadership Era*—see 1 Sam 12:23). This macro lesson— *Leaders called to a ministry are called to intercede for that ministry*—occurs in all six leadership eras. See: Ro 1:8-10; 1Co 1:4; Eph 1:15-20, 3:14-21; Col 1:3, 1:9-14; 2:1; 1 Th 1:3, 2:13; 2 Th 1:3, 11-13; 2:13. See *leadership era, prayer ministry principle*, **Glossary**. See **Articles**, *35. Macro Lessons Defined; 27. Leadership Eras in the Bible—Six Identified*.

[7] Note, Paul does not give thanks directly for gifts, a problem with this church, but for grace—probably a *metonymy*, a figure of speech in which one word is substituted for another to which it is related. Grace would emphasize gifts freely given by God. See *metonymy, grace*, **Glossary**. See **Article**, *12. Figures and Idioms in the Bible*.

[8] *Enriched* (SRN 4148) carries the sense of ample resources. Its verb action, once in time with on-going results, suggests the Corinthians need not be seeking new things (like tongues) to be fuller Christians, but that they already have everything in Christ.

[9] Note *enriched, utterance* and *knowledge*. Paul uses the *get-it-on-the agenda motivational technique* again. He is dealing with a philosophical problem. They want esoteric wisdom. They also have an overemphasis on tongues as a spiritual gift. He will later deal with these directly (ch 1, 2 for wisdom and ch 12-14 tongues). In effect this *seeking after things to fulfill some driven need* is a seed form of the Gnostic heresy occurring later in Colosse, Ephesus, and more fully in the church near the end of the first century. See *change dynamics principle, getting-it-on-the-agenda principle*, **Glossary**.

[10] See *Second Coming* as a motivating factor—especially in 2Ti 4:7,8.

1 Corinthians 1:9-15 page 13

Christ.[11] 9 God is faithful. He called you to have fellowship with His Son, Jesus Christ our Lord.[12]

10 Now I plead with you, fellow Christians, by the authority of our Lord Jesus Christ: agree in what you say so that there will be no divisions among you. Be one in your thinking and in your purpose.[13] 11 For I have heard quite plainly from some of Chloe's family, that there are quarrels among you. 12 Now here is what I hear you saying. "I follow Paul," or "I follow Apollos,"[14] or "I follow Peter,"[15] or "I follow Christ." 13 Is Christ divided? Was Paul crucified for you? Or were you baptized in the name of Paul?[16]

14 I thank God that I baptized none of you except Crispus[17] and Gaius,[18] 15 lest anyone should say

---

[11] The phrase *Day of Christ* or equivalent occurs six times (Php 1:6,10; 2:16; 2Th 2:2; 2Co 1:14 and here with slight variation). It is synonymous in Paul's thoughts with *Day of the Lord* and like phrases used nine times in 1,2Th). Paul implies a future day of accounting both for himself as a leader and for these Corinthian folks. This is a strong Pauline leadership value. *Leaders will ultimately give an account for their ministries.* See also Php 2:16 for a stronger indication. There Paul uses this fact to influence the Philippian followers as he exhorts them to live out the Christian life in an attractive manner. He deals with this issue more strongly in 2Co 5. See also: 1Co 3:13; 5:5; Php 1:6,10; 2:16; 2Co 5:10; 2Th 2:2. See also Heb 13:17. See *Day of the Lord, Leadership Value*, **Glossary**. See **Articles**, *40. Motivating Factors For Ministry; 41. Motivating Principles: Pauline Influence; 9. Day of Christ—Implications for Leadership.*

[12] This sub-context, verses 4-9, illustrates an important leadership function. Leaders, at higher levels of leadership must provide three kinds of leadership: task oriented leadership, relational oriented leadership, and inspirational oriented leadership. One way of inspiring is to motivate toward a hope in the future. Paul does this here and throughout his epistles. See also Jesus' inspirational leadership, Jn 13-17. See *task oriented leadership, relational oriented leadership, inspirational leadership*, **Glossary**. See **Article**, *28. Leadership Functions—3 High Level Priorities.*

[13] See Eph 4:1ff for comprehensive treatment of unity in the body. See Also 1Co 12, the body metaphor.

[14] It is interesting to note that Apollos was a strong leader (see 1Co 16:12). He seemed to be somewhat independent from Paul. Note also he is still running strong in the Christian race toward the end of Paul's life (Tit 3:13). See also Ac 18:24; 19:1 1Co 1:12; 3:4,5,6,22; 4:6; 16:12 Tit 3:13 for other mention of Apollos.

[15] The actual word is Cephas. He is referred to six times as Cephas, 187 times as Peter.

[16] These are rhetorical questions—questions not asking for an answer but to emphasize a statement. *Christ brings unity not divisions. Paul was not crucified for you. I did not baptize you to be my followers.* Paul is dealing with a major leadership problem—that of leaders drawing to themselves followers and creating divisions in a church. See *rhetorical questions*, **Glossary**. See **Article**, *12. Figures and Idioms.*

[17] Here is another Jewish leader who was converted. See Ac 18:8.

[18] Gaius was one of Paul's companions, a leader on his traveling team. Paul was constantly selecting and developing leaders. One of the major leadership lessons we have observed is: *Effective leaders view leadership selection and development as a priority function.* Paul exemplifies this. Gaius probably studied in the Bible institute Paul taught in during the extended Ephesus stay. See Ac 19:29; 20:4; Ro 16:23; 1Co 1:14; 3Jo 1:1. See **Articles**, *43. Paul and His Companions; 32. Leadership Selection.*

1 Corinthians 1:16-2:16   page 14

that I had baptized in my own name. 16 (Oh yes, I also baptized Stephanas[19] and family. Offhand I cannot remember any one else I baptized.)[20] 17 For Christ did not send me to baptize, but to preach the gospel[21] and not with brilliant oratory, lest I detract from the power of the cross of Christ.

Contextual Statements:[22]
1:18-20
God's wisdom is revealed in the Cross and is foolishness to the worldly wise.
1:21-25
Worldly wisdom can not know God who through Christ demonstrates wisdom and power.
1:26-31
God's wisdom will bring glory to God and not humankind.

Chapter 2
1 And I, fellow Christians, when I came to you, did not come with excellence of speech or of wisdom declaring to you the testimony of God. 2 For I determined not to know anything among you except Jesus Christ and his work on the cross. 3 I was with you in weakness, in fear, and in much trembling.[23] 4 And my speech and my preaching were not with persuasive words of human wisdom, but in demonstration of the Spirit and of power, 5 that your faith should not be in the wisdom of men but in the power of God.[24]

Contextual Statements:[25]
2:6-12
God has revealed His wisdom through His Spirit whom we believers have received.
2:13-16
Non-believers cannot understand or appreciate God's wisdom for they are discerned only by those who have the Spirit.

---

[19] Stephanus is another leader Paul developed. See 16:15-18, which indicates he was a full time worker. See also 1Co 1:16; and commentary explanation on 1 Co 15:16,17.

[20] Note the use of personal names, Crispus, Gaius, Stephanas. Paul lists some 80 or so people by name in his epistles. He thus demonstrated an important leadership value. *Ministry should be personal.* See especially Romans 16. See *leadership value*, **Glossary**. See **Article** *45. Paul—Developer Par Excellence.*

[21] This is most likely an idiom called the absolute for the relative, form—not A but B—really means some of A but much more important is B. Paul is not down playing baptism but stressing the importance of unity. See *absolute for relative*, **Glossary**. See **Article**, *12. Figures and Idioms In The Bible.*

[22] In this contextual flow about wisdom Paul basically defends God's ways of revealing wisdom, centers it in Christ, and asserts that we have in Christ that wisdom which we need.

[23] See also Php 2:12,13; 2Co 7:15; Eph 6:5. See *fear and trembling*, *idiom*, **Glossary**. See **Article**, *Fear and Trembling—The Right Attitude.*

[24] Paul models to the Corinthians what he has just said about wisdom. He himself was weak. His ministry was only successful because of God's power and not because of Paul's wisdom or oratory. God received the honor, not Paul.

[25] In this contextual flow Paul continues to deal with an epistemological problem—how one receives and knows truth. In the Corinthian church there was an overbalance of Greek philosophy and special pressure to get esoteric knowledge in unhealthy ways.

1 Corinthians 3:1-7

II. (Ch 3,4)[26] Problem About Divisions[27]

Chapter 3

1 And I, fellow Christians, could not speak to you as to spiritual people but as to worldly people, as to baby Christians.[28] 2 I fed you with milk and not with solid food. For up to now you were not able to receive it, and even now you are still not able.[29] 3 For you are still worldly in your thinking. Envy, strife, and divisions among you show that you are acting like worldly people. 4 For when one says, "I follow Paul," and another, "I follow Apollos," you are acting like worldly people.[30]

5 Who then is Paul, and who is Apollos, but ministers[31] through whom you believed. The Lord gave us each work to do. 6 I planted, Apollos watered, but God gave the increase. 7 So then neither he who plants is

---

[26] In these two chapters, Paul touches on truth concerning the responsibility side of the Stewardship Model. Leaders are accountable to God for how they develop God's work in their ministry. See **LEADERSHIP TOPIC 3. STEWARDSHIP MODEL. He also indirectly is dealing with LEADERSHIP TOPIC 7. STRUCTURE.** The Corinthians church was getting an unhealthy structure, organizing its small groups around cultic-like fascination with certain leaders. Paul deals with the structure problem also in 1 Co 12-14—but there from a giftedness standpoint and from a corporate gathering standpoint. See *accountability, structure*, **Glossary**. See **Article** 24. *Jesus' Five Leadership Models: Shepherd, Harvest, Steward, Servant, Intercessor; Accountability—Standing before God As A Leader*.

[27] Disunity is a serious problem even today. Splits abound in denominations. Divisions occur within local churches. Paul's teaching and admonition fits almost directly. This is Problem #2 of 10 problems that Paul has to deal with in the Corinthian situation. And some of the 10 have multiple issues—problems within problems. This repetitive dealing with various problems highlights the complexity macro lesson, **Macro Lesson 41:** *Leadership is complex, problematic, difficult and fraught with risk—which is why leadership is needed.* See **LEADERSHIP TOPIC 1. COMPLEXITY OF LEADERSHIP.** See **Articles**, *35. Macro Lessons Defined; 36. Macro Lessons—List of 41 Across Six Leadership Eras*.

[28] Other references on immaturity include: Heb 5:11,12; 6:1,2.

[29] The immature Corinthians need highly directive leadership styles. Paul uses them. For mature followers, spiritual authority could be used. But it depends on their sensitivity to discern and follow. Paul was a flexible leader and hence could vary his leadership style to meet the situation and maturity level of the followers. See *leadership style*, **Glossary**. See **Articles**, *49. Pauline Leadership Styles; 60. Spiritual Authority Defined—Six characteristics*.

[30] Disunity in a church is one of the prime signs of immaturity.

[31] This leadership term *ministers* (SRN 1249) is translated: as minister 20 times, as servant eight times, and as deacon three times—Php 1:1; 1Ti 3:8,12. Paul uses this term to describe himself, Phoebe, and here, Apollos. It is not clear how this role relates to that of bishop and elder. It is distinguished as a separate leadership role and probably of less influence than bishop in 1Ti 3 and possibly less influence in Php 1:1. But here it seems to refer to someone doing foundational work in a group. See **Article**, *50. Pauline Leadership Terms*.

1 Corinthians 3:8-17

anything, nor he who waters, but God who gives the increase. 8 Now he who plants and he who waters are together in this. Each one will receive his own reward according to his own labor. 9 For we are companions[32] in God's work. You are God's cultivated field; you are God's building.[33] 10 God gave grace[34] to me, as a wise master builder[35] I have laid the foundation. Another builds on it. But each one must be careful how he builds on it. 11 For no other foundation can anyone lay than that which is laid, which is Jesus Christ. 12 Anyone can build on this foundation with varying results: gold, silver, precious stones, wood, hay, or stubble. 13 Each one's work will become clear.[36] For the Day[37] will declare it. it will be revealed by fire. The fire will test each one's work, of what sort it is. 14 If anyone's work which he has built endures, he will receive a reward. 15 If anyone's work is burned, he will suffer loss; but he himself will be saved, yet so as through fire.[38]

16 Do you not know that you are[39] the temple of God and [that] the Spirit of God dwells in you? 17 If anyone defiles the temple of God, God will destroy him. For the temple of God is holy, which [temple] you

---

[32] This is a beautiful illustration of the application of *the Moses Leadership Principle—Zealous for God's Work*. A leader should be zealous for God's work no matter through whom it is accomplished. See Php 1:18; Nu 11:26-30. See also Mk 9:38-40, the incident John brought to Jesus' attention. Many leaders do not honor God's work through others if not done under their authority or using their methodologies or ideas. Frequently, they are inwardly jealous of God's work through others. Paul sees himself and others as not competing but complementing each other in ministry. See *Moses' zealous principle*, **Glossary**.

[33] Paul first uses two metaphors, *building* and *garden* (or field), to describe the work of God at Corinth and indirectly what the workers do. As a pioneer worker he was the architect for the work—designing it from the ground up. Apollos came along later and added to it—cultivated the field some more. See 1Pe 2:5,9; 5:2; Acts 20:28, 29; 1Cor 3:16 for other church metaphors—that is, right brained illustrations of the church. See *metaphor*, **Glossary**. See **Article**, *12. Figures and Idioms*.

[34] *Grace* (SRN 5485) is most likely a metonymy, a figure in which one word is substituted for another to which it is closely related. Grace here probably is standing for spiritual gifts (same root word used for gifts) and emphasizing that these gifts are by the grace of God. More on spiritual gifts in ch 12-14. See *metonymy*, **Glossary**.

[35] This word *master builder* (SRN 753) describes the one who lays out the plans for a building and supervises its construction. We get our word *architect* from it. This is an apostolic function. See **Article**, *2. Apostolic Functions*.

[36] This is metaphorically describing ministry results.

[37] This is probably another occurrence of Day of Christ; day being a shortened form. Again we are seeing a strong Pauline leadership value: *Leaders will ultimately give an account for their ministries*. See also: 1Co 1:8; 3:13; 5:5; Php 1:6,10; 2:16; 2Co 5:10; 2Th 2:2 and Heb 13:17. See *leadership value*, **Glossary**. See **Articles**, *1. Accountability—Standing Before God As a Leader; 11. Entrustment—A Leadership Responsibility*.

[38] Paul is using fire as a metaphorical description of judgment. Some things will burn up (stubble, hay, wood); other things (gold, silver, precious stones) will be purified and still shine through.

[39] This is a 2nd person plural. He is speaking corporately of the Corinthian church—the body as a whole—and not individuals.

1 Corinthians 3:18-23　　　　　　　　　　　　　　　　　page 17

are.[40]

18 Don't be deceived. Anyone among you who seems to be a wise person by this world's standards should become a fool. 19 For the wisdom of this world is foolishness with God. For it is written, "He catches the wise in their [own] craftiness";[41] 20 and again, "The LORD knows the thoughts of the wise, that they are futile."[42]

21 Therefore let no one continue boasting in men.[43] For all things are yours. 22 Paul or Apollos or Peter, or the world or life or death, or present or future—all are yours. 23 And you belong to Christ, and Christ belongs to God.[44]

---

[40] Paul has thus far described the church by three strong metaphors: *cultivated field*, *building*, now a *temple*. This temple metaphor emphasizes God's holy presence in the church. A strong lesson is given: *A leader who leads a church astray, especially with teaching and behavior which experientially results in denying the Holiness of God is subject to God's final discipline—destruction.* Presumably this is in time and not at the Day of Christ.

[41] See Isa 5:21.

[42] See Ps 94:11. Paul quotes from the O. T. nine times: 1Co 1:19 (Isa 29:14); 1Co 2:9 (Isa 64:4); 1Co 2:16 (Isa 40:13); 1Co 3:19 (Job 5:13); 1Co 3:20 (Ps 94:11); 1Co 9:9 (Dt 25:4); 1Co 10:26 (Ps 24:1 or Ex 9:29 or 19:5); 1Co 14:21 (Dt 28:49); 1Co 15:32 (Isa 22;13). He also quotes Jesus twice: 1Co 11:24, 25. Paul in the church age is the archetype of a *Bible centered leader*. The Corinthians were mainly Gentiles. So Paul does not quote too much from the O. T. Scriptures. But it is clear he was very familiar with them and used them with impact. Isa, Ps, and Dt were most likely three of Paul's core books. If there is a major weakness in today's leaders it is that they are dominantly fad leaders (looking for pragmatic tactics bringing "success") instead of Bible centered leaders. *See core books, Bible Centered Leader,* **Glossary**. See **Articles,** *6. Bible Centered Leader; 72. Vanishing Breed, Needed Bible Centered Leaders.*

[43] He is talking about the leaders dividing the Corinthian church.

[44] What is Paul saying here about leaders? By his answer that "all is yours," is he implying that various groups were claiming to have more because of their leaders? Are folks seeking something else? Is Paul saying that potentially in Christ you have all you will ever need? Is he saying you need not seek other things that these leaders are promising? My own best understanding is that Paul is emphasizing that in Christ they have all that they will ever need. They do not need to be searching around for some other better things. They belong to God in Christ. This is an *anti-fad-chasing* passage. They need to learn to live in light of what they have, that is, to appropriate what is theirs in Christ. See Eph for further comprehensive treatment of this idea.

1 Corinthians 4:1-9   page 18

Chapter 4

1 You should consider Apollos and me as Christ's leaders[45] who have been put in charge[46] of explaining God's truths not yet known. 2 Moreover it is required of leaders who are responsibly in charge[47] that they be found faithful. 3 Now I am not concerned about your evaluation of my leadership and conduct or anyone else's. In fact, I do not even judge myself. 4 My conscience is clear on this. The Lord will really judge me correctly. 5 Therefore don't jump to conclusions before the time when the Lord comes. He will show secret things for what they are. He will reveal the hidden purposes in hearts. God will give the praise that is really due.[48]

6 My Christian friends, I have used Apollos and myself as illustrations so that you may understand. Don't go beyond the Scriptures. Don't boast about your leader by comparing to other leaders. 7 For who makes anyone different from another one? And what do you have that you did not receive? Now if you did indeed receive it, why do you boast as if you had not received it?[49]

8 You already have all you need! You are already rich! You have reigned as kings even though we haven't. I could wish you did reign, that we also might reign with you![50] 9 For I think that God has

---

[45] This term *leaders* (SRN 5257) is used to describe Paul, Apollos, the Roman emperor, and other church leaders—its emphasis is responsible service as a leader. Other English words used for it: minister, servant, and officer—referring to military leaders. Here, particularly faithfulness as a leader is being stressed. See **Article**, *50. Pauline Leadership Terms*.

[46] The phrase used here, *leaders who are responsibly in charge* (SRN 3623) is one word in the Greek and translated by the word *steward*—the manager of someone's estate. This is one of the passages outside of the Gospels, which helps illustrate the Stewardship Leadership Model. See *stewardship model*, **Glossary**. See **Articles**, *11. Entrustment—A Leadership Perspective; 24. Jesus—5 Leadership Models: Shepherd, Harvest, Steward, Servant, Intercessor*.

[47] Again, *steward* (SRN 3623) occurs here. See also: Lk 12:42; 16:1,3,8; Ro 16:23; 1Co 4:1,2; Gal 4:2; Tit 1:7; 1Pe 4:10.

[48] Again, Paul stresses a leader's accountability to God. A leader is a person with God-given capacity and a God-given responsibility who is influencing specific groups of God toward God's purposes for them. The second characteristic, God-given responsibility, has a two-fold meaning, downward and upward: (1) A calling or burden from God for that leadership; (2) a responsibility to God for that leadership—accountability. That second aspect is highlighted. *Leaders will ultimately give an account for their ministries*. See *leader*, **Glossary**.

[49] Rhetorical questions implying and emphasizing that: (1) God made you different. (2) God gave you what ever you have. (3) You have no room to boast. This is an all important principle of how to treat giftedness in leaders. Giftedness comes from God. We cannot then boast about it or become proud. Nor can we really compare our giftedness with others. This is emphasizing the God-given capacity of our definition of leader. More on this in 1Co 12-14. See *rhetorical questions*, *leader* **Glossary**.

[50] Maybe an allusion to the afterlife and certainly one in which apostles will be recognized for who they are and what they have done—not like here as second-class people. See following context.

1 Corinthians 4:10-21

displayed us, the apostles, lowest on the ladder, as people condemned to death; for we have been made a spectacle[51] to the world, both to angels and to people. 10 We are seen as fools for Christ's sake, but you are wise in Christ! We are weak, but you are strong![52] You are honored, but we are dishonored! 11 Even now, we go hungry and thirsty. We are poorly clothed, beaten, and homeless. 12 We work to support ourselves. We bless those who curse us. When persecuted, we patiently endure. 13 When insulted we answer with kind words. And even right now we are treated as garbage.[53]

14 I do not write these things to shame you, but as my beloved children I warn you.[54] 15 For though you might have ten thousand Christian teachers, you only have one father in the faith.[55] For I became your spiritual father when I preached the Gospel to you. 16 Therefore I urge you, imitate me.[56] 17 For this reason I am sending Timothy[57] to you. He is my beloved and faithful son in the Lord. He will remind you of my ways in Christ, as I teach everywhere in every church.[58]

18 Now some of you are arrogant, as if I am not coming to visit you. 19 But Lord willing, I am coming to you soon. I will find out then if these arrogant leaders really have God's power. 20 For the kingdom of God is not just talk but is backed by power. 21 What do you want? Shall I come to you with a rod,[59] or in

---

[51] *Spectacle* (SRN 2302) refers to a theater, a place in which games and dramatic spectacles are exhibited, and public assemblies held. Refers not only to the public show but also to a person who is exhibited to be gazed at and made sport of at such a place.

[52] Paul uses irony here, even bordering on sarcasm. This whole context is showing the cost of apostolic ministry. Such a leader is often unappreciated, persecuted, ridiculed, looked down upon, etc. Further, there is often great sacrifice both in physical comfort and monetary reward as well as status. But there is indeed honor from God's sight. See *irony*, **Glossary**. See **Article**, *12. Figures and Idioms*.

[53] See especially 2Co 4:7-11; 11:22-28; 2Ti 3:10-17.

[54] Here is a capture of this absolute for the relative idiom. Paul is really saying, *"I am writing to shame you, (to wake you up); but much more importantly, to warn you."* See *absolute for the relative idiom*, **Glossary**. See **Article**, *12. Figures and Idioms*.

[55] Paul uses hyperbole to both denounce these leaders causing divisions by their teaching and to emphasize in contrast that he, alone, is really responsible for their faith in Christ. He is using a leadership style identified as *Father-initiator*. That is, he is influencing based on this foundational relationship. They should listen to him. They owe him. See **LEADERSHIP TOPIC 4. LEADERSHIP STYLES.** See *hyperbole, Father-initiator*, **Glossary**. See **Article**, *49. Pauline Leadership Styles*.

[56] This strong exhortation, *urge* (SRN 3870) is the same word used for the exhortation spiritual gift. This exhortation example stresses the following Pauline leadership style which is called the *Imitator* style. See Modeling concept: 1Co 4:16; 11:1; 2Th 3:7,9; 1Ti 4:12; Php 3:17; 4:9; Heb 13:7; 1Pe 5:3; Tit 2:7; 1Pe 2:21. Here in vs 16 Paul uses his imitator leadership style (indirectly appealing to the maturity leadership style). See **LEADERSHIP TOPIC 4. LEADERSHIP STYLES.** See *exhortation, imitator, modeling, leadership style*, **Glossary**. See **Article**, *48. Paul—Modeling as An Influence Means; 49. Pauline Leadership Styles*.

[57] Timothy (occurs 31 times in Scripture) is a close companion.

[58] Paul illustrates mentor sponsoring for Timothy. See *mentor sponsor*, **Glossary**. See **Articles**, *45. Paul—Developer Par Excellence; 47. Paul—Mentor For Many*.

[59] *Rod* is a metonymy, a word substituted for another word, to emphasize punishment given by a rod. Paul illustrates another strong leadership style, *Confrontation*. All styles used so far are directive or highly directive styles because strong leadership is needed when solving basic problems with immature followers. See *Metonymy, confrontation*, **Glossary**. See **Article**, *49. Pauline Leadership Styles*.

1 Corinthians 5:1-13

love and a spirit of gentleness?

III. (Ch 5) Problem on Toleration of Immorality[60]

Chapter 5
1 It is actually being said that there is sexual immorality among you so terrible that even pagans don't do it. I hear that a man is living with his father's wife! 2 And you are proud? You should be sad. The man doing this thing should be put out of the group.[61] 3 Even though I am not there physically, I am in spirit. And I have already passed judgment on him.[62] 4 In the authority of our Lord Jesus Christ, when you meet together, think of me as being there with you, with the power of our Lord Jesus Christ. 5 Deliver this man to Satan[63] for the destruction of the body, that his spirit may be saved in the day of the Lord Jesus.[64]

Contextual Statements:
Paul continues to deal with the problem of immorality.

5:6-8
If you allow this sin to remain, it will corrupt the whole church. Deal with it.

5:9-11
You need to break fellowship with church members who are openly practicing sexual immorality or the like.

5:12-13
We have a responsibility to judge within our church. God will judge those outside the church.

---

[60] This is Problem #3 of 10 problems that Paul has to deal with in the Corinthian situation. Immorality was rampant in the Corinthian culture. Paul is going against the grain in addressing this situation. This repetitive dealing with various problems highlights the complexity macro lesson, **Macro Lesson 41:** *Leadership is complex, problematic, difficult and fraught with risk—which is why leadership is needed.* Paul also reverts to two leadership styles: a confrontive style (all of ch 5 does this) and an indirect conflict style of leadership (see especially vs 4,5). See **LEADERSHIP TOPIC 1. COMPLEXITY OF LEADERSHIP; LEADERSHIP TOPIC 4. LEADERSHIP STYLES.** See *confrontation style, indirect conflict, spiritual warfare,* **Glossary.** See **Articles,** *49. Pauline Leadership Styles; 65. Sprititual Warfare—Satan's Tactics; 35. Macro Lessons Defined; 36. Macro Lessons—List of 41 Across Six Leadership Eras.*

[61] *Confrontation,* a highly directive leadership style, is seen again. Paul confronts head on, not pulling any punches. Interestingly enough, the Corinthians followed this strong advice. See *confrontation,* **Glossary.** See **Article,** *49. Pauline Leadership Styles.*

[62] See spiritual warfare: 1Ti 1:18-20; 3:6,7; 4:1; fn 1Ti 3:6. 2Ti 2:26; Eph 6:10-18.

[63] See Ro 16:20; 1Co 5:5; 7:5; 2Co 2:11; 11:14; 1Th 2:18; 2Th 2:9; 1Ti 1:20; 5:15 for Paul's awareness of Satan and spiritual warfare. See **Articles,** *65. Spiritual Warfare—Satan's Tactics; 66. Spiritual Warfare—Two Extremes To Avoid; 67. Spiritual Warfare—Two Foundational Axioms.*

[64] This rare leadership style, *indirect conflict,* realizes spiritual warfare as part of the problem and exercises power to combat it. Paul does this even though he is not present physically. The spiritual warfare is sensed as a necessary first step before any real problem solving can take place. See also 2Co 10:4,5 where Paul refers to this style. From a distance Paul gave this man over to Satan. See *indirect conflict,* **Glossary.** See **Article,** *49. Pauline Leadership Styles.*

1 Corinthians 6:1-20   page 21

IV. (Ch 6) Problem of Lawsuits Among Believers And Other Issues[65]

Chapter 6
Contextual Statements:
6:1-6[66]
Christians should settle legal matters before wise Christians in the church rather than in secular law courts.
6:7-11[67]
Legal suits are indicative of bigger issues of sinfulness and unrighteousness.
6:12-14
Freedom to do things does not mean we have to do them.
6:15-17
Our bodies are not our own but belong to Christ; therefore we should not practice sexual sin which dishonors our oneness with the Spirit.
6:18-20
Flee sexual sin. You were bought with a price and should glorify God in body and spirit.

---

[65] This is Problem #4 of 10 problems that Paul has to deal with in the Corinthian situation. And some of the 10 have multiple issues—problems within problems. This repetitive dealing with various problems highlights the complexity macro lesson, **Macro Lesson 41:** *Leadership is complex, problematic, difficult and fraught with risk—which is why leadership is needed.* This is also indirectly dealing with the problem of wisdom (ch 1,2) from another angle. Corinthians should have enough wisdom from God to deal with the legal problems they were facing. See **LEADERSHIP TOPIC 1. COMPLEXITY OF LEADERSHIP**. See **Articles**, *35. Macro Lessons Defined; 36. Macro Lessons—List of 41 Across Six Leadership Eras*.

[66] Verses 4 and 5 imply, at least informally, a leadership role needed in local churches—that of wise leaders who can judge issues between church members, and prevent public law suits.

[67] Leaders must inspire followers—one of the three major overall generic leadership functions. Paul does this indirectly in this context, 6:7-11, when in verse 11 he says, "And such were some of you." He asserts that the Gospel can free people from all kinds of dysfunctional issues. What Paul saw happen in Corinth, freeing people from sinful behaviors, gave him the impetus to exclaim in Ro 1:16, *I am completely confident* (a litotes—not ashamed) *in the Gospel of Christ. It is the power of God to deliver people.* That kind of message brings hope. See *litotes, inspirational leadership*, **Glossary**.

1 Corinthians 7:1-40   page 22

V. (Ch 7) Problems About Marriage, Separation, Divorce[68]

Chapter 7[69]

Contextual Statements:
7:1-5
These verses deal with sexual passion and marriage and marriage partners meeting each others needs.
7:6,7
Paul opts personally for singleness.
7:8,9
Singleness is good but marriage may be necessary because of physical needs.
7:10,11
Concerning separation or divorce, the basic rule is to stay together and try to work out one's situation.
7:12-16
Staying together can allow for one partner to influence the other partner toward God. But separation is not forbidden.
7:17-24
A person can operate as a Christian from the background that he/she was called in: whether married or single, circumcised or not, slave or free,
7:25-28
A person is free to marry or not marry but be aware of the pressures of a marriage in the present situation.
7:29-31
Time is short. It must be used well.
7:32-35
There is an advantage in serving the Lord in being single.
7:36-38
One can marry and it is all right. If one can stay single it is better.
7:39,40
Widows are free to remarry but staying single has its advantages.

---

[68] This is Problem #5 of 10 problems that Paul has to deal with in the Corinthian situation. It is a problem we face repetitively in the west. Without this very helpful clarification we would be limited only to the Jewish approach to marriage problems and Jesus' teaching on it. This added information from Paul gives us guidelines for dealing with the complex problems involved in hurting marriages and in mixed marriages with believers and unbelievers. This repetitive dealing with various problems highlights the complexity macro lesson, **Macro Lesson 41:** *Leadership is complex, problematic, difficult and fraught with risk—which is why leadership is needed.* See **LEADERSHIP TOPIC 1. COMPLEXITY OF LEADERSHIP.** See **Articles,** *35. Macro Lessons Defined; 36. Macro Lessons—List of 41 Across Six Leadership Eras.*

[69] In terms of leadership issues, other than a model of problem solving, chapter 7 touches indirectly on three leadership issues. One concerns the social base of a leader—the home base out of which a leader operates. A second concerns being single or married in ministry. Paul gives his own preference for remaining single to devote himself more fully to ministry. But he does not project this on others. It is not simply a matter of willpower but of an enabling from God to do so. Third, this passage emphasizes very sharply the sexual barrier to finishing well as a leader. See **Articles,** *58. Social Base Issues; 15. Finishing Well—Six Major Barriers.*

1 Corinthians 8:1-8

VI. (Ch 8-10) Problem on Disputed Practices[70]

Chapter 8
Contextual Flow:
Paul in chapter 8 deals with issues of Christian freedom and disputed practices by laying out basic guidelines for how a Christian should approach disputed practices. He then goes on in chapter 9 to demonstrate with his own life, by modeling, how he gives up his rights (one of the guidelines).[71]

8:1-3
Paul addresses a specific disputed practice, of eating meat offered to idols, which was troubling some Christians at Corinth.

8:4-6
Paul shows that God is supreme over any other supernatural power associated with the idol, thus abrogating any allegiance to the idol because of eating the meat.

8:7-8
Some Christians do not know this and hence have troubled consciences about eating meat sacrificed to these idols.

---

[70] This is Problem #6 of 10 problems that Paul has to deal with in the Corinthian situation. This repetitive dealing with various problems highlights the complexity macro lesson, **Macro Lesson 41:** *Leadership is complex, problematic, difficult and fraught with risk—which is why leadership is needed.* See **LEADERSHIP TOPIC 1. COMPLEXITY OF LEADERSHIP**. See *disputed practice, stronger brother, weaker brother,* **Glossary**. See **Articles**, *35. Macro Lessons Defined; 36. Macro Lessons—List of 41 Across Six Leadership Eras.*

[71] Christians often differ on what a Christian can do or not do in practicing Christianity in a given culture. See *disputed practices,* **Glossary**. Paul gives guidelines here and in Romans 14 on this important subject. The content of chapter 8 is important to all leaders who will be applying these guidelines many times to themselves and followers. I have written a small manual on this called, **Disputed Practices**. The central guideline, giving up one's rights (the stronger brother) in order to help others (the weaker brother), is a fundamental axiom of servant leadership.

1 Corinthians 9:1-6

9:1-6
A knowledgeable Christian has liberty to eat but can give up that freedom if such a model will cause unknowledgeable Christians to sin against their consciences.[72]

Chapter 9[73]

1 Am I not an apostle? [You bet] Am I not free? [You know it] Have I not seen Jesus Christ our Lord?[74] [Yes, I have] Are you not my work in the Lord? [You are proof of my apostleship]2 Even if others don't admit my apostleship, you must. Certainly my work among you shows I am an apostle. For you are the seal[75] of my apostleship in the Lord.

3 When people criticize my leadership, here is how I respond. 4 Don't we have a right to be given food and drink because of our work? [We sure do] 5 Don't we have the right to take along a Christian wife, like the other apostles, the brothers of the Lord,[76] and Peter? [Sure we have that right] 6 Or are Barnabas[77] and I

---

[72] From a leadership standpoint the whole process is instructive. Paul goes from a specific problem to a general principle that can be applied to other specific issues. Basic Principle: *A knowledgeable Christian, on a given disputed practice, can freely give up a practice if it causes an unknowledgeable Christian to sin against his/her conscience.* The issue is causing the other one to sin. This leaves room for the unknowledgeable Christian to grow into the freedom yet also guides the knowledgeable Christian in applying the freedom.

[73] In this chapter Paul uses 20 rhetorical questions to hammer home his points. Remember, in this literary technique, questions are not asked to get answers. They are really emphatic statements. The question itself shows the kind of answer Paul is implying. These questions are carrying a flow of ideas that defend Paul's apostleship, teach about financial support of Christian workers and teach about "giving up one's rights" as a leader so as not to impede one's influence as a leader. This is a great passage applying servant leadership. I add parenthetical comments to help you feel Paul's points. The **TEV** captures many of these rhetorical questions. See *capture*, *rhetorical question*, **Glossary**. See **Article**, *12. Figures and Idioms in the Bible*.

[74] In Ac 1, Peter and others chose a replacement for Judas. They introduce the notion that a successor must have been one who knew Jesus. This seems to have carried over to the notion of proof of apostleship for Paul, personally. He did see the Lord in his destiny experience on the road to Damascus.

[75] The word *seal* (SRN 4973) refers to a signet ring used to make an authenticating impression in a wax seal, used on official governmental papers. Paul figuratively emphasizes that the Corinthian Christians are his authentication of apostolic leadership. Here in vs 1,2 Paul uses his apostolic leadership style. See **LEADERSHIP TOPIC 4. LEADERSHIP STYLES.** See apostolic style, Glossary. See **Article**, *49. Pauline Leadership Styles*.

[76] He is referring to Jude and James, the half-brothers of Jesus, early church leaders.

[77] Barnabas was a significant early mentor of Paul's and a partner on the first missionary journey. Our present day empirical studies show that all leaders will need mentoring throughout their lifetime in order to finish well. Barnabas played an early role which opened doors for Paul's ministry. Many budding Pauls will never reach their potential because there are not enough Barnabases around. See 1Co 9:6; Gal 2:1,9,13; Col 4:10. See **Article**, *5. Barnabas—Significant Mentoring; 8. Constellation Model, Mentoring Relationships*.

1 Corinthians 9:7-18

the only ones who have to work to support our own ministry? [No] 7 Who ever goes to war at his own expense? [No one] Who plants a vineyard and does not eat of its fruit? [No one] Or who tends a flock and does not drink of the milk of the flock? [No one]

8 Is this just human reasoning? [No] Doesn't the Old Testament law say the same also? [Yes, it does] 9 For it is written in the law of Moses,

> "You shall not muzzle
> an ox
> while it treads out
> the grain."[78]

Is it just oxen God is concerned about? [No] 10 Wasn't He also speaking to us? [Yes] No doubt it is for our sakes, this is written. The person who plows and the person who reaps should do their work in anticipation of getting a share of the crop. 11 If we have sown spiritual seed among you, is it too much to expect to reap material benefits? [I don't think so] 12 If others have the right to expect benefits for ministering to you, don't we have an even greater right? [yes, we do; but here is my point!][79]

Nevertheless we have not used this right. We have had to put up with lots in order not to hinder the gospel of Christ. 13 Don't you know that those working in the temple have a share of the sacrifices brought to the altars? [for their meals] 14 In the same way, the Lord has commanded that those who preach the gospel should get their living from it. 15 But I have not used this right, nor do I now write these things in order to claim these rights. I would rather die first than impose these rights. 16 I have no right to boast because I preach the Gospel. I am compelled to do so due to my calling. What an awful thing it would be if I didn't preach the Gospel! 17 For if I did my ministry out of my own desire, I would deserve to be rewarded. But I do it because it has been given me as a trust.[80] 18 Do I get any reward then? [You bet] I get satisfaction when I preach the Gospel without charging anyone. This certainly keeps me from abusing my authority and demanding my rights.[81]

---

[78] This is instructive. Paul shows how he uses the notion of intentional selection of Scripture (the command about an ox) and the meditative reflection on it, which allows for deriving a principle compatible with the character of God and how God works. Leaders must be able to hear from God. One way of hearing from God is via truth seen in the word. This exemplifies a Bible-centered leader. See **Article**, *53. Principles of Truth*.

[79] Paul has used this large buildup of rhetorical questions to show that he has a right to expect financial remuneration from these Corinthians to whom he has done a fundamental work in bringing the Gospel to them. Now he makes his point. "I gave up this right in order not to hinder the Gospel being received by you." He thus models the guideline of giving up a right for the better good that he has just taught on in chapter 8. He will come back to this support problem in chapter 16.

[80] Again the steward concept is in mind. See **Article**, *11. Entrustment*.

[81] Paul is in this contextual flow dealing with two of the major barriers to a leader finishing well: (1) financial issues, (2) abuse of power. He is careful to avoid being trapped by either one. See **Article**, *15. Finishing Well—Six Major Barriers*.

1 Corinthians 9:19-26

19 Since I am not under obligation to anyone I am free to minister;[82] yet I have made myself a slave[83] to all in order to win as many as possible. 20 With the Jews I live like a Jew[84] to win them. When I am with those who strictly follow the law, I do too, even though I am free from the law. 21 In the same way, when I am with Gentiles who do not have the Jewish law, I identify with them as much as I can in order to win them.[85] I do not discard God's law but I do obey the law of Christ. 22 With those weak in the faith I become weak like them in order to win them. I can adapt to different situations that I might save some of them by any means.[86]

23 Now I do these things for the gospel's sake, that I may share in its blessings. 24 Don't you know that those in a race all run, but only one wins the prize? Run in such a way that you will receive the prize.[87] 25 And everyone who competes[88] for the prize exercises real discipline[89] in order to be ready. Now they do it to win a fleeting prize.[90] We do it for an eternal prize. 26 Therefore I, personally, run my course with

---

[82] There is an implication here. I am not paid by people; therefore they can't order me around. **NLT** captures this as, *This means I am not bound to obey people just because they pay me...*

[83] *Not under obligation* translates one word, *free* (SRN 1658) with connotations of not being a slave. Paul contrasts this freedom he has with his choosing to be a *slave* (SRN 1402). Quite a contrast—notice it is a willful choice and involves giving up his rights.

[84] See Acts 18:18; 21:23

[85] See Gal 2:3,5,11ff. but also note 1Co 16:8—Pentecost.

[86] Paul's flexibility in adapting to Jewish and non-Jewish situations implies: (1) He has a core (law of Christ) which he holds on to but he also has a lot of give and take in peripheral things; (2) More importantly, he can give up his rights with regards to these peripheral issues which to others may seem core. He does this in order to get the best hearing possible for the Gospel. When he speaks of being weak he means on some disputed practice on which he, himself, has freedom. But he can give up that right. See also 2Ti 2:24-26 for adaptability.

[87] I capture Paul's figures and emphasizing these key words with the following paraphrase which I use often when teaching on continuing well, a prelude to finishing well. 1Cor 9:24-27 *I am serious about finishing well in my Christian ministry. I discipline myself for fear that after challenging others into the Christian life I myself might become a casualty* (Clinton Paraphrase). See Ac 20:24; 2Ti 4:7,8 for notion of finishing his course. Here in these vs Paul models his understanding of personal discipline and the role it plays in one finishing well. See **LEADERSHIP TOPIC 6. PERSONAL DISCIPLE.** See *enhancement factors, disciplines—spiritual*, **Glossary**. See **Article**, *13. Finishing Well—Five Factors enhancing Leadership Styles*.

[88] The word translated as *competes* (SRN 75) is the word from which we get our word agonize. It means *really struggles* (to get ready and participate). Present-day marathon runners do train this rigorously.

[89] The word translated as *exercises real discipline* (SRN 1467) means to practice self-control. It described athletes who were preparing for the Olympic Games. Such an athlete abstained from unwholesome food, wine, and sexual indulgence.

[90] *Prize* (SRN 4735) is the wreath or garland, which was given as a prize to victors in public games. Status-wise today's equivalent is a gold medal from the Olympic Games or a Super Bowl ring or an NBA championship ring.

1 Corinthians 9:27-10:26

definite purpose, to win—to finish well. Thus I box, making my punches count.[91] 27 So I discipline[92] myself and exercise strict control, lest after preaching to others, I myself should become a loser.[93]

Chapter 10[94]
Contextual Flow:
Strong warnings are given in this chapter. Paul refers to Old Testament examples to draw out some lessons which he will apply to the disputed practices teaching given in Chapter 8.
10:1-5
Israelites who experienced numerous miracles of God under Moses leadership did not profit wisely from them and did not follow God wholly and were set aside.
10:6-11
These historical happenings are strong examples to us against sexual immorality and idolatry.
10:12-13
Every one will face temptations like they did, but God can deliver from them.
10:14-17
Flee idolatry. Participating in the Lord's Supper is sharing the things of Christ.
10:18-22
Sharing in sacrifices offered to demons may involve participating in the things of demons.

23 While I might have freedom to do lots of things, not all these things are helpful. I am free to do them but they are not beneficial. 24 No one should be looking out only for self-interests but for the good of others.[95]

25 [Here is my conclusion:] You can eat whatever is sold in the meat market without asking questions because of conscience.[96] 26 for

> "the earth [is] the
> LORD'S,
> and all its fullness."[97]

---

[91] Literally, as not flailing in the air.

[92] See also 1Ti 4:8 for priority of spiritual disciplines over physical disciplines.

[93] This whole context, 9:24-27, is promoting one of the important enhancements that helps leaders finish well. Discipline in the life, is one of five enhancement factors that have been identified with effective leaders who have finished well. All kinds of disciplines, especially spiritual disciplines, will be needed and used with purpose in order to continue toward the finish. Paul is in his fifties here, a time when leaders tend to plateau. Disciplines are needed. See **Articles**, *13. Finishing Well—5 Factors Enhancing; 62. Spiritual Disciplines—And On-going Leadership*.

[94] From a leadership standpoint, ch 10 is instructive for several reasons: (1) Paul shows the importance of studying and using the Old Testament; (2) he warns against sexual immorality, a major barrier for leaders; (3) all Christians face temptations, leaders even more so but God can deliver in them; (4) idolatry must be avoided—partaking of meat to idols could be participating in demon worship; (5) Paul deliberately uses modeling as a major means of influencing. See **Article**, *6. Bible Centered Leader*.

[95] See Php 2:3,4 where the notion of others is first taught.

[96] See fn 1Ti 1:5 for more on *conscience*.

[97] See Ps 24:1. Paul knew the Psalms—probably a core book of his. See *core books*, **Glossary**.

1 Corinthians 10:27-11:16　　　　　　　　　　　page 28

27 If an unbeliever invites you to a meal, and you desire to go, eat whatever is set before you without asking questions. Your conscience is clear. 28 But if that unbeliever says to you, "This was offered to idols," do not eat it for the sake of the one who told you, for conscience sake. 29 "Conscience," I say, not your own, but the other person's.

But why is my Christian freedom limited by another person's conscience [you might ask]? 30 But if I partake with thanks, why am I criticized for eating this food?

[Here is my point] 31 Therefore, whether you eat or drink, or whatever you do, do all to the glory of God. 32 Don't cause others to sin because of your freedom—Jews or Gentiles or the church of God. 33 Do as I do. I try to please all in all that I do, not seeking what is best for me but what is best for them that they may be saved. 11:1 And you should follow my example just as I follow Christ's example.[98]

VII. (Ch 11) Problem on Worship Practices[99]

Chapter 11:2 ff
Contextual Flow:
Paul in chapter 11:2ff deals with two major disturbances in public worship: (1) defiance of tradition among women—refusing to wear head coverings as they pray publicly—strong cultural implications about this; (2) improper participation in the Lord's supper.[100]
11:2-12
Tradition has its place, but remember public worship should not be upset because of cultural practices regarding head coverings or lack of for women.
11:13-16
Common practice in churches has women praying in public using head coverings. But I don't think this is

---

[98] I have included this whole last sub-context, 10:27-11:1, because of its importance concerning modeling. Paul gives his reasoning, backs it up with his own lifestyle, then urges the Corinthians to follow his example. He is deliberately using modeling as a strong means of influence. And in all of it, the notion of giving up one's rights for the good of the ministry reigns supreme. This kind of thinking is at the heart of servant leadership. See also Ro 14-15:3 for a parallel treatment of disputed practices. See Modeling concept: 1Co 4:16; 11:1; 2Th 3:7,9; 1Ti 4:12; Php 3:17; 4:9; Heb 13:7; 1Pe 5:3; Tit 2:7; 1Pe 2:21. See *modeling, disputed practices*, **Glossary**. See **Article**, *48. Paul—Modeling as An Influence Means.*

[99] This is Problem #7 of 10 problems that Paul has to deal with in the Corinthian situation. This is really several problems all flowing from worship practices the Corinthians are involved in. The Corinthians had a very free public worship time. Paul seeks to bring some orderliness into it as well as deal with issues regarding gender problems involved in the Corinthian cultural situations.This repetitive dealing with various problems highlights the complexity macro lesson, **Macro Lesson 41:** *Leadership is complex, problematic, difficult and fraught with risk—which is why leadership is needed.* See **LEADERSHIP TOPIC 1. COMPLEXITY OF LEADERSHIP**. See *disputed practice, stronger brother, weaker brother,* **Glossary**. See **Articles**, *35. Macro Lessons Defined; 36. Macro Lessons—List of 41 Across Six Leadership Eras.*

[100] This is a difficult passage, especially about the women praying publicly. There are cultural factors going on here, which are not totally clear. Paul's arguments make use of these cultural factors and cultural understandings of women and men. The one clear thing is that the worship time must not be disrupted. Going against tradition and cultural understandings may well upset unity and orderly worship. See **Article**, *17. Gender and Leadership.*

1 Corinthians 11:17-12:3

worth arguing over.

11:17-22
Your conduct at the Lord's supper is inexcusable. How can you share with divisions among you? Participate together in this meal.

11:23-26
The Lord's supper should be a sacred remembering of the Lord's death and a reminder of his return.

11:27-34
Do not participate in the Lord's supper in an improper manner but do so meaningfully or be judged by God.[101]

VIII. (Ch 12-14) Problems About Spiritual Gifts[102]

Chapter 12

1 Now, Christian friends, I want to clear up misunderstandings about spiritual gifts.[103] 2 You know that you were pagans, led astray in worshipping speechless idols. 3 [I want you to know how to discern what is from God]. No one led by the Spirit[104] of God can curse Jesus. And no one can say that Jesus is Lord unless

---

[101] Paul closes this last sub-context with the words, *"As for the other matters, I will settle them when I come."* So there were obviously other things going on in the public worship which were causing problems. Here he deals with the two most important ones: women, probably in defiance of authority or at least disrupting the public services with questions and sacrilege about the Lord's supper.

[102] This is Problem #8 of 10 problems that Paul has to deal with in the Corinthian situation. From the amount of material devoted to it, three whole chapters, it was a major problem. Paul has already alluded to it in the salutation and salutation extension. This repetitive dealing with various problems highlights the complexity macro lesson, **Macro Lesson 41:** *Leadership is complex, problematic, difficult and fraught with risk—which is why leadership is needed.* See **LEADERSHIP TOPIC 1. COMPLEXITY OF LEADERSHIP; LEADERSHIP TOPIC 2. GIFTEDNESS.** Note too, how Paul uses his own gift-mix very well in dealing with this major problem. Paul's apostolic gift, teaching gift and exhortation gift are in full view in his attempt to solve this problem. Paul is applying basic contextualization guidelines, adapted by Scriptural truth to the situation. See the leadership commentary, **Titus—Apostolic Leadership** for a full treatment of contextualization applied to a phase 2, apostolic situation. See *contextualization*, **Glossary.** See **Articles**, *35. Macro Lessons Defined; 36. Macro Lessons—List of 41 Across Six Leadership Eras; 4. Apostolic Giftedness—Multiple Gifted Leaders; Basic Ideas on Contextualizaion.*

[103] For other gifts passages see also Ro 12:6-8; Eph 4:11; 1Th 5:12-22; Heb 2:1-4; 1Co 7:7 non-example; Ro 16:1,2; 1Ti 1:18; 3:1-7; 8-13; 4:1, 14-16; 5:17; 6:20; Tit 3:8,14; 2Ti 1:6, 12-14; 4:5; 1Pe 4:10,11; 1Jn 4:1-4. See my book, **Unlocking Giftedness**, which comparatively studies these gifts passages.

[104] Some Pentecostal writers assume the somewhat confusing passage of 1Co 12:1-3 (speaking by or in the Spirit) to refer to an instance of kinds of tongues. The implication is that no person can use the gift of tongues to blaspheme, i.e. say that Jesus is accursed. This is supposedly in answer to a query about tongues with regards to this suspected abuse in the Corinthian church. It is a possible view.

1 Corinthians 12:4-15　　　　　　　　　　　　　　　　page 30

guided by the Holy Spirit.[105]

4 There are different kinds of spiritual gifts, but the same Spirit [distributes them]. 5 There are different kinds of ministries,[106] serving the same Lord. 6 Effectiveness varies also but it is the same God doing it. 7 Each one is given some spiritual gift[107] for the good of all. 8 [Here are some examples:] To one person is given a word of wisdom[108] through the Spirit; to another a word of knowledge[109] through the same Spirit; 9 to another faith[110] by the same Spirit; to another gifts of healings[111] by the same Spirit; 10 to another the working of miracles;[112] and to another prophecy;[113] to another discernings of spirits;[114] to another kinds of tongues;[115] to another interpretation of tongues.[116] 11 The same Spirit energizes all these gifts. He distributes to each one individually as He purposes.

12 The human body has many parts but it is still one body. So it is with the church, the body of Christ. 13 For by one Spirit we were all united into one body—whether Jews or Greeks, whether slaves or free—and have all received the same Spirit.[117]

14 For in fact the body[118] is not one member but many. 15 If the foot should say, "Because I am not a

---

[105] Paul emphasizes this Lordship idea further in Ro 8:9; 10:9,10.

[106] This word *ministries* (SRN 1248) is a cognate of the word deacon, one of the leadership words. See **Article**, *50. Pauline Leadership Terms*.

[107] Literally *some manifestation of the Spirit*. The **TEV** captures its essence— *given some proof of the Spirit's presence*. The entire context is on spiritual gifts so it is not wrong to translate this manifestation as a gift and simply recognize it as a special proof of the Spirit's presence. This has important implications for leaders. Every member of the body will have a spiritual gift imparted. It will differ from others. It will find different service. It will have different effectiveness.

[108] For possible examples see Ac 6:8; 15:13-21.

[109] For possible examples see Ac 5:1-10; 9:10-19.

[110] For a possible example see Ac 27:21-25.

[111] For a possible example see Ac 3:1-10.

[112] Literally—*operations of powers*. For possible examples see Ac 2:43; 4:33; 19:11,12.

[113] For possible examples see Ac 13:1; 16:9,10; 18:9,10; 21:9-12.

[114] For possible examples see Ac 5:1-10; 13:9-11; 16:16-18; 19:11,12; 1Jn 4:1-3.

[115] For possible examples see Ac 2:1-40; 10:46; 19:1-7.

[116] This is the first of six major gift lists in 1Co. These lists are: 12:8-10; 12:28; 13:1-3; 13:8; 14:6; 14:26,27; A major gift list refers to any context in which two or more gifts are listed either specifically or by a generic label and/or the passage deals with the use or abuse of a gift or gifts. Two other major lists include: Ro 12:6-8; Eph 4:11. All of these lists must be studied comparatively. 1Co 12:8-10 is sometimes called the *come-and-go gifts* (technically called *non-vested gifts*) since these manifestations may occur when a body meets and worships and does not seemingly indicate permanence. For seven of these gifts (gifts of healings, discernings of spirits, word of knowledge, word of wisdom, kinds of tongues, interpreting of tongues, faith) this is the only list on which the gifts occur. Hence there is no context to help define these gifts—only word studies, for the word or phrases, can be used. See *gifts definitions*, *vested gifts*, *non-vested gifts*, **Glossary**. See 1Co 14:13-15. See **Articles**, *63. Spiritual Gift Clusters; 64. Spiritual Gifts, Giftedness and Development; 4. Apostolic Giftedness—Multiple Gifted Leaders*.

[117] See Eph 4:1-6 for emphasis on unity by the Spirit. See also Gal 3:28 for a fuller formula; here the male/female category is left out.

[118] See also Ro 12:4,5 for a short version of the body metaphor.

1 Corinthians 12:16-31

hand, I am not part of the body," Does that mean it is not part of the body? [No]16 And if the ear should say, "Because I am not an eye, I am not of the body," Does that mean it is not part of the body? [No]17 If the whole body were only an eye, how could we hear? If the whole body were only an ear how could we smell?

18 But now God has established the members, each one of them, in the body just as He pleased.[119] 19 There would not be a body if there were only one member.[120] 20 As it is there are many members, yet still one body.

21 And the eye can't say to the hand, "I don't need you."[121] The head can't say to the feet, "I don't need you." 22 No, much rather, those members of the body which seem to be weaker are necessary. 23 Those members of the body which we think aren't worth much are the ones which we give greater care. And our body parts which don't need to be seen we cover up. 24 Some parts of our body don't need this. But God has put together the body giving greater honor to those parts that lack it. 25 Hence there should be harmony in the body. Each member should have the same care for other members. 26 And if one member suffers, all the members suffer with it; or if one member is honored, all the members rejoice with it.

27 Now you are the body of Christ and yet are individually [gifted] members. 28 And God has appointed these in the church:[122] first apostles, second prophets, third teachers, after that miracles, then gifts of healings, helps, governments,[123] varieties of tongues.[124] 29 Are all apostles? [No]Are all prophets? [No] Are all teachers? [No] Are all workers of miracles? [No]30 Do all have gifts of healings? [No]Do all speak with tongues? [No] Do all interpret? [No][125] 31 But earnestly desire the best gifts.

---

[119] In the context 12:4-11, it is the Spirit of God who purposefully gives spiritual gifts. Here God (presumably the Father) is said to put the gifts in the body as He purposes. In Eph 4:7,8 Christ is seen to be the giver of gifts. All of the Trinity is involved in giftedness.

[120] Notice I have captured the rhetorical question *If there were only one member, how could there be a body?*

[121] This is the metaphorical equivalent of 1Co 14:39.

[122] See Eph 4:11 for a fuller list. Evangelist and pastor omitted here.

[123] The word translated by *governments* (SRN 2941) is a *hapax legomena*, a one-time only occurring word. Here there is no context around it to help define it. Some Greek commentators would render it *wise counsels*. A cognate (SRN 2942) occurs in Acts 27:11, meaning helmsman or ship owner and in Rev 18:17, ship master. If *wise counsels*, it could be a manifestation of word of wisdom. Or it could be defined as some sort of lower-level leadership gift since it is not in the top three prioritized list. I have opted for this latter definition. See *governments*, **Glossary**.

[124] This list, 12:28, is the only list which prioritizes gifts—of any of the gift lists. It is obvious that these are leadership gifts and important ones. See also Eph 4:11 which repeats these and adds evangelist and pastor. Note that prophets occurs also on the *come—and—go* list. This list, the list in 12:28, and Eph 4:11 all indicate permanence (vested gifts) in gifting. They do so by referring by metonymy to the gifts via the persons having the gifts. So too, Ro 12:6-8, which contains teaching. See *metonymy*, *vested gifts*, **Glossary**.

[125] This whole list of gifts is given not to define the gifts but: (1) to illustrate the diversity of gifts just taught in 1Co 8:8-10 and the body metaphor, (2) to indicate where tongues fits in importance in the list of gifts, (3) to show that you cannot expect every person in a church to have the same gift, i.e. tongues. (4) to repeat again that it is God who sets in order the gifts. The Corinthians should not project lesser gifts on people but should seek the gifts more useful to the body. *See gift projection*, **Glossary**. See **Article, 63. Spiritual Gift Clusters**.

1 Corinthians 13:1-14:4

And yet I show you a more excellent way.[126]

Chapter 13

1 Though I speak earthly or heavenly languages, but lack love, I am just making meaningless noises like a noisy gong or a clanging cymbal. 2 And though I have the gift of prophecy, and understand all mysteries[127] and all knowledge, and though I have all faith, so that I could move mountains, but don't have love, I am nothing. 3 And though I give all my possessions to feed the poor, and even if I give the ultimate gift, my body to be burned, but I don't have love, I am nothing.[128]

4 Love perseveres patiently. Love acts kindly. Love harbors no jealousy. Love doesn't promote its own self interest.[129] Love is not proud. 5 Love does not behave rudely. Love doesn't demand its own way. Love is not irritable. It doesn't keep records of being wronged. 6 It doesn't rejoice in injustices, but rejoices when truth prevails. 7 Love never gives up but continues to patiently endure, to have faith, to have hope.

8 Love lasts forever. But gifts of prophecy, tongues, and words of knowledge—they will all cease.[130] 9 Our gifts—word of knowledge and prophecy—give us only a small part of the perspective. 10 But someday, in the end when we know fully, these gifts will not be needed. [131]

11 When I was a child, I spoke as a child, I understood as a child, I thought as a child. But when I became a man, I put away childish things. 12 For now we see imperfectly in a poor mirror but then we shall see with perfect clarity. Now I have partial knowledge. But then I shall know completely just as completely as God's knowledge of me. 13 Mean-while, three things will last: faith, hope, love. But the greatest of these is love.

Chapter 14

1 Eagerly seek love,[132] and zealously desire spiritual gifts, but especially the gift of prophecy. 2 For the one speaking in a tongue isn't speaking to people but to God. No one understands. That one may be speaking secret truths. 3 But the one who prophesies speaks to build up and urge to action and to comfort the hearers.[133] 4 A person speaking in tongues is strengthened personally. But one prophesying helps the

---

[126] Paul here gives a strong exhortation. The motivation behind the use of a gift is critical. The Corinthians are bickering about gifts. They are not exercising love so that gifts can be used with effectiveness. Paul describes love here not just to give an essay on love but to show what should be the nature of a gifted body—one in which love relationships exist.

[127] This is hidden truth known only through God *revealing* it.

[128] In 1Co 13:1-3, six gifts are referred to directly or by illustration: kinds of tongues; prophecy; word of wisdom; word of knowledge; faith; giving (here martyrdom is a supreme act of giving). Again these gifts aren't given to define gifts but to show that without love as a motivating force these gifts do not accomplish their purposes.

[129] We have a proverb—*toot one's own horn*. Love doesn't toot its own horn.

[130] 1Co 13:8,9 refers to three gifts: prophecy, kinds of tongues, word of knowledge. They are mentioned only to show their impermanence, for time only, when compared with love which will last eternally.

[131] This is an unclear verse, literally when *that which is perfect* (SRN 5046) is come. This could be the Second Coming or when the church reaches maturity in the future. Some commentators believe this is the completed canon of Scriptures. My preference—Second Coming.

[132] See topic of love in all the major gifts passages—Ro 12:9,10 and Eph 4:15 as well as 1Co 13.

[133] It is from this verse that I draw out my threefold thrust of prophecy: exhorts, admonishes, comforts. See *prophecy*, **Glossary**.

1 Corinthians 14:5-21

whole church.

5 I wish you all spoke with tongues, but even more, that you all would prophesy; for the one prophesying is more useful than the one speaking in tongues, unless someone interprets so that the church is helped. 6 But now, Christian friends, if I come to you speaking in tongues, what good is it to you? But if I speak to you by revelation—a word of knowledge, or prophecy, or some teaching, [that will help]?[134]

7 Even a lifeless musical instrument like a flute or harp must sound their notes distinctly for the tune to be understood. 8 And if the bugler doesn't give a clear call, how will the soldiers get ready for battle?[135] 9 In the same way if you give a tongue, how will anyone understand? Your words will vanish into air. 10 There are many different kinds of languages in the world which can be understood. 11 But, if I do not know the meaning of a language, I will be a foreigner to whoever speaks it, and whoever speaks it will be a foreigner to me. 12 So you are zealous for spiritual gifts. Why not then focus on the ones of greater use for the church?

13 Therefore, let the person giving a tongue pray for the gift of interpreting tongues.[136] 14 If I pray in a tongue,[137] my spirit prays, but my mind doesn't understand it. 15 What is the conclusion then? I want to pray in the spirit, and I want to also pray with understanding. [Just like] I want to sing in the spirit, and I want also to sing with understanding. 16 Otherwise, if you praise in the spirit, how can others join in your praise, since they don't understand what you say? 17 For you indeed may be personally benefited but others are not helped.

18 I thank my God I speak in tongues more than you all. 19 But in a church service I would rather speak five words that can be understood, in order to teach others, than ten thousand words in tongues.[138]

20 Christian friends, don't be childish in understanding these things. Be innocent as babies about evil.[139] But in your thinking be mature. 21 In the law it is written:

---

[134] This could be interpreted otherwise as—*unless I give a tongue which is interpreted as a word of knowledge or prophesy or teaching*. The list 14:6 gives tongues, the generic gift title—revelation, word of knowledge, prophecy, and teaching. However, these latter gifts could be aspects of tongues if the latter interpretation were held.

[135] In this Corinthian letter Paul illustrates strongly his teaching gift. He is dominantly a left-brained (very logical) teacher; but note how he uses many, many right brained pictures, illustrations, etc., in his teaching because he wants to communicate to all.

[136] My empirical giftedness research for 10 years shows it is very rare for a person to have both tongues and interpretation of tongues. In light of this prayer admonition, what does that mean? Folks today should project the gift of interpreting tongues as much as they do the gift of tongues—and hence bring some balance to this.

[137] Some Pentecostal/ Charismatic groups speak of a prayer language, "Have you got your prayer language yet?" They mean speaking in tongues and presumably use this verse as their backing for that. Frequently, they project this gift on others. When groups are ministering to others about healing or deliverance they will often be praying in tongues. See Eph 6:18; Jude 20. See *gift projection*, **Glossary**.

[138] This is another example of Paul's willingness to give up his rights in order for the good of others.

[139] See Mt 18:3.

1 Corinthians 14:22-39

> "With people of other
> languages and
> other lips
> I will speak to this
> people;
> And yet, for all that,
> they will not hear
> Me,"
> says the Lord.[140]

22 Therefore tongues are for a sign, not for believers, but to unbelievers. Prophecy is for believers, not for unbelievers.

23 So when the whole church assembles, and all speak with tongues, won't the un-informed or unbelievers think you are crazy? 24 But if all prophesy, and an unbeliever or an uninformed person comes in, they will be convicted. 25 Their secret thoughts will be laid bare. They will bow down and will worship God. They will report that God is truly among you.

26 What am I saying then, Christian friends? When you meet to worship, one of you has a psalm, another has a teaching, another has a tongue, another has a revelation, someone else has an interpretation.[141] Let all things be done for edification.[142] 27 If anyone speaks in a tongue, two or three at the most, do it one after another and let each be interpreted. 28 But if there is no interpreter, let those tongues be done privately to God. 29 Let two or three prophets speak, and let others discern. 30 But if someone else gets a revelation, the one speaking can stop. 31 Each can prophesy one by one so that all may learn and all may be encouraged. 32 People who prophesy can control what they are doing. 33 For God is not disorderly but peaceful—as in all the churches of God's people.

34 Let your women keep silent in the churches.[143] They are not permitted to speak but should be submissive, as the law also says. 35 And if they want to learn something, let them ask their own husbands at home. For it is shameful for women to speak in church.[144]

36 Or did the word of God come from you? Or are you the only ones who hear God?[145] 37 If you have the gift of prophecy or if you are spiritual you will acknowledge that what I am saying are commands from the Lord. [I have tried to clear up misunderstandings about gifts] But if anyone is ignorant now, let that one stay ignorant.[146]

39 Therefore, fellow Christians, be eager to prophesy. But do not forbid to speak with tongues.[147]

---

[140] See Dt 28:49.

[141] See Col 3:16,17—a direct exhortation to operate like this.

[142] Paul here gives some more information on the structure of the gathered church. Here the church is seen to be a gifted church in which a number of people participate in the worship by using their gifts in an orderly way, which builds up the church.

[143] Compare this with 1Ti 2:12 where *silent* used there means not disruptive (it does not mean be quiet and don't speak).

[144] I don't think Paul is talking about speaking in general, since he talks about women praying in the church with heads uncovered previously. And when talking about orderly use of gifts in v. 26 he does not limit these gifts to men only. I think here, in the context, he is talking about disruptions, asking questions that could better be answered at home. For God is a God of order. The thrust of these contexts is for orderly public worship.

[145] Paul uses a bit of irony here. He is really saying that his word from God is an apostolic one that they should heed. See *irony*, **Glossary**.

[146] See 1Co 12:1. Paul starts to address their ignorance on spiritual gifts. Now he closes as if to say, *"If you haven't got it by now you never will!"*

[147] See 1Co 12:21,—a metaphorical equivalent of this admonition.

1 Corinthians 14:40-15:19

40 Everything should be done in a proper, orderly manner.[148]

IX. (Ch 15,16) Problem[149] About Resurrection[150]

Chapter 15
Contextual Flow:
Paul in chapter 15 deals with a false teaching denying the resurrection by showing that the resurrection is the foundation of the Gospel and by answering questions about the resurrected body.[151]
5:1,2
I want to remind you of the Gospel.
15:3-7
Christ died for our sins and rose again. This is confirmed by many witnesses.

15:8-11
  8 Then last of all He was seen by me also, as though I had been born almost too late for this. 9 For I am the least of the apostles.[152] I don't deserve to be called an apostle because I persecuted God's church. 10 But by the grace of God I am what I am [an apostle]. His grace in me was not without effect. I have worked harder than all the other apostles. Yet it was not I, but the grace of God working through me. 11 So then, whether I preach it or they preach it, you have believed it.
15:12-19
Paul refutes the false teaching that there is no resurrection of the dead by showing such a doctrine also

---

[148] This entire passage, 1Co 12-14, is instructive from a leadership perspective. Leaders must be able to solve problems with regard to use and abuse of gifts. Here we see one of the major apostolic functions—correcting of doctrine and practice. We see also how important the prophetic gift is, a gift not so used today in the majority of churches. We see also that practices today, which do not allow tongues and the other so-called charismatic gifts, are in violation of this strong admonition of verse 39 and are not obeying verse 26.

[149] This is Problem #9 of 10 problems that Paul has to deal with in the Corinthian situation. The first 8 problems have been dominantly orthopraxic (related to behavioral practices in the Corinthian church) with a tad of orthodoxic issues (Paul gives revelation truth on several of these behavioral situations). But this one is largely an orthodoxic problem. Revelation is needed. Paul gives both explanation and revelation on this problem. We learn more about the resurrection and resurrection life, somewhat, than anywhere else in Scripture. Note again, this repetitive dealing with various problems highlights the complexity macro lesson, **Macro Lesson 41:** *Leadership is complex, problematic, difficult and fraught with risk—which is why leadership is needed.* See **LEADERSHIP TOPIC 1. COMPLEXITY OF LEADERSHIP**. See *disputed practice, stronger brother, weaker brother,* **Glossary**. See **Articles**, *35. Macro Lessons Defined; 36. Macro Lessons—List of 41 Across Six Leadership Eras.*

[150] From a leadership standpoint chapter 15, dealing with the false teaching on the resurrection, is instructive for several reasons: (1) it demonstrates an apostolic function—that of correcting false teaching; (2) it inspires hope—a major high level function of leadership; (3) the sub-context 15:8-11 asserts Paul's apostolic authority, a subject he will deal much more comprehensively in 2Co. See **Articles**, *28. Leadership Functions—Three High Level Generic Functions; 2. Apostolic Functions.*

[151] See 2Ti 2:18 for another false view of the resurrection.

[152] See 1Ti 1:15-16 where Paul calls himself, chief of sinners.

1 Corinthians 15:20-16:1

denies Christ's resurrection and invalidates the Gospel message.

15:20-28
Christ has risen from the dead and will triumphantly return again to rule and to raise up those who belong to him.

15:29-32
Paul gives two secondary reasons backing up the claim that there is a resurrection: (1) baptism for the dead; (2) under girding reason why he persists in his Apostolic ministry fraught with danger.

15:33-34
Don't be led astray by this false teaching—you don't know God if you believe it.

15:35-41
Paul answers questions about a resurrection body by using illustrations from everyday life: seeds and plants; different kinds of animal bodies; astronomical bodies.

15:42-49
Paul carries the seed analogy further asserting that a mortal body will be changed into a spiritual body at the resurrection—after the likeness of Christ's resurrected body.

15:50
A resurrected body which, is immortal is necessary in order to share in God's kingdom.

15:51-57
At the return of Christ our bodies will be transformed into immortal bodies—demonstrating Christ's victory over death.

15:58
Stand firm and continue working for Christ since what you do for Christ will count.

I. (Ch 16) Problem About Support[153]

Chapter 16[154]

1 Now concerning the collection for the Church in Jerusalem[155]— do what I told the churches in

---

[153] This is Problem #10 of 10 problems that Paul has to deal with in the Corinthian situation. Note carefully Paul's dealing with finances. Integrity is crucial for him when dealing with finances. He does not want to go under due to the financial barrier. Note too he is dealing with apostolic function 6, *Resource Old Ministries and New Ones*. Paul is unselfish in his carrying out of this function. Very rarely will you ever see him asking for funds for himself. Always he is collecting funds to help a corporate situation in financial need or some other apostolic workers. This repetitive dealing with various problems highlights the complexity macro lesson, **Macro Lesson 41:** *Leadership is complex, problematic, difficult and fraught with risk—which is why leadership is needed.* See **LEADERSHIP TOPIC 1. COMPLEXITY OF LEADERSHIP.** See *disputed practice, stronger brother, weaker brother*, **Glossary.** See **Articles**, *35. Macro Lessons Defined; 36. Macro Lessons—List of 41 Across Six Leadership Eras; 15. Finishing Well—Six Major Barriers Identified.*

[154] Paul's closing words usually are filled with all kinds of leadership implications. Usually they will have a series of small miscellaneous comments. Such is the case with 1Co 16. Of note, Paul subtly points out the Corinthians lack of recognition, respect for, and support of Christian workers by referring to three different cases (himself—a rare and subtle reference, and Timothy, and Stephanus).

[155] See impact of Barnabas' mentoring on Paul about giving: Ac 4:36,37; 11:29,30; Ro 15:25,26. See **Article**, *5. Barnabas—Significant Mentoring.*

1 Corinthians 16:2-12

Galatia to do. 2 On the first day of every week each one of you should put some money aside, in proportion to what you have earned.[156] That way there will be no need for special collections when I come. 3 And when I come, I will send the ones you approve,[157] along with letters of recommendation, to take your liberal offerings to Jerusalem.[158] 4 If appropriate, I may also accompany them.[159]

5 Now I will come to you after I have been to Macedonia—for I do intend to go through Macedonia. 6 And it could be that I will stay awhile, or maybe even spend the whole winter with you. And then you may send[160] me on my journey, wherever I go. 7 For I do not wish to only have a short visit. I hope to spend a longer time with you, if the Lord permits. 8 But I will stay in Ephesus until Pentecost.[161] 9 For a great opportunity for effective ministry has opened up. But there are many who oppose me.[162]

10 Now if Timothy comes, treat him with respect.[163] He is doing the work of the Lord, just like me. 11 Don't look down on him. But send him on his journey in peace, so that he will come back to me. I am waiting for him with the brothers.[164]

12 Now concerning [our] brother Apollos,[165] I strongly urged[166] him to come to you with the brothers, but he was quite unwilling to come at this time. However, he will come when it is convenient for him.

---

[156] Notice, Paul advocates proportionate giving, not a tithe. Note also the systematic giving.

[157] See also 2Co 8:18-21 for integrity in handling of finances. Paul definitely wants to avoid the financial barrier, one which derails many leaders today.

[158] Note the special care to maintain integrity with regard to finances (financial issues often waylay a leader). See **Article**, *15. Finishing Well—Six Major Barriers*.

[159] Paul is audacious—asking for money from this problem-filled church. He expands on this quick teaching on giving in 2Co 8,9. Note he implies that the Galatian church is following his orders about giving—a motivating lever to challenge the Corinthians. In 2Co 8,9 he again uses this comparative motivational technique, there using the Philippian church. See **Article**, *41. Motivation Principles: Pauline Influence*.

[160] When Paul uses *Send* (SRN 4311) he means to send him off and fit him out with the requisites for a journey—i.e. resources, money, whatever. See also verse 11 where Paul uses this same word to urge the Corinthians to back Timothy.

[161] The Pentecost festival is mentioned in Ac 2:1ff; 20:16. See also 1Co 9:20, where Paul talks about becoming a Jew to Jews. This is an example of that.

[162] A major leadership principle is embedded here. *Success always brings with it problems*. In this case success has brought about major opposition. Later in 2Co you will see that in spite of this great opportunity Paul decides to leave the scene, partially because of the tremendous pressure he feels from the Corinthians challenging his spiritual authority.

[163] See problem of younger leader with older people—1Ti 4:12.

[164] Paul is here acting as a mentor sponsor for Timothy. Not only does he strongly ask for Timothy to be treated with respect, he also asks that they *send* (SRN 4311) him off—that is, give him financial backing. Young leaders in Asian and African setting often do not get respect for their leadership since the cultures respect age and tend to want older leaders. See **Articles**, *37. Mentoring—An Informal Training Model; 47. Paul—Mentor For Many*.

[165] See fn 1Co 1:12. Apollos is a strong leader.

[166] This is another example of the gift of exhortation in action, *strongly urge* (SRN 3870). See also verse 15 where this word is used. See *spiritual gift, exhortation,* **Glossary**.

1 Corinthians 16:13-24

13 Be on the alert, persist in your Christian walk, be brave, be strong. 14 Let all that you do be done with love.

15 You know that Stephanas and his family were the first Christians in Greece. They have dedicated themselves to serving Christians. 16 I urge you, fellow Christians that you respect their leadership, and others like them who also serve.[167] 17 I am glad that Stephanas, Fortunatus, and Achaicus came. They have made up for your lack of help.[168] 18 For they have encouraged me just like they did you. These men deserve to be honored.

19 The churches in Asia greet you. Aquila and Priscilla[169] greet you heartily in the Lord along with the church that meets in their house.[170] 20 All the Christians greet you. Greet each other in Christian love.

21 And here is my own personal greeting, written by me—Paul.[171]

22 If anyone does not love the Lord Jesus Christ, let him be accursed. O Lord, come!

23 The grace[172] of our Lord Jesus Christ be with you.[173]

24 My love to all of you in Christ Jesus. Amen.[174]

---

[167] Again as with Timothy in 16:10,11, Paul acts as a mentor sponsor, this time for Stephanus. See *mentor sponsor*, **Glossary**.

[168] Paul gives a slight admonition about lack of support for himself—a problem being repeatedly dealt with in these closing remarks. Paul rarely mentions his own need.

[169] A leadership team, wife and husband, involved in hosting several house churches. Prisca, also called Priscilla seems to be the lead person (mentioned first in the majority of listings of their names). They, with Priscilla probably in the lead, grounded Apollos in the Gospel truths (see Acts 18:26). Priscilla, most likely, was teaching in the Ephesus Church at the time of Paul's writing of 1Ti. Another indication that 1Ti 2:12 and 1Co 14:34 are not prohibiting women from talking or teaching or being leaders but is dealing with disruption in the church at Corinth and heretical teaching in Ephesus. Paul has the highest regard for this couple, see Romans 16:3,4. Other references to them include Ac 18:2,18,26; Ro 16:3,4; 2Ti 4:19.

[170] This gives insights into church structure. Also note the personal names that are included in this chapter (Timothy, Apollos, Stephanas, Fortunatus, Achaicus, Aquila, Priscilla; earlier in the book, Sosthenes, Chloe, Peter, Crispus, Gaius, Barnabas). It is indicative of a Pauline leadership value: Paul felt that ministry ought to be personal. He developed lots of meaningful relationships. Personal ministry allows for a strong probability of accomplishing one of the major leadership lessons that has been identified: *Effective leaders view leadership selection and development as a priority in ministry.* See *leadership value*, **Glossary**. See **Article**, *32. Leadership Selection; 30. Leadership Lessons, Seven Major Lessons Identified; 43. Paul—And His Companions*.

[171] Paul signs off personally like this on four letters—1Co 16:21; Gal 6:11; Col 4:18; Phm 1:19—all books in which he is exerting strong influence

[172] Paul closes this epistle by blessing the Corinthians with grace, The Greek word here is *grace*, (SRN 5485). Paul uses this in 1 Ti, 2 Ti, Tit and here in the sense of the enabling presence of God in a life so as to cause that one to persevere victoriously. See *grace*, **Glossary**.

[173] One wonders if verses 22,23 are part of Paul's doing spiritual warfare: verse 22 a curse; verse 23 a blessing. If so, he is certainly using apostolic authority.

[174] Some refer to a note on some manuscript which reads: The first [epistle] to the Corinthians was written from Philippi by Stephanas and Fortunatus and Achaicus and Timotheus. That is, these were the stenographers as Paul dictated. If so, what a good Bible class! Several such postscripts are given with different epistles and are suggestive.

For Further Leadership Study--First Corinthians

General

1Co contains five kinds of leadership genre. Remember, leadership genre means sources from which to draw out leadership information. 1Co contains Leadership Acts, Biographical, Direct, Book as a Whole, Macro Lessons. 1Co is a series of leadership acts in which Paul, the outside leader who founded the church and moved on, now seeks to handle a range of major problems that have arisen. There is biographical information, leadership acts, and even some direct individual verses directed at those who are influencing in the church. This book is filled with leadership lessons because it is an example of a leader confronting typical leadership issues that do arise in local churches. See **Article**, *29. Leadership Genre—7 Types*.

Suggestions For Further Study

1. Leadership acts can be studied with great profit, both for content, methodology, principles, and values. Each of the problems can be studied as a leadership act. See **Article**, *26. Leadership Act*.

2. Paul's leadership styles should be studied, noting the variety he uses. In my leadership comments in the footnotes I have treated a number of the genre above. But further in-depth study can be done. See **Article**, *49. Pauline Leadership Styles*. See also a separate booklet I have published, See **Bibliography, Coming To Conclusions on Leadership Styles.**

3. This a major book contributing to giftedness theory. Its insights must be studied in depth and comparatively with other gifts passages for major lessons. I suggest **Unlocking Your Giftedness—What Leaders Need To Know To Develop Themselves and Others**. See **Bibliography** for information on this book. This book was developed for leaders. An in-depth comparison of all giftedness passages is given in this book.

4. Each of the problems should be studied in depth to understand the confrontation leadership style.

5. This book contributes to what apostolic leadership looks like. Apostolic workers use highly directive leadership styles to solve problems—especially with immature followers. See **Article**, *2. Apostolic Functions*.

6. Chapter 7 dealing with marriage, singleness and separation situations should be studied in depth for content since most leaders today will be facing situations with divorced people, separated people, many single people and single again people. Chapter 7 must be studied comparatively with the Gospel passages on marriage. Leaders need a clear understanding of their position on marriage, divorce, and separation—especially as it relates to emerging leaders and leaders. Many emerging leaders will arise from backgrounds of divorce and separation.

For Further Leadership Study   page 40

Special Comments

This book highlights an important doctrine—the resurrection of the Lord. That truth is essential to the whole Christian message. In it lies God's affirmation of all that Christ was and did. In it lies power that will enable. In it lies the future hope of things being made right. Chapter 15 should be studied exegetically and in-depth since it contains the most comprehensive ideas about resurrection and after- life details.

Personal Response

1. What is the most significant leadership insight you have gained from your study of 1Co?

2. What one idea from this study can you put into practice in your own leadership? How?

Your Observations.

You may want to jot down important insights you want to remember. You may wish to note follow-up intents.

BOOK	**2 CORINTHIANS**	**Author: Paul**

Characters Who To/For
People mentioned or involved: Paul, Timothy, Titus
The young church at Corinth and other churches in Achaia (Greece)

Literature Type
A letter containing teaching and exhortation

Story Line
Paul had heard back from the church in response to his first letter. They had basically responded positively to his exhortations. It was clear, however, that at least some of them had personally misunderstood Paul, his ministry, and motivations behind his actions. Understandably then one can see why this letter is so personal and emotional. Paul's character and ministry are on the line. He writes to explain himself and does so in the first section of the book. The writing of the letter is compounded by the fact that he has a delicate task—asking the Corinthians for money to help out in a sister church situation. He does this in the middle portion of the letter and thus we are given teaching on giving that nowhere else occurs in the Scriptures. Paul then goes on in the final section of the book to defend his apostolic authority with vigor.

Structure
I.   (Ch 1-7)   **Paul's Apostolic Ministry and Motives**

II. (Ch 8,9)   **Paul's Financial Appeal to the Corinthians**

III. (Ch 10-12) **Paul's Defense of His Authority**

Theme
PAUL'S APOSTOLIC DEFENSE,
- involved an explanation of his personal conduct, motives, and view of the ministry,
- was in harmony with his plea for the Jerusalem gift, and
- concluded with an overwhelming refutation of arguments opposing his Apostolic authority.

Key Words
Ministry and related words (18); personal references to Paul himself (many); apostle(s) (6); grace (25)

Key Events
None

Overview of 2 Corinthians

Purposes
- to correct the over correction the Corinthians had made in regards to the immorality problem mentioned in the 1st letter,
- to explain his motives and ministry among the Corinthians so as to correct misrepresentations being circulated about him,
- to establish his spiritual authority among them,
- to give further instruction about the offering,
- to bring to light ministry values that ought to under gird a leader.

Why Important

No other book in the Scriptures so exposes the inner life of a leader in terms of leadership values. A leadership value is an underlying assumption, which affects how a leader behaves in or perceives leadership situations. It is a mindset, which gives meaning to ourselves and explains why we do things or think things. It can relate to a belief, personal ethical conduct, personal feelings desired about situations, and ideas of what brings success or failure in ministry. Our values might be rooted in personality, is certainly related to our heritage and our experiences in leadership, which have shaped us. About 19 major Pauline leadership values (and many lesser related ones) are exposed in 2 Corinthians. These can be very instructive for today's leaders. The book also exposes the notion of spiritual authority and its ultimate aims. While other power bases are necessary in the ministry, it is this power base, spiritual authority, which should be the priority of an effective leader for God.

Where It Fits

This is a book about leadership in the Church Leadership Era—the age in which we live today. 2Co was most likely written on Paul's third missionary journey. He had been a Christian for about 21 years. So we are getting some mature leadership advice. Because Paul had been misunderstood by some in his first letter to the Corinthians he goes into personal details about his reasons, motivations, and ministry philosophy-- leadership values. This letter then unfolds for us insights into apostolic leadership, spiritual authority, and leadership values of the most prominent church leader to the Gentiles. Many of these values, though uniquely and personally Paul's, will fit many church leaders today.

General Reflections On Second Corinthians

The church leadership era is dominated by Paul's leadership. His finest hour as an apostolic church leader occurred with the crisis at Corinth. Paul had been a Christian leader about 21 or so years. He was probably in his early 50s. He was a mature leader. His whole ministry was threatened by this crisis at Corinth. If this crisis could not be solved he would have been discredited and his ministry as we now know it would never have happened. He would have been finished.

Paul had sent off his first letter to Corinth and some problems had been resolved. He perhaps sent off a second letter which we don't have. But something has happened as a result of this interplay. A sizable group at Corinth opposes Paul. Whereas in 1Co Paul addresses a number of complex problems in the church, in 2Co he is addressing mainly two: (1) the attacks against his own apostolic leadership, (2) the continued effort to raise money to help the church in Jerusalem. As frequently happens in problematic situations the issues move from problems directly to people. Instead of disagreeing with Paul's solutions to problems, a sizable group in Corinth began to attack Paul himself—his qualifications, his character, his leadership.

So then Paul is forced to write to defend his own leadership and character. Because he is defending his apostolic authority and character, Paul gives us his innermost thoughts—the motivations behind what he was doing. He tells us why he did things. He explains his reasons. He addresses their misunderstandings. Because of this we can identify the leadership values that underlie his thinking. Thus 2Co, with all its emotion, transparency, vulnerability—one of Paul's most personal letters—provides a backdrop replete with leadership findings. We learn what it means to minister out of being. For Paul's beingness is certainly exposed.

Paul is under great pressure—health problems, burdens for the churches he related to, his own reputation at stake, his life purpose and achievements on the line. And he comes through with flying colors. Read these lessons and realize you are dealing with beingness at its best. Paul, a mature Christian leader under pressure, is modeling for us and teaching us what it means to be an honest leader who has integrity. Character counts in leadership. Paul models that.

Leadership Topic/Lessons

1. MINISTRY PHILOSOPHY AND VALUES.

Ministry philosophy is key to a leader's overall influence and ultimate achievement. 2Co exposes us to Pauline leadership values and thus helps us begin to see the underpinnings of Paul's ministry philosophy. *A ministry philosophy is a strategically organized set of values. They guide a leader in his/her application of personal giftedness, calling, and influence to the leadership situations. Ultimately they move a leader to achieve God-given purposes and leave behind an ultimate contribution for a life-work.* Values learned via experience and flowing from one's beingness comprise a ministry philosophy. Below are given 19 Pauline values identified in 2Co which help explain Paul's motivations and actions in his dealing with the Corinthians. *A leadership value is an underlying assumption which affects how a leader behaves in or perceives leadership situations.* Usually, when explicitly identified and written, the statement will contain strong forceful words like should, ought, or must to indicate the strength of the value. e.g. A specific Pauline leadership value—*Paul felt he should view personal relationships as an important part of ministry, both as a means for ministry and as an end in itself of ministry.* Or generalized to all leaders—*Leaders should view personal relationships as an important part of ministry, both as a means for ministry and as an end in itself of ministry.* Stronger would be the word *ought* and even stronger the word *must*. I have generalized from specific statements applying uniquely to Paul to broader statements. These statements could easily fit leaders today. Nineteen is not a magic number. There are probably more. But these are the ones I saw and they are certainly some of the most important ones. See **Article**, *39. Ministry Philosophy; 51. Pauline Leadership Values.*

Leadership Values Suggested in 2 Corinthians:
   a. **Divine Appointment.** Leaders ought to be sure that God appointed them to ministry situations.
   b. **Training Methodology.** Leaders must be concerned about leadership selection and development.
   c. **Personal Ministry.** Leaders should view personal relationships as an important part of ministry.
   d. **Sovereign Mindset.** Leaders ought to see God's hand in their circumstances as part of His plan for developing them as leaders. See *sovereign mindset*, **Glossary**. See **Article**, *50. Sovereign Mindset.*
   e. **Integrity and Openness.** Leaders should not be deceptive in their dealings with followers but should instead be open, honest, forthright, and frank with them. See **Article**, *22. Integrity—A Top Leadership Quality.*
   f. **Ultimate accountability.** Leaders' actions must be restrained by the fact that they will ultimately give an account to God for their leadership actions. See **Articles**, *9. Day of Christ—Implications for Leaders; 40. Motivating Factors for Ministry.*
   g. **Spiritual Authority**—Its ends. Spiritual authority ought to be used to mature followers. See **Articles**, *60. Spiritual Authority Defined—Six Characteristics; 16. Followership—Ten Commandments.*

h. **Loyalty Testing.** Leaders must know the level of followership loyalty in order to wisely exercise leadership influence. See **Article,** *16. Followership—Ten Commandments.*
i. **True Credentials** (competency and results). A leader should be able to point to results from ministry as a recommendation of God's authority in him/her.
j. **True Competence** (its ultimate source). A leader's ultimate confidence for ministry must not rest in his/her competence but in God the author of that competence.
k. **Transforming Ministry.** Followers who are increasingly being set free by the Holy Spirit and who are increasingly being transformed into Christ's image ought to be the hope and expectation of a Christian leader.
l. **Prominence of Christ in Ministry.** A leader must not seek to bring attention to himself/herself through ministry but must seek to exalt Christ as Lord.
m. **Servant Leadership.** A leader ought to see leadership as focused on serving followers on Jesus' behalf.
n. **Death/Life Paradox.** The firstfruits of Jesus resurrection life ought to be experienced in the death producing circumstances of life and ought to serve as a hallmark of spiritual life for followers. In other words, Christianity ought to work in thick or thin.
o. **Motivational Force.** Leaders should use obligation to Christ (in light of his death for believers) to motivate believers to service for Christ.
p. **True Judgment Criterion.** Leaders should value people in terms of their relationship to God in Christ and not according to their outward success in the world (even in the religious world).
q. **Unequally Yoked.** Christian leadership must not be dominated by relationships with unbelievers so that non-Christian values hold sway.
r. **Financial Equality Principle.** Christian leadership must teach that Christian giving is a reciprocal balancing between needs and surplus.
s. **Financial Integrity.** A Christian leader must handle finances with absolute integrity.

These certainly do not exhaust the values implied in 2Co but do reflect a number of important contexts explaining Paul's views on ministry and motivating factors for his own leadership actions.

2. FINANCIAL SAFEGUARD.

Leaders must be open and honest with followers concerning giving and finances. Churches and parachurch organizations have financial needs just like any other organization in society. These needs must be met. How leaders influence followers with respect to meeting these needs is important. Paul demonstrates this delicate matter in 2Co 8,9. Some observations concerning his handling of financial matters include:

Leadership Principles/ Values Suggested by this concept:
a. A major motivational technique relates the issue of giving to the issue of absolute surrender. True freedom to give flows from a life given to God.

b. Another motivational technique involves competitive comparisons with others who are poorer and yet give beyond expectations.
c. Willingness to give, not the amount given, is the criterion for giving.
d. Resources in the wider body of Christ will include surplus and great need. Where there is surplus giving should shift resources to needs.
e. Integrity in the handling of money is essential.

3. SPIRITUAL AUTHORITY INSIGHTS.

Paul demonstrates the essentials of spiritual authority in his defense of his apostolic authority. *Spiritual authority is the right to influence conferred upon a leader by followers who willingly follow that leader because of their perception of spirituality in the leader as demonstrated by a godly life (character), gifted power, and deep experience with God.* Paul's entire letter emphasizes these elements: character, gifted power (both in revelation, and in application to the situation including spiritual warfare), and in deep experiences with God in which he has seen the sufficiency of Christ put to the test and proved sufficient. See **Article**, *60. Spiritual Authority—defined, Six Characteristics*.

Leadership Principles/ Values Suggested by this concept:
a. Spiritual authority comes from God.
b. The more mature that followers are, the more they recognize and follow spiritual authority.
c. Spiritual authority essentially uses modeling, persuasion, and demonstrated competence as the means to influence followers.
d. Spiritual authority is the ideal kind of authority that a leader should strive for but other authority bases must be used when followers are immature.
e. Godly character, deep experiences with God and gifted-power are indications of spiritual authority which followers relate to.
f. Spiritual authority is given in order for leaders to be able to mature followers.

4. AUTHORITY/POWER.

An apostolic leader must demonstrate God-given power, in order to validate his/her authority, when correcting major problematic/crises situations in a church. While Paul would prefer their willing response to his appeals he is prepared to enforce his analysis and solutions with God-given power. See 2Co 13. See **Article**, *2. Apostolic Functions*.

Leadership Principles/ Values Suggested by this concept:
a. Highly directive leadership styles must be used when followers are immature. That is, when they cannot recognize spiritual authority nor discern issues and underlying truth about them.
b. A leader must have a majority of followers with him/her in order to enforce discipline in a situation.
c. A leader whose character is defamed must be vindicated, preferably by God alone. Clarification, openness, identifying under lying motivations and vulnerability along with demonstrated deep experiences from God are the tools for correcting viewpoints of a leader's character.

d. Coercive authority must be backed by God-demonstrated power. That is, a leader confronting problems must have supernatural manifestations validating God's backing and actual intervention in the situation.

5. PERSONAL EXPERIENCE /SPIRITUAL AUTHORITY.

Spiritual authority is the right to influence conferred upon a leader by followers because of their perception of spirituality (God's presence, power, values, etc.) in a leader. While there is an intrinsic spirituality invested by God in a spiritual leader, immature followers will not always see it or respond to it. Spiritual authority as recognized by followers comes in several ways: (1) by going through deep experiences with God and being sustained and met by God in them; that is, knowing God's resources in Christ and experiencing the sufficiency of them. (2) by modeling of Godly character because of an understanding of God and His ways and because of an intimate relationship with God; (3) by demonstration of God's power via giftedness (God's special anointing on ministry efforts using giftedness—natural abilities, acquired skills, and spiritual gifts). A person using spiritual authority influences followers through persuasion (a power form), force of personality/charisma—a personal authority form; demonstrated expertise, moral and other—a competency authority form. Modeling is a dominant methodology that allows these various power and authority forms to influence. Paul, in 2Co demonstrates all of the power forms. See **Article, *21. Influence, Power, and Authority Forms; 48. Paul— Modeling as An Influence Means; 60. Spiritual Authority Defined—Six Characteristics.***

Leadership Principles/ Values Suggested by this concept:
a. Modeling, especially of deep experiences with God and lessons learned, is a major means of exposing spiritual authority for recognition by followers. Paul does this in several contextual units in 2Co.
b. Transparency about issues in question must be demonstrated in order to foster credibility and trust, especially where character has been defamed.
c. Exposure to truth about God and from God concerning issues must be prominent. A leader who cannot hear from God on critical issues in the life of a church or Christian organization has little to lead with. A leader is a person with God-given capacity, with a God-given burden, who is influencing a specific group of God's people toward God's purposes for them. To fail to hear from God is to not lead toward God's purposes for a group. This hearing from God is intensified in conflict and crises situations.
d. Godly character, especially integrity, must be demonstrated in a problematic situation where character assassination has happened. The response in the situation by the leader on trial is probably more important than the issues of the situation.
e. Competency in leadership must be demonstrated. While followers may not want to follow a leader for a number of reasons—they will inherently be drawn to expertise applied in a leadership situation even when they might not otherwise approve of a leader.
f. Leaders should attempt to take immature leaders to a new level of awareness of spiritual authority. While highly directive leadership styles are in order, the leader

should also offer non-highly directive alternatives (willful compliance instead of forced compliance) whenever possible.

6. MOTIVATIONAL LESSONS

Paul demonstrates several techniques for motivating the Corinthians. Leaders are people with God-given capacities and a God-given burden who are influencing a specific group of people toward God's purposes for them. Influence is the key word. And motivational techniques are means of exerting that influence. Motivation in this case is even more difficult since Paul is confronting a problem church in which a minority are not responding to him. Paul uses several means of motivating (of course including raw spiritual authority concepts described above). See **Articles, 40.** *Motivational Factors For Ministry; 41. Motivating Principles: Pauline Influence.*

Leadership Principles/ Observations Suggested by this concept:
   a. Goodwin's Expectation Principle, a social dynamic usually dealing with individuals, which recognizes that emerging leaders will usually rise to the level of expectancy of someone they respect, is applied by Paul to a group situation of followers. Paul states his personal positive outcome expectancies for the Corinthians, both concerning their giving and their following of his exhortations.
   b. Paul uses the gift of exhortation throughout the book, deliberately, openly, and with clear application to situations. See footnotes identifying the gift of exhortation in use.
   c. Paul uses a form of comparative competition. He describes what other churches have done with respect to giving (in a rather positive ideal description) in order to set expectancies for giving from the Corinthians.
   d. Paul tells the Corinthians that he has said great things about their giving to other churches. Their failure to give would make them lose face in the eyes of these other churches.
   e. Paul commissions a delegate from one of the churches which has given and been used as a model to go to Corinth to be part of the group that will administer the gift.
   f. Paul uses Jesus as a model of giving.
   g. Paul uses coercive authority (threatens to exercise spiritual power to correct situations if people do not respond voluntary) backed by a personal visit to motivate.
   h. Paul uses well reasoned out logic in giving solutions to issues and defending his own character.
   i. Paul uses irony, often, in order to force the Corinthians to see their positions on things and to challenge them to respond.

7. TEACHING ON GIVING

Chapters 8 and 9 give us the most comprehensive treatment of N.T. Church giving. I am certain that Paul was deeply affected by his mentor, Barnabas, concerning giving. See Ac 4:36,37; 11:27-30. Paul advocates giving to help fellow churches in need. He also advocates giving to help Christian workers (see fn on this in 1Co 9, 16 as well as Php

4:10-17). His strong exhortations on giving highlight a number of principles which I have identified below. See **Article**, *18. Giving—Paul's view in 2 Corinthians*.

Leadership Principles/ Values Suggested by this concept:
   a. Christians should be led of God to give (purpose in their hearts).
   b. Christians should give proportionately as God has blessed them (as opposed to the O.T.'s various tithes given out of duty).
   c. Christians should give as generously as they can.
   d. Christians should give joyfully out of what they have, fully expecting God to bless it beyond its intrinsic worth.
   e. Christians should give to those in need out of their extra that God has supplied; they can expect the same thing to happen when they have need.
   f. Christians should expect God to give them more than their needs which they can then give generously.
   g. Collections should be done systematically over time so they will be ready when needed.
   h. God will receive honor and praise and thanksgiving from many who are helped.
   h. Those helped will remember the givers in prayer with affection;
   i. There should be integrity in the handling of money given for various needs. Multiple parties of trustworthy people should be involved in the handling, helps insure integrity.

8. APOSTOLIC LEADERSHIP FUNCTIONS

Paul founded this church. He led most of these people to a saving knowledge of Christ. He does not have a formal base to operate from, i.e. a position backed by a salary, a job description, or formal structure. He therefore operates not from a formal leadership relationship with the Corinthian believers and those scattered about in Greece. Because he has founded this work, backed by God-given authentication—signs and wonders, and miraculous conversions that have changed lives—he can operate as an apostle with these people. Paul demonstrates a number of apostolic functions. See **Articles**, *2. Apostolic Functions; 3. Apostolic Functions—Comparison of Titus and Timothy; 4. Apostolic Giftedness—Multiple Gifted Leaders*.

Leadership Principles/ Values/ Suggested by this concept:
   a. Apostolic leadership must authenticate its authority by demonstrated power from God.
   b. Apostolic leadership will manifest strong burdens for works they have founded. They do not give up easily just because situations are complex and trying.
   c. Apostolic leadership must demonstrate all of the means of recognized spiritual authority (gifted power, godly character, deep experiences with God) in order to have credibility in their leadership.
   d. Apostolic authority must recognize power structures within a situation and use influence, power and authority forms in order to counteract/ and/or operate within that situation.

Key Leadership Topics/ Insights—2 Corinthians

e. Apostolic authority must distinguish between core and peripheral issues both in doctrine and practice and bring corrective issues to doctrinal and behavioral situations which are heretical.
f. Apostolic authority must recognize that problem solving is a major thrust of its ministry.
g. Apostolic authority must be confrontive in order to solve problems.
h. Apostolic authority will always have edification of churches as a long term goal, even in the midst of problem solving.

9. ACCOUNTABILITY

Paul, in 1Co and 2Co, more than any other of his books shows his awareness of a very important leadership value. It concerns leadership accountability. Leaders will ultimately give an account to God for their ministries. The value implied: *Leaders must be restrained by the fact that they will ultimately give an account to God for their leadership actions*. In Php Paul uses this value to motivate the Philippians. In 1,2Co he uses this notion to clear his character of the accusations against him. He reveals his honesty before God, declares his responsibility to God, and in general claims a clear conscience before God concerning his leadership actions. Motivations, decisions, and explanations in general are all weighed in light of God's appraisal of them. Paul was an accountable leader—constantly reminding his readers that he was aware of God's awareness and judgment of his actions as a leader. See especially fn 1Co 1:8; 3:13; 4:5; fn 2Co 1:18; 2:17; 4:2; 5:10. Other references: 1Co 1:8; 3:13,15; 4:5. 2Co 1:14,23; 2:18; 4:2; 5:10; 11:31; 12:19. Php 1:6,10; 2:16; 2Th 2:2; 1Ti 5:19,20; 2Ti 1:16; 4:8,14. See **Articles**: *1. Accountability—Standing Before God As A leaders; 11. Entrustment—A Leadership Responsibility; 24. Jesus—5 Leadership Models: Shepherd, Harvest, Steward, Servant, Intercessor.*

Leadership Principles/ Values/ Observations Suggested by this concept:
a. Leaders must be restrained by the fact that they will ultimately give an account to God for their leadership actions.
b. Leaders show burden for a ministry by recognizing their accountability to God for it.

2 Corinthians 1:1 page 51

I. (Ch 1-7) Paul's Apostolic Ministry and Motives

Chapter 1
1 Paul,[1] an apostle of Jesus Christ by the will of God,[2] and Timothy[3] our brother,[4] To the church of God which is at Corinth, with all the saints[5] who are in all Greece.[6]

---

[1] Paul authored 13 epistles. See **Article**, *68. Time-Lines—Defined For Biblical Leaders*.

[2] Paul had a strong sense of appointment to ministry from God. See also 2Co 1:21 and other Pauline salutations: Ro 1:1; 1Co 1:1; 2Co 1:1; Gal 1:1; Eph 1:1; Col 1:1; 1Ti 1:1; 2Ti 1:1; Tit 1:1. Throughout this epistle in general and 2Co 10-12 in particular Paul stresses his apostolic affirmation. He needs apostolic authority if to clear the character assassination against him in the Corinthian church. Straight away he claims this authoritative backing. This is one of the strongest wordings of his apostolic authority, he uses in any salutation. Note *by the will of God*. He had a *leadership value* which generalized says, **Value 1. Divine Appointment.** *Leaders ought to be sure that God appointed them to ministry situations.* This conviction reflects his *sense of destiny*. See **LEADERSHIP TOPIC 1. MINISTRY PHILOSOPHY AND VALUES.** See *sense of destiny, leadership value*, , **Glossary.** See also **Article**, *42. Paul—A Sense of Destiny, 60. Spiritual Authority— Defined, Six Characteristics; 51. Pauline Leadership Values.*

[3] Timothy's name occurs 31 times in the New Testament—six times as a co-author. Timothy's last mention in Heb 13:23 is instructive. He, a respected leader, has just been let out of prison. Timothy is one of some 14 people mentioned by name in 1,2 Co. Timothy as well as others named in 1,2 Co illustrate an important leadership value that Paul had. Generalized it can be stated as, *Personal Ministry—Leaders should view personal relationship as an important part of ministry.* It also illustrates the major leadership lesson: **Lesson 6. Relational Empowerment.** *Effective Leaders See Relational Empowerment As Both A Means And A Goal Of Ministry.* See **LEADERSHIP TOPIC 1. MINISTRY PHILOSOPHY AND VALUES.** See **Article**, *43. Paul and His Companions; 69. Timothy A True Son in the Faith; 30. Leadership Lessons, Seven Major Lessons Identified.*

[4] One of Paul's leadership values is in view here. Generalized, *Leaders must be concerned about leadership selection and development.* Paul developed Timothy as a leader. He here acts as a mentor sponsor for Timothy. People tend to see a lesser known leader as rising in status to the more well known leader when the two co-minister together (e.g. write together, preach and teach together, etc.).The recipients would recognize that Paul thought highly of Timothy and would in turn respect him because of Paul's sponsorship. Paul includes Timothy, like the above, in six salutations: 2Co, Php, Col, 1Th, 2Th, Phm. See **LEADERSHIP TOPIC 1. MINISTRY PHILOSOPHY AND VALUES.** See *leadership value*, **Glossary.** See **Article**, *47. Paul— Mentor For Many; 51. Pauline Leadership Values.*

[5] Paul uses saints to mean believers in general—those who want to become godly in their Christian testimony.

[6] Paul, expands his title given in 1Co, *Church of God in Corinth*, to include the area round about—*all the saints who are in all Greece*. He is still emphasizing that this is God's church. This expansion may suggest that some of the opposition was coming from house church leaders in the region more than Corinth proper.

2 Corinthians 1:2-8

2 Grace[7] to you and peace from God our Father and the Lord Jesus Christ.

3 God should be honored as the Father of our Lord Jesus Christ, a merciful Father and the God who comforts. 4 He comforts us in all our trying experiences. Then we in turn can comfort those facing like trying experiences with the help we have received from God. 5 Just as we share the many sufferings of Christ, so too we will also share much comfort from Christ.[8] 6 So when we experience trying times, you will indirectly benefit.[9] 7 And so we have an unshakable hope for you. For we know that as you go through trying times you also will get the help you need to do so.[10]

8 I want you to know, dear Christian friends, of the very trying experiences[11] which we faced in the province of Asia. I was overwhelmed,[12] beyond my ability[13] to cope with it.[14] I thought[15] I was going to

---

[7] Paul tends to use the Greek word here translated as grace, (SRN 5485), in the sense of the enabling presence of God in a life so as to cause that one to persevere victoriously. See *grace*, **Glossary**.

[8] 2Co 1:3-7 contains a major dynamic observed in God's development of leaders. *God takes leaders through shaping activities in order to teach them personally of their resources in Christ*. They learn to rely on God to meet them in these shaping activities. In turn then, they have something to offer others, lessons from God learned through deep experiences. See *deep processing*, *process items*, **Glossary**. See **Article**, *19. God's Shaping Processes With Leaders*.

[9] This indirect benefit Paul is talking about involves learning from and being helped by another's modeling. Paul will use modeling throughout this epistle as a means of influencing the Corinthians. See also Php 4:9 where one of Paul's strongest statements on modeling occurs.

[10] Every leader recognizes this truth and watches emerging leaders go through various shaping activities knowing that if they learn to trust God in the midst of the shaping, they will develop further as leaders. The Pauline value involved: *Leaders ought to see God's hand in their circumstances as part of His plan for developing them as leaders*. See **LEADERSHIP TOPIC 1. MINISTRY PHILOSOPHY AND VALUES;** see **LEADERSHIP TOPIC 5. PERSONAL EXPERIENCE/ SPIRITUAL AUTHORITY.** See **Article,** *59. Sovereign Mindset; 51. Pauline Leadership Values*.

[11] *Trying experiences* (SRN 2347) represent the same Greek word used several times in 2Co 1:3,4 and often translated as tribulation or affliction. Paul is modeling here. He has just talked about knowing that God can take a person through deep processing. Now he illustrates with his own life. See *modeling*, **Glossary**. See **Article**, *48. Paul— Modeling As An Influence Means*.

[12] *Overwhelmed* (SRN 5236) is a translation of a word meaning excessively so (**KJV** beyond measure).

[13] *Ability* (SRN 1411) is a translation of the Greek word, power.

[14] I have taken out the editorial *we* and replaced it with *I*. Paul is talking about himself. When he is really describing himself I will use the first person. When he is really including Timothy or is inclusively speaking to Corinthians as well I will use *we*.

[15] *Thought* (SRN 1820) is a very strong word meaning despaired or to be destitute. It probably would not be too strong to say Paul was depressed.

2 Corinthians 1:9-13

die. 9 I concluded[16] that I would die. But as a result I learned not to trust myself but to rely on God, who can raise the dead.[17] 10 He delivered me from that tremendous near death experience. He continues to deliver. He will do so in the future too! 11 You play a part in this by praying for us. As a result, because many prayed, many will give thanks to God for his answered prayer—our safety.[18]

12 I am proud because I have a clear conscience.[19] I have conducted myself, by the grace of God, in the world and especially in my relationship with you, free from pretense and with godly sincerity—not with earthly wisdom.[20] 13 My letters are straight forward. I mean what I say—nothing hidden or between the lines. Now I hope you will understand completely what you

---

[16] *Concluded* (SRN 610) represents the noun word usually translated as *sentence* or *judgment*. Hamel comments: 2Co. 1:9 ... the meaning is "on asking myself whether I should come out safe from mortal peril, I answered, I must die." Paul was in deep trouble.

[17] This experiential acknowledging of total dependence on God in a deep processing situation is usually a turning point in this shaping activity by God.

[18] Paul recognizes an important dynamic. *The transparency and vulnerability of a leader allows others to identify with and pray more fervently and with understanding for God's answers*. By this sharing then, God receives much more praise and honor because many are partnering with Him. Prayer backers make a big difference in the life of a leader who can share openly with them. Many leaders fear sharing vulnerably and openly. They miss out on one of God's resources for them. Paul models here the kind of open sharing that leaders need to do. See *modeling*, **Glossary**. See **Articles**, *48. Paul—Modeling As An Influence Means; 74. Vulnerability and Prayer Power*.

[19] Paul uses *conscience* (SRN 4893) some 21 times. Ministry flows out of being. Being is a complex diversity consisting of at least: intimacy with God, character, giftedness, gender, personality, destiny, learned values. For other references on *conscience* see fn 1Ti 1:5; 4:2. Conscience reflects the inner life governor of character. Leadership must have a moral foundation. See *conscience*, **Glossary**. See also **Article**, *7. Conscience, Paul's Use of*.

[20] Phillips captures this so wonderfully: *Now it is a matter of pride to us—endorsed by our conscience—that our activities in this world particularly our dealings with you, have been absolutely above-board and sincere before God*. The TEV also strongly words a part of this, *with God-given frankness*. Paul here begins defense of some of the Corinthian character assassinations. There is a *leadership value* involved here: *Leaders should not be deceptive in their dealings with followers but should instead be open, honest, forthright and frank with them*. See **LEADERSHIP TOPIC 1. MINISTRY PHILOSOPHY AND VALUES**. See *integrity*, **Glossary**. See **Article**, *22. Integrity—A Top Leadership Quality; 51. Pauline Leadership Values*.

2 Corinthians 1:14-2:4   page 54

only now know in part, 14 so that on the day of the Lord Jesus[200] you will be as proud of me as I am of you. 15,16 I made plans. I was so sure that I could see you twice, on my way to Macedonia and when I returned from there on my way to Judea. I could bless you and you could help me. 17 I did intend this but it didn't work out. I don't say one thing and mean another. I really meant it. 18 God knows what I am saying is true.[201] 19 For the Son of God, Jesus Christ, who was preached among you by us—by me, Silas,[202] and Timothy—never wavered between Yes and No. He was firmly consistent. 20 God firmly said yes through Him. For all God's promises have been fulfilled in Him. Amen!? [You bet]. God is glorified [when we assert this.] 21 Now God has anointed me [for my ministry]. He has established me and you in our lives in Christ. 22 God has identified us as His own and guaranteed this by giving us the Spirit in our hearts.

     23 Now I call God as witness—He knows my inner thoughts.[203] It was to spare you that I didn't come to Corinth. 24 I am not trying to dictate to you what you believe. You are standing in the faith. But I want to work with you for your own happiness.

Chapter 2

     1 So I inwardly reasoned, I am not going there for another painful visit. 2 For if I make you unhappy, who is left to make me glad? 3 That is why I wrote my letter as I did. I did not want to be saddened by the very people who should make me glad. My happiness depends on your happiness. 4 I wrote to you from a distressed and unhappy heart—in fact with many tears. I wrote not to make you sad but to show you how

---

[200] The phrase *Day of Christ* or variation of it occurs a total of 6 times (Php 1:6, 10; 2:16; 2Th 2:2; 1Co 1:8 and here, 2Co 1:14 with slight variation). Probably synonymous in Paul's thoughts with *the Day of the Lord* and like phrases used 9 times in 1,2Th. Paul implies in the usage of this term a future day of accounting both for himself as a leader and for these Corinthian folks. This is a strong Pauline leadership value. *Leaders will ultimately give an account for their ministries and hence leaders' actions must be restrained by the fact that they will ultimately give an account to God for their leadership actions.* See also Php 2:16 for a stronger indication of accountability as a leader. There Paul uses this fact to influence the Philippian followers as he exhorts them to live out the Christian life in an attractive manner. He deals with this issue more strongly in 2Co 5. See **LEADERSHIP TOPIC 1 MINISTRY PHILOSOPHY AND VALUES.** See *Day of the Christ, leadership value,* **Glossary**. See **Articles**, *40. Motivating Factors For Ministry; 9. Day of Christ—Implications for Leaders.*

[201] Paul is ever aware of his accountability to God. He knows God is always with him. The ultimate accountability value constantly guides him. For other references on accountability, see 2Co 1:14,23; 2:17; 4:2; 5:10; 11:31; 12:19. 1Co 1:8; 3:13,15; 4:5. Php 1:6,10; 2:16; 4:1; Heb 13:17; 2Th 2:2; 2Ti 1:16; 4:8,14. 1Ti 5:19,20. See **LEADERSHIP TOPIC 1. MINISTRY PHILOSOPHY AND VALUES.** See *accountability*, **Glossary**. See **Article**, *1. Accountability—Standing Before God As A Leader.*

[202] Silas is one of Paul's special companions as well as Peter's. See Ac 15:22,27,32,34,40; 16:19,25,29; 17:4,10,14,15; 18:5; 2Co 1:19; 1Th 1:1; 2Th 1:1; 1Pe 5:12. See **Article**, *43. Paul and His Companions.*

[203] Note again that Paul is ever aware of his accountability to God. He knows God is always with him. He is responsible to God for his leadership. See *accountability*, **Glossary**. See **Article**, *1. Accountability—Standing Before God As A Leader.*

2 Corinthians 2:5-12   page 55

much I love you.[204]

5 The man who caused this trouble has hurt your entire church more than he hurt me.[205] 6 But now I think your punishment of this man, by the majority of you, is enough.[206] 7 So now however, you should forgive and encourage him. Otherwise, he may get so discouraged that he will give up and not recover. 8 I now urge you to show your love to him.[207] 9 I wrote you to test your obedience. Would you obey me?[208] 10 Now if you
forgive this person, I do too. And when I forgive, I do so for your benefit, with Christ's authority.[209] 11 Otherwise, Satan[210] could take advantage of us. We know his tactics.[211]

12 Well, when I came to Troas[212] to preach the Good News about Christ, the Lord gave tremendous

---

[204] A leader is a person with (1) God-given ability and a (2) God-given responsibility who is influencing a (3) specific group of God's people (4) toward God's purposes for it. The God-given responsibility has a two-fold direction—upward to God, that is responsible to God for the group and leadership of the group and downward, a burden for the group. Here, the downward is in focus. Paul shows a genuine burden for the Corinthians—that of love for them. He cares deeply for them and tells them so. Again, Paul models openness, honesty and sharing of emotions. See *burden, downward burden, upward burden*, See **Article,** *40. Motivating Factors for Ministry.*

[205] See immorality problem described in 1Co 5:1-5. Leaders must expect to deal with such problems and surprisingly must also expect results.

[206] Paul uses the word translated as *majority* (SRN 4119), implying that there were others who did not agree with the punishment and did not fully support Paul in this.

[207] The Corinthians followed his advice given in 1Co and disciplined the person living in immorality. The discipline worked. Now Paul applies a redemptive twist. Lets reclaim the man. Love him back.

[208] Paul is here expressing another of his inward values as a leader which I call *Loyalty Testing.* Generalized: *Leaders must know the level of followership loyalty in order to wisely exercise leadership influence.* See *leadership value,* **Glossary**. See **Article,** *16. Followership—Ten Commandments.*

[209] Notice that Paul is quick to forgive, just as quick as he was to command the punishment. And just as he applied spiritual warfare in excommunicating the man, he here applies a spiritual blessing to forgive and restore the man. These are *apostolic functions.* See Mt 16:19. See **LEADERSHIP TOPIC 8. APOSTOLIC LEADERSHIP FUNCTIONS**. See *identificational forgiveness,* **Glossary**. See **Article,** *2. Apostolic Functions.*

[210] The name *Satan* occurs 35 times in the N.T. There are 10 Pauline direct references (Ro 16:20; see fn 1Co 5:5; 7:5; 2Co 2:11; 11:14; 12:7; 1Th 2:18; 2Th 2:9; 1Ti 1:20; 5:15.) and other indirect ones (*devil*: Eph 4:27; 6:11; 1Ti 3:6,7; 2Ti 2:26).

[211] An unforgiving heart gives Satan a hook into the person which He can use to divide Christians. See **Article,** *65. Spiritual Warfare—Satan's Tactics.*

[212] At Troas Paul had a strong ministry opportunity. The depth of his burden for the Corinthian situation is seen in that he leaves this open door. See 2Ti 4:13 for another mention of Troas which shows Paul did have a further ministry time there.

2 Corinthians 2:13-17 page 56

opportunities to me. 13 I had an inner restlessness waiting for Titus,[213] my brother; So I said goodbye and left for Macedonia.[214] 14 Now thanks be to God who always triumphantly leads us in union with Christ. Like a sweet fragrance that permeates the air everywhere, God uses us to make Christ known to all people.[215] 15 Our lives are like a sweet incense presented to God by Christ. But this aroma is perceived differently by those saved and by those perishing. For we are the fragrance of Christ among those who are being saved and among those who are perishing. 16 To some it is a death stench. To others an aroma bringing life.[216]

And who could claim sufficiency for such a task?[217] 17 For I am not like many, using God's word to make money.[218] I speak in utter sincerity[219] as one sent by God, a minister accountable to

---

[213] Titus is a very important New Testament apostolic leader to whom a whole letter was written by Paul giving us insights on apostolic leadership. He particularly exemplifies a trouble-shooting type of roving apostolic ministry. Paul used ministry tasks to develop this leader. For other references to Titus, see Ac 18:7; 2Co 2:13; 7:6,13,14; 8:6, 16, 17, 23; 12:18; Gal 2:1,3; 2Ti 4:10; Tit 1:4. See **LEADERSHIP TOPIC 8. APOSTOLIC LEADERSHIP FUNCTIONS**. See *ministry task,* **Glossary**. See **Articles,** *43. Paul And His Companions, 2. Apostolic Functions*.

[214] Success and/or opportunities alone do not mean it is God's will to do something. Here, Paul recognizes something more important even than this open door of ministry. He has sent Titus to the Corinthians and needs to hear back from him. He is hoping of course to meet him in Macedonia (referred to 26 times by Paul). Paul's whole future ministry weighed in the balance. It depends on how these Corinthians would respond to his apostolic authority and attempts to clear his character. Paul eventually returns to Troas for ministry. See reference to Carpus and Troas, 2Ti 4:13.

[215] Paul uses here an extended metaphor. He is alluding to a Roman Triumphant, a great celebration, in which a Roman general is feted by the whole nation. See Barclay's great commentary on this. The **TEV** and **NLT** both capture this idea. Note the **TEV**: "...we are always led by God as prisoners in Christ's victory procession."

[216] The metaphor continues. Both victors and vanquished marched in the triumphal parade. The aroma was life-giving to the victors but only symbolic of death to come shortly to the vanquished.

[217] This is really a *rhetorical question* which I paraphrase as, *What leader can claim sufficiency for the great challenge of presenting the fragrance of Christ everywhere?* Captured: *No leader is capable within his/her self for this great task.* A Pauline leadership value is in focus here. ***True Competence*** (its ultimate source): *A leader's ultimate confidence for ministry must not rest in his/her competence but in God the author of that competence.* See *rhetorical question, leadership value, True Competence,* **Glossary**.

[218] *Using* (SRN 2585) is a word which means peddle or sell something for profit (with negative connotations; putting something over on the buyer).

[219] See also comments on 2Co 1:12. There is a *leadership value* involved here: *Leaders should not be deceptive in their dealings with followers but should instead be open, honest, forthright and frank with them.* See **LEADERSHIP TOPIC 1. MINISTRY PHILOSOPHY AND VALUES.** See *leadership value, integrity,* **Glossary.** See **Article,** *22. Integrity—A Top Leadership Quality; 51. Pauline Leadership Values*.

2 Corinthians 3:1-7

God.[220]

Chapter 3

1 Do I need to commend myself to you? Or do I need, as some might think, a letter of recommendation to you or from you?[221] 2 You are my letter written in my heart, known and read by all people. 3 Clearly you are a letter written by Christ, through our ministry. You are a letter written not with ink but by the Spirit of the living God, not on tablets of stone but on human hearts.[222]

4 I say this because I have such confidence[223] in God through Christ. 5 Not that I am confident of doing anything in my own resources. But my sufficiency comes from God.[224] 6 He made us capable ministers of the new covenant, not one of written laws but of the Spirit. The written law kills, but the Spirit gives life.

7 But if the law etched in stone resulted in a ministry of death, and yet was so glorious that the children of Israel couldn't look steadily at the face of Moses because of his bright shining face, a glory

---

[220] A strong Pauline leadership value is implied here. *Leaders will ultimately give an account for their ministries.* Paul knows he is responsible to God for his leadership. And yet Paul had a clear conscience about his decision not to come, about not following up on the open door at Troas and in his dealings with the Corinthians, and about handling the Word of God. *Accountable to God* translates the phrase, *in the sight of God we speak*. See *ultimate accountability*, **Glossary**.

[221] Rhetorical questions. Captured: I don't need to be recommended to you. I don't need any letter of recommendation to you or from you. You alone are proof enough of my credentials. See *rhetorical questions, capture*, **Glossary**.

[222] An important Pauline leadership value is in view here which I label as *True Credentials* (competency and results). *A leader should be able to point to results from ministry as a recommendation of God's authority in him/her.* Spiritual authority is a combination of the power- form persuasion and two authority forms: legitimate authority and competent authority. Spiritual authority comes through recognition of spirituality as seen in Godly character, deep experiences with God and gifted power. Part of gifted power is competent ministry which is in view here. See *spiritual authority, True Credentials, leadership value*, **Glossary**. See **Article**, *21. Influence, Power and Authority Forms*.

[223] The three sub-contexts—3:4-6; 3:7-11; and 3:12-18—combine to portray one of the most powerful passages describing Paul's confidence and hope in the *New Covenant*. Leaders must inspire followers. It is one of the three major overall generic leadership functions. Paul does this by comparing the permanence and glory of this *New Covenant* with the *Old Covenant*. See *New Covenant, Old Covenant*, **Glossary**. See **Article**, *28. Leadership Functions—Three High Level Generic Priorities*.

[224] An important Pauline leadership value is in view here which I label as *True Competence* (its ultimate source): *A leader's ultimate confidence for ministry must not rest in her/his competence but in God the author of that competence.* See also 1Co 4:7,8. A leader trusting in his/her own competence is in for either of two snags:(1) plateauing or (2) brokenness. See *plateauing, brokenness, leadership value, True Competence*, **Glossary**.

2 Corinthians 3:8-4:4 page 58

which was fading away, 8 how much more glorious will the ministry of the Spirit be? 9 For if the ministry of condemnation had glory, the ministry of righteousness exceeds it with much more glory.[225] 10 The old glory seems almost dim when compared with the new glory. 11 So if there was glory in the old which lasted only for a while, how much more glory is there in that which lasts forever.

12 Because we have such hope, we speak freely and boldly.[226] 13 We aren't like Moses, who put a veil over his face so that the children of Israel could not see the brightness fade away.[227] 14 But their minds were blinded.[228] Even today the same veil keeps them from seeing when the Old Testament is read. This veil can only be removed by Christ. 15 But even to this day, when Moses' law is read, a veil covers their heart. 16 But when one turns to the Lord, the veil is taken away. 17 Now the Lord is the Spirit. And where the Spirit of the Lord is present, there is freedom. 18 All of us Christians with uncovered faces reflect like mirrors the glory of the Lord. That glory is from the Lord who is the Spirit and who transforms us into his likeness in an ever increasing degree.[229]

Chapter 4

1 Because God in His mercy has given me this ministry, I am not going to become discouraged and give up.[230] 2 I have rejected secret and shameful deeds. I don't act deceitfully. I don't handle the word of God deceitfully. I speak the plain truth. I thus appeal to every person's conscience, openly before God.[231] 3 If our gospel is veiled, it is veiled only to those who are lost. 4 They don't believe because [Satan] the god of this world has blinded their minds.[232] They can not see the glorious light of the Good News about Christ,

---

[225] Condemnation and righteousness are both metonymies, one word substituted for another to which it is related. In this case both are effects for causes. Captured: ministry through the law which brought such condemnation; ministry of grace through the Spirit which resulted in righteousness. See *capture*, *metonymy*, **Glossary**.

[226] Confidence in the power of the Good News about Christ is a strong motivating factor leading to bold ministry. See **Article**, *40. Motivating Factors for Ministry*.

[227] Paul alludes to a historical event in Ex 34:33. Paul knew his Old Testament.

[228] Paul later talks about Satan as one who blinds (2Co 4:4). See *spiritual warfare*, **Glossary**. See **Article**, *63. Spiritual Warfare—Satan's Tactics*.

[229] These words capture the great hope of the Good News of Christ. We Christians are transformed by the work of the Holy Spirit so that we become like Christ. This is one of the wonderful union life passages. Paul had a leadership value which I label *Transforming Ministry*: *Followers who are increasingly being set free by the Holy Spirit and who are increasingly being transformed into Christ's image ought to be the hope and expectation of a Christian leader*. See 1Co 6:17 for the union with the Spirit. See also Ro 8 for the fuller explanation of union life and the work of the Holy Spirit. See *Union life*, **Glossary**.

[230] This is one of Paul's stronger expressions of his personally embracing the stewardship model. His call from God, his anointing by God and his sense of destiny are behind these words. *See stewardship model*, **Glossary**. See **Articles**, *11. Entrustment—A Leadership Responsibility; 24. Jesus' Five Leadership Models: Shepherd, Harvest, Steward, Servant, Intercessor*.

[231] *Openly before God*—another of the indications of Paul's sense of accountability. Paul in verse 2 is denying at least three charges about his person and ministry. See *Ultimate Accountability*, **Glossary**.

[232] Paul is aware that spiritual warfare is often involved in communicating the Good News about Christ. People are blinded by Satan, the god of this world. See **Article**, *65. Spiritual Warfare—Satan's Tactics*.

2 Corinthians 4:5-15

who is the exact likeness of God. 5 And it is Christ Jesus as Lord that I preach, not myself. I am your servant for Jesus' sake.[233] 6 For the same God who commanded light to shine out of darkness, has shone in our hearts to let us understand the glory of God in the person of Jesus Christ.[234]

7 But we have this spiritual treasure in clay pots,[235] to show that it is God's power in us and not us. 8 We are hard pressed on every side, yet not crushed; we don't know which way to turn, but we don't despair; 9 we are persecuted but not abandoned; we are knocked down, but not destroyed. 10 Every day we are experiencing something of Jesus death in our human condition so that his life might be seen through us. 11 It is for Jesus' sake that this death/life process is seen in our everyday lives.[236] 12 So then death is working in us, but life in you. 13 The Scripture says,

> "I believed and
> therefore I spoke."[237]

I have this same kind of faith. I also believe and therefore speak. 14 I know that He who raised up the Lord Jesus will also raise me up with Jesus, and will present me with you.[238] 15 All of this is for your sake. And as God's grace continues spreading to more and more people, there will be many more prayers of thanksgiving and praise honoring God.[239]

---

[233] These strong words show Paul's grasp of the *servant model*, **Glossary**. See **Article**, *24. Jesus' Five Leadership Models: Shepherd, Harvest, Steward, Servant, Intercessor*.

[234] This amazing comparison shows it takes a miracle to transform a non-believer into a believer, just as big a miracle as the creation act of light in Genesis 1. But God has that power. We as leaders must remember this when we face unbelieving opposition.

[235] It is the contrast which brings out God's enabling grace in us. We as humans go through all kinds of trials in our human experience. But God works in and through these, which demonstrates a life very different from those around us who do not have Christ.

[236] A very important Pauline leadership value emerges here—*Value 14*. I label it the **Death/Life Paradox**: *The firstfruits of Jesus' resurrection life ought to be experienced in the death-producing circumstances of life and ought to serve as a hallmark of spiritual life for followers*. Other passages in 2 Co also show the deep experiences that Paul went through. See **LEADERSHIP TOPIC 5. PERSONAL EXPERIENCE/ SPIRITUAL AUTHORITY.** Paul alludes to the deep experiences he had gone through. And these experiences added to his spiritual authority, as seen in the eyes of those he ministered to. See *leadership value, firstfruits*, **Glossary**. See **Article** 51. *Pauline Leadership Values*.

[237] This is loosely drawn from Ps 116:10. Another indication of Paul's Scripture-based leadership. See *Bible Centered leader*, **Glossary**. See **Article**, *72. A Vanishing Breed, Needed Bible Centered Leaders*.

[238] Paul was strongly motivated by the resurrection. It is a dominant theme for him. Notice his personal confidence expressed here about it. See **Article**, *40. Motivating Factors for Ministry*.

[239] The dynamic of partnering with God and praise going back to God first seen in 1Co 1:8-11 is reemphasized here.

2 Corinthians 4:16-5:10

16 So now you see why I do not get discouraged and quit. Even though my physical being is deteriorating my inner spirit is renewed day by day. 17 For my present troubles are only momentary and will eventuate in an immeasurable eternal glory. 18 So I fix my attention not on things that are seen—[those things all around me], but on things that are unseen. For what I see here lasts a short time. But the unseen things will last forever.[240]

Chapter 5[241]

1 When we die and leave this temporary body we will have an eternal body in heaven made by God himself and not by human hands.[242] 2 We sigh because we so desire to wear that new heavenly body[243] like new clothing. 3 We won't be spirits without bodies. 4 We sigh impatiently in our present body, not because we don't want a body, but so that we can have that eternal body and everlasting life. 5 God has prepared us for this change. He has given us the Spirit as a guarantee[244] of this truth.[245]

6 So we are always encouraged. Even though we know that as long as we are in these bodies, we are not at home with the Lord. 7 For we live trusting [in God], not by appearances around us. 8 We are full of courage and would love to be out of this body and into our heavenly body and with the Lord. 9 But above all, we purpose to please Him always whether here in these bodies or away from them.[246] 10 For we must

---

[240] Paul closes off this chapter where he began. He asserts he won't give up in ministry. And in concluding, he gives yet another motivating factor. He views present problems, pressures, and setbacks as only momentary annoyances when seen in the light of eternity and all it holds for him. See **Article**, *40. Motivating Factors For Ministry*.

[241] This is one of the strongest passages dealing with accountability. Here it is dealing with all individuals. Several times in 1,2 Co Paul deals with accountability of leaders. Here it is for all—leaders and followers. See **LEADERSHIP TOPIC 9. ACCOUNTABILITY.** See **Article**, *1. Accountability—Standing Before God As A Leader*.

[242] I have captured two of Paul's metaphors, *house* and *tent*. See *capture*, *metaphor*, **Glossary**.

[243] For the notion of an eternal body and other references to this teaching, see 1Co 15:35-41; 42-49;50; 51-57; 1Jn 3:2.

[244] *Guarantee* sometimes translated as *earnest* (SRN 728) in daily life referred to money which in purchases is given as a pledge or down payment insuring that the full amount will subsequently be paid. It is like a present day down-payment with one major difference. The one giving the down-payment is God. He will not forfeit; He will pay off the whole thing.

[245] Leaders provide three kinds of high-level overall leadership functions: *task oriented leadership*, *relational oriented leadership* and *inspirational leadership*. This is one of those great inspirational leadership passages. A future resurrection body that lasts forever in heaven gives great hope to sustain us in our present life where we in fact may be groaning with our present disease-riddled dying bodies. See *inspirational leadership*, **Glossary**. See **Article**, *28. Leadership Functions—Three High Level Generic Priorities*.

[246] See Php 1:20,21 for Paul's own personal feelings about this.

2 Corinthians 5:11-21   page 61

all stand before Christ and be judged.[247] We will each receive what we deserve for what we have done in these bodies,—whether good or bad.[248]

11 Recognizing this judgment of the Lord and fearfully respecting it, I persuade people [to accept Christ].[249] God knows me completely and I hope deep down you do too.[250] 12 I am not recommending myself to you again. But I am giving you opportunity to brag about me. And something to say to those who boast about a person's appearance and not about inner character. 13 Am I really crazy? If it looks so it is for God's sake; or if I am sane, it is for your sake. 14 For Christ's love compels me. Here is my thinking. He died for all. Therefore all share in that death. 15 Those who receive this new life will not longer live just to please themselves. Instead, they now live to please Christ who died and was raised for them.[251]

16 So from now on I don't judge people by human standards. I once judged Christ that way but not now. 17 Therefore, if anyone is in Christ, that one has a new life; the old life has passed away. A new life has started. 18 This (transformation) has been done by God. Through Christ He has brought us back to Himself. And He has given us the ministry of reconciling other to Himself. 19 God was in Christ reconciling the world to Himself, no longer counting their sins against them. [I say it again for emphasis] God has given us this wonderful reconciling message.

20 So then, I am an ambassador[252] for Christ. God is using me to challenge you. I beg you. Be reconciled to God. 21 For He made Christ who knew no sin to be an offering for sin for us, in order that we

---

[247] Literally, stand before the *judgment seat* (SRN 968). This most likely refers to the *Day of Christ*, which Paul uses so much when talking about his own accountability as a leader. Here he is expanding accountability to everyone. See *task-oriented leadership, relational-oriented leadership* and *inspirational leadership, Day of Christ*, **Glossary**. See fn 2Co 1:14.

[248] This is Paul's strongest teaching on accountability. Here he points out that all will be held accountable, not just leaders. See also 2Co 1:14,23; 2:17; 4:2; 5:10; 11:31; 12:19. 1Co 1:8; 3:13,15; 4:5. Php 1:6,10; 2:16; 4:1; Heb 13:17; 2Th 2:2; 2Ti 1:16; 4:8,14. 1Ti 5:19,20. See *accountability*, **Glossary**.

[249] This day of accountability, for everyone, was a major motivating factor for Paul's ministry. He wanted people to be found in Christ. See **Articles**, *40. Motivating Factors For Ministry, 9. Day of Christ—Implications for Leaders*.

[250] This is another expression of that leadership value, *Integrity and Openness: Leaders should not be deceptive in their dealings with followers but should instead be open, honest, forthright and frank with them.* See **LEADERSHIP TOPIC 1. MINISTRY PHILOSOPHY AND VALUES.** See *leadership value, Integrity and Openness*, **Glossary**. See Article, *22. Integrity—A Top Leadership Quality; 51. Pauline Leadership Values*.

[251] Union Life, Ro 6-8 treats this comprehensively. See *union life*, **Glossary**. See **Article**, *70. Union Life—Intimacy With God*.

[252] *Ambassador* (SRN 4243), used only here and in Eph 6:20 is a cognate of the leadership word we have translated as elders (See Acts 20:17 et al, presbyteros). Paul sees himself with the status of a statesman speaking for Christ. That is a healthy view of a leader's status. As leaders we represent the King of Kings.

2 Corinthians 6:1-4   page 62

in union with Christ might have the righteousness of God.[253]

Chapter 6
1 As one of God's partners in His work,[254] You have received God's grace; I beg [255] you— don't let it go to waste. 2 For He says:

> In an acceptable time I have heard you,
> And in the day of salvation I have helped you.[256]

Listen, right now God is ready to help you. Right now is the day of salvation. 3 I don't want anyone to find fault with my ministry.[257] So I try not to create obstacles that may hinder them.[258] 4 Instead, I try to

---

[253] Paul concisely states the doctrine of justification in one small verse. See also Ro 3:21-31 for a comprehensive treatment of this great subject. This message inspires followers. No leader can lead well without being grounded in this great doctrinal truth.

[254] Paul, almost in an aside, gives a great perspective on leadership. *Leaders should see themselves as partners with God. Partners* (SRN 4903) is a compound word made up of an obsolete verb form (SRN 2041) meaning *to work* and a preposition (SRN 4862) meaning *together with*. As leaders, we do work for God but much more so, we work with God. Servant leadership involves first of all serving God and secondly serving those followers He brings our way. This word, *partners* with God, stresses that we are serving God as we proclaim the truths of the Gospel message. There is a dynamic tension in servant leadership: we serve those we lead and we lead those we serve. We maintain this dynamic tension best when we remember, as Paul does here, we partner with God in this leadership He has entrusted to us. See **Article**, *11. Entrustment—A Leadership Responsibility; 24. Jesus—5 Leadership Models: Shepherd, Harvest, Steward, Servant, Intercessor.*

[255] This is the verb form for exhort—another example of the gift of exhortation in action. Exhortation usually carries with it one of three emphases: admonishing, encouraging, comforting. Here it is a plea embracing both admonishment and encouragement. See **Article**, *63. Spiritual Gift Clusters.*

[256] See Isa 49:8. This again shows Paul's knowledge of the Old Testament.

[257] Paul here models what he has asserted as the bedrock qualification for leadership in 1Ti 3:2,8,11—moral integrity, that is, a character that can not be faulted from without. See also comments on 1Ti 3:2. There is a *leadership value* involved here: *Leaders should not be deceptive in their dealings with followers but should instead be open, honest, forthright and frank with them.* See **LEADERSHIP TOPIC 1. MINISTRY PHILOSOPHY AND VALUES.** See *leadership value, Integrity and Openness,* **Glossary**. See **Article**, *51. Pauline Leadership Values; 22. Integrity—A Top Leadership Quality; 6. Bible Centered Leader; 51. Principles of Truth; 72. Vanishing Breed, Needed Bible Centered Leaders.*

[258] See 1Co 10:27-11:1 for a beautiful example of how Paul views not putting obstacles in the way of others.

2 Corinthians 6:5-14   page 63

demonstrate in all that I do, that I am a servant of God.[259] I model endurance in various kinds of trouble, hardships and trying experiences.[260] 5 I have been beaten, been put in prison, have faced riots, have been overworked have gone without sleep, and have done without food. 6 My purity, knowledge, patience, kindness and my sincere love, all engendered by the Holy Spirit, speak for me. I present the truth. I demonstrate God's power.[261] Righteousness is my weapon—both for attack and defense.[262] 8 Sometimes I am honored. Sometimes I am disgraced. Sometimes I get insults; other times I get praise. I am treated as a liar yet I speak truth. 9 I am well known yet treated as an unknown. I have faced death yet I am alive. I have been severely beaten yet survived. 10 In the midst of sorrow I can still find joy. I am poor, yet I make many [spiritually] rich; I own nothing yet really havee verything.[263]

11 Dear friends in Corinth! I am speaking honestly with you.[264] My heart is wide open to you. 12 I have not closed my heart to you; but it is you who have closed your hearts to me. 13 I am talking to you as if you were my own little children. Open your hearts to me.

14 Don't form partnerships with unbelievers such that they can dominate you.[265] How can goodness

---

[259] In the next several verses Paul shows that being a servant of God, involves modeling what it means to be a Christian in all the experiences of life that come our way. So it is not so much by gifted power that we demonstrate that we serve God as leaders, but by the way we live—especially in our trying times. Note the various kinds of experiences that Paul now lists. See **Articles**, *44. Paul—Deep Processing; 19. God's Shaping Processes With Leaders*.

[260] What a leader models in a situation usually speaks louder than the issues of the situation. See **Article**, *48. Paul—Modeling As An Influence Means*.

[261] Note the emphasis— word and deed. John too emphasizes this in the book of John in Jesus' ministry. Frequently word gifts must be authenticated by power gifts. See 1Co 12-14 for a more detailed treatment dealing with giftedness. See **Article**, *63. Spiritual Gift Clusters*.

[262] This is one of the great spiritual warfare weapons—righteousness, a Spirit-empowered life. See Eph 6:10-18, especially verse 14. This was Job's major weapon (even though he didn't know spiritual warfare was going on). See **Articles**, *63. Spiritual Warfare—Satan's Tactics; 67. Spiritual Warfare—Two Foundational Axioms*.

[263] When Paul shares personal experiences like these, he is using a leadership style called *maturity appeal*, one of 10 Pauline leadership styles. The maturity appeal leadership style is the form of leadership influence which counts upon godly experience, usually gained over a long period of time, an empathetic identification based on a common sharing of experience, and recognition of the force of imitation modeling to convince people toward a favorable acceptance of the leader's ideas. Used in Phm. See also 1Pe 5:1-4 where Peter uses this style. A life which backs up what is said is a strong influence on followers. See **Article**, *49. Pauline Leadership Styles*.

[264] Paul again models an important leadership value to him. *Leaders should not be deceptive in their dealings with followers but should instead be open, honest, forthright and frank with them.* See **LEADERSHIP TOPIC 1. MINISTRY PHILOSOPHY AND VALUES.** See *integrity*, leadership value, *Integrity and Openness*, **Glossary**. See **Article**, *22. Integrity—A Top Leadership Quality; 51. Pauline Leadership Values*.

[265] My translation stresses unequally yoked. I don't think this prevents, for example, business partnerships where a believer can freely operate with Christian values. A relationship, business or social or whatever which will tarnish one's testimony and dominate it so that Jesus is not Lord in a life, is certainly prohibited here.

partner with wickedness? Light can not co-exist simultaneously with darkness. 15 Christ and the Devil can't work together. Neither can a believer partner with an unbeliever. 16 How can God's temple be compatible with idols? For you are the temple of the living God. As God has said:

> I will dwell in them
> And walk among them.
> I will be their God,
> And they shall be My people.
> 17 Therefore, come out from among them
> And be separate, says the Lord.
> Do not touch what is unclean,
> And I will receive you.
> 18 I will be a Father to you,
> And you shall be My sons and daughters,
> Says the LORD Almighty.[266]

Chapter 7

1 Because we have these promises, dear friends, we should purify ourselves from whatever might contaminate our bodies and souls. We should live completely holy lives as showing our fearful respect for God.[267]

2 Open your hearts to me. I haven't wronged anyone. I haven't corrupted anyone. I have cheated no one. 3 I don't say this to make you feel guilty. I have already said before that you are in my heart. We are together facing life and death. 4 I have tremendous confidence in you. I am proud of you. I am encouraged. I am really happy despite all our troubles.

5 Even after I got to Macedonia, I could not rest. There were troubles everywhere— outwardly actual quarrels and inwardly feelings of anxiety.[268] 6 And then God, who encourages the discouraged, encouraged me by Titus' arrival. 7 It was not just his coming but the news of how you encouraged him that encouraged me. He told me how much you want to see me. He told me how sorry you were about things, and about

---

[266] No one O.T. quote covers this entirely. Some Bible editors suggest the following references as each contributing something to this quote: Isa 52:11; Eze 20:34,41; Ex 4:22; 2Sa 7:14; 1Ch 17;13; Isa 43:6. Whether all of these are accurate or not is not the point. It does show that Paul was very familiar with the Old Testament. This is another indication of his being a Scripture-Based leader. See *Bible Centered leader*, **Glossary**. See **Article**, *72. A Vanishing Breed, Needed Bible Centered Leaders*.

[267] Verses 6:14-7:1 almost seem out of place. This problem was not addressed at all in 1Co. Paul interrupts the flow of the defense of his own character on this note of advice about this partnership problem. Perhaps Titus brought him word about this problem. The problem itself is not clear. And then he goes back to his own defense in 7:2ff. See **Article**, *54. Problems—The N.T. Church*.

[268] Paul has just left a situation of opportunity at Troas because he was restless within and was hoping to meet up with Titus in Macedonia. In Macedonia he faces other problems. Here Paul is being very human and open with the Corinthians. This is the same man who talks about stop worrying and know the God of Peace and the Peace of God in Php 4:6,7. So there will be moments when anxiety and worry are there. They will not however dominate over the whole of life. The norm will be assurance within of God's peace in the midst of distressing times. See **Article**, *44. Paul—Deep Processing*.

2 Corinthians 7:8-16

your loyalty to me.[269] So I rejoiced even more now.

8 For even though my letter made you sorry, I don't regret it now, though I did for a while. I see that it did upset you for a short time. 9 But now I am happy about it, not for the pain it caused you, but that it resulted in your remorse and your changing your ways. That sadness was used by God. It caused you no harm.[270] 10 God can use sadness to bring about a change of heart which leads to salvation—I don't regret that kind of sorrow. But sorrow without a change of heart leads to death. 11 Recognize this, you reacted sorrowfully in a godly way which produced: earnestness, a concern to clear yourselves, indignation, an alarm, a longing to see me, devotion, a readiness to punish wrongdoing. You have done all you can to make things right.[271]

12 So, although I wrote to you, I didn't do it just to point out who was right and who was wrong. But I wrote it so you would know, in the sight of God, how much you really cared for me. 13 This is why I am so encouraged.

Not only was I encouraged but so was Titus overjoyed. You all really cheered him up. 14 I had told him how proud I was of you and you didn't disappoint me. What I have spoken to you is true. And so too what I told Titus about you proved true. 15 Now he cares for you all the more, especially as he remembers how you were ready to obey. And how you received him respectfully.[272] 16 I am happy that I can really count on you completely.

---

[269] Paul earlier (fn 2Co 2:9) demonstrated a value, which I call *Loyalty Testing*. Generalized: *Leaders must know the level of followership loyalty in order to wisely exercise leadership influence.* Two of the Ten Commandments of Followership are seen in that testing and in this remark about their loyalty to Paul. *1. LOYALTY: Leadership in voluntary organizations can not be effectively exercised without followership loyalty. 2. DISCIPLINE: Leadership can not apply adequate discipline without a firm base of loyal committed followers.* See *leadership value*, **Glossary**. See **Article**, *16. Followership— Ten Commandments*. In Titus' report, Paul was overjoyed for many reasons, not the least of which was that he had a base of followers so that he could exercise leadership.

[270] Strong discipline will often result in painful experiences for those being disciplined. For a leader it is not the discipline that is in view, but the redemptive application of it to help the people being disciplined. Here, because the followers responded well, God was able to really use the discipline and pain involved to redeem the situation. . See **Article**, *16. Followership— Ten Commandments*.

[271] Note this long list of positive results that came out of this discipline, so strongly given in 1Co. Notice also that Paul openly affirms them, "*You have done all you can to make things right,*" Many leaders cannot give affirmation to others. Giving affirmation is one of the major tools a leader can use to motivate and build up followers. When people respond to God, leaders should recognize this and encourage them. See also verse 16, *I am happy that I can really count on you completely*. . See **Article**, *16. Followership— Ten Commandments*.

[272] I have captured the *fear and trembling* idiom which occurs also in Php 2:12 Eph 6:5. Titus was received with the same respect that would have been given by Paul himself. See *idiom, capture, fear and trembling*, **Glossary**. See also **Articles**, *Fear and Trembling—The Right Attitude; 12. Figures and Idioms in the Bible*.

2 Corinthians 8:1-6

II. (Ch 8,9) Paul's Financial Appeal to the Corinthians[273]

Chapter 8

1 Christian friends, God has graciously supplied the churches in Macedonia. 2 They have been going through some very trying times. Yet even in their poverty and hard times they have exhibited great joy[274] and have been extremely generous in their giving. 3 I can testify that they gave as much as they could—even more than that. They did it of their own free will. 4 They asked us strongly if they could give and help out the Christians in Jerusalem.[275] 5 They went beyond our expectations. First they gave themselves to the Lord; then they gave themselves, by God's will, to us.[276] 6 So we urged[277] Titus, who

---

[273] Chapters 8 and 9 give us the most comprehensive treatment of New Testament church giving. I am certain that Paul was deeply affected by his mentor, Barnabas, concerning giving. See Acts 4:36,37; 11:27-30. Paul advocates giving to help fellow churches in need. He also advocates giving to help Christian workers (see footnotes on this in 1Co 9, 16 as well as Php 4:10-17). His strong exhortations on giving highlight a number of items: (1) Christians should be led of God to give (purpose in their hearts); (2) They give proportionately as God has blessed them (as opposed to the Old Testament's various tithes given out of duty); (3) They should give as generously as they can; (4) They give joyfully out of what they have; (5) They should give to those in need out of their extra that God has supplied; they can expect the same thing to happen when they have need; (6) They should expect God to give them more than their needs which they can then give generously, (7) Collections should be done systematically over time so they will be ready when needed; (8) God will receive honor and praise and thanksgiving from many who are helped; (9) Those helped will remember the givers in prayer with affection. (10) There should be integrity in the handling of money given for various needs. Several of Paul's leadership values are seen in this teaching on giving: **Financial equality Principle.** *Christian leadership must teach that Christian giving is a reciprocal balancing between needs and surplus* and **Financial Integrity**. *A Christian leader must handle finances with absolute integrity.* See **LEADERSHIP TOPIC 1. MINISTRY PHILOSOPHY AND VALUES; LEADERSHIP TOPIC 7. TEACHING ON GIVING.** See *integrity, leadership value, Integrity and Openness,* **Glossary.** See **Article**, *22. Integrity—A Top Leadership Quality; 51. Pauline Leadership Values; 18. Giving—Paul's View in 2 Corinthians; 53. Principles of Truth.*

[274] It is interesting to note that the Philippian church gave joyfully. And this is even before the Philippian letter in which Paul so strongly urges them about joy.

[275] Notice two things here: (1) the Philippians had some self-initiative in this whole giving scenario; (2) they gave willingly.

[276] Paul uses the Philippian church as a model in order to motivate the Corinthian Christians to give. He has previously used the Corinthian *pledge to give* to stir up the Philippian church (2Co 9:1,2). So then Paul motivates churches to give by telling what others have done, particularly the values underlying their giving. He quickly shows that giving is not a matter of being rich. The Philippian church gave out of poverty. The key to their giving was to first surrender to the Lord. Once a group of people are surrendered to the Lord, they can give. And God will supply their needs. See **Article**, *41. Motivating Principles, Pauline Influence.*

[277] Another demonstration of the exhortation gift in action. *Urge* is the translation of the Greek verb form for exhortation. See **Article**, *63. Spiritual Gift Clusters.*

2 Corinthians 8:7-14

began this collection with you, to complete it and help you in this special ministry of giving. 7 You overflow in so many ways—in faith, in speech, in knowledge,[278] in your eagerness to help, and in your love for us. Show me that you can excel in also in this gracious ministry of giving.[279]

8 I am not ordering you to do it. But I am testing the sincerity of your love by comparing it with other churches that are giving.[280] 9 For you know the grace of our Lord Jesus Christ, even though He was rich, yet for your sakes He became poor, in order that you might become rich, profiting from His poverty.[281]

10 Let me advise you. You should finish now what you began last year. You were the first to propose this idea and the first to begin to act on it. 11 Get on with it and finish the job. Be as eager to finish as you were when you so enthusiastically started. Give from whatever you have. 12 For if you have the right attitude in giving, God will accept your gift on the basis of what you have to give, not on what you don't have.[282]

13, 14 I don't intend that you should give so much that you suffer for it. But there is an equalizing principle here. Right now you have more than you need and can help them out. Later you may have need

---

[278] *Speech* and *knowledge* are probably both metonymies, a figure of speech in which one word is substituted for another to emphasize some relationship between the two words. Here speech probably is substituted for speaker—and emphasizes gifted speakers (**NLT** so translates). Knowledge here stands for knowledgeable leaders. Paul is almost ironically chiding them about these problems which he addressed in 1Co 1,2. See *capture*, *metonymy*, **Glossary**. See **Article**, *12. Figures and Idioms in the Bible*.

[279] I have observed that churches that excel in giving, especially to the poor and to missions in general, are blessed of God. This is a real challenge to all churches and especially Christian organizations. Many Christian organizations ask and receive but don't give.

[280] Paul is open and above board even in his motivational techniques. He here tells the Corinthians that he is not commanding them (using an apostolic leadership style) but is strongly urging them and leaving the decision up to them (a form of obligation persuasion leadership style) while at the same time telling them they are being tested in their sincerity to other churches and their giving. See *apostolic style, obligation persuasion,* **Glossary**. See **Article**, *49. Pauline Leadership Styles; 41. Motivating Principles: Pauline Influence*.

[281] Another of Paul's motivational techniques is to appeal to Jesus' modeling (e.g. Php 2:5-11) which he does here. Peter (e.g. 1Pe 2:21 and John (1Jn 2:6) both also use this technique. See **Article**, *41. Motivating Principles: Pauline Influence*.

[282] In fund-raising, leaders will, like Paul, have to repeatedly exhort, since initial enthusiasm for some project don't always last. Note, however, that Paul does not badger. He gives his opinion, strongly, but leaves it up to them to obey and demonstrate their loyalty to him as well as their obedience to God. See **LEADERSHIP TOPIC 8. APOSTOLIC LEADERSHIP FUNCTIONS**. See *apostolic function 6, Resource New Ministries and Old Ones* in **Article**, *2. Apostolic Functions*.

2 Corinthians 8:15-19 page 68

and they may help you out.[283] 15 As it is written,

> He who gathered much had nothing left over,
> and he who gathered little had no lack.[284]

16 I thank God for giving Titus the same enthusiasm for you that I have. 17 He not only responded to my challenge but he did it because he himself wanted to.[285] 18 We are sending with him a brother, highly respected by all the churches for his work in proclaiming the Good News 19 He was appointed by the churches to travel with us as we take this gift to Jerusalem. This service of love brings the Lord glory and shows that we really want to help.

---

[283] A Pauline leadership value occurs here. *Financial Equality Principle: Christian leadership must teach that Christian giving is a reciprocal balancing between needs and surplus.* This equalizing principle, giving when we have abundance and others have need, and in turn receiving when we have needs and others have abundance, must be recognized, embraced, and then applied very carefully so as to not create dependencies. But for the most part western Christians don't realize just how wealthy they are when in comparison with many other non-western Christians. With no exposure to missions and churches around the world, Christians will rarely ever really embrace this principle. Leaders must raise awareness levels about needs around the world as well as teach this principle (and model it in their own lives). See also comments on 2Co 9:8. See **Articles**, *55. Promises of God; 51. Pauline Leadership Values.*

[284] See Ex 16:1-18. This is another indication of Paul's Scripture centered leadership. Paul quotes from Psalm 112, which describes a person who fears the Lord and walks with God. Such a person gives generously and can expect God's long-term blessing. This is an example of how Paul references the O.T. Scriptures a number of times in 1,2 Co. In 1,2 Co Paul quotes, or alludes to or applies some O.T. scripture some 196 times. Books involved include Ge, Ex, Lev, Nu, Dt, Jdg, 1, 2 Sa, 1 Ch, Ezr, Ne, Job, Ps, Pr, Ecc, SS, Isa, Jer, Ezek, Da, Hos, Am, Mic, Hab, Zec, Mal. Most of those times he is referring to some principle of truth underlying the quoted material or verses being referred to. See **Articles**: *6. Bible Centered Leader; 72. Vanishing Breed, Needed Bible Centered Leaders; 53. Principles of Truth.*

[285] Titus' first mission trip to Corinth illustrates a ministry task. *A ministry task is an assignment from God, which primarily tests a person's faithfulness and obedience but often also allows use of ministry gifts in a context of a task which has closure, accountability, and evaluation.* So ministry training happens and growth as well as tasks accomplished. The more a leader is already developed the more the task is to accomplish the objective, rather than training. Titus had five ministry tasks. See particularly Titus' last ministry task, an apostolic one in Crete, described in the book of Titus. See also biographical sketch on Titus in **Clinton's Biblical Leadership Encyclopedia**. This illustrates a Pauline value, which generalized is stated as: *Training Methodology. Leaders must be concerned about leadership selection and development.* Note Paul mentions several people throughout 1,2 Co who he has selected and has trained or is training. **LEADERSHIP TOPIC 1. MINISTRY PHILOSOPHY AND VALUES.** See *leadership value, leadership selection, ministry task* **Glossary**. See also **Article**, *51. Pauline Leadership Values; 47. Paul—Mentor For Many; 45. Paul—Developer Par Excellence; 32. Leadership Selection; 37. Mentoring—an Informal Training Model.*

2 Corinthians 8:20-9:5 page 69

20 We want to be very careful in handling this gift and avoid any criticism. 21 We want to do what is right, not only in the sight of the Lord but in the sight of everyone.[286]

22 And we are sending along another brother who has been thoroughly tested on many occasions. He has always been eager to help. He is now even more eager to help because of his increased confidence in you. 23 Titus is my partner in my work with you.[287] The other brothers going with him represent the churches and are honoring Christ. 24 So show them your love. Prove to all the churches that our boasting about you was justified.[288]

Chapter 9

1 I don't really need to write you about the gift being sent to Jerusalem. 2 I know you want to help. I have even bragged about you to the Macedonians—that Greece was ready to give last year. Your enthusiasm stirred up most of them.[289] 3 So I have sent these brothers—I don't want my bragging to be empty words—so that you will get the collection ready. 4 What if some Macedonians come with me and find you unprepared? I and you too would be ashamed because of my confident boasting. 5 Therefore I thought it necessary to urge these brothers to go to you ahead of time so you could prepare your generous gift ahead of time, just as you had previously promised. This will show that you gave willingly and not

---

[286] Of the Six Barriers to leaders finishing well, improper handling of finances (whether deliberately or just carelessly) is probably the number three barrier (illicit sexual relationships, abuse of power, and money problems, in that order. Usually two and three go together). Financial issues often waylay a leader. Note the special care to maintain integrity (Pauline value, **Financial Integrity.** *A Christian leader must handle finances with absolute integrity*) with regards to finances that Paul suggests in 1Co 16:3,4 and Ac 11:27-30. See **LEADERSHIP TOPIC 1. MINISTRY PHILOSOPHY AND VALUES.** See *integrity, leadership value, Integrity and Openness,* **Glossary.** See **Article,** *22. Integrity—A Top Leadership Quality; 51. Pauline Leadership Values; 15. Finishing Well—Six Major Barriers.*

[287] Paul is a mentor sponsor for Titus. Whenever he can, Paul recommends to churches his team members as competent leaders. See *mentor sponsor,* **Glossary.** See **Articles,** *47. Paul—Mentor For Many; 5. Barnabas—Significant Mentoring; 37. Mentoring—An Informal Training Model* .

[288] Again the competitive motive is used by Paul to influence. It is stronger here because there will be representatives of those other churches there to assess the Corinthians. Will they live up to Paul's appraisal of them? Or better still, did they live up to Paul's expectations? We will probably have to wait till heaven to find out.

[289] Note Paul motivated the Macedonians this way too. See **Article,** *41. Motivating Principles, Pauline Influence.*

2 Corinthians 9:6-15

because you had to.[290]

6 Consider: A farmer who plants a small crop gets a small harvest; a farmer who plants a big crop will reap a big harvest. 7 Each one should give from the heart, not unhappily or because of pressure; for God loves a cheerful giver. 8 And God is able to provide more than you need. You will have what you need with some left over for giving.[291] 9 As it is written:

> The one dispensing blessings,
> The one giving to the poor;
> That one's acts of righteousness will be remembered.[292]

10 And God, who provides seed to the sower, and bread to eat, will also supply you and multiply the results of the gift you have given. 11 You will be enriched so that you can be generous. Many will thank God for the gifts sent by us. 12 So your ministry of giving meets the needs of those in Jerusalem and will result in much thanksgiving to God. 13 Your generosity will prove your obedient response to the Good News and will give honor to God.[293] 14 And they will pray with great love for you because of the way God has worked grace into your lives.[294] 15 Let us thank God for His indescribable gift!

---

[290] In terms of leadership styles Paul is using a *modified obligation-persuasion*, that is, maintaining a delicate balance—using highly directive exhortation but still allowing for and encouraging a willingness from the heart in obedience. Another leadership style, somewhat modified—the *Father Initiator*, is also being used here. *Father-initiator* is one of 10 Pauline leadership styles—a highly directive style. The father-initiator leadership style is related to the apostolic style which uses the fact of the leader having founded the work as a lever for getting acceptance of influence by the leader. Here Paul uses highly directive exhortation but backs off to allow the Corinthians to make up their own mind. This leadership style is seen in Phm and in 1Co 4:14,15 as well as here. See *obligation-persuasion*, *father—initiator*, **Glossary**. See **Article**, *49. Pauline Leadership Styles*.

[291] I believe this to be a promise from God that is broader than just the Corinthians. When believers give cheerfully and generously and to meet God-directed needs, I believe they can expect God to enrich them to give. I also believe the equalizing principle is in effect. If they give out of their overages they can expect help when they have need. The right kind of attitude is crucial however. They don't give to get. They give because God gives them grace to give and gives them liberal and joyous hearts to give. And they surrender themselves to God for this giving ministry through them. When this is done, I believe this promise is a good as gold. See **Article**, *55. Promises of God*.

[292] See Ps 112:9 for this quote. The meaning of this Hebrew poetry is that giving to the poor is a form of ultimate contribution—a legacy that will last. See *ultimate contribution*, **Glossary**. See my manual, **Interpreting The Scriptures: Hebrew Poetry**.

[293] As a leader Paul recognizes that he must from time to time raise money for various needs. And so he does want to meet those needs. But at the same time he sees the importance of people learning about giving from a longer viewpoint—what it does for them (See also Php 4:17). See **LEADERSHIP TOPIC 8. APOSTOLIC LEADERSHIP FUNCTIONS**. See function 6 in **Article**, *2. Apostolic Functions*.

[294] Paul is well aware of how people are motivated to pray. In one sense he is demonstrating the philosophical model, *Intercessor*. For he knows that in effect, he is recruiting prayer for the Corinthians. They give to those in need and those in need will pray for them. See **Article**, *24. Jesus—5 Leadership Models: Shepherd, Harvest, Steward, Servant, Intercessor*.

2 Corinthians 10:1-12

III. (Ch 10-12) Paul's Defense of His Authority

Chapter 10

1 Now I, Paul, personally[295] plead[296] with the kind of meekness and gentleness you see in Christ. I know you say that I am bold when I write you but timid when I am present. 2 Don't force me to be bold. I certainly can and especially with those who say I act from worldly motives. 3 It is true that I do live in this world; but I do not fight from worldly motives. 4 Nor do I use worldly weapons. I use God's mighty weapons which can destroy Satanic strongholds. I destroy false arguments. 5 I tear down any and every proud argument that keep people from knowing Christ. I conquer these rebellious ideas and force them to obey Christ. 6 And I will punish those who have remained disobedient, now that you have proved your loyalty to me and are ready to punish acts of disloyalty.[297]

7 You are making your judgments based on surface level appearances. Is someone there saying he is Christ's representative? Well, let that one think again! I am more so. 8 I am confident[298] when I assert so strongly about my spiritual authority—which the Lord gave me in order to help you grow not to destroy you.[299] 9 I am not trying to frighten you with my letter. 10 Some think I write boldly but will not be able to back it up in person when I speak to you. 11 Let those persons beware. I will be just as strong in person as my writings to you.

12 But don't think that I am classifying myself like those there who think so highly of themselves.

---

[295] Emphatic pronouns, two of them, (SRN 846; SRN 1473), are used here where none have to be used normally since the verb form carries the pronoun in itself. Paul is personally laying his defense of his apostolic authority on the line with these Corinthians. He does it in as strong an apostolic manner as he can and still be gentle in doing so. See *apostolic style*, **Glossary**. See **Article**, *49. Pauline Leadership Styles*.

[296] Again *plead* is a translation of the verb form of *exhortation*. The gift of exhortation is used much in 1Co and 2Co. Leaders doing problem solving and convincing, particularly by persuasion, use this gift. See *exhortation*, **Glossary**.

[297] This is the third instance of an important Pauline value with regards to followers. See earlier (fn 2Co 2:9; 7:5). The value, **Loyalty Testing,** can be stated generally as: *Leaders must know the level of followership loyalty in order to wisely exercise leadership influence.* Two of the Ten Commandments of Followership are seen in that testing and in this remark about their loyalty to Paul. *1. LOYALTY: Leadership in voluntary organizations cannot be effectively exercised without followership loyalty. 2. DISCIPLINE: Leadership can not apply adequate discipline without a firm base of loyal committed followers.* Here Paul is threatening to deal with the minority, who have not accepted his 1Co advice. See comments on 2Co 2:5 which implies a majority accepted and some did not. And he threatens in the verses, which follow, to use strong power—this is spiritual warfare—using the indirect conflict leadership style. See *indirect conflict, leadership value, spiritual warfare,* **Glossary**. See **Articles**, *16. Followership—Ten Commandments; 60. Spiritual Authority—Defined, Six characteristics; 65. Spiritual Warfare—Satan's Tactics*.

[298] I have capturing *not ashamed* as an emphatic negative, *litotes*, really meaning, *I will not be put to shame or be disappointed or its positive opposite, I am completely confident.* See *litotes,* **Glossary**. See **Article**, *12. Figure and Idioms in the Bible*.

[299] A strong Pauline leadership value is in view here. I label it ***Spirituality Authority*** (*Its Ends): Spiritual authority ought to be used to mature followers.* See *spiritual authority,* **Glossary**. See **Articles**, *60. Spirituality Authority—defined, Six Characteristics; 16. Followership—Ten Commandments; 21. Influence, Power and Authority Forms*.

2 Corinthians 10:13-11:9   page 72

They make up their own standards to measure themselves by. And then they use them to judge themselves. That's not wise. 13 I myself am careful about boasting about my spiritual authority. I stay within the limits that God has placed on me. And that includes my work among you. 14 I am not going too far when I claim authority over you. For I was the first to bring the Good News to you.[300] 15 I do not claim credit for somebody else's work. Instead I have hope that as you grow I will have an even much greater work among you but still staying within the limits God has set for me. 16 I hope to preach the Good News in the regions beyond you. I won't be boasting about work accomplished in someone else's territory then.

17 But "the one who boasts, should boast in what the LORD does."[301] 18 When a person boasts about self it doesn't carry weight. But when the Lord commends someone, that counts.

Chapter 11
1 I wish you would put up with a little of my foolishness. 2 I have a godly jealously for you. For I have promised you in marriage to one husband, who is Christ. And I want to present you to him as a pure virgin. 3 But I am afraid, that somehow, as the serpent subtly deceived Eve, so your thinking may be corrupted from your simple openness to Christ. 4 You seem to believe what anyone teaches you about Jesus, even if it differs from what I taught. You receive this different truth and a different spirit from what you first received from me.[302]

5 Now I don't think I am inferior to your very special apostles.[303] 6 Even though I may appear unskilled in my speaking style,[304] yet I am very knowledgeable. I have made this very clear to you again and again.

7 I was certainly not wrong in preaching the Good News to you without it costing you a cent. I put you first above myself. 8 Other churches supported me financially so I could minister at no cost to you. 9 While I was with you, I had some needs; but I didn't ask you for help. The folks from Macedonia brought me persecuted me. 27 I have wearily worked on, missing sleep, sometimes

---

[300] Again the Father-Initiator leadership style is openly in view here. See *father-initiator*, **Glossary**. See **Article**, *49. Pauline Leadership Styles*.

[301] This little allusion to the Old Testament is found in several locations, not totally as is (Jer 9:24; Ps 34:2; 44:8). Again this is indicative of Paul's knowledge of and use of the Old Testament. It is another indication of his being a Scripture-Based leader. See *Bible Centered leader*, **Glossary**. See **Article**, *72. A Vanishing Breed, Needed Bible Centered Leaders*.

[302] Remember, a leader is a person with (1) God-given ability and a (2) God-given responsibility who is influencing a (3) specific group of God's people (4) toward God's purposes for it. The God-given responsibility has a two-fold direction—upward to God, that is, responsible to God for the group and leadership of the group and downward, a burden for the group. Here, as in 2Co 2:1-4, the downward is in focus. Paul shows a genuine burden for the Corinthians—he is concerned that they are being led astray by these "so-called apostles" who will subtly twist truth to deceive them. This is apostolic function 5, *Combat Heresy (both orthodoxy and orthopraxy),* which seeks to maintain doctrinal and behavioral purity. See **LEADERSHIP TOPIC 6. MOTIVATIONAL LESSONS; LEADERSHIP TOPIC 8. APOSTOLIC LEADERSHIP FUNCTIONS.** See *burden, downward burden, upward burden*, **Glossary**. See **Articles**, *2. Apostolic Functions; 40. Motivating Factors for Ministry*.

[303] This is probably a negative emphatic and is even stronger in the capture. *I am superior to these so-called apostles.* See *litotes/tapenosis, negative emphatic*, **Glossary**. See **Article**, *12. Figures and Idioms in the Bible*.

[304] Unskilled here does not infer ineffective but most likely refers to formal training in rhetoric. Paul was an effective speaker, even if occasionally he did speak too long and too late at night and put people to sleep (remember Eutychus, Acts 20:9).

everything I needed. In the past and in the future, I'm not going to ask you for my personal support. 10 So help me Christ, I won't stop pointing this out everywhere in Greece. 11 Why do I say this? Because I don't love you? No way! God knows this to be true![305]

12 And I will continue doing this. That will negate those other so-called apostles from boastfully claiming to work just as I do. 13 These are not true apostles. They are deceitful workers. They disguise themselves as apostles to fool you. 14 Is that surprising? No. Even Satan can disguise himself as God's messenger of truth.[306] 15 So it's no big thing then if his servants pretend to be godly workers. But in the end they will be found out and receive their due punishment.

16 I repeat. Don't think I am a fool. But if you must, at least consider what this fool can boast about. 17 Let me confidently boast, even though appearing foolish and not as a word from Christ. 18 Others boast for human reasons, why not me? 19 You seem to tolerate fools gladly, from your all-wise stance. 20 You put up with them even when they enslave you, take all you have, look down on you, and slap you in the face. 21 I am proud to say, I never did that.

But in whatever they boast about, foolishly speaking, I can match them boast for boast. 22 Are they Hebrews? I am too. Are they Israelites? I am too. Are they descendants of Abraham? I am too. 23 Are they Christ's servants? This may sound foolish but I have served him more than them. I've worked harder. I've been beaten much more. I've been in prison more times. I've faced death more than they have. 24 From the Jews five times I received the maximum thirty-nine lashes. 25 Three times I was whipped by the Romans. Once I was stoned. Three times I was shipwrecked—once spending twenty-four hours adrift at sea. 26 I've traveled much and faced floods and robbers. I've faced danger from my own people, the Jews. Gentiles too have threatened me. I have faced danger in cities, in deserts, and on stormy seas. Even some claiming to be Christians have persecuted me. 27 I have wearily worked on, missing sleep, sometimes

---

[305] In this interweaving context (11:1-4; 5-6; 7-11; 12-15; 16-21; 21-29; 30-33) Paul is obviously answering charges against his leadership. These charges are implied in the strong statements he makes about himself. Verse 5—He is not an apostle; these "super apostles" at Corinth are claiming more authority than Paul. Verse 6—Paul's public oratory has been criticized (remember they had some great orators there, like Apollos). Verse 7—He has been maligned by being accused of wanting finances from the Corinthians. He is probably accused of personally misusing funds requested for other needs. Verse 11—He has probably been accused of being interested in their resources but not them. Verse 22—Paul is not a pure Hebrew; his contextualization work dealing with applying truth to Gentile situations certainly could make him appear less than a strict law-abiding Hebrew. Verses 23-27—His ministry activity has been questioned. Verse 28—His concern for churches and their on-going welfare has been questioned. Probably something like this, "Ah, yes. He starts works but leaves them to flounder on their own. Look at your own case; he has promised to come back and help but hasn't, has he?" Often conflict will move from the real issues to deprecation of character. Here Paul is defending his character. Only twice in the Pauline epistles do we see Paul defending himself—here and in Galatians. Here, where the spread of the Gospel will be hindered and perhaps blocked from expanding into Europe, if the Corinthians pull away from Paul's influence. And in Galatians, where the heart of the Gospel, the work of the Cross appropriated by faith, is at stake. In both these extreme cases, Paul has to use other authority forms, in addition to spiritual authority. See **Articles**, *21. Influence, Power, and Authority Forms. 60. Spiritual Authority Defined—Six Characteristics.*

[306] I have captured, *angel of light*, as messenger of truth. A major Satanic tactic is to twist truth subtly so that it appears at first as all right but will deceive and lead astray in the end. See *metaphor, capture*, **Glossary**. See **Article**, *65. Spiritual Warfare—Satan's Tactics.*

2 Corinthians 11:28-12:8   page 74

going hungry and thirsty, often fasting. I've done without shelter and clothing to keep me warm. 28 Then besides all this, daily, I am burdened with my responsibility for the churches. 29 I feel for them when they are weak. When someone falls I'm really upset.[307]   30 If I must boast, I will boast about things which reveal my weaknesses. 31 The God and Father of our Lord Jesus Christ, who is blessed forever, knows that I am telling the truth.[308] 32 In Damascus the governor, under King Aretas, guarded the city gates with a garrison, hoping to arrest me. 33 But I was let down in a basket through a window in the wall, and got away.[309]

Chapter 12
   1 I don't like to boast, but if I must, I will talk about visions and revelations given me by the Lord. 2 About fourteen years ago—whether physically in my body or whether an out of body experience, I am not sure which—only God knows—I was snatched up to the highest heaven. 3 I repeat , I am not sure if this was real or in a vision. 4 But I was caught up into Paradise and heard sacred inexpressible words, which shouldn't be retold. 5 I could boast about that experience. Yet personally I would rather speak of my weaknesses.[310] 6 I could boast about plenty of things and wouldn't be foolish in doing so because it would be the truth. But I won't. I don't want anyone to have a higher opinion of me than what they have actually heard and seen me do.[311]
   7 But to keep me from being proud about these wonderful revelations, I was given a painful physical ailment, a reminder from Satan, to plague me and keep me from getting conceited.[312] 8 Three times I

---

[307] Again another indication of Paul's sense of burden, as a leader, for the Corinthians. See also comments on 2Co 2:4; 11:4. See **Article**, *40. Motivating Factors for Ministry*.

[308] This, again shows Paul's sense of accountability and his value *Ultimate Accountability: Leaders' actions must be restrained by the fact that they will ultimately give an account to God for their leadership actions.* See *ultimate accountability*, **Glossary**. See **Articles**, *9. Day of Christ—Implications for Leaders, 40. Motivating Factors for Ministry*.

[309] This seems an afterthought as if to say, "And oh yes, I remember something else I can boast about. I escaped by being let down in a basket out of a guarded city; let those super apostles top that!"

[310] I have captured the third-party description and made it first person. Paul is talking about himself and couches it in third-party language to make it look less like he is boasting. These kind of experiences are Type I Destiny Process Items—awe inspiring experiences with God which confirm and deepen a person's sense of destiny and commitment to follow God and to know God's powerful presence in life and ministry. See *destiny processing, Type I Destiny, Type II Destiny, Type III Destiny, Type IV Destiny*, **Glossary**. See **Article**, *42. Paul—A Sense of Destiny; 10. Destiny Pattern*.

[311] Paul implies two values here. *A leader should not take credit for the work of others as if it were his/her own.* The "super apostles" in Corinth probably were. *People should be able to validate a leader's work from first-hand experience.* See *leadership value*, **Glossary**.

[312] Inordinate pride is one of the six major barriers keeping leaders from finishing well. Strong, powerfully gifted leaders, especially those who have numerous Type I destiny experiences, often have need for God to curb pride and ambition. God uses brokenness, deep processing (like isolation, crises, conflict, etc.) and even as in this case, some physical ailment to keep on reminding these leaders of their dependence upon God. See *deep processing, brokenness, isolation, Type I destiny*, **Glossary**. See **Article**, *15. Finishing Well—Six Major Barriers*.

2 Corinthians 12:9-16

admonished the Lord about this thing—for Him to take it away. 9 His answer was, "My enabling presence is all you need. My power shows forth much stronger in your weakness." So you can see then, why I boast about my weaknesses. Christ's power will work through me. 10 So I am glad for my weaknesses: for the insults that come; my distressful times; my persecutions; my hard times for Christ's sake. For when I am weak,[313] paradoxically speaking, I am strong.[314]

11 You have made me act like a fool—boasting this way. You should be showing your approval of me, not me doing it for myself. For even though I am nothing, I am in fact superior to your very special apostles. 12 Signs and wonders and miracles, those things that are the proof of apostleship, I patiently demonstrated among you. 13 What makes you inferior to other churches? Was it that I didn't take financial support from you? My apologies for this wrong![315]

14 I am ready to come to you, for the third time. And I am not going to be a burden[316] for you. I don't want your money; I want you. For children shouldn't have to support parents. Parents should take care of their children. 15 I will very gladly spend all I have and all that I am in order to help you. Though it seems the more I love you, the less you love me.[317]

16 Whatever! You know I did not burden you. Yet some of you still think I was sneaky and trapped

---

[313] The word *weakness* or variations of it occur repeatedly in these few verses. This reiterates *The Clay Pot Principle*, previously seen in 2Co 4:7. When a leader ministers out of weakness, it is clear that what is accomplished comes from God's strength. Some leaders, more than others, will be called to minister out of weakness. Note Pauline leadership value 14 is in view: *14. **Death/Life Paradox**. The firstfruits of Jesus resurrection life ought to be experienced in the death producing circumstances of life and ought to serve as a hallmark of spiritual life for followers. In other words, Christianity ought to work in thick or thin.* See **Article**, *51. Pauline Leadership Values*.

[314] Notice how Paul always puts the best spin, i.e. has *a Sovereign Mindset*, on what is happening to him. The Pauline value involved: *Leaders ought to see God's hand in their circumstances as part of His plan for developing them as leaders.* See **LEADERSHIP TOPIC 1. MINISTRY PHILOSOPHY AND VALUES.** See **Article**, *59. Sovereign Mindset; 51. Pauline Leadership Values*.

[315] Strong irony is being used here. Captured it might sound like: *I treated you exactly like other churches, except for one difference. I didn't burden you with my financial needs. I showed a little leniency and now pay a price for it. I should have burdened you. Quit hassling me about finances!* See *irony, capture*, **Glossary**. See **Article**, *12. Figures and Idioms in the Bible*.

[316] That is, try to obtain money for my own needs. Paul was above board on any issues regarding his personal finances. Note how carefully he states over and over that he did not take finances from them. Obviously he had been accused of this by the false apostles. And probably just as obvious, he is accusing these apostles of doing that very thing. That is why he is so clear about his own finances. Pauline leadership value 19 is in view: *Value 19. **Financial Integrity**. A Christian leader must handle finances with absolute integrity.* See **LEADERSHIP TOPIC 1. MINISTRY PHILOSOPHY AND VALUES; LEADERSHIP TOPIC 2. FINANCIAL SAFEGUARD.** See *integrity, leadership value, Integrity and Openness*, **Glossary**. See **Article**, *22. Integrity—A Top Leadership Quality; 51. Pauline Leadership Values*.

[317] Again Paul shows that he has a real burden for these Corinthians. This is an important leadership concept. For without burden for a work of God a leader will give up when it gets tough. See *burden, downward burden, upward burden*, **Glossary**. See **Article 40.** *Motivating Factors for Ministry*.

2 Corinthians 12:17-21

you with lies.[318] 17 Did I take advantage of you through the messengers I sent? 18 I urged Titus to come to see you and sent another brother with him. Did Titus take advantage of you? Didn't Titus and I both have the same motives? Didn't we both act the same way?[319]

19 I am not giving excuses to defend myself to you. No, openly I speak knowing God is listening.[320] What I am doing is done to help you grow.[321] 20 I am afraid when I get there I won't like what I see. And I am afraid you might not like what you see me to be. I am afraid that I will find arguments, jealousy, angry outbursts, self-seeking political activity, insults, gossip, pride, and disorderly behavior. 21 I am afraid. When I come again, my God will humiliate me because of you. I will weep for many who have sinned in the past. For they have not repented for immoral behavior—sexual sins and lustful pleasure.[322]

---

[318] Paul is obviously being accused of lying and trapping these Corinthians with his teachings. He certainly refutes it here. Pauline leadership value 5 is in view here: *Value 5. **Integrity and Openness**. Leaders should not be deceptive in their dealings with followers but should instead be open, honest, forthright, and frank with them.* See **LEADERSHIP TOPIC 1. MINISTRY PHILOSOPHY AND VALUES.** See **Article,** *22. Integrity—A Top Leadership Quality.*

[319] Titus' consistency in teaching and behavior with Paul was a strong argument for Paul's ministry. Titus would refute the so-called *special apostles* and also back Paul's views. Pauline leadership value 9 is in view: *Value 9. **True Credentials** (competency and results). A leader should be able to point to results from ministry as a recommendation of God's authority in him/her.* See **Article,** *51. Pauline Leadership Values.*

[320] This, again as in several passages in both 1Co and 2Co, shows Paul's sense of accountability and his value of *Ultimate Accountability*: *Leaders' actions must be restrained/encouraged by the fact that they will ultimately give an account to God for their leadership actions.* See *Ultimate Accountability,* **Glossary**.

[321] Paul is giving strong leadership advice which admonishes, corrects, and clarifies his own motives for ministry (defending himself). Yet in it all, it is not the discipline that is in focus. These words, "What I am doing is done to help you grow," are at the heart of this apostolic function. Discipline is rarely an end in itself. Almost always there is the redemptive side of it: to gain back the one being disciplined, to bring about growth, to enhance relationship with God, etc. Pauline leadership value 7 is in view: *Value 7. **Spiritual Authority**—Its ends. Spiritual authority ought to be used to mature followers.* See **LEADERSHIP TOPIC 8. APOSTOLIC LEADERSHIP FUNCTIONS.** See *spiritual authority,* **Glossary**. See **Articles,** *2. Apostolic Functions; 60. Spiritual Authority Defined—Six Characteristics; 16. Followership—Ten Commandments.*

[322] Paul here uses a motivational technique called *foreshadowing*. He paints a possible scenario with undesired consequences, for both himself and the Corinthians, with a view toward motivating them to opt for the opposite positive scenario. It is a sort of reverse psychology ploy applied to the group. He lets them know he would really be disappointed if the negative scenario happened. And he strongly urges repentance for sins of some there who have not done so. Maybe these unrepentant ones are part of the minority alluded to in 2Co 2:6—see comments there. Because of his *apostolic leadership style* and his *Father-Initiator leadership style*, they would want to heed this motivational urge. This is a good example of Wrong's power form of coercive authority. Note also that Paul also emotionally reflects his burden for this Corinthian bunch. See *coercive authority apostolic style, father-initiator style,* **Glossary**. See **Articles,** *21. Influence, Power, and Authority Forms; 41. Motivating Principles: Pauline Influence.*

2 Corinthians 13:1-10

Chapter 13

1 This will be the third time I am coming to visit you. Scripturally, it is so that,

"Accusations must be upheld by the confirming evidence of two or three witnesses.[323]"

2 On my second visit I warned those who have sinned in the past. Now again I warn them and all others just as before. This next time I come nobody will escape punishment. 3 I will give you all the proof you want to show that Christ speaks through me. Christ is not weak in his dealing with you. He shows his power among you. 4 In weakness He died on the cross. Yet he lives by the power of God. In union with him we are weak yet in union with him we have power—the power we will use in dealing with you.[324]

5 Examine yourselves. Is your faith genuine? Test yourselves. If you don't know that Jesus' presence is with you, you have failed the test. 6 But I trust that you will know that I have passed the test.[325] 7 Now I pray to God that you'll not do anything wrong—not that I need your approval—but because I want you to do right, even if I have seemed to fail. 8 I want the truth to win out. 9 I will gladly be weak if it makes you strong. I pray for your maturity. 10 Therefore I write these things before I come hoping that I will not have to deal harshly with you when I do come. I do have spiritual authority from the Lord to deal with you—authority to build you up, not tear you down.[326]

---

[323] See Dt 19:15. Again this shows Paul's grasp of Scripture. He was a Scripturally-based leader. See *Bible Centered leader*, **Glossary**. See **Articles**, *6. Bible Centered Leader; 72. Vanishing Breed, Needed Bible Centered Leaders*.

[324] This is risky and courageous leadership. This is as strong an apostolic threat as you will see from Paul anywhere. He is saying that Christ will show power through him to discipline all those who are not heeding his apostolic advice. When he shows up in Corinth one of three things could happen: 1. The Corinthians will have complied with Paul's advice and corrective teaching—A great positive scenario; 2. They will not have complied and Paul will have been humiliated and will be forced to demonstrate great apostolic power with discipline via power ministry (like Moses with Korah); 3. Paul will have been humiliated and will try to discipline with power ministry but will not have power to do so. Each of these are a real possibility. Paul is putting it on the line. He will either have power or his apostolic ministry is finished. See **LEADERSHIP TOPIC 8. APOSTOLIC LEADERSHIP FUNCTIONS**. See *power ministry*, **Glossary**. See **Article**, *2. Apostolic Functions*.

[325] Paul knows that *the essential ingredient of leadership is the powerful presence of God in the life and ministry of the leader (macro lesson 9)*. Here, he applies that basic idea to the ministry and results of ministry. If people, supposedly saved and related to God in Christ, do not have the presence of Christ demonstrated in them (i.e. by changed lives and growth) then they have no guarantee that they are Christ's. Paul's Transforming Ministry value is underlying this basic admonition: *Value 11*. **Transforming Ministry**. *Followers, increasingly being set free by the Holy Spirit and being transformed into Christ's image ought to be the hope and expectation of a Christian leader*. See macro lesson, *Transforming Ministry*, **Glossary**.

[326] Paul openly states his motivation behind his letter—he definitely wants to avoid the negative scenario seen in 2Co 12:20,21. See Pauline leadership value 5: *Value 5*. **Integrity and Openness**. *Leaders should not be deceptive in their dealings with followers but should instead be open, honest, forthright, and frank with them*. See **LEADERSHIP TOPIC 1. MINISTRY PHILOSOPHY AND VALUES**. See **Article**, *51. Pauline Leadership Values; 22. Integrity—A Top Leadership Quality*.

2 Corinthians 13:11-14

11 Finally,[327] Christian friends, good bye. Rejoice. Restore yourselves. Encourage yourselves. Strive for unity and peacefulness. Then the God of love and peace will be with you.

12 Greet each other in Christian love. 13 All the Christians here send their greetings.

14 The grace of the Lord Jesus Christ, the love of God, and the communion of the Holy Spirit be with you all. Amen.[328]

---

[327] Note how short these closing remarks are. Clearly missing in the closing remarks are all the personal things Paul usually refers to. There are no names here. There are no little requests. It is as if Paul is emotionally whipped after dictating this letter with all its strong language and its defense of himself and his ministry. Only in one other book does he defend as strongly, Galatians. For the most part, Paul lets God vindicate his ministry and apostolic authority. In these two cases, Corinth and the Galatian problem, core issues are at stake and Paul is not only defending himself but essential truths that under gird apostolic ministry. If these are not clarified then his own ministry is finished as well as his contextualized view of the Gospel.

[328] Some copies have the following appended to this letter: *The second epistle to the Corinthians was written from Philippi, a city of Macedonia, by Titus and Luke*. If this is so, go back and note how Paul carefully praised the Macedonians and uses them as strong examples of giving to the Corinthians. For the Corinthians, it was a motivational technique, based on competitiveness. But for the Macedonians it was an example of a motivational technique known as *Goodwin's Expectation Principle*. This is a social dynamic which is described as, *emerging leaders tend to live up to the genuine expectations of leaders they respect*. Paul applies it corporately to a group (e.g. the Macedonians) as well as to individuals like Timothy and Titus. See *Goodwin's Expectation Principle*, **Glossary**. See **Article**, *41. Motivational Principles: Pauline Influence*.

For Further Leadership Study--Second Corinthians

General

2Co contains much of what Paul was feeling from the attack on his character. In an open, honest way he vents these feelings along with the reasons why he did or said things. This makes 2Co a valuable data base for uncovering values underlying Paul's ministry. A number of process items can be seen in the pages—shaping activities of God in the life of Paul. It is valuable for understanding when and how a leader defends his/her own ministry. When core truth of the Gospel is at stake (see Gal) or when character assassination will abrogate a work of God and God's truth, then a leader is free, with honesty and integrity, to validate leadership decisions, etc. At least that is Paul's experience.

Suggestions For Further Study

1. Some fifty process items have been codified in leadership emergence theory. Identify the kinds of process items that Paul indicates in his various relating of incidents.

2. Study the notions of influence, power, and authority to understand the basic power bases a leader has to under gird his/her leadership influence. Which kinds of power forms does Paul use in 2 Corinthians?

3. Paul's view of giving is not tithing, something many present-day leaders advocate. His view is proportionality. We give freely, not in obligation. We give liberally as we can. We give recognizing that God enables us to give. We give recognizing that we are stewards. Everything we have (not just a tenth) belongs to God. We are simply using it for His purposes in our lives. Compare these ideas with the O.T. view of the tithe.

4. Study other Pauline books with a focus on leadership values to add to the identified Pauline leadership values. It is generally accepted that Paul wrote 1,2Th before 1,2Co and over the next nine years wrote the rest of his epistles with 2Ti being the last and occurring about ten years after 2Co. Did any of these values identified in 2Co change over the rest of his lifetime? What new values do we see added as we study each of the later epistles? What leadership values are stressed in his three last books, the pastoral epistles? These especially should be informative as he is dealing specifically with leadership issues.

Special Comments

This book can be studied with great profit for leadership processing information in the life of Paul. Many process items can be identified and helpful lessons from them.

For Further Leadership Study

Personal Response

1. What is the most significant leadership insight you have gained from your study of 2Co?

2. What one idea from this study can you put into practice in your own leadership? How?

3. Immediate Application: List an idea from this study that you can share with someone today.

    a. Idea:

    b. Who?:

Your Observations.
   You may want to jot down important insights you want to remember. You may wish to note follow-up intents.

Leadership Articles For 1, 2 Corinthians Commentary[1]

Page   Articles Title

Page	#	Article Title
83	1.	Accountability—Standing Before God As A Leader
85	2.	Apostolic Functions
89	3.	Apostolic Functions—Comparison of Titus and Timothy
91	4.	Apostolic Giftedness—Multiple Gifted Leaders
98	5.	Barnabas—Significant Mentoring
103	6.	Bible Centered Leader
106	7.	Conscience, Paul's Use of
110	8.	Constellation Model, Mentoring Relationships
114	9.	Day of Christ—Implications for Leaders
115	10.	Destiny Pattern
121	11.	Entrustment—A Leadership Responsibility
123	12.	Figures and Idioms in the Bible
129	13.	Finishing Well—Five Factors Enhancing
132	14.	Finishing Well—Six Characteristics
135	15.	Finishing Well—Six Major Barriers Identified
137	16.	Followership—Ten Commandments
140	17.	Gender and Leadership
142	18.	Giving—Paul's View in 2 Corinthians
145	19.	God's Shaping Processes With Leaders
149	20.	Impartation of Gifts
151	21.	Influence, Power, and Authority Forms
156	22.	Integrity—A Top Leadership Quality
161	23.	Isolation Processing—Learning Deep Lessons from God
168	24.	Jesus—5 Leadership Models: Shepherd, Harvest, Steward, Servant, Intercessor
176	25.	Leaders—Intercession Hints from Habakkuk
181	26.	Leadership Act
184	27.	Leadership Eras in the Bible—Six Identified
187	28.	Leadership Functions—Three High Level Generic Priorities
191	29.	Leadership Genre—7 Types
193	30.	Leadership Lessons, Seven Major Lessons Identified
198	31.	Leadership Levels-Looking At a Leadership Continuum
202	32.	Leadership Selection
207	33.	Leadership Transition Concepts
212	34.	Leadership Tree Diagram
215	35.	Macro Lessons Defined
218	36.	Macro Lessons—List of 41 Across Six Leadership Eras.
221	37.	Mentoring—An Informal Training Model
224	38.	Ministry Entry Patterns
229	39.	Ministry Philosophy
234	40.	Motivating Factors For Ministry
236	41.	Motivating Principles: Pauline Influence
238	42.	Paul—A Sense of Destiny
242	43.	Paul—And His Companions
249	44.	Paul—Deep Processing

---

[1] Throughout the commentary Articles listed with numbers are included with this commentary and refer to the numbered articles listed above. Some articles, without numbers occur in other commentaries. I will be publishing a series called, **Clinton's Leadership Encyclopedia**, which will contain all the articles in all the leadership commentaries. Those articles not included in this commentary will be available also there. Some of the articles included here were written later, some time after the 1,2 Corinthians commentary was already done. But in reviewing all of the leadership articles I felt that some were very appropriate to Paul's ministry with the Corinthians. In any case, I introduce each article with a short paragraph telling how the article is relevant to the Corinthian ministry. All of these articles were revised at least somewhat for this issue of the 1,2 Corinthian Leadership Commentary.

Leadership Articles For 1, 2 Corinthians Commentary

255	45.	*Paul—Developer Par Excellence*
257	46.	*Paul—Intercessor Leader*
261	47.	*Paul—Mentor For Many*
264	48.	*Paul—Modeling as An Influence Means*
269	49.	*Pauline Leadership Styles*
275	50.	*Pauline Leadership Terms*
280	51.	*Pauline Leadership Values*
284	52.	*Prayer Macro Lesson*
285	53.	*Principles of Truth*
289	54.	*Problems—The N.T. Church*
293	55.	*Promises of God*
296	56.	*Receptor Oriented Communication*
299	57.	*Reciprocal Living—The One-Another Commands*
303	58.	*Social Base Issues*
307	59.	*Sovereign Mindset*
310	60.	*Spiritual Authority—Defined, Six Characteristics*
313	61.	*Spiritual Benchmarks*
314	62.	*Spiritual Disciplines—And On-Going Leadership*
319	63.	*Spiritual Gift Clusters*
323	64.	*Spiritual Gifts, Giftedness and Development*
326	65.	*Spiritual Warfare—Satan's Tactics*
328	66.	*Spiritual Warfare—Two Extremes To Avoid*
330	67.	*Spiritual Warfare—Two Foundational Axioms*
333	68.	*Time-Lines—Defined For Biblical Leaders*
335	69.	*Timothy A Beloved Son in the Faith*
337	70.	*Union Life—Intimacy With God*
342	71.	*Value Driven Leadership*
343	72.	*Vanishing Breed, Needed, Bible Centered Leaders*
347	73.	*Variations on His Theme—Paul's Salutations--Harbingers of His Epistles*
352	74.	*Vulnerability and Prayer*

Article 1

<u>Relevance of the Article to Paul's Corinthian Ministry</u>

Two of Paul's core passages on judgment occur in the Corinthian letters—1 Cor 3 and 2 Cor 5. Paul was very aware that leaders would have to give an account for their influence. See Leadership Topic 3 Stewardship Model, 1 Co and Leadership Topic 9 Accountability, 2 Co.

1. Accountability—Standing Before God As a Leader

Introduction

What do the following biblical quotes have in common?

> 27 Each person is destined to die; and then they will be judged by God. Heb 9:27

> 10 That at the name of Jesus every knee should bow, of those in heaven, and of those on earth, and those under the earth. 11 Further, every tongue will confess that Jesus Christ is Lord, to the glory of God the Father. Php 2:10, 11

> 10 For we must all stand before Christ and be judged. We will each receive what we deserve for what we have done in these bodies,—whether good or bad. 2Co 5:10

How do the following quotes, which are similar, differ?

> 17 Obey your leaders. Follow what they say. They diligently watch out for your spiritual welfare since they must give an account of their ministry to God. Give them occasion to lead with joy as they see you obeying. Otherwise they lead with lack of joy. And that doesn't help you either. Heb 13:17

> 5 Who then is Paul, and who is Apollos, but ministers through whom you believed. The Lord gave us each work to do. 6 I planted, Apollos watered, but God gave the increase. 7 So then neither he who plants is anything, nor he who waters, but God who gives the increase. 8 Now he who plants and he who waters are together in this. Each one will receive his own reward according to his own labor. 9 For we are companions in God's work. You are God's cultivated field; you are God's building. 10 God gave grace to me, as a wise master builder I have laid the foundation. Another builds on it. But each one must be careful how he builds on it. 11 For no other foundation can anyone lay than that which is laid, which is Jesus Christ. 12 Anyone can build on this foundation with varying results: gold, silver, precious stones, wood, hay, or stubble. 13 Each one's work will become clear. For the Day will declare it. it will be revealed by fire. The fire will test each one's work, of what sort it is. 14 If anyone's work which he has built endures, he will receive a reward. 15 If anyone's work is burned, he will suffer loss; but he himself will be saved, yet so as through fire. 1 Co 3:5-15

The first three passages, two by Paul, and one by the author of Heb talk about the general notion of accountability. All people will be held accountable before God for their lives and what they did with them. But the last two passages Heb 13:17 and 1 Cor 3:5-15 narrows this accountability to leaders in particular. It avers that leaders will give an account to God for their ministry efforts.

Paul has an underlying value regarding accountability and his ministry efforts.

1. Accountability—Standing Before God As A Leader

> **Leader's actions must be restrained by the fact they will ultimately give an account to God for their leadership.**

Paul operates always with a view that he will answer to God for his leadership influence.

Accountability

This value is seen as a motivating factor in Paul's ministry to the Philippians and the Corinthians. Paul, in 1Co and 2Co, more than any other of his books shows his awareness of this very important leadership value. In 1,2 Co he uses this notion to clear his character of the accusations against him. He reveals his honesty before God, declares his responsibility to God, and in general claims a clear conscience before God concerning his leadership actions. Motivations, decisions, and explanations in general are all weighed in light of God's appraisal of them. Paul was an accountable leader—constantly reminding his readers that he was aware of God's awareness and judgment of his actions as a leader.[2] Two leadership observations arising from this notion of accountability include:

a. Leaders must be restrained by the fact that they will ultimately give an account to God for their leadership actions.
b. Leaders show burden for a ministry by recognizing their accountability to God for it.

Stewardship Model

Jesus teaches with authority this general notion of accountability. The <u>stewardship model</u> is a philosophical model, which is founded on the central thrust of several accountability passages, that is, that a leader must give account of his/her ministry to God. These accountability parables include: Mt 20 Laborers in the Vineyard; Mt 24 The Waiting Servants; Mt 25 The Ten Virgins; Mt 25 The Ten Talents; Lk 16 The Worldly Wise Steward; Lk 19 The Pounds. Paul and the author of Heb build on Jesus' teaching in such passages as: Ro 14:11,12; 1Co 3:5-9,12-15; 4:1-5; 2Co 5:10; Php 2:10,11; Heb 9:27, 13:17; Jas 3:1; 1Pe 5:1-4.

Some of the basic values, which underlie the Harvest Model include:

1. God holds a leader accountable for leadership influence and for growth and conduct of followers. A leader must recognize this accountability.
2. Leaders must recognize an ultimate accounting of a leader to God in eternity for one's performance in leadership.
3. Leaders should recognize that they will receive rewards for faithfulness to their ministry in terms of abilities, skills, gifts and opportunities. This is one motivating factor for leading.
4. Leaders ought to build upon abilities, skills, and gifts to maximize potential and use for God.
5. Leaders ought to know that they frequently must hold to higher standards than followers due to "the above reproach" and modeling impact they must have on followers.

Paul exemplifies these Harvest Model values in his ministry.

Conclusion

Leaders should be aware of giving accountability to God for their ministry. Such a value can change day-to-day ministry. Such a value maintained over a lifetime is a springboard to a good finish for a leader. Such a value is greatly needed, especially by strong leaders.

See **Articles**, 24. *Jesus—Five Leadership Models: Shepherd, Harvest, Steward, Servant, Intercessor; 51. Pauline Leadership Values; 41. Motivating Principles—Pauline Influence; 2. Apostolic Functions.*

---

[2] See especially 1Co 1:8; 3:13,15; 4:5; 2Co 1:14,23; 2:18; 4:2; 5:10; 11:31; 12:19; Php 1:6,10; 2:16. For other references see 2Th 2:2; 1Ti 5:19,20; 2Ti 1:16; 4:8,14.

Article 2

Relevance of the Article to Paul's Corinthian Ministry

This article was written primarily for use with the Titus commentary. However, it is helpful for us to recognize the three phases of apostolic ministry and to see the Corinthian ministry as second Phase work bordering on third phase work. This article along with the two following articles detail thinking about apostolic work. You will see that Paul was performing a number of these apostolic functions with the Corinthian church.

2. Apostolic Functions

Introduction

What do apostles do? Comparative studies in Ac, 1,2Ti and Tit reveal a number of functions that are symptomatic of apostles. But before looking at what apostles do perhaps it is in order to examine some characteristics of apostolic workers such as giftedness, power bases used, leadership styles and leadership models. This will lay a good foundation for understanding apostolic functions.

Apostolic Giftedness

All apostolic workers have spiritual gifts as the focal element of their giftedness set.[3] But what spiritual gifts? First of all an apostle in this technical sense being examined in this article is one who has the gift of apostleship. Second, such leaders are often multi-gifted and include various power and word gifts. The below definitions refer to giftedness seen in apostles.

Definition   The gift of apostleship refers to a special leadership capacity to move with authority from God to create new ministry structures (churches and para-church) to meet needs and to develop and appoint leadership in these structures. **Its central thrust is Creating New Ministry.**

Definition   Power gifts refer to a category of spiritual gifts which authenticate the reality of God by demonstrating God's intervention in today's world. These include: tongues, interpretation of tongues, discernings of spirits, kinds of healings, kinds of power (miracles), prophecy, faith, word of wisdom, word of knowledge.

Definition   Word gifts refer to a category of spiritual gifts used to clarify and explain about God. These help us understand about God including His nature, His purposes and how we can relate to Him and be a part of His purposes. These include: teaching, exhortation, pastoring, evangelism, apostleship, prophecy, ruling, and sometimes word of wisdom, word of knowledge, and faith (a word of). All leaders have at least one of these and often several of these.

Frequently, in addition to power gifts which authenticate and validate an apostle's ministry, an apostle will have the gift of faith—which enables a strong projection of vision on others.[4]

---

[3] Giftedness set refers to natural abilities, acquired skills, and spiritual gifts which a leader has as resources to use in ministry. Focal element refers to the dominate component of a giftedness set—either natural abilities, acquired skills, or spiritual gifts.

[4] Apostolic workers are strong leaders who use highly directive leadership styles. Those with the gift of faith obtain vision from God and can exercise strong inspirational leadership to motivate and recruit to the vision. They attract followers to their cause.

2. Apostolic Functions

What Power Bases Enforce Apostolic Functions?

Apostles use various power bases[5] to enforce their leadership influence. While, most would recognize spiritual authority as the ideal, they frequently use other forms since they often are dealing with immature followers in new works. A prioritized list of power forms seen in apostolic ministry would include personal authority, competent authority, coercive authority, induced authority—all laced with a sense of spiritual authority. Networking power often buttresses power used by apostolic workers.

What Leadership Styles Flow From the Power Bases?

Apostles frequently use highly directive leadership styles. A prioritized list of leadership styles seen in apostolic ministry includes: apostolic style, father-initiator, father-guardian, confrontation, indirect conflict, obligation persuasion, imitator. Highly indirect styles are used basically only with loyal trusted leaders.

What Leadership Models Dominate Apostolic Work?

Apostolic workers dominantly are driven by values underlying the stewardship model and the harvest model. Apostolic workers have a strong sense of calling and desire to accomplish for God. And for the most part this is directed toward the outward functions of the Great Commission as seen in the harvest model. Servant, Shepherd, and Intercessor models are less seen in apostolic ministries.

Apostolic workers are dominantly task-oriented leaders with strong inspirational leadership. Usually apostolic workers lack relational leadership skills and must depend on others to supplement this or suffer the consequences of conflict, confrontation, and large back doors in their ministry as emerging workers leave them.

What Are Some Apostolic Functions?

Table 1,2 Co 2-1 below lists seven major headings for apostolic functions observed in the N.T. Church Leadership Era. While there may be other apostolic functions these at least are highlighted in the Ac and epistles. I subsume a number of minor apostolic functions under these higher level categories.

---

[5] Wrong sees power in terms of a power holder, a power subject and the means the power holder uses to gain compliance from the power subject. Power base deals with the means. Force, Manipulation, Authority, and Persuasion are the general categories containing various power bases.

2. Apostolic Functions

Table 1,2 Co 2-1. Apostolic Functions

Function	N.T. Indication	Description/Explanation
1. Start New Ministries	Paul and Barnabas, Ac 13; Paul Ac 16, 18	Paul and Barnabas inaugurate the missionary movement. Paul breaks open a new work in Europe and other new works in Asia. These are usually creative new approaches to ministry which challenge traditional approaches. Power ministry is often used to validate the apostle's ministry and authenticate God's existence, power, and presence. When starting new ministries whether churches, movements, organizations, apostolic workers attract followers due to their personality, competency, and power seen in ministry. Paul tried to start indigenized churches.[6] Most apostolic workers are driven by values underlying the Harvest Leadership model, though these values may be implicit.
2. Appoint Leaders	Paul and Barnabas do (1st missionary trip). Paul does this on all his missionary trips. Titus did this in Crete. Timothy does this in Ephesus.	Apostolic workers raise up leadership including selecting, developing and giving training that will develop these workers; they impart gifts as Paul did with Timothy; they appoint leaders in works. In fact, the basic message of Titus (and in 1,2Ti) concerns leadership selection and appointment. The basic message of the book of Tit (**Setting The Church In Order** involves the appointing of qualified leaders, requires leaders who are sound in teaching and who model a Christian life style, and necessitates leaders who exhort others to practical Christian living.) exemplifies this apostolic function and function 3.
3. Establish Works	Paul does this in Philippi, Corinth, Ephesus, Rome and Crete.	Apostolic workers are concerned that ministries they have begun mature in the faith. They will send workers to solve problems, help develop leaders, and to teach and help followers mature. They will send helpful materials. They will exert influence through relationships to keep works going and growing. But establishing is secondary to creating new works. See the book of Tit.
4. Intercede for Works, both new and old	Paul does this for the churches he established.	Paul had a real burden for the churches he founded and worked with. *Beside outward circumstances pressing me, there is the inward burden, i.e. the anxiety and care, I feel daily for all the churches.* 2Co 11:28. Almost all apostolic leaders will have many values of the Intercessor Leader Model and will feel the responsibility of prayer for the works they associate with.
5. Combat Heresy[7] (both orthodoxy and orthopraxy)	Paul does this somewhat in Corinth and Crete and much in Ephesus. See also the Jerusalem conference, Ac 15.	1Ti is the comprehensive example of this apostolic function (four lines of heresy dealt with). Paul deals with potential heresy both in orthopraxy and orthodoxy. The practice of Christianity as well as the beliefs of Christianity can be heretical. Apostles are concerned with this. And apostles and so-called apostles themselves, frequently not accountable to others, can easily be the source of heresy. See 1,2 Co.

---

[6] An indigenized church has its own leadership from its own people and is organized to survive independently of outside leadership from other cultures and operates with appropriate forms, rites, and ministry fitting to its own culture.

[7] Heresy refers to deviation from a standard, whether in belief (orthodoxy) or practice (orthopraxy). e.g. See 1Ti where both are present in the Ephesian church (as prophesied in Ac 20:30).

2. Apostolic Functions

6. Resource New Ministries and Old Ones	Paul and Barnabas Ac 11; Paul in 1Co, 2Co.	Apostolic workers raise finances for workers like Paul did for Timothy (1Co 16, 1Ti), Stephanus (1Co 16). They help out old works in special need. Paul had the Philippian church giving to other churches. Had Corinthian churches giving to needs in Jerusalem. They also provide workers to help out in situations like Timothy, Titus, etc. Part of the resourcing includes knowledge, wisdom and findings from related experience. They also help those with resources understand both their freedom and responsibility to use these for the kingdom (1Ti).
7. Test New Ministries for Validity	Barnabas Ac 11	Barnabas is sent on a ministry task from the apostles in Jerusalem to test the Christianity in Antioch. Titus' ministry tasks had somewhat of this flavor in Crete as well.

Conclusions

Apostolic functions involve the critical job of expanding ministry into new situations. Most apostolic workers identify strongly with values of the *Harvest Leadership model*. Without this expansion Christianity would die. Apostles exhibit strong gifts and strong leadership. Along with this strength goes the corresponding weakness of independence. Interdependence is needed—especially for accountability. Most apostolic workers do not have accountability for their ministries and hence abuses of power and heresies, both orthodox and orthopraxic, occur. A strong task-oriented leadership bias by most apostolic workers often lacks the needed balance of a relational leadership bias. Apostolic workers tend to build empires which they over control in a micro-managing manner. Needed is the indigenization function modeled by Paul, a very strong apostolic worker, which releases leadership and allows new leadership to function. But hats off to apostolic workers! They carry out the Great Commission. They want to reach the world!

See *gifts of healings; discernings of spirits; exhortation; evangelism; faith; prophecy; ruling; teaching; word of knowledge; word of wisdom; coercive authority; competent authority; induced authority; personal authority ; spiritual authority; leadership styles; apostolic style; father-initiator; father-guardian; imitator; confrontation style; indirect conflict; obligation persuasion; harvest model, stewardship model, shepherd model, servant model, intercessor model;* **Glossary**. See **Articles**, *24. Jesus-Five Leadership Models: Shepherd, harvest, Steward, Servant, Intercessor; Developing Giftedness; 63. Spiritual Gift Clusters; 64. Spiritual Gifts, Giftedness, and Development. 49. Pauline Leadership Styles; 71. Value Driven Leadership.* See For **Further Study Bibliography**, Clinton's **Leadership Styles**.

Article 3

Relevance of the Article to Paul's Corinthian Ministry
This article was written primarily for use with the Titus commentary. In reviewing the Corinthian ministry, it can be seen that it is apostolic functions 5,6, and 8 introduced in this article, which is being highlighted.

3. Apostolic Functions--Comparison of Titus and Timothy

Introduction

In a previous article I identified 7 apostolic functions.[8] As I worked on the Titus leadership commentary I identified a new function that stood out because of the Cretan situation. I also identified three phases of apostolic ministry.[9] So this article is written not only to update the former article but also to compare which of these functions is seen in Titus ministry on Crete and Timothy's ministry in Ephesus and to draw out some comparative observations. All of the apostolic functions are seen in Paul's various ministries which involved different stings in all three phases of apostolic ministry.[10]

Apostolic Functions Updated

Below in Table 1,2 Co 3-1 are given the previous 7 apostolic functions and the new function seen in Titus, function 8--Contextualization.

Table 1,2 Co 3-1 Apostolic Functions--Paul's, Timothy's and Titus

Function	Apostolic Thrust	Supplementary Gifts
1. Start New Ministries	pioneer new work	evangelism, power gifts
2. Appoint Leaders	leadership selection	basically an apostolic gifting function; sometimes word of knowledge, word of wisdom
3. Establish Works	leadership development; edification ministry with believers	teaching, exhortation, ruling
4. Intercede for Works, both new and old	release spiritual power in situations	faith, discernings of spirits, sometimes word of knowledge or word of wisdom
5. Combat Heresy[11] (both orthodoxy and orthopraxy)	correct and stabilize a deteriorating situation	exhortation, prophecy, teaching
6. Resource New Ministries and Old Ones	resource apostolic ministries; give help to needy church situations	not clear
7. Test New Ministries for Validity	authenticate God's work	not clear
8. Contextualize[12] the Gospel to Cross-cultural Situations	apply truth to complex cultural situations	teaching, exhortation, sometimes prophecy

---

[8] See **Article**, *2. Apostolic Functions*.
[9] See **Article**, *4. Apostolic Giftedness--Multiple Gifted Leaders*.
[10] Paul does have ministry in all three but dominantly in phase 1 ministries.
[11] Heresy refers to deviation from a standard, whether in belief (orthodoxy) or practice (orthopraxy). e.g. See 1Ti where both are present in the Ephesian church (as prophesied in Ac 20:30).

3. Apostolic Functions--Comparison of Titus and Timothy

Comparison of Timothy and Titus's Apostolic Ministries

Three phases of apostolic ministry will work on differing apostolic functions:

Phase I.   Ground Breaking Apostolic Work (like Paul and Barnabas in Thessalonica)
Phase II. Edification Work (like Titus in Crete)
Phase III. Corrective Work (like Timothy in Ephesus)

The Corinthian ministry is a phase two work primarily but with some Phase III effort.

Table 1,2 Co 3-2 Comparison of Apostolic Functions--Timothy and Titus

Function	Apostolic Thrust	Seen In Ministry
1. Start New Ministries	pioneer new work	neither
2. Appoint Leaders	leadership selection	seen in both
3. Establish Works	leadership development; edification ministry with believers	seen in both
4. Intercede for Works, both new and old	release spiritual power in situations	Paul models this in Timothy and commands Timothy to do so. Not seen in Titus.
5. Combat Heresy[13] (both orthodoxy and orthopraxy)	correct and stabilize a deteriorating situation	Timothy is combating at least 4 lines of heresy; Titus 2.
6. Resource New Ministries and Old Ones	resource apostolic ministries; give help to needy church situations	Paul does this in Titus. Titus does to (also did this at Corinth) gives Timothy advice on doing this in Ephesian situation.
7. Test New Ministries for Validity	authenticate God's work	neither
8. Contextualize the Gospel to Cross-cultural Situations	apply truth to complex cultural situations	Titus must do this. Cretan cultural has many values degrading from Christian testimony

Conclusion

Timothy does apostolic functions 2, 3, 4, 5 and 6. Titus does apostolic functions 2, 3, 5, 6 and 8.

Timothy's situation was complex because it involved turning around a situation that had developed over 20 years. A major problem involved turning the leadership around--getting rid of leaders who were involved in heresy--both orthodoxic and orthopraxic. Four lines of heresy had to be combated.

Titus ministry was complicated in that he had to introduce values into a Cretan culture which had many counter values. His was a primitive situation in which new believers had a relatively small church base to work from. He too had to do leadership selection--to get leaders of integrity to help him model the needed changes.

Here is an observation on both their ministries. Neither were using or admonished to use power gifts. However, both were admonished to use the gifts they had with power--dominantly teaching, exhortation, and probably prophetical gifts.

Apostolic ministries will vary due to local cultural situations and gifting of the apostolic leaders as well as the type of apostolic ministry being done, Phase 1, or 2, or 3.

---

[12] See **Article**, *Basic Contextualization Principles*.
[13] Heresy refers to deviation from a standard, whether in belief (orthodoxy) or practice (orthopraxy). e.g. See 1Ti where both are present in the Ephesian church (as prophesied in Ac 20:30).

Article 4

Relevance of the Article to Paul's Corinthian Ministry

This article was written primarily for use with the Titus commentary. However, the Corinthian ministry introduces in depth the whole question of giftedness and its place in the body. Apostolic giftedness is extremely important to the spread and edification and correction of the body of Christ. This article delves into that concept of apostolic giftedness. One can easily appreciate the multiple giftedness of Paul in dealing with the problematic situations he faced in the churches as they spread into the Gentile world.

4. Apostolic Giftedness--Multiple Gifted Leaders

Introduction

Breaking open new ground, like planting a church in a cross-cultural situation, will require a number of gifts. This can be done by a team which has the necessary gifts comprising the total needed in the situation.[14] One of the gifts needed for such new work is the apostleship gift. Another is the gift of evangelism. Sometimes power gifts will be needed in order to authenticate the work as being of God. As the work begins to succeed other gifts will be needed like teaching, exhortation, and pastoring. As a work ages it usually experiences ecclesiastical entropy--plateauing or worse, diverting from truth. Prophetical gifts, teaching gifts and exhortation gifts are desperately needed to embrace and correct this situation. Examples in the New Testament show apostolic ministries arising to help in all these situations.

Usually an apostolic leader will have multiple gifts, a gift-mix.[15] Teammates will come along side to provide other needed gifts, the apostolic support gifts.[16] In reading any of the Pauline epistles[17] or especially leadership books like Titus or 1, 2 Timothy or the book of Acts one needs an understanding of apostolic giftedness in order to read with an enlightened perspective. Such a perspective might also help to prevent certain excesses in apostolic ministries which may lead to leaders not finishing well. This article gives a quick overview of apostolic giftedness. Three phases of apostolic ministry will need differing sets of gifts:

Phase I.	Ground Breaking Apostolic Work (like Paul and Barnabas in Thessalonica)
Phase II.	Edification Work (like Titus in Crete or Paul in Corinth)
Phase III.	Corrective Work (like Timothy in Ephesus or Paul in Corinth)

---

[14] Different sets of gifts will be needed in different situations. More on this later.

[15] *Gif-mix* refers to the set of spiritual gifts that a leader is exercising at a given time in his/her ministry. the broader term is *giftedness set* which includes natural abilities, acquired skills and spiritual gifts. In this article, we are restricting ourselves to spiritual gifts. See **Article**, *Developing Giftedness*. See **Glossary**, *spiritual gifts, gift-mix, giftedness set*, each of the individual spiritual gifts named in this article.

[16] From 1973 to 1983 I did Biblical research on *spiritual gifts* and taught on spiritual gifts in a number of teaching roles. I published a book, **Spiritual Gifts**, which defined the gifts, from an exegetical and comparative study of them in the New Testament. From 1983 to 1993 we (my son began helping me in the research) did empirical research on giftedness in leaders. Around 500 contemporary leaders were studied. Out of that research came our present understanding of giftedness, a broader and more comprehensive treatment of how a leader operates. Of special interest was the whole notion of developing spiritual gifts. This research is written up in **Unlocking Your Giftedness** and forms the basis for much of this article.

[17] Paul's epistles should be studied not only for content but to see what Paul is doing and how he is doing. Paul exercises apostolic ministry throughout his missionary career. An understanding of apostolic ministry and its giftedness is instructive for appreciating Paul's leadership.

4. Apostolic Giftedness--Multiple Gifted Leaders 92

Leaders--Word Gifted

Apostleship, prophecy, evangelism, pastoring and teaching are often called the leadership gifts. Because of their nature and function, the exercising of these gifts are directly connected to exercising leadership influence. Some would not call these gifts but would call them offices. Because of the way that these gifts are listed in Ephesians 4, it is easy to see how this viewpoint is formed. In the Ephesians 4 passage, we believe that Paul is using metonymy as he wrote the text on spiritual gifts. We believe that he is referring to individuals who are gifted in apostleship, prophecy, evangelism, pastoring and teaching not just to apostles, prophets, evangelists, pastors and teachers who hold that office in the church.[18]

Is it possible to operate with these gifts without the *office* or official position? We believe that it is possible. In fact, we have observed many leaders operating in these gifts without the *official* title or position. Often, those positions were not available to these individuals because of things like denominational tradition, gender issues, or certain types of circumstances in their past. The fact that they were not in the position didn't stop them from exercising the leadership influence associated with the gift.

It is primarily these leadership gifts that have responsibility for maturing the body. Evidently they were needed to mature the church as described in Ephesians 4. Even if you don't believe them to be gifts you can ask yourself the question, what did each of these offices contribute to the maturing of the body? Even if the offices don't exist officially today, what functions did they represent? These functions will be needed today to mature the body. So what are these functions? They are essentially the thrust of certain spiritual gifts. Those central thrusts are essentially the functions that are needed to mature the body. Look at them!

1. The Apostolic Function--	**CREATING NEW MINISTRY**
2. The Prophetic Function--	**TO PROVIDE CORRECTION OR PERSPECTIVE ON A SITUATION**
3. The Evangelistic Function--	**INTRODUCING OTHERS TO THE GOSPEL.**
4. The Pastoring Function--	**CARING FOR THE GROWTH OF FOLLOWERS.**
5. The Teaching Function--	**TO CLARIFY TRUTH**

And to these we have added two other influence gifts--exhortation and ruling.

6. The Exhortive Function--	**TO APPLY BIBLICAL TRUTH**
7. The Ruling Function--	**INFLUENCING OTHERS TOWARD VISION.**

It is our contention that God is still following the Ephesians 4 mandate of equipping the body and developing it toward maturity. And these kinds of functions are still needed.

---

[18] We have some difficulties with the whole idea of these being just offices. What is the office of pastor? What kind of gifts would a person in that office have? What is the office of teacher? What kind of gifts would a person in that office have? What is the office of evangelist? What kind of gifts would a person in that office have? What is the office of prophet? What kind of gifts would a person in that office have? What is the office of Apostleship? What kind of gifts would a person in that office have? Why would these offices be in the church? If to equip and lead the body to maturity, is that not needed today? Has the church reached the full maturity described in Ephesians 4 so that we can do away with these offices and the gifts entailed in them? Why would some of them disappear and not all of them? Are just some of them needed to take the body to maturity?

4. Apostolic Giftedness--Multiple Gifted Leaders

Implications

1. All seven of the functions listed above are needed to bring a balanced maturity to the body.

2. In general, over an extended time, no one of the functions should be overemphasized to the exclusion of others.

3. For a given contextual situation and for a given time, one or more of the functions may need to be overemphasized to meet crucial needs.

Phase I Apostolic Ministry--Initial Breakthroughs

The Acts of the Apostles traces Paul's pioneering ministry in a number of places including Cyprus, Iconium, Lystra, Derbe, Phillipi, Thessalonica, Berea, Athens, Corinth, and Ephesus. In these pioneer ministries Paul demonstrates apostolic gifting supplemented with various power gifts (word of knowledge, working of powers, gifts of healings, discernings of spirits, faith) to authenticate divine backing and various word gifts (dominantly teaching and exhortation with evangelism, occasionally prophecy) to start the edification process. Paul was very multi-gifted and needed to be since he is basically ushering in the church leadership era. He is an exemplar.

In the initial stages of a new work, power gifts validate the word gifts and bring about breakthroughs. Various word gifts initiate the growth process.

Phase II Apostolic Ministry--Edification Breakthroughs

Once a work gets going, apostolic leadership will usually transition leaders from the local setting in to do the edification work (especially pastoral gifting and ruling) needed to stabilize the embryonic work. In some situations, where much contextualization of the Gospel is needed, apostolic leadership will be necessary to get edification breakthroughs. This was the case for Titus in Crete. We do not know for certain Titus' giftedness set. But we do know that the demands that Paul gave him required strong teaching and exhortation gifts as well as the ruling gift. His apostolic gift gave him authoritative backing to contextualize the Gospel into the Crete situation with its values so counter to living out Gospel truth.

Phase III. Apostolic Ministry--Correction Breakthroughs

Timothy's work in Ephesus exemplifies apostolic ministry that is corrective in nature. The Ephesian church had stagnated, in fact, deteriorated following along the lines of Paul's prophetic warning given to them in Acts 20. It was about 20 years old and had its own indigenous leaders at the time Timothy is sent in to correct the situation.[19] A number of heresies (orthopraxic and orthodoxic) needed to be countered. Timothy did this. Again we do not know for certain what Timothy's gift-mix was but we do know what was needed in addition to apostleship: teaching, exhortation, prophecy.

Apostleship Functions And Giftedness Needed

Elsewhere in two articles,[20] I have described some apostolic functions. Below I list these functions and suggest the apostleship gift and supplementary gifts needed to probably carry out the functions.

Table 1,2 Co 4-1. Apostolic Functions and Related Giftedness Needed.

Function	Apostolic Thrust	Supplementary Gifts
1. Start New Ministries	pioneer new work	evangelism, power gifts
2. Appoint Leaders	leadership selection	basically an apostolic gifting function; sometimes word of knowledge, word of wisdom

---

[19] See **Article**, *Ephesian Church--Its Time-Line*.
[20] See **Articles**, *2. Apostolic Functions; 3. Apostolic Functions--Comparison of Titus and Timothy*.

4. Apostolic Giftedness--Multiple Gifted Leaders

3. Establish Works	leadership development; edification ministry with believers	teaching, exhortation, ruling
4. Intercede for Works, both new and old	release spiritual power in situations	faith, discernings of spirits, sometimes word of knowledge or word of wisdom
5. Combat Heresy[21] (both orthodoxy and orthopraxy)	correct and stabilize a deteriorating situation	exhortation, prophecy, teaching
6. Resource New Ministries and Old Ones	resource apostolic ministries; give help to needy church situations	not clear
7. Test New Ministries for Validity	authenticate God's work	not clear
8. Contextualize the Gospel to Cross-cultural Situations	apply truth to complex cultural situations	teaching, exhortation, sometimes prophecy

In the following discussion I will suggest a basic core that is usually seen throughout apostolic ministry. Then I will show how it may be modified to fit the three phases of apostolic ministry. At this point, having discussed the apostolic functions and related giftedness, I want to suggest that frequently apostolic leaders easily recruit people to come alongside and work with them in an apostolic ministry. Such team members will usually be drawn for two very different reasons. Two patterns discovered in our giftedness research describes these reasons:

1. The Like-Attracts-Like Pattern
2. The Needs Pattern

The *like-attracts-like pattern* is a general giftedness pattern very helpful to a leader in assessing leadership selection and development. It asserts that potentially gifted emerging leaders are attracted to leaders because of gifts which they already have in potential or will receive. *The Needs Pattern*, much more rarely seen, asserts that emerging leaders recognize some glaring omissions in an apostolic leader in terms of giftedness and are drawn to help solve those needs. These emerging leaders have the needed gifts to supplement and support the apostolic ministry.

Definition   Apostolic support gifts refer to gifts that are needed in an apostolic work and are supplied by leaders drawn to the ministry.

This relieves the pressure on a given apostolic leader. Such a leader then does not have to have all the gifts needed in a situation.

---

[21] Heresy refers to deviation from a standard, whether in belief (orthodoxy) or practice (orthopraxy). e.g. See 1Ti where both are present in the Ephesian church (as prophesied in Ac 20:30).

4. Apostolic Giftedness--Multiple Gifted Leaders

Apostleship Giftedness--The Core

We can display a person's gift-mix and show the relationship between the various spiritual gifts that he/she operates in.[1] All leaders we have studied are multi-gifted. In our research we have commonly seen that certain gifts frequently supplement other gifts. Below I give the core Venn diagram for an apostolic worker. Then I modify it to fit the three phases of apostolic work.

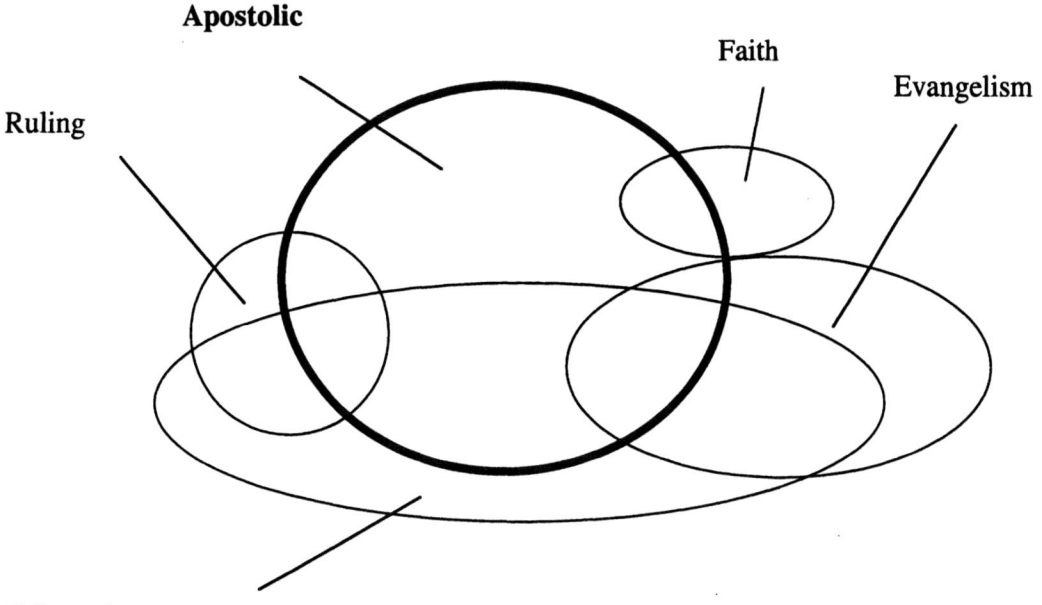

Figure 1,2 Co 4-1. Venn Diagram--Apostolic Core

Of course in team situations, one or more of the gifts shown in the apostolic core may be dominantly supplied to the situation by some other team member. Frequently, in our giftedness research, the gift of faith accompanied the apostleship gift--especially in Phase 1 ministry.

For a Phase 2 ministry, like Titus' ministry in Crete, the apostolic core would be modified somewhat. The evangelism gift would usually be dropped off. In its place would be the teaching gift. Again, any of the peripheral gifts could be supplied by a team member. The *faith gift* may or may not be seen. The *ruling gift* takes on more of an influence as indicated by the larger bold faced line. Actually the book of Titus indicates a strong exhortation and teaching gift is needed.

---

[1] These are called Venn diagrams. See chapter 9 in **Unlocking Giftedness** for a detailed explanation of a Venn diagram and guidelines for constructing.

4. Apostolic Giftedness--Multiple Gifted Leaders

Apostolic

Ruling

Teaching

Exhortation

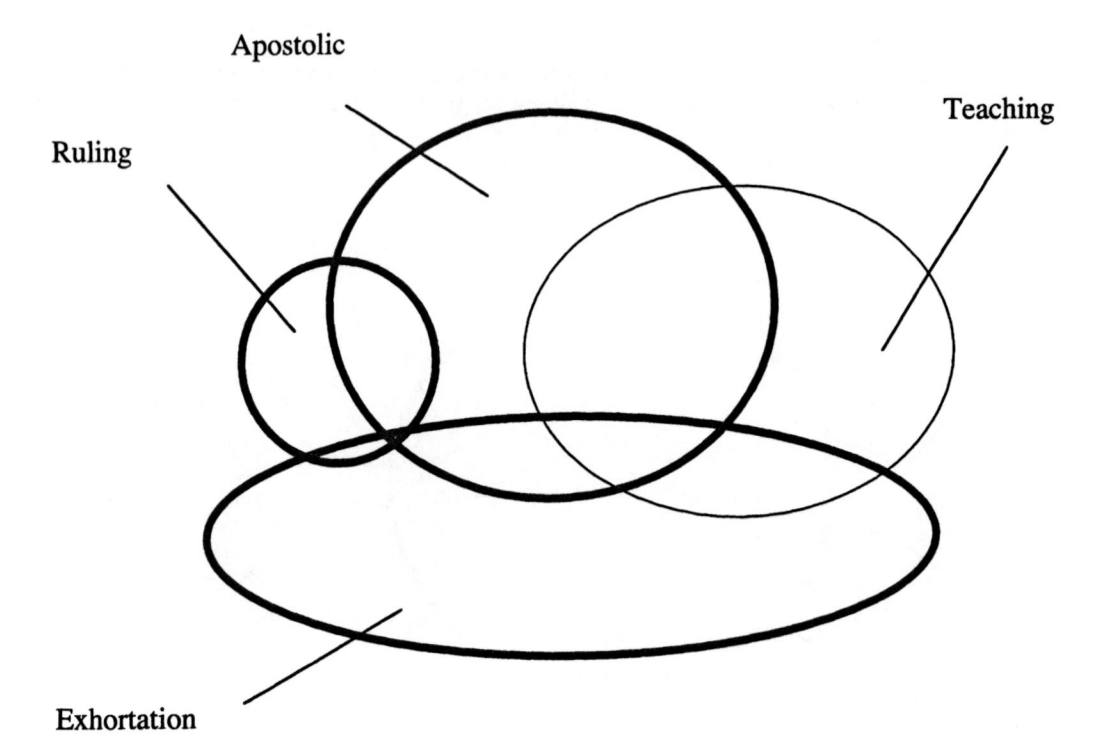

Figure 1,2 Co 4-2. Venn Diagram--Apostolic Core Modified for Phase 2

For a Phase 3 ministry like Timothy's ministry in Ephesus, the core would be modified again.

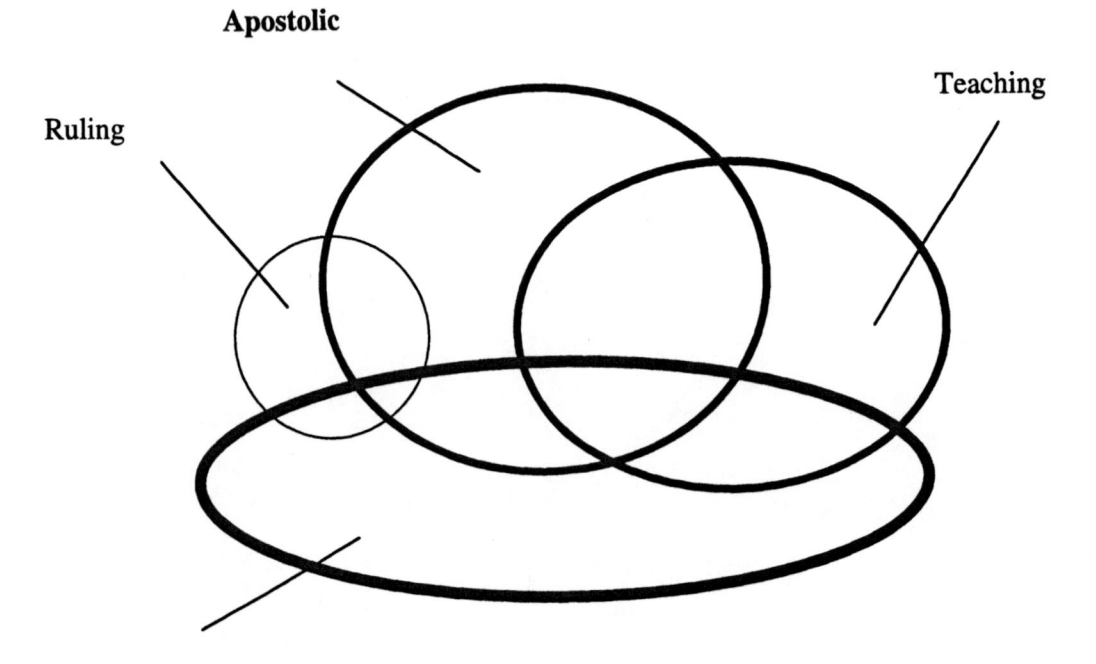

Apostolic

Ruling

Teaching

Exhortation and/or Prophecy (corrective thrust)

Figure 1,2 Co 4-3. Venn Diagram--Apostolic Core Modified for Phase 3

4. Apostolic Giftedness--Multiple Gifted Leaders

Notice the strong exhortation and/or prophetic gift. This is needed to correct the drift from known truth or practiced truth and to regain momentum. The teaching gift has to take on heightened use due to the clarification of heresy. The ruling gift drops off somewhat since there is indigenous leadership in place. However, leadership selection is usually needed to transition in leaders that can get the situation back on track. Old leaders, those immersed in the heresy and the stagnation will probably have to be moved on. The apostolic function of appointing leaders will be really needed.

Conclusion

Paul, Timothy, and Titus model for us apostolic ministries. Paul was powerfully multi-gifted as can easily be demonstrated from Luke's historical narrative in Acts. The gift-mix of Timothy and Titus is not demonstrated. But from the functions they had to perform in their ministries, certain things about gifts can be inferred.

Perspective is needed on apostolic ministry and apostolic giftedness. In the fervor of a powerful movement, like the present day emphasis on apostolic leaders, it is easy to be carried away pragmatically by tides that tug away from Biblical anchors. This article is a start to analyzing apostolic ministry and giftedness. The varying gift needs in terms of the basic three phases provides some anchors.[23] The concept of apostolic support gifts, another anchor, takes some of the pressure off of an apostolic worker. They do not have to have it all.

---

[23] In terms of the barriers to finishing well it is easy for present day apostolic ministries to fall into the traps of five of the six barriers: abuse of power, financial impropriety, family neglect, sexual impropriety, pride. This basically relates to lack of accountability of powerful apostolic leaders.

Article 5

Relevance of the Article to Paul's Corinthian Ministry

Barnabas sponsored Paul in Jerusalem and Antioch. He was the facilitator for Paul's acceptance into the Jewish community in Jerusalem and the Gentile community in Antioch. He modeled for Paul the concept of mentoring which became a major feature in Paul's ministry. Sponsor mentors are needed all over. Barnabas was a good one. And Paul was too. Note his sponsoring efforts in the Corinthian ministry. Paul mentions Barnabas in the Corinthian ministry—and basically favorably.

5. Barnabas—Significant Mentoring[24]

Introduction

There are a good number of *Pauls/Paulines* in this world who will never become effective for God because there are not enough Barnabases to go around. Who was Barnabas?

1. He is mentioned 33 times in four different books in the N.T.: 28 times in Ac, once in Col and 1Co and three times in Gal.
2. He was part of the movement called *The Way* right from the beginning.
3. He was recognized by the early church leaders as having potential for leadership.
4. He had a giving heart. Early on in his Christian life he was challenged by truth about giving and responded positively by learning to give freely and sacrificially.
5. His real name was Joseph but he was given a nickname, Barnabas—which meant one who encourages, because of his personality and ministry. He was noted for this ability to encourage others.
6. He was a Jewish Levite from Cyprus—meaning he was cross-cultural but also had deep Jewish tradition and religious beliefs.
7. He risked his own reputation to sponsor Paul with the early church leaders when they did not trust him. He was able to successfully do this.
8. John Mark was a relative of his—one whom he sponsored.
9. He was sent to Antioch to assess the Christianity of the Gentile church there.
10. He was indirectly responsible for 16 of 27 books or 59% of the New Testament

Barnabas was a significant mentor. Two people whom he mentored were important early church leaders. Are Barnabases still needed today? Consider the significance of Barnabas' mentoring.

The Situation—A Mentor Sponsor Needed

God had a problem. He wanted to introduce some change into a situation. What He wanted to introduce would bring change to beliefs, attitudes and lifestyles to a certain group of people—Jews. Now, this group of people have been cultivating the beliefs, attitudes, and lifestyles for about 2000 years. This group is not a powerful group as the world goes. They did not have a big army, economic power, or valuable resources. The only thing that separated them from any other group was their beliefs about their destiny. This belief made them hostile toward anyone who is not in their group. It was based on their view of God. They believed He loved them exclusively and was their God.

What was the change? These Jews are not the only group that God loves. He loves all the groups in the world and wants them to reach out to the other groups with this good news. God wants to bless them all.

What did God do? Well, he had a small band of Jewish folks who had accepted Messiah—who died for the whole world. He needed to convince them that they should take this message to Gentiles. They

---

[24] For a full biographical study of Barnabas, see Clinton and Raab, **Barnabas: Encouraging Exhorter—A Study in Mentoring.**

5. Barnabas—Significant Mentoring

needed to know that Gentiles were part of God's plan. So God decided to select some very strong, very gifted individuals who could convince the other Messianic believers that God wanted to bless all the people in the world with the good news about Jesus Christ, the Savior. God reviewed all the possible candidates: There was one individual who certainly had all of the necessary qualities and characteristics: strong, brilliant, persistent, relentless, etc. However, there was one small problem. Paul's only previous job experience was persecuting the very people that God wanted him to change. If God hired Paul, God was going to have to work at getting him accepted into the small group of Jewish believers. How could God do that? It would require some help from the inside. God needed someone who was respected by those Jewish believers and who was willing to take a chance. There was only one person available for this job. **Barnabas!** Why Barnabas?

Barnabas—A Brief History

Table 1,2Co 5-1 gives in brief form the story of Barnabas' life, pointing out the scant 33 times he is mentioned in Scripture. Note the implications of these occurrences of Barnabas.

Table 1,2Co 5-1. The Biblical Data on Barnabas

No.	Reference	Barnabas—How Mentioned
1	Ac 4:36	Barnabas was challenged to give. His positive response became part of his destiny. For his solid character was recognized by the Apostles. They named him with a label describing his character—*Joseph, a Levite from Cyprus, whom the apostles called Barnabas, which means Son of Encouragement* (that is, one who encourages).
2	Ac 9:27	Barnabas, with naïve trust, links Paul in. He was a mentor sponsor. But Barnabas took him and brought him to the apostles. He told them how Saul on his journey had seen the Lord and that the Lord had spoken to him, and how in Damascus he had preached fearlessly in the name of Jesus. This was risky business.
3-6	Ac 11:22, 25, 26,30	Barnabas is sent to Antioch. Why chosen? He was dependable. He had an island worldview, familiarity with Greeks, the founders of the church at Antioch were from Cyprus, Barnabas' home, etc. Barnabas performs apostolic functions at Antioch—encouraging and affirming the aspects of Christianity he saw there. He assessed the situation and brought in a strong leader who could change it. He sponsored Paul into this Christian group. The two of them had an effective ministry—*disciples called Christians*. He was recognized as a Spirit-filled man. Barnabas encouraged giving in this church and modeled giving. He mentored Paul in this.
7	Ac 12:25	Barnabas sponsored John Mark. He saw potential in this young emerging leader.
8,9	Ac 13:1,2,	Barnabas was chosen along with Paul as one of the leaders of first deliberate missionary effort to Gentiles.
10-14	Ac 13: 7, 42,43,46,50	Barnabas is part of first breakthroughs to Gentiles. He and Paul experience God's power as promised in *The Great Commission*.
15-20	Ac 14:1, 3, 12, 14, 20, 23	Barnabas has made the transition to have Paul lead. Amazing! Rarely in the Bible do you see a leader who can become the follower of one he has led. Barnabas did.
21-24	Ac 15:2, 12, 22, 25,	At the Jerusalem conference, Barnabas again takes the lead since he has more credibility with Jewish leaders. He thus again sponsors Paul.
25	Ac 15:35	Paul and Barnabas continue their furlough at Antioch.
26-28	Ac 15:36, 37, 39	Paul and Barnabas split up over taking John Mark back on the next missionary trip. Later John Mark is appreciated by Paul. But at this point in his ministry Paul was not the gentle leader he became in latter years.
29	1 Co 9:6	Paul refers to Barnabas showing that Barnabas was bi-vocational in his missionary effort. This shows Barnabas is still in ministry and still well thought of by Paul.

5. Barnabas—Significant Mentoring

30-32	Gal 2:1, 9,13	Barnabas does not take a strong stand about contextualization of Gospel for Gentiles. Barnabas is a gentle peaceful person and tends to avoid confrontation—sometimes a weakness, the other side of the coin of gentleness. Paul admonishes him and Peter in this situation.
33	Col 4:10	John Mark is identified as relative of Barnabas.

For a brief moment Barnabas is spotlighted in the N.T. He touches Paul's life at a crucial time and connects him in to the Christian story. They, together, pioneer cross-cultural ministry to the Gentiles—a world changing innovation. They have a conflict. They part company. And so Barnabas passes from the pages of the N.T. He was born into a contextual situation which fitted him to be a natural bridge to the Gentile world. By gifts, training, growth and temperament he was divinely suited to link Christianity to the Gentile world. His exhortive, apostolic gift-mix was greatly used by God *unto the full measure of faith*.

Are Barnabases still needed? Consider the notion of mentor functions in general and mentor sponsoring in particular. You will see that the answer is yes. Barnabas is a model that many can emulate—many who could never be a *Paul/Pauline*.

Mentor Functions And Mentor Sponsors

Barnabas had mentor eyes. What does mean have mentor eyes? Here are some basic mentor functions that are symptomatic of those who have mentor eyes. These are seen both in Biblical mentors and in contemporary mentors today.

Table 1,2Co 5-2. Five General Mentor Functions Underlying Sponsorship

Function	Explanation
1. Giving	They are giving people. They give to younger emerging leaders such things as: affirmation; encouragement; timely advice; finances; training materials such as tapes, books, manuals, etc.; connections to other literary information which gives timely perspective.
2. Risking	They are willing to take a risk with untried potential leaders. They are willing to stake their own reputation in order to sponsor these younger leaders with others.
3. Modeling	They model various aspects of leadership functions so as to challenge the young leaders to emulate them.
4. Bridging	They connect those young leaders to needed resources (people, finances, materials, opportunities, perspectives) that would further develop them.
5. Co-Ministering	They minister together with those young leaders in order to increase their confidence, status, and credibility.

Generally Barnabas did all the functions listed above. Particularly Barnabas was a mentor sponsor. He demonstrated the functions given below for mentor sponsors.

Table 1,2Co 5-3. Sponsor Functions And Empowerment

Functions	Empowerment	Explanation
1. Selection	confidence building, expectation, sense of eliteness	They select potential leaders and build in them a sense of confidence and a sense of eliteness— that they will bring a great contribution to the organization.
2. Encouragement	perseverance	They believe in the mentoree and encourage them to believe they will make it and will accomplish things.
3. Impart Skills	some leadership, some power skills,	They impart relational skills, how to use networking, the proper use of power, other direct leadership skills.
4. Linking To Resources	the resources	They link the mentoree to power resources including education, training, finances, and people.

5. Barnabas—Significant Mentoring

5. **Perspective**	analytical skill	Sponsors have an overall picture of the organization or movement, its structures, its power networks, its long range purposes, etc. These provide a framework for decision making not usually accessible to lower level positions.
6. **Inspiration**	sense of destiny	Sponsors usually begin with the end in mind. They see what the mentoree is capable of being and achieving and can inspire him/her to become that.

These mentor functions of Table 1,2Co 5-3 describe a mentor sponsor. What is a mentor sponsor?

Definition   A mentor sponsor is a person of influence within an organization or movement who can spot potential leaders early and help them develop along a profitable career development path that will benefit the mentoree and the organization or movement.

Definition   Sponsorship is a relational process in which a mentor having credibility, positional authority, or spiritual authority within an organization or movement relates to a mentoree not having those power resources so as to enable development of the mentoree.

The Sponsor Gap

Christian organizations, both churches and parachurches, have a big back door. That is, many of the finest potential leaders and leaders frequently leave the organization. They do so for many reasons. Frequently at the heart of the problem lies the need for people of influence in the organization to see this problem and take steps to retain these potential leaders. Sponsors—who take such potential leaders under their wing, support them, provide hope for change, advancement and an important contribution to the organization—are desperately needed in almost every large organization.

Definition   The sponsor gap refers to the need for high level leaders to intervene in a mentoring sense with potential leaders well below their levels to encourage, protect, enable, link to resources and otherwise relate to the potential leader so as to keep them in the organization or movement and to develop them.

Why is there a big back door? Why do potential leaders leave churches and parachurches?

1. They do not fit the normal leadership patterns expected or accepted in the group.
2. They have ideas that are beyond the present vision of the organization or group.
3. They have rough edges that cover up their good leadership qualities and potential.
4. They do not want to be over used and under developed.
5. They are placed in non-challenging roles, and in general do not have connections into the decision making power of the organization.

What happens to them? Those leaving organizations may:
1. quit the ministry altogether,
2. found an organization to do what they want,
3. become an effective leader and contribute to some other organization,
4. or perhaps fail to develop.

In any case those leaving do not benefit the organization or movement they left. Can this back door be shut somewhat? Yes, by mentor sponsors.

The Impact of Barnabas as a Sponsor Mentor

Where would Paul have been without Barnabas? Did Paul need Barnabas? Where would we be without Barnabas? Consider what your N.T. would be like if Barnabas had not mentored Paul. It would be comprised of Mt, Jn, Heb, Jas, 1Pe, 2Pe, 1Jn, 2Jn, 3Jn, Jude, and Rev. Note further that 16 of 27 books or

5. Barnabas—Significant Mentoring

59% are influenced by Paul—and if no Barnabas mentoring, then no Paul. We would know very little about a theology of the cross, practically nothing about the church. In fact, you and I would know nothing about God at all except what we could learn through nature.

Conclusion

Allow the life of Barnabas to impact yours! Barnabas was a giving, encouraging person. God could use you like he used Barnabas. Who knows the next *Paul /Pauline* could be waiting in the desert for a person like you to initiate a relationship and motivate toward all that Christ has planned for that one. Or perhaps you are the next *Paul/Pauline* and you need a Barnabas to come alongside of you and encourage, refine, lead and teach you about the way of Christ. Look for your *Barnabas* and start learning.

There are a good number of Pauls/*Paulines* in this world who may never become effective because there are not enough Barnabases to go around. Help close the sponsorship gap. Become a Barnabas.

See *movement; mentoring definitions; sponsorship; sponsor gap; spiritual gifts, gift-mix; apostleship; exhortation;* **Glossary**. See **Article**: Movements.

Article 6

Relevance of the Article to Paul's Corinthian Ministry

Paul demonstrates in his Corinthian ministry several aspects of a Bible Centered leader. Even though this is a Gentile context, he still strongly advocates the use of the O.T. Scriptures. In 1,2 Co Paul quotes, or alludes to or applies some O.T. scripture some 196 times. Books involved include Ge, Ex, Lev, Nu, Dt, Jdg, 1, 2 Sa, 1 Ch, Ezr, Ne, Job, Ps, Pr, Ecc, SS, Isa, Jer, Ezek, Da, Hos, Am, Mic, Hab, Zec, Mal. One of Paul's strongest Bible Centered leadership emphases comes from the following: 1 Corinthians 10:6,11 6 Now these things occurred as examples for us, so that we might not desire evil as they did. 11 These things happened to them to serve as an example, and they were written down to inform us, who live in such a momentous time. We do well to heed Paul's example of a Bible Centered Leader. Problematic leadership will always test one's grasp of God word and its use for those situations. And God will instruct us through many of the examples of the Bible, both Old and New Testaments.

6. Bible Centered Leader

Introduction

Where would you go in the O.T. if you wanted to look at a description of a Bible centered leader? Where would you go in the N.T. if you wanted to look at material about a Bible Centered Leader. Here is where I would go.

Table 1,2Co 6-1. Bible Centered Material O.T./ N.T.

Old Testament   Psalm 1, 19, 119
New Testament   2 Timothy

Glance quickly at Psalm 1 and feel its impact about how important it is to base a life on God's word.[25]

1. O, how happy is the person
   who hasn't based his conduct on the principles of the ungodly
   Nor taken his stand in the way of sinners,
   Nor taken his place with an assembly of scoffers!

2. But it is in the law of the Lord that he takes his delight;
   And on His law he keeps thinking day and night.

3. And he will be like a tree planted by the side of streams of water,
   That yields its fruit in its season;
   Its leaves also do not wither;
   And whatsoever he attempts, succeeds

4. Such is not the case with the ungodly,
   But they are like the chaff which the wind scatters.

5. Because of this, the ungodly will not be able to maintain themselves when the judgment comes,
   Nor sinners, with righteous people.

6. For the Lord watches over (knows intimately) the way of the righteous;
   But the way of the ungodly is headed toward destruction.

What is A Bible Centered Leader? According to this passage, Psalm 1, given above, here is a definition.

---

[25] An adaptation of Leupold's work. See **For Further Study Bibliography** section.

6. Bible Centered Leader

Definition A Bible centered leader[26] is one who:
1. Gets his/her counsel on life matters from other Bible centered leaders.
2. Delights in the Word of God and lets it permeate his/her soul.
3. Will persevere joyfully and with stability through out life (figure of tree/ rooted deep in water).
4. Will be watched over by God and will prosper. That is the bent of the life.

Now glance at two passages taken from 2Ti. These were given to a relatively young leader, Timothy, probably in his early 30s. I have reversed the order of these passages so you can see the challenge first and then the appropriate response next.

2 Timothy 3:16,17 The Guarantee
Every Scripture inspired of God is profitable for teaching, for setting things right, for confronting, for inspiring righteous living, in order that God's leader be thoroughly equipped to lead God's people.

That is quite a challenge for any leader. My response to that choice and one, which is encouraged by Paul himself is:

2 Timothy 2:15 The Proper Response to the Guarantee
Make every effort to be pleasing to God, a Bible Centered leader who is completely confident in using God's Word with impact in lives.

From these two passages and from reading 1Ti and 2Ti in general, I would define a Bible centered leader as,

Definition A Bible centered leader is one who:
1. studies the word of God in order to use it confidently and proficiently, and
2. recognizes that inspired Scripture will equip him/her for a productive leadership ministry.

A Bible Centered Leader Defined

Here is my own definition, derived from a comparative study of several Bible characters and numerous passages stating the importance of the **Word of God**.

Definition A Bible Centered leader
- refers to a leader whose leadership is informed by Biblical leadership values,
- has been shaped personally by Biblical values,
- has grasped the intent of Scriptural books and their content in such a way as to apply them to current situations,
- and who uses the Bible in ministry so as to impact followers.

Note carefully the meaning of each of the concepts:

---

[26] I am using Bible loosely to mean what is known of God's word; I realize the Psalmist was limited in terms of how much of God's word was available. I also am assuming that a Bible centered leader is first of all a person centered in God. The word of God becomes a central part of centering one self in God. So I am not talking about some one who is simply technically proficient in knowing the Word but one whose life is centered in God and as such wants to hear from God.

6. Bible Centered Leader

Table 1,2Co 6-2. Bible Centered Leader Components Explained

Concept	Meaning
Bible centered	A person who is centered on God and recognizes that hearing from God involves seeing the Word of God as being very important.
Leadership informed from the Bible	Recognizes that the Bible itself will have much to say about leadership (one thrust of the words equipped to lead in 2Ti 3:16,17). Further, it means recognizing leadership issues from the Bible like that which is given on the books of this Handbook of Biblical Leadership.
Has been shaped personally by Biblical values	The Bible has been used by God to change the life of the leader. That is one reason such a leader can use it confidently. He/she knows it has life changing power in it.
Has grasped the intent of Scriptural books and their content in such a way as to apply them to current situations	A thorough understanding of books in the Bible allows for the application of dynamic principles where they fit current situation.
Uses the Bible in ministry so as to impact followers	The Bible contains authoritative truth. When used it will change lives.

Conclusion

Take comfort in the **Guarantee** and **Your Response** to it.

2 Timothy 3:16,17 The Guarantee
Every Scripture inspired of God is profitable for teaching, for setting things right, for confronting, for inspiring righteous living, in order that God's leader be thoroughly equipped to lead God's people.

2 Timothy 2:15 Your Response To the Guarantee
Make every effort to be pleasing to God, a Bible Centered leader who is completely confident in using God's Word with impact in lives.

Become a Bible Centered leader. It will take a lifetime of discipline. But it is worth it. It will revolutionize your life and ministry.

See **Article**, 72. *Vanishing Breed; Daniel—Exemplar of a Learning Posture*.

Article 7

Relevance of the Article to Paul's Corinthian Ministry
    This article was originally written for use with 1,2 Ti. However, it has repercussions for the Corinthian ministry since Paul describes two aspects of conscience in the Corinthian letters. Conscience is vitally related to the inner life development of a leader. Ministry flows out of being where being is made up of: intimacy with God, conscience, character, personality, giftedness, destiny, values drawn from experience, and gender influenced perspectives. Conscience is a part of the inner-life of a leader—a part, which must be guarded. Paul makes two very strong statements about conscience in his two letters to the Corinthians. Leaders need to profit from the implications of these two statements. Note the bottom-line of these two statements. A person can model in such a way as to help another person defile his/her own conscience (1Co 8:7). Leaders should model lives and ministries that commend them to the consciences of others (2Co 4:2). I have included a new table referring to the use of conscience in 1,2 Co.

7. Conscience—Paul's Use of in 1,2Ti, Tit (and 1,2 Co)

Introduction

    Paul uses conscience (SRN 4893), some 21 times—four times in 1Ti, one time in 2Ti, one time in Tit and 15 times in his other epistles, including 10 times in 1,2 Co. His use of it in his closing letters at the end of his ministry is important. Here's why. He is connecting it to leadership issues. 1,2Tim and Tit are leadership books. And Paul is stressing to Timothy the importance of the inner life. Ministry flows out of being. Being is a complex diversity consisting of at least: intimacy with God, character, giftedness, gender, personality, destiny, learned values. Conscience, reflects the inner life governor of character. Leadership must have a moral foundation. And it is conscience which is the tail wagging the dog of character.

Definition   <u>Conscience</u> is the inner sense of right or wrong which is innate in a human being but which also is modified by values imbibed from a culture. This innate sense can also be modified by the Spirit of God.

    Integrity measures a leader's inner worth.

Definition   <u>Integrity</u> is by far the top leadership character quality. It is the consistency of inward beliefs and convictions with outward practice. It is an honesty and wholeness of personality in which one operates with a clear conscience in dealings with self and others.

Note how I connect integrity and conscience. If a leader lacks integrity you can be sure that leader also will have a shaky conscience.
    1,2Ti and Tit were the last letters Paul wrote. He was a leader finishing well. He was a leader passing on the leadership baton to his faithful co-worker Timothy. So when Paul, at the height of his mature leadership notes the importance of conscience, we should pay attention.

How Did Paul Use Conscience

    Table 1,2Co 7-1, dealing with 1,2Ti and Tit, suggests a label for the use of conscience, lists the vs reference, gives the actual vs, and gives a word of explanation.

7. Conscience—Paul's Use of in 1,2 Ti, Tit, 1,2 Co

Table 1,2Co 7-1. Paul's Use of Conscience—Relating it To Leadership Issues

Label	Vs	Scripture	Explanation
1. Ministry End Results	1Ti 1:5	Now the purpose for this strong command is to produce love that comes from a pure heart, and a clean conscience, and a genuine faith.	Paul points out that the end result of a pastoral or teaching ministry should be to produce mature believers who are characterized by love, purity, a *clean* conscience, and a genuine faith. Other words synonymous with *clean* in other versions include: *good, honorable, upright, pleasant, excellent, agreeable.*
2. Warning	1Ti 1:19	Keep faith and a clear conscience, which some having failed to listen to, have shipwrecked their faith.	Paul points out by example two leaders who did not heed their consciences with the result that they brought disaster on their lives and ministry. When a leader avoids the prompting of his/her conscience that leader is opening a door to Satanic control and eventual loss of ministry.
3. Aid to Understanding Truth	1Ti 3:9	One who has a clear understanding of the deep things of the faith with a clear conscience.	Put positively, a leader can understand, especially moral truth, when he/she has a clear conscience about that truth personally in his/her own life. Conversely, when a leader has problems of conscience with some truth he/she can not teach that truth with power.
4. Seared Conscience	1Ti 4:2	These hypocritical leaders speak lies, having their conscience seared with a hot iron.	This reference to conscience shows it can become unreliable (seared = hardened to truth) if false teaching is accepted. Conscience alone is not a totally reliable guide, but a spirit-controlled conscience is. However, one should not violate conscience—a basic principle. Here Paul shows that a person's conscience can become dead to truth and hence can not function as a governor of the inner life. Leadership must have a moral edge to it. These teachers of heresy lacked this.
5. Assurance	2Ti 1:3	I thank God, whom I serve with a pure conscience just as my ancestors did.	Paul had a clear conscience that what he was doing, following Jesus, the Messiah, was true to the tradition of his Jewish ancestors. Messianic Jews today have this same conviction.
6. Judgmental Conscience	Tit 1:15	Tit 1:15 Unto the pure all things [are] pure: but unto them that are defiled and unbelieving [is] nothing pure; but even their mind and conscience is defiled.	Leaders with a tainted conscience will tend to suspect people as having that same problem. Leaders with a pure (clear conscience) will not be judgmental of others. Conscience is here identified also with thinking or cognition. It is not just a matter of the hear but of the head too.

Some ten times Paul refers to conscience in 1,2 Co. The large majority of these are in connection with his dealing with the problem of disputed practices—eating meat that had been sacrificed to idols. Table 1,2Co 2 points out how Paul used conscience in 1,2 Co.

Table 1,2Co 7-2. Paul's Use of Conscience—in 1,2 Corinthians

Label	Vs	Scripture	Explanation
1. In Regards to Disputed Practices	1 Co 8:7,10, 12; 10:25, 27,28, 29	Numerous	Paul points out that in a disputed practice the stronger brother (one having freedom to partake in the disputed practice) should be willing to forego the practice in order not to destroy a weaker brother's conscience (the one for whom the practice seems to be wrong)
2. In Regards to Transparent Modeling/ Sharing of a Leader's Testimony	2 Co 1:12	2Co 1:12 For our rejoicing is this, the testimony of our conscience, that in simplicity and godly sincerity, not with fleshly wisdom, but by the grace of God, we have had our behavior in the world, and you especially	Paul is transparent. He reminds the Corinthians that his life was an open book before them. Paul has a clear conscience as to integrity with regards to behavior in the Corinthian situation. See also *exteriority, interiority, community* **Glossary**. Paul refers to three of the eight spirituality components—INTERIORITY, EXTERIORITY and COMMUNITY. Spirituality is the work of the Spirit in a leader's life which is indicated by the leader's growing personal relationship with Christ (CENTRALITY), inner life with God (INTERIORITY), relationships with others in the body (COMMUNITY), Spirit-led and empowered ministry (UNIQUENESS), sensitive obedience to the Spirit daily (SPIRIT SENSITIVITY, EXTERIORITY), and by a character transformation toward Christ-likeness (FRUITFULNESS, DEVELOPMENT). See spiritual guide mentoring in **The Mentor Handbook** for a full treatment of these eight spirituality components.
3. In Regards to his actual conduct regarding the Corinthians in his corrective procedures seen in 1, 2 Co.	2 Cor 4:2	2Co 4:2 But have renounced the hidden things of dishonesty, not walking in craftiness, nor handling the word of God deceitfully; but by manifestation of the truth commending ourselves to every man's conscience in the sight of God.	Paul has been accused of underhanded dealing with the Corinthians by the pseudo-apostles seeking to undermine Paul's ministry in Corinth. Here he appeals to their conscience and claims to be innocent of underhanded practices.
4. As regards motivation in evangelistic work	2 Co 5:11	2Co 5:11 Knowing therefore the terror of the Lord, we persuade men; but we are made manifest unto God; and I trust also are made manifest in your consciences.	Paul used the maturity appeal leadership style in reminding the Corinthians of his evangelistic ministry among them—particularly his motivation to evangelize. The should see this in their conscience and agree with Paul's reminder.

Other Uses

Paul also uses conscience as the inner reflector of a universal moral law that God has created in humans to help them know right and wrong (Ro 2:15). The conscience can give underlying strength and conviction to strong beliefs. The conscience of others can affect our own actions (Ro 13:5). Let me repeat these two in 1,2 Co which relate especially to leaders. A person can model in such a way as to help another person defile his/her own conscience (1Co 8:7). Leaders should model lives and ministries that commend them to the consciences of others (2Co 4:2).

Conclusion

Once, Paul made a challenging statement about his life and ministry.

> **16 I make every effort to conduct my life and ministry so as to have a conscience pleasing to God and those around me.** Acts 24:16

A leader must have a clean conscience or suffer the inability to teach and preach on certain truth with power. A leader must have a clean conscience or recognize that tainted conscience issues offer hooks for Satan to use to demoralize the leader. A leader must have a clean conscience or face the possibility of destruction of his/her Christian life or ministry. A leader must have a clean conscience to teach truth with real conviction. A leader with judgmental tendencies may well have a tainted conscience in the judgmental area himself/herself. Conscience is the governor of character. Without character a leader cannot lead.

Article 8

Relevance of the Article to Paul's Corinthian Ministry

This article was originally written for use with Paul's mentoring ministry as reflected in the books of 1,2 Ti, Philippians, Philemon and Titus. Titus, the apostle, was directly related to the Corinthian ministry. He was sent by Paul to help correct some of the Corinthian problems. Mentoring is a powerful way of training Christian workers. The constellation model depicted below gives perspective on the kinds of mentor-mentor relationships needed over a lifetime. In Table 1,2Co 8-1 depicting the 9 mentoring types, I have inserted comments showing how the letters to the Corinthians illustrates some of the mentoring types.

8. Constellation Model

Introduction

One of the major lessons[27] identified from a comparative study of many effective leaders is,

> **Effective Leaders See Relational Empowerment As Both A Means And A Goal Of Ministry.**

Both Jesus and Paul demonstrated this leadership principle in their ministries. In fact, both used mentoring as a means for applying this principle in their ministries. Jesus dominantly mentored in a small group context. Paul mentored both with individuals and in a small group context.

Definition   <u>Mentoring</u> is a relational experience in which one person, the mentor, empowers another person, the mentoree, by sharing God-given resources.[28]

Stanley researched leadership relationships for a number of years. From his observations on various kinds of mentoring relationships as well as his observations on leaders who finished well and who did not, he postulated a principle.[29]

> **Stanley's Thesis**
> **Over A Lifetime A Christian Leader Needs A Balanced Relational Network With other Christian Leaders Who Will Help Him/Her And Vice Versa.**

---

[27] Seven such lessons have been identified: (1) Effective Leaders View Present Ministry in Terms Of A Life Time Perspective. (2) Effective Leaders Maintain A Learning Posture Throughout Life. (3) Effective Leaders Value Spiritual Authority As A Primary Power Base. (4) Effective Leaders Who Are Productive Over A Lifetime Have A Dynamic Ministry Philosophy. (5) Effective Leaders View Leadership Selection And Development As A Priority Function In Their Ministry. (6) Effective Leaders See Relational Empowerment As Both A Means And A Goal Of Ministry. (7) Effective Leaders Evince A Growing Awareness Of Their Sense Of Destiny.

[28] See the nine mentor roles: mentor discipler, mentor spiritual guide, mentor coach, mentor counselor, mentor teacher, mentor sponsor, mentor contemporary model, mentor historical model, mentor divine contact, **Glossary**. The apostle Paul demonstrated many of these roles in his relationships with team members and others in his ministry. See **Articles**, *Paul— Developer Par Excellence; 47. Paul— Mentor for Many*. For further follow-up study, see Stanley and Clinton **Connecting** for a popular treatment of mentoring. See Clinton and Clinton **The Mentor Handbook** for a detailed treatment of mentoring.

[29] Paul Stanley, at this writing, is an International Vice President for the Navigators, a Christian organization heavily involved in developing laborers for the Kingdom. Mentoring is heavily used in Navigator ministries. Stanley would never call this theorem by his name, but I have taken the liberty to do so, since he was the discoverer of it and taught it to me.

8. Constellation Model

What did he mean by a balanced relational network with Christian leaders? By it Stanley was saying that four kinds of relationships are needed over a lifetime:

<u>Upward Help:</u>
A Christian Leader needs to relate to Christian Leaders more experienced in the Christian life who will help them in their growth and give needed perspective as well as help them be accountable for growth.

<u>Lateral Help:</u>
A Christian Leader needs to relate to Christian Leaders who are peers in the Christian life who will share, care, and relate so as to encourage them to persevere.

<u>Downward Help:</u>
A Christian Leader needs to relate to younger emerging leaders who he/she can help to grow.

Stanley was talking about mentoring relationships. Both he and I have observed that over a lifetime, effective leaders who finished well experienced from five to 30 or more mentoring relationships for limited periods of time in their lives. Mentoring is one of the five major enhancement factors that accompany leaders who finish well. [30]

The Constellation Model

The popular name for the graphic representation of Stanley's thesis is *The Constellation Model*. Figure 1,2Co 8-1 shows this graphic representation.

```
            Upward Mentoring

Lateral Peer                    Lateral Peer
External Mentoring              Internal Mentoring

            Downward Mentoring
```

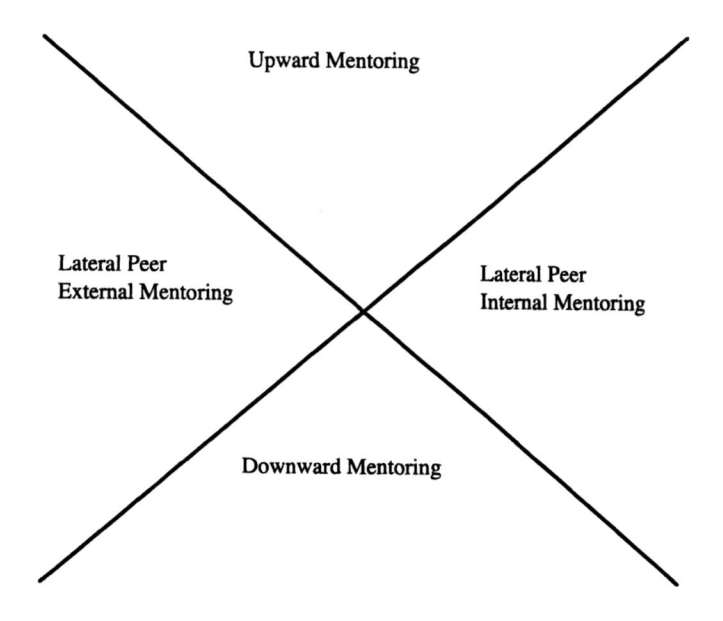

Figure 1,2Co 8-1. The Constellation Model

Upward mentors dominantly bring strategic accountability and perspective to a relationship. When you have an *upward mentor*, you are being mentored by someone else. *Lateral peer mentoring*, internal, means a mentoring relationship with someone in the same organization or someone coming from basically the same background as you. Such a mentor knows you and your organization fairly well. Confidential things

---

[30] See **Articles**, *13. Finishing Well—Five Factors Enhancing; 14. Finishing Well—Six Characteristics*.

8. Constellation Model

can be shared. Accountability for each other is expected. An internal lateral mentor is roughly at the same stage of maturity as you. Lateral peer mentoring, external, means a relationship with some one from a very different background than you and a very different ministry experience. Such a person can bring objectivity to you and you to that person, since you will frequently ask the question, "Why do you do it that way?" Accountability and perspective are expected in such a relationship. Downward mentoring means that you are helping someone not as far along as you, at least in the area of the mentoring expertise. Such a relationship benefits both participants. The person being mentored of course receives the empowerment of the mentoring. The person doing the mentoring often experiences two things: (1) reality checks (mentorees frequently ask embarrassing questions about whether or not something is true for you); (2) a fresh injection of faith—often a by-product of being around a younger Christian is that they are not so cynical about things and trust God in ways that an older mentor used to do.

Each of the nine mentoring relationships can fit into any of the quadrants of *The Constellation Model*. Table 1,2Co 8-1 briefly lists the nine relationships.

Table 1,2Co 8-1. Nine Mentoring Relationships That May Happen in the Four Quadrants

Type	Definition
mentor discipler	A mentor discipler is one who spends much time, usually one-on-one, with an individual mentoree in order to build into that mentoree the basic habits of the Christian life. It is a relational experience in which a more experienced follower of Christ shares with a less experienced follower of Christ the commitment, understanding, and basic skills necessary to know and obey Jesus Christ as Lord.
mentor spiritual guide	A spiritual guide is a godly, mature follower of Christ who shares knowledge, skills, and basic philosophy on what it means to increasingly realize Christ-likeness in all areas of life. The primary contributions of a Spiritual guide include accountability, decisions, and insights concerning questions, commitments, and direction affecting spirituality (inner-life motivations) and maturity (integrating truth with life).
mentor coach	Coaching is a process of imparting encouragement and skills to succeed in a task via relational training.
mentor counselor	A mentor counselor is one who gives timely and wise advice as well as impartial perspective on the mentoree's view of self, others, circumstances, and ministry. In a corporate sense (that is, given to the group as a whole and not an individual mentoring situation) Paul is a mentor counselor for the Corinthian situation.
mentor teacher	A mentor teacher is one who imparts knowledge and understanding of a particular subject at a time when a mentoree needs it. (Paul illustrates this in a Corporate mentoring sense in the Corinthian situation.)
mentor sponsor	A mentor sponsor is one who helps promote the ministry (career) of another by using his/her resources, credibility, position, etc. to further the development and acceptance of the mentoree. (Paul is sponsoring Titus—as his representative and one who should have spiritual authority to help correct the Corinthians.)
mentor model (contemporary)	A mentor contemporary model is a person who models values, methodologies, and other leadership characteristics in such a way as to inspire others to emulate them. (Paul is modeling for us how to handle church problems. The books of 1,2 Co stand as apt illustrations of how to deal with church problems. Paul is a literary mentor for any mentoree who wants to learn from his example.)
mentor model (historical)	A mentor historical model is a person whose life (autobiographical or biographical input) modeled values, methodologies, and other leadership characteristics in such a way as to inspire others to emulate them.
mentor divine contact	A person whose timely intervention is perceived of as from God to give special guidance at an important time in a life. This person may or may not be aware of the intervention and may or may not have any further mentoring connection to the mentoree.

8. Constellation Model

Closing Observations

1. Mentoring relationships that fill the four quadrants are usually limited in time and are not permanent. They happen and meet a need and then terminate after the empowerment. The relationship may endure and be rekindled later for mentoring effectiveness.
2. A given leader will not necessarily have mentoring relationships in all the quadrants at once. But over a lifetime mentoring in each of the quadrants brings balance.
3. Internal lateral peer mentoring usually stresses relationship, accountability and perspective rather than specific mentoring relationships.
4. Upward mentors are harder to find as a leader matures and ages in life. This is because fewer and fewer leaders are upward to a mature leader.
5. A leader with a strong learning posture will take proactive steps to find mentoring.

A closing exercise that is often used at mentoring workshops involves having leaders draw a constellation diagram and have them fill in names of mentors and types of mentoring that they have experienced in the past, even if the mentoring was not deliberate or formal. I have them try to think through each of the four quadrants. Then I ask them to re-do the diagram and put in current mentoring relationships they are experiencing. Finally I ask them to draw a final diagram with the kind of profile they would like to have over the next year or two. These diagrams are called Constellation Profiles.

What does your Constellation Profile look like now?

Article 9

Relevance of the Article to Paul's Corinthian Ministry

This article was originally written for use with 1,2 Co since Paul deals with the concept of a judgment in both of those books. And judgment will happen after Christ's return, which we should eagerly be expecting. And such a perspective ought to affect how we live as we wait for this coming.

9. Day of Christ—Implications For Leaders

The phrase *Day of Christ* brings great encouragement to believers in general. But leaders probably benefit from its implications the most.

Definition　　Day of Christ or also Day of the Lord, or That Day are phrases used by Paul to indicate the return of Christ and not only a judgment of what has gone on before in the lives of people and leaders but also a making right of things.

Leaders know that they will be judged and rewarded as well as punished for their leadership actions. This motivates them to live well and lead well. But also there is the desire to see things that have been evil and wrong and which engender hopelessness in our world to be made right. Bible centered leaders long to see the *Ancient of Days* sit in judgment, the O.T. equivalent of the N.T. Day of Christ.

See **Articles**, *1. Accountability; 40. Motivating Factors For Ministry.*

Article 10

Relevance of the Article to Paul's Corinthian Ministry

This article was originally written for use with 1, 2 Ti and 1,2 Co where Paul strongly asserts his apostolic authority. In those letters he needs that authority to bring correction. Paul's destiny is intimately tied to that apostolic calling—which was a powerful destiny experience in the life of Paul. Paul is an exemplar of the threefold destiny pattern, which this article explains. The Corinthian ministry was a challenge to the fulfillment of that destiny. It was a critical incident deeply affecting Paul. Should Paul's ministry fail in Corinth, then his whole destiny would be in jeopardy. Much can be learned from the study of Paul's life from a destiny perspective. In this article, Paul, along with Joseph and Moses, is used to show that destiny indeed is a relevant perspective to use in understanding leaders life-time contribution. A later article treats destiny more specifically for Paul. This article is basically validating the notion of sense of destiny and the three-fold pattern. Paul is included because we have so much information on him that it is easy to depict Paul as reflecting the three fold pattern.

10. Destiny Pattern

Introduction

One of the major leadership lessons[31] that emerged from a comparative study of effective leaders concerned the concept, sense of destiny.

Effective leaders evince a growing sense of destiny over their lifetimes.[32]

A young emerging leader thinks of numerous questions when confronted with that major leadership lesson.

1. What is a sense of destiny? A Destiny pattern?
2. How does one get a sense of destiny?
3. Can emerging leaders be sensitized to destiny experiences?
4. Is this a biblical concept?
5. Can these young leaders be encouraged to seek and express these experiences and rely on them as their leadership unfolds?
6. Are there dangers in promoting a sense of destiny to young leaders?
7. Do all leaders have a sense of destiny?

---

[31] Seven such lessons have been identified: (1) Effective Leaders View Present Ministry in Terms Of A Life Time Perspective. (2) Effective Leaders Maintain A Learning Posture Throughout Life. (3) Effective Leaders Value Spiritual Authority As A Primary Power Base. (4) Effective Leaders Who Are Productive Over A Lifetime Have A Dynamic Ministry Philosophy. (5) Effective Leaders View Leadership Selection And Development As A Priority Function In Their Ministry. (6) Effective Leaders See Relational Empowerment As Both A Means And A Goal Of Ministry. (7) Effective Leaders Evince A Growing Awareness Of Their Sense Of Destiny. It is this last one I am exploring in this article.

[32] This is a major key to an effective ministry. No Bible leader who had an effective ministry failed to have a sense of destiny. Paul is the exemplar in the N.T. Church Leadership Era. Over and over again in his epistles, Paul's makes statements that reflect on his understanding of his destiny with God.

10. Destiny Pattern

Comparative studies of leaders—Biblical case studies, historical case studies, and contemporary studies—have suggested answers to these questions.

Some Basic Definitions and A Fundamental Destiny Pattern

What is a sense of destiny? How does one get a sense of destiny?

Destiny experiences refer to those experiences which lead a person to sense and believe that God has intervened in a personal and special way in the leader's life. In a sense then, it is God's way of encouraging a leader toward embracing and accomplishing some purpose of God during that leader's lifetime.

Definition — A <u>sense of destiny</u> is an inner conviction arising from an experience or a series of experiences in which there is a growing sense of awareness that God has His hand on a leader in a special way for special purposes.

Definition — <u>Destiny processing</u> refers to the shaping activities of God in which a leader becomes increasingly aware of God's Hand on his/her life and the purposes for which God has intended for his/her leadership. This processing causes a sense of partnership with God toward God's purposes for the life and hence brings meaning to the life.

It is through God's shaping activities in the life of a leader that a leader gets a sense of destiny. Destiny experiences include preparation experiences, revelation experiences, and fulfillment experiences.

Sometimes the experience is awe inspiring and there is no doubt that God is in it and that the leader or emerging leader is going to be used by God. Such are the destiny revelation experiences of Moses in Ex 3 and Paul in Acts 9. But at other times it is not so clear to the individual. Over a period of time various experiences come to take on new light and an awareness of that sense of destiny dawns. For example, Moses' birth and deliverance into Pharaoh's palace was an indicator of God's hand on his life and in retrospect can be seen that way.

Bertelsen's study of sense of destiny in the scriptures pointed out that sense of destiny may be a process as much as a unique awe inspiring experience. A full blown destiny does not emerge all at once. It happens over time. The three-fold pattern describes how it happens. The idea of the destiny continuum came out of Bertelsen's[33] thinking. The destiny continuum graphically portrays the pattern Bertelsen discovered. Since Bertelsen's study the notion of destiny processing and the destiny pattern have been confirmed many times with other case studies.

Definition — A <u>destiny pattern</u> is a leadership pattern. The development of a sense of destiny usually follows a three fold pattern of destiny preparation, destiny revelation, and destiny fulfillment. That is, over a period of time God shapes a leader with experiences which prepare, reveal, and finally brings about completion of destiny. The destiny continuum shown in Figure 1,2Co 10-1 graphically portrays the destiny pattern.

---

[33] Walt Bertelsen studied with me in 1983. He did special studies throughout the scriptures, researching the concept of sense of destiny. His unpublished paper was helpful in identifying kinds of sense of destiny experiences and the notion of the destiny continuum.

10. Destiny Pattern

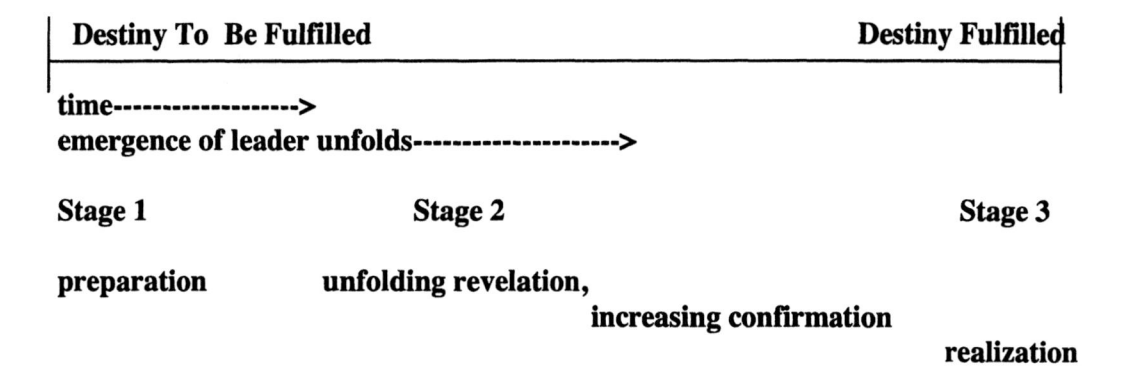

```
Destiny To Be Fulfilled                                    Destiny Fulfilled
|--------------------------------------------------------------------|
time------------------>
emergence of leader unfolds-------------------->

Stage 1                    Stage 2                         Stage 3

preparation        unfolding revelation,
                           increasing confirmation
                                                           realization
```

Figure 1,2Co 10-1. The Destiny Continuum—A Pictorial Display of the Destiny Pattern

Can emerging leaders be sensitized to destiny experiences? Yes. By knowing what a sense of destiny is and by recognizing the destiny pattern one can become sensitized to how God works and thus be able to hear and respond to God regarding one's destiny. Becoming sensitized to kinds of destiny experiences and seeing Biblical examples of them is an important next step in the process of being sensitized.

Four Categories of Destiny Experiences

Destiny processing can be categorized under four headings. Table 1,2Co 10-1 gives these categories with a brief explanation.

Table 1,2Co 10-1. Four Categories of Destiny Experiences

Category	Explanation
Type I destiny item	a destiny experience which is an awe-inspiring experience in which God is sensed directly as acting or speaking in the life. Example: Moses at the burning bush.
Type II destiny item	a indirect destiny experience in which some aspect of destiny is linked to some person other than the leader and is done indirectly for the leader who simply must receive its implications. Example: Hannah's promise to give Samuel to God.
Type III destiny item	the build up of a sense of destiny in a life because of the accumulation of providential circumstances which indicate God's arrangement for the life. See Apostle Paul's birth and early life situation.
Type IV destiny item	the build up of a sense of destiny in a life because of the sensed blessing of God on the life, repeatedly. Seen by others and recognized by them as the Hand of God on the life. See Joseph.

Are sense of destiny, the destiny pattern, and destiny processing biblical concepts? If you mean are there passages that say here is what a sense of destiny is or here is the destiny pattern or here are the four types of destiny experiences, then no. But if you mean are these concepts illustrated in the Scriptures? Do these concepts help us see things in the Scriptures? Then the answer is definitely yes. Consider the following three cases—Two O.T. and one N.T. You will see that, yes, these are certainly seen in the Bible.

10. Destiny Pattern

```
|Destiny To Be Fulfilled                              Destiny Fulfilled|
|--------------------------------------------------------------------|
time-------------------->
emergence of leader unfolds--------------------->
```

Stage 1   **Stage 2**   **Stage 3**

preparation   unfolding revelation,
                              increasing confirmation
                                                                    realization

Destiny Experiences
|
can be categorized in terms of the continuum
in three major categories
|

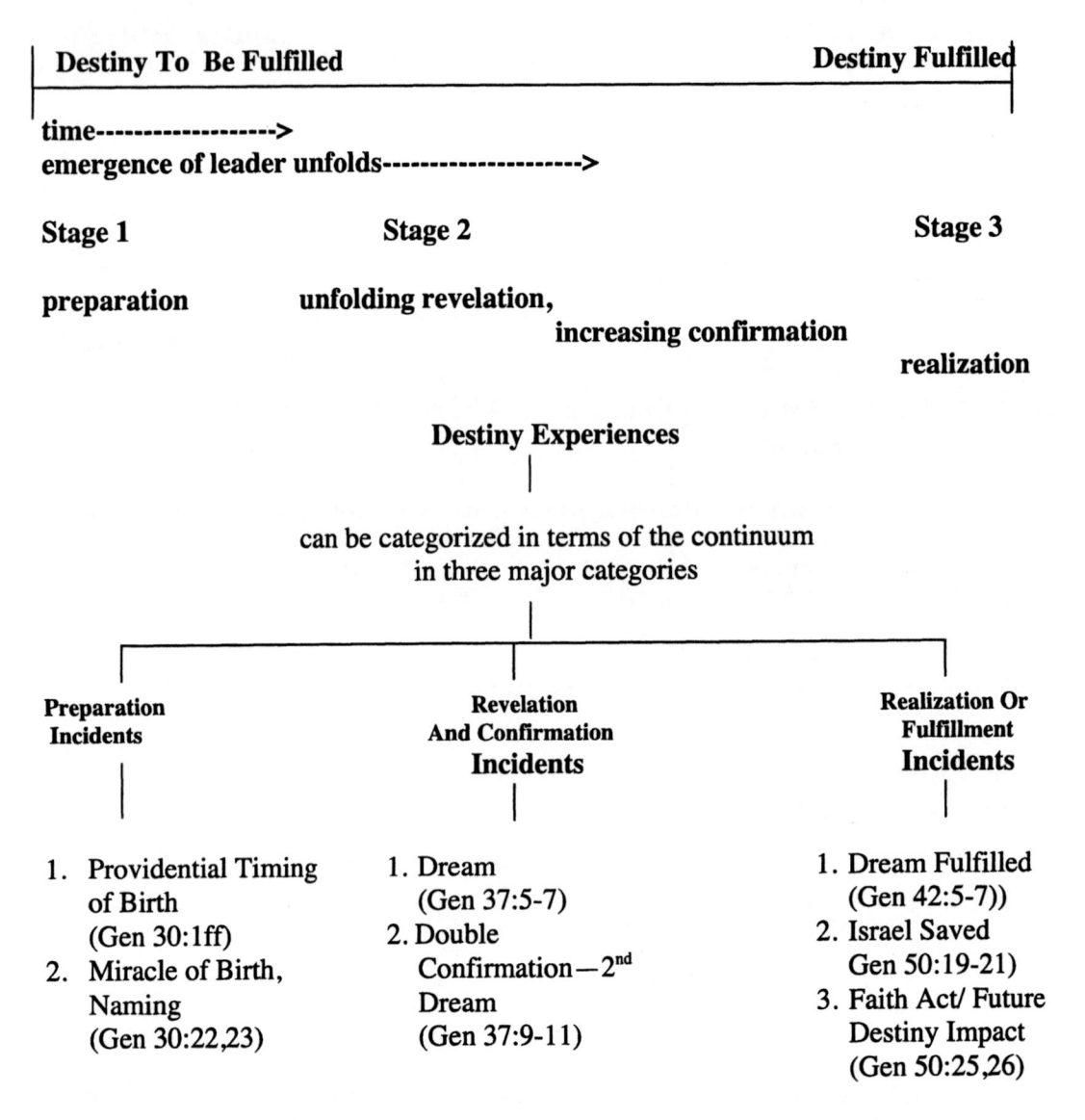

Preparation Incidents | **Revelation And Confirmation Incidents** | **Realization Or Fulfillment Incidents**

1. Providential Timing of Birth (Gen 30:1ff)
2. Miracle of Birth, Naming (Gen 30:22,23)

1. Dream (Gen 37:5-7)
2. Double Confirmation—2nd Dream (Gen 37:9-11)

1. Dream Fulfilled (Gen 42:5-7))
2. Israel Saved Gen 50:19-21)
3. Faith Act/ Future Destiny Impact (Gen 50:25,26)

Figure 1,2Co 10-2. Joseph's Destiny Processing and Three-Fold Destiny Pattern

10. Destiny Pattern

```
|Destiny To Be Fulfilled                              Destiny Fulfilled|
|                                                                      |
time------------------->
emergence of leader unfolds-------------------->

Stage 1                    Stage 2                         Stage 3

preparation         unfolding revelation,
                              increasing confirmation
                                                           realization
```

Destiny Experiences

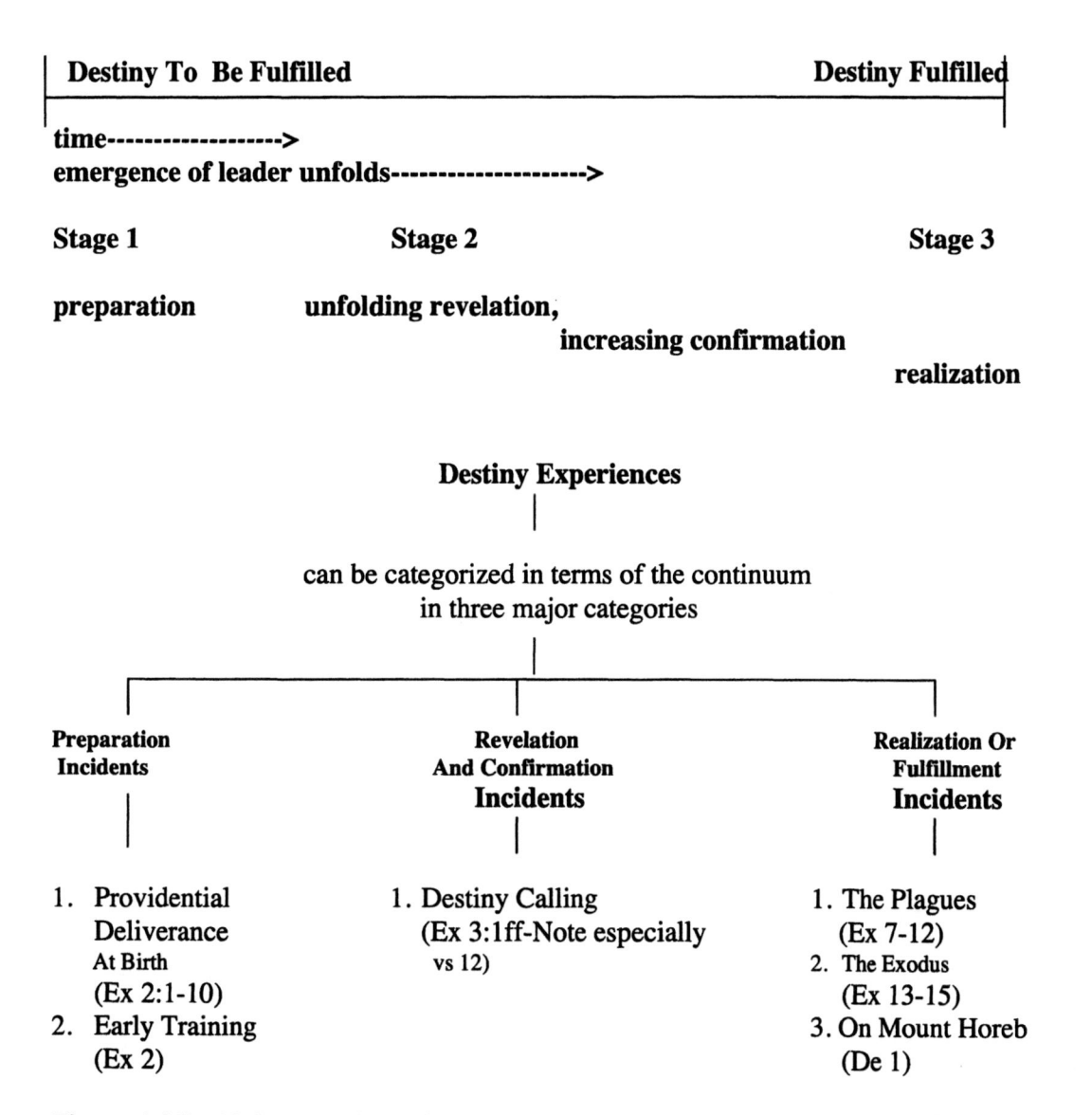

can be categorized in terms of the continuum
in three major categories

Preparation Incidents	Revelation And Confirmation Incidents	Realization Or Fulfillment Incidents
1. Providential Deliverance At Birth (Ex 2:1-10) 2. Early Training (Ex 2)	1. Destiny Calling (Ex 3:1ff-Note especially vs 12)	1. The Plagues (Ex 7-12) 2. The Exodus (Ex 13-15) 3. On Mount Horeb (De 1)

Figure 1,2Co 10-3. Moses' Destiny Processing and Three-Fold Destiny Pattern

10. Destiny Pattern

| Destiny To Be Fulfilled | | | Destiny Fulfilled |

time------------------>
emergence of leader unfolds-------------------->

| Stage 1 | Stage 2 | | Stage 3 |
| preparation | unfolding revelation, | increasing confirmation | realization |

Destiny Experiences
can be categorized in terms of the continuum
in three major categories

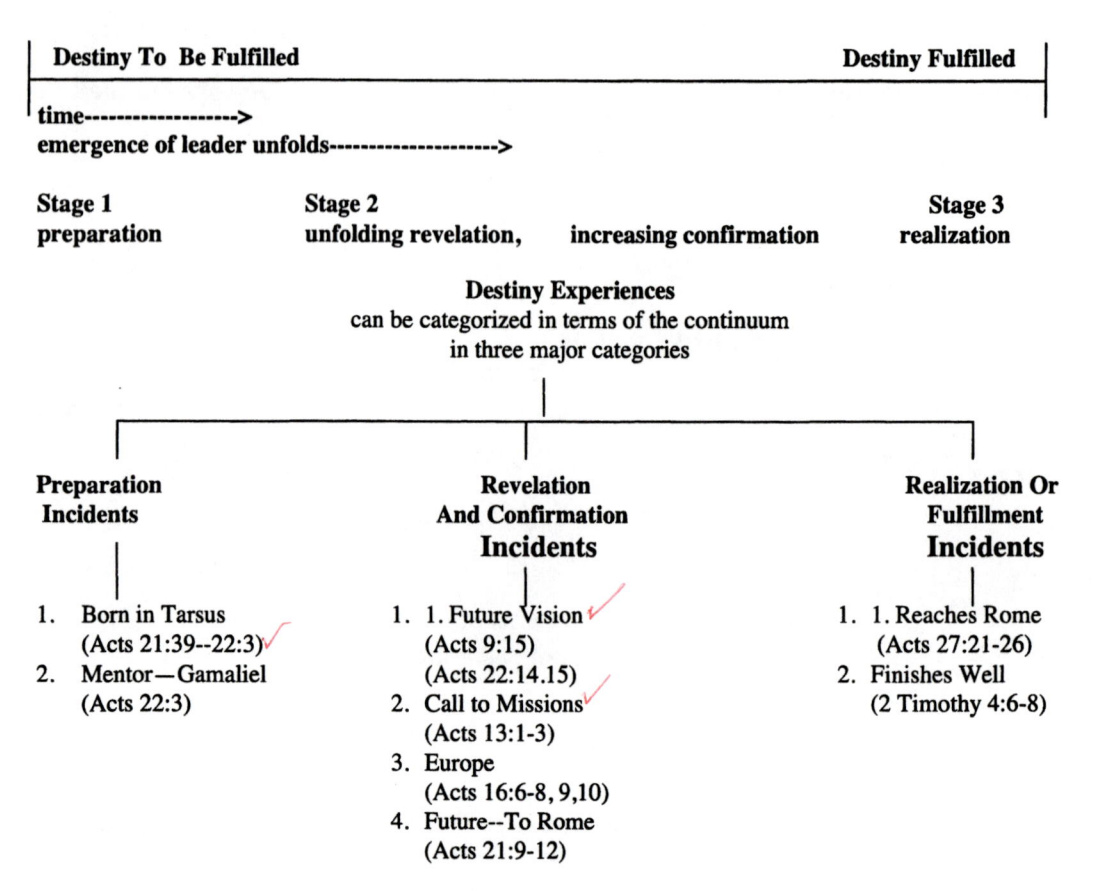

Preparation Incidents	Revelation And Confirmation Incidents	Realization Or Fulfillment Incidents
1. Born in Tarsus (Acts 21:39--22:3)	1. 1. Future Vision (Acts 9:15) (Acts 22:14,15)	1. 1. Reaches Rome (Acts 27:21-26)
2. Mentor—Gamaliel (Acts 22:3)	2. Call to Missions (Acts 13:1-3)	2. Finishes Well (2 Timothy 4:6-8)
	3. Europe (Acts 16:6-8, 9,10)	
	4. Future--To Rome (Acts 21:9-12)	

Figure 1,2Co 10-4. Paul's Destiny Processing and Three-Fold Destiny Pattern

Final Questions

Can young leaders be encouraged to seek and express these experiences and rely on them as their leadership unfolds? I noticed Joseph was young when God gave him his two dreams that foreshadowed his destiny. I have repeatedly encouraged young leaders in my classes (and older ones who have not experienced significant destiny processing) to be open to God's destiny processing. In fact, I have told them not only to be open, but I have told them to expect it. Reach out by faith and see God reveal their destiny to them. And God has done this.

Are there dangers in promoting a sense of destiny to young leaders? Yes, there are. Particularly is this true of young leaders who have strong egos and lots of ambition. They can easily impose their own desires on what they think might be their sense of destiny. But God has a way of bringing to earth those with high ambition and giving them a *Holy Ambition*. And I learned long ago that a leader can not afford to ignore some truth simply because others abuse it.

Do all leaders have a sense of destiny? All Biblical leaders who accomplished things for God did have a growing awareness of their sense of destiny. I think that leaders at higher levels of leadership responsibility will necessarily need a clearer sense of destiny since there leadership will influence so many more.

Conclusion

Remember, no leader in the Bible ever accomplished anything for God without a sense of destiny. Understanding how it develops is a good start on getting your sense of destiny.

See *life purpose*, **Glossary**. See **Articles**, *42. Paul—A Sense of Destiny; Life Purpose—Biblical Examples; Destiny Examples from Scripture*.

Article 11

Relevance of the Article to Paul's Corinthian Ministry

This article was originally written to show how Paul committed to Timothy a sense of leadership responsibility. The very existence of the two letters to the Corinthians illustrates Paul's own sense of responsibility for these two churches and by implications all the other church plants he had been involved in—indeed he stresses that in 2 Co 11:28 , Beside those things that are without, that which cometh upon me daily, the care of all the churches.

11. Entrustment—A Leadership Responsibility, The Notion of a Leadership Stewardship.

In the midst of a trial Paul makes an astonishing statement.

> Yet I am completely confident. For I know whom I have believed, and am persuaded that he is able to keep that which was entrusted[34] to me until that day.   2Ti 1:12

What was entrusted to him?

> ...which is in harmony with the glorious gospel of the blessed God, which was entrusted to me. 1Ti 1:11

> And this is why I was established[35] as a preacher, and an apostle. I speak the truth in Christ, and lie not; a teacher of faith and truth to the Gentiles. 1Ti 2:7

> So I was divinely chosen[36] as a preacher, and an apostle, and a teacher. 12 For this reason I am suffering [in prison]. 2Ti 1:11

Paul viewed his call to ministry and its ensuing destiny as a special leadership task. He would take the Gospel to the Gentiles. This task was an entrustment.

Definition   A leadership entrustment is the viewing of one's call to leadership and its ensuing ministry as a trust, something committed or entrusted to one to be used or cared for in the interest of God, who has given the trust. It is a leadership stewardship.

---

[34] Paul viewed his leadership ministry as something entrusted to him—a leadership stewardship—that he was to use and fulfill. He also recognized that God would protect him in the carrying out of that trusteeship until it was finished. Finally, he knew he would have an accounting for it (That Day). One could not have this view nor the confidence about it without a strong sense of destiny—a major *leadership committal*, see **Glossary**.

[35] Again, an assertion of divine assignment from God. established (SRN 5087) carries the sense of appointing or ordaining as was seen in putting in 1:12. See also 1:1 Apostle by the commandment of God and also the Pauline salutations: Ro 1:1; 1Co 1:1; 2Co 1:1; Gal 1:1; Eph 1:1; Col 1:1; 1Ti 1:1; 2Ti 1:1; Tit 1:1. These also strongly assert a divine calling. Leaders need a strong sense of God's calling for their lives if they are to persevere and be effective over a lifetime.

[36] The heart of a ministry that is effective begins here. This is a statement of a *leadership committal*, see **Glossary**—a response to God's call on a life for leadership. It is a *sense of destiny* experience, *a spiritual benchmark*, which a leader can always look back to and be bolstered in ministry. See **Article**, *61. Spiritual Benchmarks*.

11. Entrustment—A Leadership Responsibility

Paul ties his entrustment back to his destiny call. Further, he is certain that God will protect that entrustment. Four Pauline leadership values embedded in these forceful quotes include:

1. Paul believed that God had entrusted to him his leadership task to preach the Gospel to the Gentiles.
2. Paul believed that he was accountable to God for that entrustment.
3. Paul believed that he must guard that entrustment.
4. Paul believed that God would protect him until that entrustment was finished.

Further, Paul saw Timothy's ministry as an entrustment—an entrustment that he as an Apostolic leader had been involved in imparting.

> This command I am entrusting to you, son Timothy. It is based on the prophecies which were given about you. These words should encourage you to fight on bravely. 1Ti 1:18

> Don't keep on neglecting your spiritual gift, which was given to you by prophecy in conjunction with the laying on of the hands of the leaders. 1Ti 4:14

> Dear Timothy, guard what has been entrusted to you. Avoid worldly and fruitless discussions and false tenets of "so called science." 1Ti 6:20

> Guard carefully what was entrusted to you with the help of the Holy Spirit who lives within us. 2Ti 1:14

As leaders today, we should take away several lessons from this brief introduction of entrustment.

Lesson 1. We should be sure of our call—the stronger is our call and our sense of divine establishment in our ministry, the better.
Lesson 2. We should see our ministry as a leadership stewardship.
Lesson 3. We should confidently trust God to preserve us in our ministry till He has done what He wants to do through us.
Lesson 4. We may, with God's leading, responsibly pass on to others a leadership trust.

See Articles, *10. Destiny Pattern; 61. Spiritual Benchmarks; 42. Paul—A Sense of Destiny; 3. Apostolic Functions—Comparison of Titus and Timothy..*

Article 12

Relevance of the Article to Paul's Corinthian Ministry

This article was originally written for use with the leadership commentary which included 8 Bible books: 1,2 Ti; 1,2 Co; Php; Phm; Da; Jn. It has been used since then, however, with every leadership commentary—because all Bible books use figurative language. An understanding of figurative language helps anyone who wants to not only get the meaning of Scripture but also wants to get the emphatic meaning of Scripture. The following article has been revised to include some of the figurative passages seen in 1,2 Co.

12. Figures and Idioms In The Bible

Introduction to Figures

All language is governed by law—that is, it has normal patterns that are followed. But in order to increase the power of a word or the force of expression, these patterns are deliberately departed from, and words and sentences are thrown into and used in unusual forms or patterns which we call figures. A figure then is a use of language in a special way for the purpose of giving additional force, more life, intensified feeling and greater emphasis. A figure of speech is the author's way of underlining. He/She is saying, "Hey, take note! This is important enough for me to use a special form of language to emphasize it!" And when we remember the fact that the Holy Spirit has inspired this product we have—the Bible—we are not far wrong in saying figures are the Holy Spirit's own underlining in our Bibles. We certainly need to be sensitive to figurative language.

Definition   A figure is the unusual use of a word or words differing from the normal use in order to draw special attention to some point of interest.

For a figure, the unusual use itself follows a set pattern. The pattern can be identified and used to interpret the figure in normal language. Here are some examples from the Bible. I will make you fishers of people. Go tell that fox. Quench not the Holy Spirit. I came not to send peace but a sword. As students of the Bible we need to be sensitive to figures and know how to interpret and catch their emphatic meaning.

Definition   A figure or idiom is said to be captured when one can display the intended emphatic meaning in non-figurative simple words.

One of the most familiar figures in the Bible is Psalm 23:1. The Lord is my shepherd. I shall not lack. *Captured*: God personally provides for my every need.

E.W. Bullinger, an expert on figurative language, lists over 400 different kinds of figures. he lists over 8000 references in the Bible containing figures. In Romans alone, Bullinger lists 253 passages containing figurative language. However, we do not need to know all of those figures for the most commonly occurring figures number much less than 400. Figure 1 below list the 11 most common figures occurring in the Bible. If we know them we are well on our way to becoming better interpreters of the Scripture. In fact, you can group these 11 figures under three main sub-categories, which simplifies learning about them.

12. Figures and Idioms in the Bible

The Majority of Commonly Occurring Figures in the Bible
can be classified as

Figures of Comparison
which include
- simile
- metaphor

  Simple   Complex

Figures of Substitution
which include
- synecdoche
- metonymy

Figures of Apparent Deception
which include

Deliberate Overstatement
- hyperbole

Deliberate Understatement
- negative emphatics
- hyperbole mixtures

Deliberate Misstatement
- rhetorical questions
- irony
- personification
- apostrophe

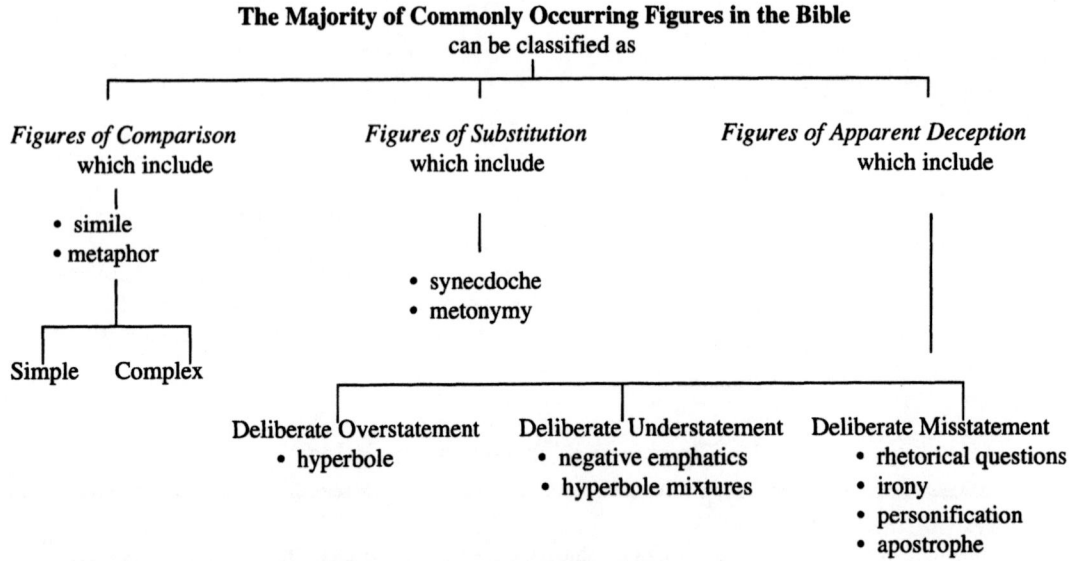

Figure 1,2Co 12-1.   11 Common Figures of Speech

Table 1,2Co 12-1 below gives these 11 figures of speech, a Scriptural reference containing the figure, and the basic definition of each of these figures.

Table 1,2Co 12-1: 11 Figures in the Bible Defined

Category/ Figure	Scriptural Example	Definition
Figures of Comparison: 1. Simile 2. Metaphor	simile—Isa 53:6 metaphor—Ps 23:1; 1 Co 3:1; 2 Co 3:18; 1 Co 3:2; 3:6-10; 11-15; 2 Co 3:2; 4:7; 5:1;	A simile is a stated comparison of two unlike items (one called the real item and the other the picture item) in order to display one graphic point of comparison. A metaphor is an implied comparison in which two unlike items (a real item and a picture item) are equated to point out one point of resemblance.
Figures of Substitution 3. Metonymy 4. Synecdoche	metonymy—Ac 15:21 Moses for what he wrote; 1 Co 14:3,12,32; 2 Co 1:14; 2 Co 5:19 synecdoche—Mt 8:8 roof for the whole house. 2 Co 7:1	A metonymy is a figure of speech in which (usually) one word is substituted for another word to which it is closely related in order to emphasize something indicated by the relationship. A synecdoche is a special case of metonymy in which (again usually) one word is substituted for another to which it is related as, a part to a whole or a whole to a part.
Figures of Apparent Deception— Deliberate Overstatement: 5. Hyperbole 6. Hyperbolic mixtures	hyperbole—1Co 4:14-16 ten thousand instructors hyperbolic mixture—2 Sa 1:23 swifter than eagles, stronger than lions	A hyperbole is the use of conscious exaggeration (an overstatement of truth) in order to emphasize or strikingly excite interest in the truth. Hyperbole is sometimes combined with other figures such as comparison and substitution. When such is the case it is called a hyperbolic mixture figure.

12. Figures and Idioms in the Bible

Figures of Apparent Deception— Deliberate understatement: 7. Negative emphatics	negative emphatics—Mk 12:34 not far = very near 2 Co 11:5	A figure of <u>negative emphasis</u> represents the deliberate use of words to diminish a concept and thus call attention to it or the negating of a concept to call attention to the opposite positive concept (I have deliberately merged two figures, litotes and tapenosis into one because of the basic sameness of negative emphasis).
Figures of Apparent Deception— Deliberate Misstatement: 8. Rhetorical questions 9. Irony 10. Personification 11. Apostrophe	rhetorical question—1Ti 3:5 irony—1 Co 9:4-10; 2 Co 3:1; 12:13 personification— Heb 4:12 apostrophe—1Co 15:55	A <u>rhetorical question</u> is a figure of speech in which a question is not used to obtain information but is used to indirectly communicate, (1) an affirmative or negative statement, or (2) the importance of some thought by focusing attention on it, or (3) one's own feeling or attitudes about something. <u>Irony</u> is the use of words by a speaker in which his/her intended meaning is the opposite of (or in disharmony with) the literal use of the words. <u>Personification</u> is the use of words to speak of animals, ideas, abstractions, and inanimate objects as if they had human form, character, or intelligence in order to vividly portray truth. <u>Apostrophe</u> is a special case of personification in which the speaker addresses the thing personified as if it were alive and listening.

I have developed in-depth explanations for all of the above figures. I have developed study sheets to aid one in analysis of them. Further I have actually identified many of these in the Scriptures and captured a number of them.[37]

Introduction to Idioms

Idioms are much more complicated that figures of speech.

Definition   An <u>idiom</u> is a group of words which have a corporate meaning that can not be deduced from a compilation of the meanings of the individual words making up the idiom.

What makes idioms difficult is that some of them follow patterns while others do not. For the patterned idioms, like figures, you basically reverse the pattern and capture the idiom. Table 1,2Co 12-2 lists the patterned idioms I have identified in the Bible.

Table 1,2Co 12-2. 13 Patterned Idioms

Idiom	Example	Definitive principle/ Description
Three Certainty Idioms: 1. Double certainty (pos/neg) 2. Fulfilled (promised/proposed) 3. Prophetic past	double certainty—1Ki 18:36 fulfilled—Ge 15:18 prophetic past—Jn 13:31	<u>double certainty</u>—a negative and positive statement (in either order) are often used to express or imply certainty. <u>fulfillment</u>—in the fulfillment idiom things are spoken of as given, done, or possessed, which are only promised or proposed. <u>prophetic past</u>—in the prophetic past idiom the past tense is used to describe or express the certainty of future action.
4. Superlative (repetitive superlative)	Ge 9:25 servant of servants Isa 26:3 peace, peace = perfect peace	The <u>Hebrew superlative</u> is often shown by the repetition of the word. Paul uses a variation of this by often using the noun form and a verb form of the same word either back to back or in close proximity. (the good struggle I have struggled).

---

[37] See my self-study manual, **Interpreting the Scriptures: Figures and Idioms**.

12. Figures and Idioms in the Bible

	2Ti 4:7	
5. Emphatic comparisons	1Pe 3:3,4	This takes three forms: absolute for relative: one thing (importance or focus item) is emphasized as being much more important in comparison with the other thing (the denial item). form not A but B really means A is less important than B. relative for absolute: One thing is positively compared to another when in effect it is meant to be taken absolutely and the other denied altogether. abbreviated emphatic comparisons: Half of the comparison is not given (either the focus item or denial items). Half of the statement is given. the half missing is an example of ellipsis and is to be supplied by the reader.
6. Climactic arrangement	Pr 6:16-19 Ro 3:10-18	To emphasize a particular item it is sometimes placed at the bottom of a list of other items and is thus stressed in the given context as being the most important item being considered.
7. Broadened kinship	Ge 29:5	Sometimes the terms son of, daughter of, mother of, father of, brother of, sister of, or begat, which in English imply a close relationship have a much wider connotation in the Bible. Brother and sister could include various male and female relatives such as cousins; mother and father could include relatives such as grandparents or great-great-grandparents, in the direct family line; begat may simply mean was directly in the family line of ancestors.
8. Imitator	Ge 6:2, 11:5	to indicate that people or things are governed by or are characterized by some quality, they are called children of or a son of or daughter of that quality.
9. Linked noun	Lk 21:15	Occasionally two nouns are linked together with a conjunction in which the second noun is really to be used like an adjective modifying the first noun.
Indicator Idioms: 10. City indicator 11. List indicator 12. Strength Indicator	city indicator La 1:16, daughter of Zion list indicator Pr 6:16, these 6 yea 7 Strength indicator 1Sa 2:1,10	city indicator—idiomatic words, daughter of or virgin of or mother of. list indicator—2 consecutive numbers—designates an incomplete list of items of which the ones on the list are representative; other like items could be included. strength indicator—a horn denotes aggressive strength or power or authority.
13. Anthropomorphism	Lk 11:20	In order to convey concepts of God, human passions, or actions, or attributes are used to describe God.

In addition, to the patterned idioms there are a number of miscellaneous idioms which either occur infrequently or have no discernible pattern. I have labeled 32. Their meaning must be learned from context, from other original language sources, or from language experts' comments, etc.

Table 1,2Co 12-3: 15 Body Language Idioms

Name	Word, Phrase, Usually Seen	Example	Meaning or Concept Involved
1. Foot gesture	shake off the dust	Mt 10:14, Lk 9:5 et al	have nothing more to do with them
2. Mouth	gnash on them	Ps 35:16;	indicates angry and cursing words given with

12. Figures and Idioms in the Bible

gesture	with teeth; gnashing of teeth	37:12 Ac 7:54 et al	deep emotion and feeling
3. Invitation	I have stretched forth my hand(s)	Ro 10:21; Pr 1:24; Is 49:22	indicates to invite, or to receive or welcome or call for mercy
4. New desire	enlighten my eyes, lighten my eyes	Ps 13:3; 19:8; 1Sa 14:29; Ezr 9:8	to give renewed desire to live; sometimes physical problem sometimes motivational inward attitude problem
5. Judgment	to stretch forth the hand; to put forth the hand	Ex 7:5; Ps 138:7; Job 1:11	to send judgment upon; to inflict with providential punishment
6. Fear	to shake the hand, to not find the hand, knees tremble	Is 19:16; Ps 76:8	to be afraid; to be paralyzed with fear and incapable of action.
7. Increase punishment	to make the hand heavy	Ps 32:4	to make the punishment more severe
8. Decreased punishment	to make the hands light	1SA 6:5	to make punishment less severe
9. Remove punishment	to withdraw the hands	Eze 20:22	to stop punishment
10. Repeat punishment	to turn the hand upon	Is 1:25	to repeat again some punishment which was not previously heeded
11. Generosity	to open the hand	Ps 104:28; 145:16	to generously give or bestow
12. Anger	to clap the hands together	Eze 21;17; 22:13	to show anger; to express derision
13. Oath	to lift up the hand	Ex 6:8; 17:16; De 32:40; Eze 20:5,6	to swear in a solemn; take an oath; an indicator of one's integrity to consider worthy to be accepted; to accept someone or be accepted by someone
14. Promise	to strike with the hands (with someone else)	Pr 6:1; Job 17:3	become a co-signer on a loan; to conclude a bargain
15. Accept	to lift up the face	Nu 6:26; Ezr 9:6; Job 22:26	to consider worthy to be accepted; to accept someone or be accepted by someone

Table 1,2Co 12-4: 14 Miscellaneous Idioms

Name	Word, Phrase, Usually Seen	Example	Meaning or Concept Involved
1. Success	tree of life	Pr 3:18; 11:30; 13:12; 15:4	idea of success, guarantee of success, source of motivation to successful life
2. Speech cue	answered and said	Mt 11:25; 13:2 and many others	indicates manner of speaking denoted by context; e.g. responded prayed, asked, addressed, etc.
3. Notice	verily, verily	Many times in	I am revealing absolute and important truth;

12. Figures and Idioms in the Bible

		Jn	give close attention (this is a form of the superlative idiom)
4. Time	__- days and __ nights	Jn 1:17; Mt 12:40; 1Sa 30:11; Est 4:16	any portion of time of a day is indicated by or represented by the entire day
5. Lifetime	forever and ever	Ps 48;14 and many others	does not mean eternal life as we commonly use it but means all through my life; as long as I live
6. Separation	what have I to do with you	Jn 2:4; Jdg 11;12; 2Sa 16:10; 1Ki 17;18; 2Ki 3;13; Mt 8:29; Mk 5:7; Lk 8:28	an expression of indignation or contempt between two parties having a difference or more specifically not having something in common; usually infers that some action about to take place should not take place
7. Reaction	heap coals of fire	Ro 12:20; Pr 25:21	to incur God's favor by reacting positively to a situation in which revenge would be normal
8. Orate	open the mouth	Job 3:1	to speak at great length with great liberty or freedom
9. Claim	you say	Mt 26:25,63,64	means it is your opinion
10. Excellency	living, lively	Jn 4:10,11 Ac 7:38; Heb 10:20; 1Pe 2:4,5; Rev 1:17	used to express the excellency of perfection of that to which it refers
11. Abundance	riches	Ro 2:4; Eph 1:7; 3:8; Col 1:27; 2:2	used to describe abundance of or a great supply
12. Preeminence	firstborn	Ps 89:27; Ro 8:29; Col 1;15, 18; Heb 12:23	special place of preeminence; first place among many others
13. Freedom	enlarge my feet; enlarge	2Sa 22:37; Ps 4:1; 18:36	freed me; brought me into a situation that has taken the pressure off, taken on to bigger and better things
14. Reverential respect for	fear and trembling	Ps 55:5; Mk 5:33; Lk 8:47; 1Co 2:3; 2 Co 7:15; Eph 6:5, Php 2:12	describes an attitude of appropriate respect for something. The something could be God, could a person, or could be a combination including some process. Sometimes indicates confronting a difficult situation or thing with a strong awareness of it and possible consequences

Again I would recommend you refer to my manual **Figures and Idioms** to see the approach for capturing the patterned idioms.

Figures and Idioms should be appreciated, understood, and should be interpreted with emphasis.

Hardly any passage, which is any one of the seven leadership genre, will be without some figure or idiom.

Article 13

Relevance of the Article to Paul's Corinthian Ministry

This article and the two immediately following articles were originally written for use with the leadership commentary which included 8 Bible books: 1,2 Ti; 1,2 Co; Php; Phm; Da; Jn. In particular, Paul is shown to be a leader who finished well in 2 Ti. The Corinthian letters depict a time in Paul's life when he could easily have been derailed from a good finish. In these epistles, especially 2 Co, Paul reveals the values that underlie his life and ministry—values that will contribute to a good finish. Paul's life illustrates a number of the enhancements for finishing well. He also lambastes the so-called pseudo-apostles. His condemnation of them highlights some of the barriers, which hinder leaders from finishing well. And the great passage in 2 Ti 4:7ff reveals a good finish. Note also 1 Co 9:24-27 in which Paul evinces his desire to continue and finish well. 1 Co 9:24-27, "I am serious about finishing well, in my Christian ministry. I discipline myself for fear that after challenging others into the Christian life I myself might become a casualty." (My paraphrase)

13. Finishing Well—Five Factors That Enhance It

Introduction to Research on Finishing Well

In 1989 in an article entitled, *Listen Up Leaders! Forewarned is Forearmed!* I summarized my research on Biblical leaders with the following opening comments.

A repeated reading of the Bible with a focus on leadership reveals four crucial observations fraught with leadership implications:

Observation 1. Few leaders finish well.
Observation 2. Leadership is difficult.
Observation 3. God's enabling presence is the essential ingredient of successful leadership.
Observation 4. Spiritual leadership can make a difference.

And what is true of Biblical leaders is equally true of historical and contemporary leaders.[38] It is the first observation to which this article speaks. Identifying the fact that few leaders finish well was a breakthrough warning for me. This led to further study. Why do few leaders finish well? What stops them? What helps them?

Five Enhancements

Comparative study of effective leaders who finished well has identified five commonalities. Not all five always appear in leaders who finish well but at least several of them do. Frequently, effective leaders who finish well will have four or five of them seen in their lives. What are these enhancements?

Enhancement 1. Perspective.

We need to have a lifetime perspective on ministry. Effective leaders view present ministry in terms of a lifetime perspective.[39] We gain that perspective by studying lives of leaders as commanded in Hebrews 13:7,8. I have been doing intensive study of leaders' lives over the past 13 years. Leadership emergence theory is the result of that research. Its many concepts can help us understand more fully just how God does shape a leader over a lifetime.[40]

---

[38] At the time of this article I have studied nearly 1300 cases with about 50 Bible leaders, perhaps 100 historical leaders and the rest contemporary leaders. The findings for enhancements and barriers generally hold true.

[39] This is one of seven major leadership lessons derived from comparative studies. See **Article**, *Seven Major Leadership Lessons*.

[40] My findings are available in two books, **The Making of A Leader**, published by Nav Press in 1988 and a lengthy detailed self-study manual, **Leadership Emergence Theory**, that I privately publish for use in

Enhancement 2. Renewal.

Special moments of intimacy with God, challenges from God, new vision from God and affirmation from God both for personhood and ministry will occur repeatedly to a growing leader. These destiny experiences will be needed, appreciated, and will make the difference in persevering in a ministry. All leaders should expectantly look for these repeated times of renewal. Some can be initiated by the leader (usually extended times of spiritual disciples). But some come sovereignly from God. We can seek them, of course, and be ready for them.

Most leaders who have been effective over a lifetime have needed and welcomed renewal experiences from time to time in their lives. Some times are more crucial in terms of renewal than others. Apparently in western society the mid-thirty's and early forty's and mid-fifty's are crucial times in which renewal is frequently needed in a leader's life. Frequently during these critical periods discipline slacks, there is a tendency to plateau and rely on one's past experience and skills, and a sense of confusion concerning achievement and new direction prevail. Unusual renewal experiences with God can overcome these tendencies and redirect a leader. An openness for them, a willingness to take steps to receive them, and a knowledge of their importance for a whole life can be vital factors in profiting from **enhancement 2** for finishing well. Sometimes these renewal experiences are divinely originated by God and we must be sensitive to his invitation. At other times we must initiate the renewal efforts.

Enhancement 3. Disciplines.

Leaders need discipline of all kinds. Especially is this true of spiritual disciplines. A strong surge toward spirituality now exists in Catholic and Protestant circles. This movement combined with an increasingly felt need due to the large number of failures is propelling leaders to hunger for intimacy. The spiritual disciplines are one mediating means for getting this intimacy. Such authors as Eugene Peterson, Dallas Willard, and Richard Foster are making headway with Protestants concerning spirituality.[41] Leaders without these leadership tools are prone to failure via sin as well as plateauing.

I concur with Paul's admonitions to discipline as a means of insuring perseverance in the ministry. When Paul was around 50 years of age he wrote to the Corinthian church what appears to be both an exhortation to the Corinthians and an explanation of a major leadership value in his own life. We need to keep in mind that he had been in ministry for about 21 years. He was still advocating strong discipline. I paraphrase it in my own words.

> **I am serious about finishing well in my Christian ministry. I discipline myself for fear that after challenging others into the Christian life I myself might become a casualty.** 1Co 9:24-27

Lack of physical discipline is often an indicator of laxity in the spiritual life as well. Toward the end of his life, Paul is probably between 65 and 70, he is still advocating discipline. This time he writes to Timothy, who is probably between 30 and 35 years old.

> **...Instead exercise your mind in godly things. 8 For physical exercise is advantageous somewhat but exercising in godliness has long term implications both for today and for that which will come.** (1Ti 4:7b,8)

Leaders should from time to time assess their state of discipline. I recommend in addition to standard word disciplines involving the devotional life and study of the Bible other disciplines such as solitude, silence, fasting, frugality, chastity, secrecy. My studies of Foster and Willard have helped me identify a number of disciplines which can habitually shape character and increase the probability of a good finish.

---

classes and workshops. In addition, my latest research is available in position papers published by Barnabas Publishers. See **For Further Study Bibliography** for full listings of these books.

[41] See also my section on spiritual guides and the appendix on the disciplines in **The Mentor Handbook**, available through Barnabas Publishers. See **Article,** *62. Spiritual Disciplines and On-Going Leadership.*

Enhancement 4. Learning Posture.

The single most important antidote to plateauing is a well developed learning posture. Such a posture is also one of the major ways through which God gives vision.

Another of the seven major leadership lessons is *Effective leaders maintain a learning posture all their lives*. It sounds simple enough but many leaders don't heed it. Two Biblical leaders who certainly were learners all their lives and exemplified this principle were Daniel and Paul. Note how Daniel observed this principle. In Da 9 when he is quite old we find that he was still studying his Bible and still learning new things from it. And he was alert to what God wanted to do through what he was learning. Consequently, Daniel was able to intercede for his people and become a recipient of one of the great messianic revelations. Paul's closing remarks to Timothy show he was still learning. "And when you come don't forget the books Timothy!" (2Ti 4:13).

There are many non-formal training events available such as workshops, seminars, and conferences covering a variety of learning skills. Take advantage of them. A good learning posture is insurance against plateauing and a helpful prod along the way to persevere in leadership. An inflexible spirit with regards to learning is almost a sure precursor to finishing so-so or poorly.

Enhancement 5. Mentoring.

Comparative study of many leaders lives indicates the frequency with which other people were significant in challenging them into leadership and in giving timely advice and help so as to keep them there. Leaders who are effective and finish well will have from 10 to 15 significant people who came alongside at one time or another to help them. Mentoring is also a growing movement in Christian circles as well as secular.

The general notion of mentoring involves a relational empowerment process in which someone who knows something (the mentor) passes on something (wisdom, advice, information, emotional support, protection, linking to resources) to someone who needs it (the mentoree, protégé) at a sensitive time so that it impacts the person's development. The basic dynamics of mentoring include attraction, relationship, response, accountability and empowerment. My observations on mentoring suggest that most likely, any leader will need a mentor at all times over a lifetime of leadership. Mentoring is available if one looks for specific functions and people who can do them (rather than an ideal mentor who can do all). God will provide a mentor in a specific area of need for you if you trust Him for one and you are willing to submit and accept responsibility.

Simply stated a final suggestion for enabling a good finish is find a mentor who will hold you accountable in your spiritual life and ministry and who can warn and advise so as to enable you to avoid pitfalls and to grow throughout your lifetime of ministry.

Conclusion

A leader ought to want to finish well. I never give this warning, few leaders finish well, and this challenge, do you want to finish well?, without an overwhelming response. Yes, I do. Then heed these five factors. Proactively take steps to get these factors working in your life. Finish well!!!

See **Articles**: *14. Finishing Well—Six Characteristics; 30. Leadership Lessons—Seven Major Lessons Identified.*

Article 14

Relevance of the Article to Paul's Corinthian Ministry
    Paul finished well. P.S. Read 2 Ti to reinforce this. He demonstrates all of the finishing well characteristics. The Corinthian ministry serves to show a number of the finishing well characteristics alive and well in the midst of great conflict.

14. Finishing Well—Six Characteristics

Introduction to Research on Finishing Well

In 1989 in an article entitled, Listen Up Leaders! Forewarned is Forearmed! I summarized my research on Biblical leaders with the following opening comments.

A repeated reading of the Bible with a focus on leadership reveals four crucial observations fraught with leadership implications:

    Observation 1.   Few leaders finish well.[42]
    Observation 2.   Leadership is difficult.
    Observation 3.   God's enabling presence is the essential ingredient of successful leadership.
    Observation 4.   Spiritual leadership can make a difference.

And what is true of Biblical leaders is equally true of historical and contemporary leaders.[43] It is the first observation to which this article speaks. Identifying the fact that few leaders finish well was a breakthrough warning for me. This led to further study. Why do few leaders finish well? What stops them? What helps them? What does it mean to finish well? This article identifies six characteristics of those finishing well.

Six Characteristics

Comparative study of effective leaders who finished well has identified six characteristics. While there may be other characteristics that I have not seen, certainly these are important ones. Not all six always appear but at least several of them do in leaders who finish well. Frequently, effective leaders who finish well will have four or five of them seen in their lives. And some, like Daniel in the O.T. and Paul in the N.T. demonstrate all of them. What are these six characteristics of those finishing well.

Characteristic 1.
They maintain a personal vibrant relationship with God right up to the end.

Example: Daniel is the classic O.T. leader who exemplifies this. In the N.T., Peter, Paul and John all demonstrate this. See their last writings—the tone, the touch with God, the revelation from God, their trust in enabling grace for their lives.

Characteristic 2.
They maintain a learning posture and can learn from various kinds of sources—life especially.

This characteristic is also one of the enhancement factors for finishing well.

---

[42] There are around 800 or so leaders mentioned in the Bible. There are about 100 who have data that helps you interpret their leadership. About 50 of these have enough data for evaluation of their finish. About 1 in 3 finished well. Anecdotal evidence from today indicates that this ratio is probably generous. Probably less than 1 in 3 are finishing well today.

[43] At the time of this article I have studied nearly 1300 cases with about 50 Bible leaders, perhaps 100 historical leaders and the rest contemporary leaders. The findings for enhancements and barriers generally hold true.

14. Finishing Well—Six Characteristics

Example: Daniel is the classic O.T. leader who exemplifies this. See Daniel chapter nine for a late in life illustration of one who continues to study and learn from the Scriptures. Paul and Peter are the classic N.T. leaders with a learning posture (see 2Pe 3:18 and 2Ti 4:13).

Characteristic 3.
They manifest Christ-likeness in character as evidenced by the fruit of the Spirit in their lives.

Example: Daniel is the classic O.T. leader who exemplifies godliness (See the summary references to him in Eze 14:14,20). In the N.T. note the evidence of character transformation in Paul's life (2Ti 2:24 and an illustration of it—the book of Phm). These were men who over a lifetime moved from strong personalities with roughness in their leadership styles to strong personalities with gentleness in their leadership styles.

Characteristic 4.
Truth is lived out in their lives so that convictions and promises of God are seen to be real.

Example: Joshua's statement about God's promises never having failed him in his closing speech demonstrate this characteristic of someone believing God and staking his life on God's truth (Jos 23:14). See the many aside truth statements that Paul weaves into his two letters to Timothy. See his famous stirring convictions echoed in Ac 27:22-25.

Characteristic 5.
They leave behind one or more ultimate contributions.

In a study on legacies left behind by effective leaders who finished well I have identified the following categories:

Table 1,2Co 14-1. Categories of Lasting Legacies—13 Specigic Types Identified

Type: Specific Legacy	Basic Notion
CHARACTER:	
1. SAINT	A Model life, not a perfect one, but a life others want to emulate.
2. STYLISTIC PRACTITIONER	A Model ministry style which sets the pace for others and which other ministries seek to emulate.
3. FAMILY	Promote a God-fearing family, leaving behind children who walk with God carrying on that Godly-heritage.
MINISTRY:	
4. MENTOR	A productive ministry with individuals, small groups, etc.
5. PUBLIC RHETORICIAN	A productive public ministry with large groups.
CATALYTIC:	
6. PIONEER	A person who starts apostolic ministries.
7. CHANGE PERSON	A person who rights wrongs and injustices in society and in church and mission organizations.
8. ARTIST	A person who has creative breakthroughs in life and ministry and introduces innovation.
ORGANIZATIONAL:	
9. FOUNDER	A person who starts a new organization to meet a need or capture the essence of some movement or the like.

14. Finishing Well—Six Characteristics

10. STABILIZER	A person who can help a fledgling organization develop or can help an older organization move toward efficiency and effectiveness. In other words, help solidify an organization.
IDEATION:	
11. RESEARCHER)	Develops new ideation by studying various things.
12. WRITER	captures ideas and reproduces them in written format to help and inform others.
13. PROMOTER	Effectively distributes new ideas and/or other ministry related things.

Examples: Daniel's ultimate contributions include: saint, (mentor), writer, stabilizer. Paul's ultimate contributions include: saint, mentor, pioneer, crusader, writer, promoter.

Of course, in addition to these standard categories there are also unique legacies that leaders also leave behind. These have to be described individually for each leader.

Characteristic 6.
They walk with a growing awareness of a sense of destiny and see some or all of it fulfilled.

Definition   A <u>sense of destiny</u> is an inner conviction arising from an experience or a series of experiences in which there is a growing sense of awareness that God has His hand on a leader in a special way for special purposes.

Over a lifetime a leader is prepared by God for a destiny, receives guidance toward that destiny, and increasingly completes that destiny. No Biblical leader who accomplished much for God failed to have a sense of destiny, one that usually grew over his/her lifetime.

Examples: Joseph's dreams and his saving of the embryonic nation; Moses' saving of the nation; Paul's vision to take the Gospel to the Gentiles.

Conclusion

The classic example in the O.T. of a good finish is Daniel who manifests all six characteristics. The classic example in the N.T. other than Christ is Paul. There are gradations of finishing well. Some finish well but not quite having all six or lesser intensity on one or the other major characteristics. This list of characteristics is probably not complete. Others may not agree totally with them. In that case, they should at least provide an alternate list. But these are certainly evident in many leaders who have finished well.

See **Article,** *Leaving Behind a Legacy.*

Article 15

<u>Relevance of the Article to Paul's Corinthian Ministry</u>
   Paul identifies a number of these barriers, especially as he deals with the sources of some of the Corinthian church problems. Paul, himself, successfully avoids these barriers in his own life.

15. Finishing Well—Six Major Barriers Identified

Introduction to Research on Finishing Well
   In 1989 in an article entitled, *Listen Up Leaders! Forewarned is Forearmed!*, I summarized my research on Biblical leaders with the following opening comments.
   A repeated reading of the Bible with a focus on leadership reveals four crucial observations fraught with leadership implications:

   Observation 1.   Few leaders finish well.
   Observation 2.   Leadership is difficult.
   Observation 3.   God's enabling presence is the essential ingredient of successful leadership.
   Observation 4.   Spiritual leadership can make a difference.

And what is true of Biblical leaders is equally true of historical and contemporary leaders.[44] It is the first observation to which this article speaks. Identifying the fact that few leaders finish well was a breakthrough warning for me. This led to further study. Why do few leaders finish well? What stops them? What helps them?

Six Barriers To Finishing Well
   Comparative study of effective leaders who finished well has identified six barriers that hindered leaders from finishing well. It only takes one of them to torpedo a leader. But frequently a leader who fails in one area will also fail in others. What are these barriers? We can learn from those who didn't finish well. We can be alerted to these barriers. We can avoid them in our own lives. Pr 22:3 tells us that,

   Sensible people will see trouble coming and avoid it, but an unthinking person will walk right into it and regret it later. Pr 22:3

Let me share with you six barriers to finishing well that I have identified. We need to look ahead in our lives and not walk right into these barriers. We need to avoid being entrapped by them.

Barrier 1. Finances—their Use And Abuse
   Leaders, particularly those who have power positions and make important decisions concerning finances, tend to use practices which may encourage incorrect handling of finances and eventually wrong use. A character trait of greed often is rooted deep and eventually will cause impropriety with regard to finances. Numerous leaders have fallen due to some issue related to money.

   Biblical Examples: O.T.: Gideon's golden ephod. N.T.: Ananias and Sapphira.

---

[44] At the time of this article I have studied nearly 1300 cases with about 50 Bible leaders, perhaps 100 historical leaders and the rest contemporary leaders. The findings for enhancements and barriers generally holds true.

15. Finishing Well—Six Major Barriers Identified

Barrier 2. Power—its Abuse

Leaders who are effective in ministry must use various power bases in order to accomplish their ministry. With power so available and being used almost daily, there is a tendency to abuse it. Leaders who rise to the top in a hierarchical system tend to assume privileges with their perceived status. Frequently, these privileges include abuse of power. And they usually have no counter balancing accountability.

Biblical Example: Uzziah's usurping of priestly privilege.

Barrier 3. Pride--which Leads To Downfall

Pride (inappropriate and self-centered) can lead to a downfall of a leader. As a leader there is a dynamic tension that must be maintained. We must have a healthy respect for our selves, and yet we must recognize that we have nothing that was not given us by God and He is the one who really enables ministry.

Biblical Example: David's numbering.

Barrier 4. Sex--illicit Relationships

Illicit sexual relationships have been a major downfall both in the Bible and in western cultures.[45] Joseph's classic integrity check with respect to sexual sin is the ideal model that should be in leaders' minds.

Biblical Example: David's sin with Bathsheba was a pivotal point from which his leadership never fully recovered. It was all downhill from there on.

Barrier 5. FAMILY--Critical Issues

Problems between spouses or between parents and children or between siblings can destroy a leader's ministry. What is needed are Biblical values lived out with regard to husband-wife relationships, parent-children, and sibling relationships. Of growing importance in our day is the social base profiles for singles in ministry and for married couples.

Biblical Example: David's family. Ammon and Tamar. Absalom's revenge.

Barrier 6. Plateauing.

Leaders who are competent tend to plateau. Their very strength becomes a weakness. They can continue to minister at a level without there being a reality or Spirit empowered renewing effect. Most leaders will plateau several times in their life times of development. Some of the five enhancement factors for a good finish will counteract this tendency (perspective, learning posture, mentor, disciplines). There again is a dynamic tension that must be maintained between leveling off for good reasons, (consolidating one's growth and/or reaching the level of potential for which God has made you) and plateauing because of sinfulness or loss of vision.

Biblical Example: David in the latter part of his reign just before Absalom's revolt.

Forewarned is forearmed. There are many other reasons why leaders don't finish well—usually all related to sin in some form. But at least the six categories are major ones that have trapped many leaders and taken them out of the race. Leaders who want to finish well, Take heed!

See Articles: *14. Finishing Well—Six Characteristics; 15. Finishing Well—Six Enhancements*.

---

[45] This is probably true in other cultures as well though I do not have a data base to prove this.

Article 16

Relevance of the Article to Paul's Corinthian Ministry

Paul knows the importance of influencing followers. He is seeking to solve major church problems in the Corinthian church. He knows that if he does not have follower loyalty, then his suggestions for solving these problems will not be heeded. Note his strong wording about followership. Once we are sure of your obedience, we shall not shrink from dealing with those who refuse to obey. 2Co 10:6. Paul is conscious of the principles embedded in these followership ideas.

16. Followership—The Ten Commandments

Leaders, followers, and situations comprise the leadership basal elements. Where ever leadership is going on around the world these three elements can be observed and analyzed. Followership describes the set of issues dealing with the follower basal element.

Definition   Followership refers to the collective relationship between a leader and those people under that leader's sphere of influence, which has at its base the voluntary acceptance of leadership by the followers and is measured by group characteristics such as:
- loyalty to leadership,
- obedience to God's vision through the leadership,
- service to carry out details of the leader's vision,
- discipline imposed upon followers not willing to be loyal, obedient, available for service or to those rebelling against God's will and direction for their lives,
- sacrifice displaying their willingness to give of what they have for the carrying out of God's vision,
- quality of relationships of followers with each other.

Paul points out (from a leadership focus) an essential of followership when he describes his prerequisites for exercising discipline.

> **Once we are sure of your obedience, we shall not shrink from dealing with those who refuse to obey. 2Co 10:6**

Three Categories of Followers in A Church Situation

Followership in a local church situation will usually be differentiated into three levels depending on intensity of the church followership measures given above:

group 1—   an inner core of followership who can be depended upon and will carry the bulk of the ministry;

group 2—   followers that have some initial commitment to the ministry and have potential to be developed into the inner core;

group 3—   fringe followers, that is, some folks who can be developed toward group 2 and some who will fall away and some who constantly need help and will never develop.

Three Categories of Followers in A Parachurch Situation

Followership in a parachurch situation will usually be differentiated into three levels also:

group 1—   an inner core followership made up of those who are the decision makers and those having close access to them;

16. Followership—The Ten Commandments

group 2— the workers who carry out the ministry in the field situation;
group 3— the support staff who administratively back up the workers.

Relating Leadership and Followership

Leadership primarily involves the efforts of leaders to motivate followers toward God's purposes for the group. Secondarily, leadership involves the development of followership, that is, for church followership moving group 1 followers into leadership, moving group 2 toward group 1, and group 3 toward group 2. It also involves recruiting outsiders into all three groups. For parachurch leadership development involves the enlargement of group 1, recruitment for group 2, and administrative affirmation for group 3.

Some Major Problems

Some problems involved in followership include:
1. leadership backlash,[46]
2. jealousy and ambition among rising leaders,
4. failure to release and other hindrances to people as they develop,
5. centralization/ decentralization cycle,
6. perseverance,
7. rebellion.

The following observations on followership came mainly from studies of two leaders and their relationships with followers—Moses and Paul.

10 COMMANDMENTS OF FOLLOWERSHIP

Label	Principle
1. LOYALTY	Leadership in voluntary organizations can not be effectively exercised without followership loyalty.
2. DISCIPLINE	Leadership can not apply adequate discipline without a firm base of loyal committed followers.
3. BACKLASH	Even in successful leadership a leader must expect follower backlash due to unforeseen ramifications[47] after the success.
4. SPIRITUAL AUTHORITY	Leaders who dominantly rely upon spiritual authority as the major power base will usually have good followership.
5. VOLUNTEERS	In most Christian organizations leaders must rely upon followership which is dominantly volunteer in nature; this directly effects power bases which can be used.
6. BALANCE	A dynamic tension must exist between centralization (which allows for direction in leadership but can weaken development of followership) and decentralization (which can allow development of followership but may lack the strong direction that is needed).
7. CORE	A wise leader recognizes that there are differing levels of commitment among followership and expects differing responses to efforts to mobilize and develop followers.
8. GOAL	Leadership must give hope to followership.

---

[46] Leadership backlash is a special term coined after repeated observations of the following cycle: 1. leaders motivate followers toward some objective, 2. leaders and followers move ahead toward the objective, 3. there is success involved in reaching the objective, 4. unforeseen ramifications also occur which are discouraging, 5. the followers who were initially for the effort now rebel against it and the leaders, 6. the leader gets discouraged, 7. the leader may give up and quit or may be driven back to God to affirm the leading, 8. God reaffirms, 9. the leader perseveres through, 10. the followers, for the most part, are convinced to accept the leadership. Many leaders bail out at 6 after the discouragement and never get to steps 7 through 10. See also Clinton's **Leadership Emergence Theory**, pages 208,209 for further details.

[47] These unforeseen ramifications occurring are called by the phrase, the *law of unintended consequences*.

16. Followership—The Ten Commandments

9.	**BIRTH**	Good followership results in birth of good leaders.
10.	**RECIPROCAL LIVING**	Good followership manifests itself in interrelationships reflecting the reciprocal commands.

Followership will differ with differing leadership situations. Do not assume that because you have led successfully in a given situation with followers that you will do so in the next situation with differing followers. Become sensitive to followership, its expectations on leadership, and its demands on leadership.

See also **Article** *60. Spiritual Authority—Defined, Six Characteristics; 57. Reciprocal Living—The One-Another-Commands.* See **For Further Study Bibliography**, Clinton's **Leadership Emergence Theory.**

Article 17

Relevance of the Article to Paul's Corinthian Ministry

Paul was way ahead of his times in seeing women as leaders. For example, note his sponsorship of Phoebe, a leader in the Corinthian church (Ro 16:1, 1 I highly recommend unto you Phoebe our sister, who is a minister of the church which is at Cenchrea). See also comments in Php where Paul talks about co-ministering with several women leaders. See also his comments in 1 Tim on qualifications for leadership where women are included. There are some problematic passages from Paul. This article treats the subject of gender and leadership from a positive approach—that of accepting gifted and called people, whether male or female, as legitimate leaders. I do not so much speak to the problematic passages in this short article. For further detail see my extended treatment of this in my article, available from Barnabas Publishers, *Gender and Leadership*.

17. Gender and Leadership

Introduction

I referred to a perspective, *the starting-point-plus-process model*, when I commented on slavery in Phm. In the article describing the *starting-point-plus-process model*, I mentioned that the model applied to women in leadership as well as to slavery and marriage, both institutions in which God moved from less-ideal held views to His ideals over long periods of time. It probably will apply as well to other issues, once they come into focus. For it describes how God works with people, graciously dealing with them to bring them to maturity. He begins where they are and moves them toward the ideal.

Basically the starting-point-plus-process model has four major assertions.

1. Assuming a valid faith-allegiance response,[48] God allows for a range of understanding of Himself and His will for people, for He starts *where people are* rather than demanding that they immediately conform to His ideals.
2. This range of understanding of God can assume a *variety of potential starting points* anywhere from sub-ideal toward ideal perception of God and His ways.
3. God then initiates a process which involves a *revelational progression* from a sub-ideal starting point toward the ideal. This on-going process often takes long time periods with small gains along the way.
4. This process of beginning with a range of sub-ideal starting points of perception and behavior and moving by revelational progression from the sub-ideal toward the ideal can be applied to any doctrine of Scripture and any Scriptural treatment of behavioral patterns.

Most of the cultures represented in the O.T. and N.T. have a sub-ideal starting point concerning leadership and the female gender. Most of these cultures were largely male-dominated cultures. This is an acceptable starting point, though sub-ideal.[49] People, who within these cultures accept God as their only God and His salvation, can be worked with to move toward the ideal. In this case of gender and leadership, that ideal is gifted leaders contributing to God's work, regardless of gender. Exceptions to the cultural norms as seen in

---

[48] That is, an acceptable starting place. By a faith-allegiance response I mean a valid decision to place God as top priority in a life—a trusting response for God's salvation and work in a life.

[49] I am assuming the ideal of a gift based leadership church in which the Holy Spirit gives gifts that are needed to people without gender bias. People with leadership gifts should lead. This is a theological argument based on the nature of the church and the ministry of the Holy Spirit in the church. I also am aware of the ideal described in Gal 3:28.

the O.T. and N.T. which are blessed by God only serve to enforce what I am saying about movement toward an ideal.[50]

Leadership and Giftedness—The Ideal

A leader is a person with God-given capacity and a God-given burden who is influencing specific groups of people towards God's purposes for them. Comparative studies of leaders identified the concept of leaders being word-gifted. Study of giftedness throughout the N.T. church era indicated that people receive word gifts without regard to gender. That is, the Holy Spirit gives leadership gifts to male and females who are part of the body of Christ. Because of the work of the Cross both males and females are accepted into the body of Christ. Both are endowed with gifts from the Holy Spirit. The ideal is simply stated.

> **A gifted body operating interdependently allows the gifts of all its people to be used by God to mature the body and to expand it by bringing in new believers from the environment around it.**

Paul—Well Ahead of His Time

By the time of Paul's ministry, God had already begun strong movement toward the ideal. Jesus' ministry, in the Pre-Church Leadership Era inaugurated the movement toward the ideal by elevating the status of women in general.[51] Paul carried it further, co-ministering with women in local church situations, and sponsoring them elsewhere.[52]

When Paul describes selection of leaders to Timothy, even in a male dominated culture, he describes the characteristics for leaders not only in male terms but also in terms allowing for females.[53] For Paul the problem of female leaders is not so much theological (he is free here) but cultural (he recognizes that cultures may not be ready for it nor women in those cultures ready for it).

The so-called objections[54] to women in leadership in 1Co and 1Ti are not dealing with women as leaders, that is, giving a theological argument against women in leadership, but represent special cultural situations in which church behavior is not proper. Paul is correcting the church situations.

Conclusion

Both males and females, who are gifted with leadership gifts, bring advantages to leadership because of their genders. Both are needed to see a full range of effective leadership in churches. Should Christ's Second Coming be delayed, we will see further movement toward the ideal in these next years. Once God has moved His people to the ideal, looking back, they wonder how they could have ever held such sub-ideal positions as were held (think back on slavery and marriage). So it will be with gender and leadership.

See *giftedness; word gifts;* **Glossary**. See **Article**, *Starting-Point—Plus—Process Model*.. **See For Further Study Bibliography**, Clinton position paper entitled, *Gender and Leadership*, an extended treatment of this subject which also gives the author's journey and paradigm shifts which brought about this present understanding.

---

[50] Deborah is a case in point in the O.T. Priscilla, Phoebe, Syntyche, Euodias, Junia, Tryphena, and Tryphosa are fellow workers with Paul and are indications of movement toward the ideal.

[51] Luke's Gospel is particularly instructive along these lines. Jesus reaches out to gentiles and women upon numerous occasions in Luke's Gospel. See also, **Article**, *Jesus—Circles of Intimacy—A Developmental Technique*.

[52] See Ro 16:1,2 where Paul sponsors Phoebe as a minister of the Gospel.

[53] See Peterson's translation, in **The Message**, of 1Ti 3 where he recognizes female leadership in the contextual flow. I agree with his interpretation.

[54] I have studied all of these objections in depth. I have also read many present day authors who come down on both sides of the fence—those dead set against women as leaders and those who see women as leaders. I would expect that Paul would have written a very clear context placing men as leaders and showing that women cannot lead if that were the nature of the case. It is not. And Paul did not. His so called anti-women-in-leadership passages are really dealing with cultural church problems specific to those situations (Corinth, Ephesus). In my comments in the **Leadership Insights** in the leadership commentary on 1 Ti, I even give a paraphrase of the 1Ti 2 passage which reflects this notion of a specific cultural problem.

Article 18

Relevance of the Article to Paul's Corinthian Ministry

Churches today need leaders who understand about giving. They need leaders who are generous in their own personal giving. Paul's teaching on the notion of giving is a must for leaders today. He also exemplifies what it means to be a high level leader who is generous. This kind of modeling is desperately needed today. It is in 1,2 Co that we get the very heart of Paul's teaching on giving.

18. Giving—Paul's View

Introduction

Barnabas was a generous giving leader. He mentored Paul in the responsibilities of giving in their co-ministry time at Antioch.[55] Paul caught the vision for *grace giving*. In his ministry from then on, where ever he went he taught people to give freely and joyfully from the heart. His comprehensive treatment on giving occurs in 2Co 8,9. In the midst of defending his apostolic authority to the problematic church at Corinth, Paul presses them to give and lays out his principles for giving. He sent Titus to that church to help them give. 2Co 8,9 portray this apostolic function.

Apostolic workers must finance ministries they initiate and care for.[56]

Today's need for resources has not lessened from the early church days. In fact, it is probably greater today than in Paul's day. Generous leaders who can influence grace givers are much in demand.

Basic Principles of Giving—10 Guidelines

While not imposing the O.T. system of tithing, Paul does use the O.T. to validate the concept of Christian workers being financed from their ministries.[57] 2Co 8,9 give Paul's teaching on giving. Paul advocates giving to help fellow churches in need. He also advocates giving to help Christian workers (see footnotes on this in 1Co 9, 16 as well as Php 4:10-17). His strong exhortations on giving highlight a number of items. Table 1,2Co 18-1 gives 10 guidelines resulting from that exhortive teaching. All of these guidelines flow from the basic notion that giving is enabled by the grace of God in the life of a giver. Grace used in 2Co 8,9 refers to that enabling presence of God in a life which frees a believer to give generously.[58]

---

[55] I am certain that Paul was deeply affected by his mentor, Barnabas, concerning giving. See Acts 4:36,37; 11:27-30.

[56] See **Article**, *2. Apostolic Functions*. Apostolic workers raise finances for workers like Paul did for Timothy (1Co 16, 1Ti), Stephanus (1Co 16). They help out old works in special need (Ac 11, 1,2Co—Jerusalem church). Paul had Philippian church giving to other churches. He had Corinthian churches giving to needs in Jerusalem. They also provide workers to help out in situations like Timothy, Titus, etc. Part of the resourcing includes knowledge, wisdom and findings from related experience. They also help those with resources understand both their freedom and responsibility to use these for the kingdom (1Ti).

[57] See 1Co 9:3-7; 8-18.

[58] Grace carries essentially the sense of freedom; when used in a context describing salvation from God it implies that God freely gave us salvation without our earning or deserving it; when used to exhort continuing in the Christian life it carries the sense of the enabling presence of God in a life so as to free (enable) one to persevere victoriously. Paul uses it especially this way in his last epistles 1Ti, 2Ti, Tit. Peter does too 2Pe 3:18. And John also, Rev 22:21. It is interesting to observe that the three great church leaders in their closing words stress the importance of grace and its value in continuing in the Christian life. It is

18. Giving—Paul's View

Table 1,2Co 18-1. 10 Guidelines Underlying Paul's Thoughts on Giving

Guideline	Vs	Explanation
1. Inner Conviction	8:3; 9:5, 7	Christians should be led of God to give (purpose in their hearts). They should freely choose to give.
2. Proportionate	8:12	Christians give proportionately as God has blessed them (as opposed to the Old Testament's various tithes given out of duty).
3. Generous	9:6-9	Christians should give as generously as they can.
4. Joyfully	8:2	Christians give joyfully out of what they have.
5. Equalization	8:13,14	Christians should give to those in need out of their extra that God has supplied; they can expect the same thing to happen when they have need.
6. Supply	9:8-10	Christians should expect God to give them more than their needs which they can then give generously.
7. Planned	9:1-5	Collections should be done systematically over time so they will be ready when needed.
8. God Centered	9:13	God will receive honor and praise and thanksgiving from many who are helped;
9. Prayer Incentive	9:11,12, 14	Those helped will remember the givers in prayer with affection.
10. Financial Integrity	8:16-24.	There should be integrity in the handling of money given for various needs.

Ten General Reflections on 2Co 8,9

(1) It is interesting to note that the Philippian church gave joyfully. And this is even before the Philippian letter in which Paul so strongly urges them about joy. Notice two things about the Philippian Church mentioned here: (1) the Philippians had some self-initiative in this whole giving scenario; (2) they gave willingly. Paul uses the Philippian church as a model in order to motivate the Corinthian Christians to give. He has previously used the Corinthian *pledge to give* to stir up the Philippian church (2Co 9:1,2). So then Paul motivates churches to give by telling what others have done, particularly the values underlying their giving. He quickly shows that giving is not a matter of being rich. The Philippian church gave out of poverty. The key to their giving was to first surrender to the Lord. Once a group of people are surrendered to the Lord, they can give. And God will supply their needs.

(2) I have observed that churches that excel in giving, especially to the poor and to missions in general, are blessed of God. This is a real challenge to all churches and especially Christian organizations. Many Christian organizations ask and receive but don't give.

(3) Paul is open and above board even in his motivational techniques. He here tells the Corinthians that he is not commanding them (using an apostolic leadership style) but is strongly urging them and leaving the decision up to them (a form of obligation persuasion leadership style) while at the same time telling them they are being tested in their sincerity to other churches and their giving.

(4) In fund raising, leaders will, like Paul, have to repeatedly exhort, since initial enthusiasm for some projects does not always last. Note, however, that Paul does not badger. He gives his opinion, strongly, but leaves it up to them to obey and demonstrate their loyalty to him as well as their obedience to God.

(5) Another of Paul's motivational techniques is to appeal to Jesus' modeling (e.g. Php 2:5-11) which he does here. Peter (e.g. 1Pe 2:21) and John (1Jn 2:6) both also use this technique.

(6) A Pauline leadership value occurs here. *Financial Equality Principle: Christian leadership must teach that Christian giving is a reciprocal balancing between needs and surplus.* This equalizing principle, giving when we have abundance and others have need, and in turn receiving when we have needs and others have abundance, must be recognized, embraced, and then applied very carefully so as to not create dependencies. But for the most part western Christians don't realize just how wealthy they are when in comparison with many other non-western Christians. With no exposure to missions and churches around

---

also used by Paul as a metonymy (Corinthians and Romans) standing for spiritual gifts given freely by God.

18. Giving—Paul's View

the world, Christians will rarely ever really embrace this principle. Leaders must raise awareness levels about needs around the world as well as teach this principle (and model it in their own lives).

(7) Of the six barriers to leaders finishing well, improper handling of finances whether deliberately or just carelessly, is probably the number three barrier (illicit sexual relationships, abuse of power, and money problems, in that order. Usually two and three go together). Financial issues often waylay a leader. Note the special care to maintain integrity with regards to finances that Paul suggests in 1Co 16:3,4 and Ac 11:27-30 as well as here, 2Co 8:16-24.

(8) I believe 2Cor 9:8, to be a promise from God that is broader than just the Corinthians.[59] When believers give cheerfully and generously and to meet God-directed needs, I believe they can expect God to enrich them to give. I also believe the equalizing principle is in effect. If they give out of there overages they can expect help when they have need. The right kind of attitude is crucial however. They don't give to get. They give because God gives them grace to give and gives them liberal and joyous hearts to give. And they surrender themselves to God for this giving ministry through them. When this is done, I believe this promise is a good as gold.

(9) Paul uses Ps 112:9 to cite an underlying principle behind this promise. The meaning of this Hebrew poetry is that giving to the poor is a form of ultimate contribution—a legacy that will last

(10) As a leader Paul recognizes that he must, from time-to-time raise money for various needs. And so he does want to meet those needs. But at the same time he sees the importance of people learning about giving from a longer viewpoint—what it does for them (See also Php 4:17).

Conclusion

Paul raised funds for ministry. He used powerful motivational techniques to do this. He was always careful and maintained integrity in the handling of funds. Funds raised were carried by more than one worker, each a check for the other. Funds were used for what they were raised for. And Paul makes a strong point of raising money for needs other than his own personal needs. He never pushes his own needs but only those of other workers and ministries. He is careful to show that funds for himself are legitimate and flow from O.T. principles of supporting workers. But he never pushes his own needs. And his needs were met.

Paul is the dominant architect of the N.T. church. His views on giving should be strongly applied by church leaders today. Paul modeled giving. He was one of the most generous N.T. church leaders. Generous leaders are needed today.

---

[59] See **Article**, *55. Promises of God*.

Article 19

Relevance of the Article to Paul's Corinthian Ministry

Ample information on God's shaping activity is given on Paul. In fact, other than Jesus, David, and Moses, more information is given about Paul than any other Biblical leader. From that information much can be learned about how a leader is shaped by God in order to carry out God's purposes. Particularly do 1,2 Co enlighten us on deep processing—that is, the hard things that happen to a leader which mold his/her inner life in a way that could not happen apart from the pain involved. We can learn much from the shaping activity seen in Paul's life in 1,2 Co. Especially is it important that we grasp the 2 Co 1:3,4 value for our lives and ministries. While this article does not specifically identify Pauline processing, it gives the labels and definitions that can help us see what happened to Paul as God developed him.

19. God's Shaping Processes With Leaders

Introduction

One major leadership lesson derived from comparative study of effective leaders states,

Effective leaders see present ministry in light of a life time perspective.[60]

This article deals with God's shaping processes with a leader.[61] It gives important aspects of perspective that all leaders need. Six observations of God's shaping processes with leaders include the following.

1. God first works in a leader and then through that leader.
2. God intends to develop a leader to reach the maximum potential and accomplish those things for which the leader has been gifted.
3. God shapes or develops a leader over an entire lifetime.
4. A time perspective provides many keys. When using a time perspective, the life can be seen in terms of several time periods, each yielding valuable informative lessons. Each leader has a unique time-line describing his/her development.[62]
5. Shaping processes can be identified, labeled, and analyzed to contribute long lasting lessons.[63]

---

[60] I have identified seven which repeatedly occur in effective leaders: 1. Life Time Perspective—Effective Leaders View Present Ministry In Terms Of A Life Time Perspective. 2. Learning Posture—Effective Leaders Maintain A Learning Posture Throughout Life. 3. Spiritual Authority—Effective Leaders Value Spiritual Authority As A Primary Power Base. 4. Dynamic Ministry Philosophy—Effective Leaders Who Are Productive Over A Lifetime Have A Dynamic Ministry Philosophy Which Is Made Up Of An Unchanging Core And A Changing Periphery Which Expands Due To A Growing Discovery Of Giftedness, Changing Leadership Situations, And Greater Understanding Of The Scriptures. 5. Leadership Selection And Development—Effective Leaders View Leadership Selection And Development As A Priority Function In Their Ministry. 6. Relational Empowerment—Effective Leaders See Relational Empowerment As Both A Means And A Goal Of Ministry. 7. Sense Of Destiny—Effective Leaders Evince A Growing Awareness Of Their Sense Of Destiny. See the **Article**, *30. Leadership Lessons—Seven Major Identified*.

[61] See also the **Article**, *32. Leadership Selection* which gives an overview across time of the major benchmarks of God's development of a leader.

[62] See **Article**, *Time-Lines: Defined for Biblical Leaders*.

19. God's Shaping Processes With Leaders 146

6. An awareness of God's shaping processes can enhance a leader's response to these processes.

Figure 1,2 Co 19-1. Describes a generalized time line and some of the processes used by God over a lifetime.

I. Ministry Foundations	II. Early Ministry	III. Middle Ministry	IV. Latter Ministry	V. Finishing Well
• character shaping	• leadership committal • authority insights • giftedness discovery • guidance	• ministry insights • conflict • paradigm shifts • leadership backlash • challenges	• spiritual warfare • deep processing • power processes	• destiny fulfillment

Figure 1,2 Co 19-1. Some Major Shaping Processes Across The Time-Line

Shaping in Early Ministry —In and Then Through

Most younger emerging leaders in their initial exuberance for ministry feel they are accomplishing much. But in fact, God is doing much more in them than through them. The first years in ministry are tremendous learning years for a young leader who is sensitive to God's working in his/her life. God works on character first, even before a leader moves into full time leadership. Table 1,2 Co 19-1 lists four major shaping processes dealing with character and four major shaping processes dealing with early ministry.

Table 1,2 Co 19-1. Early Shaping Processes Identified and Defined

Type	Name	Explanation/ Biblical Example
Character	Integrity Check	A shaping process to test heart intent and consistency of inner beliefs and outward practice./ Daniel 1:3,4.
Character	Obedience Check	A shaping process to test a leader's will for obedience to God. /See Abraham, Ge 22.
Character	Word Check	A shaping process to test a leader's ability to hear from God./ See Samuel ch 3.
Character	Ministry Task	A shaping process to test a leader's faithfulness in performing ministry./ See Titus, Corinth trip (references in both 1,2 Co).
Foundational Ministry	Leadership Committal	A shaping process, part of Guidance, to recruit a leader into ministry and to continue to engage that leader along the ministry path destined for him/her. /See Paul, Ac 9,22,26.
Foundational Ministry	Authority Insights	A shaping process to help leaders learn how to deal with leaders over them and folks under them./ See Ac 13 Barnabas and Paul.
Foundational Ministry	Giftedness Discovery	A shaping process in which a leader learns about natural abilities, acquired skills, and spiritual gifts that God wants to use through that leader./ See Phillip, Ac 8.
Long Term Ministry	Guidance	A shaping process in which God intervenes in the life of a leader at critical points to direct that leader along the ministry path destined for him/her./ See Paul, Ac 16.

[63] See **For Further Study Bibliography**, Clinton's **Leadership Emergence Theory**, a self-study manual which gives detailed findings from research on God's shaping processes with leaders. This manual describes 50 shaping processes in detail. This article touches on only a few of these shaping processes.

19. God's Shaping Processes With Leaders

Shaping in Middle Ministry —Efficient Ministry

During middle ministry the leader now sees God working through as much as in the leader. Leaders identify giftedness. They learn how to influence; they are learning to lead. They gain many perspectives that channel their ministry toward effectiveness. Table 1,2 Co 19-2 lists some of the more important shaping processes that happen during this developmental phase.

Table 1,2 Co 19-2. Middle Ministry Shaping Processes—Identified and Defined

Type	Name	Explanation/ Biblical Example
Character/ Ministry	Conflict	A shaping process in which a leader learns perseverance, surfaces defects in character, gets new perspective on issues, and learns how to influence in less than ideal conditions./ See Paul, Ac 19 Ephesus.
Breakthroughs in Ministry	Paradigm Shifts	A shaping process in which God gives breakthrough insights that allow a broadening of perspective so as to propel the leader forward in ministry. /See Paul, Ac 9.
Character/ Ministry	Leadership Backlash	A shaping process in which a leader learns about follower reactions and about perseverance, hearing from God, and inspirational leadership./ See Moses, Ex 5.
Renewal/ Long Term	Challenges	A shaping process in which a leader is induced along the lines of new ministry; a part of the guidance process to take a leader along the life path. /See Paul and Barnabas, Ac 13.

Latter Ministry And Finishing Well—Effective Ministry

The essential difference between middle ministry and latter ministry has to do with focus.[64] In middle ministry the leader learns to be efficient in ministry—that is, to do things well. In latter ministry and the finishing well time the leader learns to be effective—that is, to do the right things well. There is a further deepening of character which enhances the leader's spiritual authority. There is a growing awareness of spiritual warfare. The leader learns to minister with power. Table 1,2 Co 19-3 lists some of the shaping processes that take place in the latter part of a leader's lifetime.

Table 1,2 Co 19-3. Latter Ministry Shaping Processes—Identified and Defined

Type	Name	Explanation/ Biblical Example
Deep Processing	Crises	A shaping process in which a leader's person or ministry is threatened with discontinuation; an overwhelming time in which the leader feels intense issues which could torpedo his/her whole ministry./ See Paul, 2Co.
Deep Processing	Isolation	A shaping process in which a leader is set aside from ministry and goes through a searching time about identity and a deepening trust of God./ See Paul, Php.
Long Term Guidance	Negative Preparation	A shaping process in which an accumulative effect of a number of negative things in the life and ministry of a leader is used by God to release that leader from some previous ministry and give freedom to enter another ministry./ See Paul, 2Co.
Long Term Guidance	Divine Contacts	A shaping process in which God uses some person in a timely fashion to intervene in a leader's life to give perspective—could be directed toward personhood, ministry, or long term guidance./ See Paul and Barnabas, Ac 9:27.
Long Term Guidance	Double Confirmation	A shaping process in which God gives clear guidance by inward conviction and by external conviction (unsought)./ See Paul and Ananias, Ac 9.
Effective Ministry	Power Issues	A group of shaping processes including power encounters, gifted power, networking power and prayer power. The leader learns balance between own effort and God's enabling through him/her. The leader learns to minister effectively with God's power./ See Elijah, 1Ki 18 et al.

---

[64] See **Article**, *Focused Life*.

19. God's Shaping Processes With Leaders

Conclusion

Awareness of these shaping processes allows a leader to combat the usually overwhelming attitude of *why me?* By seeing that these shaping processes occur in many leaders lives, leaders are affirmed that they are not way off base. It is part of God's way of developing a leader. A leader who understands what is happening in his/her life stands a better chance of responding to the processes and learning the lessons of God in them than one who is blindsided by these processes.

See Integrity *Check; Obedience Check; Word Check; Ministry Task; Leadership Committal; Authority Insights; Giftedness Discovery; Guidance; Conflict; Paradigm Shifts; Leadership Backlash; Faith Challenge; Leadership Challenge; Crises; Isolation; Negative Preparation; Divine Contacts; Double Confirmation; Power Encounters; Prayer Power; Gifted Power; Networking Power;* **Glossary**. See **Articles**, *59. Sovereign Mindset; 23. Isolation Processing—Learning Deep Lessons from God; 60. Spiritual Authority—Defined, Six Characteristics*. See **For Further Study Bibliography—The Making of A Leader; Leadership Emergence Theory;** *The Life Cycle of a Leader*.

Article 20

Relevance of the Article to Paul's Corinthian Ministry

Giftedness is a subject treated in 1 Co. Paul does not say anything explicitly about how apostles can impart gifts. His emphasis in 1 Co is on the ministry of the Holy Spirit in imparting gifts. In Ephesians, he emphases the role of Jesus in imparting gifts. In Ro it is God the Father who imparts gifts. So then the trinity is involved in the notion of impartation of giftedness. But what we do see in 1 Co is the clearest teaching on what the gifts are and what they do for the body. Paul certainly points out the importance of the apostolic gift. He is also attempting to solve the problem of highly exalting certain gifts over all other gifts (tongues in particular).

20. Impartation of Gifts—An Apostolic Function

Introduction

Paul alludes to a leadership concept not generally stressed except in some Pentecostal circles and in the new apostolic church movement. Note his words of admonition to his young mentoree, Timothy.

> Don't keep on neglecting your spiritual gift, which was given you by prophecy in conjunction with the laying on of the hands of the leaders. 1Ti 4:14

He reemphasizes this admonition in a later epistle to Timothy.

> Because of this I am reminding you, fan the flame of your God-given spiritual gift, which you received when I laid hands on you. 2Ti 1:6

Paul, in his apostolic role, apparently was led of God, when setting Timothy aside for ministry, to bless Timothy with a spiritual gift. We do not know exactly which one. He prophesied about this, that is, the gift and its use.

Laying on of hands, the means indicated by Paul in the above quotes, occurs in several passages. Table 1,2 Co 20-1 groups the basic functions involved with laying on of hands and gives some representative passages.

Table 1,2 Co 20-1. Passages—Laying On Of Hands

No.	Passage	Possible Implications
1	Ac 6:6, 13:3	Anointing leaders for service; public recognition, affirmation and backing.
2	Ac 8:17, Ac 9:17 et al	Impartation of Holy Spirit
3	Ac 9:12, 28:8	For healing
4	Heb 6:2	Unclear what the purpose is
5	1Ti 5:22	Leadership selection and recognition of same publicly
6	1Ti 1:14; 2Ti 1:6	Impartation of Gifts

Four functions identified with laying on of hands include: anointing for service in a public way which affirms the emerging leader; imparting the Holy Spirit for service; for healing; for impartation of gifts. This last function should be more widely applied today.

20. Impartation of Gifts

Spiritual Gifts

In his teaching on spiritual gifts in 1Co, Paul indicates that it is the Holy Spirit who imparts gifts to believers. In Ro Paul implies that it is God, the Father, who imparts gifts. In Eph he indicates that gifts are imparted by Christ. So then the entire Trinity is involved in imparting spiritual gifts to believers.[65] But in the passages above Paul indicates that as an apostle, when prompted by the Holy Spirit (prophetic gift), he can impart a needed spiritual gift to a leader who is being set aside for ministry. These passages reveal the human side of impartation of spiritual gifts, at least one way that the Trinity imparts gifts.

Leaders today, particularly those with the gift of apostleship,[66] ought to be aware of the needed gifts for the ministry they are sending leaders into. So then, when selecting leaders and sending them into service Apostles ought to impart the needed gifts to them. This is not an abuse of power[67] but a responsibility of partnering with God in an endeavor. Speaking a word of faith about a gift for a leader ought to be the fruit of mature apostleship.

Conclusion

In any case a leader must remember Paul's final admonition to Timothy involving laying on of hands.

> Don't hastily lay hands on any person for leadership; neither be partaker of other's sins.
> 1Ti 5:22

Character in the emerging leader ought to be founded well before impartation of gifts. Nevertheless, it will take gifted power to break through in the post-modern world we face. Apostles should impart these needed break-through gifts to choice young leaders.

See *spiritual gifts, various definition of spiritual gifts*, **Glossary**. See **Article**, *Developing Giftedness*.

---

[65] In my opinion it is unclear, biblically speaking, when spiritual gifts are actually imparted. Possibilities include: at time of conversion and hence the initial receiving of the Holy Spirit; at an infilling of the Holy Spirit at some later time after conversion; when needed.

[66] The following gifts also would stimulate this impartation: faith, prophecy, word of knowledge.

[67] Motivation in this is a key. See Simon in Ac 8:18,19 who for his own use in an improper way wanted to get the power to lay hands on people and impart the Holy Spirit to them. I am talking about a mature apostleship gift which is being used in a discerning way with God's plans for the ministry involved.

Article 21

Relevance of the Article to Paul's Corinthian Ministry

Paul had tremendous spiritual authority in his ministry to the churches that he had planted. In fact, he had no positional power at all. However, when dealing with problems in the Corinthian church Paul demonstrated the use of other influence means in addition to spiritual authority. In fact, his spiritual authority was being called into question. The following adapted taxonomy from Dennis Wrong is helpful in understanding the need for all kinds of influence, power, and authority means in order to exert effective leadership. Paul does that—uses various influence means in order to get the Corinthians back on track.

21. Influence, Power, and Authority

Introduction

A major lesson concerning how a leader ought to influence states:

Effective leaders value spiritual authority as a primary power base.

To understand this important principle we need to define some terms. The terms that are used to describe leadership make a difference in how we see leadership. Three important terms are influence, power, and authority. Sometimes these important terms are used interchangeable in leadership literature. I use a simplified adaptation of Dennis Wrong's[68] basic schema for relating these concepts—though I have adapted it to fit my understanding of spiritual authority. Influence is the most embracing of the concepts. Power is intended use of influence. And authority is one kind of power usually associated with tight organizations.[69] Below, in Figure 1,2 Co 21-1, is given the adapted tree diagram.

---

[68] See Dennis Wrong, **Power--Its Forms, Bases, and Uses**. San Francisco, CA: Harper and Row, 1979. This is a brilliant treatment involving definitions of power concepts as well as recognition of how these forms change over time. His analysis gave a complicated taxonomy which I have simplified and adapted.

[69] Christian organizations operate on a continuum from tight to loose. The more loose an organization is the more it is characterized by voluntary workers who are not paid to do some job but do it because they want to. Therefore leaders in loose organizations do not have as much authority as those in tight organizations which are characterized by paid workers, structures levels of leadership, and supervisory responsibility (that is, people have bosses who can fire them if they don't submit to authority).

21. Influence Power and Authority

```
                    INFLUENCE
                     can be
            ┌───────────┴───────────┐
        Unintended            Intended = POWER
                            which has forms such as
              ┌──────────┬──────────┬──────────┐
            Force  Manipulation  Authority  Persuasion
                        ┌─────┬─────┬─────┬─────┐
                    coercive induced legitimate competent personal
                              │
                     various forms of
                     organizational
                     authority

                              Spiritual Authority
    ←──────────────→          ←──────────────→
    Involuntary Reception      Voluntary Reception
       of Influence              of Influence
```

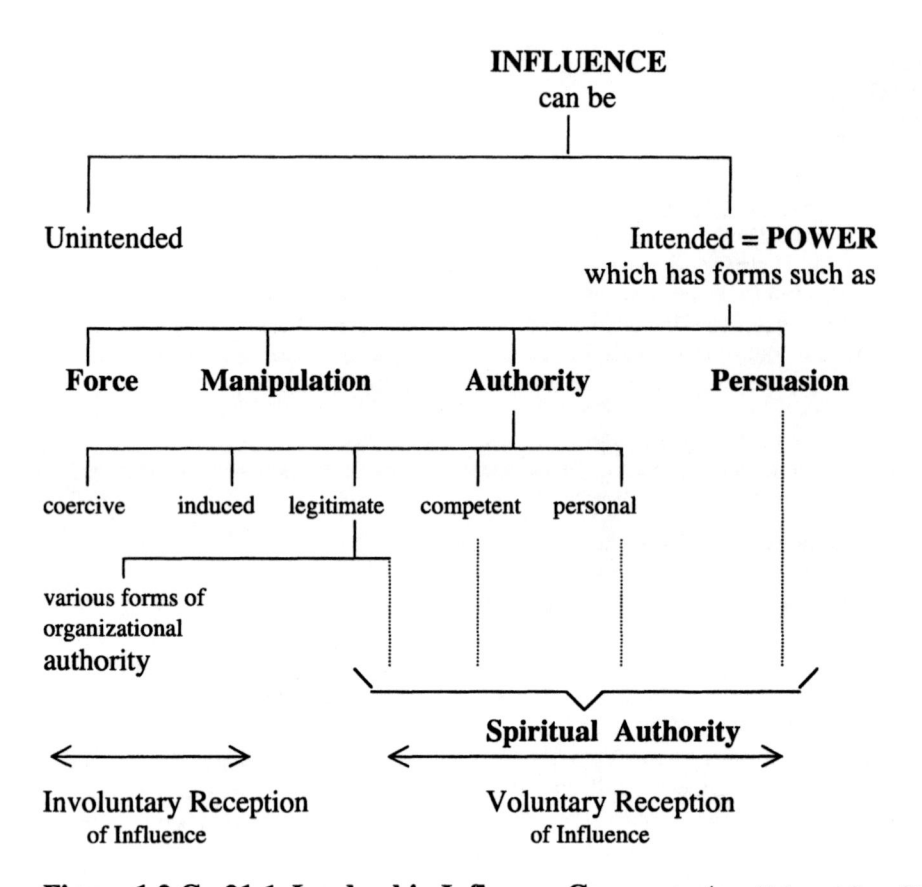

Figure 1,2 Co 21-1. Leadership Influence Components — (Adapted from Wrong)

Explanation

Leaders are people with God-given capacities and God-given responsibilities who are influencing specific groups of people toward God's purposes for them. They are intentional in their use of means to influence, meaning using deliberate power forms. When we describe such leaders we are coming down the right side of the diagram in Figure 1,2 Co 21-1. Leaders have a right to influence. The ability to influence comes through the control of power bases.

Definition   Power base refers to the source of credibility, power differential, or resources which enables a leader (*power holder*) to have authority to exercise influence on followers (*power subjects*).

Definition   Authority refers to the right to exercise leadership influence by a leader over followers with respect to some field of influence.

Power is manifested in power forms which bring about compliance. The four major power forms in our tree diagram include FORCE, MANIPULATION, AUTHORITY, AND PERSUASION. Authority is further sub-divided into coercive, induced, legitimate, competent, and personal. Spiritual authority is a hybrid combination of persuasion and legitimate, competent, and personal authority.

Power forms depend upon power bases. Bases come from power resources—those individual and collective assets such as organization, money, reputation, personal appeal, manipulative skills, interpersonal skills, kinds of knowledge, information, indwelling Holy Spirit, giftedness.

The central concept of authority is the right to exercise influence. That right is recognized both by leader and follower. It is based upon common assumptions about the *field of influence*. For a spiritual

21. Influence Power and Authority

leader the *field of influence* has to do with God's purposes and His directions for accomplishing specific aims that He reveals. Morality, corporate guidance, and clarification of truth are three aspects within the *field of influence* which define the leader's range of use of authority.

Table 1,2 Co 21-1 details a number of important concepts that help clarify how a leader influences.

Table 1,2 Co 21-1. Influence, Power, Authority Concepts Defined

Influence, Power, Authority Concepts	Description
Power forms	Power forms refer to four general terms of influence means: force, manipulation, authority, and persuasion.
Force	A force power form refers to the use of physical and psychic influence means to gain compliance. This form is now rarely used by spiritual leaders though historically it has been used.
Manipulation	A manipulative power form refers to any influence means whereby a leader gains compliance of a follower where the follower does not have awareness of the leader's intents and therefore does not necessarily have freedom to exert moral responsibility in the situation.[70]
Authority	An authority power form refers to influence means such as: coercive authority, induced authority, legitimate authority, competent authority, personal authority and spiritual authority. See definitions which follow in this Table.
Persuasion	A persuasive power form refers to any influence means such as arguments, appeals or exhortations whereby the leader gains compliance of the follower yet protects the freedom of the follower to exercise moral responsibility.
Coercive Authority	Coercive authority is the form of power in which a leader obtains compliance by using influence means such as threat of force or of punishment.
Induced Authority	Induced authority is the form of power in which a leader obtains compliance by using influence means of promise of reward or some gain for the follower.
Legitimate Authority	Legitimate authority is the form of power in which a leader obtains compliance by using influence pressure consonant with common expectations of the role or positions held by the follower and leader.
Competent Authority	Competent authority is the form of power in which a leader obtains or can expect (but not demand) compliance by virtue of acknowledged expertise in some field of endeavor. The authority is limited to that field of endeavor.
Personal Authority	Personal authority is the form of power in which a leader obtains or expects compliance (but can not demand it) by virtue of the follower's recognition of the leader's personal characteristics.

Machiavelli[71] posited two real ultimate motivations: fear and love. For him, fear was the stronger of the two and hence a vital part of effective leadership. Jesus advocated love as the stronger. On the power continuum, those forms to the left of inducement all utilize the motivation of fear—they are categorized by

---

[70] Manipulation in general usually has only negative connotations in western societies since it usually implies influencing against one's wishes. While it is true that manipulation is usually bad, it does not have to be so. The definition above is neutral. It is the motivation behind and the ultimate purpose of the influence that is the key.

[71] His views were published in the classic, **The Prince**.

the notion of involuntary reception of influence. Those from induced authority to the right all have in essence love as the primary motivation. They are categorized by the notion of voluntary reception of influence.

Hersey and Blanchard[72] give terms which help us understand further the *competent* authority form. They use the term *expert* to indicate a person who has expertise, skill and knowledge about something so as to command respect from followers. In addition, they define *information* to indicate the leader's possession of information that is valuable to followers. Competent power includes this as well. From a Christian standpoint, giftedness—a God-given capacity—fits under competent power.

Two terms from Hersey and Blanchard help us understand further the *personal* power sub-form. *Referent* power is a type of power based on the leader's personal traits. Such a leader is usually liked and admired by others because of personality, sincerity, or the like. *Modeling* describes the Christian equivalent of this form. Follower are influenced by leaders they admire. They want to emulate them. *Connection* power refers to a type of power that arises because a leader has connections to influential or powerful people. In leadership emergence theory this is called networking power.

Leaders will need the entire range of power forms and authority forms in order to lead followers. It is helpful to know this as well as the negative and positive aspects of these forms.[73]

Understanding Spiritual Authority Via Influence, Power, and Authority Concepts

Now we can examine that major trans-Biblical lesson I stated earlier.

Effective Leaders Value Spiritual Authority As A Primary Power Base.

While it will take a whole range of power forms to accomplish God's purposes to take immature followers to maturity, it should be the goal of spiritual leaders to move people toward the right on the power continuum so that they voluntarily accept leadership and follow for mature reasons.[74] So, leaders who are concerned with developing followers should be continually using spiritual authority whenever possible. From our diagram in Figure 1,2 Co 21-1, spiritual authority is defined as a hybrid power form which includes influence via persuasion and authority, especially competent and personal. Legitimate authority frequently helps supplement spiritual authority but does not guarantee it. Notice the voluntary aspect of the spiritual authority definition.

Definition   Spiritual authority is the right to influence conferred upon a leader by followers because of their perception of spirituality in that leader.

An expanded clarification of this definition describes spiritual authority further as that characteristic of a God-anointed leader, which is developed upon an experiential power base that enables him/her to influence followers through:

1. Persuasion (a major power form),
2. Force of modeling (fits under the personal authority form) and
3. Moral expertise (fits under the competent authority form).

Spiritual authority comes to a leader in three major ways. As leaders go through deep experiences with God they experience the sufficiency of God to meet them in those situations. They come to know God. This *experiential knowledge of God and the deep experiences with God* are part of the experiential acquisition of spiritual authority. A second way that spiritual authority comes is through a life which *models godliness*. When the Spirit of God is transforming a life into the image of Christ, those

---

[72] See Paul Hersey and Ken Blanchard, **Management of Organizational Behavior--Utilizing Human Resources.** Englewood Cliffs, N.J.: Prentice-Hall, 1977.

[73] See Dennis Wrong, **Power--Its Forms, Bases, and Uses.** New York: Harper and Row, 1979. He gives an excellent treatment of definitions as well as the dynamics of the forms. When certain forms are overused they tend to change to other types of forms.

[74] This is the model God uses with us as believers. He can force us to do things and sometimes does, but He always prefers for us to willingly obey.

21. Influence Power and Authority

characteristics of love, joy, peace, long suffering, gentleness, goodness, faith, meekness, temperance carry great weight in giving credibility that the leader is consistent inward and outward. Both of these sources of spiritual authority reflect themselves dominantly via the personal authority form. A third way that spiritual authority comes is through *gifted power*. When a leader can demonstrates gifted power—that is, a clear testimony to divine intervention in the ministry—there will be spiritual authority. This source of spirituality buttresses the competent authority form. While all three of these ways of getting spiritual authority should be a part of a leader, it is frequently the case that one or more of the elements dominates.

Conclusion

Some closing observations on spiritual authority are worth noting:

1. Spiritual authority is the ideal form of influence that should be used by leaders.
2. Because of the responsibility of leaders, that is, they must influence—it will require more than just spiritual authority as a power base because of immature followers who cannot recognize spiritual authority.
3. Leaders must develop followers in maturity so that they can more sensitively see God's use of spiritual authority in a leader.
4. Leaders who do not develop followers in maturity will find they have to use the less ideal forms of power (coercive, inducive, legitimate) more often.
5. These forms tend to degenerate toward the left on the continuum becoming less effective over time. This in turn often drives a leader to abuse his/her authority because of the need to force influence.
6. Spiritual authority, like any of the authority forms, can be abused.
7. Mature leaders never abuse spiritual authority.
8. Spiritual authority is ideally used to build up followers and carry out God's purposes for them.
9. Leaders should treasure deep processing with God, knowing that God will use it to develop their spiritual authority.
10. Giftedness alone, even when backed by unusual power, is not a safe source of spiritual authority. Giftedness backed by godliness is the more balanced safe source of spiritual authority.

Jesus led almost totally by spiritual authority. Paul, having to deal frequently with immature believers, uses almost the whole range of authority forms. However, whenever Paul can he uses spiritual authority. Both of these models set the pattern for Christian leaders.

An awareness of what spiritual authority is and how it relates to the basic ways a leader influences forms a solid foundation upon which to move toward spiritual authority.

Effective Leaders Value Spiritual Authority As A Primary Power Base.

Do you value spiritual authority? Are you using it to influence specific groups of God's people toward His purposes for them?

See **Articles,** *49. Pauline Leadership Styles, 60. Spiritual Authority—Defined, Six Characteristics.*

Article 22

Relevance of the Article to Paul's Corinthian Ministry
Paul demonstrates integrity in his Corinthian ministry. Integrity is the top leadership quality—see Paul's leadership lists in 1 Tim 2 and Titus 1 for his emphasis on integrity and character. In the 2 Co epistle Paul especially reveals his inner values and shows how they are consistent with his practice, both in the past with the Corinthian church and these letters written to them to help them get back on track. It is this consistency between inner values and outward behavior which is at the heart of integrity. This article should be read by every emerging leader. For it is usually some character issue, not ministry skills, that causes failure in ministry and leads to a poor finish. Integrity is at the heart of character.

22. Integrity—A Top Leadership Quality

Introduction

I have been repeating a number of times in the leadership commentary, for a number of books, a major leadership principle.

Ministry flows out of being.

Being is a term describing a number of factors which refer to the inner life and essence of a person. It refers to at least the following, but is not limited to them: (1) intimacy with God; (2) character; (3) personality; (4) giftedness; (5) destiny; (6) values drawn from experience; (7) conscience, and (8) gender influenced perspectives. The axiom, ministry flows out of being means that one's ministry should be a vital outflow from these inner beingness factors.

It is integrity, the rudder that steers character, that I want to highlight in this discussion. Consider the following two words:

1. deception noun 1.The use of deceit. 2.The fact or state of being deceived. 3. A ruse; a trick. [adapted from The American Heritage Dictionary of the English Language, Third Edition, 1992.] **Synonyms**: trickery, gulling, lying, juggling, craftiness. **Antonyms**: sincerity, frankness, honesty, openness, truthfulness, trustworthiness, genuineness, earnestness, innocence, candor, veracity, verity, probity, fidelity.

2. integrity The uncompromising adherence to a code of moral, artistic or other values which reveals itself in utter sincerity, honesty, and candor and avoids deception or artificiality (Adapted from Webster). **Synonyms**: honesty, virtue, honor, morality, uprightness, righteousness. Antonyms: deception, dishonesty, corruption, infidelity.

The words are opposite.

Few leaders finish well.[75] Most major failures in ministry are dominantly rooted in spiritual formation issues (spirituality) rather than ministerial formation and strategic formation issues.[76] Most of these failures

---

[75] Of the Biblical leaders for whom there is evidence about finishing well, about one in three finish well. Probably it is even less for contemporary leaders if anecdotal evidence means anything. What do I mean by finish well? I have identified six characteristics of finishing well from a comparative study of leaders who finished well. A given leader will not necessarily demonstrate all six but at least several. These six characteristics include the following: (1) They maintain a personal vibrant relationship with God right up to the end. (2) They maintain a learning posture and can learn from various kinds of sources—life especially.

22. Integrity—A Top Leadership Quality

can ultimately be traced to basic failures of integrity.[77] Leaders who fail often do not have integrity but instead have some sort of deception about at least some of their leadership. On the other hand, leaders who finish well, across the board are leaders of integrity.

Let me remind you of the definition of a Christian leader: A Christian leader is a person with a God-given capacity and a God-given responsibility who is influencing a specific group of God's people toward God's purposes for the group. You cannot influence a group very effectively if they don't trust you. And if you are suspected of trickery, gulling, mendacity, juggling, craftiness—they won't trust you and you won't lead them.

At the heart of any assessment of biblical qualifications for leadership lies the concept of integrity—that uncompromising adherence to a code of moral, artistic or other values which reveals itself in utter sincerity, honesty, and candor and avoids deception or artificiality. So if we want to be leaders who finish well we want to be people of integrity. What is integrity? How do we get it?

Definition	<u>Integrity</u>, the top leadership character quality, is the consistency of inward beliefs and convictions with outward practice. It is an honesty and wholeness of personality in which one operates with a clear conscience in dealings with self and others.

God develops integrity in leaders. It is at the heart of character. A repeated observation on leaders whom God developed and used for his purposes resulted in the following helpful definition.

Definition	An <u>integrity check</u> refers to the special kind of shaping activity (a character test) which God uses to evaluate heart–intent, consistency between inner convictions and outward actions, and which God uses as a foundation from which to expand the leader's capacity to influence. The word check is used in the sense of test—meaning a check or check-up.

I'll come back to this notion of an integrity check and give detailed information on it. But first think with me about Biblical leaders and the notion of integrity.

Biblical Leaders of Integrity

If I were to ask you to name the top two O.T. leaders who demonstrated integrity, who would you suggest? If I were to ask you to name the top two N.T. leaders who demonstrate integrity, who would you suggest?

My top two O.T. leaders who demonstrated integrity are Joseph and Daniel. My top two N.T. leaders who demonstrated integrity are Jesus and Paul (Barnabas is a close second behind Paul).

Both Joseph and Daniel exemplify leaders who were tested by God as to their integrity and passed with flying colors. Joseph in Gen 39 refuses to have an affair with Potiphar's wife. He sees this as wrong. In fact, he states that to do so would be sin against God. God honors this stand and later elevates Joseph to the top administrative post in Egypt (under the Pharaoh). Daniel in Da 1 is tested as to integrity with regard to eating food unacceptable to a Jew. He stands on his convictions. He too is blessed by God and becomes a

---

(3) They manifest godliness (especially Christ-like attitudes and behavior) in character as evidenced by the fruit of the Spirit in their lives. (4) Truth is lived out in their lives so that convictions and promises of God are seen to be real. (5) They leave behind one or more ultimate contributions. (6) They walk with a growing awareness of a sense of destiny and see some or all of it fulfilled.

[76] <u>Spiritual formation</u> is the shaping activity in a leader's life which is directed toward instilling godly character and developing inner life (i.e. intimacy with God, character, values drawn from experience, conscience). <u>Strategic formation</u> is the shaping activity in a leader's life which is directed toward having that leader reach full potential and achieve a God-given destiny. <u>Ministerial formation</u> is the shaping activity in a leader's life which is directed toward instilling leadership skills, leadership experience, and developing giftedness for ministry.

[77] Studies of leaders who have failed to finish well has identified six major barriers to their finishing well. These include: finances—their use and abuse; power—its abuse; inordinate pride—which leads to a downfall; sex—illicit relationships; family—critical issues; plateauing. At the very heart of most of these major barriers lies an integrity issue.

22. Integrity—A Top Leadership Quality

high administrator under Nebuchadnezzar and eventually becomes the number one administrator under Darius. Jesus throughout his whole ministry demonstrates integrity, always showing unity between outward practice and inward conviction. (See especially the Satanic temptations in Mt 4.) Paul writes a whole epistle defending his integrity. He was being accused of all kinds of deception: lying, craftiness, dishonesty, trickery. The book of 2Co reveals Paul's answers to the accusations of deception. A major Pauline leadership value emerges in 2Co.

Label	Statement of Value
Integrity and Openness	*Leaders should not be deceptive in their dealings with followers but should instead be open, honest, forthright, and frank with them.*

Paul, throughout 2Co, refutes the accusations of deception in his leadership and lays out for us many principles underlying integrity in a leader.

Paul's instruction to Timothy in 1Ti about leadership qualifications should be noted here. His qualifications for leaders includes character and conscience. Paul's list of qualifications focuses on integrity and deals mainly with character not giftedness. See his three lists[78] in 1Ti 3:1-7; 8-10; 11-13. All three lists emphasize integrity. And this integrity should be seen by those outside the church as well as those within.

Integrity Check Revisited

God uses life situations to test and build up the inner character of a leader. Integrity is one of the main qualities God shapes in a leader. The *integrity check* is a major way this happens. From comparative study (e.g. Daniel in Da 1,5; Shadrach, Meshach, and Abednego in Da 3; Joseph in Gen 39; Abraham in Gen 24; Jephthah in Jdg 11; Paul in Ac 20:22,23 and many others), a list of kinds of integrity checks can be identified. And their use by God can be suggested. Table 1,2 Co 22-1 gives the kinds of integrity checks. Table 1,2 Co 2 lists their uses.

Table 1,2 Co 22-1. Kinds of Integrity Checks

Label	Explanation
temptation (conviction test)	An integrity check frequently is given to allow a leader to identify an inner conviction and to take a stand on it. Such a stand will deepen the conviction in the leader's life. Can a leader really take a stand on some conviction?
restitution (honesty testing)	Some integrity checks force a leader to make right things done wrong in the past, particularly those with on-going ramifications. This is particularly seen in money matters where in the past someone was defrauded. Will a leader be honest, especially about the past?
value check (ultimate value clarification)	Situations frequently force leaders to think through their beliefs about something so that they can identify explicitly a value(s). This value once identified can be evaluated. It can be used more strongly. It may be modified. It may be discarded as not really valid. Can a leader identify the underlying value in a situation?
loyalty (allegiance testing)	God must be first in a life. Frequently, other things become first in a leader's life with perhaps it not even being known by the leader. God can bring to light those things which take His rightful place in our hearts and lives. Who is really first in our lives?

---

[78] These three lists are apparently list idioms in which the initial item on the list is the main assertion and other items illustrate or clarify the primary item. If so, then the major leadership trait is integrity, a moral characteristic implying a consistency between inner and outer life. The items on the list would then illustrate in the Ephesian culture what moral character, integrity, looks like. So then these items in themselves are not necessarily universal characteristics for a leader but are indicative of what moral character and integrity look like in this culture. The obligatory item is inner integrity, moral character. Paul concludes this small section in vs 7 by returning to this important idea to reemphasize it. This is repeated in descriptions of the lesser leader lists described in vs 8-10, 11-13. Note especially vs 8 and 11. See *list idiom*, **Glossary**.

22. Integrity—A Top Leadership Quality

Guidance (alternative testing—a better offer after Holy Spirit led commitment to some course of action)	Frequently a leader is led by God to declare for a certain thing (a ministry, a choice, some option). It is clear that God has led the leader to that choice. After making the choice God may well bring an alternative which looks easier or better simply to test the follow-through on the original decision. Can a leader stick to God's former sure guidance when other challenging guidance comes along?
conflict against ministry vision (guidance/faith testing)	Frequently, a leader will be led into a situation and even have follower support in it. But down the line in the midst of the decision being worked out, particularly when negative ramifications arise, followers or others will oppose the situation. Conflict arises. Note that conflict is a mighty weapon in the hand of God. Usually this integrity check will enforce faith in the leader. Can a leader maintain guidance and believe God will under gird some ministry vision?
word conflict or obedience conflict (complexity testing usually in guidance)	Sometimes a leader will get a word from God or be challenged to obey God in some particular way. Usually this has to do with guidance. Conflict arises as in the previous description. Can a leader trust in his/her ability to hear from God? Or will a leader obey, even if conflict arises?

Table 1,2 Co 22-2. The Ways that God Uses Integrity Checks

Identifying Label	Why It Is Used
Follow Through	to see follow-through on a promise or vow
Deepening Burden	to insure burden for a ministry or vision
Edification	to allow confirmation of inner-character strength
Faith Builder	to build faith
Value Clarifying	to establish inner values very important to later leadership which will follow
Lordship	to teach submission
Warnings	to warn others of the seriousness of obeying God

Often the integrity check happens completely unknown to people around the leader. That is because of its inward nature. The secondary causes may be events, people, etc. They may not even know that they are sources. The primary causal source is inward through the conscience. The Holy Spirit shapes the conscience.[79]

There is a three step pattern to an integrity check which is passed positively: (1) the challenge to consistency with inner convictions, (2) the response to the challenge, and (3) the resulting expansion. Sometimes the expansion may be delayed or take place over a period of time but it can definitely be seen to stem from the integrity check. Delayed expansion is seen in Joseph's classic test with Potiphar's wife. Immediate expansion is seen in Daniel's wine test.[80]

There is also a three part pattern to an integrity check which is failed: (1) the challenge to consistency with inner convictions, (2) the response to the challenge, and (3) the remedial testing. God will frequently repeat an integrity check until a leader gets it or will take more drastic action. Instead of remedial testing there may be discipline, or setting aside from ministry, or even death.

Conclusion

Character is crucial to leadership. Integrity is the foundational trait of character in a leader. Let me summarize some observations, principles and values suggested by the importance of integrity in a leader.

a. Ministry flows out of being of which character is a major component and integrity the dominant necessary leadership trait within character.
b. Leaders without character cannot be trusted and will be followed only to the extent that they have coercive power to back up their leadership claims.

---

[79] Conscience refers to the inner sense of right or wrong which is innate in a human being but which also is modified by values imbibed from a culture. This innate sense can also be modified by the Spirit of God. See **Article**, *7. Conscience, Paul's Use of*.
[80] See testing *patterns, positive and negative*, **Glossary**. See **Article**, *Daniel Four Positive Testing Patterns*.

22. Integrity—A Top Leadership Quality

    c. A leader must be conscious of what others think of him/her, character-wise. Integrity is universal and occurs in every culture as a notion. But it will take on cultural manifestations peculiar to a culture that demonstrate to those in the culture what integrity is.[81]

    d. A leader must seek to have a testimony respected by others (within the bounds of God's ministry assignments).[82]

    e. Even though the source of some character trial may be Satanic, a leader should use it to purge impure character traits and rest in God's overriding purposes through the testing.[83]

    f. A leader should recognize that character integrity checks will be used by God as foundational training for increased usefulness.[84]

Do the people you influence see you as deceptive or a person of integrity? Do the people outside your ministry see you as deceptive or a person of integrity? Conscience is the inner governor of character—and especially integrity. Remember Paul's challenging statement.

> **Because I believe in an ultimate accounting before God, I make every effort always to keep my conscience clear before God and man. Ac 24:16**

---

[81] For example, oath-keeping was a high value of integrity in the Hebrew O.T.

[82] Paul repeats this notion over and over in 1Ti when advising Timothy about his consulting ministry with the Ephesian church.

[83] Job shows us that behind the apparent things happening to us there may be an unseen spiritual source causing it (Satanic). But even where bad things happen, God can use them to shape character.

[84] A basic understanding of integrity checks can aid one in recognizing much earlier and giving a godly response to them. Forewarned is forearmed.

Article 23

Relevance of the Article to Paul's Corinthian Ministry

Crucial lessons, which will drastically affect forever a leader's life and ministry are learned through deep processing. One such deep process, a major shaping activity used by God is isolation processing. Paul experienced numerous isolation processing incidents. The most prominent of the isolation processing was his final imprisonment and trials that lasted for several years. Paul learned valuable lessons about dependency upon God. This article treats the notion of isolation processing in general. Paul certainly experienced it—note especially 2 Co 1 where he had a near death experience.

23. Isolation Processing—Learning Deep Lessons From God

Introduction

Leaders get set aside from ministry. Isolation is the term used to describe this process. Sometimes the leader is directly set aside by God, sometimes by others, sometimes by self. Whatever the case, isolation results in deep processing in the life of a leader. More than 90% of leaders will face one or more important isolation times in their lives. Most do not negotiate these times very well. Knowing about them and what God can accomplish in them can be a great help to a leader who then faces isolation.

Defining and Describing Isolation
   What is isolation?

Definition   Isolation processing refers to the setting aside of a leader from normal ministry or leadership involvement due to involuntary causes, partially self-caused or voluntary causes for a period of time sufficient enough to cause and/or allow serious evaluation of life and ministry.

Some notable Biblical examples include Job, Joseph, Moses, Jonah, Elijah, Habakkuk, Jesus, Paul. Usually this means the leader is away from his/her natural context usually for an extended time in order to experience God in a new or deeper way. Sometimes isolation can occur in the ministry context itself.

Isolation experiences can be short—like intensive time spent away in solitude to meet God. Or it can last up to several months and occasionally more than a year. Figure 1,2 Co 23-1 describes isolation in terms of three major categories.

23. Isolation Processing—Learning Deep Lessons From God

Three Major Categories Of Isolation
Include

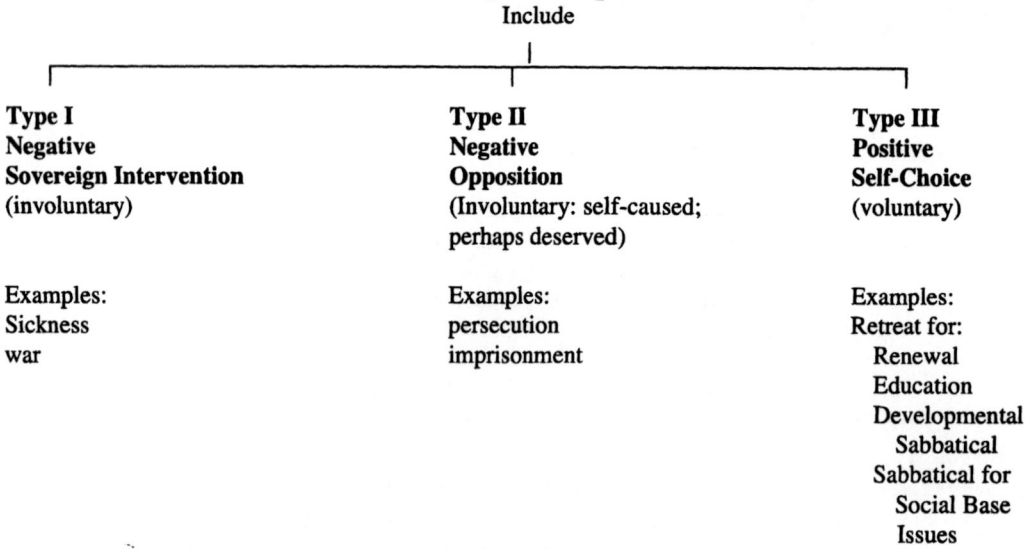

Type I	Type II	Type III
Negative	Negative	Positive
Sovereign Intervention	Opposition	Self-Choice
(involuntary)	(Involuntary: self-caused; perhaps deserved)	(voluntary)
Examples:	Examples:	Examples:
Sickness	persecution	Retreat for:
war	imprisonment	Renewal
		Education
		Developmental
		Sabbatical
		Sabbatical for Social Base Issues

Figure 1,2 Co 23-1. Three Types of Isolations

These isolation experiences can be viewed in terms of perceived intervention of God in them. Figure 1,2 Co 23-2 gives a continuum correlating the isolation experiences to a leader's understanding of God's place in them.

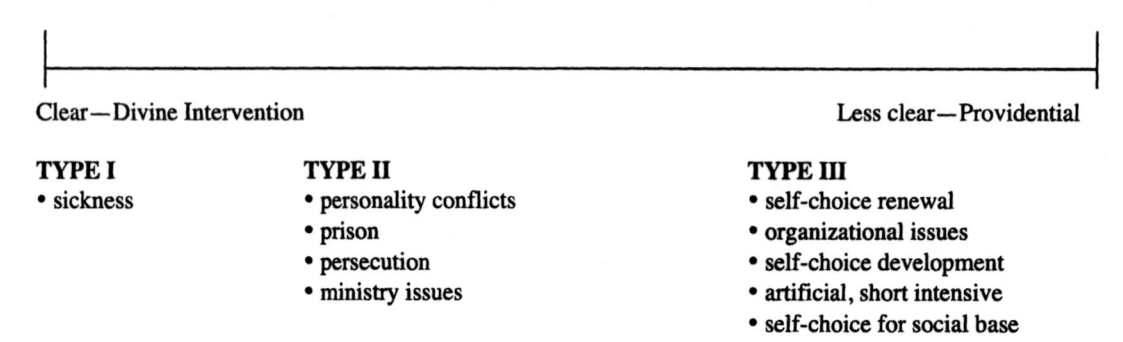

Clear—Divine Intervention　　　　　　　　　　　　　　　　　　　　Less clear—Providential

TYPE I
- sickness

TYPE II
- personality conflicts
- prison
- persecution
- ministry issues

TYPE III
- self-choice renewal
- organizational issues
- self-choice development
- artificial, short intensive
- self-choice for social base

Figure 1,2 Co 23-2. Isolation Sovereignty Continuum

Table 1,2 Co 23-1 list some results that have been observed in comparative studies of leaders in isolation.

Table 1,2 Co 23-1. Isolation Results

Isolation Type	Results or Uses of Isolation
I. Negative/ Sovereign Intervention	lessons of brokenness; learning about supernatural healing; lessons about prayer; deepening of inner life; an intensified sense of urgency to accomplish; developing of mental facilities; submission to God; dependence upon God.
II. Negative/ Opposition	lessons of brokenness; submission to spiritual authority; value of other perspectives; dependence upon God
III. Positive/ Self-choice	new perspective on self and ministry; rekindling of sense of destiny; guidance; oneself to change; upon wider body of Christ

23. Isolation Processing—Learning Deep Lessons From God

Overlapping Features in Many Isolation Experiences
Table 1,2 Co 23-2 lists some common things that happen to leaders in isolation.

Table 1,2 Co 23-2. Common Happenings in Isolation

Isolation Type	Some Happenings
I or II	1. Sense of Rejection
I or II	2. Sense of stripping away--getting down to core issues
I, II or III	3. Eventually a deep need for God
I, II or III	4. Searching for God
I, II, or III	5. Submission to God
I, II, or III	6. Dependence upon God
I, II, or III	7. Rekindling of desire to serve God in a deeper way

Bible Characters and Isolation Lessons From Their Lives
Job, Moses, Elijah, and Paul provide some important isolation lessons. See the Tables, which follow listing each of these Bible Characters and observations about isolation.

Job
Job faced sickness, loss of life, loss of wealth, loss of friends, and loss of status as an important person. Table 1,2 Co 23-3 suggests some things that can be learned from Job's Type I isolation experience.

Table 1,2 Co 23-3. Job and Type I Isolation

Step	Explanation
1.	**Begin With The End In Mind** (need a framework/ perspective). In isolation, deep-seated ideas are challenged in such a way as to capture our attention and force us to come to essential values. Maybe it is only in isolation that they could be challenged. But know that isolation will end and God will teach lessons even about deep-seated ideas.
2.	**Analyze From The Known To The Unknown.** Apart from unusual revelation, we can only search out answers in terms of what we know. That is, the first step in the isolation process— search out what is happening in terms of what you do know (e.g. paradigms).
3.	**Recognize That The Unknown Can Serve Two Functions.** When anomalies arise we must recognize that they may not really be anomalies and will be cleared up in the end (in which case it is a matter of faith and waiting), or they are real and will force us into new paradigms.
4.	Expect God's Intervention. **God may give insight if a new paradigm is needed or may require a faith response.**
5.	**Believe In God's On-Going Answer.** The book of Job shows us that God is in charge of our individual processing—no matter how or through whom it may come, even including Satanic origin. We do not have all the answers. He does. We must trust Him in them.

Moses
In Ex 2:11-15, there is an incident in which Moses kills an Egyptian and then flees (He 11:23-28 and Ac 7:23 give an interpretation of this). Then in Ex 3:7 and following, God calls Moses to a major task, the very one he had tried on his own and given up. There is a major difference in the Moses of Ex 2 and the Moses of

23. Isolation Processing—Learning Deep Lessons From God

Ex 3. Nu 12:3 describes it. Something happened. I want to suggest that it was a brokenness[85] experience. And that brokenness experience was part of isolation processing for Moses.

Moses experienced this Type II isolation processing. It included aspects of geographical and cultural isolation. Three characteristics of geographic and cultural isolation include: 1. It is more powerful in its early effects; wears off with time and as assimilation occurs. (This is seen also in the life of Daniel.) 2. In Geographic/ cultural isolation there is a loss of self-esteem. The things you were and value in the old culture are usually not so respected and valued in the new. 3. There is often a loss of momentum and vision.

Table 1,2 Co 23-4. Moses and Type II Isolation

Lesson	Explanation/ Generalized
1	**Look for leadership committal processing as a means toward ending isolation.** Often isolation involves and may terminate with God's renewal of call. See *progressive calling;* **Glossary**.
2	**God has to sometimes take a vision away in order to later accomplish that vision in his way.** Keep an open hand to plans, visions, future work.
3	**Humility is often the fruit of isolation processing--an unhealthy egotism is broken.** God can unleash great power through a broken/ humble leader without fear of that leader abusing the power.

Elijah

Elijah had two impactful isolation experiences. The first was a Type I, clearly God directed. The second was a Type II. I do not think Elijah ever fully recovered from the second experience. Table 1,2 Co 23-5 gives some observations about the Type I experience. Table 1,2 Co 23-6 gives the Type II isolation experience which arose due to persecution.

Table 1,2 Co 23-5. Elijah's Type I Isolation Experience, 1Ki 17:1-6—Some Observations

Observation	Explained
1	Isolation was God-directed (vs 2,3)
2	Success brings problems (vs 7 brook dries up--he prayed for no rain)
3	God will provide in isolation (vs 4, 9, 14)
4	God protects in isolation (I Kings 18:10).

Elijah's Type II isolation experience was the fallout from one of the most successful ministry events recorded in the O. T. He has just seen God move mightily in a power encounter[86] with the prophets of Baal on top of Mount Carmel—a true mountain top experience. When he flees from persecution he moves into an isolation experience—again a mountain top experience—this time, Mount Sinai. Note that again as with the first experience, success brings with it problems.

---

[85] See *brokenness*, **Glossary**.

[86] This is the classic power encounter which defines others. The steps of a *Power Encounter* include: 1. There is a confrontation between God and Evil. 2. The forces are recognized for that--the issues are who is more powerful and thus deserving of allegiance. 3. There is a public demonstration so that both forces can be seen by all as to who is more powerful. 4. God demonstrates publicly His power and defeats the evil forces so that there can be no doubt about to whom allegiance should be given. 5. Aftermath--God is glorified, evil forces are punished; there may be a response toward God. See *power encounter*, **Glossary**.

23. Isolation Processing—Learning Deep Lessons From God

Table 1,2 Co 23-6. Elijah's Type II Isolation Experience, 1Ki 19—Persecution—Running For His Life

Observation	Explained

1. The Situation	Vs4 Desert Isolation—
	   1. Hope gone; despair; take my life, (vs 4,5)
	   2. Angel touches him--provision (vs 5,7)
	   3. Horeb--Mountain of God--40 days/ 40 nights); cave
	What are you doing? God shows up.

2. Notice the Steps	Step 1. The feelings: I alone/ stood up for God/ persecution Step 2. Presence of God—the antidote to the feelings. Step 3. God answers--not you alone (vs11), 7000 who have not bowed the knee
3. The Price To Pay	Power encounters can be costly--they drain away energy—After mountain-top experiences expect attacks from Satan, evil forces; you may well crash hard in the valley. Elijah never again has a major ministry success?
4. Rejection/ God's Affirmation	In isolation there is a sense of personal rejection and a need for divine affirmation. Notice how God does this. **Small Still Voice.** Not the spectacular like you might expect or hope for.
5. Leadership Selection	Elijah imparted power and authority to Elisha--one who was faithful, tenacious, wanted what Elijah had. He carried on Elijah's ministry with more power than Elijah. Elijah's isolation experiences brought spiritual authority. Emerging leaders are drawn to leaders with spiritual authority.

One of the most important things to see from Elijah's isolation experiences is that isolation is frequently accompanied by a sense of personal rejection. It is divine affirmation that we need. God will meet us--maybe not in the way we expect.

Paul

Paul had numerous isolation experiences. It is from his life that the concept of repeated isolation experiences occurring in a leader's life emerged. Five are worth noting—1) his short days in Damascus with Ananias, Ac 9; 2; 2) His 2 to 3 years in Arabia mentioned in Gal; 3) His short prison experience in Philippi seen in Ac 16:23; 4) His four years in Rome (during which Eph, Col, Phm, Php were written); 5) His short few months in Rome just before his death. Table 1,2 Co 23-7 suggests nine observations drawn from a comparative study of Paul's isolation experiences.

Table 1,2 Co 23-7. Nine Observations from Paul's Isolation Experiences

Isolation Experience	Description and Observations
Galatian Isolation 1. Reflection	Paul's Galatian/Arabia--Pre-Ministry isolation was a Type III self-choice isolation. It was a time of Reflection in which he worked out his Christology. Basic Principle: **Reflection is a major goal and means of processing during isolation.** Reflection will happen in isolation. Depending on the kind of isolation there will be questions. A seeking after something—time for thinking. (2Ti is especially filled with reflection; a looking back on a lifetime given to the Gospel.)

2. Prison Isolation; Response Attitude	A. In general, the following principle makes the difference in whether the isolation is profitable or not.
	    A sovereign mindset in processing makes the difference in
	    immediate response and in long lasting results.
	Attitude is everything. Notice Paul's attitude as reflected in: Eph 3:1; 4:1; Col 4:3,9,10; Phm 1; Php 1:12; 4:22. Paul saw a God-ordained purpose behind isolation. What does it mean to have a *sovereign mindset* in processing? It means to recognize that however the isolation may have come about—unjust determination, terrible circumstances, or whatever—you must recognize that God has an ultimate purposes in it: 1) to demonstrate the sufficiency of the supply of the Spirit of Christ, 2) to do specific things fitting the

23. Isolation Processing—Learning Deep Lessons From God

	immediate situation, 3) to open up new thinking that could not have been possible, 4) to bring long-range productivity out of it (spiritual authority).
3. Intense Focus	**Critical issues come into focus during isolation processing.** Isolation forces one to focus usually first on why, causes of it, and then later on the purposes of it. And finally with a powerful concentration that allows for problem solving, new revelation to meet situations, and insights that could only come because of the situation.
4. Evaluation— Divine Perspective	**Divine evaluation of character, leadership commitment, and perspective is in focus in isolation processing.** Frequently, what happens is a recognition that God is allowing you to search your life and ministry and evaluate it in light of the situation and often with resulting paradigm shifts that will affect your ministry philosophy and the rest of your life.
5. Deepened Relationship	**A deepened relationship with god is always a major goal of isolation processing.** Philippians, the last of the first set of prison epistles and the most positive upbeat of all of Paul's letter culminates four years of isolation which have been filled with crises. It is filled with the importance of union with Christ. Its message points out what can happen in isolation processing—a grasping of the sufficiency of Christ for life.
6. Basis for Long Range Productivity	**Long lasting productivity is often rooted in isolation processing.** The prison epistles may never have been written had Paul been on the go. But set aside, reflection time produced thinking in regard to his own personal sanctification intimacy with Christians (Php), church problems (Col), the nature of the church (Eph), the solving of a problematic social institution (Phm). But not just products, attitudes and ideas are born in isolation which may come to fruition down road. 1. Specific things—people touched, saved, advise given, etc. 2. Modeling—an intangible product 3. written achievements—one product of isolation.
7. The importance of praise	**Praise is a major weapon in isolation processing.** In external isolation you probably feel less like praising than almost anything else, yet it is at that juncture that praise is probably the most important faith challenge. See Php jail experience, Ac 16, and the tone of praise in all the prison epistles--most of the opening prayers carry that note of praise. Praise will release power, new perspective in isolation.
8. Short Isolation	**Life changing and ministry changing revelation may come even in a short isolation experience.** Moses, 40 days of isolation by self-choice (divine drawing); Paul in two different times (Ac 9, Ananias, Ac 16 Philippian jail experience)
9. Intensified Prayer	**Isolation processing often presses a person into intensified prayer burdens and efforts.**

   Let me summarize what we can see in Paul's isolation experiences. Such experiences will tell a leader whether or not that leader has a sovereign mindset. They will also force reflection and evaluation of one's self in relation to: God, truth, a ministry, the past, the future. Critical issues come into focus. Peripheral issues are seen for what they are. In normal times we worry about a lot of things--many peripheral and non-essential. But in isolation times we get down to basic issues: who we are, what we really know, where we are going, who God really is, what He wants from us, etc. A leader will deepen his/her relationship with God—because that is what really matters--more than our ministry, more than the problems around us. A leader may discover the importance of praise or see an intensified outpouring of prayer, or the roots for long range productivity in our lives.
   Knowing these things, so what? How can observing these principles in the life of Paul help us as we life schedule or as we work through a present isolation experience? How can we be proactive? Here are some suggestions:

1. **Reflection**—If you are not a thinker or if you are a thinker but are confused in isolation, because you know that reflection is important, you should get with someone in the body of Christ who has either natural abilities of analytical skills, discernment, or spiritual gifts of exhortation, teaching, word of wisdom, word

23. Isolation Processing—Learning Deep Lessons From God

of knowledge and ask for help on getting an overall perspective on what the intent of God is in the isolation. In terms of mentor types, you need to get with a spiritual guide or mentor counselor.

2. **Response Attitude**—Acknowledge that God is in this isolation. By faith accept this and then move with a learning posture through it. I am going to learn great things from God. Others may be to blame but God is in it.

3. **Intense Focus**—Recognize that critical issues will be pointed out in the isolation processing.

4. **Divine Perspective Evaluation**—Do self-evaluation of your life and ministry. Some suggestions as to how to do this: Be alert to values. Expect new revelation. Know that paradigm shifts often occur in isolation.

5. **Deepened Relationship**—Spend time in intimacy disciplines with God; extended times of silence, solitude, prayer, Bible study, fasting.

Conclusion

Here are some final warnings and assurances about isolation.

1. **Expect it.** About 90% of leaders go through an isolation experience of Type I or II.
2. **Recognize that there will be a sense of rejection in it.** Because of this it is helpful to keep a log of your divine affirmation and ministry affirmation items. Review them alone with God and feel anew His acceptance.
3. **Determine beforehand to go deep with God.** He will take you into a place of more dependence, perhaps a place of intimacy that you could not have without this kind of processing.
4. **Know that God will indeed meet you in isolation** though at first He may appear remote. Do not try to move out of isolation on your own until God has met you. Otherwise, you may go through a repeated isolation experience.
5. **Know the uses of isolation** and seek to see and sense which of these God is working into your life.
6. For a Type III isolation experience **set goals** for personal growth that include dependence, intimacy, and a deeper walk with God.
7. **Talk to other Christians who have gone through deep processing.** They will give you perspective with a proper empathy.

As a leader you will face isolation. Will you meet God in it and see His purposes in it fulfilled? Remember, isolation processing comes to almost all leaders. Expect repeated isolation processing. It is needed throughout a lifetime. Don't forget, attitude is crucial. Perspective can make the difference—knowing what isolation does, that it does end, that it will accomplish many important things. If you sense you are plateauing then self-initiate an extended time of isolation—get help from mentor counselors and mentor spiritual guides.

Article 24

Relevance of the Article to Paul's Corinthian Ministry

Usually in most leadership circles, only one leadership style of Jesus is highlighted—that of a Servant Leader. And that is an important emphasis—for no culture has that leadership model as a natural leadership practice. It is something that must be learned. God will shape leaders to understand that important leadership style—if they will respond to his shaping activity. But, there are 4 other leadership models, which are equally important in carrying out the Great Commission. This article lists those models and does a comparitive study of the three major church leaders, Peter, John, and Paul. The comparison shows the need for multiple use of these models in getting the job done. Leaders will be drawn to two of the models primarily due to giftedness. They are gift-driven models. The others are models. which must be chosen. They are value-driven models. All leaders need to know how they relate to these important leadership models that Jesus exemplified.

24. Jesus—Five Philosophical Leadership Models: Servant, Steward, Harvest, Shepherd, Intercessor

Introduction to the Five Models

Jesus' ministry, in the *Pre-Church Leadership Era*, radically affected underlying notions of what leadership really was. The transition from the O.T. Leadership Eras to the N.T. Leadership Eras necessitated a new power base and new values underlying that base. No longer was leadership associated solely with national leadership as in the O.T. It was now concerned with spiritual leadership. And Jesus, while fully offering leadership to the Jewish national situation, was also introducing the bases for leadership to be expanded cross-culturally into all the world. This expansion would follow in the *Church Leadership Era*. What were the radical changes Jesus instilled? Consider the nine macro lessons identified with Jesus ministry given in Table 1,2 Co 24-1 below. All were radically different from anything seen in O.T. leadership.

Table 1,2 Co 24-1. Nine Radical Macro Lessons Seen in Jesus Ministry

Lesson Label	Statement of Lessons
28. Selection	The key to good leadership is the selection of good potential leaders which should be a priority of all leaders.
29. Training	Leaders should deliberately train potential leaders in their ministry by available and appropriate means.
30. Focus	Leaders should increasingly move toward a focus in their ministry which moves toward fulfillment of their calling and their ultimate contribution to God's purposes for them.
31. Spirituality	Leaders must develop interiority, spirit sensitivity, and fruitfulness in accord with their uniqueness since ministry flows out of being.
32. Servant	Leaders must maintain a dynamic tension as they lead by serving and serve by leading.
33. Steward	Leaders are endowed by God with natural abilities, acquired skills, spiritual gifts, opportunities, experiences, and privileges which must be developed and used for God.
34. Harvest	Leaders must seek to bring people into relationship with God.
35. Shepherd	Leaders must preserve, protect, and develop God's people.
36. Movement	Leaders recognize that movements are the way to penetrate society though they must be preserved via appropriate on-going institutions.

24. Jesus—5 Leadership Models

This article is concerned with the philosophical bases underlying the leadership models associated with macro lessons 32, 33, 34, and 35. In addition, another macro lesson originating in the O.T. is seen in minimum form in Jesus' ministry— *the Intercessor Model*. It becomes clearer that it was a significant part of Jesus' ministry philosophy with the writing of the epistle to the Hebrews—.

    8. Intercession   Leaders called to a ministry are called to intercede for that ministry.

For each of these radical macro lessons, Servant, Steward, Harvest, Shepherd and Intercessor I will describe a philosophical model. I define what I mean by ministry philosophy below. A model is simply an attempt to coherently interweave the definition, values, and implications associated with the idea.

Definition   Ministry philosophy refers to ideas, values, and principles, whether implicit or explicit, which a leader uses as guidelines for decision making, for exercising influence, and for evaluating his/her ministry.

These philosophical models are not exhaustively treated in one unified source in the N.T.. Much of the descriptive analysis comes as much from observations of practice of N.T. leaders as from explanatory passages. I will describe each of these models using the following format: introduction, definition, some supporting Biblical passages, basic values, and implications. I will also add explanatory comments. Finally, I will close by describing how the Holy Spirit applied these models into the Church.

The Servant Leader Model

introduction   Ministry philosophy refers to a related set of values that underlies a leader's perception and behavior in his/her ministry. The values may be ideas, principles, guidelines or the like. Each Christian leader will have a unique ministry philosophy that generally differs from others due to values God has taught experientially. But there will be some items in common with other leaders. The Servant Leader Model provides a set of values that should be common to the ministry philosophy of each Christian leader. Its central thrust says in essence that a leader's main focus is to use leadership to serve God by serving followers. A leader is great whose leadership capacities are used in service vertically to God and horizontally to followers.

Definition   The servant leader model is a philosophical model which is founded on the central thrust of Jesus' teaching on the major quality of great Kingdom leaders. That is, a leader uses leadership to serve followers. This is demonstrated in Jesus' own ministry.

passages   Mt 20:20-28, Mk 10:35-45.

secondary passages   Parable of the Waiting Servant—Mt 24:42-51, Lk 12:35-40, 41-48
Parable of the Unprofitable Servant—Lk 17:7-10. Isaiah's suffering Servant—Isa 52:13-53:12.

Basic Values

1. Leadership must be exercised primarily as service first of all to God and secondarily as service to God's people.
2. Service should require sacrifice on the leader's part.
3. Servant leadership ought to be dominated by an imitation modeling leadership style. That is, the dominant form of influence is modeling for the followers and setting expectancies for them to do the same.
4. Abuse of authority, Lording it over followers in order to demonstrate one's importance, cannot be compatible with servant leadership.
5. A major motivational issue for leadership must be anticipation of the Lord's return.
6. One ought to minister as a duty expected because of giftedness. Hence, there is no expectancy or demand or coercion for remuneration—no demanding one's due.

Implications

1. A servant leader does not demand rights or expect others to see him/her as one with special privileges and status.
2. A servant leader can expect God to give ministry affirmation and does not demand it from followers.
3. A servant leader expects to sacrifice. Personal desires, personal time, and personal financial security will frequently be overridden by needs of service in ministry.
4. The dominant leadership style to be cultivated is imitation modeling. While there is a place for other more authoritarian styles this style will dominate.
5. Spiritual authority, with its earned credibility, will be the dominant element of one's power-mix.
6. Leadership functions are performed always with a watchful spirit anticipating the Lord's return.
7. Finances will not dominate decision making with regard to acceptance of ministry.

comment Balance is important, for the servant leader must lead and must serve. The servant leader must maintain a dynamic tension by recognizing Butt's (1975) assertion that a leader leads by serving and serves by leading.

comment The Servant Model is a general leadership model applying to all leaders.

examples Both Peter and Paul demonstrate the values of this leadership model.

The Stewardship Model   synonym: Accountability Model

introduction Ministry philosophy refers to a related set of values that underlies a leader's perception and behavior in his/her ministry. The values may be ideas, principles, guidelines or the like which are implicit (not actually recognized but part of perceptive set of the leader) or explicit (recognized, identified, articulated). For any given leader a ministry philosophy is unique. It is dynamic and related to three major elements: Biblical dynamics, giftedness, and situation. Though a ministry philosophy is dynamic there are core issues which are stable and apply to all leaders. The stewardship model is one such set of stable Biblical values.

Definition The stewardship model is a philosophical model which is founded on the central thrust of several accountability passages, that is, that a leader must give account of his/her ministry to God.

specific passages Accountability parables: Mt 20 Laborers in the Vineyard, Mt 24 The Waiting Servants, Mt 25 The Ten Virgins, Mt 25 The Ten Talents, Lk 16 The Worldly Wise Steward, Lk 19 The Pounds.

General Ro 14:11,12; 1Co 3:5-9, 12-15; 2Co 5:10; Php 2:10,11; Heb 9:27. These passages indicate general judgment.

Special Jas 3:1, Da 12:1-3, Heb 13:17. These are special leadership passages.

Other Passages 1Co 4:1-5; 2Co 4:1-6; Ac 20:17-38; 1Pe 5:1-4. These indicate accountability/ rewards.

Basic Values

1. Ministry challenges, tasks, and assignments ultimately must be seen as from God.
2. God holds a leader accountable for leadership influence and for growth and conduct of followers. A leader must recognize this accountability.
3. Leaders must recognize an ultimate accounting of a leader to God in eternity for one's performance in leadership.
4. Leaders should recognize that they will receive rewards for faithfulness to their ministry in terms of abilities, skills, gifts and opportunities. This is one motivating factor for leading.

24. Jesus—5 Leadership Models

5. Leaders ought to build upon abilities, skills, and gifts to maximize potential and use for God.
6. Leaders should recognize that they will be uniquely gifted both as to gifts and the degree to which the gift can be used effectively.
7. Leaders should know that they will receive rewards for their productivity and for zealously using abilities, skills, gifts, and opportunities for God.
8. Leaders ought to know that they frequently must hold to higher standards than followers due to "the above reproach" and modeling impact they must have on followers.

Implications

1. Leaders must maintain a learning posture all of their lives—growing, expanding, developing.
2. Leaders must make certain of ministry tasks, challenges, and assignments in terms of God's guidance (calling) for them.
3. Leaders must perform in ministry as unto the Lord in all aspects of ministry.

comment	The Stewardship Model is the most general of the N.T. Philosophical models in that it applies to followers as well as leaders. Servant leadership applies only to leaders as does the Shepherd and Harvest Models. It is unclear about to whom the Intercessor Model applies—probably both to leaders and followers gifted with faith.
comment	Paul exemplifies this model.

Harvest Model

introduction	Ministry philosophy refers to a related set of values that underlies a leader's perception and behavior in his/her ministry. The values may be ideas, principles, guidelines or the like. Each Christian leader will have a unique ministry philosophy that generally differs from others due to values God has taught experientially. Leaders whose giftedness and calling line up with the central function of the Harvest Leader Model will find that its values are enmeshed in their own unique ministry philosophy. Leaders not so gifted may or may not have been shaped toward these particular ministry values. In any case the values are worth evaluation. Harvest leaders tend to have a leadership style bent which is fundamentally task oriented in nature.
Definition	The harvest leader model is a philosophical model founded on the central thrust of Jesus' teaching to expand the Kingdom by winning new members into it as demonstrated in the agricultural metaphors of growth in scripture.
central thrust	Its central concern is with expansion of Kingdom so as to bring new members into the Kingdom as forcefully commanded in the outward aspect of the Great Commission—Go ye into all the world and make disciples of all people groups.
primary passages	Mt 28:19,20: Great Commission—Outward Aspect. (See also Mk 16:15, Lk 24:46,47, Jn 20:21, Ac 1:8). Kingdom Growth Parables: Mt 13:24-30 Tares. Mt 13:31,32 Mustard Seed; Mk 4:30-32 Mustard Seed. Mt 13:33-35 Leaven; Lk 13:33-35 Leaven. Mk 4:26-29 Mysterious Growth of Seed. Sending Passage: Lk 10:1-12 Sending of 70.
archetype	Paul is the archetype of a harvest leader in the N.T. Peter also in his early ministry.

Values

1. Harvest leaders must have a strong concern for those outside the kingdom and want to give them a choice to hear and enter the kingdom. (Great Commission Passages)

24. Jesus—5 Leadership Models

2. Harvest leaders should have a strong desire to motivate followers to take the kingdom message to others. (Lk 10:1-12)
3. Harvest leaders must have a strong concern for power in ministry—they know the value of power to gain a hearing for the gospel of the kingdom. (Mt 28:20, Mk 16:16,17, Lk 24:49, Ac 1:8)
4. Harvest leaders must concerned with the ultimate destiny of those outside the kingdom than the present state of those in the kingdom. (Mt 28:19 emphasis on outward not inward)
5. Harvest leaders should recognize that Kingdom expansion means will not always sift out the real from the unreal but know that ultimately there will be resolution. (Mt 13:24-30)
6. Harvest leaders by and large must exercise faith. They believe God will accomplish His expansion work and hence are not afraid of small beginnings. (Mt 13:31,32, Mk 4:30-32)
7. Harvest leaders should recognize the evangelistic mandate as taking priority over the cultural mandate since the cultural mandate will require large numbers before impact on a non-kingdom society can be made. (Mt 13:33-35, Lk 13:20-21)
8. Harvest leaders ought to value receptivity testing in order to discover movements of God. (Mk 4:26-29)

comment Gift-mixes which correlate strongly with the Harvest Leader model include the various combinations of: the word gifts of apostle, faith, evangelist; the love gifts of mercy; the power gifts of healing, miracles, word of knowledge.

The Shepherd Leader Model

introduction Each Christian leader will have a unique ministry philosophy that generally differs from others due to values God has taught experientially. Leaders whose giftedness and calling line up with the central function of the Shepherd Leader Model will find that its values are enmeshed in their own unique ministry philosophy. Leaders not so gifted may or may not have had shaping experiences imparting these particular ministry philosophy values. In any case the values are worth evaluation. Shepherd leaders tend to have a leadership style bent which is fundamentally relational in nature.

Definition The shepherd leader model is a philosophical model which is founded on the central thrust of Jesus' own teaching and modeling concerning the responsibilities of leadership in caring for followers as seen in the various Shepherd/ Sheep metaphors in scripture.

central thrust Its central thrust is concern and care for the welfare of followers—that is, growth and development in the Kingdom so that they know God's rule in their lives and hence bring God's righteousness in society. This model is concerned primarily with the inward aspects of the Great Commission—teach them to obey all that I have commanded.

primary passages Mt 28:19,20, Great Commission, Inward Aspect. Mt 9:36,37 Shepherd Aspect of the Analogy. Mt 18:12 Parable of Lost Sheep, Lk 15:1-7 Parable of Lost Sheep. Jn 10:1-18 The Good Shepherd, Jn 21:15-17 Feed My Sheep. 1Pe 5:1-4 Peter's View, Shepherd Leadership. Ac 20:17-38 Paul's View, Watching for the Flock.

archetypes Peter, in his latter ministry, and Barnabas are significant examples of shepherd leaders. Paul, occasionally as in his more lengthy stays in churches.

Values

1. Shepherd leaders value personal kingdom growth in each follower. That is, they have a strong desire to see realization of kingdom truth in followers that is, they have a drive to see followers increasingly experiencing the rule of God in their lives. (Mt 28:20, Jn 21, Ac 20)
2. Shepherd leaders should have a strong empathy with followers. They seek to assess where they are and to help meet their needs so as to develop them toward their potential for the kingdom. (Mt 9:36,37)
3. Shepherd leaders value each follower as important to the whole body and want to keep them incorporated in the body. (Ac 20:28 Lk 15:1-7, Mt 18:12,13)

24. Jesus—5 Leadership Models

4. Shepherd leaders value a personal relationship with followers. (Jn 10:3, 4, 14)
5. Shepherd leaders ought to give personal guidance to followers by setting examples—particularly in the area of kingdom values. They value imitation modeling as an influence means with followers. (Jn 10:4)
6. Shepherd leaders should protect followers from deviant teaching by giving positive truth that will aid them in assessing counterfeit teaching. (Jn 10:5, 10, 12 Ac 20:28)
7. Shepherd leaders value followers experiencing abundant life in Christ. (Jn 10:10)
8. Shepherd leaders ought to be willing to sacrifice and know that personal desires, personal time, and personal financial security will frequently be overridden by needs of service in ministry. (Jn 10:11)
9. Shepherd leaders should be willing to persevere through persecution or hard times in order to better the condition of followers. (Jn 10:11)
10. Shepherd leaders must transparently expose weaknesses, strengths and their heart with followers. (Jn 10:14)
11. Shepherd leaders value unity in body and wider body. (Jn 10:16)
12. Shepherd leaders ought to willingly take responsibility for followers. (1Pe 5:2)
13. Financial gain ought to be secondary to performing ministry in the values of a Shepherd leader. (1Pe 5:2)

comment   Gift-mixes of leaders correlating strongly with the Shepherd Leader model include the various combinations of: the word gifts of pastor, teaching; the love gifts of mercy, helps and governments; the power gifts of healing, word of wisdom. The word gifts of prophecy, exhortation and leadership can operate with both Shepherd and Harvest leader models.

The Intercessor Model   synonym: Accountability Model

introduction   Ministry philosophy refers to a related set of values that underlies a leader's perception and behavior in his/her ministry. The values may be ideas, principles, guidelines or the like which are implicit (not actually recognized but part of perceptive set of the leader) or explicit (recognized, identified, articulated). For any given leader a ministry philosophy is unique. It is dynamic and related to three major elements: Biblical dynamics, giftedness, and situation. The intercessor model flows out of the prayer macro lesson and shows the concern of a leader for God's intervention in ministry. It is not clear to whom this model applies—all leaders or those leaders who have the gift of faith. It may also well apply to some who are not leaders but who have the gift of faith.

Definition   The <u>intercessor model</u> is a philosophical model which is founded on the central thrust of the prayer macro lesson (which applies to all leaders—as a role) and an additional responsibility for praying for a ministry, flowing out of the faith gift or some aspects of the prophetical gift.

general   Abraham and the macro lesson: Ge 18:16-33; Moses and the macro lesson: Ex 32:7-14; Samuel and the macro lesson: 1 Sa 12:1-25; Jesus and the macro lesson: some 44 different verses indicate Jesus praying throughout his ministry. One especially important prayer passage occurs in Jn 17.

Special   Matthew 9:36-38 links intercession with the raising up of emerging leaders. Heb 7:25 in the midst of an argument highlighting Jesus' eternal ministry as a priest, gives as an argument this phrase, "Wherefore he is able also to save them to the uttermost that come unto God by him, seeing he ever lives to make intercession for them."

Basic Values
1. A leader who is called to ministry must accept responsibility for prayer for that ministry.
2. A leader should show acceptance of responsibility for a ministry by interceding for that ministry and involving others to intercede.
3. A leader must seek God's leading in prayer, the divine initiative, as to how and what to pray for.
4. A leader should bathe major decision making in prayer.

24. Jesus—5 Leadership Models

5. A leader ought to encourage the development of emerging leaders by praying for them and telling them of prayer for them.
6. A leader should cultivate an attitude of prayer at all times and ought to break into prayer spontaneously.
7. Crises should drive a leader deeper into intercessory ministry.
8. Extended times alone in prayer should be used for intercession, for personal renewal and for revelation from God for guidance, breakthroughs in ministry, and for decision making.

Implications
1. No ministry will long endure without intercessors behind it.
2. Quantity (the number of and amount of time spent by) of intercessors is not as important as quality of intercession of the ones doing the interceding.
3. Leaders with the gift of faith will do personal intercession with a zeal, passion and fruitfulness beyond that of leaders who do this as a role.
4. Leaders should recruit faith gifted intercessors to help in the ministry.
5. Power in ministry comes from giftedness and from prayer. Both are needed.

comment   The Intercessor Model is the most specific of the leadership models. It is the most gift related. Gifts of faith, apostleship, and in general, the revelatory gifts (word of knowledge, word of wisdom, prophecy, word of faith) will usually be associated with leaders operating strongly in this model. Now all leaders have the duty to intercede for their ministries. But those who are drawn to this model will be gifted to see its impact more than just that which results from praying in general. It is not clear to what extent each leader will be involved in this model. Jesus does exhort his followers to pray for emerging leaders.

comment   Paul exemplifies this model.

Applied to The Church Era of Leadership

Four of these models, Servant, Steward, Harvest, and Shepherd, originated in Jesus' ministry in the *Pre-Church Leadership Era*. The fifth, Intercessor, is widespread across all leadership eras. It is clear with the emergence of the church and the spiritual leadership which accompanied it that the Holy Spirit applied all five of these models to the *Church Leadership Era*. Peter, John, and Paul, the leading models of church leaders strongly emphasize these models.

Table 1,2 Co 24-2. The Three Archetype Church Leaders and Philosophical Models

Leader	Models Exemplified
Peter	Early on—Harvest Later Ministry—Shepherd Steward Servant
John	Shepherd Servant
Paul	Harvest Shepherd Steward Servant Intercessor

We have much more information on Paul than either of the other two. So it is easier to see examples of each of the models in his life. With more information it is likely that all five of the models would be seen in

24. Jesus—5 Leadership Models

all three lives. Certainly John with his right brained approach and mysticism must have been involved in a intercessor model, though we do not see it in his writings, which are not autobiographical.

Conclusion

Our studies of leaders and giftedness indicate that leaders with apostleship, evangelism, and faith tend to be Harvest Model adherents. Leaders with pastoral, teaching, and governments tend to be Shepherd Model enthusiasts. Leaders with exhortation, prophecy, and leadership gifts can go in either direction—Harvest Model or Shepherd Model. However, most leaders tend to be one or the other and not both. All leaders are to be Servant Leaders (a model which does not naturally appear in most cultures). All leaders are to be Stewards. Some leaders will embrace fully the Intercessor Model personally (those faith gifted) while others will recruit people to utilize that model for them.

Leaders should be increasingly conscious of the values which under gird their ministries. Explicit understanding can increase proactive use. Value driven leaders are needed especially those who will embrace the models that Jesus instituted.

Related **Articles**: *36. Macro Lessons—List of 41 Across Six Leadership Eras; 27. Leadership Eras in the Bible—Six Identified; 71. Value Driven Leadership.*

Book Referred to: Howard Butt, **The Velvet Covered Brick: Christian Leadership in An Age of Rebellion**. 1973. New York: Harper and Row.

Article 25

Relevance of the Article to Paul's Corinthian Ministry
One of the impressive things about Paul's leadership concerns his prayer life. Paul prayed for his ministries. He knowingly perhaps, or implicitly at least, observed the Intercession/prayer macro lesson in his life. **LEADERS CALLED TO A MINISTRY ARE CALLED TO INTERCEDE FOR THAT MINISTRY.** Three other articles go hand-in-hand with this one. See **Article 46.** *Paul—Intercessor Leader,* **Article 52.** *The Prayer Macro,* and **Article 74.** *Vulnerability and Prayer.* Note too that some of the lessons seen in Habakkuk's prayer ministry are also applicable to Paul's ministry.

25. Leaders—Intercession Hints from Habakkuk

Introduction
In the small three chapter book of Habakkuk, the prophet Habakkuk is facing the crisis of his life. This crisis can make or break Habakkuk. How does he respond in this crisis—by praying? The entire book records Habakkuk's talking and listening to God about his crisis issues. The prayer goes back and forth. Here are the highlights of the dialog in my terse paraphrase.

Habakkuk Speaks.
Chapter 1:1-4
Are you there, O God? You don't seem to be taking care of the injustices I see.

God Speaks.
Chapter 1:5-11
I am doing something about this? I am raising up the Chaldeans to solve your problem.

Habakkuk Speaks
Chapter 1:12-2:1
I am waiting to hear what you will say to my accusation that your character won't let you do this.

God speaks.
Chapter 2:2b-20
What I am doing will happen. You need to trust me to work it out. But know I will also take care of punishing the Chaldeans. And I will be vindicated throughout the whole earth.

Habakkuk Sings His Response To God (A corporate celebration and prayer)
I am going to trust you and joyfully respond to the things that happen. You will enable me to do this.

Some Prayer Observations Seen in this Book of Prayer
I want to briefly comment on five observations about prayer that I see in this prayer book. Table 1,2 Co 25-1 below gives the brief statements.

Table 1,2 Co 25-1. 5 Prayer Observations Seen in Habakkuk

Observation	Topic	Statement
1.	Holiness	A proper understanding of God's holiness causes one to have a burden to pray about social injustice.

25. Leaders, Intercession Hints from Habakkuk   page 177

2.	Discerning Answers	God's answer to our prayers may be difficult to discern in our surrounding circumstances.
3.	Honesty in Prayer	A leader can be absolutely honest with God in prayer concerning how he/she feels or thinks.
4.	Dialogue	Prayer can be a dialogue in which the prayer talks and listens and God listens and speaks.
5.	Solitude	Listening for God's speaking in prayer may best be done in a time and place of solitude.

Brief Comments on Each Observation

Observation 1
A proper understanding of God's holiness causes one to have a burden to pray about social injustice.

Notice Habakkuk's words in chapter 1, verses 1-4.

2 O Jehovah, how long shall I beg for your help,
    When will you listen?
  I cry out unto you about violence,
    And you will not deliver.

3 **Why do you tolerate the iniquity I see,**
    And cause me to experience such injustice?
  For destruction and violence are before me,
    And there is strife,
    And criminal activity all about.
4 Therefore, the law is not enforced,
    And justice does not happen.
    For evil people outnumber the righteous.
  Therefore justice is distorted.

Essentially what Habakkuk is seeing around him in his situation seems to contradict what he knows of God and God's ways. How can a holy God tolerate iniquity. Why doesn't God do something to bring about justice?

What Habakkuk does is to go to God in prayer about the situation. He honestly confronts God. He demonstrates a burden for seeing God (a holy God) deal with the sin and injustice around him.[87]

Observation 2
God's answer to our prayers may be difficult to discern in our surrounding circumstances.

When God answers Habakkuk, it is clear that He wants Habakkuk to listen and discern carefully.

5 Look among the nations; look very carefully,
    There is something that will astonish you,
  For I am doing something even as you speak,
    Which, you won't believe, even when told.
6 Consider: I am raising up the Babylonians,
    That ruthless and unruly nation,
    That marches all over the land,
    To possess homes and cities that are not theirs.

---

[87] God did answer. I feel in this case, that if God had not answered, Habakkuk would have probably quit his ministry. However, sometimes God does not answer. How do we handle that?

25. Leaders, Intercession Hints from Habakkuk

Three times in this short response, God tells Habakkuk to really listen and discern: look, look very carefully; consider. Apart from this revelatory information—Habakkuk would probably never have known that God was working in the emerging of the Babylonian empire. God tells Habakkuk that He is already working. It is clear from this astounding revelation that discerning answers to our prayers about complex situations can be hard to discern. We, like Habakkuk, will be forced to get God's revelatory word on current situations.

Observation 3
A leader can be absolutely honest with God in prayer concerning how he/she feels or thinks.

Notice again Habakkuk's words in chapter 1, verses 1-4.

2   O Jehovah, how long shall I beg for your help,
        When will you listen?
    I cry out unto you about violence,
        And you will not deliver.

3   **Why do you tolerate the iniquity I see,**
        And cause me to experience such injustice?
    For destruction and violence are before me,
        And there is strife,
        And criminal activity all about.
4   Therefore, the law is not enforced,
        And justice does not happen.
        For evil people outnumber the righteous.
    Therefore justice is distorted.

These are honest words. Habakkuk is accusing God of laxity in holiness; lack of intervention in a situation needing God's touch.

Look also at the following from Habakkuk 2. It sums up Habakkuk's accusative words towards God's use of the Babylonians (Hab 2:12-17).

2:1 I will doggedly set myself to wait for God's answer,
        And station myself on the watch tower,
        And watch carefully to perceive, what He will communicate to me.
        And then I will have an answer to my **complaint**.[88]

Habakkuk certainly demonstrates this prayer observation.

A leader can be absolutely honest with God in prayer concerning how he/she feels or thinks.

This prayer observation is seen repeatedly through a number of the Psalms. Being honest with God in our prayers is a major step forward to transparency and vulnerability—needed traits by leaders.

Observation 4
Prayer can be a dialogue in which the prayer talks and listens and God listens and speaks.

---

[88] Lines 3,4 seem to indicate that Habakkuk will persistently wait till he can **perceive what God is saying**. Habakkuk is hoping for some **restorative word** (answer SRN 07725) to his **complaint** (SRN 0843) to God (the word complaint connotes rebuke—very honest expression toward God). How much time is involved in this is uncertain. But that Habakkuk is getting away from his normal way of life in order to especially hear from God is indicated.

25. Leaders, Intercession Hints from Habakkuk

Habakkuk prays honestly to God. God answers Habakkuk with what He is doing. Habakkuk challenges this solution. God defends His plans and shows how he will bring justice, both in the situation Habakkuk is in presently and to the Babylonians as well. Habakkuk then talks to God about his awe inspiring interventions in the past. He also intercedes for mercy. And finally he tells God that he has heard and accepted God's revelation. This is a back and forth dialog in prayer. What it stresses to leaders today is the necessity to develop listening skills in one's prayer time. Disciplines of silence and listening must be cultivated in order to hear God's prayerful dialog.

Observation 5
Listening for God's speaking in prayer may best be done in a time and place of solitude.

Look again at the opening verses of chapter 2.

2:1 I will doggedly set myself to wait for God's answer,
   And station myself on the watch tower,[89]
   And watch carefully to perceive, what He will communicate to me.
   And then I will have an answer to my **complaint**.

Habakkuk is seeking a place of solitude—a place where he can be alone and not distracted. He wants to hear God. Solitude is needed if a leader is to focus on God.

Closure

Now these observations are simple enough. But the real question is, do we have the outworking of these 5 observations in our life. Take a look at the five observations given below. Check on the continuum for each where you actually are with regard to using the observation in your own life.

Observation 1
My understanding of God's holiness causes me to have a burden to pray about social injustice.

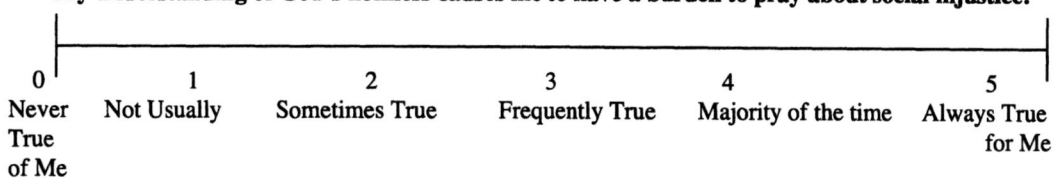

0	1	2	3	4	5
Never True of Me	Not Usually	Sometimes True	Frequently True	Majority of the time	Always True for Me

Observation 2
God's answer to my prayers is really difficult to discern in my complex situation.

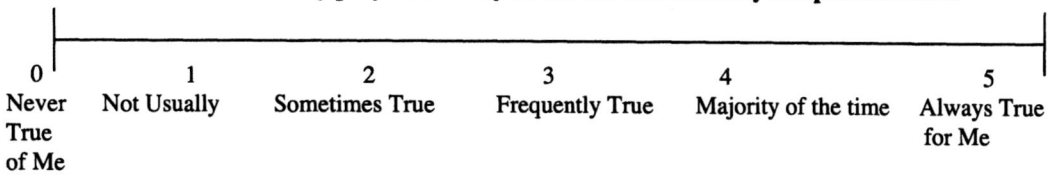

0	1	2	3	4	5
Never True of Me	Not Usually	Sometimes True	Frequently True	Majority of the time	Always True for Me

---

[89] The sense of this stanza (the four lines of verse 1) seems to be that Habakkuk will isolate himself until he perceives God's reply to his complaint that God is unfair using the wicked Babylonians to bring about judgment on Judah. Lines 1 and 2 seem to indicate that Habakkuk will go into the outlying fields where observation towers were set up with sentries to watch for enemies attacking. Habakkuk is getting away from his normal way of life in order to especially hear from God is indicated.

Observation 3

I am absolutely honest with God in prayer concerning how I feel or think or otherwise see things.

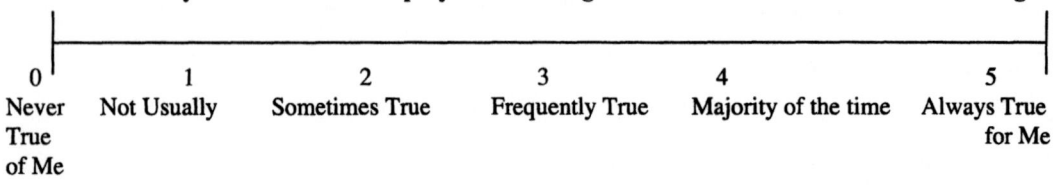

0	1	2	3	4	5
Never True of Me	Not Usually	Sometimes True	Frequently True	Majority of the time	Always True for Me

Observation 4

For me prayer is a dialogue in which God and I both talk and listen. I have developed my prayer listening skills to a high degree.

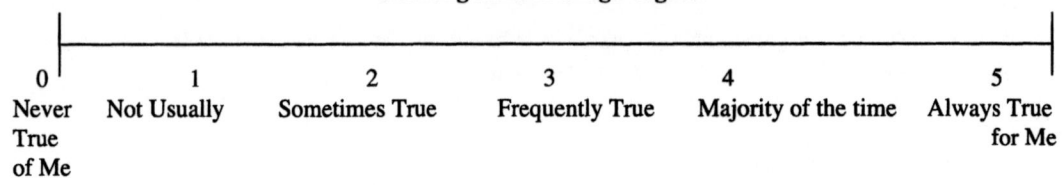

0	1	2	3	4	5
Never True of Me	Not Usually	Sometimes True	Frequently True	Majority of the time	Always True for Me

Observation 5

I have a regular time and a special place in which I practice solitude and my prayer listening skills.

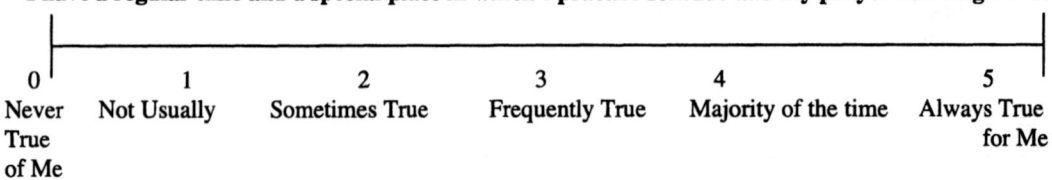

0	1	2	3	4	5
Never True of Me	Not Usually	Sometimes True	Frequently True	Majority of the time	Always True for Me

I am also modeling something in this article. When you study a Bible leader be sensitive to how that leader's prayer life is seen. Learn to draw out observations about a leader's prayer attitudes and habits. These leaders in the Bible can speak into our own lives, if we but have the eyes to see. This is especially true for Paul. In his epistles he allows us to see his prayer life for the various church situations.

Article 26

<u>Relevance of the Article to Paul's Corinthian Ministry</u>

The entire books, 1 Co and 2 Co, are major illustrations of a leadership act. Paul, the leader, seeks to intervene in the life of a church filled with problems. He seeks to correct those problems. He uses varied influence means. Note well the leadership styles being displayed: apostolic, confrontational, Father-Initiator, Father-guardian, maturity appeal, imitator, indirect conflict. See the article on Pauline leadership styles for definitions of these Pauline leadership styles. But know as you read this article, that the two letters to the Corinthians represent a major leadership act.

26. Leadership Act

Leadership Act Defined

Of the seven leadership genre[90] in the Bible, sources from which we can draw leadership insights to inform our own leadership, the three most common are biographical, books as a whole, and leadership acts. There are numerous leadership acts in the O.T. and quite a few in the N.T.

Definition   A <u>leadership act</u> is the specific instance at a given point in time of the leadership influence process between a given influencer (person said to be influencing) and follower(s) (person or persons being influenced) in which the followers are influenced toward some goal.

Examples of leadership acts include: Barnabas in Acts 9:26-30; Barnabas in Acts 11:22-24; Barnabas in Acts 11:25-26; Agabus in Acts 11:27-28; leaders and whole church in Acts 11:29-30; Paul, Barnabas, apostles, Peter, James and elders in Jerusalem, in Acts 15:1-21; almost all of the Pauline epistles.

How To Study A Leadership Act—Seven Steps

A leadership act is a vignette, usually some historical narrative, which contains a leader or leaders, followers, and some situation which demands leadership. The narrative gives enough information for one to analyze what the leader did and how he/she did it. Usually there are indications of leadership styles used, power bases used, problems being faced, solved or not, etc. Leadership lessons are very readily derived. The three major overarching leadership components—leadership basal elements, leadership influence means, and leadership value bases—provide categories which can be used to screen the data for ideas. Table 1,2 Co 26-1 lists the basic steps for studying a leadership act.

Table 1,2 Co 26-1. How To Study a Leadership Act

Step	Procedure
1	Study the passage (in this case the books, 1, 2 Co as a whole, and individual passages in them) using normal hermeneutics to get the meaning of the passage in terms of its use in the chapter, section, or book.
2	Describe the macro context and local context in order to understand the situation. See if you can identify the reason why the act is included (in this case I introduce 1,2 Co and give the structure, theme and purposes of the letters which do much to explain the macro and local contexts).

---

[90] See **Article,** *29. Leadership Genre—Seven Types.* Genre refers to a category. Hence seven *Leadership Genre* means seven types of categories of leadership information in the Bible: biographical, leadership acts, books as a whole, macros lessons, indirect contexts, direct contexts, parabolic.

26. Leadership Act

3	Use the 3 Major components of leadership to help stimulate your thinking: (1) leadership basal elements: leader, follower, situation; (2) leadership influence means both individual leadership styles and corporate leadership styles; (3) leadership value bases: underlying cultural or theological values in view). Describe what you see using those as stimulants for discovery. Look for God's shaping activities in the life of individual leaders or groups as a whole. See if any of the followership laws are present or absent and if so are significant. Describe the macro context and local context in order to understand the situation. See if you can identify the reason why the act is included. (Pauline leadership styles involved in the Corinthian intervention and his leadership value bases are very instructive.)
4	Are there leadership values that are in view? What other lessons are suggested in the act? (See especially my comments on leadership values and *Article 51. Pauline Leadership Values*)
5	At this point summarize in the form of principles. Try to raise the level of specific principles for wider application. (See the Leadership Topics for 1,2 Co where I have identified specific principles. See also the leadership comments in the commentary on the text, itself.)
6	For each statement of truth, determine where on the leadership truth continuum it is located.
7	Comment on the broader application of your findings. (Much of the leadership comments is actually implying application of the findings as do many of the leadership articles.)

Most of Paul's letters are in themselves major leadership acts (1,2 Co are). This is much easier to see in the smaller ones like Phm and Php. Books like Phm and Php serve as more than one leadership genre. For example consider Php: 1. It has *biographical information* on at least six different leaders; 2. Php can be studied as *The Book As A Whole* genre for leadership insights. I have done so in the Bible section of this book. 3. Philippians is also a *major leadership act* for which you can analyze leader, follower, situation as well as influence means (Pauline leadership styles. 4. It also validates a number of macro lessons, notably, the *prayer macro lesson* that originated in the O.T.

In summary, a leadership act occurs when a given person influences a group in terms of behavioral acts or perception, so that the group acts or thinks differently as a group than before the instance of influence. Such an act can be evaluated in terms of the three major leadership categories: 1) leadership basal elements, 2) leadership influence means and 3) leadership value bases. It should be noted that any given act of leadership may have several persons of the group involved in bringing about the influence. While the process may be complex and difficult to assess, leadership can be seen to happen and be composed essentially of influencer, group, influence means, and resulting change of direction by the group.

End Results of A Study—Example From Joshua's Ministry

The end result of the study of a leadership act is a set of observations, principles, lessons, guidelines, values, or absolutes. For example, the leadership act of Joshua's leading the people to cross the Jordan is full of leadership observations, lessons, and principles. Consider the following:

Table 1,2 Co 26-2. Lessons Drawn from Joshua 3,4—Crossing the Jordan

Lesson	Statement of Lesson
1	Spiritual authority, though conferred by people, is in the ultimate sense given (delegated) by God.
2	In leadership transition of a high level leader, the spiritual authority of the new leader must be established early.
3	In a God-directed leadership transition, the leader can expect a spiritual authority experience which will probably involve a faith challenge or conflict or crisis or isolation experience.
4	Memorials of spiritual benchmarks are important to leadership to serve as reminders of God's deliverance and to engender a faith-filled awe in the leader.
5	Leaders and followers should seek to deliberately set up "stones of remembrance" to commemorate spiritual benchmarks so as to counter tendencies to forget God's mighty power and build expectancies for the future.
6	Great faith challenges will be accompanied by great moments of divine affirmation.
7	A profound sense of God's presence revolutionizes a leader's attitude toward all of his/her leadership.
8	Leaders need a personal inward affirmation from God as well as external affirmation.

26. Leadership Act

| 9 | A Fourfold Pattern of Affirmation for a Major Faith Challenge involves the following four items: (1) A revelation of the Lord. (2) A realization that it is the Lord who will fight for us. (3) Submissive worship of the Lord. (4) M.1 Pattern--rapid response, rapid development. |

These observations will range along the leadership truth continuum all the way from suggestions on the left on to guidelines in the middle and perhaps one or two to the far right as absolutes.

Leadership acts provide an excellent source of leadership principles, if you have eyes to see the implications for leadership insights contained within them.

Final Comment

What do you think was the result of the 1,2 Co leadership act?

See **Articles** 29. *Leadership Genre—Seven Types; 16. Followership—10 Commandments, 35. Macros Lessons Defined; 34. Leadership Tree Diagram; Principles of Truth.* See the manual, **Leadership Perspectives,** which illustrates fully the use of these steps in doing the leadership act seen in 1 Sa 12.

Article 27

Relevance of the Article to Paul's Corinthian Ministry

Paul's ministry takes place in the 5th leadership era—the Church Leadership Era. He was the major architect for the Church Leadership Era. Almost 50% of the N.T. canon deals with church leadership. Paul is the dominant figure. His church planting, development of leaders, and apostolic problem solving in the new churches stands as a tour de force for which we as leaders today are extremely grateful. But recognize as you read that in each leadership era, the macro context and local context and cultural perspectives of the leaders in question play a heavy role in projecting what leadership is. Certainly this is true for Paul. Note particularly the definitive characteristics of the Church Leadership Era.

27. Leadership Eras in the Bible— Six Identified

Introduction to the Six Leadership Eras

A <u>Bible Centered leader</u> refers to a leader whose leadership is informed by the Bible, who has been personally shaped by Biblical values, has grasped the intent of Scriptural books and their content in such a way as to apply them to current situations and who uses the Bible in ministry so as to impact followers. Notice that first concept again—

whose leadership is informed by the Bible.

Two of the most helpful perspectives for becoming a Bible centered leader **whose leadership is informed by the Bible** include:

(1) recognizing the differences in leadership demands on leaders throughout the Bible, i.e. seeing the different leadership eras, and
(2) Recognizing and knowing how to draw out insights from the seven genre of leadership sources in the Bible.

This article overviews the first of these helpful perspective—seeing the leadership eras in the Bible.

The Six Leadership Eras

Let me start by giving you one of the most helpful perspectives, a first step toward getting leadership eyes, for recognizing leadership findings in the Bible. That first helpful perspective involves breaking down the leadership that takes place in the Bible into leadership eras, which on the whole share common leadership assumptions and expectations for the time period. These assumptions and expectations differ from one leadership era to the next, though there are commonalties that bridge across the eras.

Definition   A <u>leadership era</u> is a period of time, usually several hundred years long, in which the major focus of leadership, the influence means, basic leadership functions, and followership have much in common and which basically change with time periods before or after it.

An outline of the six eras I have identified follows.

    I. **Patriarchal Era (Leadership Roots)—Family Base**
    II. **Pre-Kingdom Leadership Era—Tribal Base**
        A.   The Desert Years
        B.   The War Years--Conquering the Land,
        C.   The Tribal Years/ Chaotic Years/ Decentralized Years--Conquered by the Land

27. Leadership Eras In The Bible, Six Identified

    III. **Kingdom Leadership Era—Nation Based**
        A.   The United Kingdom
        B.   The Divided Kingdom
        C.   The Single Kingdom--Southern Kingdom Only
    IV. **Post-Kingdom Leadership Era—Individual/ Remnant Based**
        A.   Exile--Individual Leadership Out of the Land
        B.   Post Exilic--Leadership Back in the Land
        C.   Interim--Between Testaments
    V. **New Testament Pre-Church Leadership—Spiritually Based in the Land**
        A.   Pre-Messianic
        B.   Messianic
    VI. **New Testament Church Leadership—Decentralized Spiritually Based**
      A. Jewish Era
      B. Gentile Era

I have used the following tree diagram[91] to provide an overview of leadership. The three overarching components of leadership include: the leadership basal elements (leader, follower, situation which make up the **What** of leadership); leadership influence means (individual and corporate leadership styles which make up the **How** of leadership); and leadership Value bases (Biblical and cultural values which make up the **Why** of leadership).

The Study Of Leadership
involves

Leadership Basal Elements	Leadership Influence Means	Leadership Value Bases
including	such as	including
• Leader	• Individual Means	• Cultural
• Followers	• Corporate Means	• Theological
• Situation	• Spiritual Means	

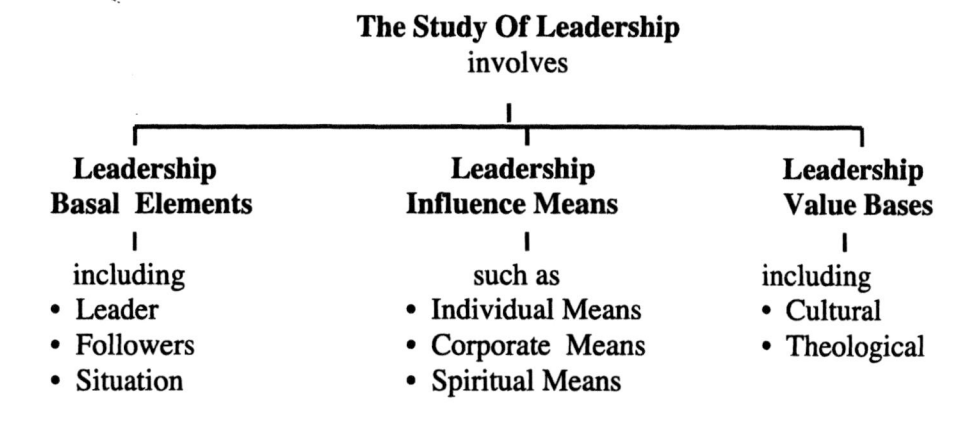

Figure 1,2 Co 27-1. Tree Diagram Categorizing the Basics of Leadership

It was this taxonomy which suggested questions that helped me see for the first time the six leadership eras of the Bible. Table 1,2 Co 27-1 below gives the basic questions/subjects/categories that helped me identify the different leadership eras. It is these categories that allows comparison of different leadership periods in the Bible.

Table 1,2 Co 27-1. Basic Questions To Ask About Leadership Eras

1. **Major Focus**—Here we are looking at the overall purposes of leadership for the period in question. What was God doing or attempting to do through the leader? Sense of destiny? Leadership mandate?
2. **Influence means**—Here we are describing any of the power means available and used by the leaders in their leadership. We can use any of Wrong's categories or any of the leadership style categories I define. Note particularly in the Old Testament the use of force and manipulation as power means.

---

[91] This was derived in a research project, the historical study of leadership in the United States from the mid 18th century to the present—for further study see **A Short History of Leadership Theory**, 1986, by Dr. J. Robert Clinton. Altadena, CA: Barnabas Publishers. See **Further Study Bibliography**.

27. Leadership Eras In The Bible, Six Identified

3. Basic **leadership functions**—We list here the various achievement/ responsibilities expected of the leaders: from God's standpoint, from the leader's own perception of leadership, from the followers. Usually they can all be categorized under the three major leadership functions of task, relational, and inspirational functions. But here we are after the specific functions.
4. **Followers**—Here we are after sphere of influence. Who are the followers? What are their relationship to leaders? Which of the 10 Commandments of followership are valid for these followers? What other things are helpful in describing followers?
5. **Local Leadership**—in the surrounding culture: Biblical leaders will be very much like the leaders in the cultures around them. Leadership styles will flow out of this cultural press. Here we are trying to identify leadership roles in the cultures in contact with our Biblical leaders.
6. **Other**—Miscellaneous catch all: such things as centralization or decentralization or hierarchical systems of leadership; joint (civil, political, military, religious) or separate roles.
Thought Questions—Here try to synthesize the questions you would like answered about leaders and leadership if you could get those answers. We are dealing here with such things as the essence of a leader (being or doing), leadership itself, leadership selection and training, authority (centralized or decentralized), etc.

Using these leadership characteristics I studied leadership across the Bible and inductively generated the Six Leadership Eras as given above.[92] Table 1,2 Co 27-2 adds some descriptive elements of the eras.

Table 1,2 Co 27-2. Six Leadership Eras in the Bible—Brief Characterizations

Leadership Era	Example(s) of Leader	Definitive Characteristics
1. Foundational (also called patriarchal)	Abraham, Joseph	Family Leadership/ formally male dominated/ expanding into tribes and clans as families grew/ moves along kin ship lines
2. Pre-Kingdom	Moses, Joshua, Judges	Tribal Leadership/ Moving to National/ Military/ Spiritual Authority/ outside the land moving toward a centralized national leadership
3. Kingdom	David, Hezekiah	National Leadership/ Kingdom Structure/ Civil, Military/ Spiritual/ a national leadership—Prophetic call for renewal/ inside the land/ breakup of nation
4. Post-Kingdom	Ezekiel, Daniel, Ezra	Individual leadership/ Modeling/ Spiritual Authority
5. Pre-Church	Jesus/ Disciples	Selection/ Training/ spiritual leadership/ preparation for decentralization of Spiritual Authority/ initiation of a movement/
6. Church	Peter/ Paul/ John	decentralized leadership/ cross-cultural structures led by leaders with spiritual authority which institutionalize the movement and spread it around the world

When we study a leader or a particular leadership issue in the Scriptures we must always do so in light of the leadership context in which it was taking place. We cannot judge past leadership by our present leadership standards. Conversely, we will find that major leadership lessons learned by these leaders will usually have broad implications for our leadership.

See **Articles**: *29. Leadership Genre—Seven Types; 35. Macros Lessons Defined; 36. Macro Lessons —List of 41 Across Six Leadership Eras.*

---

[92] I have a short form of answers to each of these questions for each of the six leadership eras. I include this in my Biblical Leadership Commentary, available on CD.

Article 28

Relevance of the Article to Paul's Corinthian Ministry

Paul was a Type E leader (international sphere of influence—that is, influence in many countries and cultural settings. See **Article 31. Levels of Leadership—Looking At a Leadership Continuum**). Paul was dominantly a task-oriented leader (the first of the 3 high level leadership priorities) who was also a powerful inspirational leader (the third of the 3 high level leadership priorities). He learned somewhat to operate as a relational leader (the second of the high level leadership priorities). This third function is seen best in his mentor/training with individuals or small groups. He went through a number of conflicts, which softened his task orientation and taught him the need for the relational function. So as you read this article, think to yourself, which of these functions are evident in the Corinthian ministry? How are they seen?

28. Leadership Functions—Three High Level Generic Priorities

Introduction

High level Christian leaders[93] perform many leadership functions. In addition to direct ministry functions based on giftedness there are those additional functions that characterize leaders simply because they are people responsible for others.

description   Leadership functions describe general activities that leaders must do and/or be responsible for in their influence responsibilities with followers.

Leadership studies in the mid-50s[94] analyzed the kinds of things leaders did in secular organizations. From a list of over a thousand they reduced them by factor analysis to two major categories. These two categories are roughly equivalent to what we would call today task-oriented leadership and relational-oriented leadership. In the early 80s and 90s leadership research began to identify another high level function, which I call inspirational leadership.[95]

Figure 1,2 Co 28-1 below groups leadership functions into three generic categories: task oriented leadership, relational oriented leadership, and inspirational leadership.

Three High Level Leadership Functions
include

| Task-Oriented Leadership | Relational-Oriented Leadership | Inspirational Leadership |

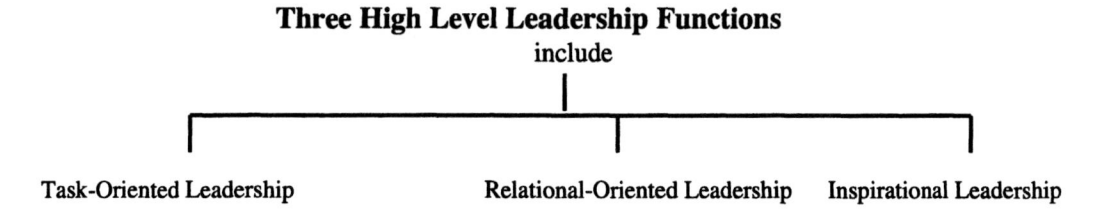

Figure 1,2 Co 28-1. Three High Level Leadership Functions

---

[93] I use a five-fold leadership typology adapted from McGavran: Type A—local internal influence in the church or Christian organization; Type B—local external influence in the church or Christian organization; Type C—local/regional influence; Type D—national influence; Type E—international influence. I am speaking mostly about Type C, D, and E leaders when I talk about generic leadership functions for high level leaders. See **Article, 31. Leadership Levels—Looking At A Leadership Continuum**.

[94] The Ohio State Leadership Research (1948-1967) reduced the many observed functions of secular leadership by factor analysis to two major generic categories: consideration and initiation of structure.

[95] McGregor and others were doing research on motivation. There was also a growing interest in values underlying why leaders did things.

28. Leadership Functions: Three High Level Generic Priorities

Task Oriented Leadership

Task oriented leadership (technically called *Initiation of structure* in the Ohio State Research) groups all of those activities which a leader does to accomplish the task or vision for which the structure exists. Task behaviors involve clarifying goals, setting up structures to help reach them, holding people accountable, disciplining where necessary and in short, to act responsibly to accomplish goals. Table 1,2 Co 28-1 displays a list of typical task oriented leadership functions.

Table 1,2 Co 28-1. Typical Task-Oriented Leadership Functions[96]

Christian leaders:
1. must provide structures which facilitate accomplishment of vision (Paul did this—e.g. missionary band/ training school in Ephesus);
2. will be involved in crisis resolution related to structural issues (the various epistles do this; the 1,2 Co epistles are actually doing this very thing as Paul solves the many church problems in Corinth);
3. must make decisions involving structures (Paul does this—note especially the notion of giftedness and its application to the Rome, Corinth, and Ephesus situations);
4. will do routine problem solving concerning structural issues (every epistle Paul wrote does this);
5. will adjust structures where necessary to facilitate leadership transitions (the Ac 15 intervention is doing this; the book of Tit and 1,2 Ti are doing this; Paul is transitioning apostolic leadership to Titus and Timothy);
6. must do direct ministry relating to maintaining and changing structures (extent depends on giftedness)(a good bit of the Ac narrative about Paul's 1 and 2 missionary journeys illustrates this).

Relational-Oriented Leadership

Relational-oriented leadership (technically called *Consideration* in the Ohio State research) groups all of those activities which a leader does to affirm followers, to provide an atmosphere congenial to accomplishing work, to give emotional and spiritual support for followers so that they can mature. In short, it is to act relationally with followers in order to enable them to develop and be effective in their contribution to the organization. Table 1,2 Co 28-2 lists some typical relational oriented leadership functions.

Table 1,2 Co 28-2. Typical Relational-Oriented Leadership Functions

Christian leaders:
1. must be involved in selection, development and release of emerging leaders (Paul was stronger in this than any other Church Leadership Era leader; Jesus was especially strong in this in the Pre-Church Leadership Era; in none of the O.T. Leadership Eras is this done well);
2. are called upon to solve crises involving relationships between people (Paul initially failed in this very area in his conflict with Barnabas. Paul somewhat does this but most of his crisis situations were corporate church crises);
3. will be called upon for decision-making focusing on people (Paul was strong in this—especially in his selection, training, and placement of leaders in various task oriented situations);
4. must do routine problem solving related to people issues;
5. will coordinate with subordinates, peers, and superiors;
6. must facilitate leadership transition—their own and others (Paul does this with Titus and Timothy);
7. must do direct ministry relating to people (extent depends on giftedness).

---

[96] The items on this list must be scrutinized from time-to-time and then contextualized to the present cultural leadership. New items may appear. Some of these may disappear. The same is true for the next two tables depicting Relational-Oriented and Inspirational Leadership Functions. These items are suggestive and must be finalized in specific contexts.

28. Leadership Functions: Three High Level Generic Priorities

Inspirational Leadership

Christian leadership is *externally directed*. That is, goals result from vision from God. Such leadership must move followers toward recognition of, acceptance of and participation in bringing about that God-given vision. Leaders will answer to God for their leadership.[97] Inspirational leadership is needed for this. Some typical inspirational functions are shown in Table 1,2 Co 28-3.

Table 1,2 Co 28-3. Typical Inspirational Leadership Functions

Christian leaders:
1. must motivate followers toward vision (Paul strong on this—see especially *Article 40. Motivating Factors For Ministry* and *Article 41. Motivating Principles: Pauline Influence*);
2. must encourage perseverance and faith of followers (Paul is very strong in this; his personal modeling alone was a great factor in accomplishing this function);
3. are responsible for the corporate integrity of the structures and organizations of which they are a part (note especially Paul's careful handling of money in every situation in which he raised or collected money);
4. are responsible for developing and maintaining the welfare of the corporate culture of the organization (Paul did this in every church situation he was involved in; note his continuing care and burden for all the churches; his intervention in the Corinthian situation especially highlights this function);
5. are responsible for promoting the public image of the organization;
6. are responsible for the financial welfare of the organization (Paul indirectly does this with his values of financial integrity and his sponsoring of other leaders in terms of financial support; his own tent making help provide financial resources for his missionary band);
7. are responsible for direct ministry along lines of giftedness which relate to inspirational functions (Paul was multi-gifted. His apostolic, teaching and exhortation gifts can be strongly sensed and felt as you read his interventions with the various N.T. church situations);
8. must model (knowing, being, and doing) so as to inspire followers toward the reality of God's intervention in lives (this is probably the strongest of the inspirational functions seen in Paul's life. Paul deliberately modeled and exhorted others to follow his modeling);
9. have corporate accountability to God for the organizations or structures in which they operate (Paul strongly advocates accountability to God for leadership influence; more than any other—excepting Jesus—he warns that we, as leaders, shall answer to God for our ministry. We will be held accountable).

Summarizing Leadership Functions

There are common activities and unique activities for the three categories of leadership functions. A single list helps pinpoint somewhat the essential activities of Christian leaders.

1. Utilize giftedness for direct ministry to those in their sphere of influence.
2. Solve crises.
3. Make decisions.
4. Do routine problem solving.
5. Coordinate people, goals, and structures.
6. Select and develop leaders.
7. Facilitate leadership transition at all levels.
8. Facilitate structures to accomplish vision.
9. Motivate followers toward vision. This usually involves changing what is, and providing/ promoting a sense of progress.
10. Must encourage perseverance and faith of followers. This usually involves maintaining what is and creating a sense of stability. This is usually in dynamic tension with activity 9.

---

[97] See **Article,** *1. Accountability—Standing Before God as a Leader.*

28. Leadership Functions: Three High Level Generic Priorities

11. Accept responsibility for corporate functions of integrity, culture, finances, and accountability.
12. Must model so as to inspire followers toward the reality of God's intervention in lives and history.

Conclusion

These three functions must be carefully tended to if an organization is to go on.[98] Yet, a given leader usually has a predilection (Paul's predilection was toward task-oriented leadership) toward either task-oriented leadership or relational-oriented leadership. It is a rare leader who can do both well. But either a task-oriented leader or a relational-oriented leader can do inspirational leadership. That is, motivational functions can be done by either a task-oriented leader or relational-oriented leader. What ever the case, it is up to a high-level leader to make sure the functions are done despite his/her own particular bent. To do this a high-level leader must be willing to delegate, to depend on and release to others functions that are not his/her own strength.

A final comment: The higher the level of leadership (Paul's level 5 is the highest level) the more the leader must powerfully demonstrate the third high level leadership function—that of inspirational leadership. Usually along the way of developing as a level 3 and level 4 leader, the task-oriented or relational-oriented leadership function will have dominated. But the higher the leader goes in development of sphere of influence—the more important is the inspirational function. Paul aptly demonstrates this.

See **Article**, *31. Leadership Levels—Looking At a Leadership Continuum.*

---

[98] Most task oriented Christian organizations simply assume that these are happening.

Article 29

Relevance of the Article to Paul's Corinthian Ministry

Six of the seven leadership genre are illustrated in 1,2 Co. The (1) biographical genre is especially informative as God's shaping activity in Paul's life is clearly seen. (2) The giftedness passages 1 Co 12-14 and the giving interlude, 2 Co 8,9 are direct leadership passages. (3) The two books, 1, 2 Co taken as a whole, illustrate in great detail a leadership act. (4) Only the parabolic leadership genre is missing. (5) This whole commentary is demonstrating the notion of book as a whole. (6) Indirect passages and (7) Macro lessons are also present. In fact, one could teach on these genre and illustrate them well by using 1,2 Co.

29. Leadership Genre—Seven Types

Introduction to the Seven Leadership Genre

A Bible Centered leader refers to a leader whose leadership is informed by the Bible, who has been personally shaped by Biblical values, has grasped the intent of Scriptural books and their content in such a way as to apply them to current situations and who uses the Bible in ministry so as to impact followers. Notice that first concept again—

whose leadership is informed by the Bible.

Two of the most helpful perspectives for becoming a Bible centered **leader whose leadership is informed by the Bible** include:

(1) recognizing the differences in leadership demands on leaders throughout the Bible, i.e. seeing the different leadership eras, and
(2) Recognizing and knowing how to draw out insights from the seven genre of leadership sources in the Bible.

This article overviews the second of these helpful perspectives—the seven leadership genres and how to get leadership information from them.

The Seven Genre—Derived From Study Across Six Leadership Eras

I have identified six periods of time, each of which characterized a major leadership era in the Bible. See Table 1,2 Co 29-1 below.

Table 1,2 Co 29-1. Six Leadership Eras in the Bible

Era	Name	Central Feature
I.	O.T. Patriarchal Era (Leadership Roots)	Family Base
II.	O.T. Pre-Kingdom Leadership Era	Tribal Base
III.	O.T. Kingdom Leadership Era	Nation Based
IV.	O.T. Post-Kingdom Leadership Era	Individual/ Remnant Based
V.	N.T. Pre-Church Leadership	Spiritually Based in the Land
VI.	N.T. Church Leadership	Decentralized Spiritually Based

29. Leadership Genre—Seven Types

Further study of each of these leadership eras resulted in the identification of seven leadership genre which served as sources for leadership findings. I then worked out in detail approaches for studying each of these genre.[99] These seven leadership genre are shown in Table 1,2 Co 29-2.

Table 1,2 Co 29-2. Seven Leadership Genre—Sources for Leadership Findings

Type	General Description/ Example	Approach
1. Biograph-ical	Information about leaders; this is the single largest genre giving leadership information in the Bible/ Joseph.	Use biographical analysis based on leadership emergence theory concepts. See **Article**, *Biographical Studies in the Bible— How To Do*.
2. Direct Leader-ship Contexts	Blocks of Scripture which are giving information directly applicable to leaders/ leadership; relatively few of these in Scripture/ 1 Peter 5:1-4.	Use standard exegetical techniques. Note the passages in 1, 2Ti and Tit which deal with leadership. These three books have more direct contexts dealing with leadership than any other books in the Bible. See my running commentary, overviews and leadership insights sections for these books.
3. Leader-ship Acts	Mostly narrative vignettes describing a leader influencing followers usually in some crisis situation; quite a few of these in the Bible/Acts 15 Jerusalem Council	Use three fold leadership tree diagram as basic source for suggesting what areas of leadership to look for. See 1,2 Co 34-1 in *Article 34. Leadership Tree Diagram* for categories helpful for analyzing.
4. Parabolic Passages	Parables focusing on leadership perspectives: e.g. stewardship parables, futuristic parables; quite a few of these in Matthew and Luke./ Luke 19 The Pounds	Use standard parable exegetical techniques but then use leadership perspectives to draw out applicational findings; especially recognize the leadership intent of Jesus in giving these. Most such parables were given with a view to training disciples.
5. Books as a Whole	Each book in the Bible; end result of this is a list of leadership observations or lessons or implications for leadership/ Deuteronomy	Consider each of the Bible books in terms of the leadership era in which they occur and for what they contribute to leadership findings; will have to use whatever other leadership genre source occurs in a given book; also use overall synthesis thinking. I have done this in this very commentary in the Leadership Insights Section for each of the 8 top leadership books of the Bible. I also have done this for each book of the Bible in another manual, **The Bible and Leadership Values**.
6. Indirect Passages	Passages in the Scripture dealing with Biblical values applicable to all; more so to leaders who must model Biblical values/ Proverbs; Sermon on the Mount	Use standard exegetical procedures for the type of Scripture containing the applicable Biblical ethical findings or values
7. Macro Lessons	Generalized high level leadership observations seen in an era and which have potential for leadership absolutes/ Presence Macro	Use synthesis techniques utilizing various leadership perspectives to stimulate observations. I have made a start on this. See **Articles**, *35. Macros Lessons Defined; 36. Macro Lessons— List of 41 Macro Lessons*.

A major step in becoming informed about leadership in the Bible is to recognize the various kinds of leadership information sources, the seven genre described above. But the more important step is to start studying these sources for leadership observations, principles, guidelines, macro lessons, and absolutes.

See **Articles**, *35. Macros Lessons Defined; 36. Macro Lessons—List of 41 Across Six Leadership Eras; 6. Bible Centered Leader*.

---

[99] These detailed approaches are given in my manual, **Leadership Perspectives—How To Study The Bible for Leadership Insights**.

Article 30

Relevance of the Article to Paul's Corinthian Ministry

Other than Jesus, Paul is the strongest leader in the N.T. in terms of these 7 lessons. And for the most part he was deliberate in using these leadership principles in his life. Many times in my comparative study of leaders it is evident that some of the lessons were known and used deliberately while others are seen but not necessarily explicitly known by the leader. However, in Paul's case it can be shown that he proactively operated with these leadership principles in mind. He models these lessons well.

30. Leadership Lessons— Seven Major Lessons Identified

From comparative study of over 1200 leader case studies, seven major leadership lessons have emerged. These leadership lessons are listed below with a brief explanation, a value suggested which flows from the lesson, reasons why important, a Biblical and a contemporary example and some suggestions for follow-up.

1. Lifetime Perspective

Effective Leaders View Present Ministry in Terms Of A Lifetime Perspective.

Explanation: Leaders who recognize the big picture for their lives have a jump start on surviving present circumstances which may be both negative and overwhelming. A leader needs to recognize the notion of developmental phases over a lifetime and boundaries transitioning between them. He/she needs to understand the shaping activity of God over a lifetime. If such a leader also knows the basic goal toward which God is moving, he/she can respond to present day shaping for maximum benefit. In general, a leader knowing what it means to finish well, determines to have that for his/her life. That leader recognizes the barriers to finishing well: 1. lack of financial integrity, 2. sexual impropriety, 3. abuse of power, 4. family related problems, 5. problems with pride, 6. plateauing. That leader recognizes the factors that will promote a good finish: 1. a learning posture, 2. mentoring help, 3. renewal experiences, 4. disciplines, 5. a lifelong perspective. A leader thus armed can perceive what is happening today from a sovereign mindset. In short, it allows the leader to go through present happenings because of the hope of the future and knowledge that God is in them.

Value Suggested: A leader ought to gain perspective on what is happening today in his/her life by interpreting it in the light of his/her whole lifetime and God's overall purposes in it.

Why Important: 1) Few leaders finish well. Perspective is one of the enhancements that can help a greater number of leaders finish well. 2) Making it through tough times in leadership may well depend on gaining perspective. Without perspective, a longer range viewpoint on what is happening, few leaders will persevere through hard times. 3) A critical difference between leaders and followers is perspective. The difference between leaders and more effective leaders is better perspective. Effective leaders will be broadening their perspective.

Biblical Examples: Jesus, Paul

Contemporary Example: Billy Graham

Suggestions for Follow-Up: Read Clinton's **The Making of a Leader** for a popular treatment of a lifetime perspective on a leader's development. See also the *Article Time-Lines—Defined for Biblical Leaders*. See Graham's autobiography, **Just As I Am**.

30. Leadership Lessons—Seven Major Lessons Identified

2. Learning Posture

Effective Leaders Maintain A Learning Posture Throughout Life.

Explanation: The ability to learn from the Bible, current events, people, reading, ministry experience, and other sources in such a way as to affect one's leadership is fundamental to being an effective leader. Flexible leaders usually do have a good learning posture (has to do with an attitude, a mental stance toward learning). Inflexible leaders are not usually active learners. God will bring into a leader's life necessary information and wisdom to meet leadership situations if that leader is open to learning. Leadership is dynamic. Changing situations demand that a leader be constantly learning. One of the five major factors identified with leaders who finish well is a good learning posture.
Value Suggested: A leader ought to be continually learning from a wide variety of sources in order to cope effectively with life and ministry.

Why Important: A good learning posture is one of the enhancements toward a good finish. It is also the key to ministry insights, paradigm shifts, and other leadership lessons that can make the difference in effective on-going leadership.

Biblical Examples: Daniel, the classic Old Testament leader, models an exemplary learning posture. The Apostle Paul does the same in the New Testament.

Historical and Contemporary Examples: Watchman Nee (Chinese church/para-church leader who died in prison in the early 70s); A. J. Gordon, Baptist pastor in Boston area and developer of one of the first flagship churches in the U.S. (1836-1895). Examples from today include Phil Yancey, Hans Finzel and Robertson McQuilkin.

Suggestions for Follow-Up: See Kinnear's book on Nee, **Against The Tide**. See **For Further Study Bibliography**, Clinton's chapter 3 on A.J. Gordon in **Focused Lives**.

3. Spiritual Authority

Effective Leaders Value Spiritual Authority As A Primary Power Base.

Explanation: Spiritual authority is the right to influence conferred by followers because of their perception of spirituality in a leader. It is that characteristic of a God-anointed leader which is developed upon an experiential power base that enables him/her to influence followers through: 1) Persuasion, 2) Force of modeling, and 3) Moral expertise. Spiritual authority comes to a leader in three major ways. First as leaders go through deep experiences with God they experience the sufficiency of God to meet them in those situations. They come to know God more intimately by experiencing Him. This experiential knowledge of God and the deep experiences with God are part of the experiential acquisition of spiritual authority. A second way that spiritual authority comes is through a life which models godliness. When the Spirit of God is transforming a life into the image of Christ, those characteristics of love, joy, peace, long suffering, gentleness, goodness, faith, meekness, temperance carry great weight in giving credibility. They show that the leader is consistent inwardly and outwardly. A third way that spiritual authority comes is through gifted power. When a leader demonstrates gifted power in ministry —that is, a clear testimony to divine intervention in the ministry—there will be spiritual authority. While all three of these means of developing spiritual authority should be a part of a leader, it is frequently the case that one or more of the elements dominates. Ideally spiritual authority is the major influence means used with mature followers. Other power bases such as coercion, inducement, positional, and competence may have to be used as well as spiritual authority because of lack of maturity in followers. Mature followers will recognize spiritual authority. Leaders who command and demand compliance are not using spiritual authority.

30. Leadership Lessons—Seven Major Lessons Identified 195

Values Suggested: 1) Leaders should respond to God's processing in their life so as to let spiritual authority develop as a by-product of the processing. 2) Leaders ought to recognize and use spiritual authority whenever they can in their ministry.

Why Important: Leaders who rely on privilege and power associated with a position tend to abuse power in their ministry. Spiritual authority counters the abuse of power. Spiritual authority honors God's maturity processes in followers.

Biblical Examples: Moses, Jesus, Paul

Historical and Contemporary Examples: Henrietta Mears, Bible teacher/ entrepreneur (1890-1963); Watchman Nee (Chinese church/para church leader who died in prison in the early 70s). John Wimber was a leader who especially had spiritual authority because of gifted power.

Suggestions for Follow-Up: See **For Further Study Bibliography**, Clinton's chapter 8 on Mears in **Focused Lives** and teaching by Nee on this subject, **Spiritual Authority**.

4. Dynamic Ministry Philosophy

> **Effective Leaders Who Are Productive Over A Lifetime Have A Dynamic Ministry Philosophy.**

Explanation: An unchanging set of core values and a changing set of peripheral values comprise a dynamic ministry philosophy. Such a ministry philosophy expands due to a growing discovery of giftedness, changing leadership situations, and greater understanding of the Scriptures. A leader's discovery of his/her giftedness and development of the same takes place over 10 to 15 years of ministry. Continued discovery will bring about issues of ministry philosophy not previously seen or anticipated. The same is true of the Scriptures. A leader will continue to master the Word over a lifetime. New input will lead to new philosophical values which will add to, clarify, or even replace earlier philosophical values which now become less important. Finally, leaders will usually move through three or four very different ministry situations over a lifetime. Each new situation will demand discovery of new leadership values. But a leader will also have some core values which continue throughout all phases. This core will also expand as new critical leadership values are added. But that leader will also have numerous periphery leadership values which will change, come and go, over a lifetime.

Value Suggested: A leader ought to identify core and peripheral leadership values under girding his/her leadership philosophy and be ready to adapt and changes these over a lifetime.

Why Important: Ministry essentially flows out of being. A conglomerate of factors make up one's being including (but not limited to): intimacy with God, personality, gender, giftedness, character, destiny and values (convictions) learned via ministry experience. One's ministry philosophy emerges from those values. Hence, if we are to operate in terms of who God has made us to be, we must increasingly become explicitly aware of the values that under gird our leadership.

Biblical Examples: Joseph, Habakkuk (generally prophetic ministry demands a ministry that is value based), Paul.

Historical and Contemporary Examples: G. Campbell Morgan, British pastor and international Bible teacher (1863-1945), Warren Wiersbe, Billy Graham.

Suggestions for Follow-Up: See **Article**, *71. Value Driven Leadership*. See also **For Further Study Bibliography**, Clinton's chapter 5 on Morgan in **Focused Lives**.

30. Leadership Lessons—Seven Major Lessons Identified

5. Leadership Selection And Development

Effective Leaders View Leadership Selection And Development As A Priority Function In Their Ministry.

Explanation: God raises up future leaders in present ministries. A major responsibility of Christian leaders is to partner with God in the on-going selection and development of leaders. The processes of identifying and developing leaders is both a means and an end. It is an end in itself by producing new leaders. But it is also a means for stimulating life in the ministry that is doing it. Emerging leaders also bring new life to a ministry. Strong leaders usually attract emerging leaders to themselves who are potentially like-gifted. Leaders should recognize this pattern and proactively respond to it by developing those potential leaders so attracted. Leaders who fail to recognize, select, and develop emerging leaders in their ministry miss out on personal growth that comes through this experience. They may almost be guaranteeing a weak future ministry that is overly dependent upon themselves.

Value Suggested: Leaders ought to be involved in the selection and development of emerging leaders.

Why Important: No work of God can last long that is not producing new leaders. Any work of God is only one generation away from nominality and mediocrity. New leadership emerging offsets nominality and plateauing ministry.

Biblical Examples: See Jesus ministry in the Gospels. See Paul's ministry. Both of these leaders selected and developed leaders.

Contemporary Examples: Robert Jaffray (1873-1945), Christian Missionary and Alliance missionary to Indo-China and Indonesia. Howard Hendricks. Paul Stanley. Alan Andrews.

Suggestions for Follow-Up: See *For Further Study Bibliography*, Clinton's chapter 6 on Jaffray in *Focused Lives*.

6. Relational Empowerment

Effective Leaders See Relational Empowerment As Both A Means And A Goal Of Ministry.

Explanation: Personal relationships between a leader and followers allow for interdependence in the body. Leaders need the feedback that comes through personal relationships with their followers. Leaders should be developing body life (reciprocal living—the one-another commands) as a major goal. This kind of behavior in a group provides a base from which all kinds of development can occur. For example, personal relationships will develop which will lead to mentoring. Mentoring is probably the best informal means for developing followers and especially emerging leaders. It is in the context of close, accountable, personal relationships that younger leaders can be encouraged and truly empowered.

Value Suggested: A leader ought to view personal relationships as a Biblical and critical priority in ministry both for developing ambiance for growth and for empowering others via mentoring methods.

Why Important: Mentoring is one of the most appropriate means of developing followers and challenging emerging leaders. Modeling, one form of mentoring, is one of the most important influence means. Personal relationships form the seedbed for both mentoring and modeling.

Biblical Examples: Jesus, Paul

Historical and Contemporary Examples: Henrietta Mears (1890-1963); Dawson Trotman (1906-1956), founder of the Navigators, Howard G. Hendricks, Paul Stanley, Bill Hull.

30. Leadership Lessons—Seven Major Lessons Identified 197

Suggestions for Follow-Up: See **Articles** *57. Reciprocal Living—The One-Another Commands; 47. Paul— Mentor For Many; 37. Mentoring—An Informal Training Model; 48. Paul—Modeling As An Influence Means.* See **For Further Study Bibliography**, Clinton's chapter 8 on Mears in **Focused Lives**. See Skinner's book, **Daws—The Story of Dawson Trotman, Founder of the Navigators.** See Clinton and Clinton, **The Mentor Handbook**. See Stanley and Clinton, **Connecting**.

7. Sense Of Destiny

Effective Leaders Evince A Growing Awareness Of Their Sense Of Destiny.

Explanation: A sense of destiny is an inner conviction arising from an experience (or a series of experiences) in which there is a growing awareness that God has His hand on a leader in a special way for special purposes. This typically happens along a three-fold destiny pattern: destiny preparation, destiny revelation, and destiny fulfillment. That is, a leader is usually unaware of preparation items as they happen, but in retrospect can reflect and see how God was preparing for a destiny. The sense of destiny deepens as God begins to unfold more clearly life purpose, role, and strategic guidance. And finally some or all of the destiny is fulfilled. Leaders become gradually aware of a destiny with God as He continues to shape them over a lifetime.

Value Suggested: A leader ought to be sensitive to destiny shaping activities in his/her past and present, and be anticipating their future implications. This awareness informs decision making reflecting partnership with God toward fulfilling that destiny.

Why Important: No Biblical leader greatly used by God failed to have a strong sense of destiny. A strong sense of destiny will buttress a leader to persevere toward a strong finish.

Biblical Examples: Abraham, Joseph, Moses, Jesus, Paul. Joseph, Moses, and Paul vividly demonstrate the threefold pattern of destiny preparation, destiny revelation and destiny fulfillment.
Contemporary Examples: Samuel Logan Brengle (1860-1936), Salvation Army Stalwart, Bill Bright.

Suggestions for Follow-Up: See **Article** *10. Destiny Pattern.* See **Glossary** for *destiny pattern; destiny processing; sense of destiny.* See also these same concepts in **Clinton's Leadership Emergence Theory Manual.** See Clarence Hall's work, **Samuel Logan Brengle, Portrait of a Prophet.** See For Further Study Bibliography, Clinton's chapter 4 on Brengle in **Focused Lives**.

Conclusion

Not all these lessons appear in a specific example of an effective leader. Some leaders exemplify three or four of them, others five or six and in a few cases all seven. But they are certainly goals for which to strive. It is not clear whether these lessons are by-products of effective leaders or causes of them being effective. Hopefully they are some of both so that if we deliberately try to put these in our lives they will improve our effectiveness.

Final Comment: Paul actually is an exemplar of each of these 7 major leadership lessons. Any one of these could be demonstrated vividly in his ministry. A number of them are evident in the Corinthian intervention.

Note: Many of the articles listed in the Suggestions for Follow-Up section are contained in this Commentary. Others occur in the Biblical Leadership Commentary CD. See the **For Further Study Bibliography** for full citations of books or manuals.

Article 31

<u>Relevance of the Article to Paul's Corinthian Ministry</u>
Even before Paul's conversion it was clear that he would have wide spread influence. He was operating in several different culture/countries as he pursued the persecution of Christians. At the critical incident—the *On the Road To Damascus revelatory Type I Awe Inspiring destiny* incident—it was clear that Paul would eventually have a Type E level influence. And Paul did. He also illustrates Types C and D and some Type A leadership in the church planting situations in which he established a longer residential ministry.

31. Leadership Levels
Looking At A Leadership Continuum: Five Types Of Leaders

Introduction

It is helpful to differentiate leaders in terms of some criteria. Several can be constructed. One typical example looks at Christian leadership in a church or denomination or parachurch organization. The primary criterion involves sphere of influence.[100] This typology of leaders along the continuum helps us pinpoint three major problems leaders face as they emerge from low level influence to high levels. These problems will repeatedly be faced around the world as the church emerges.

1. The Experience Gap,
2. The Financial (Logistics) Barrier,
3. The Strategic (Psychological) Barrier

Five Types of Leaders Along An Influence Continuum

Examine Figure 1,2 Co 31-1 which presents a continuum of leaders based on sphere of influence and shows some potential problems along the way.

---

[100] <u>Sphere of influence</u> refers to the totality of people being influenced and for whom a leader will give an account to God. The totally of people influenced subdivides into three domains called direct influence, indirect influence, and organizational influence. Three measures rate sphere of influence: 1. Extensiveness—which refers to quantity; 2. Comprehensivenes—which refers to the scope of things being influenced in the followers' lives; 3. Intensiveness—the depth to which influence extends to each item within the comprehensive influences. Extensiveness is the easiest to measure and hence is most often used or implied when talking about a leader's sphere of influence.

31. Leadership Levels

```
                          Leaders
                     can be classified into
    ┌──────────┬──────────┬──────────┬──────────┐
  TYPE A     TYPE B     TYPE C     TYPE D     TYPE E
  Local      Local      Regional   National   International
  Unpaid     Paid       Paid       Paid       Paid
```

←Low Levels of Influence   High Levels of Influence→

Problem 1. The Financial Barrier

Problem 2. The Experience Gap

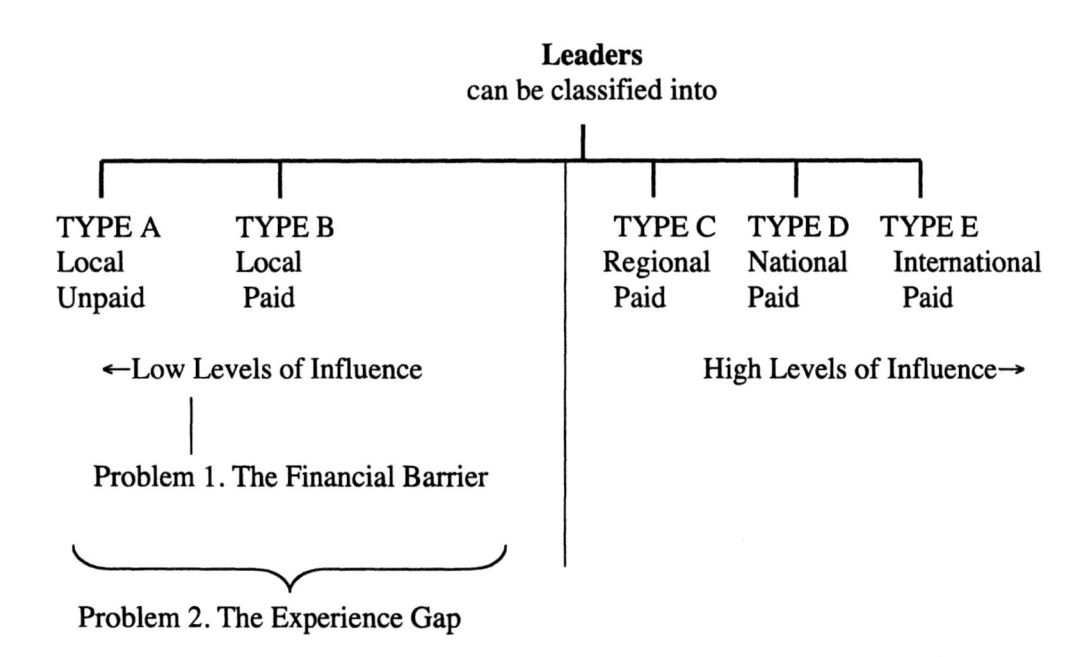

Problem 3. The Strategic Barrier

Figure 1,2 Co 31-1. Five Types of Leaders—Expanding Sphere of Influence/ Three Problems

Table 1,2 Co 31-1 further identifies each of the types of leaders.

Table 1,2 Co 31-1. Five Types of Leaders Described

Type	Description
A	These are volunteer workers who help local churches get their business done. Low level workers in a Christian organization, who do clerical work or other detailed staff administration work, fit this level of influence also.
B	Paid workers in small churches like pastors of small congregations or pastors of multi-congregations fit here. Sometimes these are bi-vocational workers having to supplement their salaries with outside employment. Associate pastors on staff in a larger church also have this same level of influence. Paid workers doing administrative work in a Christian organizations have the equivalent level of influence from an organizational standpoint.
C	This level of influence includes senior pastors of large churches who influence other churches in a large geographic area (e.g. via Radio/TV ministry, Pastor Conferences, separate organization promoting the pastor's publications, workshops, etc.). It also includes leaders in Christian organizations or denominations who are responsible for workers in a large geographic region.
D	These include senior pastors of large churches who have national influence usually via organizations created by them to promote their ministry. Denominational heads of a country would fit here too. Professors in prestigious seminaries which train high level leaders and are writing the texts which others use would fit here too. Some influential Christian writers might fit here.
E	Heads of international organizations with churches in various countries and or missionaries in many countries fit here. Some influential Christian writers might fit here. Leaders at this level dominantly do strategic thinking. Often Type E leaders will control large resources of people, finances, and facilities. They will have very broad personal networks with other international leaders and national leaders. They will often be on boards of very influential organizations.

31. Leadership Levels

It should be explicitly stated here that there is no inherent value attached to any of the types. That is, a Type E leader is not better than a Type A leader. All of the various types are needed in the church and mission organizations. More types A and B are needed than Type E leaders. The type of leader we become depends on capacity that God has given and God's development of us toward roles which use that capacity. To be gifted for Type B leadership and to aspire for Type D is a mismanagement of stewardship. So too, to be gifted for Type E and yet remain at Type C. None of the types are better than any other. All are needed. We need to operate along the continuum so as to responsibly exercise stewardship of our giftedness and God's development of our leadership. Bigger is not better. Appropriate is best.

Problem 1. The Financial Barrier

Problem 1, also called the *Logistics Barrier* or the *Lay/Clergy Dilemma*, deals with finances.[101] In most situations where a church is emerging, a need for workers who can devote their full time and giftedness to accomplish ministry goals will arise. In the Christian enterprise there are non-professional workers, people doing necessary work in churches. There are para-professional workers, those who give their most energy to church work and have some developed giftedness but who support themselves financially with some sort of secular job. And finally there are semi-professional workers. Some leaders get partial pay for their Christian work. When a worker moves from non-professional, para-professional, or semi-professional status to full time paid Christian worker, that is, workers move from Type A to Type B, he/she will face the financial barrier. How can such workers be financed? [102]Many potential leader stumbles over this barrier and never makes it in to full time ministry (and perhaps because of discouragement, drops out of ministry altogether). Paul was dealing with this problem in 1Co 16 when he exhorts the Corinthians about finances for Christian workers—his own self (subtlety given), Timothy, and Stephanus.

Additional Problems with Problem 1 Moving Across the Financial Barrier

There is a tendency, which I call, *The Projection Tendency,* to seek to pressure effective Type A leaders to *go full time*. The idea involves the subtle implication that full time Christian leaders are more dedicated to God than lay leaders.

There is another minor problem involved in moving from Type A to Type B leadership. I call it *The Expectation Problem*. When leader cross the logistics barrier, it involves a major status change for leaders. Laity perceive full time Christian workers differently than lay leaders. Movement from Type A to Type B leadership means that people will view them differently (perhaps have higher expectations of them) even though their roles may not change.

Problem 2. The Experience Gap

Problem 2, also called the pre-service training problem, basically deals with a modern problem. Where churches have spread in a given geographical area, training institutions like seminaries and Bible colleges have also emerged. Normally, as a church is emerging, leaders are trained on-the-job and take on more responsibility as they are ready for it. But once there is a large number of churches and larger individual churches, people who are untrained on the job and with little or no leadership experience go to these training institutions and in a short period of time are academically trained (sort of) for ministry. They then attempt to enter ministry at Type B or higher level if they can. They don't have the experience for it. So we have people leading at levels they are not experienced to lead. A similar but not identical problem is being dealt with in 1Ti where Paul is seeking to give Timothy, a younger worker, to be accepted by older leaders, the Ephesian elders. The problem is not exactly the same, since Timothy did have experience—but the

---

[101] Leaders who hold to the major leadership lesson on selection and development, as a value, will face this problem repeatedly as they seek to find ways to move leaders along in development. That lesson (Effective leaders view leadership selection and development as a priority function) carries with it some heavy responsibility.

[102] This is a major problem that will be faced around the world as the model which arose in the 19th and 20th centuries in countries with financial resources, that is, at least one full time paid pastor per congregation, go by the by. Bi-vocational workers will most likely dominate in the early part of the next century.

culture did not respect younger leaders. *The Experience Gap* is a double problem in some cultures since they respect age and experience, and training institutions turn out potential leaders who fit neither requirement.

Problem 3. The Strategic Barrier—Its Two Problems

Problem 3, also called the *ministry focus problem*, deals with a giftedness/ responsibility problem seen in leaders who move from Type C ministry to Type D or E ministry. That is, they become leaders who do less direct ministry and more indirect ministry. Heads of organizations with a big sphere of influence face this problem. Direct ministry means dominantly using word gifts to influence people directly. Indirect ministry means leaders who are now helping or directing other leaders in direct ministry but are themselves not primarily doing direct ministry. Usually leaders who rise to these levels do so because they were successful in direct ministry at lower levels of influence. Simply because they were effective at that lower level doing direct ministry depending on their word gifts does not insure that they will be successful at a higher level not dominantly using their word gifts. In short, they are not trained for the functions at the higher level. And what is more startling, little or no formal training exists to develop leaders to do these higher level leadership functions.

A second problem arises. It is a psychological one. It has to do with satisfaction in ministry. When one is doing direct ministry and dominantly using word gifts, there is a constant feedback of things happening in lives which gives affirmation and satisfaction. At higher levels most leaders are doing leadership functions like problem solving, crises resolution, structural planning, and strategizing. These functions do not reward one in the same way as direct ministry. They do not receive the same satisfaction in doing these things and getting little affirmation as they did when they effectively did direct ministry.

Two things can help overcome these two problems. One, leaders should be trained for the higher level functions, dominantly by mentoring from leaders who are doing them well, and then transitioned into them. Two, the psychological loss perceived by leaders crossing the strategic barrier can also be addressed in at least the following two ways that I have observed in leaders at high level. One, they can from time to time do forays back into direct ministry which bring satisfaction that was experienced previously. Two, they can learn to see that what is being accomplished has broader potential and more far reaching results than their former direct ministry which had to be sacrificed in accepting the higher level of leadership. This requires strategic thinking and an application of the servant leadership model at a higher capacity level. Paul's later ministry dealt with this strategic barrier problem. Most of his latter ministry was indirect. Note his epistles are largely indirect ministry. He is helping other leaders deal with their issues—problem solving, dealing with crises, etc. He is not out there teaching and preaching directly. Note he got strategic eyes—see 2Co 11:28,Then besides all this, daily, I am burdened with my responsibility for the churches.

Conclusion

Types of leaders, that is, levels of leadership, are distinguished not to imply that bigger is better but to indicate that problems will be faced as leaders develop to higher levels of leadership. Further, leadership issues will vary noticeably with the different types. Types D and E are much more concerned with leadership means/resources, items of organizational structure, culture, dynamics, and power. They are multi-style leaders. They are more concerned with leadership philosophy and with strategic thinking. They know they will have heavy accountability to God in these areas. They are concerned with macro-contextual factors. Because leadership functions vary greatly along the continuum, different training is needed for each type. Informal/non-formal training focusing on skills for direct ministry is needed for Types A/B and should usually be in-service. All three modes (informal, non-formal, and formal) are needed to provide skills and perspectives for Types C, D, and E. In-service and interrupted in-service should dominate for Types C, D, and E.

See *sphere of influence, pre-service training, in-service training, word gifts, mentoring definitions, leadership styles, formal training, non-formal training, informal training,* **Glossary**. See **Articles**, *49. Pauline Leadership Styles; Training Modes—When They Fit.*

Article 32

Relevance of the Article to Paul's Corinthian Ministry

Paul shines here. Read *Article 43. Paul and His Companions* to get a view of his fishing pool. Paul had a great number of personal relationships from which to ascertain potential leaders and select them for further training. See also **Articles** *45. Paul—Developer Par Excellence, 47. Paul—Mentor For Many, 48. Paul—Modeling as An Influence Means and 37. Mentoring—An Informal Training Model.* In all these articles as well as the concepts seen below in this article, you will see that Paul is an exemplar in Leadership Selection and Development. His three year training time in the Bible School at Ephesus probably is the highlight of his leadership development. His deliberate selection of the six future apostolic leaders, (from different geographical situations) stands out. He deliberately invited Timothy, Titus, Aristarcus, Segundus, Gaius, Sopater to his on-the-job training institute in Ephesus. Later Trophimus, Tychicus, and Epaphras also came and spent residential time there. This training at Ephesus really is the highpoint of Paul's leadership selection and development. It is clear he was aware of a limited time left him. He wanted to train those who could carry on his legacy. Major Leadership Lessons 5. Leadership Selection And Development (Effective Leaders View Leadership Selection And Development As A Priority Function In Their Ministry) and 6. Relational Empowerment (Effective Leaders See Relational Empowerment As Both A Means And A Goal Of Ministry) standout out in Paul's ministry. This article highlights the selection perspectives that are needed to emulate Paul's leadership and selection accomplishments.

32. Leadership Selection

Introduction

A major lesson identified from a comparative study of leaders[103] challenges to the core,

> **Effective Leaders View Leadership Selection and Development as a priority function.**

This value dominated Christ's ministry. To instill an on-going movement Christ had to inculcate his values in a band of leaders who would continue to propagate his movement. And he had to train them well in order for them to carry on. This he did. *Selection and Development* are stressed in Christ's Ministry.[104] Paul held to this value very strongly in his ministry.[105] What should we know about leadership selection and

---

[103] Seven such lessons have been identified: (1) Effective Leaders View Present Ministry in Terms Of A Life Time Perspective. (2) Effective Leaders Maintain A Learning Posture Throughout Life. (3) Effective Leaders Value Spiritual Authority As A Primary Power Base. (4) Effective Leaders Who Are Productive Over A Lifetime Have A Dynamic Ministry Philosophy. (5) Effective Leaders View Leadership Selection And Development As A Priority Function In Their Ministry. (6) Effective Leaders See Relational Empowerment As Both A Means And A Goal Of Ministry. (7) Effective Leaders Evince A Growing Awareness Of Their Sense Of Destiny. It is the fifth one I am exploring in this article.

[104] See Bruce's, **The Training of the Twelve**, a famous treatise dealing with Jesus' approach to leadership selection and development. See also, **Articles**, *Jesus—Circles of Intimacy, A Developmental Technique, Jesus—Recruiting Techniques.*

[105] Whereas both selection and development are seen equally well in Jesus' ministry, development dominates Paul's ministry. See **Articles**, *43. Paul—And His Companions; 47. Paul—Mentor For Many; 48. Paul—Modeling as An Influence Means.*

32. Leadership Selection

development if we want to have this important value in our lives? Two things will help us: (1) terminology that describes what happens and (2) an overall time perspective integrating the things that happen. [106]

Leadership Selection—The Basic Concept Defined

When God touches a life for leadership, there will be indications that can be recognized by observant Christian leaders. Mature leaders who know the importance of leadership selection and development are constantly on the lookout for just such recognition features. They want to partner with God in what He is doing to raise up emerging leadership. The process of God's selection, the recognition and affirmation by human leadership, and the subsequent development comprise what leadership selection is all about.

Definition   Leadership selection is the life-long process of divine initiative and human recognition whereby a leader[107] emerges.

Leadership selection describes a life-long recognition process which is punctuated with critical incidents, as viewed from a two-fold intermeshing perspective—the divine and the human. The process starts from earliest symptomatic indications of a leader emerging. It continues right on up to maturity. God will continue to select a leader throughout his/her lifetime. Mature selection involves God strategically guiding the leader on to a focused life. But note this is a threefold interactive process: (1) God is involved; (2) the leader is involved; and (3) other human leadership is involved. God gives confirmation to the selection of a leader via others leaders as well as directly to that leader.

The Ministry time-line is shown below in Figure 1,2 Co 32-1 highlights the three-fold interactive process. The Divine perspective involvement occurs above the time-line. The entries below the line portray some of the human interactions—both the individual leader's processing and what other human leaders see (Paul was strong here—he had eyes for potential leaders) and confirm.

---

[106] To really appreciate leadership selection over a lifetime one needs to have a thorough grasp of leadership emergence theory.

[107] The definition of leader used in this commentary pre-supposes the divine element of leadership selection. A leader is a person with God-given capacity and God-given responsibility who is influencing a specific group of God's people toward God's purposes.

32. Leadership Selection

<u>Divine Initiative/ Perspective</u>

1. (Pre-birth Call)
2. Destiny Unfolding --->
       Destiny Preparation   Destiny Revelation   Destiny Fulfillment
3. Giftedness/ Leadership
     Potential Engendered --->
           4. Call
               5. Processing: focal incidents/ strategic guidance ---------------------->

Time-Line[108] ------>

Phase I	Phase II	Phase III	Phase IV
Ministry Foundations	General Ministry	Focused Ministry	Convergent Ministry

<u>Human Recognition Vantage Point</u>

1. Response to God
  2. Potential Seen
    3. Emerging Leader Symptoms, Word Gifts/ Obedience Attitude
      4. Challenge Toward Expectations
        5. Foundational Patterns
        6. Foundational Ministry Pattern
        7. Like--Attracts-Like Gift Pattern
        8. Ministry Entry Patterns
        9. Give Affirmation
            10. Transitional Training Patterns
            11. Mentoring
            12. Giftedness Development Pattern

Figure 1,2 Co 32-1. The Leadership Selection Process Viewed Pictorially Over a Time-line

Illustrations from Jesus' and Paul's Ministry

Table 1,2 Co 32-1 illustrates important leadership selection concepts in Jesus own life, Paul's own life and in their ministry.

---

[108] See **Article**, *Time-Line, Defined for Biblical Leaders*. The time-line shown here is a generic time-line used to assess where a leader is in development over a life time. The four phases represent segments correlating to development in a life. Each phase to the right represents a more mature stage. General ministry is a time of learning for the leader. God is doing more in the leader's life than through him/her. Focused ministry is a time of efficient ministry. The leader knows his/her own giftedness and uses it well—a time of tactical ministry. Convergent ministry represents a time of strategic ministry. If Focused Ministry can be described as doing things right then Convergent Ministry means doing the right things right. It is a time of strategic accomplishment.

32. Leadership Selection

Table 1,2 Co 32-1. Leadership Selection Concepts Illustrated

Concept	Illustration
Divine 1. (Pre-birth Call)	See Gal 1:15—indication in Paul's life; See also Samuel; Samson; John the Baptist.
Divine 2. Destiny Unfolding	See **Article**, *Destiny Pattern*, for Paul's destiny unfolding.
Divine 3. Giftedness/ Leadership Potential Engendered	Php 3:4-6 Paul's advancement before conversion—indications of great potential. Apollos—Ac 18:24-26;
Divine 4. Call	Jesus ministry: See Jn 1 for call of John, Andrew, Simon Peter, James, Philip, Nathanael. For (repeated) call trace the phrase, *follow me*: see Mt 4:19; 8:22; 9:9; 16:24; 19:21; Mk 2:14; 8:34; 10:21; Lk 5:27; 9:23; 9:59; 18:22; Jn 1:43;12:26.
Divine 5. Processing: focal incidents/ strategic guidance	See Section, **Biblical Leaders Time-Lines** where critical incidents are shown along time-lines. See Paul's Time-Line; See Jesus' Time-Line. See *critical incident*, **Glossary**.
Human 1. Response to God	See Paul, Ac 9, 22, 26—conversion story; Ac 13 further ministry call; Ac 16 further call to Europe. All show Paul's response well.
Human 2. Potential Seen	See Timothy Ac 16:2.
Human 3. Emerging Leader Symptoms, Word Gifts/Obedience/Attitude	Obedience and Attitudes seen in lives of Paul's companions. But symptoms of Word Gifts not seen in a detailed way in Biblical examples. This selection observation arises from many contemporary case studies.
Human 4. Challenge Toward Expectations	See Paul's writings to Timothy for numerous illustrations of this. See especially the concept of Goodwin's Expectation principle, 2Ti 1:5;
Human 5. Foundational Patterns	See Timothy for Heritage pattern; see Titus for Radical Conversion;
Human 6. Foundational Ministry Pattern	See Lk 16:10 for Jesus teaching on this. Faithfulness in ministry leads to other ministry. Illustrated in ministry assignments given Timothy and Titus.
Human 7. Like--Attracts-Like Gift Pattern	Difficult to see in Biblical characters because of lack of details but seen repeatedly in contemporary case studies.
Human 8. Ministry Entry Patterns	The most important ministry entry pattern *self-initiated creation of new ministry structures* is seen repeatedly in Paul's life.
Human 9. Give Affirmation	This is demonstrated repeatedly in Paul's life and ministry.
Human 10. Transitional Training Patterns	The transitional training in-service pattern is seen repeatedly in both Jesus' and Paul's training of emerging leaders.
Human 11. Mentoring	Jesus mentors in a group context with occasional personal mentoring with Peter, James and John. Paul demonstrates mentoring at group level and many illustrations of individual mentoring. Both Jesus and Paul move along into partnering with God in developing leaders via deliberate proactive intervention in lives via mentoring.
Human 12. Giftedness Development Pattern	Not seen in Biblical examples because of lack of details. But seen in numerous contemporary case studies.

32. Leadership Selection

Observations on Leadership Selection

Observations flowing from this leadership selection model include:

1. The on-going operation of a movement, organization, or church require leadership selection and development. To ignore selection is to cut off the next generation of leaders. To ignore development is to provide a big back door whereby your recruited leaders leave and are developed by others.
2. To partner with God in leadership selection and development effectively, a leader needs to be very familiar with developmental theory—that is, how a leader develops over a lifetime.[109] Or to say it another way, the more familiar you are with how God develops a leader the more you will be sensitive to when you can intervene in a godly way to help develop that leader.
3. Rarely will all 17 selection elements be seen in a given individual. Some are missing altogether. Others are more prominent. The list was synthesized from comparative study of many leaders.
4. The prime responsibility for leadership selection and development is God's. But an important secondary responsibility involves God's use of other human leaders to select and develop leaders. Without human affirmation of God's call in a life, a potential leader is subject to only internal subjective discernment of God's working. Self-deception can run rampant. External human recognition and affirmation is desperately needed to protect both an individual leader and those he/she will influence.
5. Progressive calls over a lifetime (see Jesus ministry with his own and God's dealing with Paul) highlight the concept of selection taking place over a lifetime.

Conclusion

No strategic thinking leader will overlook this important leadership value,

> **Effective Leaders View Leadership Selection and Development as a priority function.**

No effective leader can carry out all the functions that need to be done to select and develop. But every leader can look for and join with other leaders who can help carry out this important function. Needed are recruiter specialists, early developer specialists, strategic developers. Recruiters hook potential leaders. Early developer specialists develop efficiency in a maturing leader. Strategic developers develop effectiveness in mature leaders.

See *progressive calling*, **Glossary**. See **Articles**, *Developing Giftedness; 10. Destiny Pattern; Divine Affirmation in the Life of Jesus; 11. Entrustment—A Leadership Responsibility; Focused Life; Foundational Patterns; 19. God's Shaping Processes With Leaders; 20. Impartation of Gifts; 22. Integrity—A Top Leadership Quality; 23. Isolation Processing—Learning Deep Lessons from God; Jesus—Circles of Intimacy—A Developmental Technique; 30. Leadership Lessons—Seven Identified; 31. Leadership Levels—Looking At a Leadership Continuum; 38. Ministry Entry Patterns; 42. Paul—Sense of Destiny; 43. Paul—And His Companions; 44. Paul—Deep Processing; 45. Paul—Developer Par Excellence; 47. Paul—Mentor For Many; 61. Spiritual Benchmarks; 64. Spiritual Gifts, Giftedness and Development; Training Models—When They Fit.*

---

[109] My leadership emergence theory has developed over the past 19 years. It views how God develops a leader over a lifetime. All of the concepts alluded to in the leadership selection model of this article are defined or described in leadership emergence theory. See **For Further Study, Bibliography**, the manual, **Leadership Emergence Theory**.

Article 33

Relevance of the Article to Paul's Corinthian Ministry

Leadership transitions in the Scripture have only a few shining examples. Most are poorly done. Seven come to mind as having some good information. You may wish to study them— Moses to Joshua, Samuel to Saul (though Saul later fails), Elijah to Elisha, Jesus to the Disciples, Barnabas to Paul, Paul to the Ephesian elders, and finally, Paul to Titus and Timothy. Paul's missionary band gave him ample opportunity to transition various pieces of his ministry to those he was training. His use of ministry tasks provided a means to gradually transition those on his traveling team into competent roles and ministry. His authoritative backing given to Titus in his ministry at Crete and Timothy in his ministry at Ephesus are his final swansongs and show a mature transition of Titus and Timothy into Apostolic ministry on their own merits. Paul did a fine job of sponsoring them so that their future ministry would be powerful.

33. Leadership Transition Concepts

Background/ Definitions

An important macro lesson discovered in the Pre-Kingdom Leadership Era is stated as:

15. [110]Transition **Leaders must transition other leaders into their work in order to maintain continuity and effectiveness.**

This lesson was discovered during Moses' leadership. His transition of Joshua into leadership over a long period of time stands out as the classical model for transitioning a leader into an important leadership role.

Transition times in movements, organizations and churches are hard, complex times. How leaders transition new leaders into leadership can make or break the on-going ministry. It is a special time of problems and opportunities. The process is best understood when viewed along a continuum.

Definition Leadership transition is the process whereby existing leaders prepare and release emerging leaders into the responsibility and practice of leadership positions, functions, roles, and tasks.

←REPLACEMENT OF LEADERSHIP				REPLACEMENT OF LEADER→	
(What the leader does; Tasks, Roles, Functions)				(The person himself/herself)	
simple task	more or complicated task(s)	role with many tasks	pick up some functions	major responsibility for functions	the leader's role

Practicing Leader increasingly RELEASES-->
Emerging Leader increasingly accepts RESPONSIBILITY---------------------->

Figure 1,2 Co 33-1. Leadership Transition Continuum

---

[110] This is number 15 of 41 macro lessons listed over the six leadership eras. See **Article**, Macro Lessons, List of 41.

33. Leadership Transition Concepts

Continuum Definitions

Definition	A *task* is an observable assignment of usually short duration.
Definition	A *role* is a recognizable position which does a major portion of the ministry. It probably has several ongoing tasks associated with it.
Definition	*Leadership functions* is a technical term which refers to the three major categories of formal leadership responsibility: task behavior (defining structure and goals), relationship behavior (providing the emotional support and ambiance), and inspirational behavior (providing motivational effort).
Comment	Each of these major leadership functions has several specific sub-functions.
Definition	*Leadership release* is the process whereby an existing leader deliberately encourages and allows an emerging leader to accept responsibility for and control of leadership positions, functions, roles, and tasks.
Definition	*Overlap* is that unique time in a leadership transition when the emerging leader and existing leader share responsibility and accountability for tasks, roles, and functions.
Definition	*Tandem training* describes the training technique during overlap used by an existing leader with an emerging leader.

Let me comment on the two extremes on the continuum. On the right of the continuum is the maximum limit of leadership transition, that is, the leader himself/ herself is replaced totally from the leadership situation. The emerging leader thus becomes the new leader and is totally responsible for the leadership situation. On the left is the minimum, the present leader turns over some small piece of leadership, e.g. a simple task. In between the two extremes, various levels of transition are experienced

The process across the continuum is simply described. As one moves across the continuum faithful performance of simple tasks leads to increasing responsibility such as a role. Faithful or successful accomplishment of a role will lead to greater responsibility—usually wider roles and responsibility for important functions of the ministry as a whole.

Two tendencies have been observed as the transition process goes on. As you move from left to right on the continuum, the present leader is increasingly releasing more tasks, functions and finally major responsibility for the ministry. This is signified by the arrow moving toward the right. The function of release is a difficult one for most leaders. The tendency is to either *over-control* on the one hand (*authoritarian defensive posture*), or to *give too much responsibility without adequate supervision* or transitional training on the other (*the quick release posture*). The first tendency suffocates emerging leaders and frustrates them in their attempt to grow and assume leadership. Such a posture usually drives them out of the organization to another ministry where they can be released. The second tendency overwhelms them and usually insures failure in their first attempt at leadership. This can be discouraging and cause some to decide not to move into leadership in ministry.

The rate at which the release should occur ought to depend on the ability of the emerging leader to pick up responsibility for it and not an authoritarian posture or a quick release posture. The arrow moving to the right demonstrates that the emerging leader should be picking up responsibility for the tasks, roles, or functions. As this is done, the leader should be releasing.

Overlap is the time in which both the leader and emerging leader are working together in an increasing way to release and accept responsibility. Overlap can occur anywhere along the continuum.

Tandem training allows the younger leader to share the learning experiences of the older leader via modeling, mentoring, apprenticeship, or internships so as to leapfrog the younger leader's development.

Leadership Transitions In The Bible

There are numerous instances in Scripture of leadership transitions. Most are not ideal as suggested by the transitional continuum. The Moses/Joshua transition, which took place over an extended time does

33. Leadership Transition Concepts

follow the description given above of the transitional continuum. It is one of the positive models of leadership transition in the Scriptures. Another positive model occurs in the New Testament -—that of Barnabas and Saul. Other leadership situations in Scripture are worthy of study, mostly for the negative lessons and identification of the items on the transitional continuum that are missing. Table 1,2 Co 33-1 lists some of the instances of Scripture that provide data for observing the positive and negative effects of leadership transitions -- be they good or bad.

Table 1,2 Co 33-1. Examples of Biblical Leadership Transitions Providing Insights

Joseph (sovereign transition)
Moses (sovereign transition)
Moses/Joshua (tandem transition)
Joshua/? (none)
Jephthah (other judges—negative)
Eli/sons (negative)
Samuel (sovereign transition)
Samuel/Saul (modified negative)
Saul/David (negative)

David/Absalom (aborted)
David/Solomon (negative)
Elijah/Elisha (minimum)
Daniel (sovereign)
Jesus/disciples
Apostles/deacons (Acts 6)
Barnabas/ Paul (leader switch)
Acts 20 Paul/Ephesian elders
Paul/ Timothy (2Ti); Titus (Tit)

Probably the best leadership transition to observe in which the continuum concepts are more readily seen involves Moses' transition of Joshua into leadership.

10 Steps In Moses/Joshua Transition

In the Moses/Joshua transition several steps, stages, or discernible events can be ordered. These give insights into why the transition was successful and led to a great leader being raised up to follow a great leader. Table 1,2 Co 33-2 lists observations which suggest why the transition was successful.

Table 1,2 Co 33-2. Observations on the Moses/ Joshua Leadership Transition

Step	Label	Description
1	Definite Leadership Selection	There was deliberate and definite leadership selection. Moses chose Joshua. Joshua came from a leading family with leadership heritage (note the march order in Exodus -- his grandfather prominent). Notice Moses Nepotism, see comment which follows these steps.

2	Ministry Task	Moses gave him ministry tasks with significant responsibility:
		  a. First, select recruits and lead battle among the Amalekites who were harassing the flanks of the exodus march.
		  b. Second, spy out the land (probably one of the younger ones to be chosen). Moses checked Joshua's: (1) faith, (2) faithfulness, (3) giftedness (charismatic ability to lead) with these increasing responsibilities.

3	Spirituality/ Tandem Training	Moses included Joshua in his own spiritual experiences with God. Joshua had firsthand access to Moses' vital experiences with God. Moses took him into the holy of holies, frequently into the tabernacle into the presence of God and up on the mountain when he was in solitude alone with God. This was tandem training in spirituality using mentoring as the means of training.
4	Leadership span	Moses recognized the complexity of the leadership situation toward the end of his life. He knew Joshua could not do it all. When transitioning him into leadership he saw that Joshua was a charismatic militaristic leader who needed a supportive spiritual leader. He set Eleazar up as the spiritual leader. He publicly did this—bolstered Eleazar in the eyes of the people, recognized Joshua's strengths and weaknesses. Moses knew that any leader coming into his position would have trouble—most likely could not fill his shoes; he would need help. Actually Joshua developed real spiritual authority and became a spiritual leader in terms of inspirational leadership.

5	Public Recognition	Moses recognized the importance of followers knowing whom he had appointed to be the next leader. No ambiguity. No scramble of leaders for that position after Moses' death. He settled it ahead of time and gave a public ceremony stipulating his backing of Joshua.
6	New Challenge	The new leader following an old leader must not look back and compare. One way of overcoming this tendency is to have a big challenge, a new task not done by the old leader. There was a big task to do. It would be his own contribution—possess the land.
7	Divine Affirmation	The new leader needed to know not only that Moses had appointed him as leader but that God had confirmed this appointment. Dt 31:14-18 and Joshua 1 point out Joshua's experiences personally with God concerning the appointment.
8	Public Ceremony	Not only must there be personal assurance that God has appointed him/her but there must be public recognition of this. God gives this in Joshua 3 (note Joshua 3:7: "What I do today will make all the people of Israel begin to honor you as a great man, and they will realize that I am with you as I was with Moses." See also Joshua 4:14: "What the Lord did that day made the people of Israel consider Joshua a great man. They honored him all his life, just as they had honored Moses.")
9	Initial Success	A leader moving into full responsibility needs an initial success that can bolster spiritual authority and demonstrate that the leader can get vision from God in his/her own right. Joshua's experience with the Captain of the Lord's Army was a pivotal point that did this. It gave him vision -- tactical plan with strategic implications. Its success came early on and stimulated followers. With it there was assurance that brought closure to the whole transition experience.
10	Initial Failure	A final thing that ensured a successful transition was the early failure at Ai. Leaders must know they are not infallible. They must trust God in their leadership. An early failure after initial success was a major deterrent to pride, showed the moral implications of godly leadership, and the notion that leaders must always move followers along toward God's purposes for them in God's way.

Commentary On Moses/Joshua Transition

Is this model transferable? Peculiar dynamics occur in this model. Its uniqueness may preclude its application in other situations. There was a long period of overlap due to the disciplining of the people in the wilderness. Joshua essentially led the next generation—not his own. A mighty expectation existed for the new task that challenged everyone. Joshua was a home-grown leader from a leadership heritage who had proved himself in many ways. He was a charismatic/military leader with a good spiritual track record of sensing and obeying God. Certain of the underlying ideas of these observations will probably be applicable even if the overall dynamics are not identical.

Notice that Moses avoids the problem of nepotism.[111] Joshua was hand-picked early for leadership. Yet when the final transition time arrived, Moses did not just assume that Joshua was the Lord's choice but sought the Lord's confirmation. And when it came *he did all he could to give Joshua the best chance of success*. This leadership transition is the most successful in Scripture. Moses was well aware that if his ministry was to be established beyond his lifetime as he wished (Psalm 90:17), providing leadership for it was necessary. He certainly exemplifies the *continuity* or *transition* macro-lesson.

Transition   **Leaders must transition other leaders into their work in order to maintain continuity and effectiveness.**

---

[111] It is not clear but it appears from hints given that Moses really had family problems and probably was separated from his family for extended times during his desert leadership. His sons are never prominently mentioned anywhere. His wife and children visit him when Jethro comes. So perhaps he was never tempted to try to place them in leadership as many charismatic leaders do today.

33. Leadership Transition Concepts

Four implications about leadership transition should be noted.

1. *Continuity*. No ministry can be expected to continue well without deliberate transition efforts.
2. *Nepotism*. Rarely can a leader replace his/her father/ mother with the same leadership effectiveness. The appropriate leader, gifted for the job, is the proper selection.
3. *Best Start*. Whenever leaving a ministry, insure that the next leader has the best possible chance of success. Note especially how Samuel did this (even though he was not for the transition itself).
4. *Models*. Study negative and positive Biblical models for guidelines. The positive models include Moses/ Joshua, Elijah/ Elisha, Jesus/ Disciples, Barnabas/ Paul, Paul/Timothy. A particularly negative one to see is Solomon/ Rehoboam.

See *leadership transition, leadership functions, leadership release, overlap, tandem training.*, **Glossary**.
See **Article**, *Regime Turnover*.

Article 34

Relevance of the Article to Paul's Corinthian Ministry

The following taxonomy was derived from a tracing of leadership in a western context. However, it became clear that the taxonomy applied to every Biblical leadership era—the four in the O.T. and the two in the N.T. And it became clearer in the School of World Mission of Fuller Theological Seminary that this taxonomy applied across cultures. It is a handy taxonomy for studying leadership issues anywhere. You can study Paul's Corinthian Intervention using this taxonomy. In fact, the leadership act approach uses this very taxonomy.

34. Leadership Tree Diagram

Introduction

The leadership tree diagram was developed from a survey of leadership history from the mid 1800s to the present. From the five leadership eras,[112] basic concepts of this tree diagram were integrated into an overall framework for evaluating leadership in any culture, including the various cultures in the Bible. Figure 1,2 Co 34-1 below gives the tree diagram. Table 1,2 Co 34-1 shows when each component was identified in terms of leadership history. Then Table 2 gives a brief description of each of the components of this tree diagram. This diagram proved especially helpful when analyzing the six Biblical leadership eras.[113] It continues to prove fruitful when analyzing leadership acts and other leadership genre in the Bible.

The Three Categories of A High Level Leadership Framework

Three categories are involved in a high level leadership framework. The first, The *Leadership Basal Elements*, deals primarily with the *What of Leadership*. The second, The *Leadership Influence Means* categorizes the *How of Leadership*. The final element, *Leadership Value Bases*, pinpoints the *Why of Leadership*. These three cross-cultural leadership components can be used to comparatively describe leadership anywhere in the world.

The Study Of Leadership
involves

Leadership Basal Elements	Leadership Influence Means	Leadership Value Bases
including	such as	including
• Leader	• Individual Means	• Cultural
• Followers	• Corporate Means	• Theological
• Situation	• Spiritual Means	

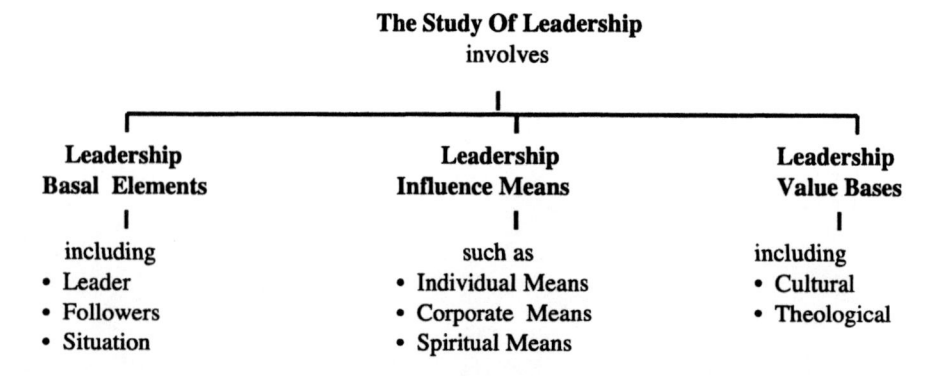

Figure 1,2 Co 34-1. Display of Three High Level Generic Leadership Components

---

[112] Five periods are identified: Phase I. Great Man Era—1841–1904; Phase II. Trait Era—1904–1948;; Phase IV. Contingency Era—1967–1980; Phase V. Complexity Era—1980–present. Each of these eras contributed to the basic elements seen in the tree diagram framework.

[113] The six Biblical leadership eras include: I. The Patriarchal Era; II. The Pre-Kingdom Era; The Kingdom Era; The Post-Kingdom Era; The Pre-Church Era; The Church Era.

34. Leadership Tree Diagram

Table 1,2 Co 34-1 When Each Component Was In Focus in Leadership Eras

Era	Element in Focus	Explanation
Phase I. Great Man Era—1841–1904	Leaders	Great Man Theory dominated. Great leaders were studied to see what could be learned about leadership. Was leadership innately a genetic thing (leaders are born)? Do they make things happen? Or do the opportunities allow one to rise to the occasion (leaders are made)?
Phase II. Trait Era—1904–1948	Leaders/ Followers	Trait Theory Dominated. Could traits of great leaders be identified at the beginning stages of development of potential leaders.
Phase III. Behavior Era—1948–1967	Individual Influence Means/	Trait theory having been debunked, theorist went on to study what leaders did and how they influenced followers. Leadership style theory emerged.
Phase IV. Contingency Era—1967–1980	Corporate means	Organizational systems begin to be studied and their impact on influence. Cross-cultural studies recognized that in other cultures corporate groups influence as much or more than individuals.
Phase V. Complexity Era—1980–present	Spiritual influence means/ cultural values/ theological values/	No one leadership theory dominates because leadership is now recognized as a very complex thing. There are numerous complex theories being studied. Motivational theory emerged. How do people influence? Christian studies looked at spiritual authority. What are the underlying theological frameworks, or cultural frameworks influence why leaders lead like they lead? Value theory began to emerge. What are the underlying concepts of one's leadership?

Table 1,2 Co 34-2. Elements of the Tree Diagram Described

Element	Description
Leadership Basal Elements	The fundamental elements of leadership anywhere are leaders, followers, situations. What leaders, followers, and situations are in different cultures will vary. Expectations will determine much. Situations will determine much. But whatever the manifestation, these three elements can be studied in any cultures.
a. leaders	All cultures recognize the right/authority of some to dominantly influence others. How they recognize, why they recognize, and how they influence others differs markedly but all cultures have leaders. They can be studied and their development analyzed.
b. followers	All cultures recognize that most people will be influenced by leaders. Those being influenced are followers. Various factors determine who followers are. Followers can be studied and the dynamics between followers and leaders can be studied. These will vary markedly in different cultures, but all cultures have dynamics underlying interplay between followers and leaders.
c. situations	Situations affect leaders, followers and the dynamics between them. The major reason trait theory was debunked was that traits of leaders varied with situations. Situations are fluid and dynamic and can even force changes in expectations on leaders and followers.
Leadership Influence Means	In every culture groups are influenced by others. Some cultures are more individualized than others and so individual influence means takes on importance. Some cultures require more conformity to group thinking. Corporate influence means carries more weight in such cultures. Spiritual influencers occur in all cultures. How they influence differs but they exist.
a. individual influence means	Individuals use leadership styles to influence followers. Leadership styles vary greatly between cultures. These can be studied.
b. corporate influence means	How groups influence, whether in formal organizations, or in cultures, can be studied. Coming to the front now is systemic theory which sees interplay between all kinds of organizational elements which exert sometimes hidden influence.

c. spiritual influence means	Spiritual leaders can influence by manipulating the spirit world power. Spiritual leaders can exert great influence because of perceived moral standards or competency or giftedness.
Leadership Value Bases	All cultures have underlying values which under gird their practices. Some are explicit. Others are highly implicit.
a. cultural value bases	Most leaders dominantly are influence by cultural values of what leaders are to be and do and how they do it.
b. theological value bases	There is a growing concern, especially among Christian leaders, that biblical leadership values ought to inform and influence Christian leaders and leadership.

Conclusion

The strength of this framework for identifying, studying, and assessing leadership is fourfold:

1. It is a framework that developed from synthesizing the best of leadership theoretical studies for the past 150 years. There is a **long-term perspective** involved.
2. It is an integrated framework manifesting the **what, how,** and **why** of leadership.
3. Its categories are generically broad enough to **guide analysis** in any culture **but allow for major differences** in what the manifestations may be.
4. Any theoretical leadership studies done today can be properly evaluated in terms of what they focus on and what they leave out.

Its basic weakness is that it is a static framework. In real life all of these elements are interacting with each other and modifying each other constantly. There is feedback and feedforward between these elements. The framework is changing constantly in terms of what is in focus and what is being defined.

However, the tree diagram depicts leadership issues that must be considered when studying leadership or training leaders.

Article 35

Relevance of the Article to Paul's Corinthian Ministry

Macro lessons, that is, major leadership observations across the various leadership eras of the Bible, provide some important guidelines for leaders today. This article defines the concept of macro lessons. The next lists them. Paul demonstrates a number of these macro lessons in his leadership influence in the Corinthian intervention.

35. Macro Lessons—Defined

Macro Lessons inform our leadership with potential leadership values that move toward the absolute. We live in a time when most do not believe there are absolutes. In my study of leadership in the Bible, I have defined a leadership truth continuum which recognizes the difficulty in deriving absolutes but does allow for them.[114] Figure 1,2 Co 35-1 depicts this.

Suggestions	Guidelines	Absolutes
May give insights	Important for most situations	Requirements

<-------------------- Macro Lessons ----------------->

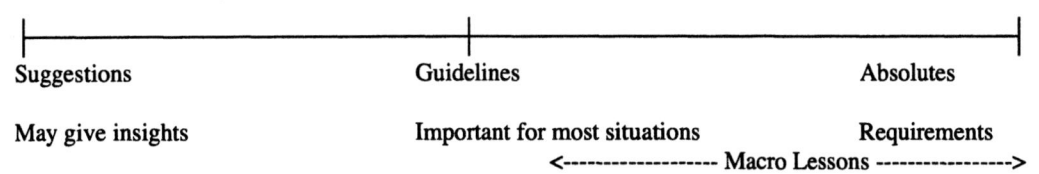

Figure 1,2 Co 35-1. Leadership Truth Continuum/ Where Macro Lessons Occur

Introduction to Macro lessons

In the *Complexity Era* in which we now live,[115] the thrust of leadership theory has moved, toward the importance of leadership values. The questions being asked today are not as much what is leadership (the leadership basal elements—leader, followers, and situations) and how does it operate (leadership influence means—corporate and individual) as it is why do we do what we do (leadership value bases). The first three eras (Great Man, Trait, and Ohio State) answered the question, "What is leadership?" The Contingency and early part of the Complexity Era answered the question, "How do we do it?" Now we are grappling with, "Why do we lead? or What ought we to do?" We are looking for leadership values. A leadership value is an underlying assumption which affects how a leader behaves in or perceives leadership situations. They are usually statements that have *ought* or *must* or *should* in them. Macro-Lessons are statements of truth about leadership which have the potential for becoming leadership values. These macro-lessons are observations seen in the various leadership eras in the Bible. Many of these became values for numerous Bible leaders. These macro-lessons move toward the right (requirement, value) of the leadership truth continuum.

What is a macro lesson?

---

[114] See Clinton, **Leadership Perspectives** for a more detailed explanation of the continuum and for my approach to deriving principles from the scriptures. See **Article,** *53. Principles of Truth*.

[115] A study of leadership history in the United States from 1850 to the present uncovered 6 Eras (an era being a period of time in which some major leadership theory held sway): 1. Great Man Era (1840s to 1904); 2. Trait Theory (1904-1948); 3. Ohio State Era (1948-1967); Contingency Era (1967-1980); Complexity Era (1980-present). See Clinton, **A Short History of Leadership Theory**. Altadena, Ca.: Barnabas Publishers.

35. Macro Lessons—Defined

Definition A <u>macro-lesson</u> is a high level generalization
- of a leadership observation (suggestion, guideline, requirement), stated as a lesson,
- which repeatedly occurs throughout different leadership eras,
- and thus has potential as a leadership absolute.

Macro lessons even at their weakest provide strong guidelines describing leadership insights. At their strongest they are requirements, or absolutes, that leaders should follow. Leaders ignore them to their detriment.

examples **Prayer Lesson**: If God has called you to a ministry then He has called you to pray for that ministry.
Accountability: Christian leaders minister ought always with a conscious view to ultimate accountability to God for their ministry.
Bible Centered: An effective leader who finishes well must have a Bible centered ministry.

Macro Lessons are derived from a comparative study of leadership in the Six Leadership Eras. These Six Leadership Eras and number of macro lessons identified are shown in Table 1,2 Co 35-1.

Table 1,2 Co 35-1. Leadership Eras and Number of Macro Lessons

Leadership Era	Number of Macro Lessons
1. Patriarchal Era	7
2. Pre-Kingdom Era	10
3. Kingdom Era	5
4. Post-Kingdom Era	5
5. Pre-Church Era	9
6. Church Era	5

I have identified 41 macro lessons, roughly 5 to 10 per leadership era. When a macro-lesson is seen to occur in varied situations and times and cultural settings and in several leadership eras it becomes a candidate for an absolute leadership lesson. When that same generalization becomes personal and is embraced by a leader as a driving force for how that leader sees or operates in ministry, it becomes a leadership value.

The top three Macro Lessons for the four O.T. Leadership Eras are listed in Table 1,2 Co 35-2. Note, Paul demonstrates all three of these in the 1,2 Co epistles.

Table 1,2 Co 35-2. Top Three Macro Lessons in O.T. Leadership Eras

Priority	Leadership Era	Label	Statement
1	Pre-Kingdom	Presence	The essential ingredient of leadership is the powerful presence of God in the leader's life and ministry. (*Therefore a leader must not minister without the powerful presence of God in his/her life.*)
2	Patriarchal	Character	Integrity is the essential character trait of a spiritual leader. (*Therefore, a leader must maintain integrity and respond to God's shaping of it.*)
3	Pre-Kingdom	Intimacy	Leaders develop intimacy with God, which in turn overflows into all their ministry since ministry flows out of being. (*Therefore a leader must seek to develop intimacy with God.*)

The top three Macro Lessons for the two N.T. Leadership Eras are listed in Table 1,2 Co 35-3.

35. Macro Lessons—Defined

Table 1,2 Co 35-3. Top Three Macro Lessons in N.T. Leadership Eras

Priority	Leadership Era	Label	Statement
1	Church	Word Centered	*God's Word must be the primary source for equipping leaders and must be a vital part of any leader's ministry.*
2	Pre-Church	Harvest	*Leaders must seek to bring people into relationship with God.*
3	Pre-Church	Shepherd	*Leaders must preserve, protect, and develop those who belong to God's people.*

Note again, all three of these are prominent in Paul's ministry.

You will notice that some of these macro lessons are already described in value language (should, must, ought) while others are simply statements of observations. I have put in italics my attempt to give the value associated with the observation.

Comparative study across the six leadership eras for macro lessons makes up one of the seven leadership genres, i.e. sources for leadership findings from the Bible.

See **Articles**, *36. Macro Lessons, List of 41 Across Six Leadership Eras; 29. Leadership Genre—Seven Types* (Macro Lessons, Biographical Material, Books as A Whole, Direct Context, Indirect Context, Leadership Acts, Parabolic). See Clinton, **A Short History of Leadership Theory.** Altadena, Ca.: Barnabas Publishers. See also Clinton, **Leadership Perspectives.** Altadena, Ca.: Barnabas Publishers.

Article 36

Relevance of the Article to Paul's Corinthian Ministry

It would be easier to mark the macro lessons not as prominent in Paul's ministry as to mark the ones that are prominent. Many of the macro lessons from the O.T. leadership era show up in Paul's ministry. All of the pre-church and church leadership era macro lessons are very evident in Paul's life. It is clear that the church macro lessons were drawn from a study of Paul's missionary career. A quick glance at each of these will readily bring to mind incidents in Paul's missionary trips in the Acts or the purposes of specific epistles he wrote. Note those church leadership era macros: 37. STRUCTURE—CHURCH LEADERS MUST VARY STRUCTURES TO FIT THE NEEDS OF THE TIMES IF THEY ARE TO CONSERVE GAINS AND CONTINUE WITH RENEWED EFFORT. Paul progressively did this as the church was carried from one Gentile situation to another. 38. UNIVERSAL—THE CHURCH STRUCTURE IS INHERENTLY UNIVERSAL AND CAN BE MADE TO FIT VARIOUS CULTURAL SITUATIONS IF FUNCTIONS AND NOT FORMS ARE IN VIEW. Paul showed that the church structure could be contextualized in the various cultures he worked with. Note especially his work with Titus on Crete in this regard. 39. GIFTEDNESS— LEADERS ARE RESPONSIBLE TO HELP GOD'S PEOPLE IDENTIFY, DEVELOP, AND USE THEIR RESOURCES FOR GOD. Paul did this. Note in 1 Co, Eph, and Ro his teaching on this and in 1,2 Ti his application in Timothy's life. 40. WORD CENTERED —GOD'S WORD IS THE PRIMARY SOURCE FOR EQUIPPING LEADERS AND MUST BE A VITAL PART OF ANY LEADERS MINISTRY. In 2 Ti he lays this principle out for Timothy—and us. 41. COMPLEXITY— LEADERSHIP IS COMPLEX, PROBLEMATIC, DIFFICULT AND FRAUGHT WITH RISK—WHICH IS WHY LEADERSHIP IS NEEDED. The Epistles, each written to deal with some areas of church problems certainly endorse this macro. However, please note that Macro lessons 40 and 41 dominate Paul's ministry. And macro lesson 40 is foundational to leaders today.

36. Macro Lessons— List of 41 Across Six Leadership Eras

Macro Lessons inform our leadership with potential leadership values that move toward the absolute. The following are the 41 lessons I have identified as I comparatively studied the six different leadership eras for leadership observations.

No.	Label	Leadership Era	Statement of Macro Lesson
1.	Blessing	Patriarchal	God mediates His blessing to His followers through leaders.
2.	Shaping	Patriarchal	God shapes leader's lives and ministry through critical incidents.
3.	Timing	Patriarchal	God's timing is crucial to accomplishment of God's purposes.
4.	Destiny	Patriarchal	Leaders must have a sense of destiny.
5.	Character	Patriarchal	Integrity is the essential character trait of a spiritual leader.
6.	Faith	Patriarchal	Biblical Leaders must learn to trust in the unseen God, sense His presence, sense His revelation, and follow Him by faith.
7.	Purity	Patriarchal	Leaders must personally learn of and respond to the holiness of God in order to have effective ministry.
8.	Intercession	Pre-Kingdom	Leaders called to a ministry are called to intercede for that ministry.
9.	Presence	Pre-Kingdom	The essential ingredient of leadership is the powerful presence of God in the leader's life and ministry.
10.	Intimacy	Pre-Kingdom	Leaders develop intimacy with God which in turn overflows into all their ministry since ministry flows out of being.
11.	Burden	Pre-Kingdom	Leaders feel a responsibility to God for their ministry.
12.	Hope	Pre-Kingdom	A primary function of all leadership is to inspire followers with hope in God and in what God is doing.
13.	Challenge	Pre-Kingdom	Leaders receive vision from God which sets before them challenges that inspire their leadership.

36. Macro Lessons—List of 41 Across Six Leadership Eras

14.	Spiritual Authority	Pre-Kingdom	Spiritual authority is the dominant power base of a spiritual leader comes through experiences with God, knowledge of God, godly character and gifted power.
15.	Transition	Pre-Kingdom	Leaders must transition other leaders into their work in order to maintain continuity and effectiveness.
16.	Weakness	Pre-Kingdom	God can work through weak spiritual leaders if they are available to Him.
17.	Continuity	Pre-Kingdom	Leaders must provide for continuity to new leadership in order to preserve their leadership legacy.
18.	Unity	Kingdom	Unity of the people of God is a value that leaders must preserve.
19.	Stability	Kingdom	Preserving a ministry of God with life and vigor over time is as much if not more of a challenge to leadership than creating one.
20.	Spiritual Leadership	Kingdom	Spiritual leadership can make a difference even in the midst of difficult times.
21.	Recrudescence	Kingdom	God will attempt to bring renewal to His people until they no longer respond to Him.
22.	By-pass	Kingdom	God will by-pass leadership and structures that do not respond to Him and will institute new leadership and structures.
23.	Future Perfect	Post-Kingdom	A primary function of all leadership is to walk by faith with a future perfect paradigm so as to inspire followers with certainty of God's accomplishment of ultimate purposes.
24.	Perspective	Post-Kingdom	Leaders must know the value of perspective and interpret present happenings in terms of God's broader purposes.
25.	Modeling	Post-Kingdom	Leaders can most powerfully influence by modeling godly lives, the sufficiency and sovereignty of God at all times, and gifted power.
26.	Ultimate	Post-Kingdom	Leaders must remember that the ultimate goal of their lives and ministry is to manifest the glory of God.
27.	Perseverance	Post-Kingdom	Once known, leaders must persevere with the vision God has given.
28.	Selection	Pre-Church	The key to good leadership is the selection of good potential leaders which should be a priority of all leaders.
29.	Training	Pre-Church	Leaders should deliberately train potential leaders in their ministry by available and appropriate means.
30.	Focus	Pre-Church	Leaders should increasingly move toward a focus in their ministry which moves toward fulfillment of their calling and their ultimate contribution to God's purposes for them.
31.	Spirituality	Pre-Church	Leaders must develop interiority, spirit sensitivity, and fruitfulness in accord with their uniqueness since ministry flows out of being.
32.	Servant	Pre-Church	Leaders must maintain a dynamic tension as they lead by serving and serve by leading.
33.	Steward	Pre-Church	Leaders are endowed by God with natural abilities, acquired skills, spiritual gifts, opportunities, experiences, and privileges which must be developed and used for God.
34.	Harvest	Pre-Church	Leaders must seek to bring people into relationship with God.
35.	Shepherd	Pre-Church	Leaders must preserve, protect, and develop God's people.
36.	Movement	Pre-Church	Leaders recognize that movements are the way to penetrate society though they must be preserved via appropriate ongoing institutions.
37.	Structure	Church	Leaders must vary structures to fit the needs of the times if they are to conserve gains and continue with renewed effort.
38.	Universal	Church	The church structure is inherently universal and can be made to fit various cultural situations if functions and not forms are in view.

39.	Giftedness	Church	Leaders are responsible to help God's people identify, develop, and use their resources for God.
40.	Word Centered	Church	God's Word is the primary source for equipping leaders and must be a vital part of any leaders ministry.
41.	Complexity	All eras	Leadership is complex, problematic, difficult and fraught with risk—which is why leadership is needed.

A Final Comment

The identification of macro lessons is not an exact science. Most likely wording can be improved. And there are probably other macro lessons than these 41 identified. However, there is good evidence for these 41 and they are certainly a good foundation to explore for our own leadership today. On-going research is underway in order to validate the notion of macro lessons and to ascertain further applicability to today's leaders. What is clear is that Paul does demonstrate the importance of many of these macro lessons, especially Pre-Church and Church macro lessons in shaping his ministry.

See Also **Article** *35. Macro Lessons—Defined.*

Article 37

Relevance of the Article to Paul's Corinthian Ministry

I personally have done much study concerning Paul's mentoring. See **Article** *45. Paul-Developer Par Excellence,* which shows Paul as a trainer—using formal, non-formal and informal means of training but with the informal methodology of mentoring dominating. Note also **Article** *47. Paul—Mentor for Many,* which specifically looks at Paul's mentor-mix—that is, the types of mentoring he did with some of his prominent leaders—like Timothy and Titus. This article describes the results of empirical research in contemporary leaders. It gives the framework for looking at mentoring in general. These categories certainly are useful in analyzing Paul's mentoring ministry. Both Timothy and Titus are being mentored, in a specific on-the-job way as they help in the Corinthian intervention.

37. Mentoring—An Informal Training Model

Training Modes

Today's training can be categorized under three modes as shown in Figure 1,2 Co 37-1.

Leadership Training
involves

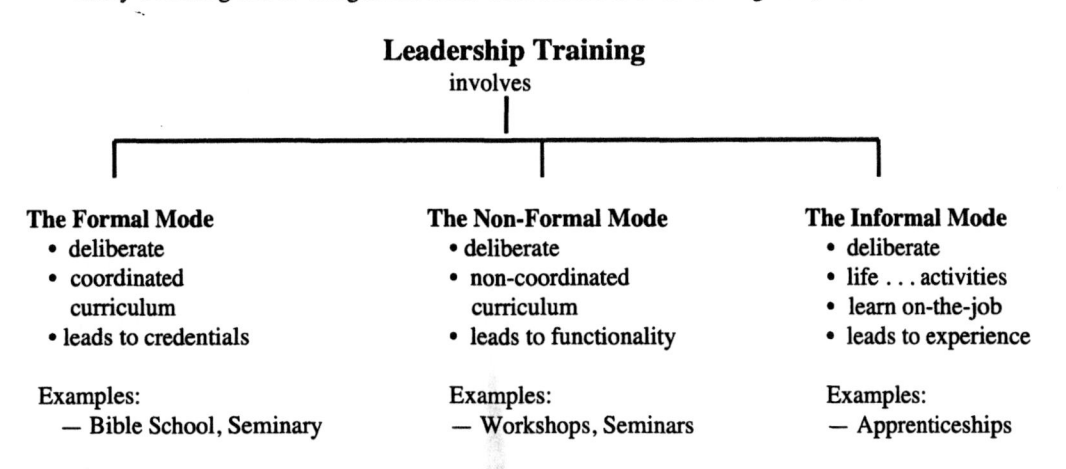

The Formal Mode	The Non-Formal Mode	The Informal Mode
• deliberate	• deliberate	• deliberate
• coordinated curriculum	• non-coordinated curriculum	• life . . . activities
• leads to credentials	• leads to functionality	• learn on-the-job
		• leads to experience
Examples:	Examples:	Examples:
— Bible School, Seminary	— Workshops, Seminars	— Apprenticeships

Figure 1,2 Co 37-1. Three Training Modes

Mentoring as a training means, while definitely informal in its essence, can be applied to any of the three modes.

Jesus and Paul used the informal training mode as their major training methodology. On-the-job training, modeling, cultural forms of apprenticeships and internships were used. But dominantly it was mentoring which was the primary informal means of training.

Mentoring Defined

Definition — <u>Mentoring</u> is a relational experience in which one person, the mentor, empowers another person, the mentoree, by a transfer of resources.

Empowerment can include such things as new habits, knowledge, skills, desires, values, connections to resources for growth and development of potential. We[116] have identified a number of mentoring functions. Table 1,2 Co 37-1 identifies nine mentoring functions we have categorized.

Table 1,2 Co 37-1. Nine Mentor Functions

Type	Central Thrust
1. Discipler	Basic habits of the Christian life dealing with hearing from God and talking with God; operating in a fellowship of Christians; learning to minister in terms of giftedness; learning to get input from God.
2. Spiritual Guide	Evaluation of spiritual depth and maturity in a life and help in growth in this.
3. Coach	Skills of all kind depending on the expertise of the coach
4. Counselor	Timely and good advice which sheds perspective on issues and problems and other needs.
5. Teacher	Relevant knowledge that can be used for personal growth or ministry or other such need.
6. Sponsor	Protective guidance and linking to resources so that a leader reaches potential.
7. Contemporary Model	Values impactfully demonstrated in a life that can be transferred and used in one's own life.
8. Historical Model	Values demonstrated in a life and inspiration drawn from that life so as to encourage ongoing development in ones own life and a pressing on to finish well.
9. Divine Contact	Timely Guidance from God via some human source.

Mentoring is a relational experience. Five dynamics are involved: attraction, relationship, responsiveness, accountability, empowerment. The more each of these dynamics are in place the more impactful is the empowerment. Table 1,2 Co 37-2 gives the essence of each of the dynamics.

Table 1,2 Co 37-2. Five Mentoring Dynamics

Dynamic	Responsibility of	Explanation
attraction	both mentor and mentoree	A mentoree must be attracted to a mentor—that is, see something in the mentor that is desired in his/her own life; A mentor must be attracted to a mentoree and see potential value in working with the mentoree—that is, development of potential for the mentoree is a worth while investment of time and energy.
relationship	both mentor and mentoree	A mentor must build the relationship with a mentoree and vice versa. The stronger the relationship the more likely that the responsiveness and the accountability functions will take place naturally instead of forced.
responsiveness	mentoree	The mentoree must respond to the mentor's suggestions and growth projects. Faithfulness in carrying out assignments is a major trait of responsiveness. The mentor is responsible to help the mentoree grow. The mentoree is responsible to respond/submit to the mentor's plan and methodology for growth.
accountability	mentor	The mentor is responsible to evaluate how the mentoree is doing and to hold the mentoree accountable for following suggestions for growth, for doing what is asked, etc
empowerment	mentor dominantly; mentoree secondarily	Both mentor and mentoree should evaluate and recognize empowerment out of the relationship. The mentor knows and has the best perspective to evaluate empowerment. But the mentoree also should recognize growth in his/her life.

All of these dynamics do not always appear in fullness in the different relationships. They are necessary for the intensive mentoring functions (heavy face-to-face time commitments are usually

---

[116] My son Dr. Richard W. Clinton, my colleague Paul Stanley and I have all been busily researching and using mentoring in our own personal ministries. See **Connecting** by Stanley and Clinton. See The **Mentor Handbook** by Clinton and Clinton.

37. Mentoring—An Informal Training Model

involved): discipling, spiritual guide, coaching. All do not have to be present in the occasional mentoring functions: counseling, teaching, sponsoring. Empowerment can happen even when all the dynamics are not present. However, the stronger the five dynamics, even in occasional mentoring, the more impactful will be the resulting empowerment. In the passive mentoring functions—contemporary modeling, historical modeling, and divine contact—attraction is present, responsiveness is present and empowerment takes place. But relationship and accountability are essentially missing.

Both Jesus and Paul used mentoring. They had individual relationships with trainees. But they also combined individual mentoring relationships with training of groups.

Mentoring relates directly to two of the seven major lessons observed in comparative study of effective leaders.

> **Effective leaders view leadership selection and development as a priority function in their ministry.**

> **Effective leaders see relational empowerment as both a means and a goal of ministry.**

Mentoring will be one of the dominant forces in the training of emerging leaders in the years to come.

See **Articles**: *30. Leadership Lessons— Seven Major Identified*; *47. Paul—Mentor For Many*. See **For Further Study Bibliography**: J. Robert Clinton and Paul D. Stanley, **Connecting—The Mentoring Relationships You Need to Succeed in Life**; J. Robert Clinton and Richard W. Clinton, **The Mentor Handbook—Detailed Guidelines and Helps for Christian Mentors and Mentorees**.

Article 38

Relevance of the Article to Paul's Corinthian Ministry
This article was done from observations of contemporary leaders and more aptly fits present ministry situations. However, you can observe in Paul's ministry that he was aware of some of the barriers involved in seeing adequate church leadership in place as well as the problems involved in his strategic leadership via his missionary band. He certainly deals with the financial problem in several different ways. His major effort with his rising apostolic mentorees was sponsoring them for higher level leadership. His use of ministry tasks with Tychicus, Titus, Timothy and others helped bridge the entry of these men into ministry.

38. Ministry Entry Patterns

Introduction

Ministry entry can refer to the initial ministry an emerging leader takes part in (all types[117] of leaders). Or it can refer to any new ministry task, assignments, or challenges that a growing leader assumes (all types of leaders). Further, it also usually refers to the first full time ministry of a Type C, D or E leader. Ministry entry patterns give perspective to any leader who is aware of and wants to put into practice two major leadership lessons:[118]

Leadership Selection	Effective leaders view leadership selection and development as a priority function.
Perspective	Effective leaders view present ministry in terms of a lifetime perspective.[119]

What can we learn from comparative study of contemporary leaders about ministry entry? Perhaps some things that will renew us to challenge people into ministry.

The Three Basic Types of Ministry Entry

Each of the three types—first attempts, new ministry, or initial entry into full time ministry—yield observations helpful to emerging leaders and those concerned with emerging leaders—leaders with a developmental perspective.

---

[117] See **Article, 31. Leadership Levels**. Briefly the types of leaders are: Type A—local, unpaid, small influence; Type B—local, paid, more influence; Type C—regional, paid, broader influence; Type D—national, paid, wide influence, indirect ministry; Type E—international, paid, widest influence, indirect ministry or direct ministry with unusual expertise.

[118] Seven such lessons have been identified: (1) Effective Leaders View Present Ministry in Terms Of A Life Time Perspective. (2) Effective Leaders Maintain A Learning Posture Throughout Life. (3) Effective Leaders Value Spiritual Authority As A Primary Power Base. (4) Effective Leaders Who Are Productive Over A Lifetime Have A Dynamic Ministry Philosophy. (5) Effective Leaders View Leadership Selection And Development As A Priority Function In Their Ministry. (6) Effective Leaders See Relational Empowerment As Both A Means And A Goal Of Ministry. (7) Effective Leaders Evince A Growing Awareness Of Their Sense Of Destiny. It is this last one I am exploring in this article.

[119] In this case, Effective leaders view present ministry in terms of a lifetime perspective—both their own ministry and other leaders' ministries.

38. Ministry Entry Patterns

Three Types of Ministry Entry
include

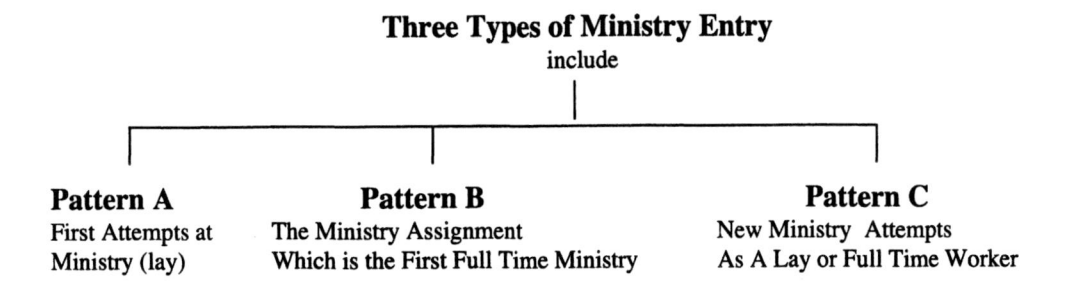

Pattern A	**Pattern B**	**Pattern C**
First Attempts at Ministry (lay)	The Ministry Assignment Which is the First Full Time Ministry	New Ministry Attempts As A Lay or Full Time Worker

Figure 1,2 Co 38-1. Three Types of Ministry Entry

description　The ministry entry patterns describe the ways that challenges come to leaders and potential leaders as they accept various ministry tasks and assignments during early, middle and latter ministry. These patterns relate three factors:
1. how the challenge comes—motivated externally or internally,
2. the structures or roles that relate to the challenge—existing structures/roles, modification of structures or role, or creation of new structures or roles,
3. the frequency of occurrence.

Tables 1,2 Co 38-1, 38-2, and 38-3 below show typical ministry challenges for the three ministry entry patterns.

Table 1,2 Co 38-1. Pattern A—Early Ministry Entry

Challenge	How The Challenge Comes	Structure or Roles It Relates To	Frequency of Occurrence
A1. Help our ministry; we need workers.	External/ existing leaders point out needs and ask for help	Work in existing ministry structures/roles	Most common
A2. I see a need in this ministry; they need …Maybe I can help.	Internal—self-initiated; maybe I can help this ministry	Work in existing ministry structures/roles	Next most common
A3. We have some needs which in our ministry are unmet; need to establish a new thing to meet these needs.	External/ existing leaders point out needs for new kind of ministry; who can do it?	Create new ministry role or structures	Rarer
A4. I see some unmet needs in this ministry; I wonder if I could do … to meet them.	Internal—self initiated; Maybe I can start something new to solve these ministry needs.	Create new ministry roles or structures	Rarest

Most leaders entering into first ministry do so as the result of challenges by leaders in ministry who need help to fill ministry slots already existing (A1). Potential leaders usually do not see needs on their own and hence volunteer for ministry (A2). Most recruiters also do not see the need for new roles or structures. (A3) They are harassed enough just to fill existing needs. Emerging leaders who create new roles or ministry structures on their own (A4) are usually: 1) brash people; 2) threaten the system; 3) won't work in the old ways which are not meeting the new felt needs. This is the rarest of pattern A. It is also an symptom of a leader who will rise to higher levels of leadership influence. The challenge to existing leaders is how to work with such potential leaders to incorporate their ideas and keep them in the system.

38. Ministry Entry Patterns

Table 1,2 Co 38-2. Pattern B—Ministry Assignment First Full Time Ministry

Challenge	How The Challenge Comes	Structure or Roles It Relates To	Frequency of Occurrence
B1. Come over and help us—fulltime?	External/ existing leaders point out needs and ask for help; we need a full time worker; who will go?	Work in existing ministry structures/roles; a slot is open for a full time worker	Most common
B2. I know God's call is on my life; I need to do…with…	Internal—I would like to do this; I wonder if they would take me.	Work in existing ministry but change structures/roles to fit the one being recruited	Very common
B3. Here is a need; I could meet it if they would…	Internal/ self initiated; this ought to be changed; if so, I would want to do this full time.	Change existing ministry structures/ roles	Very common
B4. We have a need; can you help us figure out how to change what we have to meet it?	External/ existing leaders point out needs for new kind of ministry; who can do it?	Change existing ministry structures/ roles	Not so common
B5. We have a need; can you help us start something new to meet it?	External/ We need to do some new things; can you help us innovate?	Create new ministry roles or structures	Occasional
B6. Here is a bright idea on how we could start something new. What do you think.	Internal/ They need something new; I can help them do it. Will they let me?	Create new ministry roles or structures	Rare

    Successful initial ministry entry for full time Christian workers depends upon several factors: 1. previous experience as Type A leader; 2. type of transitional training pattern; 3. degree of balanced learning in the training (cognitive, affective, volitional, experiential); 4. time/ ministry context perspectives (A-service, pre-service, in-service); 5. how to finance.

    Leaders with on-the-job experience who have learned and who have had some successful ministry move more easily into a full time ministry based on what they have been doing than otherwise. This would describe the transitional training pattern, in-service. Emerging leaders from the pre-service pattern, that is, who by-passed Type A experience, will find initial ministry entry more difficult. They face a high probability of experiencing the abbreviated entry pattern (drop out). This is especially true if the pre-service training is unbalanced toward the cognitive side rather than experiential side.

    How to finance is a question that depends on whether the emerging leader is going to existing works (primary responsibility for finances with the leaders of that work—denominational work or going on a staff of a large church or pastoral responsibility in an existing church); existing works (but primary responsibility for finances is on the new leader joining the work—most faith missions); starting a new work (primary responsibility on the emerging leader to finance the new work somehow).

38. Ministry Entry Patterns

Table 1,2 Co 38-3. Pattern C—New Ministry Attempts

Challenge	How The Challenge Comes	Structure or Roles It Relates To	Frequency of Occurrence
C1. Change to new job; learn some new skills; build on what you have.	Internal/ I see something in our group I would like to do ,different from what I am doing now	Work in existing ministry structures/roles	Very common
C2. I would like to change the job I have to better fit me.	Internal—self-initiated; maybe I could do better if we could just alter what I am doing.	Change existing ministry structures/roles	Very common
C3. You don't fit here. But if you can change to this we can use you.	External/ existing leaders point out needs for changing.	Create new ministry role or structures in the group.	Not so common
C4. More can be done here than I am doing. How can I change what is being done and me to meet these needs.	Internal—self initiated; Maybe I can start something new to challenge me to grow and to meet needs unmet now.	Create new ministry roles or structures in the group.	Rare
C5. God's call on me is to leave this ministry and start a new one.	Internal—self initiated; I have to leave to get done what needs to be done. This group is not going to do it.	Create new ministry roles or structures outside the group; in another organization; or begin one.	Rare

Ministry challenge is the shaping activity, which describes the means whereby a leader or potential leader is prompted to accept a new ministry assignment and sense the guidance of God into service. The most common pattern of entry into a ministry assignment is an external challenge to work in some existing role in a ministry situation. The rarest entry patterns involve self-initiated challenges to create new ministry roles and structures. Frequently new challenges come via a paradigm shift (see some breakthrough ministry insight that needs to be done), a renewal experience (God challenges afresh to commit to something He wants done), or a deliberate movement toward fulfilling one's destiny (recognizing one's focused life components—life purpose; major role; effective methodologies; ultimate contributions).

An important entry pattern in all three ministry entry patterns involves usually internal (self-initiated) challenges to adapt present roles or ministry structures or create new ones. This signals potential for high level leadership. Self-initiative type people rise to challenges and create new opportunities for ministry. They become leaders of influence.

Conclusions

Three implications come to mind. The first two are leadership selection insights and are for leaders selecting other leaders. The third is for any leader to consider for self-evaluation.

1. The majority of leaders will follow common entry patterns.
2. It is the self-initiation instinct which indicates strong potential for upper level leadership.
3. Plateauing is indicated by a lessening frequency of interest in ministry challenges and ministry assignments.

Application of implication 1 is straightforward. A major function of all leadership is the selection and development of potential leaders. Thus, present leaders should openly and deliberately challenge potential leaders in terms of specific roles and the needs of existing ministries. Over the years the enthusiasm of ministry often wanes as leaders move toward latter ministry processing. As a result there is a corresponding lack of challenging and recruiting. This insight should help people in ministry, whether in early, middle or latter processing to see the value of continuing to enthusiastically challenge others for ministry.

38. Ministry Entry Patterns

Self-initiated ministry tasks or assignments carry with them the seeds of higher level leadership. Leaders should recognize that this quality is important and be on the alert for those who are constantly doing this kind of thing. One problem does exist. Often those who self-initiate ministry tasks and assignments are challenging the status quo and threatening leaders over them. Often when defensiveness arises in the midst of threatening situations, the sparkling quality of self-initiative is quickly by-passed and set aside for re-enforcing the status quo. Thus, implication 2 is very important. Later, in guidance processing, the mentor process item will be stressed. Mentors tend to be alert to this predictive quality and can patiently work to see it developed.

Most initial ministry entry activities come while the emerging leader is a lay person and is usually the result of some sort of challenge. So, as an existing leader, identify the ministry opportunities in your group and challenge lay people with them. Then watch the ones who respond to God and work with them.

A Final Comment

Paul is the exemplar of self-initiated ministry at all levels of sphere of influence. We do not see this same quality in Timothy and Titus but it is easy to imagine that after Paul passed off the scene, these men too were self-initiators.

See *ministry task; ministry assignment; ministry challenge; mentor definitions;* **Glossary**. See **Article**, *Jesus Recruiting Techniques*; *Training Modes—Where They Fit*; *Focused Life*.

Article 39

<u>Relevance of the Article to Paul's Corinthian Ministry</u>
Our study of ministry philosophy is barely underway. It is fairly clear that Paul had a basic ministry philosophy. He followed certain approaches in his church planting ministry. More clear is it that Paul had underlying values which guided this church planting ministry. This is clearly seen as Paul defends his ministry in 2 Co. He explicitly identifies reasons why he did things—from which values can be derived. This article then is a tentative first try at examining ministry philosophy.

39. Ministry Philosophy

Introduction

Paul was a value driven leader.[120] He demonstrated throughout his 30+ years of ministry an important major lesson.

Effective Leaders Who Are Productive Over A Life Time Have A Dynamic Ministry Philosophy.[121]

Definition   <u>Ministry philosophy</u> is a phrase describing the leadership values which are implicit or explicit and which under gird a leader's perception of ministry and decision making and practice of ministry.

The Challenge
Leaders Must Develop A Ministry Philosophy Which Simultaneously Honors Biblical Leadership Values, Embraces The Challenges Of The Times In Which They Live, And Fits Their Unique Giftedness And Personal Development If They Expect To Be Productive Over A Whole Life Time.

I have identified a number of Pauline leadership values as I have done the leadership commentary on the various Pauline epistles. Identification of leadership values, moving from implicit to explicit is a first step in seeing one's ministry philosophy. An understanding, theoretically, about ministry philosophy can help a leader become more proactive about identifying and using it with effectiveness.

Ministry Philosophy-Like a Roadmap

Ministry philosophy refers to ideas, values, and principles whether implicit or explicit which a leader uses as guidelines for decision making, for exercising influence, and for evaluating his/her ministry. By implicit I mean not actually recognized openly but part of the perceptive set of the leader. By explicit I mean openly recognized, identified and articulated. For any given leader a ministry philosophy is unique. All leaders act, think, and make decisions, which are based on this underlying related set of guidelines. Let me describe this abstract concept by using two analogies.

---

[120] See *leadership value*, **Glossary**. See **Article**, *71. Value Driven Leadership*.

[121] This is one of seven major lessons. These include: (1) Effective leaders maintain a learning posture throughout life. (2) Effective leaders value spiritual authority as a primary power base. (3) Effective leaders recognize leadership selection and development as a priority function. (4) Effective leaders who are productive over a lifetime have a dynamic ministry philosophy. (5) Effective leaders evince a growing awareness of their sense of destiny. (6) Effective leaders increasingly perceive their ministry in terms of a lifetime perspective. (7) Effective leaders perceive relational empowerment as important in their own and their followers lives. See **Article**, *30. Leadership Lessons, Seven Major Identified*.

39. Ministry Philosophy

In terms of an analogy a ministry philosophy serves a leader like a road map serves a person going from point A to point B. A road map gives an overall perspective. At critical points in the journey, the overall perspective that the map gives allows reasonable choices to be made as to detailed routes to travel upon. Knowing where you are going, a relatively explicit notion, helps provide focus along the way as you travel. Ministry philosophy gives focus to a leader's ministry. Like a road map it allows a strategic evaluation of where he/she is at a given point in life and how much further there is still to go and the best ways to get there from where the leaders is presently. In short, it gives a *strategic evaluative component* to our ministry.

A ministry philosophy is like a recipe. There are a lot of things involved in cooking something. There are the ingredients, the way they are mixed together, the timing involved, and the way the stove is used. Sometimes when you are cooking something familiar you automatically go through these items hardly thinking. You just know what you are doing. You gather all the ingredients and put them together in the right amounts and just do it. That is like the parts of a ministry philosophy which are implicit. At other times, you do not trust your memory but get out the old recipe book and follow the instructions. You are thankful for the detailed list of ingredients and the instructions that tell you how to blend things together and what temperature to cook at, etc. That is like the explicit parts of a ministry philosophy. Where would you be without recipes? A cook will have many recipes. Each has its special time and use. So too your ministry philosophy will have all kinds of standards that you use in given situations to help you evaluate your given situation. In short, like a recipe, a ministry philosophy gives us *tactical operating instructions* and guidelines.

Understanding the Notion of Dynamic

By dynamic I mean changing. I am actually suggesting that a leader's ministry philosophy changes over a lifetime. Three basal factors define the dynamic quality of a ministry philosophy of a Christian leader: the Scriptures, giftedness, and leadership situation.

Christian leaders view the Scriptures as foundational to their understanding of God, His purposes, and what He is wanting to accomplish. Over a lifetime a Christian leader will continue to study and use the Scriptures. As life is experienced, the leader will see things in the Scriptures that were not previously seen. That is, there is a growing awareness of what the Scriptures are saying. Life gives new perspectives with which to view this important source of information for leadership. So that, while there are core values derived from the Scriptures that will not change over a lifetime, there is much that will change as new truth is grasped. So then, as God opens us up to the Scriptures we are continually adding to a core of truth which builds on our past understanding and influences our present understanding of who we are, what we are about, and how we are going about it so as to fit in with the divine shaping of our lives and ministries.

Each Christian leader is unique. As a Christian leader develops over a lifetime there is a growing understanding of giftedness and personality. In terms of giftedness, leaders are a complex bundle of natural abilities, acquired skills and spiritual gifts.[122] Over a lifetime there is a developmental movement to mature a leader so that the three elements work synergistically. At any given moment in a leader's life, he/she has an understanding of who he or she is. A person's ministry philosophy will directly be related to this understanding of giftedness. This understanding may be implicit and not readily articulated. Even so, there will be a drifting toward ministry which utilizes this implicit giftedness.[123] Or the understanding may be explicit in which there is proactive movement toward a ministry philosophy flowing from this understanding. Since ministry philosophy is so integrated with giftedness and giftedness is developmental it follows then that ministry philosophy will be dynamic--that is, changing.

---

[122]These three form the giftedness set. Usually over a life time one of the three elements (natural abilities, acquired skills, or spiritual gifts) dominates the leader. I call this the focal element of the life. This focal element is also affected by personality factors though it is not clear exactly how. See **Article**, *Developing Giftedness; 63. Spiritual Gift Clusters; 64. Spiritual Gifts, Giftedness and Development.*

[123]I have identified four giftedness patterns: a drift pattern, a like-attracts-like pattern, a forced role/ gift enabling pattern, and a standard development pattern (9 stages). In the first three of the patterns there is only an implicit understanding of giftedness. In the fourth, from stages 3 on there can be a deliberate proactive movement toward effective use of giftedness, a more explicit understanding. **See For Further Study Bibliography,** Clinton and Clinton, **Unlocking Your Giftedness.**

39. Ministry Philosophy

In all leadership, no matter where it takes place, there are leaders, followers, and situations. I have already mentioned that leaders change over a lifetime as they discover who they are. But it is also true that for most leadership there is a series of ministry assignments over a lifetime. That is, it is rare for a leader to face an unchanging core of followers and situations over a lifetime. Followers change. Leadership situations change. Some followers and some situations change more drastically and more rapidly in some cultures than others. But every leader will either gradually or radically face situations that are different. Values will have to be learned which fit the situation. Now there are a number of processes through which God will shape leaders to fit these new situations.[124] These changing situations a leader faces will force that leader to add new elements to ministry philosophy as he/she adapts what was used in the past.

Let me reiterate. There is a core of unchanging values that come from Biblical underpinnings that fit all leaders. These stem from servant leader assumptions and stewardship assumptions that apply to all leaders. To these are added values as a leader learns through processing in life. In addition, a leader learns more about his/her own identity, especially about giftedness, as he/she develops over life. The changes may be gradual over a lifetime so that they are hardly perceived. Leadership situations will change including maturity levels of followers. This will often force leaders to modify past proven ministry philosophy. Frequently, from a combination of the effect of discovery of giftedness and new leadership situations a leader will discover new ways of delivering ministry more effectively to followers. The impetus from these three factors, a growing understanding of Scriptures, a continuing discovery of who one is in terms of giftedness, and the processing that happens to us as we face leadership situations will force us to develop a growing core of principles, values, and guidelines that will affect our leadership behavior, our decision making, our ways of influencing, and our understanding of the value and effectiveness of our ministry.

Constant And Changing

A ministry philosophy is like an island amidst a sea of waves. A ministry philosophy has firm constant values, which do not change (the island) but are added to, modified, or clarified as we develop over life (the waves). Ministry philosophy will include some Biblical values that are relatively constant (a leader will have a growing appreciation for, a better understanding of them over time, and more of a buy in) such as those depicted in the N.T. *Servant Leadership model* or the N.T. *Stewardship Model*. These two general N.T. philosophy models are called value driven models. They contain values that all Christian leaders will gradually learn and use. A ministry philosophy will also involve Biblical values that are tied more to the uniqueness of the person such as those flowing from the N.T. *Harvest Model* or the N.T. *Shepherd Model*. These are gift driven models that have values that will become increasingly a part of those who have gifts which focus around one or the other of the models.[125]

Some Helpful Generalizations About Ministry Philosophy

Ministry philosophy can be characterized by the following:

1. Ministry philosophy will include Biblical values that are relatively constant, Biblical values that are tied to the uniqueness of the individual, and experiential values that are learned in a developmental way from our leadership experience.

---

[124] See **Article**, *19. God's Shaping Processes*.

[125] The phrase *value driven model* means that the model contains values that are required of all Christian leaders because the N.T. enjoins them upon leaders who are to serve God and contribute to the Kingdom. The phrase *gift driven* means that people with the appropriate gifts will agree with and appropriate the values of the model that most aptly fits their giftedness. There are some gifts which uniquely fit the *Harvest Model* and there are some gifts which uniquely fit the *Shepherd model*. There are some gifts which overlap the two models. People with *Harvest Model* gifts will buy into harvest values which will dominate their ministries. People with *Shepherd Model* gifts will buy into shepherd values which will also affect their ministries. People containing some of both (rare individuals) will embrace some values from both models. See **Article**, *24. Jesus—Five Leadership Models—Shepherd, Harvest, Steward, Servant, Intercessor*.

39. Ministry Philosophy

2. Ministry philosophy values, when identified (that is, the leader moves from an implicit understanding to a more explicit understanding) become a springboard to more effective application of them in life.[126]
3. Ministry philosophy probably can never be identified absolutely for a given individual. Because ministry philosophy values are so closely aligned to world view values and thus operate at deep level as well as surface level structures in our understanding and practice, it is probably the case that ministry philosophy is so complex that we will not be able to actually explicitly identify or define our ministry philosophy values. There will be overlap between core values and specific values. There will be inconsistency between what we state as values and our implementation means for using them in ministry. At this point identification of ministry philosophy is as much an art as a science.
4. Yet, the process of trying to identify a ministry philosophy will be invaluable in itself apart from the actual findings, which will also be valuable even if they are not absolutely certain. You will discover in the process more of who you are, who you are becoming in God's shaping process, and have a greater sense of His operating in your life to accomplish His purposes.

A Start Toward Identifying Ministry Philosophy—Four Steps

The overall approach leading to proactive development and use of a ministry philosophy can be summarized by this umbrella statement:

> **Start Where You Are And Work Backward, Then Forward, Always Identifying And Making Explicit As Much As You Can.**

Four steps are suggest for applying the umbrella statement.

1. Move From Implicit To Explicit Values

Analyze the values of your ministry philosophy that have already formed. If you are fairly young and have only a little experience, don't expect to have a full-blown ministry philosophy. More of it will come with time. If you are further along you will identify more of it. Remember a ministry philosophy develops over time. You don't have to have everything all together early on. Your reflection should especially note giftedness, destiny processing, ministry structure insights, core values, specific values, and past contributions. Where ever you can, adapt your role to fit what you are learning about yourself and your ministry philosophy. Whenever you make a decision to change a ministry assignment always move toward an assignment and role which fits more of who you are becoming as suggested by your ministry philosophy.

2. Do Future Perfect Thinking[127] By Focusing On The Possibilities Of The Future With A Full Blown Ministry Philosophy In Place.

A practical start on this involves the following four suggestions. a. *Tentatively identify your ultimate contribution* set. b. Get confirmation from God. c. *Study other* people who have a similar set. d. *Deliberately* move towards roles which focus on your *ultimate contribution set.*[128]

3. Develop A Life Purpose[129] statement Which Reflects Your Findings For Steps 2 And 3.

4. Write Yearly Goals Based On Your Life Purpose Statement.

As these goals are accomplished, you are working out your ministry philosophy in practice.

---

[126]This assumption is certainly subject to questioning based upon personality types. As it is not yet clear that there is a relationship between giftedness and personality types so it is also not clear that some types need explicit knowledge of why they do what they do. My own feeling is that even Myers-Briggs -NFP types who seem to operate fairly powerfully without explicit frameworks to guide them would be helped, at least somewhat, by a clearer understanding of their ministry philosophy. It is more easily seen that -STJ types profit from this explicit understanding.

[127]Future perfect thinking is a paradigmatic way of viewing the future as if it had already happened. Present decisions are then made with a beforemath perspective. See *future perfect*, **Glossary**. See **Article**, *Future Perfect Paradigm*.

[128]See **Article**, *Leaving Behind a Legacy*.

[129] See *life purpose*, **Glossary**. See **Article**, *Life Purpose, Biblical Examples*.

39. Ministry Philosophy

Closure

Let me close with two observations and a challenge. Leadership emergence theory posits that **ministry flows out of being**. An understanding of our beingness includes: 1. our intimacy with God, 2. knowing something about personality and character, 3. knowing ones giftedness set, 4. seeing the Divine interventions and hence recognizing the destiny processing and where it is leading, 5. knowing ones ultimate contribution set. All of these things should impact upon a ministry philosophy. I have been repeatedly emphasizing that,

> **Effective Leaders Who Are Productive Over A Life Time Have A Dynamic Ministry Philosophy.**

So we I am back to where I began the paper. I will leave you with this final challenge.

The Challenge

You must develop a ministry philosophy which honors Biblical leadership values, embraces the challenge of your situation, and flows from who you are.

Paul is the model N.T. church leader who exemplifies this challenge, accepted and accomplished.

Article 40

Relevance of the Article to Paul's Corinthian Ministry

To motivate people a leader must first be motivated himself/herself. This article delves into what motivated Paul to ministry. Certainly the Corinthian intervention illustrates much about factors involved in Paul's personal motivation. All 9 of these factors are illustrated in 1, 2 Co.

40. Motivating Factors For Ministry

Introduction

What motivated Paul to be and do—to be what God intended him to be and to accomplish what God intended him to accomplish? Some factors which motivated Paul, who is our major model for leadership in the **Church Leadership Era**, are given below. Many of these same factors should motivate leaders today.

Factors That Motivated Paul

Table 1,2 Co 40-1 list motivating factors observed in some of the Pauline epistles.[130]

Table 1,2 Co 40-1. Motivational Factors for Paul's Ministry

Factor	Where Observed	Explanation
1. Finishing Well; (Achieving/ Becoming/ Fulfilling Life Purpose)	2Ti 4:7,8; 1Co 9:24-27; 1Ti 6:11,12; 2Ti 4:6; Php 3:14.	Paul is the classic N.T. case of a leader finishing well. Christ is still Lord of His life. He is ministering looking for the return of Christ. All six characteristics of a good finish are indicated. (a) His relationship with God via Christ is still warm and personal. (1Ti 4:17). (b) He evinces a learning posture (1Ti 4:13). (c) He has been shaped by the Holy Spirit over his lifetime into the image of Christ. That is, he demonstrates Christ-likeness (1Ti 4:16). (d) He lives by Biblical convictions, his faith intact (2Ti 4:7). (e) He is leaving behind a legacy. His ultimate contributions include those associated with saint, stylistic practitioner, mentor, pioneer, writer, promoter. To finish well, go the full distance, to finish his course all were drives under lying Paul's motivation for ministry. Principles: a. Present ministry should always be seen in the light of a whole life of ministry and particularly the end of ministry a good finish. A good thought question, "In what way is my present shaping circumstances going to affect my finish?" b. One's sense of destiny guides toward and highlights a good finish. c. An anticipation of the Lord's return is a major motivating factor for a leader to minister well and finish well.
2. Return of Christ (and the Ultimate Accountability associated with it)	2Ti 4:7,8 (see also Tit 2:11-13). Php 1:6,10; 2:16; 4:1;	Paul always ministered with a conscious view to ultimate accountability to God for their ministry. Paul was conscious of a future day in which God would hold him and others accountable for their actions (see 1:16, 4:8, 4:14). This is more fully developed in 2Co and 1, 2Th but is affirmed in many epistles. (See especially He 13:17). Principles: a. Leaders will be held accountable for their ministry

---

[130] Missing would be Ro, Gal, Eph, Col, 1,2Th. Probably some new factors might emerge but the major ones will have been identified from the epistles that were studied. Originally the epistles studied were 1,2 Ti, 1,2 Co, Php, Phe. Later the epistle directing Titus work on Crete was studied.

40. Motivating Factors For Ministry

	2Th 2:2; 2Co 1:14; 5:10.,11; 11:30; 1T 6:14; 2Ti 4:8; many others	efforts. b. Leaders will be rewarded for their positive achievements in ministry. c. A final accountability is one motivating factor for a leader.
3. Giftedness (especially the Apostolic Functions with it)	1Co; 1Ti; 2Co 11:4	Paul exemplifies all of the apostolic functions. For example, a number of his epistles were written in part to correct heresy. His word giftedness dominated all that he did: apostleship, teaching, evangelism, and sometimes pastoring. His giftedness was a major factor in motivating and directing/ guiding him into ministry.
4. Confidence in the Gospel	2Co 3:12; (see also Ro 1:16); 1 Co 6:11.	Confidence in the power of the Good News about Christ is a strong motivating factor leading to bold ministry. Paul spoke boldly because he had experienced the power of the Gospel in lives. He saw people delivered from sins and from addictive sin.
5. Burden for Ministry	2Co 2:4; 2Co 11:28;	Paul, like Moses, had a heavy calling on his life. This calling gave him a burden which drove him to reach Gentiles and to do the apostolic functions he did with them. His strong concerns for those he influenced are interwoven throughout all he does. He exemplifies the double thrust of burden—downward toward ministry with those he was influencing and upward, answering to God for them.
6. Resurrection	1Co 15; 2Co 4:14; Php 3:10;	Paul was driven to know that there was a life after death. His conversion experience convinced him that it was real. From then on, he was obsessed with realizing this for his own life; particularly he wanted to experience resurrection power in his ministry.
7. Handling God's Word appropriately	2Ti 2:15; 2Co 4:2; 2Ti 3:16,17	Paul used the Word of God with great impact. He maintained integrity in how he handled the Word. Knowing the Word of God and used it properly with impact in ministry was a motivating guideline for Paul.
8. Eternal Realities	2Co 4:18	Paul viewed present problems, pressures, physical problems as being bearable in the light of eternity. He always ministered looking forward to resurrection life. He saw these kinds of things *as negative preparation* making him ready and longing for heaven and eternal reality.
9. Love	1Co 12:29; 13; 2Co 5:14	Paul believed that love should be a major underlying motivating and driving force for using giftedness and for ministry in general. His love for Christ compelled him in ministry.

Conclusion

What motivates you in ministry? Strangely absent from Paul's motivation was a drive for prestige, power, or money—factors driving numerous present day leaders.

See *negative preparation*, **Glossary**.

Article 41

Relevance of the Article to Paul's Corinthian Ministry

Paul, like Haggai, Ezra and Nehemiah, stands out as an inspirational leader who motivated people.

In the last article I examined the motivating factors, which inspired Paul to ministry. In this article I examine how these factors were worked out in his ministry as he influenced others. Leaders need to identify their own principles for motivating others. This allows more deliberate inspirational leadership to be accomplished. A study of Paul's motivating principles is a first step, perhaps, in identifying one's own motivational leadership.

41. Motivating Principles—Pauline Influence

Introduction

Paul was a powerful leader who influenced numerous people and churches in *the Church Leadership Era*. What principles or techniques did he use? Following are given some observations (some are statements of principles; others are techniques) which Paul used to motivate individuals and churches. Many of these same principles/techniques can be used by leaders today. Paul, the major model for leadership in the **Church Leadership Era**

Paul's Motivational Principles and Techniques

Table 1,2 Co 41-1 list some principles/ techniques observed in the Pauline epistles on how Paul motivated followers. Not all the Pauline epistles were considered.[131]

Table 1,2 Co 41-1. Paul's Motivational Principles and Techniques

Principle/ Technique	Where Observed	Explanation
Goodwin's Expectation Principle[132]	1Ti 6:11; 2Ti 1:5 et al	Principle: Paul uses the dynamic under lying Goodwin's expectation principle—emerging leaders tend to live up to the genuine expectations of leaders they admire.
Teach For Results	1Ti 1:5	Principle: True teaching ought to result in people who have love, a pure heart and a genuine faith. Paul contrasts this result with the heretical teachers who are producing argumentative people.
Prophecy	1Ti 1:18; 4:14	Principle: Paul recalled a prophecy about a spiritual gift made over Timothy in order to motivate Timothy to use that gift with impact. He recalled a prophecy about Timothy living the Christian life.
Touchstone	1Ti 6:11,12	Principle: Use public committals as a motivating factor for continuing on in the Christian life. Public committals on major decisions form a touchstone.
Heritage	2Ti 1:5	Principle: Paul affirmed a foundational heritage for Timothy in order to exhort him to move on in faith (like his mother and grandmother).
Get It On the Agenda	1Co 1:1, 4, 5;	Principle: Paul often subtly introduced subjects he would later deal with in depth. Later when he began to deal with the subject the hearers were already somewhat primed for it.
Future/ Hope	1Co 1:4-9;	Principle: Inspirational leaders point toward the future and what God will do in order to give followers hope.

---

[131] Missing would be Ro, Gal, Eph, Col, 1,2Th. Probably some new factors might emerge but the major ones will have been identified from the epistles included in this commentary. 1,2 Ti, 1,2 Co, Php, Phe, and Titus were the data base underlying these principles.

[132] I named this principle after Bennie Goodwin who spoke about it in his little pamphlet put out by IV press, **Effective Leadership**. Later I saw this principle identified in secular leadership theory as well.

41. Motivating Principles—Pauline Influence

Competition	1Co 16:1, 4; 2Co 8:1-5, 24; 9:1,2;	Principle: Paul compares churches with churches always pointing out the strengths of churches in order to motivate the other churches to attain that level.
Absolute Surrender	2Co 8:5	Principle: Paul challenged believers to commit themselves totally to God. From that standpoint, then he could motivate them to give freely of all kinds of their resources. Without it, at best he would get some grudging help.
Openness	2Co 8:8	Principle: Paul was open and above board even about using motivational techniques. He would sometimes explain his motivational technique.
Modeling/ Jesus	2Co 8:9; Php 2:1-11.	Principle: Paul appealed to Jesus as a model to motivate followers of Jesus to emulate that modeling.
Spiritual Authority	2Co 12:19;	Principle: Paul used strong authoritative techniques but always in line with spiritual authority which seeks the best for the ones being helped.
Foreshadowing	2Co 12:21.	Principle: Paul lays out for them a future scenario that could happen should they not follow his advice. And he promises to back this scenario up with power.
Modeling/ Jesus	See Php	Principle: One of Paul's strongest motivating means is the modeling in his own life. Over and over this is stressed throughout all his epistles. Paul knows it is a motivating force.
Accountability	Php 2:16; 3:17.	Principle: Paul uses his own ultimate accountability to motivate followers.

Conclusion

Paul demonstrates several techniques for motivating followers, especially the Corinthians. Leaders are people with God-given capacities and a God-given burden who are influencing a specific group of people toward God's purposes for them. Influence is the key word. And motivational techniques are means of exerting that influence. Motivation in this case is even more difficult since Paul is confronting a problem church in which a minority are not responding to him. Paul uses several means of motivating which I have given in the table above. However, let me summarize the more important ones. Motivational Leadership Principles/ Observations include:

a. Goodwin's Expectation Principle, a social dynamic usually dealing with individuals, which recognizes that emerging leaders will usually rise to the level of expectancy of someone they respect, is applied by Paul to a group situation of followers. Paul states his personal positive outcome expectancies for the churches (see especially the Corinthians, both concerning their giving and their following of his exhortations).
b. Paul uses the gift of exhortation throughout all his books, deliberately, openly, and with clear application to situations. See footnotes identifying the gift of exhortation in use.
c. Paul uses a form of comparative competition. He describes what other churches have done with respect to giving (in a rather positive ideal description) in order to set expectancies for giving from the churches (both Philippians and Corinthians).
d. Paul tells churches that he has said great things about their giving to other churches. Their failure to give would make them lose face in the eyes of these other churches.
e. In the Corinthian case, Paul commissions a delegate from one of the churches which has given and been used as a model to go to Corinth to be part of the group that will administer the gift.
f. Paul uses Jesus as a model of giving and as a model for humility and putting others first.
g. Paul uses coercive authority (threatens to exercise spiritual power to correct situations if people do not respond voluntary) backed by a personal visit to motivate.
h. Paul uses well reasoned out logic in giving solutions to issues and defending his own character.
i. In the Corinthian case, Paul uses irony (sometimes bordering on sarcasm), often, in order to force the Corinthians to see their positions on things and to challenge them to respond.

Paul motivated people—even in very complex and problematic situations. An awareness of some of his techniques might prove helpful to leaders today who must motivate followers in equally, if not more complex and problematic situations.

Article 42

Relevance of the Article to Paul's Corinthian Ministry

Paul is a prototype of a leader who explicitly understood and followed the major destiny leadership lesson identified earlier in **Article** *30. Leadership Lessons—Seven Major Lessons Identified.* That major lesson—Effective leaders evince a growing sense of destiny over their lifetimes—is foundational to one's persevering and finishing well. This article describes Paul's sense of destiny. Note, his sense of destiny was tied to his apostolic calling and authority for his ministry—a fact, which he underscored when dealing with church problems such as the Corinthian situation.

42. Paul—A Sense of Destiny

Introduction

The Apostle Paul had a strong sense of destiny. You see it all over the pages of his epistles. One of the major leadership lessons[133] that emerged from a comparative study of effective leaders concerned the concept, sense of destiny.

Effective leaders evince a growing sense of destiny over their lifetimes.[134]

You will notice reminders of Paul's sense of destiny sprinkled throughout my leadership commentary notes on the Pauline Epistles. He exemplifies in the N.T. Church Leadership Era the importance of a sense of destiny. Such an awareness stabilizes a leader, encourages perseverance, and becomes a Pole Star to shed directive light in major decisions about guidance.

Definition	A <u>sense of destiny</u> is an inner conviction arising from an experience or a series of experiences in which there is a growing sense of awareness that God has His hand on a leader in a special way for special purposes.
Definition	<u>Destiny processing</u> refers to the shaping incidents or means God uses to instill this growing sense of awareness of a destiny.

It is through these shaping activities of God that a leader becomes increasingly aware of God's Hand on his/her life and the purposes for which God has intended for his/her leadership. This processing causes a sense of partnership with God toward God's purposes for the life and hence brings meaning to the life.

A sense of destiny and accompanying destiny processing form the seedbed for life purpose—not only the driving force behind our lives but the defining essence of it. When a leader surrenders to God, in terms of an all out commitment to be the leader God wants, a whole process begins in which that leader begins to discover for what purposes he/she was uniquely created. **Life purpose** represents the descriptive label that characterizes the underlying motivational thrust(s) that energizes a given leader to be and do and around which life begins to center. It becomes that overall centralizing ideal or accomplishment or task to which

---

[133] Seven such lessons have been identified: (1) Effective Leaders View Present Ministry in Terms Of A Life Time Perspective. (2) Effective Leaders Maintain A Learning Posture Throughout Life. (3) Effective Leaders Value Spiritual Authority As A Primary Power Base. (4) Effective Leaders Who Are Productive Over A Lifetime Have A Dynamic Ministry Philosophy. (5) Effective Leaders View Leadership Selection And Development As A Priority Function In Their Ministry. (6) Effective Leaders See Relational Empowerment As Both A Means And A Goal Of Ministry. (7) Effective Leaders Evince A Growing Awareness Of Their Sense Of Destiny. It is this last one I am exploring in this article.

[134] This is a major key to an effective ministry. No Bible leader who had an effective ministry failed to have a sense of destiny. Paul is the exemplar in the N.T. Church Leadership Era. Over and over again in his epistles, Paul's makes statements that reflect on his understanding of his destiny with God.

42. Paul—A Sense of Destiny

all of a leader's life is committed. **Life purpose** is the most important of four focal issues which define the focused life.[135]

Definition   A <u>life purpose</u> is a burden-like calling, a task or driving force or achievement, which motivates a leader to fulfill something or to see something done.

Paul and The Destiny Pattern

Paul exemplifies the N.T. church leadership prototype for the destiny pattern.

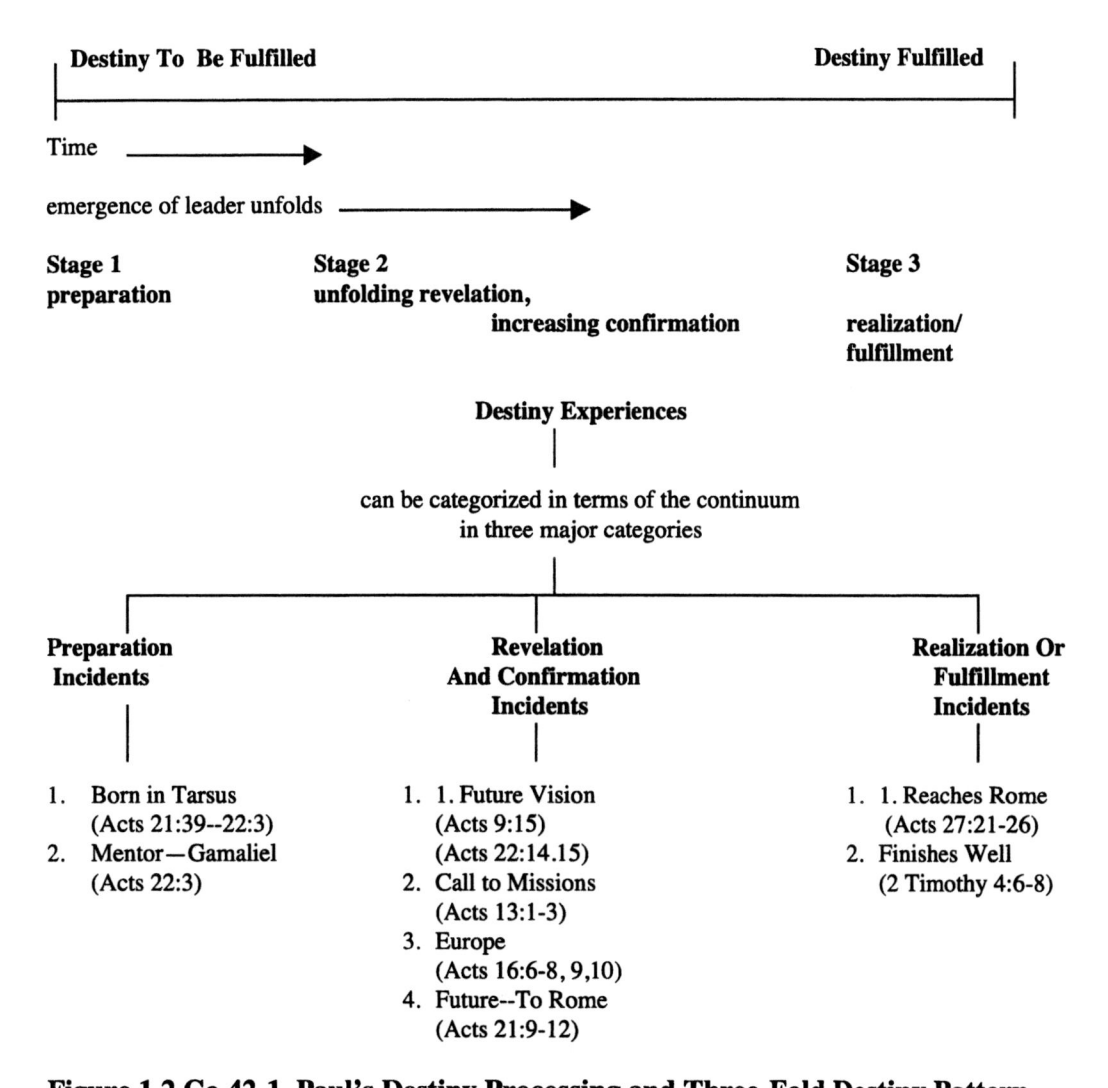

```
| Destiny To Be Fulfilled                                    Destiny Fulfilled |
|─────────────────────────────────────────────────────────────────────────────|

Time ─────────▶

emergence of leader unfolds ─────────▶

Stage 1                Stage 2                              Stage 3
preparation            unfolding revelation,
                            increasing confirmation         realization/
                                                            fulfillment
```

Destiny Experiences

can be categorized in terms of the continuum
in three major categories

Preparation Incidents	Revelation And Confirmation Incidents	Realization Or Fulfillment Incidents
1. Born in Tarsus (Acts 21:39--22:3)	1. 1. Future Vision (Acts 9:15) (Acts 22:14,15)	1. 1. Reaches Rome (Acts 27:21-26)
2. Mentor—Gamaliel (Acts 22:3)	2. Call to Missions (Acts 13:1-3)	2. Finishes Well (2 Timothy 4:6-8)
	3. Europe (Acts 16:6-8, 9,10)	
	4. Future--To Rome (Acts 21:9-12)	

Figure 1,2 Co 42-1. Paul's Destiny Processing and Three-Fold Destiny Pattern

---

[135] A <u>focused life</u> is a life dedicated to exclusively carrying out God's unique purposes through it, by identifying the focal issues, that is, life purpose, major role, effective methodology, or ultimate contribution, which allows an increasing prioritization of life's activities around the focal issues, and results in a satisfying life of being and doing. The 4 focal issues—life purpose, major role, effective methodology, or ultimate contribution—are discovered over a lifetime.

42. Paul—A Sense of Destiny

Paul's Destiny And Ensuing Life Purpose—Progressively Seen

Paul progressively grasped his sense of destiny. God used a number of special events over time to build into Paul a more detailed awareness of his sense of destiny.

Definition   A **prime critical incident** is a special intervention (could be a series over time) in which God gives a *major value* that will flow through the life or will give *strategic direction* to narrow the leader's life work.

1. Some produce a dominant value which pervades the leader's ministry philosophy.
2. Some pinpoint a key strategic directional factor.
3. Some do both.

Table 1,2 Co 42-1 gives Seven prime critical incidents in the life of Paul. I synthesize how each of these progressively fed into Paul's life purpose.

Table 1,2 Co 42-1. Paul's Life Purpose Unfolding

Incident	Label/ Scripture	Life Purpose
C_1	Damascus Road	My life purpose is to serve the risen Lord Jesus by witnessing to what he has shown me and will show me to Jews, Gentiles, and Kings.
C_2	Barnabas Sponsors Acts 9	My life purpose is to serve the risen Lord Jesus by witnessing to what he has shown me and will show me to Jews, Gentiles, and Kings. **I know I am to be a part of expanding Jesus' work begun in Jerusalem.**
C_3	Barnabas sponsors in Antioch Acts 11	My life purpose is to serve the risen Lord Jesus by witnessing to what he has shown me and will show me to Jews, Gentiles, and Kings. I know I am to be a part of expanding Jesus' work begun in Jerusalem. **It will involve working with a team and development of local groups of Christians.**
C_4	Apostolic Call/ Acts 13	My life purpose is to serve the risen Lord Jesus by witnessing to what he has shown me and will show me to Jews, Gentiles, and Kings. I know I am to be a part of expanding Jesus' work begun in Jerusalem. It will involve working with a team and development of local groups of Christians. **Further, I know that I will be in an itinerant ministry, having been sent by the Holy Spirit, confirmed by other leaders, to witness to Gentiles on Cyprus.**
C_5	Conflict and the Jerusalem Council/ Gospel Clarified Acts 15	My life purpose is to serve the risen Lord Jesus by witnessing to what he has shown me and will show me to Jews, Gentiles, and Kings. I know I am to be a part of expanding Jesus' work begun in Jerusalem. It will involve working with a team and development of local groups of Christians. Further, I know that I will be in an itinerant ministry, having been sent by the Holy Spirit, confirmed by other leaders, to witness to Gentiles on Cyprus. **I will be the primary person who will contextualize truth into Gentile situations. Occasionally, I will also speak truth into Jewish situations.**

42. Paul—A Sense of Destiny

C_6	European/ Western Gentiles Acts 16	My life purpose is to serve the risen Lord Jesus by witnessing to what he has shown me and will show me to Jews, Gentiles, and Kings. I know I am to be a part of expanding Jesus' work begun in Jerusalem. It will involve working with a team and development of local groups of Christians. Further, I know that I will be in an itinerant ministry, having been sent by the Holy Spirit, confirmed by other leaders, to witness to Gentiles on Cyprus, **Asia Minor and Europe. My ministry will thus be widespread, an itinerant ministry among Gentiles.** I will be the primary person who will contextualize truth into Gentile situations. **I know that my ministry will be pioneering, breaking open new situations to western Gentiles as well as others.** Occasionally, I will also speak truth into Jewish situations.
C_7	Destiny in Rome Via Jerusalem Persecution Acts 21	My life purpose is to serve the risen Lord Jesus by witnessing to what he has shown me and will show me to Jews, Gentiles, and Kings. I know I am to be a part of expanding Jesus' work begun in Jerusalem. It will involve working with a team and development of local groups of Christians. Further, I know that I will be in an itinerant ministry, having been sent by the Holy Spirit, confirmed by other leaders, to witness to Gentiles on Cyprus, Asia Minor and Europe. My ministry will thus be widespread, an itinerant ministry among Gentiles. I will be the primary person who will contextualize truth into Gentile situations. I know that my ministry will be pioneering, breaking open new situations to western Gentiles as well as others. Occasionally, I will also speak truth into Jewish situations. **I know I am destined to give my witness to Christ before high rulers.**

Conclusion

Paul finished well. One reason, he led a focused life. At the heart of that focus was the sense of destiny that drove him on to serve God. He struggled a good struggle. He finished his course. He fulfilled his life purpose. He stands as a model for us.

> 6 As for me, I am ready to be sacrificed. The time for me to depart this life is near. 7 I have run a good race.[136] I have fulfilled my God-given destiny.[137] I still have my faith intact. 8 And now for my prize, a crown of righteousness. The Lord, the righteous judge, will award it to me at that day. And not to me only, but unto all those who eagerly await his return.[138]

---

[136] Literally, this is *the good struggle I have struggled*, a use of the superlative repetitive idiom. The two words for struggle are the noun form and verb form from which we derive our words agony and agonize and refer to an Olympic athlete who is disciplining himself for a marathon or other event.

[137] Fulfilled my destiny, literally I have finished or completed (SRN 5758) a perfect action, i.e. already done it with on going results, my course (SRN 1408). Course, used three times in the N.T., refers to life's destiny, the pathway set before one to do. The destiny pattern usually follows a threefold pattern: destiny preparation, destiny revelation, and destiny fulfillment. This idea of already completing it is the use of a certainty idiom, the prophetic past. It is so certain that he speaks of it in the past tense as if it had already happened. See Ac 20:24 where Paul states his desire to finish his course. See also, Ac 13:25 where the same word refers to John the Baptist's having finished his course. See *certainty idiom, prophetic past, sense of destiny, destiny preparation, destiny revelation, destiny fulfillment*, **Glossary**. See **Articles**, *10. Destiny Pattern*.

[138] Vs 4:6-8 show that Paul finished well. He is the classic case of a N.T. church leader finishing well. All six characteristics of a good finish are seen: (1) vibrant personal relationship with God; (2) have a learning posture; (3) Christ-likeness in character; (4) live by Biblical convictions; (5) leave behind ultimate contributions; (6) fulfill a sense of destiny. One of the major leadership contributions of 2Ti is this challenge to finish well, which Paul models. See *modeling*, **Glossary**. *Article, 14. Finishing Well—Six Characteristics*.

Article 43

Relevance of the Article to Paul's Corinthian Ministry

Paul had a great fishing pool from which to identify and select and develop leaders. Paul, more than any other leader in Scripture identifies by name people he influenced. This article lists those people named in scripture who Paul identified with in some way or other. A number of these folks are actually listed in the Corinthian letters, 14 of them. Paul exemplifies two of the seven major leadership lessons as can be clearly seen by a study of these people associated with Paul. Lesson 5—Effective Leaders View Leadership Selection And Development As A Priority Function In Their Ministry and Lesson 6— Effective Leaders See Relational Empowerment As Both A Means And A Goal Of Ministry certainly are evident when one sees the number of people Paul related to and how he used these relationships to move many of these folks into ministry.

43. Paul—And His Companions

Introduction

Paul developed leaders. He did this through teaching, modeling, and on-the-job training. A comparative study of his relationships with numerous leaders reveals that he exemplifies a number of mentoring roles: discipler, spiritual guide, coach, teacher, contemporary model, sponsor. He operated as a mentor with individuals. He also mentored in a team context.

Several Pauline leadership values[139] under girded this drive to develop leaders.

> **Leaders Must Be Concerned About Leadership Selection And Development.**
>
> **Leaders Should View Personal Relationships As An Important Part Of Ministry.**
>
> **A Christian Leader Ought To Have Several Life Long Mentorees Who He/She Will Help Over A Lifetime To Reach Their Potential In Leadership.**

And the following two major lessons are the foundation for the above three.

> **Effective Leaders View Leadership Selection And Development As A Priority In Ministry.**
>
> **Effective Leaders View Relational Empowerment As Both A Means And A Goal In Ministry.**

This article simply points out that Paul had a personal ministry. Paul developed many leaders, his companions in ministry. It also seeks to exhort us by example.

Paul's Companions

Luke's *we sections* in Ac[140] points out that Paul frequently had a team with him. A number of the people listed below actually traveled on teams with Paul. Others were in ministry with him in various locales. Still other were acquaintances he thought highly of. But all of them had some personal relationship with Paul. Table 1,2 Co 43-1 lists the many folks Paul related to personally. Many of them were leaders.

---

[139] A <u>leadership value</u> is an underlying assumption which affects how a leader perceives leadership and practices it. Leadership values contain strong language like should, ought, or must. Must statements are the strongest.

[140] The "we" sections are chs 16:10-17; 20:5-21:18; 27:1-28:16.

43. Paul—And His Companions

Table 1,2 Co 43-1. Paul's Companions—Reflected in His Epistles

Who	Vs	Comments
Achaicus	1Co 16:17, 24	One of three men who brought Paul financial support when he was in Philippi, from the Corinthian church. Also one of three men who were present when the first letter to the church at Corinth was penned. So, he along with the other two probably supplied Paul with lots of information about the church at Corinth.
Ampliatus	Ro 16:8	A close friend in the church at Rome.
Andronicus	Ro 16:7	An apostle and Christian before Paul. Was in prison probably with Paul. Paul calls him a kinsman but whether this is a brother in Christ or physically is not certain.
Apelles	Ro 16:10	A Christian friend well thought of by Paul in the church at Rome. In his greeting he gives affirmation for this person.
Apollos	Seen 10 times in Ac, 1Co, Tit	A strong Christian worker and well known as a public rhetorician, mighty in the Scriptures. Was mentored by Priscilla and Acquilla. Associated with the church at Corinth. Late in Paul's ministry, when Titus was in Crete, Paul asked Titus to raise funds in Crete to support Apollos.
Apphia	Phm 2	A female Christian, probably the wife of Philemon. Paul loved her dearly and thought highly of her in his greeting in the Phm letter.
Aquila	Ac 18:2, 18, 26; Ro 16:3, 1Co 16:19; 2Ti 4:19.	A Jewish believer married to Priscilla. They were persecuted under Claudius and driven out of Rome. A tentmaker by trade he and his wife associated with Paul (bi-vocational; financial support) and were taught by him in the Christian faith. They were teammates with Paul and made a ministry trip with him. Paul affirmed them to the church at Rome as co-ministers with him and as those who had saved his life—putting their own lives on the line. Priscilla and Aquila apparently had house churches where ever they went. They were in Ephesus when Timothy went there to do apostolic consulting work.
Archippus	Col 4:17; Phm 1,2	A Christian worker well thought of by Paul. He ministered in the church at Colosse and in the church in Philemon's home. Paul calls him a fellow soldier—a beautiful compliment.
Aristarchus	Ac 19:29; 20:4; 27:2	A fellow preacher with Paul. He was persecuted in Ephesus. He traveled on one of Paul's teams from Ephesus to Turkey. Also accompanied Paul to Rome. Suffered in prison with Paul. Mentioned in Phm as a fellow worker.
Aristobulus	Ro 16:10	A Christian friend well thought of by Paul in the church at Rome. In his greeting he gives affirmation for this person.
Artemas	Tit 3:12	On Paul's team when he wintered in Nicopolis, late in Paul's ministry. Probably sent as a messenger to Titus on Crete.
Asyncritus	Ro 16:14	One of several Christians at Rome that Paul greeted warmly. Most likely a small group leader since he greets not only him but the Christians with him. See Ro 16:14 Salute **Asyncritus**, Phlegon, Hermas, Patrobas, Hermes, and the brethren which are with them.
Barnabas	Mentioned 33 times; Many times in Ac; 1Co 9:6, Ga 2:1,9, 13 ; Col 4:10	A mentor sponsor of Paul who brought Paul into the work at Antioch. He led the first missionary team (Paul and his nephew John Mark). Paul became the leader of that team when it moved from Cyprus to Asia minor. Barnabas continued to sponsor Paul with the Jerusalem church. His generosity and giving values impacted Paul. He and Paul had a falling out and split before Paul's second missionary journey. Paul still thought highly of him as seen by his mentioning him in 1Co.
Cephas	1Co 1:12; 3:22; 9:5; 15:5; Gal 1:18; 2:9, 11, 14.	Paul uses this name for Peter several times. Paul recognized and respected Peter as the leader of the Jewish Christian movement. He also clashed with Peter concerning contextualizing the Gospel. Peter respected Paul and recognized that God had revealed truth through him—Scriptural truth.

43. Paul—And His Companions

Claudia	2Ti 4:21	A Christian at Rome. Paul mentions her in his last words to Timothy in 2Ti. She is probably a local house church leader or small group leader since Paul singles our her name and then says also all the Christians. Probably among those Christians giving support to Paul in Rome.
Clement	Php 4:3	A fellow Christian worker with Paul in Phillipi. Paul ask the unnamed pastoral leader at Philippi to aid Clement.
Crescens	2Ti 4:10	Crescens was part of a team around Paul in his second Roman imprisonment. He is mentioned as having left Paul. The context is not clear whether he was on some mission or left for some other reason.
Crispus	Ac 18:8; 1Co 1:14	He was the chief ruler of the Jewish synagogue at Ephesus. Paul led him to Christ. And Paul baptized him. Crispus led his family to the Lord, always a difficult thing with Jewish people.
Demas	Col 4:10; Phm 24; 2Ti 4:10	Demas was part of a team around Paul in his second Roman imprisonment along with Luke and Titus. He is mentioned as having deserted Paul to go to Thessalonica. The context indicates this was not pleasing to Paul. He loved this present world (does that mean he didn't want to be martyred with Paul or that he loved worldliness?)
Epaphroditus	Php 2:25; 4:18	Took a gift from the Php church to Paul while Paul was in prison. He helped Paul while Paul was imprisoned. Nearly died of some sickness. He was a fellow Christian worker with Paul. Paul sponsored him to the Philippians.
Epaphras	Col 1:7; 4:12; Phm 23.	A fellow minister of the Gospel, from the church in Colosse and probably sent out by them. Paul speaks very highly of him calling him a faithful servant of Christ, an intercessor praying for the maturity of the church at Colosse. He was also a fellow prisoner with Paul.
Epenetus	Ro 16:5	Paul speaks highly of this Christian calling him beloved and identifying him as the first Christian in the Achaia (region surrounding Corinth). Probably was in Rome at the time of Paul's writing the Roman epistle.
Erastus	Ac 19:22; Ro 16:23; 2Ti 4:20	He was a missionary with Paul, on one of his traveling teams on his third missionary journey. He was a city treasurer at Corinth so a man of influence. He is mentioned as staying in Corinth when Paul was in prison the second time in Rome. He was one of several people, probably a support team for Paul, who heard Paul dictate the letter to the Romans. One of the team took the dictation.
Eubulus	2Ti 4:21	A Christian at Rome. Paul mentions him in his last words to Timothy in 2Ti. He is probably a local house church leader or small group leader since Paul singles our his name and then says also all the Christians. Probably among those Christians giving support to Paul in Rome.
Eunice	2Ti 1:5	Timothy's mother. A woman of real faith whom Paul highly respected. She gave Timothy a foundation in the O.T. Scriptures and modeled a life of faith and piety for him.
Euodias	Ph 4:2,3	A woman who co-labored in the Lord with Paul at Philippi. She was having problems with another woman, Syntyche, in the church at the time Paul wrote the Php epistle. He spoke highly of her as he entreated her to make up her differences with Syntyche.
Fortunatus	1Co 16:17,24	One of three men who brought Paul financial support when he was in Philippi, from the Corinthian church. Also one of three men who were present when the first letter to the church at Corinth was penned. So, he along with the other two probably supplied Paul with lots of information about the church at Corinth.
Gaius	Ro 16:23; 1Co 1:14	Gaius was led to Christ and baptized by Paul in the city of Corinth. Later Paul stayed in his home, at the time of the writing of the epistle to the Romans. Gaius was part of a small group of people that heard Paul dictate the letter to the Romans.
Hermas	Ro 16:14	A Christian at Rome that Paul greeted warmly. Most likely a small group leader since he greets not only him but the Christians with him.

43. Paul—And His Companions

Hermes	Ro 16:14	A Christian at Rome that Paul greeted warmly. Most likely a small group leader since he greets not only him but the Christians with him.
Hermogenes	2Ti 1:15	He is described as one who has turned away from Paul.
Herodion	Ro 16:11	A Christian at Rome that Paul greeted warmly. Paul identified him as a kinsman (spiritual or other, it is not clear).
Jason	Ro 16:21	Maybe a relation of Paul. One of a privileged group who heard Paul dictate the letter to the church in Rome (Timothy, Lucius, Jason, Sosipater, Tertius, Gaius, Erastus and Quartus).
John Mark (Marcus)	Ac 12:25; 13:5, 13; 15:37, 39; Col 4:10; Phm 24; 2Ti 4:11; 1Pe 5:13	Also called Mark or John. John Mark was a relative of Barnabas (most likely a cousin or nephew). He was on Barnabas and Paul's missionary team which went to Cyprus. He quit the team when it went on to Asia minor. Paul would not have him on his second missionary journey. Paul and Barnabas split over this. Later he went with Barnabas back to Cyprus and Paul took Silas with him on his 2nd missionary journey. Later Paul received him back and sponsored him. Mark also served with Peter and is the author of the Gospel of Mark.
Julia	Ro 16:15	A Christian woman at Rome greeted warmly by Paul. Probably a local church leader since Paul also mentions the saints that are with her.
Junia	Ro 16:7	A female apostle and Christian before Paul. Was in prison probably with Paul. Paul calls her a kinsperson but whether this is a sister in Christ or physically is not certain.
Linus	2Ti 4:21	A Christian at Rome. Paul mentions him in his last words to Timothy in 2Ti. He is probably a local house church leader or small group leader since Paul singles our his name and then says also all the Christians. Probably among those Christians giving support to Paul in Rome.
Lois	2Ti 1:5	Timothy's grand mother. A woman of real faith whom Paul highly respected. She along with Timothy's mother Eunice gave Timothy a foundation in the O.T. Scriptures and modeled a life of faith and piety for him.
Lucius	Ro 16:21	One of a privileged group who heard Paul dictate the letter to the church in Rome (Timothy, Lucius, Jason, Sosipater, Tertius, Gaius, Erastus and Quartus). He could possibly be the prophet who was at Antioch in Ac 13:1 when Paul and Barnabas received their great sense of destiny call to missions.
Luke	2Co 13:14; Col 4:14; 2Ti 4:11; Phm 24	Luke was called the beloved physician. He was on one of Paul's traveling teams, the second missionary journey. He went to Rome with Paul (including the shipwreck). He ministered faithfully to Paul in his imprisonments. He authored the Gospel of Luke and the book of Acts. Both these writings reflect the deep impact that Paul made on Luke. 2 Co 13:14 postscript (The second [epistle] to the Corinthians was written from Philippi, [a city] of Macedonia, by Titus and Lucas.)
Mary	Ro 16:6	A Christian at Rome who was noted for her ministry of helps to Paul.
Narcissus	Ro 16:11	A Christian at Rome who Paul greeted warmly. Probably a small group leader or house church leader as Paul also mentions his household (could be only his kin or a house church set up).
Nereus	Ro 16:15	A Christian at Rome that Paul greeted warmly. Probably a local church leader since Paul also mentions the saints that are with him.
Nymphas	Col 4:15	Said to have been a wealthy and zealous Christian in Laodicea. Hosted a house church and was probably a small group leader.
Olympas	Ro 16:15	A Christian at Rome that Paul greeted warmly. Probably a local church leader since Paul also mentions the saints that are with them.
Onesimus	Col 4:9, 18; Phm 10, 11;	A runaway slave whom Paul led to the Lord while he was in prison in Rome. After some mentor discipling, Paul sent him back to his master, Philemon, a Christian who had a church in his home. This was a challenge both to Onesimus and Philemon, showing the power of the Gospel to break up a major social institution, slavery. Tradition had it that Onesimus became a very influential church leader in the region.

43. Paul—And His Companions

Onesiphorus	2Ti 1:16; 4:19	This man ministered unashamedly to Paul during his second imprisonment. He was probably a small group leader or elder in the work at Ephesus.
Patrobas	Ro 16:14	A Christian at Rome that Paul greeted warmly. Most likely a small group leader since he greets not only him but the Christians with him.
Persis	Ro 16:12	A Christian woman at Rome. Paul uses the word beloved in describing her and that she labored much in the Lord's work.
Philemon	Phm 1. See whole book.	A wealthy landowner in the Colosse region. He became a Christian under Paul's two year teaching ministry at Ephesus. Philemon hosted a house church. Paul asked him a special favor—to take back a runaway slave named Onesimus. He gave strong affirmation to Philemon for his Christian testimony.
Philologus	Ro 16:15	A Christian at Rome that Paul greeted warmly. Probably a local church leader since Paul also mentions the saints that are with him.
Phlegon	Ro 16:14	A Christian at Rome that Paul greeted warmly. Most likely a small group leader since he greets not only him but the Christians with him.
Phoebe	Ro 16:1	A fellow leader, female, in the church at Corinth. Paul sponsored her to the church in Rome.
Phygellus	2Ti 1:15	He is described as one who turned away from Paul.
Priscilla	Ac 18:2, 18, 26; Ro 16:3, 1Co 16:19; 2Ti 4:19.	A Jewish woman, a believer married to Acquila. They were persecuted under Claudius and driven out of Rome. A tentmaker by trade he and his wife associated with Paul and were taught by him in the Christian faith. They were teammates with Paul and made a ministry trip with him. Paul affirmed them to the church at Rome as co-ministers with him and as those who had saved his life—putting their own lives on the line. Priscilla and Aquila apparently had house churches where ever they went. Their final ministry was in Ephesus. They were in that church when Timothy went there to do apostolic consulting work. Priscilla was apparently the word gifted person of the pair.
Pudens	2Ti 4:21	A Christian at Rome. Paul mentions him in his last words to Timothy in 2Ti. He is probably a local house church leader or small group leader since Paul singles our his name and then says also all the Christians. Probably among those Christians giving support to Paul in Rome.
Quartus	Ro 16:23	One of a privileged group who heard Paul dictate the letter to the church in Rome (Timothy, Lucius, Jason, Sosipater, Tertius, Gaius, Erastus and Quartus).
Rufus	Ro 16:13	A Christian at Rome. Paul makes a strong destiny statement about him. He also praises Rufus' mother whom he addresses as his own mother—so close was the relationship.
Sosipater	Ro 16:21	One of a privileged group who heard Paul dictate the letter to the church in Rome (Timothy, Lucius, Jason, Sosipater, Tertius, Gaius, Erastus and Quartus).
Sosthenes	1Co 1:1	Co-authored 1Co with Paul. A respected leader in Corinth. He most likely filled Paul in on many issues of the church situation at Corinth.
Stachys	Ro 16:9	A Christian in Rome greatly loved by Paul.
Stephanas	1Co 16: 15, 17, 24	One of three men who brought Paul financial support when he was in Philippi, from the Corinthian church. Also one of three men who were present when the first letter to the church at Corinth was penned. So, he along with the other two probably supplied Paul with lots of information about the church at Corinth. Paul asks the Corinthian church to support this man who has gone into full time ministry.
Silvanus	2Co 1:19; 1Th 1:1; 2Th 1:1	A Roman citizen and fellow missionary. A part of Paul's traveling team. Co-authored two books, 1,2Th. A respected leader by Paul.
Syntyche	Php 4:2,3	A woman who co-labored in the Lord with Paul at Philippi. She was having problems with another woman, Euodias, in the church at the time Paul wrote the Php epistle. He spoke highly of her as he entreated her to make up her differences with Euodias.

43. Paul—And His Companions

Tertius	Ro 16:22	One of a privileged group who heard Paul dictate the Roman epistle (Timothy, Lucius, Jason, Sosipater, Tertius, Gaius, Erastus and Quartus).
Timothy	Occurs 31 times; 1Co 4:17; 16:10, 24 2Co 1:1, 19	The most intimate follower of Paul. Traveled with him on many missionary trips. Was sent on ministry trips for Paul. Best known for his apostolic consultation ministry at Ephesus. One of a privileged group who heard Paul dictate the letter to the church in Rome (Timothy, Lucius, Jason, Sosipater, Tertius, Gaius, Erastus and Quartus). Received two special letters while at Ephesus which reveals the mentoring relationship between Paul and Timothy. These two letters are the top two leadership books in the N.T. Church Leadership Era. In 2Ti Paul passes the baton of leadership over to Timothy. [1 Co 16:24 is a postscript]
Titus	Occurs 15 times; 2Co 2:13; 7:6, 13, 14; 8:6, 16, 17,23; 12:18; 13:14	Next to Timothy, Paul's closest worker. He was given some of the toughest ministry assignments including one at Corinth dealing with finances and authority problems. He also was given an apostolic assignment in Crete. The book of Tit written to sponsor him is the third most important book on leadership in the N.T. Church Leadership Era. 2 Co 13:14 postscript (The second [epistle] to the Corinthians was written from Philippi, [a city] of Macedonia, by Titus and Lucas.)
Trophimus	2Ti 4:20	He was one of a small group of people close to Paul during Paul's second imprisonment. He became sick and was left at Miletum.
Tryphena	Ro 16:12	A Christian woman in Rome who was described as a worker for the Lord.
Tryphosa	Ro 16:12	A Christian woman in Rome who was described as a worker for the Lord
Tychicus	Eph 6:21, 24; Col 4:7, 18; 2Ti 4:12; Tit 3:12	A Christian worker, part of Paul's support team during his second imprisonment. He also was involved in transcribing and carrying the Ephesian and Colossian letters and traveled with Onesimus as he carried the Philemon letter. Tychicus was well thought of by Paul—described as a beloved brother. He was sent on a mission to Ephesus during the time of the writing of 2Ti.
Urbanus	Ro 16:9	A Christian worker in Rome who had helped Paul in the past (financially or ministry wise—unclear).
Zenas	Tit 3:13	A lawyer whom Titus was to bring to Paul.

Some Observations

Several important observations from Paul's co-ministry and relationship with others should be noted.

1. Paul believe in affirmation both public and private. Affirmation is one of the strongest means a leader has in encouraging emerging workers. Frequently, affirmation involves use of Goodwin's Expectation Principle: *Emerging leaders tend to live up to the genuine expectations of leaders they respect*. Paul not only affirms but challenges through the affirmation.

2. Paul personally related to leaders all up and down the levels of leadership: local church members, lay leaders in general, bi-vocational leaders at small group level, local church elders, fellow bi-vocational workers, full time workers of regional influence, leaders of Christian movement in Jerusalem, etc. He was at home with kings, ambassadors, and with common folk.

3. Paul used networking power as a means of strong influence in numerous leadership ways. He could not have accomplished all that he did with out all kind of help from people whom God had given to him in relationships.

4. Most of Paul's companions, whom he knew at one time or another and supported him, stayed faithful to him. Only a very small few are said to have fallen away from him.

43. Paul—And His Companions

5. A number of Paul's companions were women who ministered in local church situations. Paul did not have a problem with women in ministry (at least from a giftedness or theological standpoint; yes, there were cultural problems).

Conclusion

Paul certainly sets a standard for those who would invest personally in the lives of others. He exemplifies one who held this important value.

Leaders Should View Personal Relationships As An Important Part Of Ministry.

Leaders today with their thoughts on bigness and success may well miss this most important aspect of ministry.

See *mentor; mentoree; mentoring; mentor discipler; mentor spiritual guide; mentor coach; mentor teacher; mentor contemporary model; mentor sponsor;* **Glossary**. See **Articles**, *47. Paul—Mentor For Many; 45. Paul—Developer Par Excellence; 69. Timothy—A Beloved Son in the Faith.*

Article 44

Relevance of the Article to Paul's Corinthian Ministry

1,2 Co, more than any other of Paul's epistles shows the hard shaping activities that God used to develop this great leader. The Corinthian intervention was **the crisis** of Paul's ministry. If the church at Corinth failed to abide by his apostolic rulings given in the letters 1,2 Co, then Paul's ministry was finished. It was a very difficult time from a church standpoint but as well from a personal standpoint. Paul faced a major illness. 2 Co especially reveals the deep soul searching Paul did as God took him through this difficult time. All leaders will face deep processing, if not directly, then via vicarious learning as they minister to others in the crises situations of life. Forewarned is forearmed. Knowing that we, as leaders, will face very difficulty times in our lives and ministries is an important perspective that can keep us from being blind-sided by it. Further, seeing how Paul responded to it (see also especially **Article 59.** *Sovereign Mindset*) can be very instructive for our own lives. This article helps us identify with Paul in a way that may eventually save us later in our own ministry.

44. Paul—Deep Processing

Introduction

Do you know someone who has quit the full time ministry? Have you ever felt like quitting the full time ministry? Did you know that there is a large dropout from full time ministry? Well if ever a Christian worker had reasons to quit, it was Paul at the time he wrote 2Co. He was in his mid-fifties and had over 20 years of tough ministry experience behind him.

Here is what he faced. Paul's first letter to Corinth was probably written at Ephesus.[141] Shortly after writing it, he was forced to flee because of the hubbub caused by the shrine makers honoring the goddess Diana.[142] Paul went on to Troas to revisit churches in Macedonia. He intended to travel south to Corinth and visit churches in Achaia.[143] He did eventually get there and stayed about three months.[144] It was in the interval between leaving Ephesus and reaching Corinth that he wrote again to the Corinthians. At the time he was going through deep processing. What he was going through was enough to make any Christian worker give up?

What was he facing? No news from Titus.[145] He had sent Titus to Corinth to deal with some of the problems there. He was anxious about what was happening there. He describes this time in Macedonia as a time when he had *no rest within and deeply troubled from without* as well. The church at Corinth appeared to be in revolt against his leadership. The churches in Galatia were falling away to another Gospel. He had narrowly escaped with his life from the uproar in Ephesus. In addition to disappointment and apprehensiveness, Paul had a physical illness which was almost fatal. Paul described it in his own words,

> 8 I want you to know, dear Christian friends, of the very trying experiences[146] which we faced in the province of Asia. I was overwhelmed,[147] beyond my ability[148] to cope with it. I thought[149] I was going to die. 9 I concluded[150] that I would die. 2Co 1:8,9.

---

[141] See 1Co 16:8.

[142] See Ac 19 for the vignette.

[143] See Ac 20:1,2.

[144] See Ac 20:3.

[145] See 2Co 2:13.

[146] *Trying experiences* (SRN 2347) represents the same Greek word used several times in 2Co 1:3,4 and often translated as tribulation or affliction.

[147] *Overwhelmed* (SRN 5236) is a translation of a word meaning excessively so (**KJV** beyond measure).

[148] *Ability* (SRN 1411) is a translation of the Greek word, power.

44. Paul—Deep Processing

But look at what he learned.

> But as a result I learned not to trust myself but to rely on God, who can raise the dead. 10 He delivered me from that tremendous near death experience. He continues to deliver. He will do so in the future too! 11 You play a part in this by praying for us. As a result, because many prayed, many will give thanks to God for his answered prayer—our safety.[151]

This experiential acknowledging of total dependence on God in a deep processing situation is usually a turning point in this shaping activity by God. Paul was at death's door. To all outward appearances his life and work were coming to an end—and not on a good note. His life, his work, and the fate of the potential of the worldwide movement of Christianity in the Gentile world all hung in the balance. Probably never before had he felt himself so helpless, so beaten down and disconcerted, as he was on that journey from Ephesus to Macedonia. He was laid up sick, unto death, and awaited Titus, not even sure he would last long enough to see Titus. And Titus came. And the news was not all good. For whatever Titus shared prompted a further letter to Corinth. Paul's apostolic authority was in question and with it the whole of the future ministry to the Gentiles. So I do not overstate it when I say Paul knew about deep processing.

If Paul ever felt like quitting, and I am sure he did, this Corinthian thing was top of the list for quitting time. If he wasn't gray headed before I am sure he had gray hairs after this thing. Now listen carefully. This was Paul's finest hour. Two other times run a close second: the Philippian epistle—he is isolated and in jail. 2 Timothy—he is in jail and awaiting death, near the end of his life. But this is his finest hour. What you are in deep processing is what you really are!

| Definition | <u>Deep processing</u> refers to a collection of process items which intensely work on deepening the maturity of a leader. The set includes the following process items: conflict, ministry conflict, crisis, life crisis, leadership backlash and isolation. |

Paul knew what deep processing was. He also knew the benefits of it.

Deep Processing—Some Shaping Activities

While God may use a number of things to take a leader deep with himself, several occur so often with leaders that they can be labeled and described. Six common deep processing items are given.

| Definition | The <u>conflict process item</u> refers to those instances in a leader's life-history in which God uses conflict, whether personal or ministry related to develop the leader in dependence upon God, faith, and inner-life. |

| Definition | The <u>ministry conflict</u> process item refers to those instances in a ministry situation, in which a leader learns lessons via the positive and negative aspects of conflict with regards to: 1. the nature of conflict, 2. possible ways to resolve conflict, 3. possible ways to avoid |

---

[149]*Thought* (SRN 1820) is a very strong word meaning despaired or to be destitute. It probably would not be too strong to say Paul was depressed.

[150]*Concluded* (SRN 610) represents the noun word usually translated as *sentence* or *judgment*. Hamel comments: 2Co. 1:9 ... the meaning is "on asking myself whether I should come out safe from mortal peril, I answered, I must Die" Paul was in deep trouble.

[151] Paul recognizes an important dynamic. *Transparency and vulnerability, in sharing by a leader, allows others to identify with and pray more fervently and with understanding for God's answers*. By this sharing then, God receives much more praise and honor because many are partnering with Him. Prayer backers make a big difference in the life of a leader who can share openly with them. Many leaders fear sharing vulnerably and openly. They miss out on one of God's resources for them. Paul models here the kind of open sharing that leaders need to do. See **Article**, *Daniel—Leaders and Prayer Backing*.

44. Paul—Deep Processing

conflict, 4. ways to creatively use conflict, and 5. perception of God's personal shaping through the conflict.

Definition — Crisis process items refer to those special intense situations of pressure in human situations which are used by God to test and teach dependence

Definition — A life crisis process item refers to a crisis situation characterized by life threatening intense pressure in human affairs in which the meaning and purpose of life are searched out with a result that the leader has experienced God in a new way as the source, sustainer, and focus of life

Definition — Isolation processing refers to the setting aside of a leader from normal ministry involvement in its natural context usually for an extended time in order to experience God in a new or deeper way.

Definition — The leadership backlash process item refers to the reactions of followers, other leaders within a group, and/or Christians outside the group, to a course of action taken by a leader because of various ramifications that arise due to the action taken. The situation is used in he leader's life to test perseverance, clarity of vision, and faith.

Paul and Deep Processing

Paul faced all of these kinds of deep processing—these shaping activities of God which make a person of God. How did Paul face these kind of shaping activities and not give up? Let me suggest several under girding values that made the difference. They are contained in the following verses.

1. 2Co 4:1
   1 Because God in His mercy has given me this ministry, I am not going to become discouraged and give up.

Let me paraphrase it emphatically.

Therefore since God put me in this ministry I am not going to quit!

2. 1Co 9:24-27
   24 Don't you know that those in a race all run, but only one wins the prize? Run in such a way that you will receive the prize. 25 And everyone who competes[152] for the prize exercises real discipline[153] in order to be ready. Now they do it to win a fleeting prize.[154] We do it for an eternal prize. 26 Therefore I, personally, run my course with definite purpose, to win—to finish well. Thus I box making my punches count. 27 So I discipline myself and exercise strict control, lest after preaching to others, I myself should become a loser.[155]

---

[152] The word translated as *competes* (SRN 75) is the word from which we get our word agonize. It means really struggles (to get ready and participate). Present day marathon runners do train this rigorously.

[153] The word translated as *Exercises real discipline* (SRN 1467) means to practice self-control. It described athletes who were preparing for the Olympic Games. Such an athlete abstained from unwholesome food, wine, and sexual indulgence.

[154] *Prize* (SRN 4735) the wreath or garland which was given as a prize to victors in public games.

[155] This whole context, 9:24-27, is promoting one of the important enhancements that helps leaders finish well. Discipline in the life, is one of five enhancement factors that have been identified with effective leaders who have finished well. All kinds of disciplines, especially spiritual disciplines, will be needed and used with purpose in order to continue toward the finish. Paul is in his 50s here, a time when leaders tend to plateau. Disciplines are needed. See **Articles**, *13. Finishing Well—5 Factors Enhancing; 62. Spiritual Disciplines—And On-Going Leadership*.

44. Paul—Deep Processing

3. 2 Co 12:9
   9 His answer was, "My enabling presence is all you need. My power shows forth much stronger in your weakness." So you can see then, why I boast about my weaknesses. Christ's power will work through me. Therefore I will boast all the more gladly about my weaknesses, so that Christ's power may rest on me.

4. Acts 26:15-20
   "Then I asked, `Who are you, Lord?' "`I am Jesus, whom you are persecuting,' the Lord replied. 16 `Now get up and stand on your feet. I have appeared to you to appoint you as a servant and as a witness of what you have seen of me and what I will show you. 17 I will rescue you from your own people and from the Gentiles. I am sending you to them 18 to open their eyes and turn them from darkness to light, and from the power of Satan to God, so that they may receive forgiveness of sins and a place among those who are sanctified by faith in me.' 19 "So then, King Agrippa, **I was faithfully obedient to this heavenly mandate**. 20 First to those in Damascus, then to those in Jerusalem and in all Judea, and to the Gentiles also, I preached that they should repent and turn to God and prove their repentance by their deeds."

Let me suggest four reasons why Paul persevered in ministry. The first two are from the human side. Paul took responsibility. The last two are from the divine side. Paul counted on God taking responsibility too.

1. He had a sense of responsibility.

1 Because God in His mercy has given me this ministry, I am not going to become discouraged and give up.[156] 2Co 4:1

2. He was Disciplined With A Purpose. He wanted to finish well.

Listen to my paraphrase of 1Co 9:24-27. It was the motivational secret underlying one great leader's sustaining his life and ministry.

I am serious about finishing well in my Christian ministry. I discipline myself for fear that after challenging others into the Christian life I myself might become a casualty. 1Co 9:24-27.

Paul was aware that many did not make it. He was in his 50s; a time when Christian leaders tend to plateau. He didn't want that. So he did something about it. Did it work? More on this later.

3. He counted on Experiencing The Grace Of God.

There are three great leaders during the Church Era of leadership: Peter, John, Paul. All three knew this under girding principle. Their final words confirm it.

But grow in the **grace** and knowledge of our Lord and Savior Jesus Christ. To him be glory both now and forever! Amen. 2Pe 3:18

The **grace** of the Lord Jesus be with God's people. Amen. Rev 22:21

The Lord be with your spirit. **Grace** be with you. 2Ti 4:22

---

[156] This is one of Paul's stronger expressions of his personally embracing the stewardship model. His call from God, his anointing by God and his sense of destiny are behind these words. *See Stewardship Model*, **Glossary**. See **Articles**, *11. Entrustment—A Leadership Responsibility; 24. Jesus— Five Leadership Models: Shepherd, Harvest, Steward, Servant, Intercessor.*

44. Paul—Deep Processing

It is interesting how each of them came to the same inescapable conclusion. You will not make it in the Christian life without grace. Now grace as described here is not unmerited favor—not referring to our standing before God. It is referring to an enabling energy of God.

Definition **Grace** is the inspirational, enabling presence of God in a life which encourages one to persevere in Victory throughout life's circumstances.

So Paul was not just talking lightly when he said in 2Co 12:9,

> 9 His answer was, "My enabling presence is all you need. My power shows forth much stronger in your weakness." So you can see then, why I boast about my weaknesses. Christ's power will work through me. Therefore I will boast all the more gladly about my weaknesses, so that Christ's power may rest on me. 2Co 12:9.

You will not make it apart from knowing and counting upon this grace. The second reason Paul profited from deep processing and made it through it was that he knew how to experience the grace of God, that enabling presence of God.

4. He had a strong Sense Of Destiny Integrated Into A Life Purpose.

So then, King Agrippa, I was faithfully obedient to this heavenly mandate. Ac 26:19.

But the most important reason for not giving up, not dropping out of ministry, not quitting: a strong sense of destiny that imparted a **life purpose**.[157] His life was tightly integrated, that is, extremely focused around a solid life purpose. In a nutshell, Paul had a sense of destiny. And that destiny focused his life and enabled him to make it through deep processing. Notice his triumphant finish.

> 6 As for me, I am ready to be sacrificed. The time for me to depart this life is near. 7 I have run a good race. I have fulfilled my God-given destiny.[158] I still have my faith intact. 8 And now for my prize, a crown of righteousness. The Lord, the righteous judge, will award it to me at that day. And not to me only, but unto all those who eagerly await his return.[159] 2Ti 4:6-8.

---

[157] A life purpose is a burden-like calling, a task or driving force or achievement, which motivates a leader to fulfill something or to see something done. This is the core focal issue and around which a life is integrated over a lifetime. See **Articles**, *Life Purpose, Biblical Examples; 42. Paul—A Sense of Destiny; 10. Destiny Pattern*.

[158] Fulfilled my destiny, literally I have finished or completed (SRN 5758) a perfect action, i.e. already done it with on going results, my course (SRN 1408). Course, used three times in the N.T., refers to life's destiny, the pathway set before one to do. The destiny pattern usually follows a threefold pattern: destiny preparation, destiny revelation, and destiny fulfillment. This idea of already completing it is the use of a certainty idiom, the prophetic past. It is so certain that he speaks of it in the past tense as if it had already happened. See Ac 20:24 where Paul states his desire to finish his course. See also, Ac 13:25 where the same word refers to John the Baptist's having finished his course. See *certainty idiom, prophetic past, sense of destiny, destiny preparation, destiny revelation, destiny fulfillment*, **Glossary**. See **Articles**, *10. Destiny Pattern; 42. Paul—A Sense of Destiny*.

[159] Vs 4:6-8 show that Paul finished well. He is the classic case of a N.T. church leader finishing well. All six characteristics of a good finish are seen: (1) vibrant personal relationship with God; (2) have a learning posture; (3) Christ-likeness in character; (4) live by Biblical convictions; (5) leave behind ultimate contributions; (6) fulfill a sense of destiny. One of the major leadership contributions of 2Ti is this challenge to finish well, which Paul models. See *modeling*, **Glossary**. **Article**, *14. Finishing Well—Six Characteristics*.

44. Paul—Deep Processing

A Major Insight—Paul's Inner-Life Attitude

Paul had a particular attitude about deep processing which made all the difference in his life and ministry. I have labeled it a *Sovereign Mindset*.

Definition A sovereign mindset[160] is an attitude demonstrated by the Apostle Paul in which he tended to see God's working in the events and activities that shaped his life, whether or not they were positive and good or negative and bad. He tended to see God's purposes in these shaping activities and to make the best of them.

There were four keys to Paul's getting and maintaining a sovereign mindset:

1. Paul recognized God's hand in life happenings--no matter who or what the immediate cause.
2. Paul submitted to God's deeper purposes in life happenings.
3. Paul learned and used the lessons derived from these life happenings.
4. Paul shared those lessons (and God's provision in them) with others.

Conclusion

Some one has said, "All great leaders walk with a limp!" The allusion is to Jacob's deep experience with God, wrestling with the Angel of God, and thereafter always walking with a limp due to the injury sustained. Now this of course is a hyperbolic description of something important. Stated in less colorful language,

God matures leaders He uses via shaping activities that deepen their walk with God and increase their effectiveness for God.

These activities for the most part are not pleasant. They may involve physical suffering, or persecution, or crises in the life. In short they will force the leader to go deep with God in order to survive in ministry. Or to say it another way, all leaders will go through some deep processing as they serve the Lord. Some leaders will be repeatedly shaped with deep processing. A very few leaders will experience it to an extent not seen in ordinary leaders. Such a leader was Paul. He was greatly used by God. He was greatly shaped by deep processing.

Two common reactions by leaders in deep processing include:

1. **Turn away from God** (Well, if this is the way God is I don't need or want God!).
2. **Turn toward God. Go deep with God** (God will meet me and take me into more intimacy in this processing and I will walk away from it with God's lessons in my life. I will benefit from this!).

Don't wait till you are in deep processing to make up your mind which of these you will do. In deep processing you most likely will not be able to think clearly. Decide now, as an act of the will, that when deep processing comes, you will go deep with God. And don't forget the basic lessons Paul gives in 2Co 1:3-7, a foundational passage for deep processing.

1. God will meet you in deep processing.
2. You are helped in order to help.
3. Deep processing tests your own belief in the sufficiency of Christ.
4. Your own development through deep processing gives hope that your followers can also know the sufficiency of Christ in their deep processing.

You are modeling and never with more impact than when you are in deep processing.

---

[160] Sovereign Mindset is a Pauline leadership value seen all through 2Co. *Leaders ought to see God's hand in their circumstances as part of His plan for developing them as leaders.* See **Article**, *59. Sovereign Mindset.*

Article 45

Relevance of the Article to Paul's Corinthian Ministry

The Corinthian intervention illustrates how Paul used ministry situations to develop leaders. Titus was charged with several ministry tasks related to the Corinthian problems. Paul believed in on-the-job training. He also took risks in doing this. Titus could have failed. But he didn't. He lived up to the expectations Paul had of him as a leader. Paul developed people. This article examines some of Paul's approaches to developing leaders. Mentoring was certainly involved. Training in a team context was too.

45. Paul —Developer Par Excellence

Introduction

Paul selected and trained leaders. No matter where he was or what actual ministry he was actively pursuing he was always developing those around him. He demonstrates, forcefully, two of the major leadership lessons observed from comparative studies of effective leaders.[161]

> **Effective leaders view leadership selection and development as a priority in their ministry.**
>
> **Effective leaders see relational empowerment as both a means and a goal of ministry.**

Paul was a developer of leaders.

Two Pauline leadership values explain this bent for Paul. A leadership value is an underlying assumption which affects how a leader perceives leadership and practices it. Let me state them first as Pauline leadership values and then generalize them for possible application in other leader's lives.

Value 1	Leadership Development
Statement of Value	Paul felt he must identify potential leadership and develop it for ministry in the church.
Generalized	Leaders must be concerned about leadership selection and development.
Value 2	Personal Ministry
Statement of Value	Paul saw that in his own life he should use personal relationships as a strong means for doing ministry.

---

[161] I have identified seven which repeatedly occur in effective leaders: 1. Life Time Perspective—Effective Leaders View Present Ministry In Terms Of A Life Time Perspective. 2. Learning Posture—Effective Leaders Maintain A Learning Posture Throughout Life. 3. Spiritual Authority—Effective Leaders Value Spiritual Authority As A Primary Power Base. 4. Dynamic Ministry Philosophy—Effective Leaders Who Are Productive Over A Lifetime Have A Dynamic Ministry Philosophy Which Is Made Up Of An Unchanging Core And A Changing Periphery Which Expands Due To A Growing Discovery Of Giftedness, Changing Leadership Situations, And Greater Understanding Of The Scriptures. 5. Leadership Selection And Development—Effective Leaders View Leadership Selection And Development As A Priority Function In Their Ministry. 6. Relational Empowerment—Effective Leaders See Relational Empowerment As Both A Means And A Goal Of Ministry. 7. Sense Of Destiny—Effective Leaders Evince A Growing Awareness Of Their Sense Of Destiny. See the **Article**, *30. Leadership Lessons—Seven Major Identified*.

45. Paul—Developer Par Excellence

Generalized — Leaders should view personal relationships as an important part of ministry.

These two values are at the heart of being a developer.

Defining a Developer

What is a developer? Let me define it.

Definition — A <u>developer</u> is a person with a mentoring bent who readily sees potential in an emerging leader and finds ways to help move that emerging leader on to becoming an effective leader.

Developers are mentors who have a variety of mentoring methods. Mentoring is a relational experience in which one person, the mentor, empowers another person, the mentoree, by a transfer of resources. The resources which empower can be habits, skills, perspectives, specific advice, training, connection to other resources, etc..

What does it take to be a developer? It takes the ability to do several key mentoring functions. A developer is a mentor who usually uses three or more of the following mentoring functions effectively in developing people:

Mentor Function	Basic Empowerment
Discipler	basic habits of Christian living
Spiritual Guide	perspective on spiritual growth
Coach	basic skills usually related to doing ministry
Counselor	perspective and advice to meet situational and growth needs
Teacher	basic information that applies to the emerging leader's situation
Model	demonstrates values and skills for possible emulation
Sponsor	watches over the mentorees development and makes sure doors are open for development to potential

Paul operated in all the above mentor functions. This is best seen in his developing ministry with Timothy. Frequently, his development involved a traveling team ministry using on-the-job experience. Leaders whom he worked with and developed include: Priscilla, Acquila, Timothy, Titus, Luke, Silas, Epaphras, Archippus, John Mark, Aristarchus, Philemon, Onesimus and many others.

Developers are concerned about the future of ministry. Paul was. Paul represents the most prominent leader in the Church leadership Period. He is an important model. We need to learn from his life. Paul The Developer sets the pace for us, concerning leading with a developmental bias.

No organization or church will last long with effectiveness if it is not developing people. Churches and Christian organizations, without exception, need developers. What should they do? They should identify developers, reward developers, help the developers develop themselves, and help promote mentoring relationships so that these developers not only have access to emerging leaders but are encouraged in behalf of the organization or church to develop people. And keep it simple. No programs. Just relationships.[162]

See Also **Articles**, *30. Leadership Lessons—Seven Major Identified; 51. Pauline Leadership Values; 37. Mentoring—An Informal Training Model; 69. Timothy A Beloved Son of the Faith; 43. Paul—and His Companions; Leading With A Developmental Bias.*

---

[162] Most developers need the freedom to move a mentoring relationship along the most natural lines for developing it. They can work within programs of development which are broad enough to let them freely identify mentoring needs and pursue them.

Article 46

<u>Relevance of the Article to Paul's Corinthian Ministry</u>

Paul exemplifies the prayer macro lesson—IF A LEADER IS CALLED TO A MINISTRY THEN HE/SHE IS CALLED TO INTERCEDE FOR THAT MINISTRY. Paul prayed for the Corinthian church as well he did for all the churches he was involved with. Paul, then, relates well to the philosophical leadership model introduced by Jesus—The Intercessor Model. See **Article 24**. *Jesus—5 Leadership models; Shepherd, Harvest, Steward, Servant, Intercessor*.

46. Paul—Intercessor Leader

Introduction

A prayer macro lesson identified in every leadership era, and specifically highlighted in Moses', Samuel's, Jesus', and Paul's ministries states,

    Intercession   Leaders Called To A Ministry Are Called To Intercede For That Ministry.

Paul interweaves this throughout his ministry. Paul mentions praying in every single Church epistle except one.[163]

The Leader Intercessor Model

Ministry philosophy refers to a related set of values that underlies a leader's perception and behavior in his/her ministry. The values may be ideas, principles, guidelines or the like which are implicit (not actually recognized but part of the perceptive set of the leader) or explicit (recognized, identified, articulated). For any given leader a ministry philosophy is unique. It is dynamic and related to three major elements: Biblical dynamics, giftedness, and situation. The intercessor model flows out of the prayer macro lesson and shows the concern of a leader for God's intervention in ministry. It is not clear to who this model applies—all leaders or those leaders who have the gift of faith. It may also well apply to some who are not leaders but who have the gift of faith.

    definition   The <u>intercessor model</u> is a philosophical model which is founded on the central thrust of the prayer macro lesson (which applies to all leaders—as a role) and an additional responsibility for praying for a ministry, which flows out of the faith gift or some aspects of the prophetical gift.

Biblical examples reflecting the prayer macro lesson and intercession occur in every leadership era.[164] Abraham and the macro lesson: Ge 18:16-33; Moses and the macro lesson: Ex 32:7-14; Samuel and the macro lesson: 1 Sa 12:1-25; Daniel and the macros lesson: Dan 9; Jesus and the macro lesson: some 44 different verses indicate Jesus praying throughout his ministry. One especially important prayer passage occurs in Jn 17. Paul and the macro lesson: see this article.

Basic Values Underlying the Intercessor Model

1. A leader who is called to ministry must accept responsibility for prayer for that ministry.

---

[163] He mentions pray, prayer, praying, etc. 60 times in his epistles. Only Gal of his epistles to churches has prayer references left out. Paul hits the ground running in Gal to correct a fundamental heresy. Apart from a possible veiled allusion to prayer in Gal 4:19 (travail SRN 5605) Paul does not speak of praying. He is angry with the Galatians and bent on correcting a fundamental heresy. Paul also omits prayer references in his personal letter to Titus.

[164] There are six leadership eras in the Bible: 1. Patriarchal; 2. Pre-Kingdom; 3. Kingdom; 4. Post-Kingdom; 5. Pre-Church; 6. Church.

46. Paul—Intercessor Leader

2. A leader should show acceptance of responsibility for a ministry by interceding for that ministry and involving others to intercede.
3. A leader must seek God's leading in prayer, the divine initiative, as to how and what to pray for.
4. A leader should bathe major decision making in prayer.
5. A leader ought to encourage the development of emerging leaders by praying for them and telling them of prayer for them.
6. A leader should cultivate an attitude of prayer at all times and ought to break into prayer when prompted to do so.
7. Crises should drive a leader deeper into intercessory ministry.
8. Extended times alone in prayer should be used for intercession, for personal renewal and for revelation from God for guidance, breakthroughs in ministry, and for decision making.

Some Implications Flowing From the Model
1. No ministry will long endure without intercessors behind it.
2. Quantity (the number of and amount of time spent by) of intercessors is not as important as quality of intercession of the ones doing the interceding.
3. Leaders with the gift of faith will do personal intercession with a zeal, passion and fruitfulness beyond that of leaders who do this as a role.
4. Leaders should cultivate relationships with faith gifted intercessors and recruit them to help in the ministry.
5. Power in ministry comes from giftedness and from prayer. Both are needed.

The Intercessor Model is the most specific of the leadership models. It is the most gift related. Gifts of faith, apostleship, and in general, the revelatory gifts (word of knowledge, word of wisdom, prophecy, word of faith) will usually be associated with leaders operating strongly in this model. Now, all leaders have the duty to intercede for their ministries. But those who are drawn to this model will be gifted to see its impact more than just that which results from praying in general. It is not clear to what extent each leader will be involved in this model. Paul exemplifies this model.

Prayer Concerns of Paul for the Churches
Paul had a burden for the churches that he had founded and was associated with.

> Beside outward circumstances pressing me, there is the inward burden, i.e. the anxiety and care, I feel daily for all the churches. 2Co 11:28

He expresses this burden so beautifully in his prayers for the churches. Table 1,2 Co 46-1 lists just a few of his references to prayer for the various churches. Notice the thrust of his burden for the churches.

Table 1,2 Co 46-1. Paul's Prayer Concerns for the Churches

Church	Passage	Prayer Thrust
At Rome	Ro 1:8-10 12:12	(1) Thankfulness for this church's strong testimony of faith toward God—its worldwide impact. (2) That God would take him to this church for ministry there.
At Corinth	1Co 1:4	That the Corinthian church respond to his admonitions so that he would not have to come and discipline them in person.
At Ephesus	Eph 1:15-20; 3:1, 14-21	(1) Continuously gives thanks for them. (2) Holy Spirit imparted wisdom. (3) Intimacy with God. (4) Perspective, especially promises, which will give hope. (5) Recognize and appropriate the resurrection-like power available in them. (6) Gentile acceptance into God's kingdom. (7) Inward strength via the Holy Spirit. (8) Realization of the indwelling Christ in their inner selves. (9) Know more fully the love of God.
At Philippi	Php 1:3	(1) Thankfulness for this church—the joy it brings and for its support of Paul and for its co-ministry with him. (2) God's continued work in their midst.

46. Paul—Intercessor Leader

At Colosse	Col 1:3 1:9-14; 2:1	(1) Thankfulness for faith toward God and love for God's people. (2) Fruit of the Spirit, love. (3) knowledge of God's will. (4) Spirit given wisdom. (5) Lead lives pleasing to the Lord. (6) Enabled by God's power to endure. (6) That these believers would be thankful to God.
At Thessalonica	1Th 1:3, 2:13; 5:23; 2Th 1:3,11- 13; 2:13	(1) Thankfulness to God for them. (2) Put their faith into practice. (3) Thankfulness for response to Gospel. (4) Thankfulness for a growing faith. (5) Thankfulness for greater expression of love. (6) Thankfulness for the way they are bearing up in persecution. (7) That their lives may express God's work. (8) Entire final and full sanctification. (9) That they might be enabled by God's power to complete their walk and honor Jesus. (10) Thankfulness for them in that they responded first to the Gospel.
In Philemon's home	Phm 4-6	(1) Thankfulness for Philemon's love and faith. (2) Realization of union with Christ in everyday life. (3) Thankfulness for joy resulting from Philemon's testimony.

What Can We Learn From Paul's Prayers And His Teaching on Prayer?

Here are a few observations that may help us see more of what an intercessor leader is all about.

1. Paul shows how important thankfulness is in praying. Over and over again he is thankful to God for individuals and for churches (see references in table above).
2. Paul operates daily with a spirit of prayer which bursts into praying. He openly states that he prays continually for people and churches (see 1Th 5:17; see Ro 12:12 and many others).
3. Paul prays specific requests for individuals and tells them what he is praying (2Ti 1:3 et al, see *prayer encouragement principle*, **Glossary**).
4. Paul prays for churches almost always giving thanks for them and almost always praying for their growth and appropriation of resources they have in Christ.
5. Intercessory prayer is hard agonizing work (see Ro 15:30, Col 2:1; 4:12. Note especially SRN 4865 used both in Ro 15:30 and Col 2:1, a word meaning agonize, strive at).
6. Paul shares vulnerably concerning his own situation so that people can pray knowingly and with empathy for him (Ro 15:30,31; 2Co 1:11 and many others).
7. Paul prays for believers to know God's power; that the Holy Spirit might enable them to live strong Christian lives.
8. Paul admonished that believers lift holy hands (that is, come to God with clean consciences and an awareness of what the Gospel has done for them) as they pray.
9. Paul admonishes believers to pray for governmental leaders (1Ti 1:1,2).
10. Paul exhorts believers to pray in the Spirit—meaning led of the Spirit in what and how to pray (Eph 6:18; see also Jude 20). He also speaks of praying in the Spirit meaning praying in tongues (and singing in tongues). Both are talked about. Paul also recognizes a praying in which the Spirit prays through us (Ro 8:26) in utterances that express what we should pray for even when we may not know what it is about or what we ought to pray.
11. Paul, not only prays for his own ministry, but prays for others' ministry (i.e. the Jews, see Ro 10:1).
12. Paul recognizes that believers will need to exercise disciplines involving fasting and praying—though he never commands believers to do this (1Co 7:5).
13. Paul suggests that believers should pray for needed giftedness (1Co 14:1, 13).
14. Paul prays for financial resources for needy churches, for individual Christian workers, and for his own self (2Co 8:14; 9:14 et al).
15. Paul asks prayer for himself for God-given opportunities for ministry and for effective impactful ministry (Col 4:3,4; 2Th 3:1).

Paul was an intercessor leader.

Conclusion

Apostolic leaders (especially Harvest leaders) need intercession for their ministries. Pastors (especially

46. Paul—Intercessor Leader

Shepherd leaders) need intercession for their ministries. God can gift them for this and/or provide others in their sphere of influence to carry this out. The prayer macro is still valid today.

Intercession Leaders Called To A Ministry Are Called To Intercede For That Ministry.

See *modeling*, **Glossary**. See **Article**, *74. Vulnerability and Prayer Power*; *24. Jesus—Five Leadership Models: Shepherd, Harvest, Steward, Servant, Intercessor.*

Article 47

Relevance of the Article to Paul's Corinthian Ministry
Paul developed leaders in ministry. One prominent way he did that was by mentoring. This article identifies his mentor-mix and gives some observations about his mentoring work.

47. Paul—Mentor for Many

Paul was an outstanding mentor. He used mentoring as a major means of developing leaders. Mentoring is a relational experience in which one person, called the mentor, empowers another person, called the mentoree, by a transfer of resources. Empowerment can include such things as new habits, knowledge, skills, desires, values, connections to resources for growth and development of potential. We[165] have identified a number of mentoring functions. Usually any given leader will not be an ideal mentor and perform all of the mentoring functions. Instead a given leader will usually be proficient in three or four of the mentor functions. The set of mentoring functions that a leader uses in ministry is called his/her mentor-mix. It is easiest to demonstrate that Paul was an outstanding mentor by illustrating his mentoring relationship with Timothy.

Table 1,2 Co 47-1 identifies the nine mentoring functions:

Table 1,2 Co 47-1. Nine Mentor Functions

Type	Central Thrust
1. Discipler	Basic Habits of the Christian Life dealing with hearing from God and talking with God; operating in a fellowship of Christians; learning to minister in terms of giftedness; learning to get input from God.
2. Spiritual Guide	Evaluation of spiritual depth and maturity in a life and help in growth in this.
3. Coach	Skills of all kind depending on the expertise of the coach.
4. Counselor	Timely and good advice which sheds perspective on issues and problems and other needs.
5. Teacher	Relevant knowledge that can be used for personal growth or ministry or other such need.
6. Sponsor	Protective guidance and linking to resources so that a leader reaches potential.
7. Contemporary Model	Values impactfully demonstrated in a life that can be transferred and used in one's own life.
8. Historical Model	Values demonstrated in a life and inspiration drawn from that life so as to encourage on-going development in ones own life and a pressing on to finish well.
9. Divine Contact	Timely Guidance from God via some human source.

Paul over the course of his 30+ years in ministry demonstrated almost all of the nine functions. With Timothy, as seen in the Acts and the two epistles to Timothy, several of the mentoring functions can be seen. Figure 1,2 Co 47-1 gives Paul's Mentor-Mix[166] in a pictorial format. This is called a Venn diagram. Each separate oval represents a mentor function. The larger the size of a symbol the more important it is. Overlap of symbols indicates some of both functions taking place. Non-overlap of a symbol with other symbols indicates exclusive manifestation of the symbol. Table 1,2 Co 47-2 takes these mentor functions and indicates where the mentoring function is indicated in the Scriptures and perhaps some empowerment.

---

[165] My son Dr. Richard W. Clinton, my colleague Paul Stanley and I have all been busily researching and using mentoring in our own personal ministries.
[166] Mentor-mix refers to the set of mentoring functions that a leader demonstrates in his/her ministry over time—not necessarily seen at any one given time but over a lifetime.

47. Paul—Mentor for Many

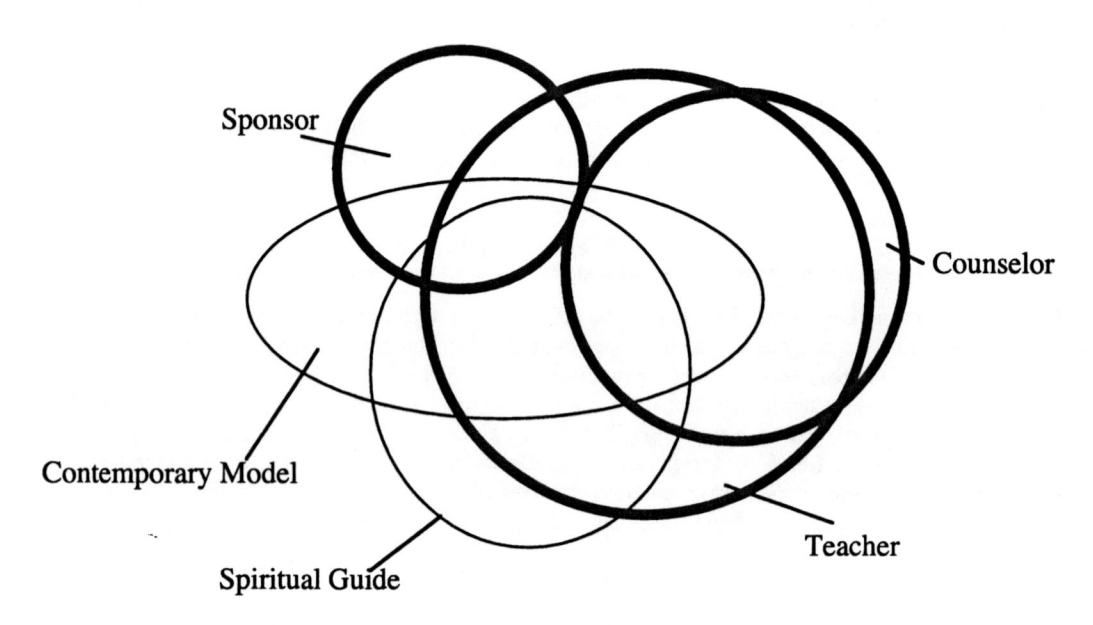

Figure 1,2 Co 47-1. Paul's Mentor-Mix with Timothy

From the Venn diagram in Figure 1,2 Co 47-1 it can be seen that the three most important mentor functions (indicated by the heavier lines) that Paul did with Timothy were teacher, counselor, and sponsor. He also models and gives spiritual advice for Timothy's own growth.

Table 1,2 Co 47-2. Mentor Functions of Paul With Timothy

Kind	Where Seen	Empowerment
Teacher	Ac 16, 17, 18, 19, 20; 2Ti 3:10 Ro 16:21; 1Co 4:17; 2Co 1:19	Timothy was familiar with all of Paul's teaching from the Scriptures. For example, he heard the teaching on the material that was later incorporated as Romans given at Corinth; he was present for the dictation of the book of Romans. He spent hours on the road with Paul and chatted with him.
Counselor	1,2Ti are laced with words of advice	1Ti ch 1,2 Paul's advice on major problems in the church, 1Ti ch 3 Paul's advice on local leadership selection, 1Ti ch 5 Paul's advice on the problem of widows and discipline of leaders.
Sponsor	1,2Ti	He is listed by Paul as co-author (a sponsoring function) of six epistles (See 2Co 1:1; Php 1:1; Col 1:1; 1Th 1:1; 2Th 1:1, Phm 1:1). The material in 1,2Ti is dominantly written with a view to the church there reading it and knowing that Paul was giving Timothy instructions for that church.
Model	2Ti 3:10-17; Php	Philippians gives Paul's comprehensive treatment of his use of modeling.
Spiritual Guide	1,2Ti	See especially 1Ti 4 Paul's personal advice to Timothy on How to Handle Himself.—especially maintaining the balance of developing self and developing ministry.. See also 2Ti 1:3-10 on developing giftedness.

Five Features of Paul's Mentoring

Table 1,2 Co 47-3 below lists five features noticeable in Paul's mentoring or that supplemented his mentoring.

47. Paul—Mentor for Many

Table 1,2 Co 47-3. Five Features About Paul's Mentoring

Feature	Explanation
Personal Value	Paul often talked straight from the heart to those he ministered to. He illustrates one of his strongest leadership values when he does that. And this is even more true in his mentoring relationships. A leadership value is an underlying assumption which affects how a leader behaves in or perceives leadership situations. Paul felt ministry ought to be very personal. Stated more generally for all leaders, *Leaders should view personal relationships as an important part of ministry both as a means for ministry and as an end in itself of ministry*. In his epistles Paul names almost 80 people by name—most of whom he ministered with or to or in some way they ministered to him. Of the five dynamics of mentoring (attraction, relationship, responsiveness, accountability, empowerment) relationship was Paul's strong suit. And with Timothy relationship is seen more clearly than any of Paul's companions. See **Article**, *Timothy, A Beloved Son in the Faith*. Principle: *The development of a personal relationship between a mentor and mentoree will increase the effectiveness of the mentoring*.
Took People With Him; On-the-Job training.	Whenever possible, Paul never went into ministry alone. He almost always took someone with him—frequently, one he had a mentoring relationship with, one who he was developing as a leader. Principle: *Modeling as a major means of influencing or developing emerging leaders best happens in on-the-job training*.
Teams	Whenever possible, Paul took more than one person with him. He used teams of people. And he would send various team members on important errands. See **Article**, *Paul and His Companions*. Note especially the *we sections* in Acts 16 etc.. See also the number of folks around in Romans 16:20-22 (Timothy, Lucius, Sosipater, Tertius, Gaius, Erastus, Quartus) when he dictated the letter.
Little/Big; Ministry Tasks	Paul used the basic principle of the Luke 16:10 little/ big: *The one faithful in little things will be faithful in bigger things*. Give people little things to do and if they are faithful in them, give them bigger things to do. This was especially true of the ministry tasks given Titus and Timothy. A ministry task is an assignment from God which primarily tests a person's faithfulness and obedience but often also allows use of ministry gifts in the context of a task which has closure, accountability, and evaluation. See Titus' five ministry tasks (3 in Corinth 1 in Crete and 1 in Dalmatia). As the person grows the ministry task moves more from the testing of the person's faithfulness toward the accomplishment of the task.
Goodwin's Expectation Principle	Goodwin's expectation principle states, *Emerging leaders tend to live up to the genuine expectations of leaders they respect*. A well respected leader can use this dynamic to challenge younger leaders to grow. The challenge embodied in the expectation must not be too much or the young leader will not be able to accomplish it and will be inoculated against further challenges. The challenge must not be too little or it will not attract. It must be a genuine expectation. Paul uses this with Timothy, Philemon, and Titus several times (see fn 1Ti 6:11 . See fn 2Ti 1:5).

The end result of mentoring is the empowerment of the mentorees. Luke, Titus, Timothy, Philemon, Onesimus, Archippus, Priscilla, Phoebe and many others attest to the power of Paul's mentoring. And of all of Paul's mentoring functions, probably the most effective was the modeling. Note in his mentor-mix how modeling subtly interweaves itself throughout every other mentoring function. Paul personally related to numerous leaders to develop them. He left behind a heritage—men and women who could continue to lead and carry out his life purpose and use his values in their lives and ministry.

See **Articles**: *45. Paul— Developer Par Excellence; 43. Paul and His Companions*. For more detailed study see **Bibliography for Further Study**, Stanley and Clinton 1992, **Connecting**. Clinton and Clinton 1993, **The Mentor Handbook**.

Article 48

Relevance of the Article to Paul's Corinthian Ministry

It is clear from the personal sharing of Paul about his own values in 2 Co that Paul is deliberately using his own life to model for the Corinthians. He actually makes two statements to the Corinthians about his modeling: (1) For this reason I strongly invite you, use me as a model. 1Co 4:16; (2) Use me as a model, just as I also follow Christ as my model. 1Co 11:1. But his strongest assertions on modeling come via the Php letter where he actually models through the whole epistle and closes off by explicitly exhorting the believers at Philippi to follow his modeling.

48. Paul—Modeling As An Influence Means

A discovery of an important macro lesson emerged from the Post-Kingdom Leadership Era.[167] In that leadership era, leaders had little or no structure through which to influence other followers of God. They were shut up by sovereign circumstances to influence dominantly with their lives. Their convictions and beliefs must be seen in how they lived and acted and talked. Respected leaders, like Daniel, set examples for other to follow. Because they were respected and had integrity in their lives, others wanted to emulate them. Out of this kind of situation, particularly demonstrated by Daniel, the modeling macro lesson emerged.

Modeling—A Post-Kingdom Macro Lesson

Leaders can most powerfully influence by modeling godly lives, the sufficiency and sovereignty of God at all times, and gifted power.

Remember, a leader is a person who has God-given capacity, and God-given responsibility to INFLUENCE specific groups of people toward God's purposes for them. Modeling is a powerful way of influencing.

Modeling

Definition   Modeling is the use of various life situations to impress upon followers godly behavioral responses, values, convictions, paradigms, and leadership lessons in order to impact their lives with these same items.

Effective leaders recognize that followers who respect their leadership are deeply impacted by their life examples, their beliefs, their behavior, and their desires or expectations. These followers will have a tendency to emulate what they see in these leaders—even if it is not recognized explicitly.

Paul, Philippians and Modeling.

Probably more than any other of Paul's writings the book of Philippians deliberately invokes modeling as a major means of influence both by deliberate example and by teaching it plainly (3:15-17, 4:8,9). Modeling is a technique whereby a leader is transparent with followers concerning life and ministry with a view toward influencing them to imitate him/her. In fact, followers do imitate leaders whether the leaders want them to or not. Leaders should take advantage of this and deliberately strive to model in such a way as to demonstrate what Christian living is all about. A contemporary model is a mentor who uses modeling in order to set ministry examples for emerging leaders. Listen to Paul's admonition and the promise attached to it. There is no doubt, he knew he was a contemporary model.

---

[167] See **Article 27.** *Leadership Eras in the Bible—Six Identified.*

48. Paul—Modeling As An Influence Means

> Those things that you have both learned and received and heard and seen in me do. And the God of Peace shall be with you. Php 4:9

A secret to having the God of Peace with you is a simple one. Find some good models to imitate. Get some mentor models for your life. Put their values into your life. And Paul says, the God of Peace shall be with you. That is a blessing Paul promises. I believe any good contemporary model can echo that blessing.

Our studies have shown that one of the enhancements for finishing well is to have some good mentors. My advice is for you to get some good mentors and imitate those God-honoring qualities in their lives. You will be disappointed some times in them. But on the whole if you put those God-honoring qualities in your life you can count on the God who gives peace being with you.

The Apostle Paul knew the power of modeling as an influence means. No where is this seen more clearly than in the life of his closest associate Timothy. Consider the story of their meeting and Paul's modeling influence in his life. Notice how Paul knew that the impact of modeling increased with an increase in relationship. That is, the deeper the relationship between a mentor and mentoree the more likely it is that modeling will impact profoundly.

The Story-Reflecting Back on A Relationship

There were tears in his eyes as he said good-bye. Paul knew that hardships, conflict, and troublesome people awaited him. Yet Paul knew God would use those in Timothy's life. Paul was proud of Timothy. Today he was sending him off to the toughest assignment he had ever given him. He was going to Ephesus—a church having subtle heresies and power issues; a church needing the Word of God in a fresh way; a church with social problems, leadership problems, financial problems. But Paul was confident. Timothy would do just fine. Paul knew that because Paul knew his heart. He knew how he had been trained on the job. He knew how Timothy had seen God work on behalf of the team—over and over. Paul's mind wandered back. He saw himself along the road leading to Derbe. And the past events, the selection of Timothy, his training—they all flashed before his eyes. He remembered ...

The First Visit

They had trudged along all day and finally arrived in Derbe. Paul had had much time to think over his split with Barnabas. He and Silas had decided to return and follow-up on the converts in Asia minor. He wondered how Barnabas and Mark were doing in Cyprus. Paul knew that personality conflicts and disagreements were sometimes an on-going thing with Jewish people. But somehow he did not feel right about the whole Barnabas and Mark controversy. After all Barnabas had been the sponsor who promoted him in Antioch and then stood up and defended his work at the Jerusalem council. He dearly loved Silas and was glad for the opportunity to minister with him. But he wished that his dispute with Barnabas had not been so final.

After an overnight stay the next morning they went on Lystra. As he neared Lystra Paul remembered how just a few short years ago he and Barnabas had in desperation fled from Iconium–just in front of a mob bent on stoning them. They had some success there including authentication of their ministry by God's miraculous working. But still a number of Jews had forced them out. It was on that journey, that frightening race away from persecution, that they had been led to Derbe and Lystra just a few short years ago. And as was often the case after a frightening experience, God had affirmed them.

It was at Lystra that Paul had seen God accomplish an amazing healing. Paul remembered it as if it were only yesterday. The man was crippled and sat listening to Paul as he explained the Way and talked about the person Jesus. Paul, as he looked at the man, suddenly knew within that this man could be healed—there was healing faith there. On the spot, Paul looked him directly in the eye and commanded him to stand up on his own two feet. This man, in a moment of time, leaped to his feet. He was healed. All who knew him were instantly amazed. Paul remembered that this man's healing led everyone immediately to believe that Paul and Barnabas were divine beings—incarnate beings representing Hermes and Zeus. Paul had immediately stopped that. A good ministry then followed.

But after some time the Jews from Antioch and Iconium who had opposed Paul's ministry earlier came to Lystra to stir up folks against Paul and Silas. And they did. Paul and Silas left for Derbe to escape the persecution. Not again, Paul had thought. Will it always be this way?

48. Paul—Modeling As An Influence Means

However, Paul thought back to the fruit in that town. During their stay Paul was impressed with a number of Jewish people who both demonstrated faith in the living God but also knew their Old Testament Scriptures. He wondered why it was so often the case that women were the more spiritual. Women responded to the Gospel eagerly, frequently sooner than Jewish men. Eunice and Lois were just such women. These Lystran women knew the Scriptures very well. When Paul began to teach Christ from the Old Testament Scriptures, their background allowed them to enter in quickly to Paul's explanation. They had opted to become followers of the Way. Paul was looking forward to seeing Eunice and Lois and others who had responded to the Gospel.

Much had happened since their last visit. There was the great Jerusalem council dealing with the essence of the Gospel. There was the controversy with Barnabas which centered on the young disciple, John Mark. That had led to the split. Time had gone by. Paul was anxious to see the growth in the believers at Lystra. He was particularly interested in Lois' son, Timothy. For he had heard good things about him.

The Return Visit To Lystra

Paul knew that to get the Gospel out he would need help. He constantly had his eyes open for potential leaders. At Iconium the assembly there had spoken about Timothy—the son of Lois. High on their list were two things: his character, he was a person of integrity and sincerity, and his love for the Scriptures. His own mother and grand mother, so alive to the Word, had been teaching Timothy since he was a small lad. Paul would assess Timothy himself. But if all went well Paul was going to ask Timothy to come along with the team. And right now that was just Silas.

And so it happened. Paul met Timothy. He invited him to come along. Because he was the son of a Greek father and a Jewish mother Paul had him circumcised. For there was much Jewish opposition in the area. And so a relationship began—Paul and Timothy.

A mentoring relationship—what does it take? time and sharing of experiences. A growing respect for one another. Paul made sure these happened with Timothy.

A Close Relationship

How close was their relationship?

> 19 But I trust in the Lord Jesus to send Timothy shortly unto you, that I also may be encouraged when I know what is happening to you. 20 For I have no one like-minded, who will naturally care for what is happening to you. 21 For all seek their own, not the things which are Jesus Christ's. 22 But you know his proven character, that, as a son with the father, he has served with me in the gospel. 23 So I hope to send him shortly, as soon as I shall see how it will go with me. 24 But I trust in the Lord that I myself shall also come shortly. Php 2:19-24

> 2 To Timothy my true son in the faith: Grace, mercy and peace from God the Father and Christ Jesus our Lord. 1Ti 1:2

Their Experiences Together

> 10 But you have fully known my teaching, manner of life, purpose, faith, longsuffering, love, patience, 11 Persecutions, afflictions, which happened in Antioch, in Iconium, in Lystra; what persecutions I endured: but out of them all, the Lord delivered me. 12 You can be sure that all that will live godly in Christ Jesus will also suffer persecution. 13 But evil men and seducers shall grow worse and worse, deceiving, and being deceived. 14 But you continue in the things which you have learned and have been assured of, knowing of whom you have learned them; 15 I know that from a child you have known the holy scriptures, which are able to make you wise unto salvation through faith which is in Christ Jesus. 16 Every scripture given by inspiration of God is profitable for teaching, for reproof, for correction, for instruction in righteousness: 17 That the man of God may be mature, throughly equipped for all good works. 2Ti 3:10-17

48. Paul—Modeling As An Influence Means

The Training
Follow along with me as I relate some of the things Timothy experienced. Remember Timothy experienced first hand these things and watched Paul in these situations:
- The Macedonian happenings,
- The evangelization efforts at Thessalonica,
- The particularly word oriented efforts at Berea,
- The tumultuous exits from both those places caused by the opposition and persecution.
- The ministry with Priscilla and Aquila in Corinth, including the Bible school ministry and all of the tremendous teaching that Paul gave,

I could go on and on. There is nothing like on-the-job training with a person with a mentoring heart.

The Main Mentor Functions Seen Here
Overwhelmingly the dominant mentoring function seen here was contemporary modeling. A strong secondary mentoring function especially at Corinth was teacher. I will say a word about the teaching mentoring function even though this article is concentrating on modeling.

> 10 But you have fully known my **teaching**, manner of life, purpose, faith, longsuffering, love, patience, 11 Persecutions, afflictions, which happened in Antioch, in Iconium, in Lystra; what persecutions I endured: but out of them all, the Lord delivered me. 2Ti 3:10,11

> 8 And he went into the synagogue, and spoke boldly for three months, disputing and persuading the things concerning the kingdom of God. 9 But when different ones were hardened, and believed not, but spoke evil of *The Way* before the multitude, he departed from them, and separated out the disciples, disputing daily in the school of one Tyrannus.10 And this continued by the space of two years; so that all they which dwelt in Asia heard the word of the Lord Jesus, both Jews and Greeks. Ac 19:8-10

Let me suggest that Paul's teaching was not confined to his public lectures. I am sure that in his tent making time with Priscilla and Acquilla, there was lots of time to talk as you cut the cloth and sew. And on the road—lots of time when walking from place to place. And I guarantee you that Paul would be sharing. He would be explaining about Christ, his updating of his own theology, his understanding of God's great plan of salvation. And even in this teaching he was modeling and important methodology—you teach in the context of every day life as well as in public situations.

The Contemporary Mentor Modeling, Was It Deliberate?
Was this modeling deliberate? Was this modeling intentional? Probably not at first. But it became increasingly clear to Paul as he traveled with his team, spent much time with them, demonstrated the effectiveness of the Gospel in the lives of others and himself that his modeling was an important part of his training methodology.

In general, this is a biblical concept.

> Remember your leaders, who spoke the word of God to you. Consider the outcome of their way of life and imitate their faith. Heb 13:7

> We do not want you to become lazy, but to imitate those who through faith and patience inherit what has been promised. Heb 6:12

But does that mean that we as leaders can deliberately use this to impact and influence. Yes! For Jesus himself deliberately modeled as a means of influence. The two top New Testament leaders, Jesus and Paul demonstrated the importance of modeling as a means of influence.

Jesus Ministry—The Prime Example
John 13 is the pre-eminent example of deliberate intentional modeling to impact.

48. Paul—Modeling As An Influence Means

> 3 Jesus knowing that the Father had given all things into his hands, and that he was come from God, and went to God; 4 rose from supper, and laid aside his garments; and took a towel, and girded himself.12 So after he had washed their feet, and had taken his garments, and was set down again, he said unto them, Do you Know what I have just done to you?...14 If I then, your Lord and Master, have washed your feet; you also ought to wash one another's feet. 15 For I have given you an example, that you should do as I have done to you. Jn 13:3-15

Paul's Deliberate Modeling—Almost From the Very Beginning

I think that fairly early on in his ministry Paul became aware of this dynamic.

> 6 And you became imitators of us, and of the Lord, having received the word under much affliction, yet having the joy of the Holy Spirit: 7 So that you yourselves were models to all that believe in Macedonia and Achaia. 1Th 1:6,7

> 7 For you know how you ought to imitate us: for we did not behave ourselves disorderly among you; 8 Neither did we eat any man's bread for nothing; but worked hard night and day, that we might not be chargeable to any of you: 9 Not because we have not power, but to make ourselves as models so you could follow us. 2Th 3:7-9

> For this reason I strongly invite you, use me as a model. 1Co 4:16

> Use me as a model, just as I also follow Christ as my model. 1Co 11:1

> Christian followers, join in following my example and observe those who walk according to the pattern you have seen in us. Php 3:17

> The things you have learned and received and heard and seen in me, practice these things; and the God of peace shall be with you. Php 4:9

Yes, Paul deliberately used modeling as a strong means of influencing followers. The essential empowerment of modeling, this indirect mentoring relationship, is the embodiment of values in such a way as to challenge the observing mentoree into emulation of these values.

Closure—What About You and Modeling

Let me go back to where I began this article. A discovery of an important macro lesson occurred in the Post-Kingdom Leadership Era.

> **Leaders can most powerfully influence by modeling godly lives, the sufficiency and sovereignty of God at all times, and gifted power.**

Some questions for you:
Have you discovered modeling as a powerful means of influencing?
Are you conscious that in situations you are modeling?
Who is imitating you?

As you consider who you are and what you do, what are the things you really want people to imitate? Remember, if you are a leader, you are modeling. People are going to imitate you. Why not take advantage of this! Model for them in your various life situations so as to impress upon followers godly behavioral responses, values, convictions, paradigms, and leadership lessons. And pray that God would use this in order to impact their lives with these same items.

See also **Articles** *35. Macro Lessons, 49. Pauline Leadership Styles; 27. Leadership Eras in the Scriptures—Six Identified.*

Article 49

<u>Relevance of the Article to Paul's Corinthian Ministry</u>
Paul was seeking to influence the Corinthian church. In fact, he was desperate to influence them to deal with the many problems he saw in their midst. How a leader influences followers involves what is known as leadership styles. Most leadership styles are imbibed from one's observations of leaders around him/her during one's foundational years—up to age 20 or so. Cultural leadership styles will dominate a church leader. Various leadership styles are needed as a leader faces unique situations. This article defines leadership styles, identifies a leadership style continuum to help identify some of the factors in exercising a leadership style and finally looks at leadership styles Paul used as he influenced followers. In the Corinthian intervention, Paul exercise at least 7 of the 10 leadership styles introduced in this article: apostolic, confrontational, Father-Initiator, Father-guardian, maturity appeal, imitator, indirect conflict.

49. Pauline Leadership Styles

Introduction

Consider the fundamental definition for leader that permeates this commentary.

Definition   A <u>leader</u> is a person with God-given capacity and God-given responsibility who is influencing a specific group of people toward God's purposes.

How does one influence? Leadership style is one measure of how a leader influences. Paul again sets an example for leaders in the N.T. Church Leadership Era.

In Php, I point out that Paul uses the maturity appeal (opening salutation) and imitation modeling leadership styles (throughout the book, see especially Php 4:9). In Phm, I show how Paul uses several leadership styles: father-initiator (Phm 19), maturity appeal (Phm 9), and obligation persuasion (Phm 8-21). In 1Co and 2Co I repeatedly make comments on Paul's leadership styles. In 1Co I point out his Father-initiator style (4:14,15), his Apostolic leadership style (9:1,2), his confrontation style (1Co 5:1-5), his indirect conflict leadership style (1Co 5:1-4) and his imitator leadership style (1Co 4:16). In 2Co I point out maturity appeal (6:9,10), obligation persuasion (8:8), Father-initiator (2Co 10:14). Paul is a multi-style leader—a very modern concept in leadership style theory. What is a multi-style leader? Some definitions are needed in order to understand leadership style. Then I will move on to examine Pauline leadership styles.

Definition: The <u>dominant leadership style</u> of a leader is that,
1. highly directive or 2. directive or 3. non-directive or 4. highly non-directive
consistent behavior pattern that underlies specific overt behavior acts of influence pervading the majority of leadership functions in which that leader exerts influence.

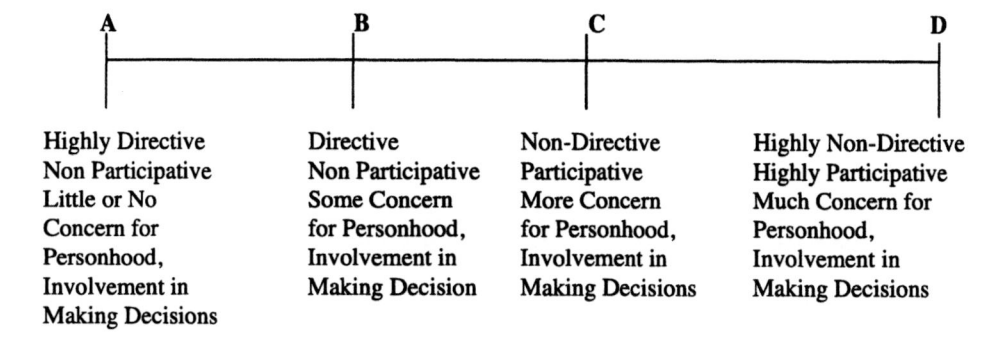

A	B	C	D
Highly Directive	Directive	Non-Directive	Highly Non-Directive
Non Participative	Non Participative	Participative	Highly Participative
Little or No Concern for Personhood, Involvement in Making Decisions	Some Concern for Personhood, Involvement in Making Decision	More Concern for Personhood, Involvement in Making Decisions	Much Concern for Personhood, Involvement in Making Decisions

Figure 1,2 Co 49-1. Influence Behavior Along a Continuum

49. Pauline Leadership Styles

Leadership style, deals with the individual behavioral expression a leader utilizes in influencing followers. This individual expression includes methodology for handling crises, methodology for problem solving, methodology for decision making, methodology for coordinating with superiors, peers and subordinates, methodology for handling leadership development. The individual methodology for a specific leadership act or series of acts can often be labeled as well as identified on the Directive—Non-Directive continuum.

My study of Paul's influence identified ten styles. These were given specific labels. Paul was multi-styled[168] in his approach to influencing followers. The styles are not defined exclusively. That is, there is some overlap of concepts between different styles. Let me describe the ten styles I labeled.

Ten Pauline Styles Observed

1. Apostolic Style

Where a person demonstrates with self-authenticating evidence that he/she has delegated authority from God—that is, there is a sense of spiritual authority about the leadership—then that person can use the apostolic leadership style.

Definition: The <u>apostolic leadership style</u> is a method of influence in which the leader
- assumes the role of delegated authority over those for whom he/she is responsible,
- receives revelation from God concerning decisions, and
- commands obedience based on role of delegated authority and revelation concerning God's will.

A synonym for this style is the command/demand style. This style is implied in 1Th 5:12, 13. "And I want you, fellow Christians, to personally know the leaders who work among you, and are over you in the Lord, and warm you. Lovingly honor them for their work's sake." It is implied in 1Ti 5:17: "Church leaders that are exercising good leadership should be evaluated as worthy of double pay—especially the ones who are working hard teaching the word." Another example implying this style is seen in Heb 13:17: "Obey those leaders who are set over you. Submit to their leadership. For they watch for your souls, as those who must give account. And they want to do so with joy and not with grief. Make it worth their while." This style is also seen in 1Th 2:6; even though Paul chooses not to command obedience, he asserts that he could have done so as was his apostolic right. The essence of the apostolic style is the legitimate right from God to make decisions for others and to command or demand their compliance with those decisions.

This style with its top-down command/demand approach is considered the most highly directive leadership style.

2. Confrontation Style

Many leaders try to avoid problems, particularly those involving troublesome people and those carrying heavy emotional ramifications. The basic rationale seems to be, "this is a tough problem; if I try to do anything about it I'm going to incur wrath, maybe have my character maligned, lose some friends and be drained emotionally. Perhaps if I just ignore it, it will go away by itself." For some problems, perhaps this is a good philosophy; time does give opportunity for a clearer perspective, for healing, and for indirect conflict to occur. But for most problems, leaders must confront the problem and parties involved directly. At least this seems to be the approaches exemplified in Jude, John, Peter, and Paul in their Scriptural writings.

Definition: The <u>confrontation leadership style</u> is an approach to problem solving
- which brings the problem out in the open with all parties concerned,
- which analyzes the problem in light of revelational truth,

---

[168] Doohan, a noted author on Pauline leadership also concludes that Paul is multi-styled. See Helen Doohan, **Leadership in Paul**. Wilmington, Del.: Michael Glazier, Inc., 1984.

- and which brings coercion to bear upon the parties to accept recommended solutions.

This style is usually seen in combination with other styles. Seemingly, the majority of cases emphasize *obligation-persuasion* as the force for accepting the solution, but *apostolic* force is also seen in the Scriptures. The book of Jude is an example. Several of the leadership acts in the book of 1Co utilize this style. Paul also uses this style in the Philippian church. See the problem between Euodia and Synteche. This style, like the apostolic style, is highly directive since the solutions to the problems are often the leader's solutions.

3. Father-Initiator Style

Paul resorts to this leadership style when exerting his influence upon the Corinthian church. He is establishing his authority in order to suggest solutions to some deep problems in the church.

Definition: The father-initiator leadership style is related to the apostolic style which uses the fact of the leader having founded the work as a lever for getting acceptance of influence by the leader.

In 1Co 4:14, 15 Paul writes, "14 I do not write these things to shame you, but as my beloved children I warn you. 15 For though you might have ten thousand Christian teachers, you only have one father in the faith. For I became your spiritual father when I preached the Gospel to you." Paul uses the father-initiator style in this case." Note in this example the force of the two powerful figures: the absolute for the relative in verse 14 and the hyperbole in verse 15.

The father-initiator style is closely related to the obligation-persuasion style, in that obligation (debt owed due to founding the work) is used as a power base. However it differs from obligation-persuasion in that more than persuasion is used. The decision to obey is not left to the follower. It is related to the apostolic style in that it is apostolic in its force of persuasion.

This style is highly directive/directive style.

4. Obligation-Persuasion Style

One method of influencing followers over which you have no direct organizational control involves persuasion. The leader persuades but leaves the final decision to the follower. A particularly powerful technique of persuasion is obligation-persuasion in which normal appeal techniques are coupled with a sense of obligation on the part of the follower due to past relationship/experience with the leader. Such a leadership style is seen with Paul's treatment of the Onesimus/Philemon problem.

Definition: An obligation-persuasion leadership style refers to an appeal to followers to follow some recommended directives which

- persuades, not commands followers to heed some advice;
- leaves the decision to do so in the hands of the followers, but
- forces the followers to recognize their obligation to the leader due to past service by the leader to the follower;
- strongly implies that the follower owes the leader some debt and should follow the recommended advice as part of paying back the obligation; and finally
- reflects the leader's strong expectation that the follower will conform to the persuasive advice.

The classic example of this is illustrated in the book of Philemon. Paul uses this style in combination with other styles in 1,2 Co also.

This is a directive style. The expectation is high, though the actual decision to do so passes to the follower.

5. Father-Guardian Style

This style, much like the nurse style, elicits an empathetic concern of the leader toward protection and care for followers.

Definition: The <u>father-guardian style</u> is a style which is similar to a parent-child relationship and has as its major concern protection and encouragement for followers.

Usually this style is seen when a very mature Christian relates to very immature followers. 1Th 2:10, 11 illustrates this style. "You know it to be true, and so does God, that our behavior toward you believers was pure, right, and without fault. You know that we treated each one of you just as a father treats his own children. We encouraged you, we comforted you, and we kept urging you to live the kind of life that pleases God, who calls you to share in his own Kingdom and glory."

Usually this style is directive, but because of the caring relationship between leader and follower and the follower maturity level it does not seem directive, since influence behavior always seem to have the follower's best interest at heart.

6. Maturity Appeal Style

The book of Proverbs indicates that all of life is an experience that can be used by God to give wisdom. And those who have learned wisdom should be listened to by those needing yet to learn. Maturity in the Christian life comes through time and experience and through God-given lessons as well as giftedness (see *word of wisdom gift*, **Glossary**). Leaders often influence and persuade followers by citing their *track record* (learned wisdom) with God.

Definition: A <u>maturity appeal leadership style</u> is a form of leadership influence which counts upon
- Godly experience, usually gained over a long period of time,
- an empathetic identification based on a common sharing of experience, and
- a recognition of the force of imitation modeling in influencing people

in order to convince people toward a favorable acceptance of the leader's ideas.

Heb 13:7 carries this implication: "Remember your former leaders who spoke God's message to you. Think back on how they lived and died and imitate their faith."

See also 1Pe 5:1–4, 5–7 where Peter demonstrates maturity appeal. "I, an elder myself, appeal to the church elders among you. I saw firsthand Christ's sufferings. I will share in the glory that will be revealed. I appeal to you to be shepherds of the flock that God gave you. Take care of it willingly, as God wants you to, and not unwillingly. Do your work, not for mere pay, but from a real desire to serve. Do not try to rule over those who have been put in your care, but be an example to the flock. And when the chief Shepherd appears, you will receive the glorious crown which will last."

Paul's description of his sufferings as an Apostle (2Co 11:16–33) and experience in receiving revelation (2Co 12:1–10) are exemplary of the maturity appeal style leadership.

This style moves between the categories of directive to non-directive depending on how forcefully the desired result is pushed for.

7. Nurse Style

In 1Th 2:7, Paul uses a figure to describe a leadership style he used among the Thessalonian Christians. The figure is that of a nurse. It is the only use of this particular word in the N.T., though related cognates do occur. The essential idea of the figure is the gentle cherishing attitude of Paul toward the new Christians in Thessalonica with a particular emphasis on Paul's focus on serving in order to help them grow.

Definition: The <u>nurse leadership style</u> is a behavior style characterized by gentleness and sacrificial service and loving care which indicates that a leader has given up "rights" in order not to impede the nurture of those following him/her.

49. Pauline Leadership Styles

The primary example is given in 1Th 2:7, "But we were gentle among you, even as a nurse cherishes her children." Paul commands an attitude of gentleness to Timothy in 2Ti 2:24–25. "24 The Lord's servant must not quarrel; instead be gentle unto all, skillfully teaching and being patient, 25 gently instructing those opponents. Perhaps God will give them opportunity to repent and see the truth."

The nurse style is similar to the father-guardian style in that both have a strong empathetic care for the followers. It differs in that the father-guardian style assumes a protective role of a parent to child. The nurse role assumes a nurturing focus which will sacrifice in order to see nurture accomplished.

The nurse style is non-directive.

8. Imitator Style

Paul seemed continually to sense that what he was and what he did served as a powerful model for those he influenced. He expected his followers to become like him in attitudes and actions. It is this personal model of *being* and *doing* as a way to influence followers that forms part of the foundational basis for spiritual authority.

Definition: The imitator style refers to a conscious use of imitation modeling as a means for influencing followers. It reflects a leader's sense of responsibility for what he/she is as a person of God and for what he/she does in ministry with an expectant view that followers must and will and should be encouraged to follow his/her example.

Paul emphasizes this in Php 4:9 which illustrates this leadership style. "9 Those things, which you have both learned, and received, and heard, and seen in me, do—and the God of peace shall be with you. A second Pauline illustration is seen in 2Ti 3:10,11. 10 "But you fully know my teaching, my lifestyle, my purpose in life, my faith, my steadfastness, my love, my endurance. 11 I was persecuted at Antioch, at Iconium, at Lystra; I endured those persecutions. Yet the Lord delivered me out of them." Paul goes on to give the response he expects of Timothy based on this imitation modeling and maturity appeal.

The whole book of Php emphasizes this influential methodology as being one of the most powerful tools a leader can use to influence followers. This style is highly non-directive.

9. Consensus Style

Decisions which affect people's lives and for which leaders must give account require careful spirit-led consideration. One leadership style approach to decision making involves consensus decision making. This style is often used in coordination situations where ownership is desired. Cultures which stress group solidarity, such as many of the tribes in Papua New Guinea, see this style used frequently by leaders.

Definition: Consensus leadership style refers to the approach to leadership influence which involves the group itself actively participating in decision making and coming to solutions acceptable to the whole group. The leader must be skilled in bringing diverse thoughts together in such a way as to meet the whole group's needs.

In a consensus style there is much give and take in arriving at decision. Unless there is a *check in the spirit* which prohibits an agreement, the final decision carries the weight of the entire group and thus will *demand* all to follow through on implications and ramifications which follow. James apparently gives a consensus decision reflecting the entire group's corporate will in the Ac 15 decision. Note this decision was identified as Spirit-led. The Ac 6 decision concerning distribution of good to widows is an example of both of consensus (within the plurality of Apostles) and apostolic (commanded to the followers) leadership styles.

This style is highly non-directive.

10. Indirect Conflict Style

A powerful style for dealing with crises and problem solving involves the concept of dealing with *first causes*, that is, the primary motivating factors behind the problem rather than the problem itself. This style recognizes that spiritual conflict is behind the situation and must be dealt with before any solution will take hold. The parties directly involved may not be aware that the leader is even doing problem solving. A leader who uses this approach must be skilled in prayer, understand spiritual warfare and either have the gift of discernings of spirits or access to a person with that gift.

> Definition The indirect conflict leadership style is an approach to problem solving which requires discernment of spiritual motivation factors behind the problem, usually results in spiritual warfare without direct confrontation with the parties of the problem Spiritual warfare is sensed as a necessary first step before any problem solving can take place.

See the context of Mt 16:21–23 especially verse 23: "Get away from me Satan. You are an obstacle in my way, because these thoughts of yours don't come from God, but from man." This is an example of indirect conflict leadership style. Mk 3:20–30 gives the underlying idea behind this style. See especially verse 27: "No one can break into a strong man's house and take away his belongings unless he first ties up the strong man; then he can plunder his house." See also Eph 6:10–20, especially verse 12: "For we are not fighting against human beings but against the wicked spiritual forces in the heavenly world, the rulers, authorities, and cosmic powers of this dark age."

Conclusions

I think the following are worth noting because they point out what I have been attempting to do in this section dealing with biblical styles, most of which come from Pauline material.

1. I have demonstrated how to use the generic (directive/non-directive continuum) as the overarching umbrella on which to pinpoint specific leadership-style behaviors.
2. I have identified 10 different Pauline leadership styles.
3. These 10 models of specific styles are transferable to many situations which we as leaders face today.
4. I have indicated that Paul's leadership style was multi-styled.
5. I have pointed out that Paul was a flexible leader who matured in his leadership as he grew older and was able to change to meet changing situations.

Current leadership style theories differ on whether or not a leader can actually change his/her leadership style. My own observations recognize that some leaders are flexible and can change. Others are not. Perhaps the ideal is a flexible leader who can change. But where this is not possible, then a leader who dominantly uses a certain leadership style should be placed in a situation where that style fits. Directive styles fit best with immature followers who need that direction. As followers mature the leadership styles should move to the right on the directive-non-directive continuum. This allows for follower maturity and for emerging leaders to arise.

Article 50

Relevance of the Article to Paul's Corinthian Ministry

Paul demonstrated both macro lesson 37. STRUCTURE—LEADERS MUST VARY STRUCTURES TO FIT THE NEEDS OF THE TIMES IF THEY ARE TO CONSERVE GAINS AND CONTINUE WITH RENEWED EFFORT and macro lesson 38. UNIVERSAL—THE CHURCH STRUCTURE IS INHERENTLY UNIVERSAL AND CAN BE MADE TO FIT VARIOUS CULTURAL SITUATIONS IF FUNCTIONS AND NOT FORMS ARE IN VIEW. In accordance with the ideas behind these two macros, as his ministry expanded into more and more Gentile cultures, he continually identified and met varying leadership needs. As a result leadership terms were added as needed. The following article seeks to identify the leadership terms seen in Paul's epistles and define them in terms of the time in which they were used.

50. Pauline Leadership Terms

One of the interesting questions that I ask of my leadership classes in seminary is, "What terms do you have for leaders and leadership in your cultures?" Since students in the School of World Mission come from 60 or more countries, in a given leadership class 10-20 different cultures will be represented. And the answers tell a lot about a cultures views of leaders. This article looks at the terms that Paul uses for leaders with a view toward:

1. identifying the different terms for leaders and implications of them,
2. understanding levels of leadership and the responsibility of leadership,
3. suggesting implications concerning leaders and giftedness.

1. Different Leader Terms in the Bible

Paul uses the following terms when talking about leaders.

Table 1,2 Co 50-1. Pauline Terms for Leaders

Term	Scripture	Referring To	Description/ Definition
apostle	Eph 4:11 et al	A leader given to the church; unclear if local, regional, or international church.	An apostle (SRN 652) is a leader who has capacity to move with authority from God to found works of God to meet needs and to develop and appoint leadership in these structures as well as preserve doctrinal purity.
bishop	1Ti 3:1, 2Tit 3:2	a local church leader; in the New Testament it is synonymous with elder.	a leadership term (SRN 1985) used in Php 1:1, 1Ti 3:2, Tit 1:7 and 1Pe 2:25. Occurs as the word overseer in Ac 20:28 and which probably best describes its function. As used in Paul's life time a person responsible for the spiritual welfare of others in a local church situation. Also used simultaneously with shepherd (pastor).
deacon	1Ti 3:8,12; Php 1:1	a local church leader probably under an overseer or elder.	a leadership term (SRN 1249) translated: as deacon three times—Php 1:1, 1Ti 3:8, 3:12; as minister 20 times; as servant 8 times. Paul uses this to describe his own self and Phoebe. It is not clear how this role relates to that of bishop or elder. It is distinguished as a separate leadership role from bishop in 1Ti 3 and probably of less influence.
elder	15 times in Ac, 1Ti, Tit	1. Jewish leaders along with Scribes and Pharisees; 2. elderly	a leadership term (SRN 4245) used by Paul and Luke 14 times in Scripture to refer to local church leadership in Ephesus. It is unclear as to how this leadership role, elder, differs from bishop. In the book of Tit the word bishop and elder is used synonymously. They are also used

50. Pauline Leadership Terms

		people in the church (male and female); 3. local church leaders.	simultaneously in Ac 20. In 1Ti elders are described as ruling and teaching in the local congregation. Also used once to describe elderly women in a local church and one time to possibly describe elderly men in the congregation (could be speaking of a local church leader).
evangelist	Eph 4:11, Ac 21:8; 2Ti 4:5	1. a leader who proclaims the Gospel—probably an itinerant leader; 2. Timothy's role to play out in Ephesians church; 3. Philip.	a leadership term (SRN 2099) used to describe Phillip the Evangelist, and to leaders given to the church to help build it up, and to the role Timothy must do in Ephesus as part of his ministry straightening out that church. The emphasis in the Eph 4:11ff passage is the building up (making mature) of the body. This is a gift given to the church.
minister	many	a general term applied to various leaders local or otherwise— the thrust of it is not on positional leadership or role but on the service involved in leading.	Three different Greek words are translated as minister: 1. a leadership term (SRN 1249) translated: as minister 20 times; as servant 8 times and as deacon three times—Php 1:1, 1Ti 3:8, 3:12. Paul uses this to describe his own self and Phoebe. It is not clear how this role relates to that of bishop and elder. It is distinguished as a separate leadership role and probably of less influence than bishop in 1Ti 3 and possibly less influence in Php 1:1. 2. a leadership term (SRN 5257) used to describe Paul, Apollos, the Roman emperor, and other church leaders—its emphasis is responsible service as a leader. 3. a leadership term (SRN 5257) literally an under rower, that is, someone who is a leader under the authority of someone else. Ananias describes Paul with this term.
overseer	Ac 20:28	a local church leader; used as such in Ephesus church and Philippian church.	a leadership term (SRN 1985) Occurs as the word overseer in Ac 20:28 and which probably best describes its function. As used in Paul's life time a person responsible for the spiritual welfare of others in a local church situation. Probably synonymous with the term elder. Also used in Php 1:1, 1Ti 3:2, Tit 1:7 and 1Pe 2:25 where it is translated by bishop.
pastor	Eph 4:11	unclear, could be a local church leader as in 1Pe 5:1-4 or Ac 20:28 but also a regional or national or international itinerant leader as in Eph 4:11.	a leadership term (SRN 4166) occurs as the English word shepherd or tend referring metaphorically to a leader who tends a flock (Christian followers); used simultaneously with bishop and elder in Ac 20.
prophet	Eph 4:11	A leader given to the church; unclear if this means local church, regional church, international church to bring	a leadership term (SRN 4396) describing strong spokespersons in the Old Testament and New Testament. In the New Testament Silas and Agabus illustrate this kind of leadership. Agabus worked in a local situation but also traveled about in his prophetic ministry. Silas traveled also as a missionary.

50. Pauline Leadership Terms

		corrective truth to situations; probably itinerant.	
rule, ruler	1Ti 3:4, 5,12; 5:12; 5:17; Ro 12:5-9	one who functions over others; most likely a local church leader.	Several Greek words underlie this leadership descriptive word. 1. a leadership term (SRN 4291) describing one who is placed over another. Used in 1Ti 3:4,5 to describe a characteristic of a bishop; Used in 1 Th 5:12 to describe a leader who is over others; used in 1Ti 3:12 describing a characteristic of a deacon; used in 1Ti 5:17 to describe the function of an elder. 2. a leadership term (SRN 2233) meaning to rule, command, have authority over. Also used in the Ro 12:5-9 gifts passage to describe a gift.
Servant (bond slave)	Php 1:1	specially committed leaders to the cause of Christ.	A special leadership term which Paul uses to describe himself and Timothy (SRN 1401). It is used of one who gives himself up to another's will, those whose service is used by Christ in extending and advancing his cause among people. It emphasizes leadership wise the vertical aspect of servant leadership. A leader first of all serves Christ. Secondly, he/she serves those being influenced or led. Peter uses this term to describe himself. Paul uses it several times when speaking of leaders in a church setting. Also used of Jesus (Php 2).
shepherd	Ac 20:28 1Pe 5:1	a local church leader caring for those under his/her influence.	a leadership term (SRN 4165) relating to a leader who cares for and protects a group of followers; used simultaneously with bishop and elder in the Ac 20 and simultaneously with bishop in 1Pe 2:25. Occurs both in noun and verb form.
teacher	Eph 4:11	A leader given to the church;	a leadership term (SRN 1320) describing a major function needed in a local church, that of teaching or explaining truth about God and His ways and His will for followers. **Need for clarification here:** In the Eph context it is unclear if this means local church, regional church, international church. Regional and international would be needed to bring corrective truth to situations—probably via itinerant ministry.

2. Understanding Levels of Leadership/ Accountability

A leader is a person with a God-given capacity and a God-given burden (responsibility) who is influencing a specific group of people toward God's purposes for the group. Now all members of the body influence each other when ever they use their gifts. But a leader is one who not only influences but has a responsibility from God to do so and who will answer to God for it. So then there is a distinction between leaders, in this sense, and followers. These leaders are set over (i.e. get a burden for and have responsibility for) the followers (in the sense of Heb 13:7, 17 and the use of rule in 1Th 5:12 and 1Ti 5:17). Further, these leaders will give an account for them (see **Article 1. Accountability**). So then there is a major distinction between followers and leaders.

Within the category of leaders in a local church there is a distinction between elders, bishops, pastors (basically used synonymously) and deacons (see 1Ti 3 where characteristics of these two different leaders are distinguished). The Ephesians 2 passage seems to indicate that apostles and prophets at least in the early church are foundational and a cut above other leaders because of their inaugural work in getting the church going.

50. Pauline Leadership Terms 278

The gifts passage in 1Co 12:27-31 apparently lists the spiritual gifts given there in a priority order: apostles, prophets, teachers which are described higher than other gifts.

The Ephesians giftedness passage (also leadership passage) also distinguishes a group of leaders from followers: apostles, prophets, evangelists, pastors, teachers. These leaders are obviously different in their responsibility from the other members of the body.

The most important thing to recognize from this section is simply that leaders are distinguished from followers and will give an account for their leadership. Thus passages like Php 2:16 (that my ministry efforts have been worth while, not wasted effort) and 4:1 (my joy and crown), Heb 13:17 (must give an account for you).

A second thing to recognize is that the terms bishop, pastor, elder, shepherd as seen in the N.T. are essentially used synonymously. They do not carry the connotations that have emerged over history of hierarchical positions. The present day use of the Pauline terms bishop, elder, and pastor have taken on traditional and historical meaning that was not true of them in New Testament times.

3. Leadership and Giftedness

From the Scriptures it seems clear that at least apostleship, prophecy, evangelism, pastoring, and teaching are leadership gifts. From my own empirical study of over 1200 contemporary case studies of leaders I have deduced the following leadership observation.

All leaders have at least one word gift and most have more than one in their gift-mix.

I define word gifts as a category of spiritual gifts used to clarify and explain about God. These gifts when used in the body highly influence those receiving the ministry. And leaders are those who influence. These word gifts help us understand about God including His nature, His purposes and how we can relate to Him and be a part of His purposes. Word gifts include: teaching, exhortation, pastoring, evangelism, apostleship, prophecy, ruling, and sometimes word of wisdom, word of knowledge, and faith (a word of). All leaders have at least one of these and often several of these.

Let me defined these gifts:

apostleship   one of the 19 spiritual gifts. The gift of apostleship refers to a special leadership capacity to move with authority from God to create new ministry structures (churches and para-church) to meet needs and to develop and appoint leadership in these structures. **Its central thrust is Creating New Ministry.**

teaching   one of the 19 spiritual gifts. It belongs to the Word Cluster. A person who has the gift of teaching is one who has the ability to instruct, explain, or expose Biblical truth in such a way as to cause believers to understand the Biblical truth. **Its central thrust is To Clarify Truth.**

ruling   one of the 19 spiritual gifts. It is in the word cluster. A person operating with a ruling gift demonstrates the capacity to exercise influence over a group so as to lead it toward a goal or purpose with a particular emphasis on the capacity to make decisions and keep the group operating together. **Its central thrust is Influencing Others Toward Vision.**

prophecy   one of the 19 spiritual gifts. It is in the word cluster and power cluster. A person operating with the gift of prophecy has the capacity to deliver truth (in a public way) either of a predictive nature or as a situational word from God in order to correct by exhorting, edifying or consoling believers and to convince non-believers of God's truth. **Its central thrust is To Provide Correction Or Perspective On A Situation.**

pastoring   one of the 19 spiritual gifts. It belongs to the Word Cluster and the Love Cluster. The pastoral gift is the capacity to exercise concern and care for members of a group so as to encourage them in their growth in Christ which involves modeling maturity, protecting

50. Pauline Leadership Terms

them from error and disseminating truth. **Its central thrust is Caring For The Growth Of Followers.**

governments — one of 19 spiritual gifts occurring primarily in the Love Cluster. <u>The gifts of governments</u> involves a capacity to manage details of service functions so as to support and free other leaders to prioritize their efforts. **Its Central Thrust Is Supportive Organizational Abilities.**

exhortation — one of the 19 spiritual gifts. It is a spiritual gift belonging to the word cluster. The <u>gift of Exhortation</u> is the capacity to urge people to action in terms of applying Biblical truths, or to encourage people generally with Biblical truths, or to comfort people through the application of Biblical truth to their needs. **Its central thrust is To Apply Biblical Truth.**

Closure

Some implications of this study include the following:

1. The large range of terms show us that leadership in terms of the many functions needed is complex. We as leaders can not perform all these functions. And our giftedness will direct us to those that are ours to perform. Thus, we need the interdependent help of others.
2. Leaders are those who see themselves as serving God (bondslave) first of all and ministering (servant) to others secondly.
3. Leaders do have responsibility to influence others with authority.
4. Leaders must care for those being led.
5. Leaders will give an account for their leadership.
6. Leaders are gifted to lead.
7. The functions of leadership are much more important than the status, privilege, or position of leaders.
8. The higher level leadership functions (apostle, prophet, evangelist, pastor, teacher) are given to equip the body. The implication being that each of these level gifted leaders are raising up others to do these functions in the body.

Remember, in closing, three important verses:

> **Listen, this is an important fact, "If a person is eager to be a Church leader, that is a good thing." 1Ti 3:1**

It is a good thing to desire leadership. This desire should be backed up by calling and giftedness and should be recognized by others in the body.

> **Remember your former leaders. Imitate those qualities and achievements that were God-Honoring, for their source of leadership still lives -- Jesus! He, too, can inspire and enable your own leadership today. Heb 13:7,8**

As a leader you will be modeling for others. And you will be following those leaders who have gone before you. And you have the same source of leadership as they—Jesus Christ.

> **Obey them that have the rule over you, and submit yourselves: for they watch for your souls, as they that must give account, that they may do it with joy, and not with grief: for that [is] unprofitable for you. Heb 13:17**

You will give an account for your leadership. You will be rewarded for those things in your leadership which were good. You will also account for those things not so good.

See accountability, **Glossary**. See **Articles**, *1. Accountablity—Standing Before God As A Leader; 2. Apostolic Functions.*

Article 51

Relevance of the Article to Paul's Corinthian Ministry

Because Paul's spiritual authority is being questioned in Corinth—especially being denounced by the pseudo-apostles there—Paul defends his personal character and rationale for making decisions. We learn more about Paul's personal life and thinking in the Corinthian intervention (especially 2 Co) than in all of the other epistles taken together. Values, which affect our perspective or behavior are important. In 2 Co we see many of the values that underlie Paul's thinking and actions. We are seeing the base of his ministry philosophy.

51. Pauline Leadership Values

Introduction

One of the six characteristics[169] of a leader who finishes well is described as,

> **Truth is lived out in their lives so that convictions and promises of God are seen to be real.**

A leader who has values and lives by them will exemplify this characteristic. Paul did. All during the leadership commentary for Paul's epistles, I have indicated Pauline values. Some of these values are unique to Paul and are at best only suggestive for other leaders. And some are guidelines that can help leaders today. But many are possibly absolutes that must be considered carefully as required of leaders today.[170]

Definition   A <u>leadership value</u> is an underlying assumption which affects how a leader perceives leadership and practices it.

Leadership values contain strong language like should, ought, or must. Must statements are the strongest.

Definition   A leader's ministry is said to be <u>value driven</u> if that leader consciously attempts to identify, make explicit, and explain leadership values that under gird his/her ministry and deliberately operates his/her ministry based on these values.

Paul was a value driven leader. 2Co is the pre-eminent book demonstrating this. Because Paul had to defend his ministry and his apostolic authority, he gave the underlying reasons why he operated the way he did. This article simply summarizes in one place statements which attempt to describe the Pauline leadership values I have identified all through his epistles. There is no attempt made here to evaluate the certainty with which these values should be applied along the principle of truth continuum. I will list the 2Co values first since that book is basal for understanding leadership values. I will number the values for later reference purposes only. These numbers do not indicate any kind of priority. Repeated listing of a value occurs just for emphasis.

---

[169] The six characteristics include: 1. They maintain a personal vibrant relationship with God right up to the end. 2. They maintain a learning posture and can learn from various kinds of sources—life especially. 3. They manifest Christ-likeness in character as evidenced by the fruit of the Spirit in their lives. 4. Truth is lived out in their lives so that convictions and promises of God are seen to be real. 5. They leave behind one or more ultimate contributions. 6. They walk with a growing awareness of a sense of destiny and see some or all of it fulfilled.

[170] See **Article, 53. *Principles of Truth***, which define principles along a continuum of suggestions, guidelines, requirements (absolutes).

51. Pauline Leadership Values

Table 1,2 Co 51-1. Pauline Leadership Values Summarized—2 Corinthians

Value Name. Statement of Value.
1. **Divine Appointment.** Leaders ought to be sure that God appointed them to ministry situations.
2. **Training Methodology.** Leaders must be concerned about leadership selection and development.
3. **Personal Ministry.** Leaders should view personal relationships as an important part of ministry.
4. **Sovereign Mindset.** Leaders ought to see God's hand in their circumstances as part of His plan for developing them as leaders. See *sovereign mindset*, **Glossary**. See **Article 59**, *Sovereign Mindset*.
5. **Integrity and Openness.** Leaders should not be deceptive in their dealings with followers but should instead be open, honest, forthright, and frank with them. See **Article 22**, *Integrity—A Top Leadership Quality*.
6. **Ultimate accountability.** Leaders' actions must be restrained by the fact that they will ultimately give an account to God for their leadership actions. See **Articles,** *9. Day of Christ—Implications for Leaders; 40. Motivating Factors for Ministry*.
7. **Spiritual Authority**—Its ends. Spiritual authority ought to be used to mature followers. See **Articles,** *60. Spiritual Authority Defined—Six Characteristics; 16. Followership—Ten Commandments*.
8. **Loyalty Testing.** Leaders must know the level of followership loyalty in order to wisely exercise leadership influence. See **Article,** *16. Followership—Ten Commandments*.
9. **True Credentials** (competency and results). A leader should be able to point to results from ministry as a recommendation of God's authority in him/her.
10. **True Competence** (its ultimate source). A leader's ultimate confidence for ministry must not rest in his/her competence but in God the author of that competence.
11. **Transforming Ministry.** Followers, increasingly being set free by the Holy Spirit and being transformed into Christ's image ought to be the hope and expectation of a Christian leader.
12. **Prominence of Christ in Ministry.** A leader must not seek to bring attention to himself/herself through ministry but must seek to exalt Christ as Lord.
13. **Servant Leadership.** A leader ought to see leadership as focused on serving followers in Jesus' behalf. See **Article,** *24. Jesus—Five Leadership Models*.
14. **Death/Life Paradox.** The firstfruits of Jesus resurrection life ought to be experienced in the death producing circumstances of life and ought to serve as a hallmark of spiritual life for followers. In other words, Christianity ought to work in thick or thin.
15. **Motivational Force.** Leaders should use obligation to Christ (in light of his death for believers) to motivate believers to service for Christ.
16. **True Judgment Criterion.** Leaders should value people in terms of their relationship to God in Christ and not according to their outward success in the world (even in the religious world).
17. **Unequally Yoked.** Christian leadership must not be dominated by relationships with unbelievers so that non-Christian values hold sway.
18. **Financial Equality Principle.** Christian leadership must teach that Christian giving is a reciprocal balancing between needs and surplus.
19. **Financial Integrity.** A Christian leader must handle finances with absolute integrity.

Table 1,2 Co 51-2. Pauline Leadership Values Summarized—1 Timothy

20. A Christian leader ought to have several life long mentorees who he/she will help over a lifetime to reach their potential in leadership.
21. Giftedness must be developed.
22. Giftedness should receive less stress in leadership selection and development than character building. Leadership selection must be based primarily on character.
23. Leaders should avoid prejudging a problematic situation without careful investigation.
24. Leaders should be disciplined with a view toward recovery.
25. Leaders must expect heresy both as to belief (orthodoxy) and practice (orthopraxy) to arise both from within the church and without it.
26. Integrity, as reflected in a purse conscience, should be the goal of every leader for himself or herself personally (Ac 24:16).
27. Money ought to be a strong power base useful to do good for people.

51. Pauline Leadership Values

28. Every leader ought to know about and be able to deal with spiritual warfare problems in the church.

Table 1,2 Co 51-3. Pauline Leadership Values Summarized—2 Timothy

29. Present ministry should always be seen in the light of a whole life of ministry and particularly the end of ministry—a good finish.
30. One's sense of destiny ought to guide a leader toward a good finish.
31. An anticipation of the Lord's return should be a major motivating factor for a leader to minister well and finish well.
32. Recognition of giving a final accountability for one's leadership ought to be a strong motivating factor for a leader to minister well and finish well.
33. Leaders should be responsible for prayer for their ministries. A leader should pray personally for those in his or her ministry. A leader should seek God for specific prayers for those in his/her ministry. A leader should tell those in his/her ministry about those prayers and thus encourage them to believe also that God will answer those prayers.
34. Leadership selection and development should be a responsibility of a leader.
35. Emerging leaders should be taught how to handle correctly God's written word.
36. Gentleness ought to be a primary trait of a leader who wants to persuade (as opposed to one who wants to prove he/she is right).
37. A leaders should proactively use modeling to influence followers.
38. A leader ought to have a strong learning posture all of life.

Table 1Co 1,2 51-4. Pauline Leadership Values Summarized—1 Corinthians

39. Gifts, operating harmoniously together, each contributing its function, should have as its purpose the edification of the church as a whole.
40. The proper attitude behind exercising gifts ought to be that of love. This attitude is essentially more important than the exercise of the gifts or results coming from those gifts.
41. Orderliness in public worship, which is consistent with the way God does things, ought to be the norm for churches.
42. A leader ought to see his/her leaders as a responsibility entrusted by God.
43. Leaders should vary their leadership styles according to the situation, personal ability, and follower maturity.
44. Leadership must be exercised primarily as service first of all to God and secondarily as service to God's people.
45. Leaders who want to finish well must maintain disciplines during the stressful middle stages of leadership in order to continue well.
46. Bible study and prayer are major disciplines that a leaders should maintain, especially during the plateauing years (40-60).

Table 1Co 1,2 51-5. Pauline Leadership Values Summarized—Philippians

47. A leader must recognize God's sovereignty in deep processing.
48. A leader should seek, in deep processing, to ask what the Lord is doing in it both in a personal way and in the ministry, with a view toward the whole of life, not just the specific time it is happening.
49. A leader in deep processing must be transparent and vulnerable enough to share with others in his/her community so as to garner support and prayer backing.
50. A leader must be aware of the fact that his/her response to deep processing will be a model for those being influenced.
51. A leader must, in deep processing, reevaluate life purpose and affirm it, modify it, or add to it, recognizing that God will often use deep processing to expand one's horizons as to life purpose.
52. A leader should proactively use modeling to influence followers.
53. A leader who models must be transparent and vulnerable to share God's working in the life both in the positive and negative shaping activities of life. It is God's working in the negative shaping activities of life that often has more impact than even the positive.
54. Effective leaders view relational empowerment as both a means and a goal in ministry.

51. Pauline Leadership Values

55. An effective leader must learn to vary his/her leadership style to fit the situation and people being influenced.
56. An effective leader should view spiritual authority as a primary power base but recognize that other bases will be needed to influence.
57. A leader should have a life purpose which serves as a guidance check for decisions about ministry and for doing ministry. Does what I am doing enhance my life purpose?
58. A leader ought to demonstrate union life for followers to see what a Christ-centered life looks like.

Table 1Co 1,2 51-6. Pauline Leadership Values Summarized—Philemon

59. Obligation-persuasion is a leadership style in harmony with spiritual authority and should be used with mature followers with whom a leader has a good relationship.
60. An effective leader must learn to vary his/her leadership style to fit the situation and people being influenced.
61. An effective leader should view spiritual authority as a primary power base but recognize that other bases will be needed to influence.
62. Sensitivity to God's shaping processes must be cultivated in a leader.

Conclusions

These Pauline leadership values are not posited as final statements. They are first attempts at getting at the driving ideas behind Paul's ministry. The are given to stimulate thought. They should be assessed and then modified, reworded, or even discarded depending on the assessment.

See **Article**, *71. Value Driven Leadership.*

Article 52

Relevance of the Article to Paul's Corinthian Ministry

Paul vividly demonstrates this macro lesson throughout his ministry. Note the strong prayer emphasis in 2 Cor.

52. The Prayer Macro Lesson

Samuel makes a strong statement in his last public ministry act, his farewell address, 1 Sa 12:1-25.

> 23 Moreover as for me, God forbid that I should sin against the LORD in ceasing to pray for you: but I will teach you the good and the right way: 24 Only fear the LORD, and serve him in truth with all your heart: for consider how great [things] he has done for you. 1 Sa 12:23,24

At the heart of this statement is the fact that Samuel feels responsibility to pray for his ministry. And he sees this as a responsibility coming from God (note sin against God). Such a gracious attitude, Samuel is being eased out of leadership by these people, becomes this great leader. From this context, also verified strongly in Abraham's leadership (Gen 18) and Moses leadership (Ex 32) a macro lesson emerges, an observation on leadership and responsibility to pray.

Leaders called to a ministry are called to intercede for that ministry.

This macro lesson occurs in many leaders' ministry across the six leadership eras. It is seen most fully developed in Jesus' ministry and Paul's ministry. This macro lesson appears on the far right of the *Leadership Truth Continuum*, most likely an <u>absolute</u>. Written in value language it becomes,

A leader must pray for the ministry he/she is responsible for.

How a leader does this, actually praying and/or taking responsibility for it and making sure it is done is unclear in the Bible. But it should be done. It is this macro lesson which forms the underlying value for the *Intercession Philosophical Leadership Model*.

See **Articles**, *35. Macro Lesson Defined; 36. Macro Lessons—List of 41 Across Six Leadership Eras; 24. Jesus—Five Leadership Models: Shepherd, Harvest, Steward, Servant, Intercessory; 46. Paul—Intercessor Leader; 74. Vulnerability and Prayer.*

Article 53

Relevance of the Article to Paul's Corinthian Ministry

Paul references the O.T. Scriptures a number of times in 1,2 Co. In 1,2 Co Paul quotes, or alludes to or applies some O.T. scripture some 196 times. Books involved include Ge, Ex, Lev, Nu, Dt, Jdg, 1, 2 Sa, 1 Ch, Ezr, Ne, Job, Ps, Pr, Ecc, SS, Isa, Jer, Ezek, Da, Hos, Am, Mic, Hab, Zec, Mal. Most of those times he is referring to some principle of truth underlying the quoted material or verses being referred to. This article describes my own approach to drawing out principles of truth from the Scriptures.

53. Principles of Truth

Introduction

Leaders who finish well are described by six characteristics.[171] Two of these claim that,

> **They maintain a learning posture and can learn from various kinds of sources—life especially.**
>
> **Truth is lived out in their lives so that convictions and promises of God are seen to be real.**

How does a leader get truth from the scriptures—one of the sources for learning? How does a leader get truth, form convictions, and arrive at promises from God?

Further, this leadership commentary has described a Bible centered leader.

> A <u>Bible Centered leader</u> refers to a leader whose leadership is being informed by the Bible and who personally has been shaped by Biblical values, has grasped the intent of Scriptural books and their content in such a way as to apply them to current situations and who uses the Bible in ministry so as to impact followers.

How does one get informed by the Bible on leadership? How does a leader get values which shape him/her?

This article suggests perspectives that help answer these questions. It details my own framework—the perspectives that have guided me as I comment on the Scriptures, suggest observations, guidelines, values, principles of truth, macro lessons, etc.

Principles

Observations of truth provide one useful result of leadership studies. These truths help us understand other leadership situations and predict what ought to be. They also help us in the selection and training of leaders since they give guidelines that have successfully been applied in past leadership situations. These truths are usually seen first as specific statements concerning one leader in his/her situation. They are then generalized to cover other leaders and like situations. The question of how generally they can be applied to others is a genuine one. The certainty continuum and screening questions provide cautions about this.

---

[171] Six characteristics of a good finish include the following. Leaders ho finish well have: (1) a vibrant personal relationship with God; (2) a learning posture; (3) Christ-likeness in character; (4) lived by Biblical convictions; (5) left behind ultimate contributions; (6) and fulfilled a sense of destiny.

53. Principles of Truth

Definition — <u>Principles</u> refer to generalized statements of truth which reflect observations drawn from specific instances of leadership acts or other leadership sources.

God's processing of leaders includes shaping toward spiritual formation, ministerial formation, and/or strategic formation. Analyzing formational shaping, serves as an important stimulus for deriving principles.

A few examples will help clarify. Analysis of God's use of the integrity check, word check, and obedience check to develop spiritual formation in numerous young leader's lives led to the following three principles.

> **Integrity is foundational for leadership; it must be instilled early in a leader's character.**
>
> **Obedience is first learned by a leader and then taught to others.**
>
> **Leadership gifts primarily involve word gifts which initially emerge through word checks**

Analysis of Samuel's final public leadership act in 1 Sa 12 (see especially vs 23) led to the following truth.

> **When God calls a leader to a leadership situation he calls him/ her to pray for followers in that situation.**

The Certainty Continuum and Related Definitions

Attempts to derive statements of truth from leadership studies meet with varied success. Some people seem to intuitively have a sense of generalizing from a specific situation a statement which apparently fits other situations. Others are not so good at this skill. This part of leadership theory is in is infancy stage. In the future we hope to delineate more structured approaches for deriving statements and for validating them. But for now we need to recognize that these statements often can not be proved as truth (in the sense that physical science can prove truth) hence we, as researchers, need to be careful of what we say is truth. Below is given the certainty continuum and the major generalization concerning the derivation of *truth* statements. These are an attempt to make us as researchers cautious about applying our findings.

Principles of truth are attempts to generalize specific truths for wider applicability and will vary in their usefulness with others and the authoritative degree to which they can be asserted for others.

description — The <u>certainty continuum</u> is a horizontal line moving from suggestions on one extreme to requirements on the other extreme which attempts to provide a grid for locating a given statement of truth in terms of its potential use with others and the degree of authority with which it can be asserted.

The basic ideas are that:
1. Principles are observations along a continuum.
2. We can teach and use with increasing authority those principles further to the right on the continuum.

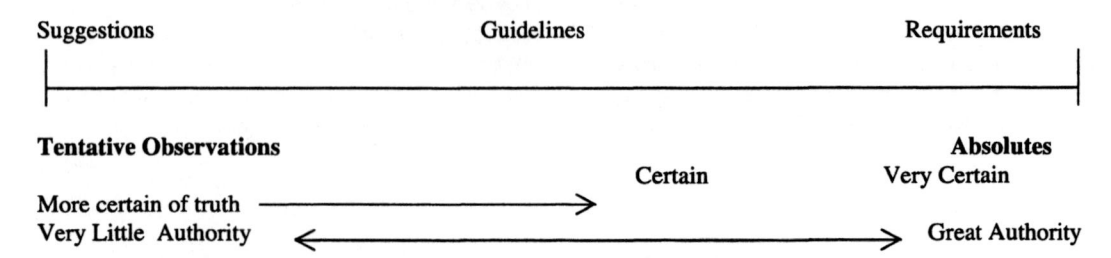

Suggestions	Guidelines	Requirements
Tentative Observations	Certain	**Absolutes** Very Certain
More certain of truth ⟶		
Very Little Authority ⟵――――――――――――⟶		Great Authority

Figure 1,2 Co 53-1. The Certainty Continuum

53. Principles of Truth

I am identifying principles as a broad category of statements of truth which were true at some instant of history and may have relevance for others at other times.

There is little difference between *Suggestions* and *Guidelines* on the continuum. In fact, there is probably overlap between the two. Some *Guidelines* approach *Requirements*. But there is a major difference from going from *Suggestions* to *Requirements*—the difference being *Suggestions* are optional but *Requirements* are not. They must be adhered to.

Definition   Suggestions refers to truth observed in some situations and which may be helpful to others but they are optional and can be used or not with no loss of conscience.

Definition   Guidelines are truths that are replicated in most leadership situations and should only be rejected for good reasons though their will be no loss of conscience.

Definition   Absolutes refer to replicated truth in leadership situations across cultures without restrictions. Failure to follow or use will normally result in some stirrings of conscience.

Absolutes are principles which evince God's authoritative backing. All leaders everywhere should heed them.

Suggestions are the most tentative. They are not enjoined upon people. They may be very helpful though.

Remember that a *Suggestion* or *Guideline* may move to the right or left if more evidence is found in the Bible to support such a move. If a *suggestion* or *guideline* identified in one place in the Scriptures is found to be abrogated, modified or somehow restricted at a later time in the progressive flow of revelation then it will move most likely to the left. However, if later revelation gives evidence of its more widespread usage or identifies it more certainly for everyone then it will move to the right.

Six Assumptions Underlying Derivation Of Principles

Principles are derived from Biblical leadership situations as well as from life situations. Several assumptions underlie my approach to deriving principles of truth. The following six assumptions underlie my approach to getting truth.

1. **Truth Assumption:** All truth has its source in God.

I need not fear the study of secular material (social science materials, leadership theory, present day situations, etc.). If there is any truth in it I can be certain it is of God. For there is no truth apart from God. I don't have to limit truth to the Bible. The Bible itself shows how God has revealed truth by many different means. These means were certainly not just limited to ancient written revelation. The problem then lies in how to discern if something is truth.

2. **Source Assumption:** All of life can be a source of truth for those who are discerning.

The central thrust of Proverbs 1:20-33 and in fact the whole book of Proverbs is that God reveals wisdom in life situations. The book of Proverbs is more than just content for us to use; it is a modeling of how that content was derived over time and in a given society. We can trust God to reveal wisdom in the life situations we study (whether from the Bible or today). Truth that evolved in Israeli history came to take on at least guideline status and much of it became absolutes.

3. **Applicability Assumption.** Just because a statement of truth was true for a specific given situation does not mean the statement has applicability for other leaders at other times. Wider application must be determined via comparative means.

A statement of truth is an assertion of fact drawn from a specific situation. The dynamics of the situation may well condition the statement. That is, the truth itself may apply only in situations which contain the same dynamics. The fact that the truth did happen means it is at least worthy of study for potential wider use. Because of the consistency of God's character we know that the truth can not violate His nature. But its happening is not sufficient justification for its use anywhere at anytime by any leader.

53. Principles of Truth

4. **Dogmatic Assumption.** We must exercise caution in asserting all truth statements as if they were absolutes.

Fewer truths will be seen as absolutes if screened with applicability criteria. The use of applicability criteria, especially that of comparative study, will force one to identify a higher level function behind a given principle. Thus a statement of truth at some lower level when compared with other situations and similar statements of truth might lead to a higher order generic statement of truth. These higher level statements of truth, though more general in nature, preserve the function intended rather than the form of the truth. Such statements will allow more freedom of application. Statements which do not carry wide applicability or have attached to them dynamics of situations which can not be fully assessed will most likely have to be asserted with less dogmatism.

5. **Dependence Assumption.** We are forced more than ever to depend upon the Holy Spirit's present ministry to confirm truth we are deriving.

Because of the sources (life as well as Biblical) from which we are drawing truth, we will need more dependence upon the ministry of the Holy Spirit. That is, we will be forced to situationally rely on and become more sensitive to the Holy Spirit's leading and voice. We will need to recognize giftedness in the body and learn to trust those who have spiritual gifts which expose, clarify, and confirm truth (discernings of spirits, word of knowledge, word of wisdom, teaching, exhortation, etc.).

6. **Trust Assumption.** Because we are following Biblical admonitions (Heb 13:7,8; 1 Co10:6,11, Ro 15:4) in our attempts to derive truth we can expect God to enable us to see much truth.

God does not command us to do things that are impossible. God's commands contain within in them the promise of enablement. Because there are great needs for more and better leadership and because we need leadership truth to develop that leadership and because God has told us to study leaders to learn from their lives, we can expect God to lead us to truth that will greatly affect our lives. By faith we can trust Him to do this.

Conclusion

For each of the **Key Leadership Insight** sections for individual books I have listed statements called observations, principles, values, lessons. Each of these will need to be assessed on the certainty continuum to determine their level of applicability.

See *integrity check, word check, and obedience check, spiritual formation, ministerial formation, strategic formation,* **Glossary**.

Article 54

Relevance of the Article to Paul's Corinthian Ministry

Paul demonstrates how an apostolic leader should confront problems in a church setting in his intervention in the Corinthian situation. Numerous problems are dealt with in 1 Co. Both the solutions given and the method used to arrive at them are worth knowing and emulating, when properly contextualized to a modern situation. This article details the problems seen in the Corinthian church as well as some of the other New Testament churches. Apostolic leaders beware—one of your major functions is dealing with complex problems.

54. Problems—The N.T. Church

Introduction

The final macro lesson identified summarizes what is seen about leadership across six leadership eras.[172]

> **Leadership is complex, problematic, difficult, and fraught with risk—which is why leadership is needed.**

Because there are problems, there is a need for leaders. And there will always be problems in ministry. I have frequently heard leaders say, "If we could only get back to the N.T. church. That would solve our problems." I always smile and ask, "Which one?" Cause all of the N.T. churches had problems. Which problems do you want to deal with? The N.T. Leadership Era was filled with problems. As Jesus' initiating work broke forth from a movement into an institution that could be transferred into multi-cultural situations, problems arose. The book dealing most comprehensively with church problems is 1Co. This article will simply list some church problems as seen in the N.T. Church Leadership Era.

My basic assumption is that awareness of problems is a first start toward avoiding them or solving them in one's own situation. And awareness of the N.T. church problems with possible N.T. advice about them goes a long way toward solving these problems. Knowing that problems can be solved is a great encouragement.

Problems With the Corinthian Church

Table 1Co 1,2 54-1 Summarizes problems in the Corinthian church.

Table 1,2 Co 54-1. Problems in the Corinthian Church

Problem	Ch	Explanation/ Paul's Advice
Wisdom	Ch 1,2	*Problem*—over emphasis on secular wisdom. *Advice*—wisdom is centered in Christ; appropriate it. God reveals wisdom. Avoid tendency to want esoteric knowledge and to get it in unhealthy ways.
Divisions	Ch 3,4	*Problem*—over emphasis on following different leaders causing divisions and cultic like groups; claims of having more of whatever Christianity is because of belonging to one group and leader. *Advice*—disunity is a symptom of an immature church; Grow up; recognize different leaders are gifted by God for different functions in the church; Respect all of them. But do not become divided over them. Paul introduces stewardship model to describe responsibility of a leader.

---

[172] See *macro lesson*, **Glossary**. See **Articles**, *35. Macro Lessons Defined; 36. Macro Lessons—List of 41 Across Six Leadership Eras; 27. Leadership Eras in the Bible—Six Identified.*

54. Problems—The New Testament Church

Toleration of Immorality	Ch 5	*Problem*—in the surrounding culture there was moral laxity; The church had a couple living in immorality—involving at least an in-law relationship and maybe even . *Advice*—excommunicate the offending party for discipline sake, hoping to bring about repentance.
Lawsuits Among Believers	Ch 6	*Problem*—Christians were bringing lawsuits against Christians. *Advice*—Christians should settle legal matters before wise Christians in the church rather than in secular law courts.
Marriage	Ch 7	*Problem*—sexual passion and illicit sexual activity; separation and divorce. *Advice*—Singleness is good but marriage may be necessary because of physical needs. Concerning singleness or divorce, the basic rule is to stay together and try to work out one's situation. Staying together can allow for one partner to influence the other partner toward God. But separation is not forbidden. A person can operate as a Christian from the background that he/she was called in, whether married or single, circumcised or not, slave or free. A person is free to marry or not marry but be aware of the pressures of a marriage in the present situation. Time is short it must be used well. There is an advantage in serving the Lord in being single. One can marry and it is all right. If one can stay single it is better. Widows are free to remarry but staying single has its advantages.
Disputed Practices	Ch 8-10	*Problem*—Disputed Practices, Christian lifestyle, and Christian freedom. *Advice*—A Christian should recognize that some lifestyle practices are legitimate but may cause problems for other Christians who do not see them as legitimate. On the one hand, a Christian should be willing to forego these practices so as not to cause the Christian not having freedom to violate his/her conscience. But on the other hand, the Christian not having freedom can mature and recognize the other's freedom.
Worship Practice	Ch 11	*Problem*—Two specific disturbances included defiance of tradition among women—refusing to war head coverings as they pray publicly (strong cultural implications about this) and improper participation in the Lord's supper. *Advice*—Tradition has its place but remember public worship should not be upset because of cultural practices regarding head coverings or lack of for women. Common practice in churches has women praying in public using head coverings but it isn't worth arguing over. The Lord's supper should be a sacred remembering of the Lord's death and a reminder of his return. Do not participate in the Lord's supper in an improper manner but do so meaningfully or be judged by God.
Spiritual Gifts	Ch 12-14	*Problem*—tongues; Lack of order in public worship gatherings like multiple tongues without interpretation and inappropriate talking and questions, all causing confusion and not communicating to unbelievers visiting these services. *Advice*— There is a God-given diversity of gifts. Each has its place in the body. None should be highly exalted over others. Do things decently and in order. Let your gifts demonstrate your love for one another. Revelatory gifts should be controlled by those having them. Tongues should be done one at a time and interpreted. Prophecy should be done one at a time and evaluated. Communicate to bring about growth and to reach those needing to know the Gospel.
Doctrinal—Resurrection	Ch 15	*Problem*—false teaching which denied the resurrection. *Advice*—Paul refutes the false teaching that there is no resurrection of the dead by showing such a doctrine also denies Christ's resurrection and invalidates the Gospel message. Christ has risen from the dead and will triumphantly return again to rule and to raise up those who belong to him. A resurrected body which is immortal is necessary in order to share in God's kingdom. At the return of Chris our bodies will be transformed into immortal bodies—demonstrating Christ's victory over death.
Financial Support—Relief funds; Christian workers	Ch 16	*Problem*—the Corinthians lack of recognition of, respect for, and supporting of Christian workers; need for relief fund. *Advice*—The Corinthians should systematically put aside money for the relief fund. They should send off the Christian workers with finances.

Problems In Other Churches

Table 1,2 Co 54-2 lists in very brief form problems implied in other churches.

Table 1,2 Co 54-2. Problems in the Other Churches

Church	Possible Problems
At Rome	Understanding of Gospel both for initial salvation and for growth / Sovereign working of God—Jews and Gentiles; Giftedness; Disputed Practices.
Galatian Church	Understanding of Gospel—fundamental work of Cross/ legalism; strategic level spiritual warfare; work of Holy Spirit in a life; recovery of those who sin;
At Ephesus	At least 4 heresies—two of which are not clear (see Leadership Topics for 1,2Ti); improper conduct in worship; heretical teachings given by women; improper leadership selection criteria; acceptance of Timothy in this church setting; problems in Timothy's own life; social problem—how to help widows in need; lack of discipline of leaders falling short; conduct of slaves; rich people and their use of money; conscience; heresy causing arguments and dividing; social pressure toward negative character traits.
At Phillipi	Reaction of a leader under persecution and pressure; lack of unity in the body; specific disagreement of two women; need for joy as an expression of Christian reality.
Colosse	Seeds of Gnostic heresy—legalism in church; understanding of strategic level warfare/ place of the Cross in it; maturity issues for the body.
Thessalonica	Doctrinal problems about the second coming; misunderstanding of spiritual gifts of prophecy; lack of respect for leaders; failure to work.
On Crete	Lack of understanding of fundamental Biblical truth; in appropriate lifestyle behaviors by men and women; need for leadership selection criteria; understanding of 2nd Coming and its impact on present behavior.

Conclusion

Let me summarize and give a challenge. A major macro lesson occurring across all the leadership eras can be simply stated as: *Leadership is complex, problematic, difficult and fraught with risk—which is why leadership is needed.* Leadership is complex. Paul deals with a whole range of problems including moral issues, philosophical issues, practical everyday issues, social issues, theological issues, conceptual issues, methodological issues. Problems in a leadership situation are a main reason for the existence of leaders. Leaders must see problems not as hindrances to leadership but as the warp and woof of leadership responsibility. Problems actually can become challenges to those who can carry a positive attitude. It is in the midst of problem solving that much creative thinking emerges. Two observations are worth meditation.

a. Problems are opportunities for creative leadership to take place.
b. Problems are part of the responsibility of leaders. They come with the territory. If you are a leader you must expect to constantly deal with problems.

Here is the challenge! Paul had a burden for the churches.

> 28 Then besides all this, daily, I am burdened with my responsibility for the churches.
> 29 I feel for them when they are weak. When someone falls I'm really upset. 2Co 11:28,29

So rather than be daunted by the many problems in these churches, he did three things:

1. He sent advice to help solve problems.
2. He sent people to them to help out.
3. He prayed about them regularly.

54. Problems—The New Testament Church

I will comment on all three.

On sending advice—note the theme of 1Co. This alone should be encouraging to us who face complex problems in our leadership.

> **Theme**   **Church Problems, In Corinth,**
> - involve multiple/ complex issues: Problem about wisdom; Problem About Divisions; Problem on Toleration of Immorality; Problem of Lawsuits Among Believers; Problems About Marriage; Problem on Disputed Practices; Problem on Worship Practices; Problems About Spiritual Gifts; Problem About Resurrection; Problems in supporting Christian workers.
> - were dealt with by Paul in highly directive leadership styles, and
> - are seen as solvable if people respond to God's revelation about them.

But further, study the Pauline epistles from this perspective: What were the problems being dealt with and how did Paul deal with it?

On Sending People to Help Out—study especially Titus and Timothy's ministries.

On praying—note the following.

> First, I **thank** my God through Jesus Christ for you all, that your faith is spoken of throughout the whole world. Ro 1:8

> I **thank** my God always on your behalf, for the grace of God which is given you by Jesus Christ. 1Co 1:4

> Cease not to give **thanks** for you, making mention of you in my prayers. Eph 1:16

> I **thank** my God upon every remembrance of you. Php 1:3

> We give **thanks** to God and the Father of our Lord Jesus Christ, praying always for you. Col 1:3

> We give **thanks** to God always for you all, making mention of you in our prayers. 1Th 1:2

> We are bound to **thank** God always for you, Christian friends, as is appropriate, because your faith is really growing and your love reaches out all toward each other. 2Th 1:3

It is not enough just to pray about the needs and problems in churches. As leaders we must have a real note of thankfulness for these churches, which have many problems. My final word on problems in N.T. churches is, be thankful for these churches.

Article 55

Relevance of the Article to Paul's Corinthian Ministry

Paul, in dealing with one of the problems at Corinth—the lack of follow-through on financial obligations—talks about the importance of a promise from God. This article explains that as well as talks about the notion of promises. Leaders, who hear from God and by faith accept promises, have a foundation upon which to look with future perfect vision. See *future perfect*, **Glossary**.

55. Promises of God

Introduction

Paul makes the following wonderful statement in the midst of a challenge to the Corinthians to give to a relief fund to help out Jerusalem Christians.

> 8 And God is able to provide more than you need. You will have what you need with some left over for giving. 2Co 9:8

I believe this to be a **promise** from God that is broader than just the Corinthians. When believers give cheerfully and generously and to meet God-directed needs, I believe they can expect God to enrich them to give. The right kind of attitude is crucial however. They don't give to get. They give because God gives them grace to give and gives them liberal and joyous hearts to give. And they surrender themselves to God for this giving ministry through them. When this is done, I believe this promise is as good as gold.

I also believe the equalizing principle is in effect.

> 13 I don't intend that you should give so much that you suffer for it. But there is an equalizing principle here. Right now you have more than you need and can help them out. Later you may have need and they may help you out.

If they give out of their surplus they can expect help when they have need. A Pauline leadership value occurs here.

> **Financial Equality Principle: Christian leadership must teach that Christian giving is a reciprocal balancing between needs and surplus.**

This equalizing principle, giving when we have abundance and others have need, and in turn receiving when we have needs and others have abundance, must be recognized, embraced, and then applied very carefully so as to not create dependencies.[173]

What I have just done is introduce you to the notion of a promise from God, but one that has conditions. God will supply. But we must generously give. We can give out of our surplus. Later there will be times when we don't have enough. Others will give to us. Some promises are unconditional and are for all who want to appropriate them. Others promises are for a special group or person. Other promises have conditions. A leader must be able to discern promises of God, both for himself/herself, for the leadership

---

[173] This principle is difficult for western Christians to see. For the most part western Christians don't realize just how wealthy they are when in comparison with many other non-western Christians. With no exposure to missions and churches around the world, Christians will rarely ever really embrace this principle. Leaders must raise awareness levels about needs around the world as well as teach this principle (and model it in their own lives).

55. Promises of God

situation, and for followers within his/her influence. This article defines a promise and gives some general guidelines about promises and introduces the image of God as *The Promise Keeper*.

Promises of God

When I was a little boy my friends and I would often say, "I promise." And the other person would say, "Cross your heart and hope to die?" The meaning was, "Do you really mean it?" Now little boys make and break promises about as fast as can be. But with God it is not so. One, He does not promise helter-skelter-like. And when He does promise He can be trusted. Our problem is learning to hear Him promise and being sure what we heard was a promise from Him, for us.

Definition A <u>promise from God</u> is an assertion from God, specific or general or a truth in harmony with God's character, which is perceived in one's heart or mind concerning what He will do or not do for that one and which is sealed in our inner most being by a quickening action of the Holy Spirit and on which that one then counts.

There are three parts to the promise:

1. the cognitive part which refers to the assertion and its understanding, and
2. the affective part which is the inner most testimony to the promise, and
3. the volitional act of faith on our part which believes the assertion and feelings and thereafter counts upon it.

A leader can err in three ways, concerning promises. One, the leader may misread the assertion. That is, misinterpret what he/she thinks God will do or not do. Or two, the leader may wrongly apply some assertion to himself/herself which is does not apply. It may even be a true assertion but not for that leader or that time. Or the leader may misread the inner witness. It may not be God's Spirit quickening of the leader.

Sometimes the assertion comes from a command, or a principle, or even a direct statement of a promise God makes. The promise may be made generally to all who follow God or specifically to some. It may be for all time or for a limited time. Commands or principles are not in themselves promises. But it is when the Holy Spirit brings some truth out of them that He wants to apply to our lives that they may become promises. Such truths almost always bear on the character of God.

One thing we can know for certain, if indeed we do have a promise from God, then He will fulfill it. For Titus 1:2 asserts an important truth about God.

God can not lie.

He is the promise keeper. This is an image of God that all leaders need.

Examples of God As The Promise Keeper

God keeps his promises. He is the Promise Keeper. Table 1,2 Co 55-1 gives some examples to shore up our faith in **The Promise Keeper**. I could have chosen 100s of promises.[174]

---

[174] Over the years I have kept a listing of promises I felt God has made to me and my wife. Many of these have been fulfilled. In December of 1997 I reviewed all of these—an encouraging faith building exercise.

55. Promises of God

Table 1,2 Co 55-1. God The Promise Keeper—Examples

To Whom	Vs	Basic Promise/ Results
Abraham	Gen 12:1,2	Bless the world through Abraham. Give descendants. Spawn nations. Give a land. / This has happened and continues to happen.
Nahum	Whole book	Judgment on Nineveh/ Assyria. Promises fulfilled.
Obadiah	Whole book	Judgment on Edom. Promises fulfilled.
Habakkuk	Ch 2	Judgment on Babylon. Promises fulfilled. See Da 5.
Zechariah	Lk 1:13	Birth of John the Baptist. Promise fulfilled.
Mary	Lk 1:35	Birth of Jesus. Promise fulfilled.
Hezekiah	Isa 39:1ff, especially vs 5-7	Babylonian captivity. Royal hostages taken (Daniel was one of these). Promise fulfilled.
Daniel	Ch 2	The broad outlines of history/ nations and God's purposes. Promise fulfilled in part with more to come.
Daniel	Ch 9	Messiah and work of cross. Promise fulfilled.
Daniel	Ch 10-11:35	Again the broad outline of history particularly with reference to Israel. Everything up to 11:35 has taken place in detail as promises. The rest is yet to come.

Conclusion

The dictionary defines a promise as giving a pledge, committing oneself to do something, to make a declaration assuring that something will or will not be done or to afford a basis for expectation. Synonyms for promise include: covenant, engage, pledge, plight, swear, vow. The central meaning shared by these verbs is *to declare solemnly that one will perform or refrain from a particular course of action*. God is **The Promise Keeper**. As children of His we should learn to hear His promises and to receive them for our lives. As a leader you most likely will not make it over the long haul if you do not know God **as The Promise Keeper**.

One of the six characteristics[175] of a leader who finishes well is described as,

> **Truth is lived out in their lives so that convictions and promises of God are seen to be real.**

A leader who has God's promises and lives by them will exemplify this characteristic. Paul did. Paul, the model N.T. church leader knew God as **The Promise Keeper**. Do you?

See *cognitive; affect; volitional*; **Glossary**. See **Article**, *53. Principles of Truth*.

---

[175] The six characteristics include: 1. They maintain a personal vibrant relationship with God right up to the end. 2. They maintain a learning posture and can learn from various kinds of sources—life especially. 3. They manifest Christ-likeness in character as evidenced by the fruit of the Spirit in their lives. 4. Truth is lived out in their lives so that convictions and promises of God are seen to be real. 5. They leave behind one or more ultimate contributions. 6. They walk with a growing awareness of a sense of destiny and see some or all of it fulfilled.

Article 56

Relevance of the Article to Paul's Corinthian Ministry

Paul's Corinthian letters illustrate many of the two communication models outlined below. Leaders who wish to impact their followers must be increasingly learning about and interacting with the underlying concepts of these two models. Paul's epistles in general and 1,2 Co in particular, show his awareness of these basic communication ideas.

56. Receptor-Oriented Communication Model; Communication With Impact Model

Introduction

John makes it very clear that he has a definite purpose in writing his Gospel. He is writing in order to communicate who Jesus is, what faith is, and what it means to have eternal life.[176] This is a book which was designed to communicate. It is a model of communication. John carefully and intentionally selected whatever he included in this book in order to reach his communication goals.

The book begins with a philosophical description in which Jesus is metaphorically identified (*The Divine Word*) as the eternal God who has appeared in human form in order to communicate and reveal God to human beings. Thus the very incarnation is a strong model of communication. It is reinforcing receptor-oriented communication. One must use others' language and cultural forms if meaning is to be communicated.

Receptor oriented communication is stressed throughout. It also exemplifies impact communication. Even though Jesus is a master communicator, still not all will understand or perceive or receive his message. There are those who refuse to receive his message for their own reasons. John illustrates this in the many specially selected vignettes.

This article defines two models of communication helpful to leaders. Leaders are word gifted people. They should be concerned with effective communication. They should know the communication principles of these two models. John's Gospel illustrates both of them. Jesus was a master communicator.

The Receptor-Oriented Communication Model

Below is the conceptual make-up of the receptor-oriented communication model.

Description   The Receptor-Oriented communication model[177] describes a context made up of seven communication items, three assertions and four communication principles.

   a. The seven communication items include: a communicator, a receptor, the message, meaning slippage, paramessages, and range of acceptable variation.
   b. The three assertions are:
      (1) The aim of each communicational interaction must be to bring about a substantial correspondence between the intent of the communicator and the understanding of the receptor.
      (2) The receptor is the final formulator of the meaning of the message.

---

[176] See Jn 20:30,31.

[177] Both models given in this article were described first by Charles H. Kraft in his ground breaking work on ethnotheology, **Christianity and Culture**, 1979, published by Orbis Books, Maryknoll, N.Y. I have adapted them and made explicit the assertions and communication principles. Hopefully I have clarified these models. My work on these models was done as part of my doctorate in missiology.

56. Receptor Oriented Communication

        (3) Meanings that ultimately are formulated by the receptor are dependent primarily upon perspective influences already resident in the receptor's interpretive paradigms.

   c. The four communication principles include:
       (1) The purpose of communication is to bring a receptor to understand a message presented by a communicator in a way that substantially corresponds with the intent of the communicator.
       (2) What is understood is at least as dependent on how the receptor perceives the message and paramessages as on how the communicator presents it.
       (3) Communicators present messages via cultural forms that stimulate within the receptor's perceptive paradigms meaning and the actual message received.
       (4) The communicator, to communicate effectively, must be receptor oriented for meaning is always evaluated at the receptor's end even more than the communicators end.

The Communication with Impact Model

Jesus communicated to impact the hearers. His ministry was not just to give information but to impact the hearers and change their lives. He illustrates the basic concepts of the communication with impact model.

While communication always involves information, the focus on the following model is not primarily about communicating information but on how the receptor responds to it. The impact principles seek to enhance desired response. Three of the principles focus on the communicator and his/her choice of actions. One focuses on the message and one focuses on the recipient. In terms of John's Gospel it is evident that God wants to communicate a life-giving message with a high degree of impact. Leaders need this kind of communication in their ministries.

Description   The <u>communication with impact model</u> contains three assertions dealing with response oriented communication and five principles for enhancing impact.

   a. The three assertions are:
       (1) Messages may be used to simply convey information or to influence behavior or some combination. This model is primarily dealing with communication that influences behavior.
       (2) Messages intended primarily to influence the behavior of the receptor are determined effective in terms of the response of the receptor to the message.
       (3) There are five factors which enhance impact communication. If principles based on the five factors are used there will be high impact communication. If these principles are violated there will be low impact communication.
   b. The five impact communication principles include:
       (1) If person to person communication is used where there is high identification prolonged over time, then likelihood of impact is maximized.
       (2) If communicator, receptor and message occupy the same cultural, linguistic, and experiential frame of reference in common settings then likelihood of impact is maximized.
       (3) If the communicator has earned credibility as a respected person in the receptor's frame or reference, then likelihood of impact is maximized.
       (4) If the message is understood by the receptor to relate specifically to the life-situation of the receptor, then likelihood of impact is maximized.
       (5) If communicators present themselves and their message with high impact so as to stimulate the receptor to discover for himself/herself the value of the message to own felt needs, then likelihood of impact is maximized.

Paradigms

John's Gospel is a book about paradigms. A paradigm is a controlling perspective for viewing **REALITY**. A paradigm shift is a change in a controlling perspective so that **REALITY** is perceived

56. Receptor Oriented Communication

differently. There is difficulty in paradigm shifts because of entrenched old paradigms. Leadership frequently has vested interest in old paradigms and therefore oppose new paradigms and their implications. John intentionally selects materials that will show the new paradigm being introduced about who Jesus was and what Jesus did. He shows that it will take a supernatural breakthrough to see the new paradigm. The conflict passages show how the entrenched paradigms with vested interest oppose the new. A negative response to a paradigm will drive one deeper into the old paradigm (12:37-41). The contrast is also given with many who go through the paradigm shift and see Jesus for who he is. Need is the key driving force for accepting a new paradigm and is the main lesson for leaders in this book. Leaders must create or utilize need in followers in order to get new paradigms accepted. John shows how paradigms can blind one to receiving communication. But paradigms can change. This book is written to do that. And it shows how Jesus brought about paradigm shifts in people's lives. Jesus was a master communicator. That is what is needed to bring about paradigm shifts. But still the receptors control the understanding and use of the message. And so there are those who accept Jesus' impact communication and have life-changing paradigm shifts. And there are those who refuse to accept Jesus' impact communication and miss out on that life.

Major Intent—To Communicate, The Word Metaphor
Note John's very first words.

> 1 At the beginning of the world, the Word already existed. And the Word was with God. and the Word was God. Jn 1:1

John begins his Gospel by referring to Jesus as the eternal Word— a communication metaphor. He is referring to Jesus as God's divine communication to human beings. John begins then with God who is receptor-oriented (incarnational) in His communication. Thus we have modeled for us, both by John in his method of communicating by intentional selection with a purpose to impact readers, and with the opening content, the need for leaders to communicate with impact and to communicate in terms of the hearers.

Supreme Example of Receptor-Oriented Communication—The Incarnation
Jn 1:14-18 climaxes the extended metaphor of *The Word*. This is receptor-oriented communication at its best. God became incarnate as a human being in order to communicate about God in terms that humans could understand. Note *has readily explained* (SRN 1834) is the root word from which we get exegesis. Exegesis is a technical term in theological training referring to the careful explanation or interpretation of a passage. Jesus exegeted God for us. He explained Him so we could know and understand Him and our relationship to Him. God has crossed communication barriers to communicate to us, his followers. Can we do any less as leaders in communicating to our followers? Communication is a major function that leaders are involved in. Communication is a major means of influence for leaders

Conclusion
Note the four observations given below.

a. Jesus used receptor-oriented awareness in all his communication.
b. A leader must constantly communicate with the receptors in mind.
c. The incarnational model serves as a paradigm which reinforces the importance of communicating to followers in their language and forms.
d. The major leadership value,

Leaders Should View Personal Relationships As An Important Part Of Ministry,

takes on increased meaning when viewed in light of receptor-oriented and impact oriented communication models. Personal relationships with prolonged interaction form the seedbed for enhancing communication. That is at least one reason why three years personally spent with the disciples fomented a world-wide movement that has lasted to this day.

Article 57

Relevance of the Article to Paul's Corinthian Ministry

The essence of Christian behavior in community—that is, living out the teaching of Christ so that they are seen and recognized both within and without the Christian community—are contained in the reciprocal commands that are given. Most of these reciprocal commands, the one-another commands, are given in Paul's epistles. At least three of these commands are given explicitly in the Corinthian letters. Several more are implied as Paul seeks to solve problems in the Christian community there.

57. Reciprocal Living—The One-Another Commands

Ray Steadman started something when he wrote **Body-Life** in the 70s. There was such a hunger for fellowship in churches that his work caught on among many. At the time I was with the West Indies Mission where we also had caught that same fever. Harold Alexander had been teaching in the French world of missions a concept that was akin to Ray Steadman's basic intent. The English translation of Alexander's work was called *Reciprocal Living* since it had to do with the one-another commands in the N.T. Sue Harville, also with the West Indies mission did a scholarly analysis. She then put her analysis into a self-study format. The resulting manual containing these N.T. commands was called **Reciprocal Living**.[178] I am attempting to reduce her outstanding manual to a simple article. These third person imperatives (at least they carry that kind of force) describe a number of relationships which, if in a local church, make that church a body-life church. The hunger for fellowship, so needed in the younger generation of today, could be filled if leaders saw the creation of a fellowship who lived out the reciprocal commands as a major leadership responsibility.

Reciprocal living refers to the mutual obligations and relationships which believers have as a result of their common relationship to Christ as members of His body. It may be defined as the outward manifestation of fellowship in which each believer puts all that he/she is and all that he/she has at the disposal of all other believers and that others do the same for him/her in order to enable one another in Christian living.

I will use Harville's categorization of the reciprocal commands which includes four major categories.

Table 1,2 Co 57-1. Harville's Four Categories of Reciprocal Commands

Commands	Number In New Testament
Command Bearing Upon Inter-Relationships	8
The Negative Commands	7
The Mutual Edification Commands	5
The Mutual Service Commands	5

Commands Bearing Upon Inter-Relationships

There are certain commands which seem to be basic to the practice of reciprocal living. These are the commands that tell Christians how they should relate to one another. These commands govern relationships. The first and foremost command is to love one another. Without love, the church is nothing and does little or nothing of value. Therefore, mutual relationships of love must be the background of mutual edification and mutual service. The eight commands of this category are summarized below in a very abbreviated form. Because of the length limitations of this article I have left off implications, Biblical

---

[178] **Reciprocal Living** by Sue Harville. Published in 1976 by the West Indies Mission of Coral Gables, Florida. This is now out of print as is her small groups manual, **Walking In Love**, which was used as a simplified 13 part study of the reciprocal commands. I am negotiating to get these fine materials reprinted. I have copied directly Harville's definitions of each of the reciprocal commands.

57. Reciprocal Living—The One-Another Commands

examples, restrictions and other information for each command. I am simply identifying these commands and commending them for your further study.

Table 1,2 Co 57-2. Commands Bearing Upon Inter-Relationships

Command	Biblical Reference	Explanation/ Description/ or Definition
Love One Another	Jn 13:34	Love is an inward attitude of affection, expressed in benevolent behavior or action, which seeks the ultimate welfare of another. Loving one another is allowing this inward attitude to control our behavioral relationships with other Christians—so that we indeed seek their ultimate welfare. (also the basic idea occurs indirectly in: Jn 15:12,17; Ro 12:9,10; 13:8; Gal 5:14; 1Th 3:11,12; 4:9,10; Jas 2:8; 1Pe 1:22; 3:8; 1Jn 3:11,23; 4:7, 11, 12, 21; 2Jn 5)
Receive One Another	Ro 15:7	Receiving one another is taking to ourselves our brothers or sisters in Christ, freely and without constraint and reserve, in full recognition of our equal and mutual fellowship in Christ.
Greet One Another	Ro 16:16 1Co 16:20 2Co 13:12 1Pe 5:14	Greeting one another is an outward acknowledgment of our mutual life in Christ and our brotherly love for one another.
Have The Same Care for One Another	1Co 12:24,25	Having the same care for one another is showing an impartial and equal interest in the welfare and ministry of every believer based on the full recognition and appreciation of that one's God-given position and function in the body of Christ.
Submit To One Another	Eph 5:18-21	Submitting to one another is inwardly considering oneself to be under the authority of fellow Christians and willingly complying with their decisions, instructions, or wishes.
Tarry One for Another	1 Cor 11:33	Tarry one for another refers to waiting patiently for folks in order to partake together of a love feast (often associated with the Lord's Supper)
Forbear One Another	Eph 4:1-3; Col 3:12-14	Forbearing one another is graciously enduring and putting up with the displeasing, offensive, or sinful attitudes and actions in others. It includes the idea that rebuke, discipline, or correction be delayed as long as possible in hope that the offender recognize his/her offense and take steps to correct it.
Confess Your Sins To One Another	Jas 5:16	Confessing sins to one another is acknowledging to fellow-believers one's sins as an outward sign of sorrow for the offense, intent to change, and desire for reconciliation. It presupposes a previous or simultaneous acknowledgment of the particular sin to God.
Forgive One Another	Eph 4:31,32	Forgiving one another is regarding a fellow-believer who has wronged or offended you without contempt or resentment but rather with compassion, not holding that one accountable for the wrong or its consequences.

The Negative Commands

Just as the Scriptures tell Christians how to relate to one another, it points out and forbids several sins that are destructive to Christian fellowship. These negative commands serve to remind believers that they are still influenced by the old sinful nature and must make an active and conscious effort to yield themselves to God rather than to sin.

Table 1,2 Co 57-3. The Negative Commands

Command	Biblical Reference	Explanation/ Description/ or Definition
Do Not Judge One Another	Ro 14:13	Judging one another is reckoning one's own position on a disputed practice or doctrinal question as superior to others' positions and expressing criticism, condemnation, or displeasure at their disagreement.
Do Not Speak Evil of One Another	Jas 4:11	Speaking evil of one another is speaking of a fellow-believer in such a way as to discredit, dishonor, depreciate or belittle his/her character or actions.
Do Not Murmur Against One Another	Jas 5:9	Murmuring against one another is expressing discontent, impatience, or displeasure with one believer to other believers, usually in a secret or in a covert manner.
Do Not Bite and Devour One Another	Gal 5:14,15	Biting and devouring one another is showing hostility and ill-will to fellow-believers through attacks on their character, worth, motives, beliefs, or actions in order to establish one's own advantage or superiority.
Do Not Provoke One Another	Gal 5:25,26	Provoking one another is challenging the work, reputation, position or belief of a fellow-believer by words or actions in an effort to assert oneself or gain recognition.
Do Not Envy One Another	Gal 5:25,26	Envying one another is desiring for oneself the position, ability, achievement, or possessions of a fellow believer, usually with a sense of resentment that the other has the advantages one desires.
Do Not Lie To One Another	Col 3:9,10	Lying to one another is telling as true that which is known to be false, distorting the truth in any way, or conveying a false impression of oneself or something, with the intent to deceive another believer.

Commands Bearing Upon Mutual Edification

When something is edified, it is built up, strengthened or fortified. The N. T. uses this term of building up and strengthening of believers in their faith so that they live lives that are pleasing to God in every way. One of the ways that God has chosen to edify His people is through the ministry of believers themselves. Christians are to edify one another. Mutual relationships of love form the basis for this ministry of edification. In fact, Paul tells us that love edifies (1Co 8:2). But the Christian life is more than relationships: It is obedience to all of God's will which He has revealed in His Word. This mutual edification begins, but does not stop, with love. To edify one another in the Biblical sense of the term, believers must also help one another to learn and apply the Word of God in their daily lives. And this task is not meant only for pastors and teachers. All Christians are to be involved. These mutual edification commands tell Christians how they can help one another, out of love for one another, learn and apply the Word of God in daily living.

Table 1,2 Co 57-4. The Mutual Edification Commands

Command	Biblical Reference	Explanation/ Description/ or Definition
Building Up One Another	Ro 14:19; 1Th 5:11	Building up one another is a process of interaction among believers by which they promote, by teaching or example, the development of Christ-like character and behavior in one another.
Teach One Another	Col 3:16	Teaching One Another is instructing, explaining, or exposing Biblical truth to fellow believers in such a way that they may understand the truth and are enabled and encouraged to apply it in their own lives.
Exhort One Another	1Th 5:11; Heb 3:12,13	Exhorting One Another is a three-fold ministry in which believers urge each other to action in terms of applying Scriptural truth, encourage each other generally with Scriptural truth, and comfort each other through the application of Scriptural truth to their needs. The main thrust of the command is that believers should strive to

		help each other understand the implications of the word of God for daily living.
Admonish One Another	Ro 15:14; Col 3:16	Admonishing one another is a disciplinary ministry in which believers bring to each other's attention their sinful attitudes and practices or unmet obligations, and offer corrective instruction that will enable and encourage them to bring those areas of their lives into conformity with the Word of God.
Speak to One Another in Psalms, Hymns, and Spiritual Songs	Eph 5:18-20; Col 3:16	Speaking to one another in psalms, hymns, and spiritual songs, or singing to one another, is a means of teaching, exhorting or admonishing others, and joining others in praise to God, in words set to music.

Commands Bearing Upon Mutual Service

The thought of being a servant is not appealing to most people. Serving is a hard and sometimes thankless job. And servants must continually put the needs and interests of others before their own. But this is just what Christians are supposed to do—be servants to one another, not grudgingly, but out of love for one another. Because Christ loved us He made Himself a servant to us throughout His life and finally in His atoning death on the cross. Because we love Him and His people, we are to make ourselves servants—to Him, but also to one another. Just as Christians who truly love one another will seek to edify one another, they will also seek to serve one another. These mutual service commands deal with ways that Christians can express their love to one another in practical and down-to-earth service.

Table 1,2 Co 57-5. Mutual Service Commands

Command	Biblical Reference	Explanation/ Description/ or Definition
Be Servants To One Another	Gal 5:13,14	Being servants to one another through love is freely and voluntarily obligating oneself to undertake for fellow-believers any work or task which may be necessary, helpful, or advantageous to their spiritual, physical, or mental welfare.
Bear One Another's Burdens	Gal 6:2	Bearing one another's burden is taking upon oneself a fellow-believer's difficulty, problem, or oppressive circumstance as if it were our own and taking any possible action to alleviate it.
Use Hospitality To One Another	1Pe 4:7	Using hospitality to one another is receiving into one's home fellow-Christians, especially strangers and those in distress, and providing for their physical and material needs as for one's own.
Be Kind To One Another	Eph 4:31,32	Being kind to one another is expressing love and benevolence to fellow-Christians in gestures of generosity, helpfulness, and thoughtfulness, without regard to circumstances and expecting nothing in return.
Pray For One Another	Jas 5:16	Praying for one another is making known to God the sins, needs, or concerns of fellow-believers, asking Him to act on their behalf so that His will might be accomplished.

Closure

These reciprocal commands need to be studied in depth in order to further clarify them, to identify implications, to see limitations of them, to see Biblical examples and non-examples of them. Simply reading them challenges a leader. But once you understand them you will want to be part of a fellowship which practices them, that is, enjoys Ray Steadman's body-life. No Christian leader can expect to see these one-another commands lived out among his followers apart from the powerful ministry of the Holy Spirit.

Article 58

Relevance of the Article to Paul's Corinthian Ministry

Social base issues refer to the four basic social needs that are needed by a leader in his/her home base situation: (1) emotional support; (2) economic support; (3) strategic support, and (4) basic physical needs. Frequently when these needs are unmet or met poorly they become barriers for leaders to finish well. Social base issues can relate to several of the barriers that torpedo leaders along the way. Paul deals in the 1 Co letter with at least two major problems related to social base issues—immorality and the whole question of separation and divorce. Paul is strict, yet merciful in his approach to both problems. Leaders need to be aware of social base issues. Many leaders in my own generation, while undoubtedly doing good work for God missed it in terms of some of these social base issues. It shows up in their generational problems. This article is a condensation of a much longer position paper, Social Base Processing, available in the **Clinton Reader—Life Long Development Concepts.**

58. Social Base Issues

Introduction

All leaders operate out of some home base environment. The more stable that environment is the more likely the leader is to move toward a focused ministry. A weak or ineffective social base setting can detract from a focused life. Below are given some minimum constructs about social base issues.

Social Base, Social Base Processing, and Social Base Needs

Definition   Social base refers to the personal living environment out of which a leader operates and which provides: (1) emotional support; (2) economic support; (3) strategic support, and (4) basic physical needs.

Definition   Social base processing is a very general category referring to the means God uses to lead to a given social base configuration as well as His use of critical incidents with regard to social base issues and their effect upon leaders.

The simple fact is that all leaders have personal social needs that must be met. Social base processing has to do with God's shaping with regards to those needs. Here are some basic needs I have identified. Perhaps there are others.[179] Perhaps a different taxonomy could be developed. This is simply what I have seen and I have found it useful in talking to leaders about what is happening in their lives. Table 1,2 Co 58-1 lists the four social base needs.

---

[179] Perhaps a psychologists or sociologist majoring in this field would have a more integrated typology. Perhaps Maslow's taxonomy could be probed in terms of this definition. Not being an expert in these fields I have simply described what I have seen. I am certainly open to more rigorous identification of such a taxonomy. My criterion is simply, "Will it help us as leaders to understand ourselves more and to become better leaders?"

58. Social Base Issues

Table 1,2 Co 58-1. 4 SOCIAL BASE NEEDS

Component	Explanation/ Details of Component
1. Emotional Support	Companionship, Listener, Recreational Outlets, Empathetic Understanding, Affirmation of Personal Worth, etc.
2. Economic Support	Financial Base which covers living expenses, medical, educational, basic physical needs like food, clothing, and transportation, recreational reprieves, etc.
3. Strategic Support	The backup for giving meaning to life; affirming that what we do is important. The sharing of ministry or career ideas, philosophy, problems, personal development--in short giving the big picture which encompasses our major choices in life.
4. Social Support--Basic Physical Needs	The necessities of life--how do we eat, sleep, have clean clothes, meet our physical drives. Where do we stay? Are we safe? Is it a place of retreat, refreshment, etc.?

Social Base Patterns

Various leaders meet these needs in various ways. In western cultures the social base revolves around singleness and its support elements or the nuclear family, and various other family patterns that are emerging in modern society. In western missions, spouses are often very influential in the development of the partner. Many relational lessons and other important insights crucial to development of a leader come via the causal source of a spouse or other important member of the social base and relates to social base needs.

In non-western society the social base may relate very strongly to an extended family or other kinship network. Various societies meet social base needs in culturally specific ways. The four social base needs (economic, emotional, strategic, and physical) will vary in terms of importance. In one culture one may have priority. In another culture a different need may have priority.

Social Base Patterns For Singles--3 Elements

Comparative study of single leaders in ministry identified three elements seen over and over in various combinations—that is, forming patterns of how singles meet their social base needs. Social base patterns for singles involve various configurations over time of the three basic elements shown in Table 1,2 Co 58-2.

Table 1,2 Co 58-2. Three Elements Involved In Singles Social Bases

Element	Explanation
1. Isolation	a. Solo Isolation--live alone, provide own emotional, economic, strategic, and social support needs primarily by one's self. b. Quasi-Isolation--same as solo isolation with aperiodic retreats into some other friendly social setting.
2. Partnerships	a. Same Sex--develop a partnership with another member of the same sex, following along the lines of patterns for married couples. b. Opposite Sex--this can be dangerous, but partnerships along the lines of the co-ministry pattern with the exception of totally meeting the social support--basic physical needs.
3. Groups	a. Part of a Team--be part of a team committed to each other and to providing social base needs. b. Part of a Family--be adopted into a family (seen in missionary situations on field)--more deliberate proactive use of forays. c. Live in Community--groups formed with singles and couples who opt to live out of the same physical set-up.

Social Base Patterns For Married--Three Major Combinations

Table 1,2 Co 58-3 lists several potential profiles focusing on how spouses arrange roles to meet the four social base needs--with a primary focus on economic and physical needs. I do not attach values to

58. Social Base Issues

these profiles. I simply describe them. I believe all are legitimate--that is, one is not necessarily more Biblical than the other. I do not indicate which are more prevalent today. There are real illustrations in life which I have seen of all of these though I admit that several of them are rarer. These combinations will vary over time.

Table 1,2 Co 58-3. Social Base Profiles—Three Major Ones for Marrieds

Name of Combination	Explanation
1. Internal/ External Ministry Profile (synonym: release pattern)	*The basic idea: This profile applies to a married couple with children. One spouse concentrates on external ministry (career) providing economic support; the other spouse concentrates on internal ministry to the family including a special care for the social thus <u>releasing the first</u> to freely engage in external ministry; both dabble in the other needs.* Spouse #1: <u>heavy engagement in external ministry</u>, emotional support, <u>economic support</u>, (strategic support) Spouse #2: not heavy external ministry--some on the side, sees children as a focused ministry--internal ministry, emotional support, (economic support), (strategic support), <u>social</u>.

2. Co-Ministry/ Partnership Profile	*The Basic Idea: There are two profiles for this. One when the couple has no children and one when the couple has children. Both spouses see themselves operating in the same ministry (career) setting together. Each has a significant role in the setting.*
	  a. No Children--each spouse has a full time external ministry focus
	    Spouse #1: <u>heavy direct ministry</u>, share economic, provide strategic support, share social, emotional
	    Spouse #2: <u>heavy direct ministry</u>, share economic, provide strategic support, share social, emotional
	  b. Children--each spouse views ministry as a partnership in external and internal ministry
	    Spouse #1: part time <u>direct ministry</u>, share economic, provide strategic support, share social, emotional
	    Spouse #2: part time <u>direct ministry</u>, share economic, provide strategic support, share social, emotional

3. Independent Ministry Profile	*The Basic Idea: Both spouses give themselves to full time ministry (career) in different settings which are relatively independent of each other.*
	    Spouse #1: heavy direct ministry in different area from spouse's ministry, share social and economic support, (strategic)
	    Spouse #2: heavy direct ministry in different area from spouse's ministry, share social and economic support, (strategic)

Conclusion

Few leaders finish well. Comparative studies revealed six major barriers to leaders finishing well. One of those barriers included social base issues. A social base in proper order enhances a ministry. Problems involving the social base can eventually take a leader out of ministry.[180] Four important observations about social base issue include:

1. Over A Lifetime Social Base Profiles And Patterns Will Change. We Need To Anticipate These Changes.

---

[180] I have only touched the basic ideas about social base. See **For Further Study Bibliography**, Dr. J. Robert Clinton, *Social Base Processing--The Home Base Environment Out of Which A Leader Works* (1993). This is a position paper, which treats this subject in detail, including time/lines showing patterns. Three of the barriers (Sexual—Illicit Relationships; family—Critical Issues; Finances—Their Use and Abuse) to finishing well relate directly to social base issues. Two of the other three are frequently overlapped with social base issues (Power—Its Abuse; Pride—Inappropriate).

58. Social Base Issues

2. We Need To Be Proactive About This Rather Than Reactive.
3. We Need To Be Aware That Social Base Needs Not Being Met Are The Seed Plot Of A Dysfunctional Pattern.
4. There Are No Value Judgments On Which Profiles And Patterns Are Better Or Not--These Are Unique Profiles And Patterns Which Flow Out Of Foundations, Beingness, Giftedness, And Destiny Processing.

A leader who does not work on social base issues by choice may well find himself/herself working in desperation, not by choice, to save a social base and ministry.

Article 59

Relevance of the Article to Paul's Corinthian Ministry

Of all the things that Paul modeled for his followers, and yes, us too, the sovereign mindset stands out as representative of what he meant in his Ro 8:28-30 sanctification concept. Paul viewed the happenings in his life through a God-lens, which always saw God's shaping activity involved. Such an attitude allowed him to make the best of his situations and to persevere on to a good finish. We do well to understand this concept—a sovereign mindset. If we do, we will find ourselves asking more *what questions* (what is God doing?) and fewer *why questions* (why me?) when deep processing comes our way. Hence, deep processing, difficult as it may be, will not blindside us. And we will have additional experiential resources (2 Cor 1:3,4) to help others out as they go through deep processing.

59. Sovereign Mindset

Mindset burst upon our English language scene in the mid-eighties. So it is a relative newcomer to English speakers. Not all English speakers even know it. But its definition is as old as the Bible itself. What is a mindset? A mindset is a fixed mental attitude or disposition—formed by experience, education, prejudice, or the like—that predetermines a person's responses to and interpretations of situations. One of the great Bible leaders, Paul the Apostle, demonstrated a special kind of mindset. I call it a sovereign mindset. A sovereign mindset represents one leadership value[181] that can make the difference for a Christian leader.[182] And I want to suggest that if you do not have this mindset you probably won't make it in ministry—at least not as an effective leader who will finish well.

A leadership value is an underlying assumption a leader holds which affects how the leader acts or perceives in leadership situations. It is a mindset, an underlying controlling force, which gives meaning to ourselves and explains whey we do things or think things. It can relate to a belief. It can relate to personal ethical conduct. It can relate to personal feelings desired about situations. It can relate to ideas of what brings success or failure in ministry. It can be rooted in personality shaping. It can be rooted in heritage. It can be rooted in the critical shaping activities that describes our personal history of leadership development.

Paul models this leadership value, a sovereign mindset, more than any other New Testament Church leader.[183] Quickly glance through the two passages below to catch the flavor of this important leadership insight. Pay special attention to the boldfaced words.

> 3 Blessed [be] God, even the Father of our Lord Jesus Christ, the Father of mercies, and
> the God of all comfort; 4 Who comforts us in all our tribulation, **that we may be able to**

---

[181] See also the **Article**, *51. Pauline Leadership Values*, which touches on 19 important leadership values derived from the book of 2Co. Values are desperately needed today in our world of tolerance for anything except absolutes. This article describes one important Christian leadership value.

[182] It can for a secular leader too. A Christian leader believes that God is involved in the events of life and therefore looks to learn what God has for him/her in the happenings of life. A secular leader who does not believe that God is or is involved in life's events can still also profit greatly from the happenings in life if that leader has a learning posture and believes that life's experiences can be used to teach lessons. The learning posture needed is simply, All of life is preparing us for all of the rest of life. We can be better leaders if we learn from life's experiences and let that learning inform our leadership. See also the **Article**, *30. Leadership Lessons, Seven Major Identified*, one of which deals with learning posture, "Effective leaders maintain a learning posture all of their lives."

[183] Paul is a major model for a Christian leader in the N.T. Leadership Era. We have more biographical information on Paul than any other Church leader. He himself recognizes the importance of modeling. See Php 4:9 and other cross-references.

59. Sovereign Mindset

comfort them which are in any trouble, by the comfort wherewith we ourselves are comforted of God. 5 For as the sufferings of Christ abound in us, so our consolation also abounds by Christ. 6 And whether we be afflicted, [it is] for your consolation and salvation, which is effectual in the enduring of the same sufferings which we also suffer: or whether we be comforted, [it is] for your consolation and salvation. 7 And our hope of you [is] steadfast, knowing, that as you are partakers of the sufferings, so [shall you be] also of the consolation. 2 Corinthians 1:3-7

8 For we would not, brethren, have you ignorant of our trouble which came to us in Asia, that we were pressed out of measure, above strength, inasmuch that we despaired even of life: 9 But we had the sentence of death in ourselves, **that we should not rely on ourselves, but in God which raises the dead: 10 Who delivered us from so great a death**, and does deliver: in whom we trust that he will yet deliver [us]; 11 You also helping together by prayer for us, that for the gift [bestowed] upon us by the means of many persons thanks may be given by many on our behalf. 2 Corinthians 1:8-11

Once you know what a sovereign mindset is, you can easily see it in the these two previous quotes. But this sovereign mindset just leaps out from the pages in the following quotes.

For this cause I Paul, the **prisoner of Jesus Christ** for you Gentiles, Eph 3:1

I therefore, the **prisoner of the Lord**, implore you to walk worthy of your Christian calling. Eph 4:1

So that my **bonds in Christ** are manifest in all the palace, and in all other [places]. Php1:13

Don't be ashamed of the testimony of our Lord, nor of me **his prisoner**: but share also in the afflictions of the gospel according to the power of God; 2Ti 1:8

Paul, a **prisoner of Jesus Christ**, and Timothy [our] brother, unto Philemon our dearly beloved, and fellow laborer, Phm 1:1

Yet for love's sake I rather implore you, being such an one as Paul the aged, and now also **a prisoner of Jesus Christ**. Phm 1:9

Paul don't you have that wrong? Aren't you a prisoner of the Roman empire? Why do you say a prisoner of Jesus Christ. What a strange way to make your point! Its all in how you see it. Yes, Paul was a prisoner of the Roman Empire. But no matter what they intended, Paul knew God would use it for God's purposes. For you see, You Paul operated under a sovereign mindset?

Definition   A <u>sovereign mindset</u> is a way of viewing life's activities so as to see and respond to God's purposes in them.

Remember, a mindset is a 1. A fixed mental attitude or disposition that predetermines a person's responses to and interpretations of situations. Paul had a fixed mental attitude toward the things that happened to him. He saw God in them. Or as he says in 2Ti 3:11, "...out of them all God worked."

God was sovereignly and providentially working through all of life's circumstances to shape Paul, guide him, and make him the great leader he became. Four keys to Paul's sovereign mindset include:

1. Paul recognized God's hand in life happenings—no matter who or what the immediate cause.
2. Paul submitted to God's deeper purposes in life happenings.
3. Paul learned and used the lessons derived from these life happenings.
4. Paul shared those lessons (and God's provision in them) with others.

59. Sovereign Mindset

His deep experiences with God were at the heart of the spiritual authority[184] he had with followers.

Let me come back to the two passages I first cited as indicating a sovereign mindset. I want to draw out some leadership observations that directly apply to Christian leaders.

From 2Co 1:3-7:

1. God will meet us in deep processing.
2. We are helped in order to help.
3. Deep processing tests our own value in the sufficiency of Christ.
4. Our own development through processing gives us hope that our followers can also know the sufficiency of Christ in their deep processing.

From 2Co 1:8-11

1. We really trust in God when we come to the end of our own resources.
2. Deep processing is meant to be shared.
3. Deep processing shared brings partnership in prayer.
4. God receives much more praise when our situation is solved.

A leader with a sovereign mindset recognizes that at the heart of all God's shaping activities is the idea that processing is never just for himself/herself alone. We as leaders are shaped by critical incidents and shaping activities for our development, yes! But our processing is also for our followers. It is this confidence in God's meeting us in deep processing that gives us confidence in His sufficiency. And a by-product of that confidence is spiritual authority, the dominant power base of a Christian leader.

Stated as a leadership value, the sovereign mindset strikingly challenges us.

Value   **Leaders Ought To See God's Hand In Their Circumstances As Part Of His Plan For Developing Them As Leaders.**

Paul had a sovereign mindset. He kept it till the end. It was one of the secrets of his finishing well. This leadership value is fundamental to a Christian view of the development of a leader.

See **Articles**, *51. Pauline Leadership Values; 30. Leadership Lessons—Seven Major Identified; 71. Value Driven Leadership.*

---

[184] See also the **Article**, *60. Spiritual Authority*, which describes a major power base for a Christian leader.

Article 60

Relevance of the Article to Paul's Corinthian Ministry

Paul had no positional authority with the Corinthian church. He depended on spiritual authority. If that wasn't to be honored then he was in deep trouble. As you read through these six characteristics, think of whether Paul does or does not demonstrate them in the Corinthian situation. See also **Article** *21. Influence, Power, and Authority* Forms as you ascertain how Paul used his power base to influence the Corinthian church.

60. Spiritual Authority—Six Characteristics

A Biblical leader is a person with God-given capacities and with God-given responsibility who is influencing specific groups of God's people toward God's purposes for them. To influence, a leader must have some power base. I am indebted to Dennis Wrong[185] for helping me identify a taxonomy of concepts dealing with power. Wrong has influence as the highest level on his taxonomy, power next, and authority third. Influence can be unintended or intended. In terms of leadership we are interested in intended influence. Intended influence can be subdivided into four power forms, the second level: Force, Manipulation, Authority, and Persuasion. All of these are important for Christian leaders with the final two being the most important—authority and persuasion—since spiritual authority is related to both. Authority, the third level, can further be sub-divided into coercive, inducive, legitimate, competent, personal. A leader will need to use various combinations of these power forms to influence people. However,

Effective leaders value spiritual authority as a primary power base.

This is one of seven major leadership lessons that I have identified from comparative study of effective leaders. This article defines spiritual authority and gives some guidelines about its use.

Spiritual Authority—What Is It?

Spiritual authority is the ideal power base for a leader to use with mature believers who respect God's authority in a leader. A simplified definition focusing on the notion of maturity of believers is:

Definition Spiritual authority[186] is the
- right to influence,
- conferred upon a leader by followers,
- because of their perception of spirituality in that leader.

An expanded definition focusing on how a leader gets and uses it is:

Definition Spiritual authority [187] is that
- characteristic of a God-anointed leader,
- developed upon an experiential power base (giftedness, character, deep experiences with God),

that enables him/her to influence followers through
- persuasion,
- force of modeling, and
- moral expertise.

---

[185] See Dennis H. Wrong, **Power—Its Forms, Bases, and Uses**. 1979. San Francisco, CA: Harper and Row.

[186] This is labeled as extrinsic spiritual authority by Crowe in his PhD dissertation on Sprtiual Authority.

[187] Crowe calls this intrinsic spiritual authority. See bibliography for Crowe's work.

60. Spiritual Authority—Six Characteristics

Spiritual authority comes to a leader in three major ways. As leaders go through deep experiences with God they experience the sufficiency of God to meet them in those situations. They come to know God. This experiential knowledge of God and the deep experiences with God are part of the experiential acquisition of spiritual authority. A second way that spiritual authority comes is through a life which models godliness. When the Spirit of God is transforming a life into the image of Christ those characteristics of love, joy, peace, long suffering, gentleness, goodness, faith, meekness, temperance carry great weight in giving credibility that the leader is consistent inward and outward. A third way that spiritual authority comes is through gifted power. When a leader can demonstrate gifted power in ministry—that is, a clear testimony to divine intervention in the ministry via his/her gifts—there will be spiritual authority. Now while all three of these ways of getting spiritual authority should be a part of a leader, it is frequently the case that one or more of the elements dominates. From the definitions and description of how spiritual authority comes you can readily see that a leader using spiritual authority does not force his/her will on followers.

What Are Some Guidelines—To Maximize Use and Minimize Abuse

The following descriptive characteristics about spiritual authority sets some limits, describe ideals, warn against abuse and in general gives helpful guidelines for leaders who desire spiritual authority as a primary means of influence.

Six Characteristics And Limits Of Spiritual Authority

These six descriptions were derived from my own observations of leaders and from adaptations made from several writers on power such as Watchman Nee, R. Baine Harris, and Richard T. De George. Nee was a Chinese Christian leader. The other two are secular authorities on power and authority in leadership.

Table 1,2 Co 60-1. Six Characteristics of Spiritual Authority

Characterization	Statement
1. Ultimate Source	Spiritual authority has its ultimate source in Christ. It is representative religious authority. It is His authority and presence in us which legitimates our authority. Accountability to this final authority is essential.
2. Power Base	Spiritual authority rests upon an experiential power base. A leader's personal experiences with God and the accumulated wisdom and development that comes through them lie at the heart of the reason why followers allow influence in their lives. It is a resource which is at once on-going and yet related to the past. Its genuineness as to the reality of experience with God is confirmed in the believer by the presence and ministry of the Holy Spirit who authenticates that experiential power base.
3. Power Forms	Spiritual authority influences by virtue of persuasion. Word gifts are dominant in this persuasion. Influence is by virtue of legitimate authority. Positional leadership carries with it recognition of qualities of leadership which are at least initially recognized by followers. Such authority must be buttressed by other authority forms such as competent authority, and personal authority.
4. Ultimate Good	The aim of influence using spiritual authority is the ultimate good of the followers. This follows the basic Pauline leadership principle seen in 2Co 10:8.
5. Evaluation	Spiritual authority is best judged longitudinally over time in terms of development of maturity in believers. Use of coercive and manipulative forms of authority will usually reproduce like elements in followers. Spiritual authority will produce mature followers who will make responsible moral choices because they have learned to do so.
6. Non-Defensive	A leader using spiritual authority recognizes submission to God who is the ultimate authority. Authority is representative. God is therefore the responsible agent for defending spiritual authority. A person moving in spiritual authority does not have to insist on obedience. Obedience is the moral responsibility of the follower. Disobedience, that is, rebellion to spiritual authority, means that a follower is not subject to God Himself. He/she will answer to God for that. The leader can rest upon God's vindication if it is necessary.

60. Spiritual Authority—Six Characteristics

Remember,

Effective leaders value spiritual authority as a primary power base.[188]

See *power forms* (various definitions), **Glossary**. See **Articles**, *21. Influence, Power, and Authority Forms; 30. Leadership Lessons—Seven Major Identified.*

---

[188] They also know that it will take varied forms of power including coercive, inducive, positional, personal, competence and others to influence immature believers toward maturity. But the ideal is always there to use spiritual authority with mature believers.

Article 61

Relevance of the Article to Paul's Corinthian Ministry

When Titus arrived with the news of the Corinthian response to Paul's letter, you can rest assured that it was a spiritual benchmark. It brought great rejoicing for Paul and reassured him of God's continuing miraculous work in his life. This article points out the importance of spiritual benchmarks in a leader's life (and also by implication in a corporate group's life; see Joshua's stones of remembrance incident). All leaders need spiritual benchmarks to remember, especially as they move into and through deep processing.

61. Spiritual Benchmarks

A benchmark provides a point of reference from which future measurements can be made. A spiritual benchmark represents a point of reference for a leader. It refers to something that happens in the life of the leader, which serves as positive proof of God's activity in that life. It is something that a leader can look back upon and thus be encouraged to continue when confused or in a discouraging situation. Because it is foundational, sure and certain, and had the distinct imprint of God's Hand on the life.

Joseph's two dreams when he was 17 years old were spiritual benchmarks. Over the next 22 years he clung to them through thick and thin. Finally, they were realized when Joseph was 39 years old. But it was Joseph's remembering them and trusting God because of them that made them noteworthy spiritual benchmarks.[189]

Isaiah's encounter with God in the year that King Uzziah died was a spiritual benchmark that forever shaped his ministry.[190]

Paul's experience on the road to Damascus and the subsequent encounter with Ananias was the spiritual benchmark which shaped Paul's whole life purpose. He referred to it several times along the way to validate his ministry.[191] The Corinthian crisis—eventually resolved by Paul's epistles, served as a major spiritual benchmark for Paul.

Spiritual benchmarks usually represent destiny events. They are reminders of God's intervention in a life. Spiritual benchmarks serve several functions:

1. they frequently serve as encouragement later in ministry when things are tough,
2. they often are prophetic and hence help give perspective later in ministry,
3. they usually are key to understanding destiny shaping (destiny preparation, destiny revelation, destiny fulfillment).

All leaders need one or more spiritual benchmarks that they can look back to in order to remember God has worked in their life; He will continue to work just as he did at that benchmark time.

See *critical incident; sense of destiny; destiny processing; leadership committal;* **Glossary**. See **Articles**: *42. Paul—A Sense of Destiny; 10. Destiny Pattern; Divine Affirmation in the Life of Jesus.*

---

[189] See Ps 105:19.
[190] See Isa 6.
[191] See Ac 9, 22, 26.

Article 62

Relevance of the Article to Paul's Corinthian Ministry

Note Paul's strong statement in 1 Co 9:24-27. "I am serious about finishing well in my Christian ministry. I discipline myself for fear that after challenging others into the Christian life I myself might become a casualty"—Clinton Paraphrase. At this stage of his life, probably early 50s, he was aware of the need for willful choices of discipline in his life. As you read through this article clarifying various kinds of spiritual disciplines—think through the record of Paul's ministry, not only with the Corinthians, but others. Which of these disciplines do you see in Paul's life? Disciplines are one of the 5 Major Enhancements frequently seen in leaders' lives, who finished well. Leaders who want to finish well do well to deliberately choose needed spiritual disciplines in their life.

62. Spiritual Disciplines—And On-going Leadership

Introduction

Comparative study of effective leaders who finished will unearthed five factors[192] which enhanced their perseverance and good finish. One of those was the presence of spiritual disciplines in the life

> Leaders who have disciplines in their lives are more likely to persevere and finish well than those who do not.

Leaders need discipline of all kinds. Especially is this true of spiritual disciplines.

Definition   Spiritual disciplines are activities of mind and body purposefully undertaken to bring personality and total being into effective cooperation with the Spirit of God so as to reflect Kingdom life.

When Paul was around 50 years of age he wrote to the Corinthian church what appears to be both an exhortation to the Corinthians and an explanation of a major leadership value in his own life. We need to keep in mind that he had been in ministry for about 21 years. He was still advocating strong discipline. I paraphrase it in my own words.

> I am serious about finishing well in my Christian ministry. I discipline myself for fear
> that after challenging others into the Christian life I myself might become a casualty. 1
> Co 9:24-27

Lack of physical discipline is often an indicator of laxity in the spiritual life as well. Toward the end of his life, Paul is probably between 65 and 70, he is still advocating discipline. This time he writes to Timothy, who is probably between 30 and 35 years old.

---

[192] The list of five enhancement factors includes the following. Enhancement 1—Perspective. Leaders need to have a lifetime perspective on ministry. Effective leaders view present ministry in terms of a lifetime perspective. Enhancement 2—Renewal. Special moments of intimacy with God, challenges from God, new vision from God and affirmation from God both for personhood and ministry will occur repeatedly to a growing leader. Enhancement 3—Disciplines. Leaders who have disciplines in their lives are more likely to persevere and finish well than those who do not. Enhancement 4—Learning Posture. The single most important antidote to plateauing is a well developed learning posture Enhancement 5—Mentoring. Leaders who are effective and finish well will have from 10 to 15 significant people who came alongside at one time or another to help them.

62. Spiritual Disciplines—And On-going Leadership

> 7 But avoid godless legends and old wives' fables. Instead exercise your mind in godly things. 8 For physical exercise is advantageous somewhat but exercising in godliness has long term implications both for today and for that which will come. 1Ti 4:7,8

Certain practices are assumed in the Scriptures as valid for developing spirituality and have been proven empirically in church history to aid development of spirituality. The scriptures do not define most of the disciplines that have come to be accepted but do mention most of them.

Three Major Categories of Disciplines

The following two categories have proved helpful in describing spiritual disciplines.

Spiritual Disciplines Involve

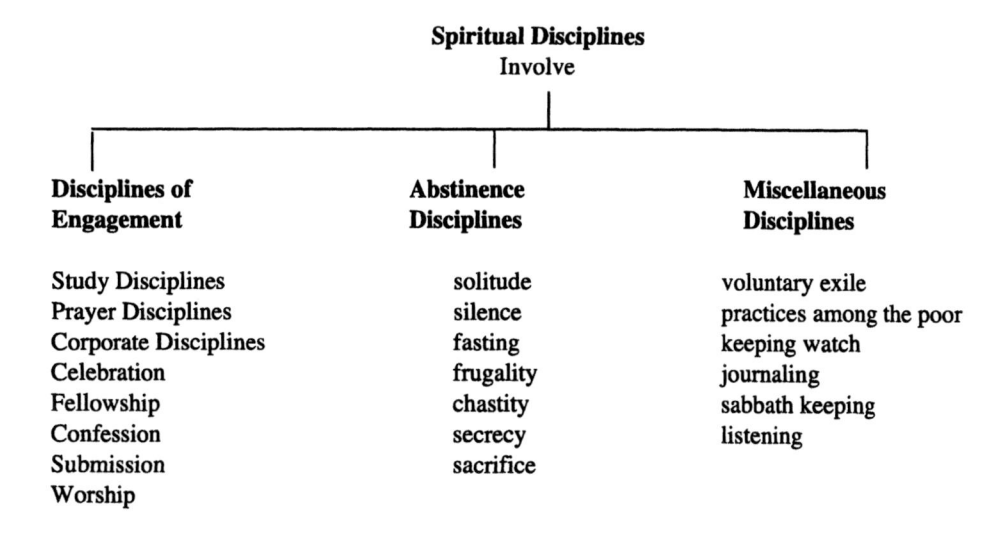

Disciplines of Engagement	Abstinence Disciplines	Miscellaneous Disciplines
Study Disciplines	solitude	voluntary exile
Prayer Disciplines	silence	practices among the poor
Corporate Disciplines	fasting	keeping watch
Celebration	frugality	journaling
Fellowship	chastity	sabbath keeping
Confession	secrecy	listening
Submission	sacrifice	
Worship		

Figure 1,2 Co 62-1 Tree Diagram Of Spiritual Disciplines

Most leaders are somewhat familiar with the disciplines of engagement. I will define the abstinence disciplines since less is known about them.

Table 1,2 Co 62-1 defines the disciplines. Table 1,2 Co 62-2 lists purposes/applications of them.

Table 1,2 Co 62-1. Abstinence Disciplines Defined

Discipline	Defined
solitude	The discipline of Solitude is a purposeful abstention from interaction with other human beings and the denial of companionship and all that comes from interaction with others with a view toward focusing on spiritual things.
silence	The discipline of silence is the practice of not speaking and closing oneself off from all kinds of sounds.
fasting	The discipline of fasting is the deliberate abstinence from food and possibly drink for a period of time.
frugality	The discipline of frugality is the abstention from using money or goods at our disposal in ways that merely gratify our desires or our hunger for status, glamour, or luxury.
chastity	A chaste person (whether married or single) is one who manifests the qualities of sexual wholeness and integrity in relationship to oneself, to persons of the same sex and to persons of the opposite sex.
secrecy	The practice of secrecy results from disciplined activities in which one seeks to abstain from causing ones good deeds and qualities to be known.
sacrifice	The discipline of sacrifice is the abstention from the possession or enjoyment of what is necessary for our living and involves forsaking the security of meeting our own needs with

62. Spiritual Disciplines—And On-going Leadership

| | what is in our possession. |

Table 1,2 Co 62-2. Abstinence Disciplines—Some purposes

Discipline	Defined
solitude	to free us from routine and controlling behaviors in order to gain God's perspective—to hear better; teach us to live inwardly; teach us to slow down; gain a new freedom to be with people.
silence	to cause us to consider our words fully before we say them so as to exercise better control over what we say; to listen to people more attentively; to observe others and other things; to allow life-transforming concentration upon God.
fasting	teaches self-denial; physical well being—cleanse body; releases power; increased sense of the presence of God in intercessory prayer; increased effectiveness; revelation from God; increase of spiritual authority; guidance in decisions; deliverance for those in bondage; increased concentration; brings intensive focus in Bible study.
frugality	frees us from concern and involvement with a multitude of desires; frees from the spiritual bondage caused by debt; teaches us respect for responsible stewardship; lessens the importance of things as essential to life; teaches us empathy for those who do not have resources; can lead toward simplicity as a way of life—the arrangement of life around a few consistent purposes, explicitly excluding what is not necessary to human well-being.
chastity	as an aid to total concentration while having extended times of fasting and praying; in marriage, bring proper focus so that sexual gratification is seen not to be the center of a relationship; recognize the importance of persons as persons; point out the power of lust in a life; teach positive relationships with those of opposite sex.
secrecy	to help us control a desire for fame, justification, or the attention of others; to help us center on God's affirmation; to learn to love to be unknown and even accept misunderstanding without the loss of peace, joy, or purpose; experience a continuing relationship with God independent of the opinions of others; teaches love and humility before God and others; help us see our associates in the best light; to help us see our egocentricity; help us appreciate a breadth of ideas related to competition; teach us to trust God in a deeper way.
sacrifice	learn to trust in God and not our own means of security; enables us to meet others needs; teach us the risk of faith.

1,2 Co 62- 3. Abstinence Disciplines—Applicational Ideas

Discipline	Defined
solitude	1. Learn to take advantage of little solitudes during the day. 2. Find places that are conducive to solitude and deliberately set out to spend time in them. 3. Have special repetitive times during the year which you set aside to be alone for evaluation and reorientation of life goals. 4. If you go on a retreat for solitude remember the basic outline of such a retreat: entry, listening time, closure. Entry may require an unwinding. Sleeping may well be in order. The actual time of solitude will force inward reflection. Finally, seek to understand what has happened.
silence	1. Arise for a time alone in the middle of the night in order to experience a period of silence. 2. Go away to a retreat center for a day or so of silence. Some retreat centers are set up for silence. 3. Refrain from turning on the radio or TV or CD or whatever at times you usually do so. Instead observe silence. 4. When riding in your car do not turn on the radio but instead meditate. 5. Buy some earplugs or "Jet ears" to use to shut out sound when you study or meditate or read or pray. 6. If you go on a retreat for silence remember the basic outline of such a retreat: entry, listening time, closure. Entry may require an unwinding time--sleeping may well be in order. In your silence learn to listen for God.

62. Spiritual Disciplines—And On-going Leadership

	Seek when you finish to understand what happened in the time of solitude.
fasting	<u>Kinds of Abstention in terms of what denied</u>: absolute—without water and food (up to three days); no food, water only—up to 40 days; no food, some liquids other than water (no stimulants)--up to 40 days. <u>Kinds of Abstention in terms of purpose</u>: *Working Fast*—a fast done secretly while maintaining regular working habits. This usually has some goal attached to it. *Isolation fast*--a fast done in which the faster isolates himself/ herself from others concentrating wholly on God and spiritual matters. This usually has some goal. o *Power Fast*—a fast done primarily to increase awareness of spiritual warfare and to release God's power to accomplish victory in power encounters. *Discipline Fast*—a fast done in obedience to conviction from God that it should be done even though there is no apparent goal. *Apostolic ministry Fast*—a fast, which has as its major goal the beginning of some new ministry. This can be done solo or in concert with some team.
frugality	1. Learn to eat simply (fewer meat meals). Healthy eating usually leads to less expense for medical and dental care. 2. Learn to opt for leisure activities, which do not cost (reading, walking, etc.). 3. Walk instead of riding when feasible. 4. Make knowing choices in buying for home (don't have to choose top of line). 5. Respect the environment (like saving water, preserving plant life, trees, etc.). 6. Pass on clothing to others (that you no longer use). 7. Learn to get by without amassing the latest technological gadgets. 8. Learn to say no to advertising, which promotes things you do not need. 9. Learn to budget and stick to it. 10. Recycle whatever you can. 11. Exercise discipline with credit cards (never charge what you can not pay off) or get rid of credit cards altogether. 12. Learn to depend on and utilize fully the resources you do have. 13. Practice "community" thinking (without living in a commune): covenant with one or two other families and/or singles for mutual accountability and encouragement in living responsible life-styles; own jointly some of the more expensive items—lawn tools, shop tools, books, journals; shop in bulk together and share; car pool whenever feasible. 14. Think homegrown: more letters, fewer long distance phone calls; purchase/make inexpensive gifts and then add a home-made personalization to give it a special touch; hand-made or hand-adapted clothing and furniture. 15. Churches and responsible living: our churches can purchase less than "top of the line" organs or other items and use the extra to share generously to the building fund of a 3rd world church. less focus on expensive entertainment and recreation at church outings; learn to get excitement and re-creation from outreach, evangelism, work projects for the needy. Occasionally go without coffee and snacks at group fellowships; use the time to talk about the hungry and give the usual expense money to the hungry. 16. Occasionally fast. 17. Hospitality—invite other to eat at your home rather than eating out; open home to out-of-towners and stay in homes when you are traveling.
chastity	1. Learn to value highly your own personhood and sexuality. 2. Learn to value highly the personhood and sexuality of others--male or female, young or old. 3. Guard thought life. 4. Abstain from any form of entertainment which might indulge improper sexual thoughts. 5. If married, abstain from sexual activity (with consent of partner) for extended times of praying and fasting. 6. Deliberately develop positive relationships with those of opposite sex which are healthy and do not focus on sexuality. 7. Deliberately seek the good of those of the opposite sex that you come in contact with in daily life. 8. Don't allow yourself to be put in potentially compromising situations with an individual of the opposite-sex.
secrecy	1. Refrain in the presence of others of discussing your accomplishments or good qualities. 2. Accept compliments graciously without much ado. 3. Recognize inwardly when accomplishments come of God's grace in giving you abilities or opportunities to accomplish. 4. Do not defend when you are attacked. 5. Trust God to both vindicate character if that is needed or to promote character if that is needed.
sacrifice	1. Respond to some other person's need by giving that which you had allocated to meet that same need for yourself. 2. After paying off all your bills at the end of the month give

62. Spiritual Disciplines—And On-going Leadership

	whatever is left over away to some needy cause. 3. Save all your loose change for a month and give it away.

Conclusion

Examples abound in the Scriptures for most of these disciplines. But what do we gain from these disciplines.

Writers on the disciplines often see the discipline of **solitude** as primary and prior to other disciplines. Its lessons are frequently necessary in order to insure profit from them.

We do not realize how much we depend on noise around us to shield out loneliness and to keep us from dealing with the distortions we have of our inner self. **Silence** helps us to separate out the false self from the true self. The practice of silence enables one to deal with loneliness in a constructive way that builds up the interior life. Silence forces evaluation of ones inner self. It helps one learn inward concentration. It will teach us to think before speaking and to choose our words well.

Fasting is a practice, which many Christian's are discovering is for today and not relegated to the Bible or historic Christianity. Not to be practices by all, this abstinence almost more than any of the others teaches the value of discipline itself.

Debt is one reason that some Christians are not available to God for service. In II Timothy 2:4 Paul warns Timothy not to become entangled in the things of the world. In Romans 13:8 Paul admonishes Christians at Rome to owe no person anything save love. **Frugality** helps one learn the discipline of wise control of finances and other resources.

Sexuality is one of the most powerful and subtle forces in human nature. Its abuse can be destructive. Discipline in the area of sexuality can be foundational to other disciplines. Some distortions of sexuality are fornication, adultery, lusting, obsessive sexual activities, homosexuality, pornography and sexism. **Chastity** helps one learn about these things.

Proverbs 27:2 cautions a person about praising oneself. "Let other people praise you—even strangers; never do it yourself. The natural tendency of the heart is to be recognized for qualities and good things done. The proverb "tooting ones own horn" occurs in numerous languages and shows the recognition of this desire. **Secrecy** as a discipline counters this natural desire.

Sacrifice goes beyond frugality. Frugality is the careful stewardship of what we have. Sacrifice uses some of what we need for others. It is a discipline which focuses on giving beyond ones means.

Leaders who have disciplines in their lives are more likely to persevere and finish well than those who do not.

Article 63

Relevance of the Article to Paul's Corinthian Ministry

Paul was strongly word gifted. But from time-to-time he saw power gifts demonstrated in needful situations. In the Corinthian ministry his word-giftedness abounds—apostolic, prophetic, teaching, exhortation. As you read through these important descriptive concepts think through the 1,2 Co letters and observe Paul's use of his giftedness-set.

63. Spiritual Gift Clusters

Introduction

All Christians have at least one spiritual gift.

Definition — A spiritual gift is a *God-given* unique capacity imparted to each believer for the purpose of releasing a Holy Spirit empowered ministry via that believer.

While this is true for the body in general, leaders usually are multi-gifted. Over their time of ministry experience, at any one given time, they will be repeatedly exercising a combination of gifts. The set of gifts that a leader is demonstrating at any given time is important. It has a special label.

Definition — A gift-mix is a label that refers to the set of spiritual gifts being used by a leader at any given time in his/her ministry.

Just as most leaders leader are multi-gifted and have a gift-mix, so too churches as a whole and Christian organizations as a whole corporately reflect gift-mixes. One way to assess this corporate gift-mix is to use a three fold category of giftings. These categories originated out of a study of Paul's affirmation to churches (corporate groups) for their impact on their surrounding communities. These affirmations occurred in an almost formula-like way in many of his salutations in his epistles. His full affirmation formula included faith, love, and hope. With some churches he would give partial affirmation. And with one church, with which he was extremely displeased he gave no affirmation at all. A study of these affirmations led to the identification of the functions implied in them: faith—the ability to believe in the unseen God (the function of the POWER gifts), love—the manifestation of the reality of the unseen God in the lives of those who know Him (the function of the LOVE gifts), hope—the expectation of what He is doing; that is, the clarification of who He is, what He desires and what He is doing.(the function of the WORD gifts).

The identification of clusters of gifts that did those functions followed as did the actual naming of them as **WORD, POWER,** and **LOVE** clusters. This identification of clusters led to the correlation between Word gifts and leadership. *All leaders we had studied always had at least one word gift in their gift-mix; many had more than one*. This idea is a powerful implication for the selection and development of leaders.

The notion of spiritual gift clusters provides a special perspective, in fact a tool, that can aid strategic planning for a corporate group.

Three Corporate Functions Of Gifts: Word, Power, Love

These three crucial corporate functions were called power gifts, word gifts and love gifts and are described and illustrated as follows.

description — Power gifts demonstrate the authenticity, credibility, power and reality of the unseen God.

examples — miracles, kinds of healings, word of knowledge

63. Spiritual Gift Clusters

description — Love gifts are manifestations attributed to God through practical ways that can be recognized by a world around us which needs love. They demonstrate the reality of relating to this God.

example — mercy, helps, pastoring

description — Word gifts clarify the nature of this unseen God and what He expects from His followers. People using these gifts both communicate about God and for God.

example — exhortation, teaching, prophecy

Pictorial View of the Three Corporate Functions: Word, Power, Love

Below in Figure 1,2 Co 63-1, given in pictorial form,[193] are the three clusters, along with the individual gifts that aid these functions. Notice some gifts operate in more than one cluster while some are exclusive to the cluster in which it primarily operates.

The following lists the three clusters in terms of spiritual gifts listed in the gifts passages of the New Testament.

Power gifts = faith, word of knowledge, discernings of spirits, miracles, tongues, interpretation of tongues, healing, word of wisdom, prophecy. These all help demonstrate the reality of the unseen God.

Love gifts = governments, giving, mercy, helps, pastoring, evangelism, healing, word of wisdom, word of knowledge. These all demonstrate the beauty of that unseen God's work in lives in such a way as to attract others to want this same kind of relationship.

Word gifts = exhortation, teaching, apostleship, ruling, prophecy, faith, pastor, evangelism, word of wisdom, word of knowledge. These all help us understand about this God including His nature, His purposes and how we can relate to Him and be a part of His purposes.

---

[193] This is technically called a Venn diagram. All of the gifts listed in a circle belong to that circle. Where there is overlap, it means that the gifts in the overlap belong to both circles involved in the overlap (or all three circles as the case may be).

63. Spiritual Gift Clusters

Power Gifts

Faith
Word of Knowledge
Discernings of spirits
Miracles
Kinds of Tongues
Interpretation of Tongues

Healing

Prophecy (faith)

Word of Wisdom
(Word of Knowledge)

Governments
Giving
Mercy
Helps

Exhortation
Teaching
Apostleship
Ruling

Pastoring
Evangelism

Love Gifts

Word Gifts

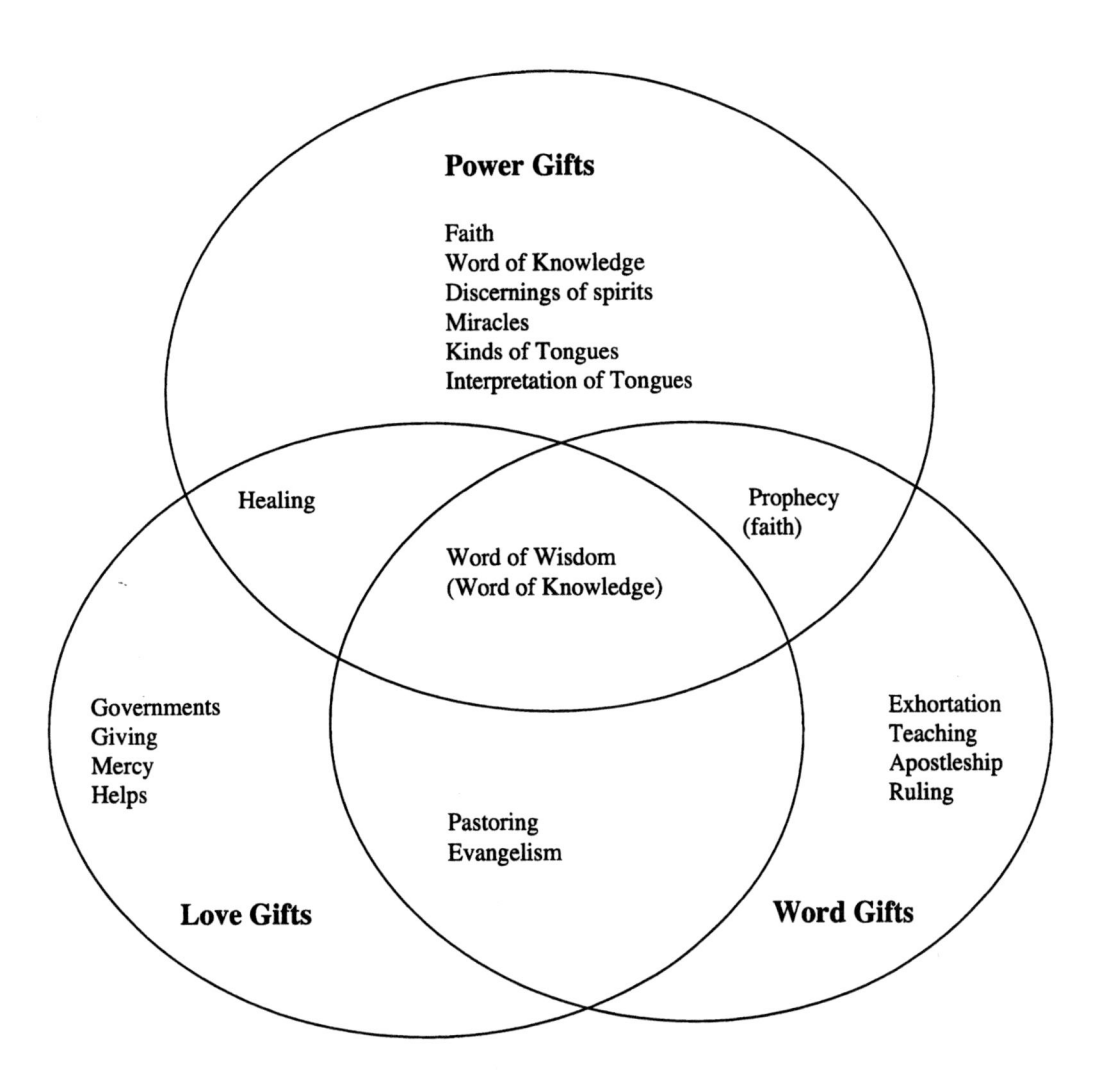

Figure 1,2 Co 63-1. Power, Love And Word Gifts Pictured

The Notion of Balance

Balance describes a proper relationship between manifestations of love, word, and power clusters operating in a given context so that God's witness in that situation can be adequate. Balance does not mean equality or equal amounts of gifts. Balance means having the appropriate mix of word, power, and love gifts for God to accomplish His purposes through the group to the people of its geographic and cultural situation.

63. Spiritual Gift Clusters

In the three profiles shown below an oval labeled with **A** means a **Word cluster**. An oval with **B** means a **love cluster**. An oval with C means a **power cluster**.

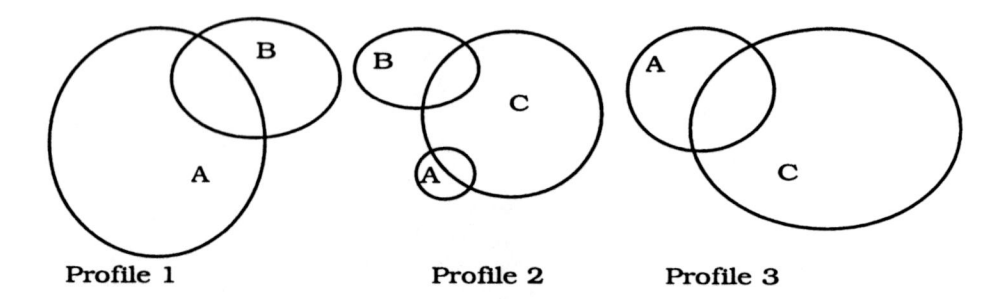

Figure 1,2 Co 63-2. Three Example of Corporate Mixes of Word, Power, Love

Profile 1 represents a church with a strong word ministry—since there is absolutely no power it means dominantly teaching and exhortation gifts. This would be a typical Bible Church. It has some compassion ministry but it is clear that it is dominantly a classroom type of church. The love cluster is about half within and half without the church. This means that there are probably a number of helps and governments gifts operating in the church doing service ministries and a number of mercy, helps types reaching out of the church. This church could use some power gifts in order to break through and reach new people for Christ. Its leadership gifts are probably pastoral and teaching. There could be some evangelism. No apostolic or prophetic types would probably be welcome here.

Profile 2 is a church which has strong power gifts. Since it has power gifts there will be some word ministry through the prophetical, word of knowledge, word of wisdom gifts. It has very little word gifts which, means that for the most part there will be little teaching and any exhortation would be in terms of the power gifts. It also has some love gifts working both in and out of the church--more outside than in. But its minimum word gifts means probably no Sunday School ministries so it probably doesn't need as many helps and governments inside the church. The question is how to get word gifts in here. There will probably be a big back door in this church. The leadership gifts in this church are probably apostolic, maybe evangelistic, maybe prophetic. There is probably a need for pastoral ministry and certainly a need for a teaching/ discipleship ministry.

Profile 3 is a church dominated with power gifts but one which has some ministry in the word. This means the leadership gifts in the church are probably apostolic and prophetical with possibly some teaching and a little pastoring. What is probably missing is an evangelistic thrust—no love gifts working. This church probably is having a hard time getting people to do ministry jobs in the church.

If I were to ask you how would you assess balance in each of the three profiles? What would you say? You could say it is unfair to ask. Balance determines whether or not the cluster fits the situation. You would need to know the contextual situations. For example, if Profile A was in the highlands of Papua New Guinea it would extremely out of balance—for power gifts are needed to get a hearing. But if it were in an early start-up church plant in a bedroom community of middle to upper middle class business types it would be appropriate. Profile 3 might be appropriate for early ministry in an inner-city location since power is needed to get breakthroughs. But later on this church will not keep its members till it develops a teaching/ discipleship thrust which need word gifts.

Conclusion

Spiritual gift clusters provide a tool for assessing development in a church. A church should know its people in terms of their gifts. Strategic planning will need this kind of assessment.

See gift*edness set, spiritual gifts, various gift definitions*, **Glossary**. See **Article**, *Developing Giftedness*.

Article 64

Relevance of the Article to Paul's Corinthian Ministry

Paul's teaching on spiritual gifts in 1 Co along with a comparative analysis of his mentioning of spiritual gifts in Ro and Eph forms the base for the biblical research of this article. Empirical comparative studies of many contemporary leaders lives over a ten-year span from 1983 to 1993 formed the basis for the application of giftedness concepts to development of leaders.

64. Spiritual Gifts, Giftedness, and Development

Introduction

All Christians have at least one spiritual gift.

Definition   A spiritual gift is a *God-given* unique capacity imparted to each believer for the purpose of releasing a Holy Spirit empowered ministry via that believer.

While this is true for the body in general, leaders usually are multi-gifted. Over their time of ministry experience, at any one given time, they will repeatedly exercise a combination of gifts. The set of gifts that a leader is demonstrating at any given time is important. It has a special label

Definition   A gift-mix is a label that refers to the set of spiritual gifts being used by a leader at any given time in his/her ministry.

My research on leaders and giftedness and my Biblical studies on *The Stewardship Leadership Model* resulted in the concept of the giftedness set.

Definition   The giftedness set describes natural abilities, acquired skills, and spiritual gifts which a leader has as resources to use in ministry. Sometimes shortened to giftedness.

Ministry flows out of beingness. Beingness describes the inner life of a person and refers to intimacy with God, character, conscience, personality, giftedness, destiny, values drawn from experience, gender influenced perspectives. The axiom, ministry flows out of being means that one's ministry should be a vital outflow from these inner beingness factors. Giftedness is a strong factor in beingness.

Out of my study also emerged also emerged the following observation,

> **When Christ Calls Leaders To Christian Ministry He Intends To Develop Them To Their Full Potential. Each Of Us In Leadership Is Responsible To Continue Developing In Accordance With God's Processing All Our Lives.**

This article deals with the notion of the giftedness set and suggests that a leader can develop himself/herself over a lifetime—a strong value flowing from the Stewardship model.[194]

---

[194] Stewardship values which relate to giftedness include: 1. Leaders ought to build upon abilities, skills, and gifts to maximize potential and use for God. 2. Leaders should recognize that they will be uniquely gifted both as to gifts and the degree to which the gift can be used effectively. 3. Leaders should know that they will receive rewards for their productivity and for zealously using abilities, skills, gifts, and opportunities for God. See **Article**, *24. Jesus—Five Leadership Models: Shepherd, Harvest, Steward, Servant, Intercessor.*

64. Spiritual Gifts, Giftedness, and Development   page 324

Giftedness Set

God endows a leader with natural abilities and later spiritual gifts. Along the way leaders pick up acquired skills. Comparative studies[195] resulted in a time-line which describes how the process develops over time. Figure 1,2 Co 64-1 shows this.

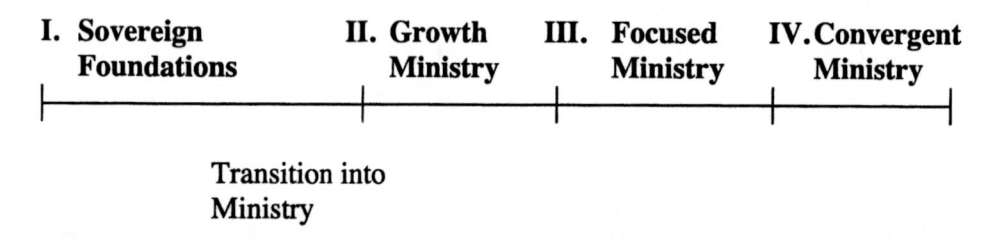

I. Sovereign Foundations	II. Growth Ministry	III. Focused Ministry	IV. Convergent Ministry
	Transition into Ministry		
Natural Abilities		Occasional Late Blooming Natural Ability	
Acquired Skills	Acquired Skills	Occasional Important Acquired Skill	
		Occasional Spiritual Gift Needed for Effective Ministry	
	Early Indications Spiritual Gifts	Dominant Spiritual Gifts Emerge	Gift-Mix Firmed Up Giftedness Set Firmed Up	Giftedness Set Developed and Used With Great Effectiveness

Figure 1,2 Co 64-1. Giftedness Development Over Time

As the giftedness set begins to emerge, a leader soon finds that one component of the set dominates the others. The other two components supplement or synergize with the dominant element.

Definition   The dominate component of a giftedness set—either natural abilities, acquired skills, or spiritual gifts is called the <u>focal element</u>.

About 50% of leaders studied in the research have spiritual gifts as focal. Another 35% have natural abilities as focal. About 15% have acquired skills as focal. This is important self-knowledge for a leader who wants to develop and wants ministry to flow out of beingness.

It is toward the notion of giftedness set developed and used effectively that I am talking when I say that Christ intends to develop a leader to full potential.

Development—What Does It Mean

A leader cannot develop natural abilities. These are givens, innate with their personhood. Though a leader may discover some latent natural ability later in life due to circumstances of ministry. Can a leader develop a spiritual gift?

---

[195] For almost 10 years, 1985-1995, I studied leaders with a focus on giftedness analysis. The heart of this article flows out of that research. See **For Further Study Bibliography**, Clinton and Clinton, **Unlocking Your Giftedness—What Leaders Need To Know To Develop Themselves and Others**.

64. Spiritual Gifts, Giftedness, and Development

The answer is not certain from Biblical evidence. But certainly a leader can develop acquired skills and can develop synergizing issues related to spiritual gifts and natural abilities.

Definition   <u>Development</u> of a leader means an increase in efficiency and effectiveness in ministry due to addition of skills or other issues which enhance the leader's use of natural abilities, acquired skills, or spiritual gifts in ministry.

My research studies show that leaders develop their giftedness due to programmatic means (designed training), happenstance (day-to-day learning in the normal course of life's activities and processes), and by deliberate development (disciplined self-initiated learning).

Deliberate development takes place through formal or informal apprenticeships or other mentoring relationships, personal growth projects, and/or some identified plan of growth. Deliberate development ought to be the norm for a leader who has a developmental bias.

Studies into each of the leadership gifts[196] (Apostleship, Pastoral, Evangelism, Teacher, Prophecy, Exhortation) from a developmental perspective have resulted in numerous suggestions for development for each of the gifts.[197]

Conclusion

Leaders can develop over a lifetime. It happens. But with an awareness of how development can happen, a leader can much more efficiently develop, when self-knowledge and self-initiative are taken.

---

[196] These are the primary gifts in the Word Cluster. All leaders have at least one of these words gifts and usually are multi-gifted. See **Article,** *63. Spiritual Gift Clusters*.

[197] See **For Further Study Bibliography,** Clinton and Clinton, **Unlocking Your Giftedness,** ch 10, pages 251-280, where suggestions for developing spiritual gifts of the Word Cluster are given. It is beyond the scope of this article to give these suggestions since the suggestions run to 30 pages by themselves.

Article 65

Relevance of the Article to Paul's Corinthian Ministry

Paul applies spiritual warfare tactics as he applies discipline from a distance with the immoral situation in Corinth. At first glance, you may not notice much of Paul's activity in terms of spiritual warfare as seen in his epistles. You do see it in his activity as described in Ac in several situations. However, careful scrutiny of the Pauline epistles uncovers lots of implications of Satanic tactics in Spiritual Warfare. See Table 1,2 Co 65-1 below for these references to spiritual warfare in the Pauline epistles. Note, quite a few occur in 1,2 Co. A leader must be aware of Satanic involvement. This article seeks to expose issues involved in spiritual warfare.

65. Spiritual Warfare—Satan's Tactics

Introduction

A simple listing of times when Paul refers to Satan or the Devil and or demonic work is instructive. Seeing these kind of verses in their weaving context suggests tactics used by Satan in spiritual warfare. And to be aware of such tactics allows a leader to combat them.

Pauline Passages on Satan, the Devil or Demons

Table 1,2 Co 65-1 lists some Pauline passages dealing with spiritual warfare instigated by Satan and lists some suggestions as to tactics involved.

Table 1,2 Co 65-1. Spiritual Warfare—Satanic Tactics

Passage	Satanic Tactic
Ro 16:20	Satan upsets Christians' inner life attitudes, taking away peace due to divisions in the church. **Antidote**: Strive for unity and maintain inward peace as God works through the relationships.
1Co 5:5	Satan can destroy a life by controlling a person through immoral sexual addiction. **Antidote**: Avoid situations that can lead to sexual addiction.
1Co 7:5	Satan can gain inroads into the life of a married person when sexual needs are not being met. **Antidote**: Keep lines of communication open in a marriage relationship, concerning sexual needs.
2Co 2:11	Satan can use lack of forgiveness and failure to receive one who repents to control a church situation. **Antidote**: Accept those back who God has forgiven and who have shown genuine repentance.
2Co 11:14	Satan can counterfeit good things that attract believers (e.g. apparent good teaching; false apostles). Satan can appear like a messenger from God to deceive Christians. **Antidote**: Get discernment on apparent good teaching, apparent dynamic leaders. This may involve having to depend on people with revelatory gifts (discernings of spirits; word of knowledge; word of prophecy; word of wisdom, etc.).
2Co 12:7	Satan can use a physical sickness or disability to prey upon a believer and instill doubts about God and His enabling grace. But God can also use these things to prevent abuse of power and pride in a leader's life. **Antidote**: Don't let sickness rob you of your trust in God. Seek His enabling grace (whether or not He chooses to heal you).
Eph 4:27	Satan can use anger in a life to gain inroads into a life and eventually control that life through the anger. **Antidote**: Get help if anger controls you. This may require inner healing. Also recognize the benefits of anger.

65. Spiritual Warfare—Satan's Tactics

Eph 6:10-20	Satan uses lies or half-truths to trick believers and give unreliable perspectives on their lives and situations. Satan uses lack of righteousness (on-going unrighteous things in a believer's life) as an inroad into the life. Satan uses lack of presentation of testimony in a believer's life to weaken that believer's stand. Satan causes a believer to doubt God (character, dealings, truth, etc,). Satan robs believers from the impact of salvation in their lives. Satan keeps believers from using the Word of God in their lives and in combating his tactics. Satan keeps believers from praying in the Spirit as they confront him in his tactics. Satan keeps people from being alert to his tactics and from discerning his involvement. **Antidotes**: See the imperatives in the Eph 6:10-20.
1Th 2:18	Satan can block a believer's guidance. So closed doors are not always clear guidance. **Antidote**: Get certainty guidance. Let all of the major guidance elements give weight to your guidance: God's Voice in the Word; God's Voice in the Heart; God's Voice in Circumstances; God's Voice in the Church.
2Th 2:9	Satan can do signs and wonders through a leader so that the leader looks as if he/she is empowered of God (apostolic workers also do signs and wonders). **Antidote**: Get discernment on apparent good teaching, apparent dynamic leaders. This may involve having to depend on people with revelatory gifts (discernings of spirits; word of knowledge; word of prophecy; word of wisdom, etc.).
1Ti 1:20	Satan can use a lack of responsiveness to one's conscience to eventually destroy a leader and take them out of ministry and further cause them to blaspheme what they once believed. The antidote, keeping a clear conscience and holding on to the truths of the Christian faith. **Antidote**: On the one hand, don't go against your conscience. On the other hand, allow God to impact your inner life and correct wrongly held ideas that affect your conscience.
1Ti 3:6	Satan can take an young leader out of ministry due to pride. **Antidote**: Potential young leaders should not placed into leadership responsibility too soon.
1Ti 4:1	Satan use demons to influence teachers to give false doctrines that appeal to people. They are actually described as seducing spirits, hypocritical liars with no conscience. **Antidote**: A Bible centered leader like Timothy should teach the truth about these evil doctrines countering these heresies.
2Ti 2:26	Satan blinds people to truth. **Antidote**: Gently persuade people winning them over by manner as well as truth.

Conclusion

I have only barely touched on Satanic tactics. I have limited myself to Pauline input in this article. Each of the passages above should be studied in a detailed way in their context. And the other passages in the N.T.[198] need to be comparatively studied along with these.

---

[198] Some 89 passages mention the Devil or Satan. Other passages talk about demonic influence. But at least the above form a core of truth to start with in observing Satanic tactics.

Article 66

Relevance of the Article to Paul's Corinthian Ministry

Paul walks the balance presented in this article concerning the two extremes to avoid. It is clear in his epistles that he was constantly aware of spiritual warfare and dealt with it when needed. But it is also clear that he did not attribute all conflict and opposition to spiritual warfare. He operated with discernment and models for us how to maintain a balance with regard to these two extremes.

66. Spiritual Warfare—Two Extremes To Avoid

Introduction

Did Paul ever engage in spiritual warfare? Oh, yes! But when you read his epistles there is very little up front information, i.e. direct teaching, on doing spiritual warfare. There is Eph 6:10-17 and Col 2:13-15. But for the most part, spiritual warfare is incidental and remarks about it are asides simply woven into the fabric of a letter.[199] In my opinion, you can draw implications from them but not solid models that can be passed on authoritatively as to how to do spiritual warfare. And herein lies a model—two basics—that can help us approach spiritual warfare.

Two Extremes To Avoid

From a comparative study of all of Paul's epistles looking for spiritual warfare information I have drawn the following implications for leaders.

1. Spiritual warfare exists.
2. The spirit world is real and impinges on our world.
3. Leaders should be aware of spiritual warfare and their strengths[200] and limitations about it.
4. Paul is a model for how leaders ought to approach spiritual warfare in their ministries.

Paul deals with many problematic situations and people in ministry. Occasionally he will assert something about spiritual warfare as being involved in a problem or as the source of some person's situation. But for the most part Paul avoids two extremes:

Extreme 1. Overemphasis on Spiritual Warfare
Paul does not assign blame for everything that happens on spirit beings, demons, and spiritual warfare.

He sees the human side of things as being heavily involved in many of the problems.

Extreme 2. Under Emphasis on Spiritual Warfare
Paul does recognize that some problems and issues have at their heart spiritual warfare. Demonic influence must be countered.

Yes, there is spiritual warfare and it must be discerned and dealt with. But, no, not everything is spiritual warfare. Paul has a healthy balance.

---

[199] For example if you trace spiritual warfare content through 1,2Ti you will see only several asides: 1Ti 1:18-20; 3:6,7; 4:1; 2Ti 1:6. You will see little or none in most of Paul's epistles. The omissions speak loudly.
[200] See especially the **Article**, *67. Spiritual Warfare—Two Foundational Axioms*.

66. Spiritual Warfare—Two Extremes to Avoid

Conclusion

In most of the evangelical world I have dealt with (Bible teaching ministries), **Extreme 2** is the norm. And most of those ministries do not discern or deal with spiritual warfare, even when most needed in their people or situations.

In a little, but not as much, the charismatic or pentecostal circles I deal with, **Extreme 1** is the norm.

When **Extreme 2** is the norm—great needs go unmet. When **Extreme 1** is the norm, abuse of power can abound. Frequently such a leader involved will fall by the wayside (many due to overpowering from the demonic world; many due to the power and pride barriers.)

Balance! How much we need it as leaders. Consistency in maintaining a middle ground and heeding both these dynamic extremes at the same time is needed. And Shakespeare said it well, "Consistency, thou art a jewel!"

See **Article**, *15. Finishing Well—Six Major Barriers*.

Article 67

Relevance of the Article to Paul's Corinthian Ministry

Having acknowledged that spiritual warfare is real in the previous article and that a careful balance must be maintained as we deal with our leadership situations, nevertheless we will face these situations in which spiritual warfare must be dealt with. These simple but clear truths from Scripture will under gird us as we do so. And John realized it. Both of these axioms flow directly from John's ministry/teaching. You will note that Paul certainly rested on them—at least implicitly.

67. Spiritual Warfare—Two Foundational Axioms

Introduction

Spiritual warfare is real. All leaders engage in it, knowingly or not. Spiritual warfare was introduced in the book of Da.[201] There we learned some initial truth about spiritual warfare.

1. The unseen spirit world is real and does affect a leader's world.
2. Leaders seemingly unanswered prayers may be delayed because of spiritual warfare in the unseen spirit world.
3. Leaders can know that God does protect them with supernatural beings.
4. Some renewal experiences can be via supernatural beings who will affirm, encourage, give physical strength and reveal God's working to leaders.
5. Progressive revelation[202] is needed before spiritual warfare in the heavenlies and our participation in it can be understood. That is, Daniel does not give the full picture or information about human leaders intervening in spiritual warfare.

Definition   Spiritual warfare refers to the unseen opposition in the spirit world made up of Satan and his demons and their attempts to defeat God's forces, angelic beings, and God's people, today called believers. It also involves the response by believers to these attempts.

This article identifies two fundamental axioms concerning spiritual warfare which are part of the progressive revelation given in the N.T. An axiom refers to a maxim widely accepted on its intrinsic merit. It is a statement accepted as true as the basis for argument or inference. It is an established rule or principle or a self-evident truth. To engage in spiritual warfare without these fundamental axioms is to invite defeat. To engage in spiritual warfare with these fundamental axioms lays the foundation for victory over those unseen spiritual forces representing Satan.

---

[201] I refer to the commentary on Daniel. In the Bible spiritual warfare is introduced in Gen 3 with Satan's influence over Adam and Eve. It is explained further in Job which points out how the unseen spiritual world can influence the seen world. There are occasional allusions to it in other books (see 2 Kings 6:8-23; Note especially vs 16). Spiritual forces on God's side are mentioned throughout the Bible (Angels). And Da gives more information on spiritual warfare.

[202] Progressive revelation is a concept noted in the O.T. and N.T. that God is a God who continues to communicate and over time clarifies earlier revelation, expanding on it, filling in more details, helping later leaders see the relevance of it, etc. See especially prophetic ministry. Example: Daniel's prophecies in ch 2, 7, 8, 9, 10-12. There is progress in both content and methodology as observed in various genre in Old and New Testaments. See Job for further references to spirit world intervention in human affairs. See also Eph 6:10ff for basic teaching on spiritual warfare, particularly what human leaders can do. See also Jn 16:11 and Col 2:15 for the strategic basis of spiritual warfare.

67. Spiritual Warfare—Two Foundational Axioms

Axiom 1. Strategic Warfare

Jesus makes an unusual statement in Jn 16:11 as he looks forward to the Cross.

> 11 Judgment is certain, because the ruler of this world is judged."[203] Jn 16:11

Removing the figurative language and expressing the meaning in a powerful statement we have the foundation for Axiom 1 on Strategic Warfare.

> **11 At the Cross I will defeat Satan and his forces; this judgment on them is sure. Jn 16:11**

This aside on spiritual warfare concerns an aspect of the Cross not usually stressed. Besides dealing with sins, sin and righteousness, the Cross also was a strategic victory over Satanic forces. This is the single most important truth for leader's using power ministry in spiritual warfare.

Paul gives the basic teaching on this foundational axiom in Col 2:13-15.

> 13 And you, Gentiles, were dead in your sins. God gave you life through Jesus' death, having forgiven you all your wrongdoings; 14 All our failures to meet the law's demands were taken care of at the Cross. 15 At the same time He openly triumphed over those spirit beings which powerfully oppose God. They are defeated. Col 2:13-15

Axiom 1. **Strategically, Jesus Has Already Defeated All Spiritual Forces Opposed To God. The War Was Won At The Cross. It Only Remains That This Strategic Victory Be Appropriated And Won Tactically.**

This is fundamental to any believer's spiritual warfare. It is a truth that must be believed and acted upon.

Axiom 2. Tactical Warfare

Though the Commander-in-Chief has declared the overall war won there are still battles going on all around us. It doesn't always appear won. A defeated army can still inflict many casualties. So it is in spiritual warfare. Satan has not acknowledged defeat and still fights on. A fundamental axiom basic to this continued warfare is introduced by John.

> 1 Beloved, believe not every spirit, but try the spirits whether they are of God. Because many false prophets are gone out into the world. 2 But here is how you can know the source is by the Spirit of God: Every spirit that affirms that Jesus Christ is come in human form is of God: 3 And every spirit that does not affirm that Jesus Christ came in human form is not from God. Such a source is a spirit against Christ and already is in the world. 4 You are of God, little children, and have overcome these spiritual forces, **because greater is he that is in you, than he that is in the world.**

In a context dealing with spiritual warfare (trying the spirits) John gives the encouraging statement which enables tactical victory.

Axiom 2. **A believer has within himself/herself, the Spirit of God which is much more powerful than Satanic forces.**

---

[203] This is a certainty idiom, the *prophetic past*. A future event is spoken of as if it had already happened (the **TEV** and **NLT** translate—*has already been judged*) because it is so certain, in this case the Cross and one result of it. *Captured: At the Cross I will defeat Satan and his forces; this judgment on them is sure*. See *capture*, certainty idiom, **Glossary**. See **Article**, *12. Figures and Idioms in the Bible*.

67. Spiritual Warfare—Two Foundational Axioms

Conclusion

Victory is certain, it was potentially won at the Cross. It will be won totally in history. In the meantime, a believer has the indwelling Holy Spirit who will enable victory in everyday skirmishes over spirit forces. Count on these axioms.

See **Articles**, *65. Spiritual Warfare—Satan's Tactics; 66. Spiritual Warfare—Two Extremes to Avoid; Daniel—Supernatural Beings and Spiritual Warfare.*

Article 68

Relevance of the Article to Paul's Corinthian Ministry

This article describes the methodology for synthesizing a time-line for a biblical character. It is helpful when studying the Pauline epistles to know where in the developmental time-line, Paul was. This article gives the time-line for Paul. You should note that Paul was probably in his 50s and had around 25 years of ministry experience when he dealt with the Corinthian situation.

68. Time Lines—Defined for Biblical Leaders

A major leadership genre is the biographical source. Below is given 12 steps to use for studying this source. Notice step two in Table 1,2 Co 68-1 below.

Table 1,2 Co 68-1. 12 Steps For Doing Biographical Study

Step	General Guideline
1	Identify All The Passages That Refer To The Leader.
2	Seek To Order The Vignettes Or Other Type Passages In A Time Sequence
3	Construct A Time-Line If You Can. At Least Tentatively Identify The Major Development Phases In The Leader's Life.
4	Look For Shaping Events And Activities (technically called process items, or critical incidents).
5	Identify Pivotal Points From The Major Process Items Or Critical Incidents
6	Seek To Determine Any Lessons You Can From A Study Of Process Items Or Pivotal Points.
7	Identify Any Response Patterns Or Any As You Analyze The Life Across A Time-Line.
8	Study Any Individual Leadership Acts In The Life.
9	Use The Three Overall Leadership Categories To Help Suggest Leadership Issues To Look For (leadership basal elements, leadership influence means, leadership value bases).
10	Use The List Of Major Functions (task functions, relationship functions, and inspirational functions) to Help Suggest Insights. Which were done, which not.
11	Observe Any New Testament Passages Or Commentary On The Leader. Especially Be On The Lookout For Bent Of Life Evaluation.
12	Use The Presentation Format For Findings On Bible Leaders To Help Organize Your Results.

This article briefly describes step two. A time-line is the end result of applying step 2. Time-lines provide an integrating framework upon which to measure development in the life, to organize findings, and to pinpoint when shaping activities occur in a life.

Important Definitions for Time-Lines

Definition   The time-line is the linear display along a horizontal axis which is broken up into development phases.

Definition   A unique time-line refers to a time-line describing a given leader's lifetime which will have unique development phases bearing labels expressing that uniqueness.

Definition   A development phase is a marked off length on a time-line representing a significant portion of time in a leader's life history in which notable development takes place. Example Below has 4 development phases indicated by Roman Letters I, II, III, IV.

Definition   A sub-phase is a marked off length on a time-line within a development phase which points out intermediate times of development during the development phase. In the Example below Development phase III. has 3 sub-phases indicated by A, B, and C.

68. Time Lines—Defined for Biblical Leaders   page 334

All leaders can describe a time-line that is unique to them. A unique time-line is broken up into divisions called development phases which terminate with boundary events. Development phases can themselves be subdivided into smaller units called sub-phases which have smaller boundary terminations.

Below is given the Apostle Paul's time-line with several findings about his life displayed. Paul's life, ministry, and development. I have also numerous other findings about Paul's life, ministry and development located on his time-line. Such things as; pivotal points, mentoring, development of life purpose, development of major role, isolation processing, other process items such as—paradigm shift, leadership committal, double confirmation, divine contact, conflict, crises, ministry conflict, word, obedience, integrity check. Time-lines are very useful to give perspective and force one to see across a whole lifetime of development.

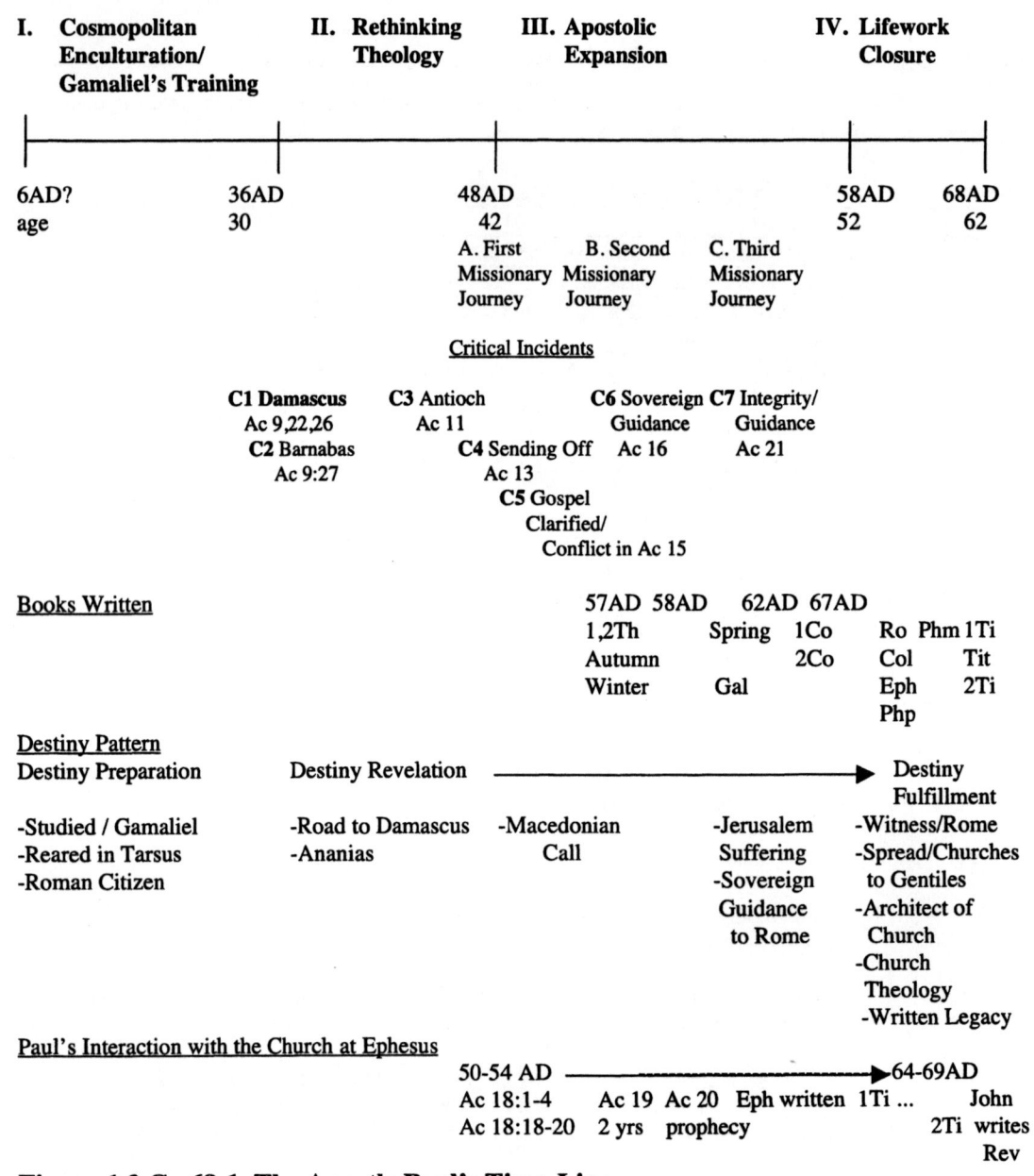

I. Cosmopolitan Enculturation/ Gamaliel's Training	II. Rethinking Theology	III. Apostolic Expansion	IV. Lifework Closure
6AD? age	36AD 30	48AD 42	58AD 52 — 68AD 62

III. A. First Missionary Journey   B. Second Missionary Journey   C. Third Missionary Journey

Critical Incidents

C1 Damascus Ac 9,22,26
C2 Barnabas Ac 9:27

C3 Antioch Ac 11
C4 Sending Off Ac 13
C5 Gospel Clarified/Conflict in Ac 15

C6 Sovereign Guidance Ac 16

C7 Integrity/Guidance Ac 21

Books Written

57AD	58AD	62AD	67AD
1,2Th Autumn Winter	Spring Gal	1Co 2Co	Ro Col Eph Php
			Phm 1Ti Tit 2Ti

Destiny Pattern
Destiny Preparation — Destiny Revelation ————————————→ Destiny Fulfillment

- Studied / Gamaliel
- Reared in Tarsus
- Roman Citizen

- Road to Damascus
- Ananias

- Macedonian Call

- Jerusalem Suffering
- Sovereign Guidance to Rome

- Witness/Rome
- Spread/Churches to Gentiles
- Architect of Church
- Church Theology
- Written Legacy

Paul's Interaction with the Church at Ephesus

50-54 AD ————————————————————→ 64-69AD

Ac 18:1-4   Ac 19   Ac 20   Eph written   1Ti ...   John
Ac 18:18-20   2 yrs   prophecy   2Ti writes
                                                                                 Rev

Figure 1,2 Co 68-1. The Apostle Paul's Time-Line

Article 69

Relevance of the Article to Paul's Corinthian Ministry

Paul's use of mentoring is probably best illustrated with his training of Timothy. His on-going and deliberate training of Timothy remind one of the tremendous example in the O.T. of Moses tandem training with Joshua. This article points out that Paul allowed himself to come close relationally to his mentorees. In fact, three are called sons. One of those is Timothy and one is Titus. Both were involved in the Corinthian ministry. It is surprising that the other is Onesimus. That should alert us to the importance of the Philemon epistle.

69. Timothy—A Beloved Son in the Faith

Effective leaders view relationships in ministry as both a means and an end.

This is one of seven major lessons that I have derived from comparative study of effective leaders. Probably in no leader in the Bible, other than Jesus, is this seen any plainer, than in the life and ministry of Paul the Apostle. Paul was a strong task oriented leader. But he knew the value of relationships. In his epistles he lists almost 80 people by name whom he had personal relationships with. Paul believed that he ought to personally relate to those around him in ministry. It was good in itself. It was good to accomplish ministry too. Paul indicates this notion of a strong relationship when he uses the phrases: *my own son in the faith, my beloved son, as a son with the father, son, dearly beloved son, my son, own son after the common faith, my son*. For three—Timothy, Titus, and Onesimus—it meant strong intimate relationships.

Table 1,2 Co 69-1 lists the instances and uses of these strong, special, intimate relationships by Paul.

Table 1,2 Co 69-1. Paul and Intimate Relationships

Reference	Phrase	Who	Use
1Co 4:17	who is my beloved son	Timothy	Sponsoring Timothy to the Corinthians so they will receive him with respect as Paul's representative.
Php 2:22	as a son with the father	Timothy	Sponsoring Timothy to the Philippians so they will receive him with respect as Paul's representative.
1Ti 1:2	[my] own son in the faith	Timothy	Greeting of encouragement to Timothy personally.
1Ti 1:18	son	Timothy	Exhortation to Timothy to boldly act as a leader in a tough situation remembering the prophecies and operating with a clean conscience.
2Ti 1:2	[my] dearly beloved son	Timothy	Greeting of encouragement. The most intimate of all the phrases.
2Ti 2:1	my son	Timothy	An exhortation to go on, drawing on the enabling grace found in union with Christ
Tit 1:4	[mine] own son after the common faith	Titus	A word of encouragement; a word sponsoring Titus before the Cretian believers.
Phm 1:10	my son	Onesimus	Sponsoring of Onesimus to Philemon. Shows how strongly Paul believed in him.

Let me suggest an exercise for you. Go back and read each of the references listed in Table 1,2 Co 69-1. Read the surrounding context as well. And imagine you are Timothy hearing those words or Titus or Onesimus. How would you feel to hear such words? Paul knew the motivational importance of affirmation. And a personal strong intimate relationship expressed openly to the person not only affirms but motivates them.

69. Timothy—A Beloved Son in the Faith

Table 1,2 Co 69-1 shows that Timothy was Paul's closest associate. He was a beloved and true son in the faith. Leaders need to pass on their heritage. They need to leave behind ultimate contributions. One sure way of doing this is to have relationships with those to whom they minister and with whom they minister. Values are passed on. Ministry methodology, though adapted lives on. Vision is caught and lives on.

Effective leaders view relationship as both a means and an end in ministry.

Paul did. Who are your true sons and daughters? Who will carry on your values, ministry philosophy, and vision?

Article 70

Relevance of the Article to Paul's Corinthian Ministry

Throughout all of Paul's epistles and especially in Ro, 2 Co and Php, he emphasizes that his living of the Christian life involves a unique relationship with the living Christ. It is this relationship, and an ever progressing realization of it that eventuates in practical sanctification in everyday life for Paul. I use the term union life to express the notion that Christ lives in us and through us uniquely in terms of who we are personality wise, our giftedness, and our values that He has instilled in us. This article seeks to give an overview of my understanding of union life. Note the tremendous passages in 2 Co, which reveal Paul's understanding of union life—especially the clay pot illustration and the transformation from one degree of glory to another.

70. Union Life

Introduction

One of the most famous union life verses appears in Col 1:27.

> 27 To whom God would make known what is the riches of the glory of this mystery
> among the Gentiles—**Christ in you**, the hope of glory. Col 1:27

Note the phrase **Christ in you**. Paul uses this concept of being **in Christ**[204] many times in his epistles. It is the essential phrase describing union life. What is union life?

Definition   Union life is a phrase which refers both to the fact of the spiritual reality of a believer joined in spirit with the resurrected Spirit of Christ and the process of that union being lived out with Holy Spirit power so that the person is not dominated by sin in his/her life.

In essence, it is the life of a believer who is living above the controlling authority of sin in a life, not a perfect life, but also not controlled by sinful habits, tendencies, sinful addictions, the sinful self. It is a believer walking sensitively to the Holy Spirit's leading and moving inexorably to being conformed to the image of Christ. That is the life of Christ in and through the believer—in fact, it is not to strong to say Christ in the believer as that person. Christ in me as me.

Today, with our modern emphasis on dysfunctionality, 1000s are bound by a past which will not allow them to live freely. Without wanting to negate the complexities of these foundational shaping events and people in our pasts I do want to say that there is provision for victory in Christ. That is what union life is all about. Union life is certainly part of the answer to that need and maybe perhaps the answer.

Throughout Christian history people serious about their Christianity have longed for a more zealous life-style expression of it. They have longed to have a deeper walk with God. They have sought to appropriate that walk with God. Union life has been the experience of many a saint who has sought this deeper walk. Different names have been used to describe this mystical union and its effect in life. Such terms as the exchanged life, replaced life, deeper life, victorious life, normal Christian life and life on the highest plain can be found in the literature. Various methodologies have been tried to attain that "more committed" expression. Numerous movements have sprung up. The phrases listed above convey rather esoterically what these various believers have discovered.

Paul comprehensively explains this kind of life in Ro 1-8. He models it in Php. He also shows its power in his own life in 2Co. John treats the concept in metaphorical fashion—living water, vine and branches. The Bible also deals with the concept using the term, *New Covenant*. This article will give an

---

[204] Paul uses the phrase *in Christ* 74 times, *in Jesus* six times and *in him* eight times referring to aspects of union life.

70. Union Life

overview of this important concept.[205] I as a believer living in Union Life can know this beautiful union—Christ in me as me. It is entered into simply by faith by knowing and appropriating what Christ has already done at the cross.

Bible Passages Dealing With the Union Life Concept

Union life is promised in the O.T. God reveals the New Covenant in the O.T. and then points to its realization in the book of Heb. Essentially the New Covenant, a promise made to corporate Israel becomes individualized in its N.T. application shown in Heb.

> 31 Behold, the days come, says the LORD, that I will make a new covenant with the house of Israel, and with the house of Judah. 32 Not according to the covenant that I made with their fathers in the day [that] I took them by the hand to bring them out of the land of Egypt; which my covenant they brake, although I was an husband unto them, says the LORD. 33 But this [shall be] the covenant that I will make with the house of Israel; After those days, says the LORD, **I will put my law in their inward parts**, and **write it in their hearts**; and will be their God, and they shall be my people. 34 And they shall teach no more every man his neighbor, and every man his brother, saying, Know the LORD: for they shall all know me, from the least of them unto the greatest of them, says the LORD: for I will forgive their iniquity, and I will remember their sin no more. Jer 31:31-34.

Heb applies union life to the N.T. church as part of what Christ has done.[206]

> 8 For finding fault with them, he says, Behold, the days come, says the Lord, when I will make a new covenant with the house of Israel and with the house of Judah: 9 Not according to the covenant that I made with their fathers in the day when I took them by the hand to lead them out of the land of Egypt; because they continued not in my covenant, and I regarded them not, says the Lord. 10 For this [is] the covenant that I will make with the house of Israel after those days, says the Lord; I will put my laws into their mind, and write them in their hearts: and I will be to them a God, and they shall be to me a people: 11 And they shall not teach every man his neighbor, and every man his brother, saying, Know the Lord: for all shall know me, from the least to the greatest. Heb 8-10

Paul describes union life by the phrase in Christ, in Jesus, the supply of the Spirit of Jesus or joined unto the Lord. Some of his most famous union life verses include the following:

> 15 But when it pleased God, who separated me from my mother's womb, and called me by his grace, 16 To **reveal his Son in me**, that I might preach him among the heathen. Gal 1:16

> 20 I am crucified with Christ: nevertheless I live; yet not I, but Christ **lives in me**: and the life which I now live in the flesh I live by the faith of the Son of God, who loved me, and gave himself for me. Gal 2:20

> 26 [Even] the mystery[207] which hath been hid from ages and from generations, but now is made manifest to his saints. 27 To whom God would make known what is the riches of the glory of this mystery among the Gentiles—**Christ in you**, the hope of glory. 28 Whom we preach, warning every person, and teaching every person in all wisdom; that

---

[205] Theologically we are dealing with the notion of sanctification when we talk about union life.

[206] Thematically, Heb is teaching that **God's Redemptive Revelation in Christ** is superior to any other, is final, and therefore demands a continued faithful allegiance. Part of its superiority is the realization of the New Covenant through Christ.

[207] A mystery, in Pauline language, means something not previously revealed by God but now revealed by God and opened up so people can see its truth. Union life is such a concept.

70. Union Life

we may present every person grown up and mature in Christ Jesus: 29 Whereunto I also labor, striving according to his working, which works in me mightily. Col 1:27

17 But he that is joined unto the Lord is one spirit. 1Co 6:17

Peter describes the foundation for union life in breath taking language.

Whereby are given unto us exceeding great and precious promises—that by these you might be **partakers of the divine nature,** having escaped the corruption that is in the world through lust. 2Pe 1:4

Most believers can read these verses and still not know anything about union life. What does it look like? Paul models it for us in all of his epistles. But it is most clearly seen in Php.

What Does Union Life Look Like? See Philippians.

Whereas Paul teaches conceptually about union life in the book of Ro, he demonstrates it in the book of Php. Table 1,2 Co 70-1 describes seven characteristics of union life as modeled by Paul in Php.

Table 1,2 Co 70-1. Seven Characteristics of Union Life Modeled By Paul in Php

Characteristic	Vs	Explanation
Christ-centered	1:20-22	Paul's daily life involved a centeredness in Christ and a desire to have this Christ impact his everyday testimony.
Inner Resources	1:19; 3:9,10; 4:13.	Paul knew that the Spirit of Christ indwelled and that Spirit was his source of power. It was the same kind of power as that which raised Jesus from the dead—resurrection power.
Joy	1:4, 25, 26; 2:2, 17, 18, 2:29; 4:1.	Joy in the midst of hard, shaping life experiences, should be the hallmark of a believer in union with Christ. Joy is a fruit of the Spirit that distinguished a believer from an unbeliever, particularly in distressing circumstances. Joy is referred to throughout Php. Paul uses five different words for joy.
Relationships	2:1-3; 4:2 and general tone throughout	A believer in union with Christ recognizes also that he/she is related to every other believer in the body. Such a recognition longs for unity with them—like mindedness, good relationships.
Sovereign Mindset	1:12; 2:17; 4:11,12.	Sovereign mindset refers to an attitude demonstrated by the Apostle Paul in which he tended to see God's working in the events and activities that shaped his life, whether or not they were positive and good or negative and bad. He tended to see God's purposes in these shaping activities and to make the best of them. A person in union life sees God's activities through life's experiences (Ro 8:28-30) as shaping toward the image of Christ.
Destiny/ Growth To Maturity	3:10-14; 15-16.	Paul has a driving goal to move toward maturity in Christ. (see also Ac 20:24 and 2Ti 4:7,8). A believer in union life presses on toward growth an maturity.
Peace	4:6,7.	Paul speaks of the God of peace and the peace of God. A believer can know this fruit of the Spirit, this aspect of victory in the life, in the midst of pressing life circumstances. In fact, it like joy, is a hallmark of a believer in union life.

Explanation—The Left Brained Approach—Logical Presentation Given in Ro 1-8.

Until a believer fully enters into the notion that Christ has indeed paid the full penalty for all his/her sins, those committed in the past, those being commuted in the present (known or unknown), and those to be committed in the future, it is very unlikely that that believer will enter into and experience *Victory* in the Christian life. The Ro 3:21-31 passage (dealing with justification—that is, God's means of justifying a sinner deserving of punishment by the sacrificial death of Christ for him/her—technically called the vicarious atonement) is the foundation for believing truth about *Victory in Christian living*. Some will by faith accept this truth without any preamble and enter into it, forever being freed from guilt. Others will perhaps need deliverance from some past dysfunctional hold as a preamble to seeing guilt forever gone.[208] In any case, a guilt free past is a pre-requisite or co-requisite to moving on to *Victory*.

The Christian life from beginning to end, Ro 1:16-18, is by faith. We accept what Christ did for us on the **Cross** to pay for our sins and make us guilt-free before a just God. We must also accept by faith what He has provided for *Victory in our lives*—that it is true that we can live increasingly knowing that sin does not control our lives. We do not claim perfection but we can live knowing we do not have to be dominated by some controlling sin in our lives. And we can experience this so as to encourage us as we move toward Christ-likeness in our lives.

The second look at the work on the **Cross** provides us with the revelation from God, the factual basis, which we accept by faith just like we did forgiveness of sins. We **KNOW** (Ro 6:6,7) it to be true, that we were mystically included with Christ in his death so as to break the controlling authority of sin in our lives and to be raised with him to know a resurrected life, free from this controlling authority of sin. It is a done deed.

We habitually **COUNT** (Ro 6:11) on it both implicitly and explicitly, moment by moment, as we sensitively follow the Spirit's leading. We know we can count on it. We give ourselves to this kind of life. It is by **FAITH** that we totally **SURRENDER** ourselves to this process, longing and wanting it in our lives.

And we know that it will take **SPIRIT FREEDOM**. But just in case we think it is us doing it we come face to face with the reality of the power of sin in our lives. And we are driven by deep need to want the **SPIRIT FREEDOM** and to know without it we are helpless and hopeless to experience that Victory in our lives.

And **SPIRIT FREEDOM** is there—again we know guilt free exposure before God and we recognize that without it we are helpless and hopeless to experience that *Victory* in our lives. And **SPIRIT FREEDOM** can be. We are assured within of our **Adoption** into the family—heirs with Christ. We will grow up to be like Christ. The Spirit stands ready always to point out our need and take care of giving us *Victory* in that need. It is a process over time for the total full perfection to be. But it will happen. It is an inevitable process moving forward to completion. We will become Christ-like. It is so certain that the whole process is **spoken of in the past** (prophetic past idiom). We were saved, we are being perfected, we will be totally perfected. Or another way of saying it: we were saved from sins, we are being saved from sin's control, we will be freed forever from its presence. We were saved. We are being saved. We will be yet totally saved.

Summarizing, Paul teaches logically that a believer's sins were taken care of at the **Cross**. Such a believer can be freed of guilt for those sins. But not only were sins dealt with at the **Cross** but also the controlling authority of sin in a life, the sin principle, was dealt with. A believer can accept this provision of enabling power to live above the controlling authority of sin in a life simply by faith. And a believer can continue to count on this enabling power. It is the Holy Spirit who will sensitively lead that believer to experience the power of the inward Christ life over sin. Such a believer, walking sensitively with the Holy Spirit will increasingly know more of this enabling power over time. Such a believer, in this life, will inexorably move toward experiencing this Christ life. It is an on-growing, ever increasing, process of growth.

Conclusion

Throughout this leadership commentary I have used the notion of,

Ministry flows out of being.

I have described being as comprised of at least the following: intimacy with God, character, personality, giftedness, destiny, values drawn from experience, gender influenced perspectives. Now I want to take it one step further. Ministry flows out of what being? I want to suggest that in addition to these characteristics

---

[208] Inner healing in which God miraculously provides knowledge about something enslaving from the past and breaks that hold or the Catholic approach of mediated authority (confession, penance, absolving) are two approaches I have seen effective in breaking past holds. For others, the Good News of the Gospel alone is sufficient. The passage in 1 Corinthians 6:9-11 shows experientially that such holds can be broken.

70. Union Life

ultimately I am talking about being involving the *union life being*—a person's beingness is complete when that person realizes intimacy as union with Christ.

Have you discovered this mystery, Christ in you as you—union life?

See **Articles**, *59. Sovereign Mindset; Abiding—Seven Symptoms*.

Article 71

Relevance of the Article to Paul's Corinthian Ministry

2 Co more than any of Paul's epistles provides the data base for deriving values that permeated his life and ministry. His was a value driven ministry.

71. Value Driven Leadership

A leader's ministry is said to be <u>value driven</u> if that leader consciously attempts to identify, make explicit and explain leadership values that under gird his/her ministry and deliberately operates his/her ministry based on these values.

Definition

A <u>leadership value</u> is an underlying assumption which affects how a leader perceives leadership and practices it.

Most leaders operate with underlying implicit values. To identify such values allows for several advantages:

1. The leader can have an increased effectiveness and consistency in his/her use of them by proactively applying them.

2. The leader can adapt or change or discard those which are not so good—as long as they are implicit, this can not be done.

3. The leader can better teach these values to others.

4. The leader can pass on the values to selected leaders who will carry them on as part of his/her heritage.

Jesus and Paul are the prime N.T. examples for explaining values underlying their ministry. See all the Gospels where Jesus is constantly explaining why he does what he does and why he says what he says. I have especially studied the Sermon on the Mount for values underlying Jesus authoritative teaching. See especially 1,2 Co and Gal where Paul explains the motivational reasons (values) behind his leadership behavior. I have identified and made explicit 19 Pauline leadership values from 2Co. See the **Article *51. Pauline Leadership Values*.**

Article 72

Relevance of the Article to Paul's Corinthian Ministry

This article describes my own pilgrimage in discovering a paradigm that has under girded my life long study of the Bible. Today we need those kind of leaders. Paul demonstrates this king of leadership—a Bible Centered Leader. This is my own journey toward grasping what Paul advocated and modeled.

72. Vanishing Breed

The concept of a vanishing breed is a relatively modern idea. For example, in the latter third of the 19th century, the buffalo became so hunted as to become an endangered species—a vanishing breed. As applied to the Christian scene the concept of a vanishing breed, in one sense, is a modern concept but in another is quite old concept. Until the mid 19th century and the proliferation of printed materials only a relatively few leaders were very familiar with the entire Bible. But with the Bible becoming a perennial best seller as has been the case in the 20th century, you would expect that many leaders would be Bible Centered leaders. But actually that is not the case. And it is growing worse, relatively speaking, because a rising generation of leaders is basically a non-reading group of people. But the notion of being a *Bible Centered Leader* is as old as the N.T. Church Leadership Era. Paul, the Apostle, stressed it to Timothy his younger co-worker. His two epistles, 1Ti and 2 Ti fairly bristle with Bible Centered Leadership insights. I suppose that you are not really surprised when I say the endangered specie I am concerned about is a little known animal—*A Bible Centered Leader*. Let me stress some ideas about that concept that I want to cover in this article:

We need Bible centered leaders.
You can become one.
Here are some helpful suggestions to become a Bible centered leader.

Shortly I will define for you a Bible centered leader. Let me first give my credentials.

I have been studying and using the Bible for 34 years. I have some deep convictions about that Bible. And I have learned some things about how to habitually ground oneself in this Bible. Three of my fundamental convictions are simple. They are captured in the following Biblical references.

A Lasting Source
The grass withers, the flower fades; but the Word of our God will stand forever. Isaiah 40:8

Fads, helpful as they may be, will come and go.[209] Effective leaders will recognize and use fads which are appropriate to the times and situations in which they lead. But there is more. My personal conviction about lasting effective ministry flows from the following two verses.

2 Timothy 3:16,17 The Guarantee About That Source
Every Scripture inspired of God is profitable for teaching, for setting things right, for confronting, for inspiring righteous living, in order that God's leader be thoroughly equipped to lead God's people.

---

[209] I consider a fad as a fashion that is taken up with great enthusiasm for a brief period of time; a craze. Frequently, behind a fad is some dynamic principle. If we can identify the dynamic underlying principle we can re-engineer other *fads* which will work later after the original fad dies out (e.g. seeker sensitive churches, various church growth fads, etc.) But the Word of God will always be eternally fresh for any time if its dynamic principles are unlocked.

72. A Vanishing Breed

> **2 Timothy 2:15 The Proper Response to the Guarantee**
> Make every effort to be pleasing to God, a Bible Centered leader who is completely confident in using God's Word with impact in lives.

In my opinion we have only one guarantee for an effective life time experience as a leader. We must be people of the Word. Seminaries are good. But a seminary degree does not guarantee an equipped leader. Short term training in leadership institutes is good and helpful. But institutes that offer various leadership emphases cannot guarantee equipping. Retreats, workshops, seminars, and conferences, all good in themselves and helpful in our development, cannot guarantee equipping. But God does guarantee it. He insures us that this unfading Word, which will stand forever, can equip us. If we center our lives and ministry in the Word we have a guarantee from God that it will equip us to lead. Our job is to respond and make every effort to please God in our mastery and use of this Word for our own lives and for those we serve. Let me suggest then, that,

> Effective leaders should have an appropriate, unique, lifelong plan for mastering the Word in order to use it with impact in their ministries.

I want to share with you four discoveries I have personally learned in my own thirty-four year pilgrimage of mastering the Word and using it with impact in my ministry.

1. A Guiding Paradigm Helps

Few leaders master the Word without a proactive, deliberate approach which plans to do so. I was challenged early on, shortly after my *Lordship committal* in 1964, to begin a lifelong mastery of the Word of God—an overwhelming task I thought at that time. Pastor L. Thompson, the challenger, had been in the Word almost 30 years at that time. He was my model that it could be done. My Navigator trained friend, Harold Dollar, gave me my first paradigm for doing that. The Navigators were using an illustration called *The Hand* to challenge people to study and use God's Word. The little finger represented listening to God's Word. The ring finger stood for reading God's Word. The middle finger indicated studying God's Word. The index finger reminded of memorizing God's Word. The thumb represented Meditating on God's Word. I immediately set out to use this paradigm. I learned to listen well (using *Sermon Listening Sheets*). I started to get tapes from Bible teachers. I started my yearly read through the Bible program. I began to memorize three verses per week. I set a goal to study one book thoroughly each year (if a long book or more if shorter books). I learned techniques for analyzing verses and doing word studies which helped me learn how to meditate. In short, I made this paradigm really work for me. I used this paradigm for 15 years with one or more of the components having more prominence from time-to-time.

During the next 10 years I found that not all the components were important to me. By this time I was well into my leadership research and was not actively teaching the Bible in a local church context. I did continue to use several of *The Hand* components as guidelines. Essentially I was struggling for a better paradigm that both fit me and my ministry.

During the last seven years I have been working from my new paradigm. And that is what I want to share with you. It has given me new life. Every where I go I try to share it—one on one, in groups, in seminars, and in classes. I find that people really respond to it. They react with a fresh new excitement about studying the Bible. I know that some of my readers have really plateaued in their mastery of the Word. I know that some of you are not seeing the Word impacting your leadership. Some of you are probably seeing impact, but are looking for more. Maybe what I have found may help you.

But even if my new paradigm may not work for you, I still contend that you need some plan to move toward life long mastery.

2. The Breakthrough Insight—The Notion of Core

I stumbled on to this new paradigm as I studied giftedness of leaders.[210] In my research of leaders developing over a lifetime, I found that:

---

[210] These first three observations which follow came as a result of 10 years research in giftedness among contemporary leaders at the School of World Mission. See **Unlocking Your Giftedness** from Barnabas Publishers which gives the results of studies of giftedness among leaders.

(1) all leaders have at least one word gift; most have a set of word gifts. Word gifts include teaching, exhortation, prophecy, pastoring, evangelism, apostleship, and ruling (leadership). Sometimes either word of knowledge, word of wisdom, discernings of spirits or word of faith functions as a word gift.
(2) all leaders have core items in the Bible which are important to them.

It was this last item that was the *breakthrough insight*. This observation can prove extremely valuable to one who has a desire to establish a life long habit of mastering the Word and wants to use it impactfully in ministry. The observation, expanded a bit:

Leaders usually have favorite Bible books, or special passages, which God has used mightily in their own lives to spur their growth or solve their problems or otherwise meet them. It is these books or special passages which form the basis for much of what they share with others in their ministry.

And they usually do so with added impact since these core items have meant something to them personally. This interest in and repetitive use of core items suggests a selection criterion. We can limit what should be mastered in-depth over a life time to our core items. These core items provide a definite starting place for mastery of the Bible. From this observation I have drawn two important definitions.

Definition — A <u>Core Set</u> is a collection of very important Bible books, usually from 5-20, which are or have been extremely meaningful to you in your own life and for which you feel a burden from God to use with great power over and over in your ministry in the years to come.

Definition — A <u>Core Selection</u> refers to important passages, important biographical characters, special psalms, special values or key topics which are or have been extremely meaningful to you in your own life and for which you feel a burden from God to use with great power over and over in your ministry in the years to come.

It is this breakthrough insight which makes mastery of the Bible a realizable potential for word gifted leaders. The *Equipping Formula* suggests one paradigm a leader can use to focus his/her mastery of the Bible.

3. The Equipping Formula—four components

My new paradigm, which I call the *Life Long Bible Mastery Paradigm*, has four components.

Component 1. **Mastery** of one's Core Books or other core material,
Component 2. **Devotional Input** (from Core Books and other Bible portions as well)
Component 3. When needed, **Familiarity Reading** of weak Bible Portions.
Component 4. **Situational Study**

The first two components are obligatory and should be going on all the time. The next two are contingent upon need.

All leaders need to be working on mastering core material continually. All leaders need to have God speak to them personally through the Word. All leaders need to have some minimum familiarity with the whole Word, even though they are moving toward mastery of a limited number of core items in the Bible. From time to time leaders will have situations in their leadership setting which demand a searching study of the Bible for special findings. These will come and go as prompted by situations. The *Equipping Formula* takes in to account these various needs. Its four components form the basis for planning, short term and long term.

4. Impact Communication—Studying for Ideas that Change Lives

Core items are important to a leader. They have already impacted that leader personally. Because of this, a leader can usually use the core items in ministry to impact others. I teach those who want to use this *Life Long Bible Mastery Paradigm* to identify the key ideas in a core book, a core Psalm, a core passage, a

72. A Vanishing Breed   page 346

core topic, core biographical characters or core values. Then as part of the plan of mastering that core item, I teach them to design communication events to present these key ideas.

Effective leaders should have an appropriate, unique, lifelong plan for mastering the Word in order to use it with impact in their ministries. We need Bible centered leaders. The *Life Long Bible Mastery Paradigm* is simply one of many that can be used. You may use others. I am happy if you do. The real questions are, "Do you have a Bible centered ministry? Are you a Bible Centered leader?" Well, I promised earlier to define this endangered specie.

Definition   A Bible Centered leader refers to a leader whose leadership is informed by the Bible, who has been shaped by Biblical leadership values, who has grasped the intent of Scriptural books and their content in such a way as to apply them to current situations and who uses the Bible in ministry so as to impact followers.

Join the *Save the Bible Centered Leaders Association*! At least save one of them. You! Be a Pauline fan and appropriate 2 Ti 3:16,17 for your life and ministry. Don't let *Bible Centered Leaders* become a vanishing breed!

Article 73

Relevance of the Article to Paul's Corinthian Ministry

Paul usually followed the epistolary format of his times. He opened his letters with a salutation. The important thing about this is that Paul usually foreshadowed what he wanted to deal with in the epistle by carefully worded, sometimes almost cryptic phrases. I have studied comparatively all of Paul's salutations to see what are the functions he carries out in them. I have identified seven functions. In the epistles to the Corinthians Paul touches on six of the seven. The most important concerns his reference to his apostolic calling. He will need the spiritual authority of that apostolic calling in dealing with the problems in Corinth. He also does the foreshadow function (a good motivating technique) of identifying some major concept(s) he will deal with in the epistle; And note that he does the sponsor function—Sosthenes in the first epistle and Timothy in the second epistle. The salutation extensions are very important in the two Corinthian letters. Paul lays out more explicitly some of the issues he will deal with.

73. Variations on His Theme: Paul's Salutations—Harbingers of His Epistles

Introduction

I distinctly remember in my eleventh grade English class when I first ran into the word harbinger. It was in a poem by now long forgotten,

> A robin is the harbinger of spring.

I had learned from my eighth grade English class to look up new words I encountered, a habit I am now very grateful for. So I looked up harbinger. Here is my simplified paraphrasing of its definition.

definition   A <u>harbinger</u> is one that foreshadows what is to come.

Usually it refers to a person. But I am applying it in my title of this article to a thing--Paul's salutation.

I think it was in my study of Romans, years ago, that I first noticed the connection between special phrases in the salutation[211] and thematic treatment of topics in the book.

Over the years as I have continued to study more and more of Paul's epistles as core books I have been very aware of Paul's salutations. A careful reading of his salutations puts you well on the way to focusing on important thematic ideas in his books.

Paul's Salutations

In our world, salutations in letters are very brief and contain only a few words or two like Dear Mom, Dear Sirs, To Whom It May Concern, etc. Not so with epistles in Paul's time. And I am thankful for the very wordy difference.

---

[211] Alford specifically identifies the doctrinal inserts in Paul's salutations and calls them fore-announcements. See bibliography for Alford entry.

73. Variations on His Theme—Paul's Salutations

definition	A <u>salutation</u> is the opening line of a letter which describes to whom the letter is addressed.
definition	A <u>Pauline Salutation</u> is the opening paragraph in any of Paul's letters which follows the form of from /to with some greeting words thrown in and some qualifying phrases tucked here and there.
definition	A <u>Pauline salutation extension</u> refers to the immediate paragraph which follows the salutation and which often links the salutation to the body of the letter as well as leads into the body itself as part of the body of the epistle. It functions to extend the thematic intent of the salutation.

Paul's salutations are intriguing. Comparative study of them identifies several functions that Paul accomplishes in his salutations.

Function 1.	He claim's apostolic authority;
Function 2.	He qualifies, in a terse explanatory way, his ministry;
Function 3.	He foreshadows (a good motivating technique) some major concept(s) he will deal with in the epistle;
Function 4.	He does sponsoring of mentorees;
Function 5.	He identifies the recipient(s)--usually with a unique name or phrase if a church;
Function 6.	He sometimes gives his own personal state;
Function 7.	Greets, usually with some form of a blessing.

Not all of these occur in every salutation. But all of them do occur in some salutation or salutation extension. A recognition of these functions can alert us to read the rest of the epistle with a focus.

Paul's Salutations Displayed

Glance quickly through each of Paul's salutations. I will highlight some important features. I will then identify the functions accomplished by each and will identify the foreshadowing phrases. Finally I will try to correlate between the foreshadowing phrases and the overall theme of each book.

Romans 1:1-7
1 Paul, a servant of Jesus Christ, called to be an apostle, separated unto the gospel of God, 2 Which he had promised before by his prophets in the holy scriptures, 3 Concerning his Son Jesus Christ our Lord, which was made of the seed of David according to the flesh; 4 And declared to be the Son of God with power, according to the spirit of holiness, by the resurrection from the dead: 5 By whom we have received grace and apostleship, for obedience to the faith among all nations, for his name. 6 Among whom you are also the called of Jesus Christ: 7 To all that are in Rome, beloved of God, called to be saints: Grace to you and peace from God our Father, and the Lord Jesus Christ.

1 Corinthians
1 Paul, called as an apostle of Jesus Christ as God willed it, and Sosthenes, our brother, 2 To the church of God which is at Corinth, to those who are especially set apart in union with Christ Jesus, to live holy lives, with all who in every place call on the name of Jesus Christ our Lord, and theirs too. 3 Grace to you and peace from God our Father and the Lord Jesus Christ.

2 Corinthians
1 Paul, an apostle of Jesus Christ by the will of God, and Timothy our brother, To the church of God which is at Corinth, with all the saints who are in all Greece. 2 Grace to you and peace from God our Father and the Lord Jesus Christ.

73. Variations on His Theme—Paul's Salutations

Galatians
1 Paul, an apostle, not of men, neither by man, but by Jesus Christ, and God the Father, who raised him from the dead; 2 And all the believers which are with me, unto the churches of Galatia: 3 Grace be to you and peace from God the Father, and [from] our Lord Jesus Christ, 4 Who gave himself for our sins, that he might deliver us from this present evil world, according to the will of God and our Father:
5 To whom be glory for ever and ever. Amen.

Ephesians
1 Paul, an apostle of Jesus Christ by the will of God, to the saints which are at Ephesus, and to the faithful in Christ Jesus: 2 Grace be to you, and peace, from God our Father, and from the Lord Jesus Christ.

Philippians
1 Paul and Timothy, the servants of Jesus Christ, to all the saints in Christ Jesus which are at Philippi, with the bishops and deacons. 2 Grace be unto you, and peace, from God our Father, and from the Lord Jesus Christ.

Colossians
1 Paul, an apostle of Jesus Christ by the will of God, and Timotheus our brother, 2 To the saints and faithful brethren in Christ which are at Colosse: Grace be unto you, and peace, from God our Father and the Lord Jesus Christ.

1 Thessalonians
1 Paul, and Silvanus, and Timotheus, unto the church of the Thessalonians which is in God the Father and in the Lord Jesus Christ: Grace be unto you, and peace, from God our Father, and the Lord Jesus Christ.

2 Thessalonians
1 Paul, and Silvanus, and Timotheus, unto the church of the Thessalonians in God our Father and the Lord Jesus Christ: 2 Grace unto you, and peace, from God our Father and the Lord Jesus Christ.

1 Timothy
1 Paul, an apostle of Jesus Christ by the commandment of God our Savior, and the Lord Jesus Christ, which is our hope; 2 Unto Timothy, my own son in the faith: Grace, mercy, and peace, from God our Father and Jesus Christ our Lord.

2 Timothy
1 Paul, an apostle of Jesus Christ by God's design, to proclaim the promised life which is in Christ Jesus, 2 To Timothy, my dearly beloved son. May you have Grace, mercy, and peace, from God the Father and Christ Jesus our Lord.

Titus
1:1 I, Paul, am ministering as a servant of God and an apostle of Jesus Christ to help mature God's own chosen followers. I want them to know the truth that leads to godliness. 2 I want them to have a faith and a knowledge grounded in an expectation of eternal life. God, who can not lie, promised this eternal life before the beginning of time. 3 At His appointed time, He revealed His truth about this. God our Savior entrusted me with this task and commanded me to preach it. 4 I write to you, Titus, one who is like my very own son because of our common faith.

Philemon
1 Paul, a prisoner of Jesus Christ, and Timothy our brother, to Philemon our dearly beloved, and fellow laborer. 2 Hello also to our beloved Apphia, and Archippus our fellow soldier, and to the church in your house. 3 Grace to you, and peace, from God our Father and the Lord Jesus Christ.

73. Variations on His Theme—Paul's Salutations

Table 1,2 Co 73-1 Functions Identified in Paul's Salutations

Book	Fn 1	Fn2	Fn3	Fn4	Fn5	Fn 6	Fn7
Rom	√	√	√		√		√
1 Co	√		√	√	√		√
2 Co	√		√	√	√	√	√
Gal	√		√		√		√
Eph	√				√		√
Php		√		√	√		√
Col	√			√	√		√
1 Th				√	√		√
2 Th				√	√		√
1 Ti	√		√	√	√		√
2 Ti	√		√	√	√		√
Tit	√	√	√	√	√		√
Phm		√		√	√	√	√

Table 1,2 Co 73-2 Foreshadowing Phrases

Book	Phrases
Rom	1....gospel of God, ... 2. promised before by his prophets in the holy scriptures, 3. Concerning his Son Jesus Christ our Lord, ... the seed of David according to the flesh; 4. declared to be the Son of God with power, according to the 5. spirit of holiness, by the resurrection from the dead: 6. ...obedience to the faith among all nations, for his name. 7...called of Jesus Christ: ...called to be saints:
1 Co	1. set apart in union with Christ Jesus, to live holy lives (Paul is going to deal with immorality problems) In the extension: 2. Grace of God (by metonymy the notion of spiritual gifts, which he will deal with in depth, especially the problems regarding projection of the tongues gifts on all) 3. enriched in everything (dealing both with the wisdom problem and the projection of certain gifts as being more important) 4. not lacking any spiritual gift (projection problem again foreshadowed) 5. without fault (dealing with the whole immorality problem and other problems—From a confidence that God can solve them) 6. day of our Lord Jesus Christ (they will be held accountable for their beliefs and actions) Note: Paul prays for the Corinthians.
2 Co	1. saints who are in all Greece In the extension: 2. with all the Saints who are in all Greece (reminds them of their needed holy behavior and that the church is bigger than their little groups in Corinth) 3. you will indirectly benefit (uses maturity appeal as well as gives expectation for the shaping activity of God through deep processing) 4. unshakeable hope (using Goodwin's Expectation Principle).
Gal	1. apostle, not of men, neither by man, but by Jesus Christ, and God the Father, 2. who raised him from the dead 3. Who gave himself for our sins, 4. that he might deliver us from this present evil world, according to the will of God and our Father:

73. Variations on His Theme—Paul's Salutations

Eph, Php, Col, 1,2 Th, Phm	none; extension yes
1 Ti	which is our hope
2 Ti	to proclaim the promised life which is in Christ Jesus
Tit	1. to help mature God's own chosen followers. 2. I want them to know the truth that leads to godliness. 3. I want them to have a faith and a knowledge grounded in an expectation of eternal life. 4. God, who can not lie, promised this eternal life before the beginning of time. 5. At His appointed time, He revealed His truth about this. 6. God our Savior

When you do detailed study of each of the books and are aware of these foreshadowing elements you will see them reflected in the theme of the book as a whole, in various parts of the structure of the book, and the emphasis of small contextual units as well as even larger contextual units.

Conclusion

I want to suggest 4 ways that an awareness of Paul's salutations and his use of them can help us as we read and study his epistles.

1. We always read better when looking for things. In our study of effective readers[212] we uncovered the basic principle that when you read looking for something you read much more alertly and discover much more than if you are reading just generally looking for things.
2. In his salutations, Paul stresses some important things to him. If they are important to Paul we want to know why.
3. It should make us aware of the basic principle of intentional selection. The Spirit of God superintended the writing of the inspired word and has not given us all that could be given but has selected that which we need. So we should recognize the importance of words. They are there not by happenstance but for reasons. This should also make us more conscious of our own words. We should use words that count.
4. Paul's use of phrases to describe God is important. He uses phrases to describe God in terms of God's revealing Himself to Paul to meet certain needs Paul faced. When we experience God, we should use language that describes God in terms of those experiences.[213] As leaders our language describing God will influence our followers. We should use our titles and phrases for God proactively so as to affect our followers.

Paul's salutations foreshadow what he will deal with in his epistles. We should read them with extra care, knowing that they will help unfold truth in the epistles.

Final Comment:

Paul introduced—not all the problems in the Corinthian church that he would deal with—but certainly some very important ones.

---

[212] See my booklet, **Reading on the Run.**
[213] The archetype of this in the Bible is Daniel. His use of names and phrases to describe God captures who God was for him.

Article 74

Relevance of the Article to Paul's Corinthian Ministry
 This is the third of three articles mentioned concerning Paul and prayer. It is an important one for it reveals the necessity of transparency in a leader—if that leader wants to experience the effects of other's powerful praying in his/her life and ministry. Obviously the Corinthian ministry serves as one of those powerful illustrations of transparency and prayer in the life of Paul.

74. Vulnerability and Prayer—As Seen In Paul's Life

Introduction

As a young Christian I frequently heard strange words at the Wednesday night prayer meetings. Some one would lift a hand for prayer but say it was an unspoken request. Now I wondered about that. How could I pray for an unspoken request? When I knew really nothing about the request? What difference would such a prayer make? Later, as I saw this more often, I became personally convinced that unspoken requests basically engender unspoken prayers. On the other hand, when I read Paul's pleas for prayer for himself I recognized something else. A Christian leader who is vulnerable, open and transparent in sharing about life and ministry with caring supporters will get empathetic, caring, intercessory prayer. Paul recognized an important dynamic.

> **Transparency and vulnerability, in sharing by a leader, allows others to identify with and pray more fervently and with understanding for God's answers.**

Prayer backers make a big difference in the life of a leader who can share openly with them. Many leaders fear sharing vulnerably and openly. They miss out on one of God's resources for them. Paul models the kind of open sharing that leaders need to do.

Kinds of Things Paul Shared

Consider the kinds of things that Paul shared with close individuals or churches.

Table 1,2 Co 74-1. Paul's Sharing

To Whom	Where	What
Philippian believers	1:3-11	His **feelings** toward them—joy because they had shared in the ministry of the Gospel; Paul openly shares his **emotions**: he tender affection for them; he has them in his heart; they stood behind him in his imprisonment.
	1:12-26	His situation while in prison; **pressures** from groups with wrong motivations about sharing Christ; his **need for the Philippian prayers** to see the Supply of the Spirit in his situation; his **feelings** about living or dying.
Corinthian believers	2Co passages: 1:3-7	His **value** underlying how and why he can face trying situations—Christ can meet him and prove sufficient, which in turn gives him a firm conviction about Christ meeting anyone in trying times.
	1:8-11	His **near death experience** and his feelings of being **overwhelmed** as a result. And his deliverance in that situation. His view on sharing this with many who prayed and in return their rejoicing in answered prayer.
	1:12-23	His **reasons** why he did not visit the Corinthians. These are open—no holding back.
	4:1-6	Why he doesn't **give up** in ministry.
	6:11-13	His **heart relationship** toward the Corinthians and there lack of.
	7:2-4	His **innocence** toward them. His desire for a **heart relationship** with them.

74. Vulnerability and Prayer—As Seen In Paul's Life   page 353

	7:5-7 7:13-15 11:21-29	**Troubles** he faced in Macedonia. His **inner feelings** about them. His joy at their **receiving** Titus. Paul shares the many things he has **suffered** in his ministry for Christ. All throughout this Corinthian epistle Paul levels with the Corinthians both as to his motivations, his values, his reasons why he did things and what he sees are wrong with them.

Conclusion

Leaders need at least some supporters with whom they can be transparent, open, and vulnerable. Paul shares attitudes, inner feelings, values, reasons why he does things, his own inadequate responses to some situations, his emotions, his affections for those he writes to, issues between them, his need of specific and special prayer, etc. He is an open leader.

It is probably not wise to share this way all the time with all followers. But this kind of sharing should go on. To admit need. To show how God meets that need. This kind of sharing actually encourages followers.

There will be mature followers who can discern, understand, and intercede wisely in prayer for a leader who does share this way. I recommend that every leader should have a close-in group of prayer supporters with whom they can share this way all the time.

See **Articles**, *Daniel—Leaders and Prayer Backing*.

74. Vulnerability and Prayer—As Seen In Paul's Life   page 354

(This page is deliberately left blank.)

Glossary—Leadership Definitions

The following leadership related definitions occur throughout the 1,2 Co commentary. They are listed here alphabetically for convenience in referencing. SRN stands for Strong's Reference Number. These numbers can be used to look up the definitions of these words in the **Strong's Exhaustive Concordance** containing Hebrew and Greek dictionaries. These numbers are now also used by many other Bible study aids.

Item	Definition
abiding	a term used in Jn 15 which refers to an on-going intimate relationship between a believer and Jesus in which the believer is identified with the life of Jesus. This is John's equivalent of union life as given by Paul.
absolute for relative	A comparative idiom of the form not A but B given absolutely. But it is really a relative comparison which really means B is much more important than A and used to emphasize how important B really is. Example 1Pe 3:3,4.
accelerated pattern	a pattern describing the early developmental foundational phase of a leader; that leader has an early rapid development sometimes flowing from generational models, a family heritage of leadership; the leader responds positively very early in life to doing ministry (often co-ministering with parents).
accountability	a term used to describe the fact that a leader will answer to God for his/her ministry. Paul has a major leadership value concerning this. See Ultimate Accountability.
affect	a learning domain, that is, a term describing learning which primarily moves the feelings and emotions.
affirmation	a personal inner need that leaders have for approval from God (sometimes via others) for personhood and for ministry.
anthropomorphism	a special idiom. Human language and illustrations are used to talk about God and His ways so that humans can grasp things about God in terms of things they do know. They are not literally true about God but point analogously to spiritual things which are true.
a-periodic scheduling	refers to a mentoring technique which stresses repeated meetings between mentor and mentoree but not on a fixed time schedule. Meetings occur when mentorees are ready—that is, they have responded to the developmental tasks given to them and are ready for feedback on it, perhaps affirmation as well, and new assignments.
apocalyptic literature	a special prophetic genre of literature. Ralph Alexander's definition of apocalyptic is technically helpful. <u>Apocalyptic literature</u> is symbolic visionary prophetic literature, composed during oppressive conditions, consisting of visions whose events are recorded exactly as they were seen by the author and explained through a divine interpreter, and whose theological content is primarily eschatological. According to this technical definition the following Old Testament passages are classified apocalyptic: Eze 37:1-14; Eze 40-48; Daniel's vision in ch 2, 7, 8 and 10-12; Zec 1:7-

6:8. Alexander's research was on the Old Testament so I have no list of New Testament apocalyptic literature.

Apostolic ministry, Phase I	Phase I. Ground Breaking Apostolic Work (like Paul and Barnabas in Thessalonica) refers primarily to evangelistic work, that is, to the expansion of Christianity into people groups not familiar with or embracing Christianity.
Apostolic ministry, Phase II	Phase II. Edification Apostolic Work (like Titus in Crete) refers to the building up of the body of Christ in people groups in cultures not familiar with or embracing the biblical revelation. It involves application/ contextualization of Scriptural truth/principles in cross-cultural situations.
Apostolic ministry, Phase III	Phase III. Corrective Apostolic Work (like Timothy in Ephesus) refers to the correction of doctrinal error or behavioral error in church situations that are beyond the initial phases of evangelism and establishing of the body based on Biblical truth, that is, dealing with orthodoxic and orthopraxic heresy.
apostolic style	one of ten Pauline leadership styles—the most highly directive style. The apostolic leadership style is a method of influence in which the leader assumes the role of delegated authority over those for whom he/she is responsible, receives revelation from God concerning decisions, and commands obedience based on the role of delegated authority and revelation concerning God's will. The essence of the apostolic style is the legitimate right from God to make decisions for others and to command or demand their compliance with those decisions.
apostleship	one of the 19 spiritual gifts. The gift of apostleship refers to a special leadership capacity to move with authority from God to create new ministry structures (churches and parachurch groups) to meet needs and to develop and appoint leadership in these structures. **Its central thrust is Creating New Ministry.**
apostrophe	a figure of speech. Apostrophe is a special case of personification in which the speaker addresses the thing personified as if it were alive and listening. e.g. 1Co 15:55 O death, where is your sting? O grave, where is your victory.
apprenticeship	refers to a leadership training model, dominantly done in the informal training mode. It represents a model in which an expert in something, technically called the master, teaches a learner to master that same subject or skill. There is usually some set time over which the learning will occur. The learner is called an apprentice.
artist	a label given to the ultimate contribution of a Christian leader who has creative breakthroughs in life and ministry and introduces innovation. e.g. John the Apostle, C. S. Lewis.
a-service	a training term which refers to when training is given—describes the fact that training does not relate directly to when ministry happens.
authority insights	from leadership emergence theory. One of 51 process items that God uses to shape a leader. Authority insights describes those instances in ministry in which a leader learns important lessons, via positive or negative experiences, with regards to: submission to authority, authority structures,

Glossary of Leadership Definitions—1,2 Co Commentary page 357

	authenticity of power bases underlying authority, authority conflict, how to exercise authority.
beingness	a term describing the inner life of a person and referring to intimacy with God, character, personality, giftedness, destiny, values drawn from experience, gender influenced perspectives. The axiom, ministry flows out of being means that one's ministry should be a vital outflow from these inner beingness factors.
benchmarks, spiritual	this refers to something that happens in the life of the leader which serves as positive proof of God's activity in that life. It is something that a leader can look back upon and be encouraged to continue when confused or in a discouraging situation. Because it is foundational, sure and certain, and had the distinct imprint of God's Hand on the life. See also destiny processing.
Bible Centered leader	a leader (1) whose leadership is being informed by the Bible and (2) who personally has been shaped by Biblical values, (3) who has grasped the intent of Scriptural books and their content in such a way as to apply them to current situations and (4) who uses the Bible in ministry so as to impact followers.
bishop	a leadership term (SRN 1985 episkopo" v)used in Philippians 1:1, 1 Tim 3:2, Titus 1:7 and 1 Pet 2:25. Occurs as the word overseer in Acts 20:28 and which probably best describes its function. As used in this time Paul's life time a person responsible for the spiritual welfare of others in a local church situation. Probably synonymous with the term elder.
broadened kinship, idiom	Sometimes the terms son of, daughter of, mother of, father of, brother of, sister of, or begat, which in English imply a close relationship, have a much wider connotation in the Bible. Brother or sister could include various male or female relatives such as cousins; mother and father could include relatives such as grandparents or great-great-grandparents, in the direct family line. Begat may simply mean was directly in the family line of ancestors.
brokenness	a state of mind in which a person recognizes that he/she is helpless in a situation or life process unless God alone works. It is a state of mind in which a person acknowledges a deep dependence upon God and is open for God to break through in new ways, thoughts, directions, and revelation of Himself that was not the case before the brokenness experience. Example: Jacob in Genesis 32 faced a life threatening situation in which he was forced to desperately depend upon God.
browse	a technical term taken from continuum reading which refers to the reading of a book in which whole contexts of the book are read such as chapters, units within chapters but not the whole book. See continuum reading. See For Further Study Bibliography—**Reading on the Run**.
burden	a technical term in leadership emergence theory referring to the sense of responsibility a leader has toward some ministry for accomplishing God's purposes for that ministry and/or a sense of giving account for that ministry to God. See also downward burden, upward burden.
capture	a technical term used when talking about figures of speech being interpreted. A figure or idiom is said to be captured when one can display

the intended emphatic meaning of it in non-figurative simple words. e.g. not ashamed of the Gospel = captured: completely confident of the Gospel.

central truth	when referring to parables, mini-parables, parabolic illustrations or the like, one uses the notion of central truth which is the main truth which the entire parabolic teaching is intending to convey. It is a statement which exhibits the meaning intended by the parabolic material which is using comparisons to teach this central truth.
change dynamics principle, getting it on the agenda	*Getting it on the agenda* is a basic motivational technique used by a change person. It means to get an idea before a people without them yet knowing it will be important later on in the change process. Frequently, in bringing about change it is better to get an idea out there, subconsciously, where it can start to take root, than to bring it up directly and have it voted down. Once voted down, an idea will be very difficult to later get action on.
change participants	when change is being introduced into some situation, one can analyze the people in the situation in terms of how they will respond to change as they participate in the change process. Usually they can be grouped into three types: favorable, neutral, unfavorable. In John's Gospel we see particularly in the religious leaders two basic type of unfavorable change participants—maintainers and resistors.
change person	a label given to the ultimate contribution of a Christian leader who rights wrongs and injustices in society and in church and mission organizations. e.g. Amos, Micah, John the Baptist.
chiasmus	a figure of speech in which two pairs of items are listed in a text. The first item really refers to the fourth item and the second really refers to the third. e.g. Philemon 5. Literally, your love and faith toward the Lord Jesus and toward all saints = your faith, which you have in the Lord Jesus, and love for all the saints.
Church Era	shortened form of Church Leadership Era. The leadership era associated with Peter, Paul, and John and to the present. Ushered in at Pentecost. It is a time of spiritual leadership exercised around the world in many cultures.
coercive authority	one of five power forms, identified by Dennis Wrong, which a leader may use to influence followers. In essence the power holder threatens to punish the follower.
cognitive	a learning domain, that is, a term describing learning which primarily focuses on the transmittal and understanding of knowledge and ideas.
competent authority	one of five power forms, identified by Dennis Wrong, which a leader may use to influence followers. In essence the leader has influence with followers because they perceive the leader has having expertise and worthy to be followed.
conative	a learning domain, that is, a term describing learning which primarily focuses on the influencing a person to commit to the things being learned; it wants to bring about volitional compliance—a willingness to use what is being learned. Jesus stresses this emphasis in Jn 7:17 and Jn 13-17.

conflict	from leadership emergence theory. One of 51 process items that God uses to shape a leader. The conflict process item refers to those instances in a leader's life-history in which God uses conflict, whether personal or ministry related to develop the leader in dependence upon God, faith, and inner-life.
confrontation style	one of ten Pauline leadership styles—a highly directive style. The confrontation leadership style is an approach to problem solving which brings the problem out in the open with all parties concerned, which analyzes the problem in light of revelational truth, and which brings authority to bear upon the parties to accept recommended solutions.
conscience	the inner sense of right or wrong which is innate in a human being but which also is modified by values imbibed from a culture. This innate sense can also be modified by the Spirit of God.
consensus	one of 10 Pauline leadership styles. A highly non-directive style. The consensus leadership style refers to the approach to leadership influence which involves the group itself actively participating in decision making and coming to solutions acceptable to the whole group. The leader must be skilled in bringing diverse thoughts together in such a way as to meet the whole group's needs. See Acts 15 for use of this.
contextualization	the process of taking something meaningful in one context and making it relevant to a new context. e.g. the Christian movement which began in a Jewish context had to be reinterpreted by Paul to a non-Jewish context, the Gentiles.
continuum reading	an approach to reading which recognizes: 1) that a book does not have to be read word for word in its entirety in order for a person to profit from it; 2) that different books should be read in different ways. This approach recognizes that books can be read at different levels with each level to the right on the continuum becoming more detailed. The levels include scan, ransack, browse, pre-read, read, and study. It also recognizes that few books will be read to the right of the continuum and many will be read to the left. Leaders with a learning posture must master this approach or have some equally functional equivalent. See manual, **Reading on the Run,** listed in **For Further Study—Bibliography section** for detailed introduction to these concepts.
core books	Bible centered leaders usually have a set of Bible books that have impacted their lives and which they repeatedly use in their ministry to impact others. Such books are called core books.
crash time	time after intensive ministry in which a leader deliberately rests. This involves lots of sleep and recovery of physical strength, maybe exercise, no deliberate ministry, and lots of non-ministry things such as reading and other recreational things, in order to regain physical strength, mental agility, spiritual stamina. Failure to get crash time and to schedule intensive ministries back to back will eventually lead to some form of burnout.
crisis	from leadership emergence theory. One of 51 process items that God uses to shape a leader. Crisis process items refer to those special intense situations of pressure in human situations which are used by God to test and teach dependence.

critical incident	a leadership emergence term referring to a specific shaping event in which a major value is taught which permeates on-going ministry from that time or major direction results which guides a leader onto accomplishment of his/her destiny. Or the event could be a combination of a major value and guidance. See Phm. See Jn 21 for Peter.
Day of Christ	or also Day of the Lord, or That Day. A phrase used by Paul to indicate among other things that leaders will be held accountable in the future at this special time for their leadership influence. Paul had a strong value, *Leaders will ultimately give an account for their ministries.* In 2Co 5:10 Paul extends this accountability to all, not just leaders. See Php 1:6, 10; 2:16 and others in 1, 2Th. See also Heb 13:17 for another strong indication of this accountability a leader will face.
deacon	a leadership term (SRN 1249 diakono" v) translated: as deacon three times—Philippians 1:1, 1 Tim 3:8, 3:12; as minister 20 times; as servant 8 times. Paul uses this to describe his own self and Phoebe. It is not clear how this role relates to that of bishop and elder. It is distinguished as a separate leadership role and probably of less influence from bishop in 1 Tim 3.
Death/Life Paradox	a Pauline leadership value seen in 2Co. *The firstfruits of Jesus resurrection life ought to be experienced in the death producing circumstances of life and ought to serve as a hallmark of spiritual life for followers.*
deep processing	refers to a collection of process items which intensely work on deepening the maturity of a leader. The set includes the following process items: conflict, ministry conflict, crisis, life crisis, leadership backlash and isolation.
delayed pattern	a pattern flowing from the foundational developmental phase; describes the developmental pattern of generational Christian leaders (emerging leaders who have a family heritage of Christian leadership) who initially rebel against ministry very early in life but who eventually experience a deep leadership committal process item and though entering the ministry phase late experience rapid acceleration in their development.
destiny item Type I	a destiny experience which is an awe-inspiring experience in which God is sensed directly as acting or speaking in the life. Example: Moses at the burning bush.
destiny item Type II	a indirect destiny experience in which some aspect of destiny is linked to some person other than the leader and is done indirectly for the leader who simply must receive its implications. Example: Hannah's promise to give Samuel to God.
destiny item Type III	the build up of a sense of destiny in a life because of the accumulation of providential circumstances which indicate God's arrangement for the life. See Apostle Paul's birth and early life situation.
destiny item Type IV	the build up of a sense of destiny in a life because of the sensed blessing of God on the life, repeatedly. Seen by others and recognized by them as the Hand of God on the life. See Joseph.

destiny pattern	a leadership pattern. The development of a sense of destiny usually follows a three fold pattern of destiny preparation, destiny revelation, and destiny fulfillment. That is, over a period of time God shapes a leader with experiences which prepare, reveal, and finally brings about completion of destiny.
destiny processing	refers to the shaping activities of God in which a leader becomes increasingly aware of God's Hand on his/her life and the purposes for which God has intended for his/her leadership. This processing causes a sense of partnership with God toward God's purposes for the life and hence brings meaning to the life. See also Type I, II, III, IV destiny items.
developer	a concept seen in Paul's life. A developer is a person with a mentoring bent who readily sees potential in an emerging leader and finds ways to help move that emerging leader on to becoming an effective leader.
developmental solution	refers to the process in a regime turnover in which the new regime seeks a developmental solution for old regime leaders, that is, it does its best to develop the old regime leaders so that they can fit in the new regime or moves them on to roles which best fit who they are.
direct ministry	as opposed to indirect ministry. <u>Direct ministry</u> refers to use of spiritual gifts, i.e. word gifts, to influence a face-to-face basic target group in terms of the word gifts themselves—a tactical function.
discernings of spirits	one of the 19 spiritual gifts belonging to the power cluster. The <u>discernings of spirits gift</u> refers to the ability given by God to perceive issues in terms of spiritual truth, to know the fundamental source of the issues and to give judgment concerning those issues; this includes the recognition of the spiritual forces operating in the issue. **Its Central Thrust Is A Sensitivity To Truth.**
disciplines, spiritual	one of five enhancement factors seen in the lives of effective leaders. <u>Spiritual disciplines</u> are activities of mind and body purposefully undertaken to bring personality and total being into effective cooperation with the Spirit of God so as to reflect Kingdom life. Three categories are frequently used to describe spiritual disciplines: <u>abstinence disciplines</u> like solitude, silence, fasting, frugality, chastity, secrecy, sacrifice; <u>engagement disciplines</u> like study, worship, celebration, service, prayer, fellowship, confession, submission; other <u>miscellaneous disciplines</u> like voluntary exile, keeping watch, sabbath keeping, practices among the poor, journaling, listening.
discourse marker	a technical term from linguistic theory which refers to a particular phrase which breaks up a discourse into major sections. The phrase can be summary-like; repeated in other places or in some way enough different from the general flow of context to show that it is concluding something. Examples: Dan 1:21, 6:28.
disputed practice	a practice for which a Christian has freedom to do, from a Biblical and conscience standpoint, but for which other Christians feel is wrong for whatever reasons, a matter of conscience for them. Essentially it deals with the notion of Christian liberty. Some would see the practice as legitimate for a Christian, others would not. Paul gives guidelines on how to approach disputed practices in 1Co 8-10 and Ro 14.

divine affirmation	a concept from leadership emergence theory. The shaping activity of God whereby God makes known to a leader his approval of that leader. This is a major motivating factor to keep one serving the Lord.
Divine Appointment	a Pauline leadership value seen in 2Co. *Leaders ought to be sure that God appointed them to ministry situations.*
divine contact	from leadership emergence theory. One of 51 process items that God uses to shape a leader. A <u>divine contact</u> is a person whom God brings in contact with a leader at a crucial moment in a development phase in order to accomplish one or more of the following to: affirm leadership potential, encourage leadership potential, give guidance on a special issue, give insights which may indirectly lead to guidance, challenge the leader God-ward, open a door to a ministry opportunity, other insights helping the emerging leader to make guidance decisions.
double confirmation	from leadership emergence theory. One of 51 process items that God uses to shape a leader. <u>Double confirmation</u> refers to the unusual guidance in which God makes clear His will by giving the guidance directly to a leader and then reinforcing it by some other person totally independent and unaware of the leader's guidance.
downward burden	that aspect of burden which senses the call of God on a life for a ministry; a deep sense of having to do the ministry because God is directing and involved in it for that leader.
effective methodology	a focused life concept; one of 4 focal issues; <u>An effective methodology</u> is some ministry insight which a leader uses to effectively deliver some important ministry which will contribute to life purpose and achievement of ultimate contributions.
elder	a leadership term (SRN 4245 presbuterosv) used by Paul 6 times in Scripture of which 4 refer to local church leadership in Ephesus. It is unclear as to how this leadership role, elder, differs from bishop or deacon. In the book of Titus the word bishop and elder is used synonymously. In Timothy elders are described as ruling and teaching in the local congregation.
enhancement factors	comparative study of effective leaders who finished well has identified five things that enhance their perseverance and ability to finish well. These include: 1. Seeing present day ministry in terms of a life time perspective and in terms of God's perspective for the ages; 2. Experiencing repeated renewals throughout their ministry—some sought, others serendipitous; 3. Maintenance of disciplines in the life, especially spiritual disciplines; 4. Having a learning posture throughout their whole ministry; 5. Having mentors from time-to-time, who enable them in various ways.
entrustment, leadership	the concept of a lifetime of leadership ministry viewed as a gift from God which is entrusted to the leader to manage as a stewardship. Paul is strong on this concept both in 1 Timothy and 2 Timothy. Viewing leadership this way, requires a strong sense of destiny. It also heightens the responsibility a leader feels for carrying out that ministry so as to give an account of it on *That Day*.

Glossary of Leadership Definitions—1,2 Co Commentary   page 363

eunuch	an emasculated male. Men serving in the palace of powerful rulers were often made eunuchs. Daniel and Nehemiah were most likely eunuchs.
exhortation	one of the 19 spiritual gifts. It is a spiritual gift belonging to the word cluster. The <u>gift of Exhortation</u> is the capacity to urge people to action in terms of applying Biblical truths, or to encourage people generally with Biblical truths, or to comfort people through the application of Biblical truth to their needs. **Its central thrust is To Apply Biblical Truth.**
experiential	an integrative learning domain which involves cognitive, affect, and conative domains so that the things being learned are put into the life and used—they are understood (cognitive), appreciated or valued (affect) and have affected the desires to use (conative). Jesus consistently taught so as to move people toward experiential learning.
evangelism	one of the 19 spiritual gifts belonging to the Word Cluster and the Love Cluster. The <u>gift of evangelism</u> in general refers to the capacity to challenge people through various communicative methods (persuasion) to receive the Gospel of salvation in Christ so as to see them respond by taking initial steps in Christian discipleship. **Its central thrust is Introducing Others To The Gospel.**
faith	(also called word of faith). one of the 19 spiritual gifts. It is in the Word Cluster and power cluster. The <u>gift of faith</u> refers to the unusual capacity of a person to recognize in a given situation that God intends to do something and to trust God for it until He brings it to pass. Sometimes the recognition is in the form of a word to challenge others about a future thing God will do. **Its central thrust is A Trusting Response To A Challenge From God.**
faith check	from leadership emergence theory. One of 51 process items that God uses to shape a leader. A <u>faith check</u> is a process item God uses to shape a leader so that the leader can learn to trust God, by faith, to intervene in his/her life or ministry.
faith challenge	from leadership emergence theory. One of 51 process items that God uses to shape a leader. A <u>faith challenge</u> refers to those instances in ministry where a leader is challenged to take steps of faith in regards to ministry and sees God meet those steps of faith with divine affirmation and ministry affirmation and often with guidance into on going ministry leading to a focused life.
father-guardian	one of 10 Pauline leadership Styles. A directive style. The <u>father-guardian style</u> is a style which is similar to a parent-child relationship and has as its major concern protection and encouragement for followers. 1Th 2:10,11 illustrates this style which is usually seen when a very mature Christian leader relates to very immature followers. Usually this style is directive, but because of the caring relationship between leader and follower and the follower maturity level it does not seem directive, since influence behavior always seems to have the follower's best interest at heart.
father-initiator	one of 10 Pauline leadership Styles. A highly directive style. The <u>father-initiator leadership style</u> is related to the apostolic style which uses the fact of the leader having founded the work as a lever for getting acceptance of influence by the leader. Seen in Philemon and in 1 Corinthians 4:14,15.

fear and trembling (idiom)	The <u>fear and trembling idiom</u> is the use of words to describe an attitude of appropriate respect for something. The something could be God, could a person, or could be a combination including some process. It occurs in 2 Co 7:15; Php 2:12.13; Eph 6:5. The definitive passage was 2 Co 7:15.
figure	the unusual use of a word or words differing from the normal use in order to draw special attention to some point of interest. The more important figures (100s used in Bible) include: metaphor, simile, metonymy, synecdoche, hyperbole, irony, personification, apostrophe, negative emphatics (litotes and tapenosis), rhetorical question. See individual definitions for each of these. See **For Further Study Bibliography, Figures and Idioms** by Dr. J. Robert Clinton.
Financial Equality Principle	a Pauline leadership value seen in 2Co. *Christian leadership must teach that Christian giving is a reciprocal balancing between needs and surplus.*
Financial Integrity	a Pauline leadership value seen in 2Co. *A Christian leader must handle finances with absolute integrity.*
firstfruits	a term indicating a display of something which guarantees something in future. Used of Jesus as being the first to be resurrected and a guarantee of the resurrection of other believers. Also used of transforming work in a life. We shall be like him, the firstfruits. Life out of death producing circumstances for us are the results of Jesus' life out of death.
flesh act	from leadership emergence theory. One of 51 process items that God uses to shape a leader. A <u>flesh act</u> refers to those instances in a leader's life where guidance is presumed and decisions are made either hastily or without proper discernment of God's choice. Such decisions usually involve the working out of guidance by the leader using some human manipulation or other means and which brings ramifications which later negatively affect ministry and life. See Genesis 16 for an example in Abraham's life. See Joshua's treaty with Gibeonites in Jos 9. See Isa 39:4 for Hezekiah's action with Babylonian envoys.
focal element	the dominate component of a giftedness set—either natural abilities, acquired skills, or spiritual gifts. About 50% of leaders have spiritual gifts as dominant. Another 35% have natural abilities as dominant. About 15% have acquired skills as dominant.
focused life	A <u>focused life</u> is a life dedicated to exclusively carrying out God's unique purposes through it, by identifying the focal issues, that is, the major role, life purpose, unique methodology, or ultimate contribution, which allows an increasing prioritizing of life's activities around the focal issues, and results in a satisfying life of being and doing.
formal training	one of three modes of training; recognized training, usually programmatic, and accepted socially as the means for preparing someone for something. Training which generally has a set curriculum and leads to some credential or formal recognition of completion.
founder	a label given to the ultimate contribution of a Christian leader who starts a new organization to meet a need or capture the essence of some movement

	or the like. e.g. Peter, James and John and others of Jesus disciples (Eph 2:20).
future perfect	The future perfect paradigm refers to a way of viewing a future reality as if it were already present which in turn, inspires one's leadership, challenges followers to the vision, affects decision making, and causes one to persevere in faith, which finally results in the future reality coming into being. For leaders who move in revelatory gifts, especially futuristic prophecy and apostolic types, especially with the gift of faith, who must get vision and motivate followers toward it, this is a very necessary paradigm.
generational Christian leaders	refers to emerging leaders who have a family heritage of Christian leadership; often indirect destiny influence comes from the heritage.
giftedness discovery	from leadership emergence theory. One of 51 process items that God uses to shape a leader. Giftedness discovery refers to instances in which a leader becomes aware of natural abilities, or acquired skills, or spiritual gifts so as to use them well in ministry. This is a significant advance along the giftedness development pattern.
giftedness set	a term describing natural abilities, acquired skills, and spiritual gifts which a leader has as resources to use in ministry. Sometimes shortened to giftedness.
gifted power	refers to the empowerment of the Holy Spirit when using giftedness; 1Pe 4:11 gives the basic admonition for this to the use of word gifts. It is naturally extended to other areas of giftedness.
gift-mix	refers to the collection of spiritual gifts that a leader demonstrates repeatedly in ministry over time.
gifts of healings	one of 19 spiritual gifts occurring primarily in the Power Cluster and secondarily in the Love Cluster. Gifts of healings refer to the supernatural releasing of healing power for curing all types of illnesses. **Its Central Thrust is Releasing God's Power To Heal.**
gift projection	the tendency of certain leaders and/or groups to promote certain gifts and require them of all. Strong gifted leaders tend to do this about their own strong gifts (e.g. teachers over emphasize teaching; evangelists over emphasize evangelism; prophets over emphasize prophecy; healers over emphasize healing; word of knowledge people over emphasize word of knowledge). The list of rhetorical questions in 1Co 12:29,30 addresses this issue.
giving	one of 19 spiritual gifts occurring primarily in the Love Cluster. The gift of giving refers to the capacity to give liberally to meet the needs of others and yet to do so with a purity of motive which senses that the giving is a simple sharing of what God has given. **Its Central Thrust Is A Sensitivity To God To Channel His Resources To Others.**
Goodwin's Expectation Principle	Bennie Goodwin in a small booklet on leadership published by InterVarsity Press identified a social dynamic principle which is helpful in developing leaders. In my own words, *Emerging leaders tend to live up to the genuine expectations of leaders they respect.* The challenge embodied in the expectation must not be too much or the young leader will not be able to

Glossary of Leadership Definitions—1,2 Co Commentary   page 366

	accomplish it and will be inoculated against further challenges. The challenge must not be too little or it will not attract. It must be a genuine expectation. Paul uses this with Timothy several times (see fn 1Ti 6:11; 2Ti 1:5).
governments	one of 19 spiritual gifts occurring primarily in the *Love Cluster*. The gifts of governments involves a capacity to manage details of service functions so as to support and free other leaders to prioritize their efforts. **Its Central Thrust Is Supportive Organizational Abilities.**
grace	carries essentially the sense of freedom; when used in a context describing salvation from God it implies that God freely gave us salvation without our earning or deserving it; when used to exhort continuing in the Christian life it carries the sense of the enabling presence of God in a life so as to free (enable) one to persevere victoriously. Paul uses it especially this way in his last epistles 1Ti, 2Ti, Tit. Peter does too 2Pe 3:18. And John also, Rev 22:21. It is interesting to observe that the three great church leaders in their closing words stress the importance of grace and its value in continuing in the Christian life. It is also used by Paul as a metonymy (Corinthians and Romans) standing for spiritual gifts given freely by God.
guidance	from leadership emergence theory. One of 51 process items that God uses to shape a leader. Guidance is the general category which refers to the many ways in which God reveals information that informs a leader about decisions to be made.
hapax legomena	a word occurring only one time in the original text of the Bible. Its meaning must be determined from the surrounding context or from other documents other than the Bible which were extant at the time of the writing of the Bible book containing the word.
harvest model	one of five philosophical leadership models introduced by Jesus and one which focuses on a leader's responsibility to extend the Kingdom by reaching out to those not in it and challenging them to enter it. See **Article**, *Five Philosophical Leadership Models in the Gospels*.
helps	one of 19 spiritual gifts occurring primarily in the Love Cluster. The gifts of helps refers to the capacity to unselfishly meet the needs of others through very practical means. **Its Central Thrust Is The Attitude And Ability To Aid Others In Practical Ways.**
heresy	refers to deviation from a standard, whether in belief (orthodoxy) or practice (orthopraxy). e.g. See 1Ti where both are present in the Ephesian church (as prophesied in Ac 20:30).
heritage pattern	refers to the early development of a leader in the foundational phase; a foundational pattern which describes the background situation out of which a leader grew up and which describes at least a nominal understanding of God and his ways. Timothy is a positive example of one who had a good heritage. He was grounded in the Scriptures and saw faith modeled by his mom, Eunice, and his grandmother, Lois.
hook	a term used in spiritual warfare and referring to some flaw or internal character weakness in the inner life of a person such as greed, lying, sexual promiscuity or the like, lack of integrity, which provides a starting point for Satan to exert pressure and eventually leading to Satan's control of the

person. Jesus refers to this kind of thing in Jn 13:2, pointing out that Satan had no hook within him.

hyperbole	a figure of speech which uses conscious exaggeration (an overstatement of truth) in order to emphasize or strikingly excite interest in the truth. e.g. 2 Sam 1:23 swifter than eagles,...stronger than lions.
identificational forgiveness	an apostolic function. An apostolic-gifted person can pronounce forgiveness in the authority of Christ for a follower under that leadership which is binding. See Mt 16:19 and Paul's use of this power in 2Co 2:10,11.
identification repentance	a leadership function. A leader can identify with the sins of followers in the past and genuinely repent for them in such a way as to break the ongoing power those sins may be influencing. See Daniel's example in chapter 9.
idiom	the use of words to imply something other than their literal meanings. People in the culture know the idiomatic meaning of the words. Example: *I smell a rat*. Some idioms are patterned in which case you can reverse the pattern to get the meaning. Others must simply be learned in the culture from contextual usage of them.
imitator	one of 10 Pauline leadership Styles. A highly non-directive style. The imitator style refers to a conscious use of imitation modeling as a means for influencing followers. It reflects a leader's sense of responsibility for what he/she is as a person of God and for what he/she does in ministry with an expectant view that followers must and will and should be encouraged to follow his/her example. 2 Timothy 3:10,11 illustrates this style.
indigenized church	A church which has its own leadership from its own people and which is organized to survive independently of outside leadership from other cultures and operates with appropriate forms, rites, and ministry fitting to its own culture. According to Roland Allen, it will be self-supporting, self-governing, and self-propagating. Others, however, see a combination of these three items along a continuum moving from dependency to interdependency where differing levels are appropriate for different times in the life of the church. Timothy in 1 Timothy is coming as an outside consultant to an indigenized church having its own leadership.
indirect conflict	one of 10 Pauline leadership Styles. A highly non-directive style. The indirect conflict leadership style is an approach to problem solving which requires discernment of spiritual motivation factors behind the problem, usually results in spiritual warfare without direct confrontation with the parties of the problem. Spiritual warfare is sensed as a necessary first step before any problem solving can take place. Matthew 16:21-23 illustrates this style.
indirect ministry	as opposed to indirect ministry. Whereas, direct ministry refers to use of spiritual gifts, i.e. word gifts, to influence a face-to-face target group in terms of the word gifts themselves, indirect ministry means influencing those who are doing direct ministry—a strategic function.
induced authority	one of five power forms, identified by Dennis Wrong, which a leader may use to influence followers. In essence the leader promises rewards to followers in order to entice them to follow.

Glossary of Leadership Definitions—1,2 Co Commentary

informal training	one of three modes of training; usually refers to learning taking place on-the-job or via mentoring or apprenticeships or self-initiated learning. Jesus was trained primarily this way. See Jn 7:15.
in-service	a training term which refers to when training is given—describes the fact that training is given to the trainee while the trainee is doing ministry and the training relates to what the trainee is doing. Jesus and Paul both trained using this timing.
inspirational leadership	a description of one of three major high level generic leadership functions that a leader of an organization is responsible for producing. It describes the motivational force for developing the relational base and for achieving the task. The ability to get and motivate toward vision, the ability to see God's presence in a work, and to believe and challenge toward hope—God's future working in the organization—are all part of inspirational leadership. Whereas some leaders are by personality either task-oriented or relationally-oriented in their leadership, inspirational leadership appear both in task and relationally oriented leaders. All three functions are necessary for healthy ministry.
integrity	the top leadership character quality. It is the consistency of inward beliefs and convictions with outward practice. It is an honesty and wholeness of personality in which one operates with a clear conscience in dealings with self and others.
integrity check	from leadership emergence theory. One of 51 process items that God uses to shape a leader. The integrity check refers to the special kind of process test which God uses to evaluate heart –intent, consistency between inner convictions and outward actions, and which God uses as a foundation from which to expand the leader's capacity to influence. The word check is used in the sense of test—meaning a check or check-up. See also testing patterns.
Integrity and Openness	a Pauline leadership value seen in 2Co. *Leaders should not be deceptive in their dealings with followers but should instead be open, honest, forthright, and frank with them.* See **Article**, *Integrity—A Top Leadership Quality*.
internship	a training model in which a trainee gets on-the-job training under the watchful eye of a supervisor. Theoretically, the trainee is practicing things already learned and getting advice during the experience. This model is sometimes used in conjunction with the formal training mode and also with the informal training mode.
interpretation of tongues	one of the 19 spiritual gifts. It belongs to the power cluster. The gift of interpretation of tongues refers to the ability to spontaneously respond to a giving of an authoritative message in tongues by interpreting this word and clearly communicating the message given. **Its Central Thrust Is Interpreting A Message Given In Tongues.**
Interrupted in-service	a training term which refers to when training is given—describes the fact that training is given to the trainee while the trainee is doing ministry but the trainee is isolated from ministry responsibility for the period of time that the training involves. Probably one the most effective means/timing for training.
intimacy	synonym: vertical intimacy. Intimacy with God refers to a close, private, and personal relationship with God in which there is mutual affection, a

sharing of interests, and a sense of growing familiarity with God based upon an accumulation of experience with God. Such a relationship is indicated by intimate times like: times in which God's presence is sensed, times of revelation of truth—when God shows something or shares it, times of affirmation by God, times of fulfillment of God's purposes in our lives (destiny fulfillment), moments of faith, in which we sense God is doing business with us and we accept it, crises—in which God delivers, times of committal, repentance, renewal (fresh starts).

intimacy, horizontal	Intimacy, which ultimately is a gift of God, is an on-going process of reciprocal sharing between two people in which there is transparency in which each feels safe to be open, vulnerability flowing from some kinds of transparency which is respected and not taken advantage of, empathy—a caring affirming reflection on what is shared together, and acceptance of the other without necessarily an agenda for change, and which results in a feeling of belonging and significance in both parties. Nine categories around which horizontal intimacy can be build include: work intimacy, recreational intimacy, intellectual intimacy, emotional intimacy, proper physical intimacy outside of marriage, conflict intimacy, crises intimacy, physical intimacy in marriage, spiritual intimacy. See resources for further study, Hershey.
intimacy instance	a term referring to a given moment in which a believer's intimacy with Jesus is seen through some symptomatic outward indication such as obeying his truth, having joy, loving other believers, answered prayer upon Jesus' authority. These symptoms show that a believer is "abiding." See John 15.
invincibility principle	protection of a leader by God till He is finished with that leader; this principle was derived because of the observed confidence that Jesus and Paul asserted based on their relationship with God and their understanding of their destiny and an awareness of timing in their lives such that they sensed that God would protect them until their accomplishment of their destiny was completed. See Jn 7:30; see Paul's shipwreck in Ac 27.
irony	a figure of speech, the use of words by a speaker in which his/her intended meaning is the opposite (or in disharmony with) the literal use of the words. e.g. Jas 5:5 you have heaped treasures for the last days. capture: Your life here on earth has been full of pleasure.
isolation	from leadership emergence theory. One of 51 process items that God uses to shape a leader. Isolation processing refers to the setting aside of a leader from normal ministry involvement in its natural context usually for an extended time in order to experience God in a new or deeper way.
Jews, the	a phrase, *the Jews*, used in John's Gospel to identify a set of Jewish religious leaders who were opposed to Jesus' ministry.
Kingdom Era	a shortened form of The Kingdom Leadership Era. the leadership era ushered in by Samuel when he anointed Saul and associated with the kings of Israel and Judah. This era was ended by the Babylonian captivity.
Kingdom of God	an idiom expressing analogously the concept of God's rule on earth and among His people. Used by Gospel writers (euphemistically by Matthew as Kingdom of Heaven) and Paul.

last days	a term used by Paul to describe the end times before the coming of Christ.
leader	in terms of Biblical leadership a leader is a person with God-given capacity, God-given responsibility who is influencing a specific group of people towards God's purposes for it.
leadership backlash	from leadership emergence theory. One of 51 process items that God uses to shape a leader. The leadership backlash process item refers to the reactions of followers, other leaders within a group, and/or Christians outside the group, to a course of action taken by a leader because of various ramifications that arise due to the action taken. The situation is used in the leader's life to test perseverance, clarity of vision, and faith.
leadership basal elements	leaders, followers, and situations are the major components of leadership basal elements.
leadership challenge	a leadership emergence theory term referring to the shaping process God uses to give a leader an on-going renewal experience about leadership and to direct that leader to some new leadership task.
leadership committal	a special shaping activity of God observed in leadership emergence theory which is usually a spiritual benchmark and produces a sense of destiny in a leader. It is the call to leadership by God and the wholehearted response by the leader to accept and abide by that call. Paul's Damascus road experience, the destiny revelation given by Ananias, and Paul's response to it as a life calling provide the New Testament classic example of leadership committal.
leadership development	the term referring to the process whereby a given leader develops over a lifetime toward that potential God has placed in him/her. This can include non-deliberate processes of life as well as informal, non-formal, and formal training which focuses deliberately on development.
leadership era	A period of time in Biblical history which describes a certain kind of leadership differing from the other eras preceding and following it. Six leadership eras are identified in Scripture. See Patriarchal Leadership Era, Pre-Kingdom Era, Kingdom Era, Post-Kingdom Era, Pre-Church Era, Post Church Era.
leadership functions	Leadership functions is a technical term which refers to the three major categories of formal leadership responsibility: task behavior (defining structure and goals), relationship behavior (providing the emotional support and ambiance), and inspirational behavior (providing motivational effort).
leadership labels	See elder, minister, bishop, deacon, servant.
leadership release	Leadership release is the process whereby an existing leader deliberately encourages and allows an emerging leader to accept responsibility for and control of leadership positions, functions, roles, and tasks.
leadership selection	the life-long process of divine initiative and human recognition whereby a leader emerges. The process is punctuated with critical incidents, as viewed from a two-fold intermeshing perspective—the divine and the human. God selects a leader as indicated by various kind of shaping activities and human leadership affirms that selection, recognizing the shaping activities of God and working with God in that processing.

leadership stewardship	see entrustment, leadership viewed as a stewardship from God.
leadership style	the individual tendency of a leader to influence followers in a highly directive manner, directive manner, non-directive manner, or highly non-directive manner. It is that consistent behavior pattern that underlies specific overt behavior acts of influence pervading the majority of leadership functions in which that leader exerts influence. The style is the means that the leader uses in influencing followers toward purposes. I identify 10 Pauline leadership styles. See Clinton **Coming To Conclusions on Leadership Styles.**
leadership training	the deliberate use of means either formally, non-formally, or informally to develop a leader.
leadership transition	Leadership transition is the process whereby existing leaders prepare and release emerging leaders into the responsibility and practice of leadership positions, functions, roles, and tasks.
leadership value	an underlying assumption which affects how a leader behaves in or perceives leadership situations. Usually when explicitly identified and written the statement will contain strong forceful words like should, ought, or must to indicate the strength of the value. e.g. A specific Pauline leadership value—*Paul felt he should view personal relationships as an important part of ministry, both as a means for ministry and as an end in itself of ministry.* Or generalized to all leaders—*Leaders should view personal relationships as an important part of ministry, both as a means for ministry and as an end in itself of ministry.* Stronger would be the word ought and even stronger the word must.
learning posture	an attitude of willingness to learn even though what may be learned may differ and expand or even contradict what has been previously learned. Such an attitude reflects what has been noted as a major leadership lesson: *Effective leaders maintain a learning posture all of their lifetimes.*
left hand of God	in contradistinction to the phrase *the right hand of God* which refers to an evident manifestation of God's power in a situation, usually through His people or His leaders, this phrase, *the left hand of God,* refers to God's use of people, nations, events not necessarily recognizing Him or what He is doing for His own purposes (e.g. Cyrus). See also Jn 11:49-51.
legitimate authority	one of five power forms, identified by Dennis Wrong, which a leader may use to influence followers. In essence the leader has a position recognized by followers as one to which they owe loyalty, submission and obedience due to the position and their relationship to it.
life crisis	from leadership emergence theory. One of 51 process items that God uses to shape a leader. A life crisis process item refers to a crisis situations characterized by life threatening intense pressure in human affairs in which the meaning and purpose of life are searched out with a result that the leader has experienced God in a new way as the source, sustainer, and focus of life.
life purpose	a focused life concept; one of 4 focal issues; A life purpose is a burden-like calling, a task or driving force or achievement, which motivates a leader to

	fulfill something or to see something done. This is the core focal issue and around which a life is integrated over a lifetime.
list idiom	an idiomatic use of a list of items. The initial item on the list is the main assertion and other items illustrate or clarify the primary item.
litotes/tapenosis	a negative emphatic figure of speech. It is used quite a bit by Luke and also by Paul. Something is diminished in order to emphatically stress just its opposite. e.g. *not ashamed of the Gospel* in Romans 1:16 means emphatically—completely confident in the Gospel. While technically different, I group *litotes* and *tapenosis* together as a class of negative emphatics. They essentially emphasize the opposite of what is denied.
love gifts	a category of spiritual gifts which are used to demonstrate the effects of God's transformation of lives and His care for people. Love gifts demonstrate the beauty of the unseen God's work in lives in such a way as to attract others to want this same kind of relationship. These include: pastoring, evangelism, gifts of healings, governments, helps, giving, mercy, (word of knowledge, word of wisdom sometimes).
Loyalty Testing	a Pauline leadership value seen in 2Co. *Leaders must know the level of followership loyalty in order to wisely exercise leadership influence.* See **Article**, *Followership—Ten Commandments*.
Luke 16:10 Principle	an application principle drawn from Luke 16:10. An emerging leader who is faithful in small tasks will be faithful later in larger tasks.
macro-lesson	is a high level generalization of a leadership observation (suggestion, guideline, requirement), stated as a lesson, which repeatedly occurs throughout different leadership eras, and thus has potential as a leadership absolute. Macro lessons even at their weakest provide at least strong guidelines describing leadership insights. At their strongest they are requirements, that is absolutes, that leaders should follow. Leaders ignore them to their detriment. Example: *Prayer Lesson: If God has called you to a ministry then He has called you to pray for that ministry.*
major role	a focused life concept; one of 4 focal issues; A major role is the job platform which basically describes what a leader does and which allows recognition by others and which uniquely fits who a leader is and lets that leader effectively accomplish life purpose(s). It is broken up into two components: base (more formal) and functional (more informal). See **Article** *A Focused Life*.
maturity appeal	one of 10 Pauline leadership styles. A non-directive to directive type of style. The maturity appeal leadership style is the form of leadership influence which counts upon godly experience, usually gained over a long period of time, an empathetic identification based on a common sharing of experience, and recognition of the force of imitation modeling in influencing people in order to convince people toward a favorable acceptance of the leader's ideas. Used in Phm. See also 1Pe 5:1-4 where Peter uses this style.
mentor	in a mentoring relationship the person helping the mentoree. This is also a label given to the ultimate contribution of a Christian leader whose has a major focus in ministry of personal ministry to individuals as opposed to

	public ministry. e.g. Jesus, Paul the Apostle. Mentoring is also one of the five enhancement factors enabling effective leaders to finish well.
mentor-mix	the set of mentoring roles that a leader functions in. e.g. spirituality mentor, counselor, contemporary model.
mentoree	in a mentoring relationship the person being helped by a mentor.
mentoring	a relational experience in which one person, the mentor, empowers another person, the mentoree, by sharing God-given resources. See the 9 mentor roles: mentor discipler, mentor spiritual guide, mentor coach, mentor counselor, mentor teacher, mentor sponsor, mentor contemporary model, mentor historical model, mentor divine contact. e.g. The apostle Paul demonstrated many of these roles in his relationships with team members and others in his ministry. See Stanley and Clinton **Connecting** for a popular treatment of mentoring. See Clinton and Clinton **The Mentor Handbook** for a detailed treatment of mentoring.
mentor coach	one of nine mentor roles. Coaching is a process of imparting encouragement and skills to succeed in a task via relational training.
mentor discipler	one of nine mentor roles. A mentor discipler is one who spends much time, usually one-on-one, with an individual mentoree in order to build into that mentoree the basic habits of the Christian life. It is a relational experience in which a more experienced follower of Christ shares with a less experienced follower of Christ the commitment, understanding, and basic skills necessary to know and obey Jesus Christ as Lord.
mentor divine contact	one of nine mentor roles. A person whose timely intervention is perceived of as from God to give special guidance at an important time in a life. This person may or may not be aware of the intervention and may or may not have any further mentoring connection to the mentoree.
mentor spiritual guide	one of nine mentor roles. A spiritual guide is a godly, mature follower of Christ who shares knowledge, skills, and basic philosophy on what it means to increasingly realize Christlikeness in all areas of life. The primary contributions of a spiritual guide include accountability, decisions, and insights concerning questions, commitments, and direction affecting spirituality (inner-life motivations) and maturity (integrating truth with life).
mentor sponsor	one of nine mentor roles. A mentor sponsor is one who helps promote the ministry (career) of another by using his/her resources, credibility, position, etc. to further the development and acceptance of the mentoree.
mentor teacher	one of nine mentor roles. A mentor teacher is one who imparts knowledge and understanding of a particular subject at a time when a mentoree needs it.
mentor model (contemporary)	one of nine mentor roles. A mentor contemporary model is a person who models values, methodologies, and other leadership characteristics in such a way as to inspire others to emulate them.
mentor model (historical)	one of nine mentor roles. A mentor historical model is a person whose life (autobiographical or biographical input) modeled values, methodologies, and other leadership characteristics in such a way as to inspire others to emulate them.

mercy	one of 19 spiritual gifts occurring primarily in the Love Cluster. The <u>gift of mercy</u> refers to the capacity to both feel sympathy for those in need (especially the suffering) and to manifest this sympathy in some practical helpful way with a cheerful spirit so as to encourage and help those in need. **Its Central Thrust Is The Empathetic Care For Those Who Are Hurting.**
metaphor	a figure of speech which involves an implied comparison in which two unlike items (a real item and a picture item) are equated to point out one point of resemblance. e.g. *The Lord is my shepherd*. These can be simple (all elements present) or complex (verbal metaphor, some element may be missing and has to be supplied). 2Ti 1:6 stir up the gift is complex, a verbal metaphor. Gift is compared to a flame which has gotten low. Timothy is urged to develop and use with power that gift.
metonymy	a figure of speech in which one word is substituted for another word to which it is related. This is to emphasize both the word and call attention to the relationship between the two words. e.g. Philemon 6 *communicate your faith* to *communicate what you believe and on which you have strong convictions*.
minister	a leadership term (SRN 1249 diakono") synonymous with deacon, actually translating the same Greek word. Paul uses it to describe himself and several of his companions. It is unclear when Paul uses it to describe himself and others of the leadership role implied.
ministerial formation	the shaping activity in a leader's life which is directed toward instilling leadership skills, leadership experience, and developing giftedness for ministry.
ministry affirmation	a concept from leadership emergence theory. The shaping activity of God whereby God makes known to a leader his approval of that leader's ministry efforts. This is a major motivating factor to keep one serving the Lord.
ministry conflict	from leadership emergence theory. One of 51 process items that God uses to shape a leader. The ministry conflict process item refers to those instances in a ministry situation, in which a leader learns lessons via the positive and negative aspects of conflict with regards to: 1. the nature of conflict, 2. possible ways to resolve conflict, 3. possible ways to avoid conflict, 4. ways to creatively use conflict, and 5. perception of God's personal shaping through the conflict.
ministry entry patterns	a leadership emergence theory pattern which describes how leaders move from non-involvement in ministry to involvement in ministry. Of importance in the process is the recognition of God's challenges to ministry and of self-initiative in attempting to do something about the challenges.
ministry philosophy	a phrase describing the leadership values which are implicit or explicit and which undergird a leader's perception of ministry and decision making and practice of ministry.
ministry task	one of 51 process items that God uses to shape a leader. A ministry task is an assignment from God which primarily tests a person's faithfulness and obedience but often also allows use of ministry gifts in the context of a task

Glossary of Leadership Definitions—1,2 Co Commentary

	which has closure, accountability, and evaluation. e.g. Barnabas trip to Antioch; Titus had 5 ministry tasks.
miracles	also called working of powers. One of the 19 spiritual gifts. It belongs to the Power Cluster. The <u>workings of powers</u> (gift of miracles), refers to the releasing of God's supernatural power so that the miraculous intervention of God is perceived and God receives recognition for the supernatural intervention. **Its Central Thrust Is The Releasing Of God's Power To Give Authenticity.**
modeling	a means a leader can use to influence followers; it involves openly demonstrating in one's life the attitudes and actions desired in others. It counts on the followers admiring and wanting what the leader has in their own lives.
Moses, zealous principle	a leadership principle which states that *a leader should not be jealous of another leader's accomplishments but should be zealous for God's work being done no matter who does it.* First seen in Moses' ministry (Numbers 11:26-30); also seen in Jesus' ministry (Mark 11:26-30) and Paul's ministry (Philippians 1:18).
Motivational Force	a Pauline leadership value seen in 2Co. *Leaders should use obligation to Christ (in light of his death for believers) to motivate believers to service for Christ.*
movement	a groundswell of people committed to a person or ideals and characterized by five important commitments:[1] 1. commitment to personal involvement; 2. commitment to persuade others to join; 3. commitment to the beliefs and ideals of the movement; 4. commitment to participate in a flexible, non-bureaucratic cell-group organization; 5. commitment to endure opposition and misunderstanding.
negative emphatic	a figure of speech which negates some concept in order to draw special attention to its opposite (see litotes). e.g. Romans 1:16.
negative preparation	from leadership emergence theory. One of 51 process items that God uses to shape a leader. <u>Negative preparation</u> refers to the special guidance process involving God's use of events, people, conflict, persecution, or experiences, all focusing on the negative, so as to free up a person from the situation in order to enter the next phase of development with a new abandonment and revitalized interest.
networking power	a leadership emergence theory term. One of 51 processing items used by God to shape a leader's ministry. It describes how God can connect a leader to resources of all kinds which can come from contacts with people. People provide a bridge, connecting a given leader with other persons or needed resources.
New Covenant	a Pauline phrase used in 1Co 11:25 and 2Co 3:6 to represent a relationship with God in Christ—salvation through faith in Christ and given by the grace

---

[1] These five commitments are taken from Gerlach and Hines research. Gerlach, L.P. and Hine, V.H., **People, Power, Change: Movements of Social Transformation.** New York: Bobbs-Merrill Co. (1970).

	of God. This is opposed to salvation via works and obedience to the law system.
non-formal training	one of three training modes; it usually refers to non-programmatic training leading to more immediate application of the training; today this is represented in workshops, seminars, and conferences. In Jesus day, his large public teachings did some of this kind of training. See Jn 7:15.
non-vested gifts	a concept from leadership emergence theory. When the body meets the Spirit of God may manifest gifts through individuals which are not seen repeatedly over their lifetime. These are situational uses (see 1Co 12:7-13 contrast with Ro 12:3ff which are vested) of spiritual gifts, sometimes called *come and go* gifts. John Wimber called this phenomena *the dancing hand of God*.
normative value	a leadership value which tends toward an absolute and should be required for any leader.
nurse	one of 10 Pauline leadership styles. A non-directive style. The nurse leadership style is a behavior style characterized by gentleness and sacrificial service and loving care which indicates that a leader has given up "rights" in order not to impede the nurture of those following him/her. 1Th 2:7 illustrates this style.
obedience check	from leadership emergence theory. One of 51 process items that God uses to shape a leader. An Obedience checks refer to that special category of process items in which God tests personal response to revealed truth in the life of a person.
obligation persuasion	one of 10 Pauline leadership styles. A non-directive style. The obligation persuasion style uses an appeal to a follower toward some recommended directive and which persuades, not commands that the follower heed the advice; but it leaves the decision up to the follower though the follower has some obligation to the leader and will thus feel the pressure to voluntary accept the directive.
Old Covenant	a Pauline phrase used in 2Co 3:14 and Ro 9:4 and indirectly in Gal to represent the law system of salvation as seen in the Old Testament Scriptures. It represents God's promises to Israel. This is opposed to salvation via faith in Christ given freely by God.
overlap	Overlap is that unique time in a leadership transition when the emerging leader and existing leader share responsibility and accountability for tasks, roles, and functions. Seen beautifully in the Moses to Joshua leadership transition.
parable	a true-to-life story, pictorial illustration, or other figurative comparison which teaches a central truth by means of one or more comparisons. This was one of Jesus' favorite means of doing non-formal training.
paradigm	a controlling perspective in the mind which allows one to perceive and understand REALITY.
paradigm shift	a change of a controlling perspective so that one perceives and understands REALITY in a different way than previously.

pastoring	one of the 19 spiritual gifts. It belongs to the Word Cluster and the Love Cluster. The pastoral gift is the capacity to exercise concern and care for members of a group so as to encourage them in their growth in Christ which involves modeling maturity, protecting them from error and disseminating truth. **Its central thrust is Caring For The Growth Of Followers.**
Patriarchal Era	shortened form of Patriarchal Leadership Era. The leadership era covering the period of time associated with Abraham, Isaac, Jacob, Joseph, Job and lasting till Moses' leadership. This was mainly family oriented leadership beginning to shift over to tribal leadership in its closing stages.
pattern	pattern is the term used in leadership emergence theory to describe a repetitive cycle of happenings (observed in comparative analysis of case studies on leaders) and may involve periods of time, stages of something happening, combinations of process items, or combinations of other identifiable leadership concepts, all of which serve to give perspective. 23 identifiable patterns have been described.
perceived reality	in paradigmatic theory this refers to the interpretive understanding of REALITY (ontological existence of things) existing in a person's mind and constrained by screening grids such as: physical, focus, reflections, paradigms or other frameworks for interpreting—existing in the mind.
perspective	a term referring to one of five enhancement factors for effective leaders who finish well. Effective leaders view present ministry in terms of a life time perspective. Further, they see their lifetime in terms of God's bigger perspective in the redemptive drama.
personal authority	one of five power forms, identified by Dennis Wrong, which a leader may use to influence followers. In essence the leader has charisma, personality, and leader traits recognized by the culture so the followers are drawn to the leader and voluntary want to follow the leader.
Personal Ministry	a Pauline leadership value seen in 2Co. *Leaders should view personal relationships as an important part of ministry.*
personification	a figure of speech which uses words to speak of animals, ideas, abstractions, and inanimate objects as if they had human form, character, or intelligence in order to vividly portray truth. e.g. Luke 7:35 Wisdom is justified of all her children.
Pharisees	a group of religious leaders, who for the most part opposed Jesus' ministry. They were fundamentalists who legalistically observed the law of Moses and its interpretations by various Rabbis.
pilot project	a phrase used to describe a minimum leadership strategy for implementing change in a situation. A pilot project is a low key attempt to do something without calling any attention to it so that after it has worked it can be used as a model for further more widespread change.
pioneer	a label given to the ultimate contribution of a Christian leader who starts apostolic ministries. e.g. Paul.
pivotal point	A pivotal point is a critical time in a leader's life in which processing going on will be responded to in such a way that one of three typical things may happen: The response to this processing can: 1. curtail further use of the

	leader by God or at least curtail expansion of the leader's potential. 2. limit the eventual use of the leader for ultimate purposes that otherwise could have been accomplished, 3. enhance or open up the leader for expansion or contribution to the ultimate purposes in God's kingdom, that is, it may be a springboard to future expanded use by God of the leader.
plateauing	a condition in the development of a leader in which that leader has ceased to grow in one or more important areas of his/her life. The growth may be blocked due to some disobedience to something God has shown, a general condition of loss of drive or energy due to an extended time of pressured ministry, or in general a lack of learning posture.
Post-Kingdom Era	shortened form of Post-Kingdom Leadership Era. The leadership era associated with Daniel, Ezekiel and others who exerted influence after the fall of Jerusalem and the deporting of Israel. This was dominantly a leadership by modeling under trying conditions.
power base	a term referring to the means which enable a leader's influence. Force, manipulation, authority, and persuasion enfold various power means.
power encounter	A phrase first defined by a missiological anthropologist, A. R. Tippett, which identifies a situation in which the power of God is tested over against some other god's power. Several elements that should be present in classical power encounters: a) A crisis between people representing god and other people must be differentiated clearly. b) There must be recognition that the issue is one of power confrontation in the supernatural realm. c) There must be public recognition of the pre-encounter terms (If...Then...). d) There is an actual crisis/ confrontation event (the more public usually the better will be the aftermath). e) There must be confirmation that God has done the delivering as the power encounter resolves. f) Celebration to bring closure and insure continuation of God's purpose in the power event. Examples: Jephthah, Jdg 11:12-32. Da 3.
power gifts	a category of spiritual gifts which authenticate the reality of God by demonstrating God's intervention in today's world. These include: tongues, interpretation of tongues, discernings of spirits, kinds of healings, kinds of power (miracles), prophecy, faith, word of wisdom, word of knowledge.
power ministry	refers to use of the power gifts to demonstrate God's intervention and often to validate or vindicate a leader's spiritual authority in a situation.
power shift	a term describing the paradigm shift in which a leader moves from not believing in God's supernatural intervention in ministry to believing it and using it. See Jn 6:1-15; 16-21.
prayer encouragement principle	The deliberate sharing by a leader with followers of specific prayer requests being prayed for them, in the will of God, in order to encourage them.
prayer ministry principle	A macro lesson first seen in Abraham's intercession for Sodom, then in Moses intercession for Israel up on the mountain, and most fully amplified by Samuel's ministry (1Sa 12:23,24). It is stated as, *Leaders called to a ministry are called to intercede for that ministry*.

prayer model	one of five philosophical leadership models introduced by Jesus and one which focuses on a leader's responsibility to intercede for ministry. See **Article**, *Five Philosophical Leadership Models in the Gospels*. Sometimes called *Intercessory Model*.
prayer power	from leadership emergence theory. One of 51 process items that God uses to shape a leader. Prayer power refers to the specific instance in which God uses the situation to answer prayer and demonstrate the authenticity of the leader's spiritual authority.
preferred value	a helpful leadership value which some leaders choose to follow but which is not necessarily applicable for all leaders.
Pre-Church Era	shortened form of Pre-Church Leadership Era. The leadership era associated with Jesus leadership. It was a transitional time moving from national leadership to spiritual leadership.
Pre-Kingdom Era	shortened form of Pre-Kingdom Leadership Era. The leadership era associated with Moses, Joshua, and the Judges and lasting until Samuel anointed Saul and began the Kingdom Era. This leadership involved an amalgamation of tribes into a commonwealth. It was moving toward a centralized national leadership but was derailed during the judges time.
pre-read	a technical term drawn from continuum reading; this level of reading assumes that scan, ransack, and browse reading have preceded it. A pre-read browses every chapter and seeks to integrate the book via overall structure and theme. See continuum reading.
pre-service	a training term which refers to when training is given—describes the fact that training is given to the trainee before the trainee is doing ministry and the training hopefully will be relate to what the trainee might do later on when in ministry.
prison epistle	Ephesians, Philippians, Colossians, Philemon and 2 Timothy are called the prison epistles since Paul penned them while being in prison. The first four were probably written in 62 A.D., Paul age 56, in Paul's first imprisonment. The last one, 2 Timothy, when Paul was about age 61 and just shortly before his martyrdom. Out of those isolation experiences we see a depth of leadership advice and wisdom born out of the experience of a leader who is mature and is fulfilling his destiny.
process item	a technical name in leadership emergence theory describing actual occurrences in a given leader's life including providential events, people, circumstances, special divine interventions, inner-life lessons and other like items which God uses to develop that leader by shaping leadership character, leadership skills, and leadership values. These shaping things indicate leadership capacity and/or potential; they expand this potential; they confirm appointment to roles or responsibilities using that leadership capacity; they direct that leader along to God's appointed ministry level for realized potential. Some 51 different shaping activities (process items) have been identified in leadership emergence theory. Synonym: shaping activities of God.
progressive calling	the recognition that most leaders will receive on-going leadership challenges from God throughout their lifetimes and not just some initial call; such challenges will bring renewal, divine affirmation, ministry

	affirmation and will continue to give strategic guidance to a leader's ministry.
progressive revelation	A concept noted in the Old Testament and New that God is a God who continues to communicate and over time clarifies earlier revelation, expanding on it, filling in more details, helping later leaders see the relevance of it, etc. See especially prophetic ministry. Example: Daniel's prophecies in ch 2, 7, 8, 9, 10-12. There is progress in both content and methodology as observed in various genre in Old and New Testaments.
Prominence of Christ in Ministry	a Pauline leadership value seen in 2Co. *A leader must not seek to bring attention to himself/herself through ministry but must seek to exalt Christ as Lord.*
promise	or more specifically, a promise from God is an assertion from God, specific or general or a truth in harmony with God's character, which is perceived in one's heart or mind concerning what He will do or not do for one, and which is sealed in that one's inner most being by a quickening action of the Holy Spirit, and on which that one then counts. See Jn 14 where six such promises are used to inspire the disciples in a crisis moment.
promoter	a label given to the ultimate contribution of a Christian leader who effectively distributes new ideas and/or other ministry related things so as to inspire others to use them. e.g. Jesus, Paul.
prophecy	one of the 19 spiritual gifts. It is in the *Word Cluster* and *power cluster*. A person operating with the gift of prophecy has the capacity to deliver truth (in a public way) either of a predictive nature or as a situational word from God in order to correct by exhorting, edifying or consoling believers and to convince non-believers of God's truth. **Its central thrust is To Provide Correction Or Perspective On A Situation.**
public rhetorician	a label given to the ultimate contribution of a Christian leader who has as a major focus in ministry a productive public ministry with large groups, as opposed to a personal ministry with individuals and small groups. e.g. Jesus, Apollos, Peter.
radical committal pattern	refers to the early development of a leader in the foundational development phase who comes from a non-Christian background or at best a very nominal Christian background in which the leader is more or less processed into whatever values the environment supports; then that leader makes a radical adult decision for Christ which involves significant paradigm shifts in terms of those early values and life-goals.
ransack	a technical term drawn from continuum reading. Ransacking is the second lightest level of reading. A book can be open ransacked or closed ransacked. Ransacking means going through the book looking for anything new (open ransacking) on a given subject or looking only for a special item (closed ransacking).
read	a technical term drawn from continuum reading. Reading is the second heaviest level of reading. Reading assumes that all the previous levels—scan, ransack, browse, pre-read—have been done. Reading requires not only evaluation of the book at structure and theme level but analysis of its import.

Glossary of Leadership Definitions—1,2 Co Commentary

reading buddy	a model for lateral peer mentoring which involves two people committing themselves to learning by reading. In an alternate fashion each person chooses the reading material and setting of assignments. Each holds the other accountable.
reality	in paradigm shift language, the perception of REALITY a person has in the mind.
REALITY	in paradigm shift language, the ontological existence of what is whether or not it is perceived (reality, little r) in the mind. Symbolized by big R.
reciprocal commands	the label referring to the one-another commands in the epistles which describe some of the strong relationships and behaviors that should be part of the church community. e.g. love one another; forebear one another.
recruitment	refers to the deliberate efforts to challenge potential leaders and to engage them in on-going ministry so that they will develop as leaders and move toward accomplishment God's destiny for them.
regime turnover	Regime turnover refers to the process and practices involved in transitioning an old staff recruited under a former regime until it fits the new leadership's idea of what its people should be and do.
relational oriented leadership	a description of one of three major high level generic leadership functions that a leader of an organization is responsible for producing. It describes the creation of community, of ambiance, development of people, building of a base from which the task can be accomplished. Some leaders by personality and processing are relationally oriented and tend to prioritize everything in terms of getting the relational perspective; this means frequently not getting the task done. All three functions are necessary for healthy ministry.
relationship insights	from leadership emergence theory. One of 51 process items that God uses to shape a leader. Relationship insights refers to those instances in ministry in which a leader learns lessons via positive or negative experiences with regard to relating to other Christians or non-Christians in the light of ministry decisions or other influence means: such lessons are learned so as to significantly affect future leadership.
renewal	one of five enhancement factors helping effective leaders to finish well. Such leaders will experience repeated renewals throughout their ministry. Renewal is a specially meaningful encounter with God in which He communicates with *freshness* various kinds of things needed by a leader such as insights about Himself, affirmation--both personal and ministry, inspiration to continue, breakthrough concepts which inspire one to try them in ministry, a sense of His personal presence and/or power, an unusual sense of intimacy--can be tied to some symbolic thing (like a place, physical object, etc)., perspective on time, now and/or the future so that ones faith is increased to see God in what is happening and will happen, so as to give the leader another anchor upon which to build a sense of a new start, a beginning again, and a desire to rededicate and continue on in following God. Type I renewals refer to renewal serendipitously engendered externally by God and Type II renewals refer to renewals which come because the leader is seeking them, usually through exercise of spiritual disciplines.

researcher	a label given to the ultimate contribution of a Christian leader who studies various aspects of Christianity, analyzes it, and develops new ideation or furthers thinking about it. e.g. Luke.
rhetorical question	a figure of speech in which a question is <u>not</u> used to obtain information but is used to indirectly communicate an affirmative or negative statement, the importance of some thought by focusing attention on it, and/or one's own feeling or attitudes about something. 1 Tim 3:5 For if anyone knows not how to rule his own house, how shall that one take care of the church of God. Captured: A person who can not lead his/her own family can't lead people in a church.
ruling	one of the 19 spiritual gifts. It is in the word cluster. A person operating with a <u>ruling gift</u> demonstrates the capacity to exercise influence over a group so as to lead it toward a goal or purpose with a particular emphasis on the capacity to make decisions and keep the group operating together. **Its central thrust is Influencing Others Toward Vision.**
role enablement	a pattern observed in leadership emergence theory concerning giftedness. A leader in a situation which warrants it may be given a spiritual gift needed for that situation. After completing or leaving that situation the leader in a new place or ministry may not see the gift in the new situation. That is, it was a temporary enablement for a specific role which needed it. See vested gifts. Probably the case with Timothy (2Ti 4:5).
saint	a label given to the ultimate contribution of a Christian leader who models a Godly life in such a way as to demonstrate Christ-likeness, the fruit of the Spirit, union life and which draws others to want to emulate it. e.g. Paul the Apostle.
salutation	A <u>salutation</u> is the opening line of a letter which describes to whom the letter is addressed.
salutation, Pauline	A <u>Pauline Salutation</u> is the opening paragraph in any of Paul's letters which follows the form of from /to with some greeting words thrown in and some qualifying phrases tucked here and there.
salutation, Pauline Extension	A <u>Pauline salutation extension</u> refers to the immediate paragraph which follows the salutation and which often links the salutation to the body of the letter as well as leads into the body itself as part of the body of the epistle. It functions to extend the thematic intent of the salutation.
scan	a technical term from continuum reading. This is the lightest type of reading and involves a short time spent in a book in order to categorize the book and determine the level at which it should be read on the continuum.
sense of destiny	an inner conviction arising from an experience or a series of experiences in which there is a growing sense of awareness that God has His hand on a leader in a special way for special purposes. See destiny pattern.
sentness	a term capturing the divine backing of Jesus' intervention in the world to represent and reveal God to our world. It carries the notion of anointing and appointment by God for a mission, but in Jesus' case—more since it was the incarnation of God in human form. The closest functional equivalent for leaders today is divine appointment.

Glossary of Leadership Definitions—1,2 Co Commentary   page 383

servant (leader)	A special leadership term which Paul uses to describe himself and Timothy (SRN 1401 doulov"). It is used of one who gives himself up to another's will, those whose service is used by Christ in extending and advancing his cause among people. It emphasizes leadership wise the vertical aspect of servant leadership. A leader first of all serves Christ. Secondly, he/she serves those being influenced or led.
Servant Leadership	a Pauline leadership value seen in 2Co. *A leader ought to see leadership as focused on serving followers in Jesus' behalf.*
servant model	one of five philosophical leadership models introduced by Jesus and one which focuses on a leader's inward attitude to see ministry as service to God and service to those being ministered to. See **Article**, *Five Philosophical Leadership Models in the Gospels.*
shepherd model	one of five philosophical leadership models introduced by Jesus and one which focuses on a leader's responsibility to relate to, protect, care for and develop those being ministered to. See **Article**, *Five Philosophical Leadership Models in the Gospels.*
simile	a figure of speech which involves a stated comparison of two unlike items (one called the real item and the other the picture item) in order to display one graphic point of comparison. The words like or so or as or than are used to indicate the stated comparison between the real and picture items. e.g. 1 Pet 2:24 All flesh is as grass.
slain in the spirit	a description of one who has lost strength and usually is flat on one's face or back and who is consciously aware of God's supernatural working or revelation being given. It is an awesome experience in which the direct hand of God is sensed. See Daniel 10 especially. Usually such an experience communicates divine affirmation.
sovereign mindset	an attitude demonstrated by the Apostle Paul in which he tended to see God's working in the events and activities that shaped his life, whether or not they were positive and good or negative and bad. He tended to see God's purposes in these shaping activities and to make the best of them.
Sovereign Mindset	a Pauline leadership value seen in 2Co. *Leaders ought to see God's hand in their circumstances as part of His plan for developing them as leaders.* See **Article**, *Sovereign Mindset.*
sphere of influence	refers to the totality of people being influenced and for whom a leader will give an account to God. The totally of people influenced subdivides into three domains called direct influence, indirect influence, and organizational influence. Three measures rate sphere of influence: 1. Extensiveness—which refers to quantity; 2. Comprehensiveness—which refers to the scope of things being influenced in the followers' lives; 3. Intensiveness—the depth to which influence extends to each item within the comprehensive influences. Extensiveness is the easiest to measure and hence is most often used or implied when talking about a leader's sphere of influence.
spiritual authority	from the standpoint of the follower, Spiritual authority is the right to influence, conferred upon a leader by followers, because of their perception of spirituality in that leader. From the leader's perspective Spiritual Authority is that characteristic of a God-anointed leader, developed upon an

Glossary of Leadership Definitions—1,2 Co Commentary   page 384

	experiential power base (giftedness, character, deep experiences with God), that enables him/her to influence followers through persuasion, force of modeling, and moral expertise.
Spiritual Authority— Its ends	a Pauline leadership value seen in 2Co. *Spiritual authority ought to be used to mature followers.* See **Articles**, *Spiritual Authority—defined, Six Characteristics.; Followership—Ten Commandments.*
spiritual authority insights	from leadership emergence theory. One of 51 process items that God uses to shape a leader. Spiritual authority insights refers to any discovery a leader learns about his/her own spiritual authority—its existence or its use.
spiritual benchmarks	see benchmarks, spiritual—for a description of foundational events which are touchstones or watermarks for a lifetime of ministry.
spiritual formation	the shaping activity in a leader's life which is directed toward instilling godly character and developing inner life.
spiritual gift	a God-given unique capacity which is given to each believer for the purpose of releasing a Holy Spirit empowered ministry either in a situation or to be repeated during the Church Leadership Era. I identify 19 such gifts from a comparative analysis of the 8 major and 16 minor passages about gifts in Scripture. I categorize these 19 in terms of major purposes for the church as Word gifts, Power gifts, and Love gifts. The 19 include: teaching, exhortation, pastoring, evangelism, apostleship, prophecy, ruling, word of wisdom, word of knowledge, faith, miracles, gifts of healings, governments, helps, giving, mercy, tongues, interpretation of tongues, discernings of spirits. All leaders have at least one word gift. See word gifts. See Clinton and Clinton **Unlocking Your Giftedness** for detailed explanation of leadership and spiritual gifts.
spiritual warfare	refers to the unseen opposition in the spirit world made up of Satan and his demons and their attempts to defeat God's forces, including believers. It also involves the response by believers to these attempts.
stabilizer	a label given to the ultimate contribution of a Christian leader who can help a fledgling organization develop or can help an older organization move toward efficiency and effectiveness. e.g. Timothy, Titus.
strategic formation	the shaping activity in a leader's life which is directed toward having that leader reach full potential and achieve a God-given destiny.
stewardship model	one of five philosophical leadership models introduced by Jesus and one which focuses on a leader's responsibility to recognize, develop, and use resources given to that leader. See **Article**, *Five Philosophical Leadership Models in the Gospels.*
stronger brother	A term used by Paul in 1 Co 8-10 and Ro 14 to describe a person who has a view on a disputed practice which allows freedom to do that practice without violating one's conscience.
structure	a term in organizational theory which refers to how an organization groups its workers to accomplish its functions. Paul deals with structure in the Corinthian church in addressing problems #2 Divisions and #8 Spiritual Gifts.

study	a technical term drawn from continuum reading. Study is the highest level of reading and involves all previous levels of reading (scan, ransack, browse, pre-read, read). This level not only evaluates the book internally for structure, theme, import and relevance but compares it to other equivalent works in the field. Very few books are read at this level.
stylistic practitioner	a label given to the ultimate contribution of a Christian leader who models a unique ministry style that others want to emulate. e.g. Peter, Paul.
superlative idiom	the Hebrew superlative is often shown by the repetition of a word. e.g. Hebrew of the Hebrews. See Php 2:27, 3:5; 1Ti 1:18; 6:12, and others.
symbol	a symbol is a visible object, quality of an object, or acted out object lesson which is used to teach a truth by a striking resemblance to the truth for which it stands. There can be visionary objects (7 Golden Lampstands), material objects (bread and wine in the Lord's Supper), and external miraculous (burning bush in Ex 3).
synecdoche	a figure of speech closely related to a metonymy. It is a figure of speech in which one word is substituted for another to which it is related as a part to the whole or whole to the part. e.g. Mt 8:8 come under my roof (roof for house).
tag question	a grammatical construction (signaled by a Greek particle) which proposes a question and expects a negative answer—you didn't catch anything, did you? See Jn 21:5-7 and others.
tandem training	Tandem training describes the training technique during overlap used by an existing leader with an emerging leader whom he is transitioning into leadership.
task oriented leadership	a description of one of three major high level generic leadership functions that a leader of an organization is responsible for producing. It describes the thing to be accomplished by the organization, its raison d'être, reason for being. Some leaders by personality and processing are highly task oriented and tend to prioritize everything in terms of getting the task done; this means frequently using people. All three functions are necessary for healthy ministry.
teachable moment	a life situation which is conducive to learning and which can be used by a mentor/developer to develop an emerging leader. The life situation itself prompts learning and catches the attention of the learners. Jesus used this technique many times. e.g. see Mt 21:19,20.
teaching	one of the 19 spiritual gifts. It belongs to the Word Cluster. A person who has the gift of teaching is one who has the ability to instruct, explain, or expose Biblical truth in such a way as to cause believers to understand the Biblical truth. **Its central thrust is To Clarify Truth.**
testing patterns	from leadership emergence theory, one of 23 fairly common patters observed in the development of leaders. The pattern involves three aspects: test, response, resultant action. Two sub-patterns occur. The success pattern, also called the positive testing pattern, involves test, positive response, and expansion. The failure pattern, also called the negative testing pattern, involves test, negative response, and remedial action.

testing, negative pattern	The <u>negative testing/ remedial pattern</u> describes God's use of the testing cluster of items (integrity check, obedience check, word check, faith check, ministry task) to point out lack of character traits through a three step process which includes: 1) presentation of a test of character through a given incident in life experience, 2) a failure response in which the leader either does not perceive the incident as God's dealing and makes a poor choice or a failure response in which the leader deliberately chooses to go against inner convictions or that which pleases God's desires in the situation, 3) remedial action by God which tests again the leader on the same or similar issue, restricts the leader's development until the lesson is learned, or disciplines the leader.
testing, positive pattern	The <u>positive testing/ expansion pattern</u> describes God's use of the testing cluster of items (integrity check, obedience check, word check, faith check, ministry task) to form character in a leader via a three step process: 1) presentation of a test of character through a given incident in life experience, 2) response of the leader first to recognize the incident as God's special dealing with him/her and then the positive response of taking action which honors inner convictions and God's desires in the situation, 3) expansion in which God blesses the positive response by confirming the inner conviction as an important leadership value and by increasing the leader's capacity to influence or situation of influence.
That Day	a phrase used by Paul especially in Php and both 1,2Ti (same concept somewhat phrased differently in 1,2Th) to describe the fact that there will be leadership accountability for a lifetime of ministry before God some day. See also Heb 13:17.
time-line (leader)	a horizontal display of a leader's life broken up into developmental phases which use labels to identify the major development in a phase. This time-line can serve then to integrate all kinds of findings about a leader over his/her lifetime.
time-line (leadership)	a horizontal display of the six Biblical leadership eras which lists the basic times involved and describes the sub-phases or intermediate leadership times as well as the key leaders and labels for macro-lesson.
tongues	technically called kinds of tongues. One of the 19 spiritual gifts. It belongs to the Power Cluster. The <u>gift of tongues</u> refers to a spontaneous utterance of a word from God in unknown words (to the individual giving the word) to a group of people. **Its Central Thrust Is Speaking A Spontaneous Message In An Unknown Language.**
Training Methodology	a Pauline leadership value seen in 2Co. *Leaders must be concerned about leadership selection and development.*
Transforming Ministry	a Pauline leadership value seen in 2Co. *Followers who are increasingly being set free by the Holy Spirit and who are increasingly being transformed into Christ's image ought to be the hope and expectation of a Christian leader.*
True Competence	a Pauline leadership value seen in 2Co. *A leader's ultimate*

Glossary of Leadership Definitions—1,2 Co Commentary

(its ultimate source)	*confidence for ministry must not rest in his/her competence but in God the author of that competence.*
True Credentials (competency and results)	a Pauline leadership value seen in 2Co. *A leader should be able to point to results from ministry as a recommendation of God's authority in him/her.*
True Judgment Criterion	a Pauline leadership value seen in 2Co. *Leaders should value people in terms of their relationship to God in Christ and not according to their outward success in the world* (even in the religious world).
Ultimate Accountability	a Pauline leadership value seen in 2Co. *Leaders actions must be restrained by the fact that they will ultimately give an account to God for their leadership actions.* See **Articles**, *Day of Christ—Implications for Leaders, Motivating Factors for Ministry.*
ultimate contribution	a focused life concept; one of 4 focal issues; <u>An ultimate contribution</u> is a lasting legacy of a Christian worker for which he or she is remembered and which furthers the cause of Christianity by one or more of the following: setting standards for life and ministry; impacting lives by enfolding them in God's kingdom or developing them once in the kingdom; serving as a stimulus for change which betters the world; leaving behind an organization, institution, or movement that will further channel God's work; the discovery of ideas, communication of them, or promotion of them so that they further God's work. 12 categories have been identified. Paul indicates a 12th—that of giving to the poor. See **Article**, *A Focused Life.*
Unequally Yoked	a Pauline leadership value seen in 2Co. *Christian leadership must not be dominated by relationships with unbelievers so that non-Christian values hold sway.*
union life	a phrase which refers both to the fact of the spiritual reality of a believer joined in spirit with the resurrected Spirit of Christ and the process of that union being lived out so that the person is not dominated by sin in his/her life. Synonym: exchanged life, replaced life, deeper life, victorious life, normal Christian life. Paul comprehensively explains this kind of life in Romans 1-8. He models it in Philippians. He also shows its power in his own life in 2 Corinthians.
upward burden	that aspect of burden which senses not only the responsibility for a ministry because it comes from God but also the accountability for that ministry to God. Paul especially demonstrates this in 1,2Co. See also accountability.
vested gifts	a concept from leadership emergence theory. Leaders operate repeatedly over a lifetime with certain gifts. These are called vested gifts. There is the implication of development and use of the gift (see 2Ti 1:6 fn 8). Most of the word gifts are vested gifts. See also non-vested gifts.
vicarious confession	sometimes called identificational repentance, this concept involves the confession of sins past by a present day leader as if he/she had committed those sins. The confession is done on the behalf of people in the past who did not confess this sin. The result is the on-going work of God, which may have been blocked due to this unrepentant sin. See Daniel 9 for an excellent application of this concept.

weaker brother	A term used by Paul in 1 Co 8-10 and Ro 14 to describe a person who has a view on a disputed practice which does not allow freedom to do that practice. To do the practice would violate such a person's conscience—hence, causing them to sin.
word check	from leadership emergence theory. One of 51 process items that God uses to shape a leader. A <u>word</u> <u>check</u> is a process item which tests a leader's ability to understand or receive a word from God personally and to see it worked out in life with a view toward enhancing the authority of God's truth and a desire to know it.
word gifts	a category of spiritual gifts used to clarify and explain about God. These help us understand about God including His nature, His purposes and how we can relate to Him and be a part of His purposes. These include: teaching, exhortation, pastoring, evangelism, apostleship, prophecy, ruling, and sometimes word of wisdom, word of knowledge, and faith (a word of). All leaders have at least one of these and often several of these.
word of knowledge	one of the 19 spiritual gifts. It is primarily in the *Power Cluster* but can be in the Word Cluster and Love Clusterde pending upon what is revealed. The *word of knowledge gift* refers to the capacity or sensitivity of a person to supernaturally perceive revealed knowledge from God which otherwise could not or would not be known and apply it to a situation. **Its central thrust is Getting Revelatory Information.**
word of wisdom	one of the 19 spiritual gifts. It is primarily in the Power Cluster but can be in the Word Cluster and Love Cluster depending upon what is revealed. **The word of wisdom gift** refers to the capacity to know the mind of the Spirit in a given situation and to communicate clearly the situation, facts, truth or application of the facts and truth to meet the need of the situation. **Its central thrust is Applying Revelatory Information.**
writer	a label given to the ultimate contribution of a Christian leader who captures ideas and reproduces them in written format to help and inform others. e.g. Paul, Luke, John.

Bibliography—For Further Study

Alford, Henry
    1871   **The Greek Testament in Four Volumes, Vol II, III.** 5th Edition. London: Deighton, Bell, and Co.

(Bratcher, Robert G. et al)
    n.d.   **Good News Bible—Today's English Version.** New York: American Bible Society.

Bruce, A. B.
    1929   **The Training of the Twelve.** 3rd Edition. Garden City, N.Y: Doubleday, Doran & Co.

Butt, Howard
    1973   **The Velvet Covered Brick: Christian Leadership in An age of Rebellion.** New York: Harper and Row.

Clinton, Dr. J. Robert
    1977   **Disputed Practices.** Redone in 1994. Altadena, Ca: Barnabas Publishers.

    1977   **Interpreting The Scriptures: Figures and Idioms.** Altadena, Ca: Barnabas Publishers.

    1983   **Interpreting The Scriptures: Hebrew Poetry.** Altadena, Ca: Barnabas Publishers.

    1986   **A Short History of Leadership Theory.** Altadena,Ca: Barnabas Publishers.

    1986   **Coming to Conclusions On Leadership Styles.** Altadena,Ca: Barnabas Publishers.

    1987   **Reading on the Run—Continuum Reading Concepts.** Altadena,Ca: Barnabas Publishers.

    1988   **The Making of A Leader.** Colorado Springs, Co: Navpress.

    1989   **Leadership Emergence Theory.** Altadena,Ca: Barnabas Publishers.

    1989   *The Ultimate Contribution.* Altadena,Ca: Barnabas Publishers.

    1993   *Getting Perspective—By Using Your Unique Time-Line.* Altadena,Ca: Barnabas Publishers.

    1993   **Leadership Perspectives.** Altadena,Ca: Barnabas Publishers.

    1993   **The Bible and Leadership Values.** Altadena,Ca: Barnabas Publishers.

    1993   *Social Base Processing—The Home Environment Out of Which A Leader Works.* Altadena,Ca: Barnabas Publishers.

    1994   **Focused Lives—Inspirational Life Changing Lessons from Eight Effective Christian Leaders Who Finished Well.** Altadena,Ca: Barnabas Publishers.

    1995   *Gender and Leadership.* Altadena,Ca: Barnabas Publishers.

    1995   **Strategic Concepts That Clarify A Focused Life.** Altadena,Ca: Barnabas Publishers.

    1995   *The Life Cycle of A Leader.* Altadena,Ca: Barnabas Publishers.

    1998   **Having Ministry That Lasts.** Altadena,Ca: Barnabas Publishers.

Bibliography—For Further Study

Clinton, Dr. J. Robert and Dr. Richard W.
    1991   **The Mentor Handbook—Deatiled Guidelines and Helps for Christian Mentors and Mentorees**. Altadena,Ca: Barnabas Publishers.

    1993   **Unlocking Your Giftedness—What Leaders Need To Know To Develop Themselves and Others**. Altadena,Ca: Barnabas Publishers.

Clinton, Dr. J. Robert and Raab, Laura
    1997   **Barnabas: Encouraging Exhorter—A Study in Mentoring** (1985—revised 1997). Altadena,Ca: Barnabas Publishers.

Davis, Stanley B.
    1982   Transforming Organizations: The Key To Strategy Is Context in Organizational Dynamics, Winter, 1982.

    1987   **Future Perfect**. New York: Addison Wesley.

Doohan, Helen
    1984   **Leadership in Paul**. Wilmington, Del.: Michael Glazier, Inc.

Gerlach, L.P. and Hine, V.H.
    1970   **People, Power, Change: Movements of Social Transformation**. New York: Bobbs-Merrill Co.

Goodwin, Bennie
    1981   **The Effective Leader—A Basic Guide to Christian Leadership.** Downer's Grove, IL: InterVarsity Press.

Hall, Clarence
    1933   **Samuel Logan Brengle**—Portrait of a Prophet. Atlanta: Salvation Army.

Harville, Sue
    1976   **Reciprocal Living**. Coral Gables: West Indies Mission.

    1977   **Walking in Love.** Coral Gables: West Indies Mission.

Hersey, Palul and Ken blanchard
    1977   **Management of Organizational Behavior—Utilizing Human Resources**. Englewood Cliffs, N.J.: Prentice-Hall, 1977.

Kraft, Charles H.
    1979   **Christianity and Culture**. Maryknoll, N.Y.: Orbis Books.

Kuhn, Thomas
    1974   **The Structure of Scientific Revolutions**. Chicago: University Press.

Leupold, H. C.
    1959   **Exposition of the Psalms**. Grand Rapids: Baker Book House.

Machaivelli
    1950   **The Prince and Other Discourses**. New York: McGraw Hill.

Morgan, G. Campbell
    1903, 1936   **The Crises of the Christ**. Old Tappan, N.J.: Fleming H. Revel Co.

    1990   **Handbook for Bible Teachers and Preachers**. 5th Printing. Original 4 Volume Series, 1912. Grand Rapids, Michigan: Baker Book House.

Bibliography—For Further Study

Peterson, Eugene H.
   1993   **The Message—The New Testlament in Contemporary Language**. Colorado Springs, Co: Navpress.

Stanley, Paul and J. Robert Clinton
   1992   **Connecting—The Mentoring Relationships You Need to Succeed in Life**. Colorado Springs, Co: Navpress.

Steadman, Ray
   19??   **Body Life. ????**   ???

Strong, James
   1890   **The Exhaustive Concordance of the Bible** (with Dictionaries of the Hebrew and Greek Words). Nashville: Abingdon Press.

(Taylor, Ken did original version; other Bible scholars the new version)
   1996   **Holy Bible—New Living Translation**. Wheaton, Il: Tyndale house Publishers, Inc.

Tippett, A. R.
              Solomon Island Christianity. Pasadena: William Carey Library.

Wrong, Dennis
   1979   **Power—Its Forms, Bases, and Uses**. San Francisco, CA: Harper and Row

(This page deliberately left blank)

BARNABAS PUBLISHERS

BARNABAS PUBLISHER'S MINI CATALOG

Approaching the Bible With Leadership Eyes: An Authoratative Source for Leadership Findings — Dr. J. Robert Clinton
Barnabas: Encouraging Exhorter — Dr. J. Robert Clinton & Laura Raab
Boundary Processing: Looking at Critical Transitions Times in Leader's Lives — Dr. J. Robert Clinton
Connecting: The Mentoring Relationships You Need to Succeed in Life — Dr. J. Robert Clinton
The Emerging Leader — Dr. J. Robert Clinton
Fellowship With God — Dr. J. Robert Clinton
Finishing Well — Dr. J. Robert Clinton
Figures and Idioms (Interpreting the Scriptures: Figures and Idioms) — Dr. J. Robert Clinton
Focused Lives Lectures — Dr. J. Robert Clinton
Gender and Leadership — Dr. J. Robert Clinton
Having A Ministry That Lasts: By Becoming a Bible Centered Leader — Dr. J. Robert Clinton
Hebrew Poetry (Interpreting the Scriptures: Hebrew Poetry) — Dr. J. Robert Clinton
A Short **History of Leadership Theory** — Dr. J. Robert Clinton
Isolation: A Place of Transformation in the Life of a Leader — Shelley G. Trebesch
Joseph: Destined to Rule — Dr. J. Robert Clinton
The Joshua Portrait — Dr. J. Robert Clinton and Katherine Haubert
Leadership Emergence Theory: A Self Study Manual For Analyzing the Development of a Christian Leader — Dr. J. Robert Clinton
Leadership Perspectives: How To Study The Bible for Leadership Insights — Dr. J. Robert Clinton
Coming to Some Conclusions on **Leadership Styles** — Dr. J. Robert Clinton
Leadership Training Models — Dr. J. Robert Clinton
The Bible and **Leadership Values:** A Book by Book Analysis — Dr. J. Robert Clinton
The Life Cycle of a Leader: Looking at God's Shaping of A Leader Towards An Eph. 2:10 Life — Dr. J. Robert Clinton
Listen Up Leaders! — Dr. J. Robert Clinton
The Mantle of the Mentor — Dr. J. Robert Clinton
Mentoring Can Help—Five Leadership Crises You Will Face in the Pastorate For Which You Have Not Been Trained — Dr. J. Robert Clinton
Mentoring: Developing Leaders...Without Adding More Programs — Dr. J. Robert Clinton
The Mentor Handbook: Detailed Guidelines and Helps for Christian Mentors and Mentorees — Dr. J. Robert Clinton
Moses Desert Leadership—7 Macro Lessons
Parables—Puzzles With A Purpose (Interpreting the Scriptures: Puzzles With A Purpose) — Dr. J. Robert Clinton
Paradigm Shift: God's Way of Opening New Vistas To Leaders — Dr. J. Robert Clinton
A Personal Ministry Philosophy: One Key to Effective Leadership — Dr. J. Robert Clinton
Reading on the Run: Continuum Reading Concepts — Dr. J. Robert Clinton
Samuel: Last of the Judges & First of the Prophets–A Model For Transitional Times — Bill Bjoraker
Selecting and Developing Those Emerging Leaders — Dr. Richard W. Clinton
Social Base Processing: The Home Base Environment Out of Which A Leader Works — Dr. J. Robert Clinton
Starting Well: Building A Strong Foundation for a Life Time of Ministry — Dr. J. Robert Clinton
Strategic Concepts: That Clarify A Focused Life – A Self Study Guide — Dr. J. Robert Clinton
The Making of a Leader: Recognizing the Lessons & Stages of Leadership Development — Dr. J. Robert Clinton
Time Line —Small Paper (What it is & How to Construct it) — Dr. J. Robert Clinton
Time Line: Getting Perspective—By Using Your Time-Line, Large Paper — Dr. J. Robert Clinton
Ultimate Contribution — Dr. J. Robert Clinton
Unlocking Your Giftedness: What Leaders Need to Know to Develop Themselves & Others — Dr. J. Robert Clinton
A **Vanishing Breed:** Thoughts About A Bible Centered Leader & A Life Long Bible Mastery Paradigm — Dr. J. Robert Clinton
The Way To Look At Leadership (How To Look at Leadership) — Dr. J. Robert Clinton
Webster-Smith, Irene: An Irish Woman Who Impacted Japan (A Focused Life Study) — Dr. J. Robert Clinton
Word Studies (Interpreting the Scriptures: Word Studies) — Dr. J. Robert Clinton

(Book Titles are in Bold and Paper Titles are in Italics with Sub-Titles and Pre-Titles in Roman)

BARNABAS PUBLISHERS

*Unique Leadership Material that will help you answer the question:
"What legacy will you as a leader leave behind?"*

*"The difference between leaders and followers is perspective. The difference between leaders and effective leaders is better perspective."
Barnabas Publishers has the materials that will help you find that better perspective and a closer relationship with God.*

BARNABAS PUBLISHERS
Post Office Box 6006 • Altadena, CA 91003-6006
Fax Phone (626)-794-3098